ERLING BOE

W9-DFE-998

Introduction to
Educational Research

CARTER V. GOOD

Dean, School of Education

University of Cincinnati

Introduction to
Educational Research

METHODOLOGY OF DESIGN IN THE
BEHAVIORAL AND SOCIAL SCIENCES

SECOND EDITION

 New York

APPLETON - CENTURY - CROFTS

Division of Meredith Publishing Company

Copyright © 1963 by
MEREDITH PUBLISHING COMPANY

All rights reserved. This book, or parts
thereof, must not be used or reproduced
in any manner without written permission.
For information address the publisher,
Appleton-Century-Crofts,
Division of Meredith Publishing Company,
34 West 33rd Street, New York 1, New York

616-8

Library of Congress Catalog Card Number: 62-17505
Copyright © 1959 by Appleton-Century-Crofts, Inc.

PRINTED IN THE UNITED STATES OF AMERICA

E-37182

Preface

THIS IS an introductory book on research methods for field workers, graduate students in the early stages of their work, and seniors in the undergraduate college. It is intended to serve the purposes of both producers and consumers of research, with research presented as a method of problem-solving or of finding answers to significant hypotheses or questions. For those who like the term "design," the title might well be "The Design of Educational Research" or "Research Designs in Educational Research," with applications to the behavioral and social sciences.

The extensive updating of the second edition includes many new illustrations and references from the research literature of the past few years, complete revision of the chapter bibliographies, and additional subheadings for new content throughout the book, although the basic structure or organization of the original chapters has been retained.

The series of chapters follows the sequence or steps of reflective thinking or problem-solving, although it is recognized that there is frequently a shuttle-like movement from hypothesis to data to tentative conclusions and often back to formulation and testing of a new hypothesis until the correct answer or interpretation is found. These steps in research and in development of a graduate thesis or project include formulation of the problem, together with a survey of the pertinent literature; selection and use of an appropriate data-gathering procedure, including analysis and interpretation of the evidence; and preparation of the research or technical report. In this book analysis and interpretation of data are presented in the functional setting of the chapters on research methods rather than as separate discussions.

By delimitation of scope, this text has left to the many specialized graduate courses and books the quantitative details of testing, statistics, computers, and data processing (except as mentioned briefly from time to time for illustrative purposes). In the field of education generally and in educational research particularly there is room for courses and books dealing with different procedures or methods of investigation. When a student, professor, or author seeks to determine the most effective approach to evidence on a particular problem, inevitably a choice must be made between different methods and procedures for assembling and interpreting necessary data. Many graduate departments of education offer at least three types of research "methods" courses, in an attempt to provide students with the tools of problem-solving, with this book representing the first option:[1]

1. A general introduction or orientation through consideration of such topics as formulation of the problem and hypothesis, the several basic approaches to problems (historical, descriptive-survey, clinical-case, experimental), and technical or research reporting

2. Appraisal, evaluation, and measurement: intelligence tests and measures of general mental ability, measurement and prediction of special abilities or aptitudes, personality and character tests, measures of attitudes and interests, projective methods and other devices for the study of personality, psychometric and sociometric techniques with emphasis on standardized testing and statistics, and educational or accomplishment tests in schools and elsewhere

3. Statistics, data processing, and experimental design.

This is not a "rule book" of research methods, but is a discussion of concepts, principles, and procedures. Under each chapter on a particular research method the typical plan of presentation is to define briefly the appropriate concepts or principles of research, to identify areas appropriate for investigation, to characterize the research procedure or data-gathering technique, and to summarize illustrative studies. Many details must remain for treatment in the voluminous literature, as listed in the chapter bibliographies and in footnotes, since it is common for a book of several hundred pages to be devoted to a single data-gathering technique or procedure. For graduate students, professors, and other research workers who sometimes express an interest in a book of "research readings" or an "anthology" of scientific method, we have included a large number of summaries, extracts, and references from a wide range of sources, presented as an integral part (as illustrations and applications) of the basic theory and techniques of research. This unified approach to the literature, concepts, and tools of investigation has proved functional and effective in the author's classes and seminars. Sometimes the biographies or life histories of scientists and scholars are more revealing than reports of research investigations in characterizing the hallmarks of scientific method. We have drawn from these life-history sources hundreds of

---

[1] Quoted from Carter V. Good, "Methods of Research." *School and Society* 88:364; October 8, 1960.

illustrations or episodes relating to the investigator or scholar at work, in terms of training, experience, motivation, creativity, attitudes, personal traits, rewards, hazards, and working conditions. The sometimes discouraged graduate student or investigator will find inspiration in these an · ecdotes and may be surprised to discover even in a parody of Omar Khay-yam encouragement to work and study rather than despair of learning:

> Awake, for Learning, in the Bowl of Night,
> Can Fling the Stones to put the Dark to Flight:
> And Lo! Already Hunters, for each other
> Flint and Steel, strike Sparks of Light.
> Stir, stir the Mind—E'er boots it to repeat
> How time is slipping underneath our Feet:
> Unborn Tomorrow and dead Yesterday,
> Think now and let Today be sweet!

The author has not strained at creating artificial dichotomies in research approaches: the scientific versus the philosophical, the quantitative versus the qualitative, the mathematical versus the descriptive, or the statistical versus the clinical. These are complementary procedures in problem-solving, probably different aspects of the purposes of inquiry or research. If we are ever tempted to establish a "pecking order" for problem-solving approaches or research methods, it is well to remember the words of Yellowhand, the Great Chief of the South Cheyenne, at the close of the Sioux War. The Indians had agreed to go on the reservation, they held their powwow on a bluff in southeastern Wyoming with the United States Commissioners, they passed the pipe, and the treaty was made. It was a moment of great sadness for the Indians and Chief Yellowhand spoke thus:

> Many kinds bird—
> Blue bird, yellow bird,
> Black bird, red bird,
> All birds!
>
> Many kinds horses—
> Black horses, white horses,
> Brown horses, gray horses,
> All horses!
>
> Many kinds men—
> White men, black men,
> Yellow men, red men,
> All men!
>
> Yellowhand has spoken.

Since an interdisciplinary view of research now recognizes the increasing interdependence of problems and procedures in education, psychology, sociology, and certain other social areas, a number of illustrative studies and techniques have been drawn from these fields. In a sense, a common pattern of research methodology has been presented for the educational, psychological, sociological, and related social fields, with primary emphasis on education.

The footnotes and bibliographies of this revised edition indicate the indebtedness of the author to hundreds of research workers and writers on investigational procedures.

C.V.G.

Contents

CHAPTER ONE

The Hallmarks and Social Obligations of Science and Research

This chapter deals with the major characteristics of science and research, interdisciplinary cooperation in the social and behavioral fields of inquiry, role of values in science and research, hallmarks or traits of the scientist, freedom and responsibility for research, and scientific progress and social responsibility.

CHARACTERISTICS OF SCIENCE AND RESEARCH

Varying Frames of Reference

The characteristics of science have been analyzed in terms of varying frames of reference. One description of science, both as substantive theory and as methodology, uses such phrasing as empirical, propositional, logical, operational, public (subject to communication to other scientists), problem-solving, abstract, tending toward a system, and on-going.[1] Other current interpretations of the term *science*, or notions about the scientist and his work, are in relation to subject-matter fields, complicated gadgets, universal laws, systematic procedures, technical methodology, and pseudo-scientific schemes (for example, astrology, phrenology, physiognomy, palmistry, and graphology).[2]

[1] John T. Doby, Editor, *An Introduction to Social Research*. Harrisburg, Penn.: The Stackpole Co., 1954. p. 6–10.
[2] Clarence W. Brown and Edwin E. Ghiselli, *Scientific Method in Psychology*. New York: McGraw-Hill Book Co., 1955. p. 3–4.

1

Such attempts to characterize or define science or research, particularly basic research, have not proved generally successful. One discussion of the problem of definition cites a list of research terms (without definitions) and concludes that, instead of futilely trying to define a long list of terms, it may seem better to relax about definitions and to concentrate on the quality of research, regardless of its setting or purpose. The terminology mentioned by way of example, in each instance preceding the word research, includes: academic, ad hoc, applied, basic, borderline, developmental, directed, experimental, theoretical, exploratory, industrial, nondirected, pot-boiling, pure, technological, long-term, and short-term.[3]

Attempts to Define Research

An older description or definition of science and research during the present century was in terms of mathematical precision and accuracy, objectivity, verifiability, impartiality, and expertness, with the first letters of these five characterizations spelling out the word *movie*. We now recognize, however, that many historical, descriptive-survey, and case-clinical studies cannot be phrased or reported in mathematical terms, and that precision may be in either mathematical or verbal terms. In many instances the criteria of objectivity and verifiability can be only partially satisfied in the educational, psychological, and social areas.

It may be that the following bit of verse will not take us too far afield. Moving up the page, the letters in bold-face type spell out the word *movie*. (It was written by a graduate student with tongue in cheek.)

M–O–V–I–E

Deep, how deep
The wisdom of Old China!
Unfathomable,
Illuminating;
Wisdom gained by reflection,
Introspection,
Conversation with sages
Long lost in sleep;
Expertly data all arrived at,
Ergos cunningly connived at,
Fallacies fully contrived at,
Impartial in their scope
And comprehension;
Verifiable in their minutest dimension
By laws of calculation
And mensuration;

[3] Dael Wolfle, "Taxonomy of Research." *Science* 130: 1163; October 30, 1959.

Objectively observed
By millions contemplative;
Mathematically demonstrable
Before and after Euclid
That VIRTUE consists simply
In being
TU-YUNG-TU.

By Ira L. Harrison, Leitchfield, Ky.

Although man has used other than scientific methods or sources through the centuries for arriving at answers to his questions or problems, including mythology and personification, supernatural explanation, personal experience, custom and tradition, the voice of authority, and syllogistic reasoning, it has been well said that "The greatest invention of the nineteenth century was the invention of the method of invention. . . . One element in the method is just the discovery of how to set about bridging the gap between the scientific ideas, and the ultimate product."[4] A striking illustration of the validity of Whitehead's statement is found in the development of instruments to explore outer space.

In recognizing the importance of "invention" and scientific method generally, we note that over the years a stereotype has developed in both the scientific and the public mind as to what constitutes serious research, especially by way of psychological investigation and scientific proof. The generally approved pattern has been as follows: crucial experiments growing out of previous findings and performed with great precision, results subjected to the closest scrutiny and alternative interpretations accepted or rejected in accordance with canons of scientific rigor, and finally, confirmed discovery inserted in a systematized lattice of already available knowledge. This type of investigation is thought to be possible only with the aid of intellectual equipment that includes logic, theory, broad and scholarly knowledge, technical proficiency in mathematics and statistics, and a background of the history and philosophy of science. This investigational stereotype, however, is only a small part of the process of active research and is more commonly found in the terminal phases, especially in controlled experimentation. The activities and the task of the individual scientist or the research psychologist are not mainly those of designing a study, collecting data, analyzing the results, and drawing conclusions, although this is probably the formal picture that many people have of the research process. Actually the process of conducting research, of creating and developing a science of psychology or of education, is a rather informal, sometimes illogical, and occasionally a disorderly-appearing affair. It includes considerable floundering around in the empirical

---

[4] Quoted from Alfred N. Whitehead, *Science in the Modern World.* New York: The Macmillan Co., 1950. 296 p.

world, and is sometimes dignified by names like "pilot studies" and "exploratory research." Somehow in the process of floundering the research worker will get an idea, or many ideas; on largely intuitive grounds he will reject some ideas and accept others as the basis for more extended work. If the idea chosen happens to be a poor one, the investigator may waste time, but if the idea proves to be a good one, he may make a significant contribution to his field of science or scholarship, the positive nature of the contribution depending on persistence, originality, intuition, and hard work. The productive investigator spends much of his time and effort on this type of activity, as compared with the more orderly and systematic phases of scientific work.[5]

Expressing himself in overly simple terms, Kettering said of his own work:

Research is a high-hat word that scares a lot of people. It needn't. . . . It is nothing but a state of mind—a friendly, welcoming attitude toward change. . . . It is the problem-solving mind as contrasted with the let-well-enough-alone mind. It is the composer mind instead of the fiddler mind. It is the "tomorrow" mind instead of the "yesterday" mind.[6]

While man has ordinarily found many of his answers to perplexing or interesting questions through other than research methods, he is engaged in research if he follows a procedure substantially as follows:[7]

If he questions his explanations, the stage is set for research. If he goes further and challenges the methods by which he arrived at his conclusion; if he critically and systematically repeats his observations; if he devises special tools for taking, recording, and analyzing his observations; if he tests the reliability and the validity of these tools and evaluates his data in other ways; if he scrutinizes the thought processes by which he passes from one step of his logic to another; if he gradually refines his concept of what it is he is trying to explain and considers anew the necessary and sufficient conditions for proof; if at every step he proceeds with the utmost caution, realizing that his purpose is not to arrive at an answer which is personally pleasing, but rather one which will stand up under the critical attacks of those who doubt his answer—if he can meet these criteria and steadfastly hold to his purpose, then he is doing research.

The characteristics of research have been identified concretely in an analysis (of two studies) made to determine whether research was represented rather than a more casual or routine piece of work. The major

---

[5] Donald W. Taylor and Others, "Education for Research in Psychology." *American Psychologist* 14: 167–79; April 1959.

[6] Quoted from T. A. Boyd, *Professional Amateur: The Biography of Charles Franklin Kettering.* New York: E. P. Dutton and Co., 1957. p. 216.

[7] Quoted from Carter V. Good and Douglas E. Scates, *Methods of Research:* Educational, Psychological, Sociological. New York: Appleton-Century-Crofts, 1954. p. 11.

characteristics of research, as identified, were: inclusion in the report of a description of methodology and sources, original observations, careful planning step by step in gathering and evaluating data, systematic organization and summarization of data, and a background of general competence on the part of the investigator.[8]

Steps or Sequence in Research

To comment more specifically on procedural sequence, it should not be assumed that any given list (series) of steps in scientific or reflective thinking (research or investigation) follows some invariable sequence. In actuality, the steps in research or problem-solving may move backward and forward in a "shuttle-like" fashion. The investigator may go from the hypothesis to the data and, if the hypothesis proves invalid, he will return to formulation of a new hypothesis. With the possibility of this shuttle-like movement always present in research, it it helpful to identify the more important steps in problem-solving. Although the temporal order is substantially as enumerated below, we should recognize that these steps in scientific investigation represent a somewhat idealized account of how the scientist actually does his work:[9]

1. Selection of problem area
2. Acquaintance with current theory and knowledge in the area
3. Definition of the problem
4. Development of hypothesis
5. Development of the formal argument
6. Delineation of the source of data
7. Creation of the instrument
8. Writing a "dummy argument"
9. Pretest of the instrument, and possible revision
10. Formal acquisition of data
11. Analysis of the data
12. Formal write-up of conclusions reached.

A briefer, consolidated list of steps in research, similar to the sequence of chapters in this book, is as follows:

1. Definition and development of the problem, including the survey of the related literature and formulation of the working hypothesis
2. Selection or creation of appropriate data-gathering techniques and actual collection of data
3. Classification and analysis of data
4. Conclusions, generalizations, and applications (with due attention to reporting).

[8] *Ibid.*, p. 269–71.
[9] John T. Doby, Editor, *op. cit.*, p. 12–15.

Science, Theory, and the Model

We expect of the broadly equipped educator, psychologist, or surgeon competence in the science, the theory and philosophy, and the art of his field of specialization. The able surgeon knows the latest research in his field, practices a humanitarian code of ethics, and has the skill of an artist in his fingertips. The psychologist, especially the practicing or clinical psychologist, must know the evidence in his field, must abide by a strict code of ethics for the profession, and must use the arts of interviewing and consultation effectively. Science, theory and philosophy, and art share certain common grounds.[10] On the wall of a university physics building is the inscription: "In this philosophy propositions are based on phenomena and laws are derived by induction."

It is maintained that men who would engage in the complete act of research must of necessity be rare, since the complete act of research includes:

1. Formal theory construction, with no empirical dimension
2. Empirical theory construction, with an empirical dimension, in the sense that it could be checked out through events
3. Checking out of theory in events, which is yet another empirical dimension.

We regard theory construction as a phase of research, and men engaged in it do research. Logicians, mathematicians, theoretical scientists, and laboratory scientists are all researchers.[11] This view answers the question of why so much talk about theory, since science *is* theory, with generalizations induced from observed particulars, and scientists in their technical writing should talk about science (or theory).

Is there possibly—this is the perception that *Contemporary Psychology* is trying right now to spin into its web—a difference between *a posteriori* theories, on the one hand, theories that summarize, with different degrees of success, observed facts and are firmly offered for what they are worth, and *a priori* theories, on the other, theories that are hypotheses put out for testing, trial balloons of systematization, presented falteringly, without a secure factual basis obtained with experimental control, hopeful contestants for success, like a picture in an exhibition or a girl in a beauty contest?

There are, of course, all sorts of well-recognized theories: (1) purely descriptive theories that summarize facts, (2) analytical theories that reduce a complex to its component conditions, (3) physiological factual theories like Helmholtz's theory of hearing, (4) conceptual theories that introduce imaginary

---

[10] Joseph Turner, "Science and Art." *Science* 129: 687; March 13, 1959.

[11] Elizabeth S. Maccia, "The Complete Act of Research." *Graduate School Record* 14: 9–10; Spring 1961.

entities like intervening variables, (5) physiological imaginary models that involve neural concepts not founded on observation, (6) physical models like isomorphism between brain fields and perceptual fields, and (7) the mathematical models. The first three tend to be *a posteriori*, to generalize what happens. The history of science is partly the story of such theories' being wrong; nevertheless they are the stuff of which science is made, and their change is its progress. But the models make less claim to be true. They are hypotheses hoping to be confirmed, the contestants in the beauty pageant. Why are they so important? Could it be because psychology is intent upon being scientific, fears that it has not yet arrived, insists on theory simply because theory is the hallmark of science?[12]

Psychologists and specialists in the field of experimental education talk a great deal about models, although many graduate students and readers of the technical journals are not very clear about the meaning of the term "model." A globe is a replica model of the earth because, in some respects, it "looks like" the earth. Today another type of model (symbolic) is what might have been called a theory several decades or more ago, and makes use of ideas, concepts, and abstract symbols to represent the object being modeled. The Helmholtz theory of hearing was a model that proved to be fact only in part. The Hering theory of vision was a speculative physiology of imaginary processes in the retinal cones that was satisfactory as a model for certain phenomena and probably not true. McDougall's drainage theory of attention and learning was a physiological speculation that now seems almost ridiculous to the sophisticated student of neurology. Physiological models always had a chance of turning out to be true; that is, a physiological explanation that accounts for conscious or behavioral phenomena might be independently confirmed by physiological observation. Today we have other kinds of models: conceptual (intervening variables), physical (electrical brain fields, the topological dynamics of life-space), mathematical (equations for the learning function).[13]

It is positive and encouraging to recognize that the model represents a habitual form of thinking, one of man's devices for bringing his enormously complex experience within the compass of his limited cognitive facilities. Science, as one such device, with a basic function of economy of thinking, uses models to reduce nature's complexity to the much lesser scope of human comprehension. In thus limiting the area of consideration, the investigator deals with the universe piecemeal; for example, the universe may be a desire to promote peace in an aggressive world. The model for a limited area of this universe may be a plan for a federalized

    [12] Quoted from Edwin G. Boring, "Theory." *Contemporary Psychology* 4: 45; February 1959.
    [13] Edwin G. Boring, "The Model." *Contemporary Psychology* 4: 385; December 1959.

world union, with a constitution for the union, a system of organization, a budget, and a plan to turn all arms and military forces over to it—a model of how the world would work if its peoples could be induced to want the new mechanism. This is a useful model of limited scope, even though it omits the facts of human egoism and man's need for aggression (other parts of the universe of peace in an aggressive world).[14]

To cite another example of the model, one of the methods for preparing to meet ethical issues is to develop descriptive models of the "ideal man," that is, models of what we think people should be like and what we hope they some day will be like, and perhaps expressed more simply, we might construct negative models describing the kind of people we hope will not emerge.

These models might be constructed from philosophical thinking, past and present, and scientific knowledge of man gained primarily through the social sciences. As long as we do not have some notion of the model man and some notion of the kind of person we would not prefer, we are especially vulnerable to selling our services, unwittingly, to support endeavors which contribute to producing ends we do not wish achieved. . . .

By developing model men we should also be in a better position to enlighten the public to the dangers involved in the use of psychological power and to present the public with clearer choices in matters concerning the public welfare.[15]

Although models are useful, especially in engineering and scientific work, they are subject to important sources of error and their limitations should be clearly recognized:[16]

1. Models invite overgeneralization.
2. Models entice us into committing a logical fallacy.
3. The relationships between variables may be incorrect.
4. The constants assumed in the model may be incorrect.
5. Models are too often not validated.
6. Model building diverts useful energy into nonproductive activity.

Psychologists and other scientists and scholars should not be discouraged, however, about their models as piecemeal approaches to evidence. Although the size of a single thought or idea is relatively small, with the aid of symbolism and language a thought's implication can be enormous, and progress can be made, even though many or most of the models may not turn out to be "true."

[14] Granville Clark and Louis S. Sohn, *World Peace through World Law*. Boston: Harvard University Press, 1958. 540 p.

[15] Quoted from David B. Lynn, "A Model Man for Applied Psychology." *American Psychologist* 14: 630-32; October 1959.

[16] Alphonse Chapanis, "Men, Machines, and Models." *American Psychologist* 16: 113-31; March 1961.

Basic Research, Applied Research, and Development

The National Science Foundation has formulated a three-fold classification of research activities—"basic research," "applied research," and "development":

Basic research includes original investigation for the advancement of scientific knowledge. The primary aim of the investigator is achievement of fuller knowledge or understanding of the subject matter under study, rather than making practical applications of new knowledge. Applied research is directed toward practical applications of scientific knowledge. Development is the systematic use of scientific knowledge for the production of useful materials, devices, systems, methods, or processes, exclusive of design and production engineering. It is evident that the sequence from research to action is in that order. An invention of a device, procedure, or method cannot be made until the key, or last essential, fact is discovered: for example, a television set could not be produced until all the basic discoveries of electromagnetic radiation and synchronization of transmitted impulses had been made.[17]

A similar classification of research activities and analysis of the characteristics of scientific method as applied to education emphasize these features:

1. *Purpose*—Scientific method deals with problems to be solved. It is therefore highly purposive since there are specific goals that guide the activities of persons who engage in it.
2. *Theory*—There is usually a step which involves a "theory," or as sometimes might be said, an hypothesis or hypotheses concerning the explanation of a phenomenon or a solution of a problem.
3. *Verification*—The establishing of an hypothesis or of a theory is followed by observation and/or experiment. Scientific method is distinct from speculation by this step consisting of tests in reality.

The more that educational research possesses characteristics such as the above, the more it contributes to one category of research which some people have called "basic research." However, since education deals to a very great extent with day-to-day matters and real phenomena, it is expected to bear on the solution of practical problems. Therefore, all educational research need not be "basic" nor of a type which is directed toward the solution of generalizable theory. Much of what is considered educational research would be classified as "development," "demonstration," or "operations research." Since education is certainly an applied field this must be an important area. This is research of a type which works day in and day out to help the teacher, or the principal or agencies in authority over school systems. Then whether our orientation is science or practice, desiring as researchers to be orderly and systematic we

17 Quoted from Nicholas A. Fattu, "The Role of Research in Education—Present and Future," in "The Methodology of Educational Research." *Review of Educational Research* 30: 413; December 1960.

justifiably examine the paraphernalia with which we work. As long as such examination of our techniques, our instruments of measurement, our devices of analysis, or other activities of research is guided by their usefulness in the solution of problems, we are certainly justified in this process. We could easily unbalance our view of the scope of educational research by limiting our discussion to techniques and methods.[18]

Brief reference has been made earlier to the "pure" or basic and to the practical or applied aspects of research. In pure research the investigator may attack any problem anywhere that appeals to his fancy. After he has selected his problem he need only apply scholarly methods to its solution and publish the results, with no concern about any practical social use of his findings. In practical (applied) research the problem is localized within practice, and the results are to be applied to the improvement of practice.

Both pure or basic and applied research should be encouraged and supported. While pure research, at the time the particular investigation was made, may have been evaluated chiefly in terms of the satisfaction afforded the research worker, at a later date the same pure research may have practical and social value. The work of Benjamin Franklin, as he played with his kite and key in studying electricity, probably would be regarded as pure research that did not take on practical and social values until Thomas A. Edison much later worked out his numerous inventions utilizing electricity. In attempting to classify pure research and practical research, we do not have a dichotomy but a continuum. The efforts of the extreme purist and of the extreme technologist are complementary, contributing to a range of research and a diversity of attitude beneficial to society.[19] An inscripton on the wall of a university mathematics building reads, "In our most theoretical moods we may be nearest to our most practical applications." (During recent years the term *action research* has become widely accepted, as discussed in the chapter on descriptive-survey studies.)

To characterize the rewards for pure and practical research in a lighter vein, in the form of verse, Ned Landon, with tongue in cheek, has produced what he calls "The Chief Executive's Utterly Exact Method for Measuring Scientific Research":[20]

I multiply your projects by the words I can't pronounce,
And weigh your published papers to the nearest half an ounce;

[18] Quoted from Francis G. Cornell, "Research and Science in Education," *Report of the First International Conference on Educational Research*. Educational Studies and Documents, No. 20. Paris: UNESCO, 1956. p. 26–30.

[19] Benton J. Underwood, *Psychological Research*. New York: Appleton-Century-Crofts, 1957. p. 8–13.

[20] Quoted from Guy Suits, "Education and Science." *American Scientist* 47: 60–67; March 1959.

I add a healthy bonus for research that's really pure
(And if it's *also* useful, your job will be secure.)

I integrate your patent-rate upon a monthly basis
And I figure what your place in the race to conquer space is;
Your scientific stature I weigh upon some scales
Whose final calibration is the company's net-to-sales.

And so I create numbers where there were none before;
And thus have facts and figures and formulae galore—
And these volumes of statistics make the whole thing very clear:
Our research should cost *exactly* what we've budgeted this year!

Educational investigators are cautioned against overemphasis on the desire to solve practical problems:[21]

1. One of the most harmful effects of the overly practical emphasis in educational research is to convert education to a more or less elaborate dogma, based on experience, informal observation, and personal preference or whim.

2. Overconcern with practicality and with practical results in educational research acts as a strong social pressure on the staffs in the universities and the public schools.

3. Educational research may have a generally unscientific bias.

4. The practical investigator may have a spurious sense of adequacy.

5. Many talented workers may be channeled into such practical efforts as action research.

6. Funds from sources outside the university may be devoted largely to practical research projects.

7. Graduate students may lack competence and confidence in handling important theoretical issues and complex research designs and projects.

SOCIAL AND BEHAVIORAL FIELDS OF INQUIRY

Procedures in Social Science

The physical sciences have constantly invented new methods of dealing with new sorts of data, as when the biochemists found that methods used in the analysis of simple inorganic compounds would not work in dealing with complex organic substances and went on to discover methods for a respectable science of the chemistry of living beings. The biochemists invented new methods as well as new techniques for the understanding of organic part-whole relationships. "In the same manner, those who aim to be social scientists are entitled to invent their own ways of mastering their materials, and to challenge the skeptic to doubt the reliability

[21] Fred N. Kerlinger, "Practicality and Educational Research." *School Review* 67: 281–91; Autumn 1959.

of their results."[22] There are difficulties to be overcome, however, as we seek to develop procedures suitable for the social areas of inquiry, since the self-consciousness of science was increased when scientific study was extended vigorously to human behavior itself, and the social sciences (including psychology) posed anew questions about the range and the effects of science that had lingered since its beginnings.

These questions are of two types. The first is, can science deal with human beings as it can with the rest of nature? That is, is the behavior of people as predictable (and by analogous methods) as the behavior of other physical bodies and organisms? Are the social sciences, then, as scientific as, say, physics? (This question, of course, requires an answer, at least by implication, to the question: what makes science scientific?) The second type of question is, can the social sciences solve the problems besetting humanity in the same way in which chemistry solves a chemical problem? Or, what, precisely, is the potential role of the social sciences in the direction of human behavior, particularly in controlling the social changes which the progress of the natural sciences has made more necessary than ever?

Just as the scientific purpose and method of the natural sciences were thought at first to be impious and immoral, so were those of the social sciences. With regard to the social sciences, however, this objection is still with us, though usually in disguised form. . . .

Even if the social sciences could predict with the degree of probability which characterizes the natural sciences, there are difficulties in applying such knowledge for purposes of control, which, though not altogether peculiar to them, are harder to overcome in the social sciences than in the natural ones. In physics, for instance, controlling energy means to utilize our knowledge so as to arrange matters in such a way as to produce the energy wanted. But in the social sciences we would have to arrange, not matters, but ourselves, so as to produce the desired result: we are not only the manipulators but also the manipulated. To some extent the natural sciences when applied also involve the manipulation of human beings, for instance in medicine. Usually, however, the individual is free to take the physician's prescription or pour it down the drain. Moreover, people are fairly agreed on what they wish to achieve with the physician's help. In contrast, in the social sciences, the measures needed to change social phenomena require collective, rather than individual, acquiescence. And we are not agreed on what changes are worthwhile.[23]

To cite another illustration of how studying people in the social sciences differs from investigating things in the natural sciences, people may resent what they interpret as another person poking his nose in their business, and the subjects selected may refuse to cooperate with the investigator. In Texas, for example, 5000 answer sheets in a student test-

---

[22] Harold A. Larrabee, *Reliable Knowledge.* Boston: Houghton-Mifflin Co., 1945. p. 485.

[23] Quoted from Ernest van den Haag, "Man as an Object of Science." *Science* 129: 243–47; January 30, 1959. Reprinted from *Science* by permission.

ing program were destroyed by a city because some parents objected to certain questions designed to measure attitudes and background. Among these questions were a few items undergoing evaluation for use in a coming nationwide program of testing. The possible contribution of the test program to the more effective use of the nation's talents was great, but success required circumspection in choosing the questions, as well as a cooperative attitude on the part of the students and their families.[24]

To comment specifically on the possibilities of sociology as a field for scientific study, there is no reason to suppose that the sociology of the future will be exactly the same as that of the present, nor does it have to imitate the models of the physical and biological sciences:

The most tenable definition of "science," in any case, is a range definition based on the history of the very diverse special sciences. Whether we approve or disapprove of it, it is a fact that sociology today contains both the scientific aspiration to derive analytical laws explaining relations among precisely indexed abstract variables, and the historical intent to communicate a part of the experimental richness of concrete human action. It may be predicted, without too much daring, that for the foreseeable future both emphases will be with us.[25]

Mistaken Image of Social Science. In spite of encouraging progress in the several fields of social investigation, mistaken notions are common in secondary school, college, and elsewhere. Among the wrong attitudes and misconceptions concerning social science, as held by many college freshmen (and others), are six common fallacies:[26]

1. Science is techniques and gadgetry. The average student judges the merits of a particular scientific endeavor by certain superficial "techniques" which are easily grasped. He sees the scientist as a man in a white coat, working alone in a laboratory full of test tubes, gurgling retorts, and flashing electronic signals. This concept would rule out most physical scientists, more biological scientists, and all social scientists.

2. In some cases he has the stereotyped idea that a scientific law must be an algebraic equation. This would rule out many biological and social generalizations. For example, the principle of blood constancy (homeostasis) can be stated clearly in words. It applies to all human beings and has many useful applications in "life and death" problems.

3. Then there is the misconception that "it must be infallible or it isn't science." We have found that the student rejects the I.Q. test as a social invention because it has certain flaws. But he does not reject the products of the

24 Joseph Turner, "More Talent for the Asking." *Science* 130: 475; August 28, 1959.

25 Quoted from Robin M. Williams, Jr., "Continuity and Change in Sociological Study." *American Sociological Review* 23: 619–33; December 1958.

26 Quoted from Raymond L. Gorden, *Antioch Notes* 33: 1–8; May 1956.

physical sciences on the same grounds. Yet anyone who has a TV set knows that it distorts reality and breaks down on occasion.

4. The social scientist is perceived as "studying people" as unique person-alities and "the basic units of society"; therefore, to predict anything which will happen in society, we must know all of the unique characteristics of each individual. But to expect any social scientist to know what Mary Jones will be doing on her twenty-first birthday is as hopeless as asking the physical scientist when a cork thrown in the Mississippi River will arrive in New Orleans. Pure scientific investigation is more likely to focus on such basic variables as con-formity, rumor, decision-making, role conflict, attitude, etc.

5. Another interesting belief is that, in the physical sciences, the basic theoretical concepts are more "real" and tangible than in the social sciences. For example, the majority of the freshmen classify the atom as something that has been proven beyond a shadow of a doubt, but the "subconscious mind" as having never been proven to exist—"It's just a theory." Yet, it is simpler to demonstrate the existence of the subconscious mind than the concept of the atom.

6. A large proportion of the freshmen share the misconception that "sci-ence is successful insofar as it contributes to the manufacturing of more gadgets."

Interdisciplinary Research and Cooperation

Understanding Between Physical and Social Scientists. It has been urged that we have a broad base of mutual understanding between physical scientists and social scientists, in the interest of interdisciplinary co-operation:

The same science that is the source of so much of today's progress could also lead to mankind's destruction in the years to come. There are many things we must do in a material way for the survival of our civilization, but all of them will avail us nothing unless we somehow learn to live with each other. That's why *all* the bright young men and women must not become scientists. We need, somehow, to achieve advances in the social sciences comparable with those that have been made in the physical sciences. And I am certain that, to an increasing extent, knowledge of *physical science* will be an essential part of the education of every *social scientist.* . . .

We will be hard put to find many single individuals who can simultane-ously grasp all the complexities of today's social, political, economic, and scientific problems. What we need is not so much a *universal genius* as a broad base of *mutual understanding* between *all* physical scientists and *all* social scientists. I think it is evident that education must play the key role in achiev-ing this understanding. I speak, of course, as a physical scientist. For us it is essential to remember that man's future destiny will be achieved not *by* science alone, but *with* science as part of the whole.[27]

[27] Quoted from Guy Suits, "Education and Science." *American Scientist* 47: 60–67; March 1959.

This need for teamwork between scholars and scientists representing different disciplines has been expressed in question form. "Is it in fact true that scientists and 'literary intellectuals' now represent two poles of culture so remote that they have lost all real communication with one another, and live in different worlds? Are the misunderstandings that separate us irreconcilable?"

To this extent I must agree: that the major problem of higher education today is the need to cure this growing schizophrenia. The sciences must become the core of a liberal education, as I have argued elsewhere, although "in teaching science we must not forget . . . that it is simultaneously social study and creative art, a history of ideas, a philosophy, and a supreme product of esthetic ingenuity." The humanities and social sciences, on their part, must do more than merely recognize that the natural sciences exist. They must become permeated with the knowledge and spirit of science if they are to be more than relics of a departed age.

The academic scientist represents more than a growing proportion of the teaching profession. He will be, whether we like it or not, the dominant figure in higher education in a very few decades. He is a strange, harsh figure to many of us, a figure tormented by a growing world-conscience, aware of dawning power but blind to his own limitations. The scientist passionately defends the freedom of science and fails to perceive that it and academic freedom are one. Academic scientists have been rather ordinary participants in the defense of academic freedom and the elevation of the standards of their profession. They are under-represented in general organizations with these aims, and they do not support their own special organizations and societies with either the vigor or the funds that physicians, lawyers, and members of labor unions expend in support of theirs. This growing and awakening giant, the academic scientist, has indeed much to learn as he moves toward leadership. As Bertrand Russell has so well said, science can enhance among men two great evils, tyranny and war. And which, I wonder, is preferable, to perish in a nuclear holocaust or to live under a scientific tyranny?[28]

Unification of Knowledge in the Physical and Biological Sciences. Intellectual boundaries have virtually disappeared in science, especially in chemistry, physics, and biology. The interests and problems of science are related to politics, economics, the humanities, and the arts.

This vanishing of intellectual boundaries has, in particular, occurred inside science. About 1920 the line between chemistry and physics began to disappear. At superficial levels of application—the cookery level of chemistry and the hardware level of physics—one can still tell the two subjects apart. But fundamentally they have now become one.

Even more spectacular and surprising is the fact that biology is now in the process of becoming completely absorbed into and merged with all the

[28] Quoted from Bentley Glass, "The Academic Scientist, 1940–1960." *Science* 132: 598–603; September 2, 1960. Reprinted from *Science* by permission.

rest of science. The modern molecular biologist is a chemist, a physicist, a mathematician, a submicroscopic cytologist—in short, a *scientist*. The origin of the elements, the origin of life, and the origin of species—these have now become interrelated parts of one grand problem. . . .

We now know that science is intertwined not only with political and economic problems but with all the concerns of the humanists and artists. We now know that the mind and spirit of man approaches reality from many directions, appreciates order and beauty in many manifestations, and by joining all forces brings creative imagination and revealing insight to bear on all aspects of nature, of life, and of living. We now know that the poet and the physicist, the musician and the mathematician, the artist and the statesman, and the philosopher and the astronomer attack their problems with essentially the same intellectual and spiritual resources.[29]

To comment further on interdisciplinary trends, interactions among the physical and biological sciences indicate that unification is progressive and that formal lines of demarcation between the several fields of biology have disappeared, just as in the physical sciences (chemistry, physical chemistry, and physics):

This revolution in the life sciences has produced results almost as remarkable and as unexpected as those of the revolution in the physical sciences that was initiated by the discovery of radio-activity. The formal lines between the several disciplines have disappeared in biology just as they were broken down in the physical sciences. It is no more possible now to make a clear distinction among cytologists, geneticists, immunologists, and virologists than to make one among chemists, physical chemists, and physicists. They attend each other's meetings, present papers on associated problems, and utilize materials, techniques and instruments that, ten years ago, they either had no interest in or had not heard of. Most important, they have come to speak a nearly common language, and thus to understand one another.[30]

We are cautioned, however, that science in its several stages is both compartmentalized (or specialized) and unified. Research in its early stages may be highly particularized, seeking to answer one question to the neglect of all other questions, but in its later stages in striving toward unity it may seek to break down the very barriers that made earlier progress possible.

Besides the posing and testing of hypotheses, science is also characterized by its procedure of not attempting to answer all questions at once. Scientific knowledge is possible because it is compartmentalized, because it is possible to discover truths about one question and at the same time ignore other ques-

[29] Quoted from Warren Weaver, "The Moral Un-Neutrality of Science." *Science* 133: 255–56; January 27, 1961. Reprinted from *Science* by permission.

[30] Quoted from Frank L. Horsfall, Jr., "On the Unity of the Sciences." *Science* 133: 1059–60; April 7, 1961. Reprinted from *Science* by permission.

tions. Hydrodynamics, for example, can be studied independently of thermo-dynamics, and the two disciplines together have nothing to say about the sensory qualities of a cold drink of water on a hot day. It may well be that freedom of the most complete sort in one part of knowledge is entirely compatible with total bondage in another part.

Research in its later stages, it is true, has a way of breaking down the very barriers that made earlier progress possible. If science is compartmentalized, it also strives toward unity. The turn of the century saw how increased knowledge about the structure of the atom broke down the barriers between chemistry and physics, and we are now watching our growing knowledge of the structure of the gene break down the barriers between biology and the physical sciences. But unity, in turn, produces new compartments. If where once stood a fence there is now a house, the house itself is a kind of enclosure and within it lives a new group of specialists.[31]

Interdisciplinary Research in Social Fields. Examples of interdisciplinary research and cooperation may apropriately be cited from the several areas of social and behavioral inquiry. Hallenbeck designates five types of specialties (disciplines) or specialists appropriate as resources or teams for interdisciplinary research:[32]

Interdisciplinary research is a team job in which specialists in different areas, using different approaches to their study, work together on a problem requiring research in order to analyze various aspects of the problem in their relationships. This raises two important questions: first, what are the disciplines from which specialists might be selected for such research; and second, what are the principles of selection and operation?

Looking only at the practical problem of resources for the team of specialists which interdisciplinary research requires, it is possible to designate five different types of specialties or specialists—some would say disciplines.

1. There are the traditional disciplines of the social sciences, long recognized and established—history, economics, anthropology, psychology, sociology, and perhaps a few others. Usually the major line of study will fall into one of these more general areas. Perhaps all of the team could be made up of what would now be called generalists in these fields. This would depend upon the focus of the study, the relationship of breadth to depth in what was planned. The particular fields to be represented would be dictated by the requirements of the particular research.

2. A great number of specialties come within each of these general areas. These are perhaps most likely to be needed when the research is directed toward a clearly defined problem. Such specialists as demographers, labor economists, criminologists, child psychologists, specialists in government or in family life, and dozens of others are of great use in building teams.

[31] Quoted from Joseph Turner, "How Helpful Is Freedom?" *Science* 133: 1393; May 5, 1961. Reprinted from *Science* by permission.

[32] Quoted from Wilbur C. Hallenbeck, "Interdisciplinary Research in the Social Sciences." *Teachers College Record* 58: 129–36; December 1956.

3. Cross-disciplines have come into prominence recently. In the social sciences, social psychology and social anthropology are best known, but there are other combinations only one side of which is social science, such as psychiatry or home economics.

4. There are specialists in each of the general disciplines who are concerned with technical processes. These fields have in some cases been followed with such intensive study that the techniques have lost contact with the purposes for which they were developed, but they can be exceedingly useful when teamed up with other specialties. There are many of these—a few of which are sociometry, polling, propaganda analysis, psychological measurement, group dynamics, statistics.

5. Finally, there are what are sometimes called the applied disciplines. These are the operational areas within which, through experience and experiment, conceptual frameworks, organizations, and techniques for carrying on the social services have developed. There are more of them than would at first be thought and they cover a wide range. Public administration, city planning, community organization, public relations, social case work, group development, guidance, personal administration, psychological counseling, and education in its many phases and divisions are particularly important.

Psychology and Interdisciplinary Effort. To use psychology as an illustration, we recognize that there have always been cross-currents between the sciences and the humanities, and it is indeed only a century since natural philosophy counted as literature. Since both breadth and depth are needed in science, modern psychology, in spite of ardent dedication to science and aggressive repudiation of anything nonexperimental in origin, may well move toward humanism, and strengthen rather than weaken its proficiency. The cultivated psychologist knows, in addition to other subjects, the psychology and psychologists of other lands, in order to think wisely in the atmosphere of other men's thinking, thus attaining wisdom as well as skill and competence. It is recognized that the dedicated experimentalist commonly would substitute, as more important tools, statistics and electronics for the languages. We need to know of other times as well as other lands, and thus get wisdom from a knowledge of the history of psychology, rather than facts as such. "One sees how thought works itself out, how human nature operates in the social institution to generate discovery and also sometimes to prevent it."[33] Science requires both objectivity and enthusiasm, and the good scientist oscillates between the two, now checking his enthusiasm with criticism, now bursting restraints in a flight of fancy.

Contemporary Psychology feels, as it views the steady stream of psychology's books and the reviews of them, that the psychologists resist the

[33] E. G. Boring, "Humanizing Psychology." *Contemporary Psychology* 3: 361–2; December 1958.

humanizing deviations that would bring their science over toward scholarship and wisdom and understanding, resist them sometimes because they are dedicated to a narrow empiricism and sometimes because they have accepted a model for rigid theorizing. Their science could go deeper and broader, becoming more objective as a consequence, and so gain strength and importance and significance. True, it would not be much of a step toward the humanities, but it would be a move in that direction; and the new psychologists who grew up in this altered atmosphere, being better educated, wiser, and no less proficient, would throw America less out of balance as it seeks to multiply its scientific competence.[34]

In the debate concerning the relations between science and the humanities, psychologists have been strangely silent, whereas psychological questions and modes of analysis really merit central attention in assessing the actual relations between the work of science and of the humanities.

Physicist-philosophers have addressed the theme. Physicist-literary critics have not been silent. Physicist-novelists have joined the issue. Physicist-administrators have not gone unheard. Sociologists have spoken. From the other side of the fence, historians, literary critics, and philosophers have been vocal. And more and more stridently there have of course been the educators, politicians, and last, but not least, military men. Psychologists have been strangely silent. That in itself is a fact worth pondering. . . .

In any consideration of the science-humanities antinomy, the position of psychology must be given special, if not central attention. In any assessment of the actual relations—similarities, differences, interpenetrations—of the work of science and of the humanities, psychological questions and modes of analysis must almost as a matter of definition be paramount. In any creative redefinition of the relations between science and the humanities, in any readjustment of the images, lay or technical, of these two great areas of the human cognitive adventure, which might more justly and precisely convey the essential unity of knowledge, psychological questions are again paramount. If psychology is to live up to the purview of its very definition, then it must be that science whose problems lie closest to those of the humanities; indeed, it must be that area in which the problems of the sciences, as traditionally conceived, and the humanities intersect. Relative to the present divisive situation in the world of knowledge, psychology, then, might be seen as a third force. It could be seen as a third force whose ranks, when they arrive in no man's land in sufficient numbers, would fill up the gap separating the contenders and reveal all three forces for what they really are: detachments from the same army which had forgotten that there was a common enemy.[35]

[34] Quoted from *ibid.*

[35] Sigmund Koch, "Psychological Science Versus the Science-Humanism Antinomy: Intimations of a Significant Science of Man." *American Psychologist* 16: 629–39; October 1961.

Psychologists and other investigators of human behavior are greatly concerned about methodology (which is drawn from a number of disciplines), in part because of the difficulties in studying people:[36]

1. Man is a complex organism.
2. The scientific study of man has a short history.
3. Man is not a good observer of complex events.
4. Man does not think of himself objectively.
5. Some human experiments are dangerous to do.
6. Some experiences are not accessible for study.

It is pointed out that current psychological research and modern logical and methodological analysis may have much to offer to each other:

We have made a promising start in the collaboration between creative science and critical, clarifying methodology. The time has come to emancipate ourselves from the radical empiricism of the operationists and the behaviorists. A more liberal view of the nature of scientific theory will help us more adequately and clearly to assign to psychology its proper place in the uniting sciences and to remove many of the philosophical embarrassments that have stood in the way of scientific progress.[37]

Sociology, Psychology, Education and Interdisciplinary Progress. It should prove especially profitable to bridge some of the remaining gaps between sociology and psychology. Although differences in the historical roots of psychology and sociology in the realms of assumption, theory, and method have often prevented effective communication and collaboration between these two disciplines, relations are now so mature that it is profitable to make explicit some of the remaining gaps between sociology and psychology. From the beginning, sociology has considered as its central problem the question of how individuals learn to act together and to adjust to one another, while the basic question posed by psychologists about social factors is what effect they have on individual behavior. Typically the psychologist has adopted the experimental method as his basic research approach, and the sociologist has emphasized observation, frequently in the form of diaries and other personal documents, questionnaire responses, scales, and similar procedures, as basic techniques of gathering evidence. Psychologists and sociologists need to give further study to differences in their approaches to problems in such areas as heredity and environment, intelligence, learning, and personality.[38]

[36] Alphonse Chapanis, *Research Techniques in Human Engineering.* Baltimore: Johns Hopkins Press, 1959. pp. 11–15.

[37] Quoted from Herbert Feigl, "Philosophical Embarrassments of Psychology." *American Psychologist* 14: 115–28; March 1959.

[38] Arnold M. Rose, "The Hiatus Between Sociology and Psychology," *Theory and Method in the Social Sciences.* Minneapolis: University of Minnesota Press, 1954. p. 220–27.

In recognizing the benefits to be derived from closer alignment between sociology and education, and in identifying the sociologist's major contribution to education, certain dangers must be avoided:

1. Overgeneralization of sociological research findings that apply to a single case or a small population so as to apply them to American education or society, when there is no logical basis for such induction
2. Uncritical acceptance of unverified pronouncements of sociologists as verified propositions
3. Acceptance of sociological research findings without critical examination of assumptions, adequacy of research methods, and conclusions.

What the sociologist has to offer is basically a series of sensitizing and analytic concepts and ideas based on theoretical and empirical analysis that will allow the practitioner to examine in a more realistic and more incisive way the multiple forces operating in his social environment. The sociologist cannot make the educational practitioner's decisions for him, nor can the sociologist's research findings based on one population be applied to any educational population indiscriminately. The practitioner's task is to assess the various forces that have a bearing on the achievement of his objectives, assign them relative weights, and make a decision based on these calculations. The basic sociological contribution is to add to the educator's kit of intellectual tools a set of sociological insights and concepts that will allow him to take account in his decision-making organizational, cultural, and interpersonal factors at work in his environment.[39]

By way of interdisciplinary progress, as the result of co-operative work on certain common problems, a number of theoretical concepts and propositions are now more or less the shared property of psychology, sociology, anthropology, and education, or, at least, such concepts are reasonably meaningful in theoretical discussions of an interdisciplinary nature that cross departmental boundaries. Certain interdisciplinary agreements in these fields may be found with respect to the human organism, human behavior, interaction, grouping, culture, social structure, personality, and symbolization and communication.

Thus we must admit that there are difficulties, technical and of a psycho-socio-cultural nature, along the way toward the achievement of general theory and wider collaboration among specialists in the study of social man. But we do not regard such difficulties as insuperable. Already we have a vast amount of data and understanding concerning mankind. On the basis of the science we already have we know that time after time men have reached their goals in the face of what seemed to be insurmountable obstacles. It would be ironic indeed if we as scientific students of man should in our own case remain paralyzed in the face of difficulties that are actually rather trivial and that we should thereby

[39] Quoted from Neal Gross, "Some Contributions of Sociology to the Field of Education." *Harvard Educational Review* 29: 275–87; Fall 1959.

be blocked from our goal—which after all, is nothing more and nothing less than a reliable understanding of social man, an understanding constantly increasing in breadth, in truth, and in clarity.[40]

Interdisciplinary Cooperation in Behavioral Science, Human Engineering, and Medicine. The present national and international scene makes imperative an evaluation of the role and potential contribution of the interdisciplinary area known as behavioral science, which is characterized as follows by a special committee:

This is the combined endeavor of many fields investigating all aspects of behavior, leading to understanding of human beings as individuals and in social relations. Behavioral science therefore includes many studies in the fields of anthropology, biochemistry, ecology, economics, genetics, geography, history, linguistics, mathematical statistics, neurology, pharmacology, physiology, political science, psychiatry, psychology, sociology, and zoology. Applications ramify into advertising, business administration, education, government, human engineering, labor relations, law, medicine, military science, operations research, personnel selection, public relations, and many other aspects of human endeavor. Some of these sciences are still in early stages of development, but American research in them at the moment has a clear lead over Russian, which is constricted by Communist dogma.

Behavioral science has demonstrated its usefulness to human welfare and national security. Its further development could increase its contribution in areas of international relations, military defense, and national vigor.[41]

According to this same committee, applications of basic research in behavioral science have led to significant advances that already have had an impact on society:

Intelligence and aptitude testing; techniques to speed learning and increase the effectiveness of education; use of drugs in alleviating or curing certain mental illnesses; sample survey methods using mathematical statistics for measuring and predicting social trends; development of increasingly reliable economic indicators fundamental to planning in government and industry; use of group dynamics to improve the efficiency of face-to-face working groups; and many others. Such achievements make for widespread general acceptance —sometimes too enthusiastic and uncritical—of behavorial science.

Throughout the ages when man has gained more knowledge he has gained more freedom. His understanding of physical laws increasingly has enabled him to control the natural environment, protect himself from heat and cold, and travel speedily and comfortably. Expanding biological science has freed

[40] Quoted from John Gillin, Editor, *For a Science of Social Man:* Convergences in Anthropology, Psychology, and Sociology. New York: The Macmillan Co., 1954. p. 263–76.

[41] Quoted from James G. Miller and Others, *National Support for Behavioral Science,* February 1958. 24 p. At time of publication, obtainable from James G. Miller, 1025 Connecticut Avenue, N.W., Washington 6, D.C.

him from pestilences, most of the terrors of childbirth, the feebleness of malnutrition, many forms of pain and physical misery. His life span has been prolonged and made more healthy.

Similarly behavioral science, directly probing man's central nature, gives promise of increasing his degrees of freedom and expanding his effectiveness and creativity. He can be released from the constriction of life by neurosis and feeblemindedness and the tragedy of psychosis; the limitation of opportunity from inadequate education, associated prejudice and bias; the diminishing of contentment and effectiveness from marital strife, industrial unrest, crime and delinquency; and perhaps most of all, the fear of international conflict which constrains the free expression of the world's peoples. To these central problems of human existence the sciences of man ultimately address themselves.

We are coming to accept as likely in the future a sort of physical existence which would have been unimaginable a few years ago. But the potential benefits which can flow from basic study of our behavior are not so clearly seen.[42]

Interdisciplinary cooperation is essential in the relatively new field of human engineering or "human factors" as a branch of modern technology that deals with ways of designing machines, operations, and work environments so that they match human capacities and limitations or, in other words, the engineering of machines for human use and of human tasks for operating machines.[43] This rapidly growing professional specialty of "human factors" is making contributions in personnel, training, human engineering, and other areas where there is man-machine interaction. Acceptance of system concepts has made the "human part" of any system a focal point for system planning, as when a system is required to collect and input information, process this information, or display data for action or decision-making, thus involving "human factors" knowledge and techniques. The fields of specialization include experimental psychology, human engineering, computer programs, design and computer engineering, statistics, and operations research. (In these areas the programs of research in business and industry have expanded rapidly, as illustrated by General Electric, IBM, and Westinghouse.)

Professional collaboration is a form of interdisciplinary cooperation, as illustrated by the field of medicine:

There are other ways, worth-while no doubt, in which the professions may be brought to a better understanding of one another. It is not necessary that they be brought to a full understanding of one another's subject matter; that would be impossible. For, if they grasp one another's mores and traditions, methods of thought, deep convictions, and motivations, there will be no further

42 *Quoted from ibid.*
43 Alphonse Chapanis, *Research Techniques in Human Engineering.* Baltimore: Johns Hopkins Press, 1959. p. vii.

need to stimulate collaboration of the highest sort. It will occur automatically. And from it will result a surge forward on that complex task of understanding life, where the skill of all professional groups will be strained to the utmost, a new accomplishment which will place a firmer foundation under the keystone of that honorable profession to which medical men belong, ministry to the people. May that ministry always be conducted with pride and dignity. And may the gratitude of humble men always remain the primary compensation and reward.[44]

THE ROLE OF VALUES

During the 1950's and 1960's the interrelationships of science and public policy were recognized as increasingly important, with major efforts on the part of government, philanthropic foundations, universities, and other research agencies to help science and technology serve the best interests of the nation. This view includes a place for the great human- ities, the spiritual ends of life, faith, and values, as presented in succeed- ing paragraphs.

Science and Human Values

To begin with engineering as an example, and then continue with other illustrations, if American science is to continue to prosper and to attract to it an appropriate complement of creative and gifted minds, we must combat the notions that science and engineering (or other technical fields) are incompatible with the great humanities or are narrowly mate- rialistic and destructive of human values:

In the face of the practical responsibilities which rest in science and engineering for our security and our material welfare, it is all too easy for people to conclude that science is inimical to the spiritual ends of life and for them to fail to understand that in reality it is one of man's most powerful and noble means for searching out truth and for augmenting man's dignity by augmenting his understanding. Scientists have an obligation to make this true character of science better understood, not by an arrogant advocacy of science and technology as the only objective means to increase our under- standing and well-being, but by the balanced and tolerant practice and pre- sentation of science as one of the powerful means by which man can increase his knowledge and understanding and still remain humble and ennobled before the wonder and the majesty of what he does not understand. When thus per- ceived and practiced, and when not misused for ignoble ends, science and engineering are major means for "making gentle the life of mankind." When

[44] Quoted from Vannevar Bush, "Professional Collaboration." *Science* 125: 49– 54; January 11, 1957. Reprinted from *Science* by permission.

so practiced and used, they become one of the great humanistic forces of our time.[45]

What is to be the future of science? Extrapolation of history is impossible, perhaps in principle, certainly in practice. The equations of the present allow three possible types of solution for the future. Decline and catastrophe have been predicted on one ground or another, in spite of science, by overpopulation and starvation, or, through the agency of science, by wholesale destruction in nuclear warfare. Continued and accelerated progress have been confidently foretold, the curve sweeping upward faster and faster as each advance in knowledge multiplies the possibilities of further discovery, and as man more consciously assumes control of his own further evolution. Between lies the third and less spectacular solution, that the curve will level out or gently undulate. But the equations are insoluble, at least by any means we know. The uncertainty afflicts and inhibits some people, but their timidity is hardly justified or useful. There has seldom if ever in the world's history been a time when existence was not in some degree precarious, yet the right response to danger lies in action. Faith in the future has indeed a very great survival value. The better equipped are certainly more likely to survive than the worse equipped, and not only to save themselves but to save others.

The task of the men of science is therefore clear. It is to go ahead undeterred by any of the uncertainties. Faith in science is not incompatible with or exclusive of any other kind of faith. Indeed there would seem to be no inconsistency in believing that scientific knowledge is itself one of the great instruments of higher ends. However that may be, duty, expediency, and the zest of living unite their voices in calling for unremitting effort, not in the certainty but in the hope and faith that knowledge may advance, mastery over environment increase, drudgery be abolished, sickness healed, the people fed and life made happier. If social and moral problems are raised they are not essentially new but part of an age-old drama, and should neither be allowed to cause despondency nor to justify obstruction or abstention. The ancient choice between good and evil is in principle unchanged by the scale or fullness of existence. Men have always had to struggle with their environment, with one another and with themselves. Not exemption from danger, hostility or temptation but the power to sustain their impact has made men what they are. The great weapons have been the things of the mind, and among the greatest of these is knowledge. While the old men dream dreams and the young men see visions we should go forward undeterred, that the dreams may become reality and the visions be fulfilled.[46]

The reason that science—every science—has to be regarded as a social institution is not only that its ultimate sanction lies in its use to man, that it was the threat of the sputniks that moved America at least one just noticeable

---

[45] Quoted from James R. Killian, Jr., "Science and Public Policy." *Science* 129: 129–36; January 16, 1959. Reprinted from *Science* by permission.

[46] Quoted from Cyril Hinshelwood, "Dreams and Visions." *Science* 132: 321; August 5, 1960. Reprinted from *Science* by permission.

difference away from its previous level of anti-intellectualism, but also that scientific "truth" depends upon value judgments, and that the "good" is what people—any in-group large enough to have a culture or a creed—want. When automation has made human beings unnecessary, science will be different. It can go on observing, recording, grinding out consequent inferences, but the decision as to what dimension of events to observe (all description is analytical), and at what level of automated confidence to stop grinding on this so as to begin on that, will depend on the scientific public opinion of all the grinding machines, as polled by a special automatic value-assessor. You cannot, however, undertake polling unless you have variability, but undoubtedly there would be individual differences among these human surrogates simply because there'd be accidents in their reproductive process, when one machine (or would it still take two to turn the trick?) begets another. Every scientific theory is just the best opinion of what it is a good idea to believe—for the date of the belief, for the place where the believing happens, and sometimes for the in-group that first got the belief in circulation. That is how social a science is.[47]

Psychology, Behavioral Science, and Values

Educational research and social investigation in general, including the behavioral sciences, owe a prominent place to certain concepts that are common in our culture: purpose, motive, teleology, values, feelings, and emotions. These values are basic to human living, a view that has received greatly increased support since the 1930's. At that earlier time, there was an overemphasis in many graduate departments of education and psychology on statistical and measurement techniques, to the partial exclusion of certain other problem-solving procedures. There were even some graduate bulletins where the term *philosophy* was not permitted to appear in a course title or description. That this view has changed materially can be amply documented in the literature of education, psychology, and sociology.[48]

The "pure" scientist traditionally prided himself on his concern for fact and his indifference to value, an attitude that influenced Titchener, who imitated the classical physicist in his zeal to make psychology scientific and excluded value, along with meaning and utility, from the then new science of psychology. It is true that some schools of psychology have centered their problems around purpose, personality, adjustment, or *Gestalten*, rather than around sensation, with at least some place for value in their world of facts, and yet other psychologists have reserved for

---

[47] Quoted from Edwin G. Boring, "Nothing-But and Something-More." *Contemporary Psychology* 5: 124–25; April 1960.

[48] Carter V. Good, "The Role of Values in Educational and Social Research." *Peabody Journal of Education* 33: 259–71; March 1956.

Carter V. Good and Douglas E. Scates, *op cit.*, p. vii.

M. B. Smith, " 'Mental Health,' Reconsidered: A Special Case of the Problem of Values in Psychology." *American Psychologist* 16: 299–306; June 1961.

values a central place in their system. From this varied background psychology in the 1930's developed applications of the scientific method in attacking various aspects of the problem of values. A comprehensive review of psychological studies of values, based on a bibliography of 211 items, covers the following problems.[49]

1. Measuring the values of groups of individuals and relating the results to other data concerning the groups (individual differences)
2. The origin and development of values within the individual
3. The influence of an individual's values on his cognitive life.

By way of definition and delimitation, Dukes concludes from his review that such terms as attitude, interest, motive, need, sentiment, or valence are often used interchangeably with value, or at least refer to some aspect of value, and that investigations of level of aspiration, character, or the superego almost necessarily involve evaluations.

As pointed out earlier in this chapter, in discussing the interdisciplinary aspects of research, scientists and scholars are coming to recognize that there is really no essential conflict between the problem-solving procedures of science, philosophy, logic, history, statistics, and case-clinical study, whether our concern is with values or some other major question. Therefore, in offering graduate instruction, particularly in research courses, and in our discussions of research, we should make only moderate use of the term *scientific*. The methods of science (and technology) and of philosophy (and logic) are complementary techniques, perhaps different aspects of the general purpose of a single discipline of inquiry, in the development of problem or concept and in the gathering of evidence with which to test or modify the concept. It is held that science without philosophy is blind, while philosophy without science is empty.

This point of view is in keeping with evidence of an interdisciplinary approach and of close cooperation between the different areas of behavioral and human and social science, as emphasized in this chapter and as found in the literature and in certain graduate programs and research centers that utilize the combined resources of psychology, sociology, anthropology, education, and a number of other social fields. This larger movement toward cooperation in all the human sciences makes it possible to develop a common pattern of research methodology (and to some extent theory, as well as background for study of values), with appropriate applications to each special field of investigation.

Today an ethical dilemma of value orientations confronts the psy-

[49] William F. Dukes, "Psychological Studies of Values." *Psychological Bulletin* 52: 24–50; January 1955.

chologist as he plays a new role in leaving his laboratory and moving out into the world to be of practical service to mankind:

While the psychologist must of necessity play this new role, he does so with certain difficulties, for he must divest himself of the robes of scientific impartiality. The psychologist as a scientist limits himself to what is; his choice of field of inquiry in his quest for truth involves values whch are purely personal. But as a practitioner, the psychologist must be concerned with what should be; his personal tastes now affect the lives of others and so become social values.

The point is that the involvement of the psychologist's own values in the applied field creates an ethical dilemma. The dilemma exists because the psychologist as a scientist cannot know to which of mankind's brave new worlds he is to be beholden. The educational psychologist facilitates learning; but learning involves understanding, whose nature is determined only by a philosophy of education. The industrial psychologist is employed by a company which seeks a profit, and only personal choice can help him reconcile loyalty to the employer with a broader loyalty to society as it is represented by the consumer and by the fellow employee.

With the counselor and the clinician, the ethical dilemma becomes more severe, for they serve not an organization but rather a particular individual. The clinician is of service by striving to bring back one who is mentally unhealthy to psychic health, and yet his science can scarcely tell him what mental health and psychological maturity really are. The counselor provides guidance for effective living, and yet it is scarcely as a psychologist that he describes the good life.

In therapy, the psychologist works toward ends which he calls "adjustment," "self-realization," "relearning," etc. These words do not even approximately describe the same thing. Further, it is impossible for research to enter the breach and describe the ends of effective counseling. . . .

In the counseling interview, it does not matter whether or not the therapist is consciously aware of a value orientation. If he is aware of his value orientation, he finds it often impossible to be loyal both to his own highest values and those of the client. If he has not systematized his beliefs, the therapist will assume his own values to be self-evident, and in ignorance he will project his own values onto the client.

The dilemma of the practicing psychologist is compounded by the existence of a multiplicity of competing sets of values, for one value orientation tends to exclude all others. . . .

If the psychologist is by definition to be ethical, he must conform to professional standards of conduct. Having described different value orientations, we can now conclude that there is no single professional standard to which his values can conform. If psychology declares by fiat that one set of values is to become absolute, it ceases to be science and becomes a social movement. If it chooses a syncretistic blend, it has arbitrarily decided in favor of a culturalism that attempts to adapt to as many viewpoints as possible. But when a value is compromised, it has become the means to some other end.

Finally, psychology can choose to hide its head in the sand of scientific research. However, the only result of such a move would be a regression to ethical superstitions exceeding even those of the so-called primitives. To do research without intending it to serve a particular value orientation is to build a high speed automobile without any steering wheel.

[A start has already been made] in untieing the ethical knot by suggesting that value orientations be removed from under the proverbial bushel and, once out in the open, be dealt with as objectively as possible. We would suggest in addition that each area in psychology become more fully aware of the implications of its efforts, much as education does through a philosophy of education. We would further suggest that, as psychologists familiarize themselves with the value orientation under which they operate, they confess their philosophic biases and then turn those biases to fullest advantage by being of professional assistance to the special interest groups with which their values coincide. In such ways as these the public will receive more of what psychology has to contribute and, dealing with psychology at a more objective level, will be able to put that contribution to better use.

We conclude that differences in value orientations cannot be resolved, each orientation having adherents whose beliefs should be respected. We suggest that each counselor have an understanding of the values both of himself and others and that his values be known by all who are personally affected by his professional behavior.[50]

By way of an illustration of research in the realm of values, as summarized by a reviewer, Morris studied the preferences of college students in several countries with respect to "ways to live."

The larger conceptions of the good life—the "schemata of value" as Gordon Allport has called them—have seemed either so complex and shifting, or so vaguely transcendental as to resist empirical study. Their analysis and dynamics traditionally have been left to the humanist, the professional philosopher, or the theologian. In the main the social scientist has avoided them. The psychologist, it is true, has achieved a certain methodological rigor and elegance in the study of such molecular phenomena as motives, attitudes, beliefs, goals, ethical judgments, and the like, all of which are, however, peripheral to the larger problem.

There have been some notable attempts to study values in the global sense. Witness the widely contrasting value patterns identified in various cultures by Ruth Benedict and Margaret Mead, and the democratic and antidemocratic polarities isolated by Adorno, Else Frenkel-Brunswik et al. in the study of authoritarian personality. The clinical psychologist has become increasingly aware that, as a matter of therapeutic strategy, implicitly or explicitly he must commit himself to some broad conception of the good life, and such a shrewd observer as Erich Fromm raises the disturbing question of the universality of the value norms by which mental health and ill health are to be judged.

[50] Quoted from C. Marshall Lowe, "Value Orientations—An Ethical Dilemma." *American Psychologist* 14: 687–93; November 1959.

A study of values which is intended to make an empirical contribution to a science of man must take into account the nature and extent of cultural influences. Although anthropologists are not in complete agreement as to its interpretation, there is an impressive amount of evidence indicating that all experience, including values, is partially or wholly culturally determined. The basic requirement of Professor Morris' research is a measuring instrument capable of use across cultural boundaries.

In the present study the basic instrument consisted of thirteen summaries of "ways to live," and the respondents rated their preferences of each Way on a sevenfold scale. The Ways were given no formal labels, but they embody the conceptions of the good life as expressed in various religious and ethical systems. The respondents were approximately 6,000 college students in the United States, Canada, China, India, Japan, and Norway.[51]

Social Science and Values

The social sciences especially are concerned with values, including social decisions, interests, desires, beliefs, prejudices, and moral implications:

The social sciences can nonetheless assist in making social decisions. They can ascertain who wants what; they can ascertain what makes people want what they do want, and how their desires may be fulfilled, or changed. Such desires may arise from wrong beliefs—prejudices. If this is so, knowledge provided by science can change the desires. Unfortunately, the desire leads to the prejudice more often than conversely. And if this is so, the desire will not change with increased knowledge. On the contrary, though available, such knowledge is unlikely to be absorbed. Further, the desire itself—apart from its rationalization—cannot be proved to be right or wrong by any science. The one thing the social sciences cannot do—the one thing, indeed, no science can decide—is whether desires ought to be fulfilled or changed or frustrated. . . .

As for the "truth" of such moral implications of values, of ends and purposes of life, though science cannot establish it, one may well allow that there is such a truth—even though people disagree on where and how to find it. A difference of beliefs does not imply that there is no truth or that it cannot be found. It implies only that it has not been found. The situation is not very different from the situation in art: it is probably impossible to prove that one composer is a great musician and another is not. Yet, I shall continue to hold very strong convictions on the value of their respective works; and I shall not regard them as matters of taste but of esthetic truth. Analogously, I hold moral values to be matters of moral truth. Science will help somewhat— it will clear the underbrush—but reason and faith cannot be dispensed with, if we wish to map a transcendent road.[52]

[51] Quoted from review by Franklin Fearing, Contemporary Psychology 2: 157–59; June 1957, of Charles Morris, Varieties of Human Value. Chicago: The University of Chicago Press, 1956. xv + 209 p.

[52] Quoted from Ernest van den Haag, "Man as an Object of Science." Science 129: 243–47; January 30, 1959. Reprinted from Science by permission.

Lasswell suggests four types of contributions needed in political science, as related to problems of values:[53]

One professional contribution, it appears, is to project a comprehensive image of the future for the purpose of indicating how our overriding goal values are likely to be affected (if current policies continue).

A closely related contribution consists in clarifying the fundamental goal values of the body politic. We are accustomed to confront political ideologies with new factual contingencies and to suggest appropriate specific interpretations. We also confront political doctrines with rival doctrines and with comprehensive theological and metaphysical systems. I have called attention to the point that the basic value systems of European civilization, in particular, are likely to be exposed to sweeping challenge as biology and engineering narrow the obvious differences between man and neighboring species and between man and centrally operating machines. The crisis will be peculiarly sharp if we create or discover forms of life superior to man in intellect or instinctual predispositions. Our traditions have not been life-centered, but man-centered. We possess various paranoidlike traditions of being "chosen." Clearly a difficult task of modifying these egocentric perspectives lies ahead.

The third task is historical and scientific. It is historical in the sense that by mobilizing knowledge about the past we are enabled to recognize the appearance of new patterns and the diffusion or restriction of the old. It is scientific in the sense that we summarize the past in order to confirm (or disconfirm) propositions about the interplay of predisposition and environment. If we are to serve the aims of historic recognition and of scientific analysis, one of our professional responsibilities is to expedite the development of more perfect institutions specialized to continual self-observation on a global scale. Self-observation requires guidance by a system of theoretical models of the political process in which a continuing graduation is maintained between the most inclusive model and submodels adjusted to more limited contexts in time and space. Continual self-observation renders it necessary at each step through time to reevaluate the appropriateness of the operational indices for the variables and concepts employed at the most recent step. In this way, all the concepts that figure in systematic, descriptive political science can be kept chronically pertinent to the ordering of political events as the future unfolds.

The fourth task is inventive and evaluative. It consists in originating policy alternatives by means of which goal values can be maximized. In estimating the likely occurrence of an event (or event category), it is essential to take into account the historical trends and the scientifically ascertained predispositions in the world arena or any pertinent part thereof.

Graduate Education and Values

In the interest of recognizing and emphasizing meaning and values in our graduate schools and in science generally, it is urged that we effect

[53] Quoted from Harold D. Lasswell, "Political Science of Science." *Scientific Monthly* 84: 34–44; January 1957.

a new infusion in science of a sense of society and human values, in social science a realistic understanding of human behavior, and in the humanities devotion to shaping a more compelling ethics and to designing better patterns for human living. These human needs are the joint responsibility of the scientist, the social scientist, and the scholar in the humanities. While it is natural that graduate education in its early stages of development historically has been concerned with the basic techniques for accurate discovery of fact and for critical study of evidence, this approach should be broadened to provide communicable understanding of the meaning and value of facts.[54]

We need new science, a new science of society and a new humanism. There is no area of scholarship in which we do not need fresh conceptualizations, new and daring hypotheses based on new or reconditioned knowledge. In science, we need a new infusion of a sense of society and human values. In social science, we need a realistic understanding of human behavior, the behavior of individuals, of groups small and large, of great societies, of the relationship between personality and culture. We cannot understand society if we do not know the individual and we can never know the individual if we study him in a vacuum.

Above all, we need a new humanism. The students of the humanities must relax their obsession with syntax, and mysterious forms of criticism and analysis, unless they learn to discover their meaning and communicate it in terms understandable by the society which supports them. It is essential, I believe, that students of the humanities, who should be most aware of human values, should devote themselves to shaping a more compelling ethics and designing better patterns for human living.

But do not misunderstand me, these latter responsibilities are not the exclusive charge of those in the humanities. May I repeat, there are no real quadrant or division boundaries in the world of scholarship. These human needs are as much the responsibility of the scientist, or of the social scientist, as they are of the student of the humanities. Some seem to feel that there is a basic division, that as the scientist seems so adept in providing the means for our destruction, he can do nothing constructive and that the social scientists and those engrossed in the humanities must save us. This I do not believe. Scientists should be just as concerned over human values as their fellows. There should be a unity of purpose among scholars, and the sooner graduate students grasp this unity the better will be the fate of mankind.

We all face a great problem. We are presumed to know how to conserve the spiritual energy of society and each individual. Do we know enough of humane values? What is, as we say, "good," what is "bad"? Do we know when to exercise control, when not to act? In ancient ethics there were stern pronouncements "Thou Shalt Not." Do we today, inflated by our own sense of power, say "Do anything you like"—there is no need for denial or self-control?

[54] Roy F. Nichols, "The Stimulus of Confusion." *Graduate School Record* 12: 3–8; Winter 1959.

What is the significance of all this to you graduate students, to you who, at least for the nonce, dwell in the cloister? It means we need new science and new art, new knowledge about ourselves in the light of better defined values, a dedication to new applications of old principles and new discoveries in the realm of ethics and humane values. We need to make stern resolves that we will reëxamine our standards of scholarly purpose and performance. We must not be satisfied merely with the discovery of facts, we must wrestle mightily with the problem of meaning and of value; we must seek not only knowledge but communicable understanding. And here I wish to place the greatest emphasis that I can muster on what I believe to be the great responsibility of those who are designing the graduate programs of the future.

Graduate work, graduate schools, as we define them and know them, are really in their infancy. None in America has yet reached its centennial. In this period of infancy and youth, graduate education has logically and correctly devoted itself largely to getting started, and consequently it has been absorbed in basic techniques. It is obvious that most of the efforts of its teaching have been in the direction of the accurate discovery of fact and in the critical study of evidence. But in the future this approach should be broadened. Too many graduate students leave the universities of this land with only the capacity to find facts. But society needs more than facts, it needs to know their meaning and their value. And it must have this meaning and this value placed before it in terms which it can understand.[55]

As indicated in the preceding paragraphs, we may overemphasize at times the scientific approach in fields where problems of values are prominent. A psychologist was surprised to hear an associate in psychology say that he did not really care what a person was interested in, just so he was enthusiastic about something—anything! The first man then recalled that as a beginning graduate student he had heard with astonishment a professor's advice on selecting a thesis topic: "Pick something close to your heart." To a first-year graduate student such an unscientific phrasing seemed appalling, although he had discovered that many students wished to belong to some group which championed a theory and desired to have an enthusiastic identification with some "issue" in their chosen field, even though they remembered admonitions from some quarters "to be eclectic and sample all the points of view while remaining detached and unimpressed." It may be that a strong purpose or goal is a form of dedication and a mark of professional maturity.

A specific way to implement the above suggestions is through the use of research teams comprised of a faculty member and those students who share the faculty member's objectives. The research teams seem to give a graduate department a more spirited atmosphere through the stimulation that comes from the exchange of ideas and the competitive spirit generated by such

[55] Quoted from *ibid.*

groups. Another plan is to have a departmental research project which provides a rallying point for faculty and students and a valuable outlet for rivalries and other interpersonal tensions.[56]

Educational research in many areas involves value judgments, even moral value judgments, in connection with such problems as manipulating experimental subjects appropriately and in interpretation of results as a basis for action within the profession:

Examples are work on the "gifted" student, "adequate representation" of lower economic classes in the parentage of the high-school groups, the "appropriateness" of counseling and guidance procedures, the evaluation of colleges and high schools on a comparative or an absolute basis, the construction of effective disciplinary procedures, the introduction of automatic teaching machines, the "obligation" of the states or the federal government to finance or desegregate education, the separation of superior students into different sections and the associated acceleration procedures, and the interpretation of "creativity."[57]

HALLMARKS OF THE SCIENTIST

What are the major characteristics or hallmarks of the scientist and scholar?[58] Although at times some investigators may fail to recognize urgent problems pressing for attention, or may lack essential training for undertaking a particular study, or may hesitate to pay the full price for an unusually time-consuming or complex investigation, most scientists and research workers possess in some form or measure the characteristics described below. (Many additional illustrations of these traits of the scientist or scholar may be found in the chapter on the formulation and development of the problem. We recognize that science as lived by its practitioners, especially in its human and social aspects, bears but little resemblance to the stereotypes of science as described in print.)

The scientist, specifically the natural scientist, is said to be of superior intelligence, with above average ability to think quantitatively, to state problems mathematically, and to reason verbally, and in most instances he possesses a high reading speed and a useful vocabulary. The

[56] Quoted from Malcolm H. Robertson, "The Student's Need for an Issue." *Journal of Psychology* 49: 349–52; April 1960.

[57] Quoted from Michael Scriven, "The Philosophy of Science in Educational Research," in "The Methodology of Educational Research." *Review of Educational Research* 30: 422; December 1960.

[58] Carter V. Good, "The Hallmarks of Scholarship and Research," *The Good Education of Youth*. Forty-fourth Annual Schoolmen's Week Proceedings. Edited by Frederick C. Gruber. Philadelphia: University of Pennsylvania Press, 1957. p. 101–110.

scientist has originality, imaginativeness, and analytic ability, plus above average manual dexterity, spatial visualization, and mechanical aptitude.[59]

Open-Mindedness and Problem Awareness

In discussing the importance of open-mindedness on the part of the scientist and scholar, Whitehead has expressed himself forcefully on what he terms "the fallacy of dogmatic finality":

> The Universe is vast. Nothing is more curious than the self-satisfied dogmatism with which mankind at each period of its history cherishes the delusion of the finality of its existing modes of knowledge. Sceptics and believers are all alike. At this moment scientists and sceptics are the leading dogmatists. Advance in detail is admitted; fundamental novelty is barred. This dogmatic common sense is the death of philosophic adventure. The Universe is vast.
>
> I was in Cambridge in the 1880's, first as an undergraduate, later as one of the staff. It was from two hundred to two hundred and fifty years since mathematics had had its fresh impetus from men like Descartes and Sir Isaac Newton; there were certain borderlands where affairs in that science were considered indefinable, but in the main, mathematical physics looked sound and solid. . . . By the turn of the century, nothing, absolutely nothing was left that had not been challenged, if not shaken; not a single major concept. This I consider to have been one of the supreme facts of my experience.[60]

The alert scholar or scientist has a sensitivity to problems, or a problem awareness, although at times even able scientists and inventors overlook problems and solutions close at hand. All too frequently the beginner in research suffers from the handicap of "problem blindness." In investigating his problem, the scientist may see fit to duplicate an experiment, may extend his study in time or scope, or may follow an "offshoot" of an investigation in progress that "buds out."

Appropriate Specialization

In modern times sound scholarship requires considerable specialization, although a caution against overspecialization is in order. It was much easier in Helmholtz's day, however, for him to consider all experimental physical science as his field and to attribute much of his success to this breadth of interest and talent: "Possessing some geometrical capacity, and equipped with a knowledge of physics, I had, by good fortune, been thrown among medical men, where I found in physiology a virgin soil of

[59] Paul F. Brandwein and Others, "Creativity and Personality in the Scientist," *Rethinking Science Education.* Fifty-ninth Yearbook of the National Society for the Study of Education, Part 1. Chicago: University of Chicago Press, 1960. p. 63–81.

[60] Quoted from *Dialogues of Alfred North Whitehead.* As Recorded by Lucien Price. New York: New American Library of World Literature, 1954. p. 12, 175.

great fertility; while, on the other hand, I was led by the considerations of the vital processes to questions and points of view which are usually foreign to pure mathematicians and physicists."[61]

It should be pointed out, however, that we can lose freedom in research through excessive and unwise specialization, which can eventually leave us no alternatives to choose among:

At any moment any man should be better able to cope with the problems he is currently working on than with others. However, the problems in a field can be made to last forever, but the real need for and value of research in a narrow field may dry up and vanish. Or, a man may be a fine pioneer in a field but may not be suited to do the refined and mathematically difficult work which becomes necessary as time passes. Wisdom and good sense may dictate that he stop what he is doing and turn to something else. But he is scarcely free if he has lost the ability to do so.

A man can lose the freedom to change his work by allowing himself to become intellectually incompetent to deal effectively with anything outside of his current narrow field of specialization, or he can lose this freedom of choice by becoming so emotionally involved in his field that he cannot bear to leave it. He can also lose any real freedom of choice by convincing himself that he has some commercial and social stake in a field, a stake he cannot afford to lose; he can convince himself that he is valuable only because of his expert knowledge, or is looked up to only because of it.

Still, just as we must have responsibility and apparatus, so too we must have some degree of specialization, even if this does cut into our freedom.[62]

Relationships with associates are important in developing a field of teaching or research. In moving from the University of Michigan to the University of Chicago in 1894, John Dewey was free to pursue his work in philosophy and also in pedagogy. There was not the same opportunity in pedagogy at Michigan, since B. A. Hinsdale held the chair in the Science and Art of Teaching. At Michigan Dewey could not have offered courses in pedagogy without Hinsdale's consent or, failing that, without trespassing upon Hinsdale's academic area, and the two men did not agree on some subjects. At Chicago Dewey had a free hand to develop the field of education.[63]

Acquaintance with Related Research

In all scientific endeavor, research workers have recognized their interdependence in the identification and solution of problems. In spite of

[61] Howard Gruber and Valmai Gruber, "Hermann von Helmholtz: Nineteenth-Century Polymorph." *Scientific Monthly* 83: 92–99; August 1956.

[62] Quoted from J. R. Pierce, "Freedom in Research." *Science* 130: 540–42; September 4, 1959. Reprinted from *Science* by permission.

[63] Robert L. McCaul, "Dewey's Chicago." *School Review* 67: 258–80; Summer 1959.

difficulties in securing the works of other scholars, even such early investigators as Roger Bacon and Leonardo da Vinci reveal an extensive knowledge of the writings of other scholars in their special fields of interest. On the other hand, it must be admitted that certain able scientists and scholars have considered it undesirable or even unwise to study closely the related literature dealing with the particular problem under study, fearing that these earlier studies would condition the investigator's mind to see the problem in the same way and thus overlook a new or more promising approach. It would seem essential and reasonable to read critically in the related literature as a stimulus to thinking.

Intellectual Curiosity and Drive

The pages of the history of science and scholarship are filled with the names of workers led or driven to their discoveries by consuming intellectual curiosity or by some compelling drive. Historians especially have been prodigious workers with remarkable powers of concentration. Pavlov's parting advice to young investigators was to become familiar with the groundwork of the science, to become accustomed to simple scientific tools, to penetrate beneath the surface of things, to remain modest, and to develop a compelling intellectual curiosity: "And lastly, science must be your passion. Remember that science claims a man's whole life. Had he two lives they would not suffice. Science demands an undivided allegiance from its followers. In your work and in your research there must always be passion."[64]

Willingness to Pay the Price

Research workers frequently encounter certain costs and hazards (financial, physical, or otherwise). Wallin tells of the early difficulties of clinical psychologists in securing recognition and prestige, as compared with the M.D. In one of his early clinical positions he did all the individual and group testing, scored the papers, made the records, compiled the results, did the transcribing (as much as could be done), and the clerical work (filing, indexing, typing case reports, letters, write-ups of results, articles, and answering phone calls). He did not even have the use of a typewriter but had to purchase his own machine, on which he did all of the official typing. He paid for his own stationery and stamps. Wallin encountered serious obstacles in the early days of his clinical work, an experience that he shared with many other psychologists, in securing recognition as a professional staff member, in studying psychological phenomena of certain patients, in freedom of movement on the grounds of

[64] Ivan Pavlov, *Scientific Monthly* 81: 129; September 1955.

the institution, in association with medical members of the staff, and in freedom of publication and attendance at professional meetings.[65]

Creativity and Ingenuity

As to technique and equipment, the most important instrument or element in research is the mind of man. Although adequate methods, techniques, equipment, and working conditions are important in many types of research, ornate laboratory equipment and complex measuring and recording instruments will not of themselves guarantee soundness of thinking or valid evidence. Great discoveries have been made in unexpected places and in improvised laboratories by equally great men. A century ago the French scientist Bernard spoke of "giants and pygmies" in research.

In the experimental sciences, great men are never the promoters of absolute and immutable truths. . . . Great men may be compared to torches shining at long intervals, to guide the advance of science. They light up their time, either by discovering unexpected and fertile phenomena which open up new paths and reveal unknown horizons, or by generalizing acquired scientific facts and disclosing truths which their predecessors had not perceived. . . . Great men have been compared to giants upon whose shoulders pygmies have climbed, who nevertheless see further than they. This simply means that science makes progress subsequent to the appearance of great men, and precisely because of their influence. The result is that their successors know many more scientific facts than the great men themselves had in their day. But a great man is, none the less, still a great man, that is to say, a giant.[66]

Three kinds of creativity have been identified:[67]

1. When creation is clearly an expression of the inner states of the creator; for example, composers, expressionist painters, sculptors, and creative writers
2. When the creator acts largely to meet externally defined needs and goals and produces a novel and appropriate product, but adds little of himself to the result; for example, experimental physicists, engineers, inventors, and research scientists
3. When creativity cuts across the other two types, in that the product is both an expression of the creator and at the same time a meeting of the

[65] J. E. Wallace Wallin, *The Odyssey of a Psychologist*: Pioneering Experiences in Special Education, Clinical Psychology, and Mental Hygiene with a Comprehensive Bibliography of the Author's Publications. Wilmington, Del.: The Author, 1955. p. 43–51.

[66] Quoted from Claude Bernard, *L'introduction à l'étude de la médecine expérimentale* (*Introduction to the Study of Experimental Medicine*). Paris: J. B. Bailliére et Fils, 1865. 400 p.

[67] "Creativity." *Carnegie Corporation of New York Quarterly* 9: 1–7; July 1961.

demands of some external problem; for example, architects, certain kinds of writers, representational painters, and musical performers.

Scientists commonly find beauty and esthetic joy in the creativity of their discoveries, as does the poet, novelist, or composer. The history of science provides many examples of this esthetic joy in scientific discovery.

Bolyai's great yell of triumph when he saw he could construct a self-consistent, non-Euclidean geometry; Rutherford's revelation to his colleagues that he knew what the atom was like; Darwin's slow, patient, timorous certainty that at last he had got there—all these are voices of esthetic ecstasy.[68]

Earlier in this chapter, we pointed out that a stereotype has developed over the years regarding what constitutes serious research, over-emphasizing the formal aspects of research and too often overlooking the importance of the individual's creativeness. At least two factors have contributed to this confusion:

First, the formal picture has developed on the basis of what the finished product looks like and not on the basis of how it is achieved. A scientific contribution, after it is finished, tends (as it should) to look neat, logical, finished. There has been an unfortunate confusion between this finished product and the art of manufacturing the product. Secondly, if one attempts to describe something complex, one is frequently seduced into describing those aspects of it which are easily visible and easily verbalized. It is easy to measure and talk about design, statistics, scholarship, and the like. It is difficult to talk meaningfully about origination, choice, and development of ideas. We know how to teach people to do an analysis of variance, but we are much less expert at teaching people how to think creatively. It is easy to be misled into thinking that the easily measurable, verbalizable, and teachable aspects of research are the most important ones.

The implication of what has been said thus far seems clear. Education for research must do more than develop competence in designing, executing, and interpreting experimental or other studies. Development of such competence is important, but much more important is the development of the individual's creativeness—his ability to discover new relations, to reformulate or systematize known facts, to devise new techniques and approaches to problems.[69]

In identifying and evaluating creativity, we find in the history of science that the truly creative person or "dreamer" frequently has been labeled as a "crackpot" during his time, and a generation later as a genius:

If I were to conclude that crackpot ideas are to be encouraged, I should probably be told that psychology has already had more than its share of them.

[68] Quoted from Charles P. Snow, "The Moral Un-Neutrality of Science." *Science* 133: 256–59; January 27, 1961. Reprinted from *Science* by permission.

[69] Quoted from Donald W. Taylor and Others, "Education for Research in Psychology." *American Psychologist* 14: 167–79; April 1959.

If it has, they have been entertained by the wrong people. Reacting against the excesses of psychological quackery, psychologists have developed an enormous concern for scientific respectability. They constantly warn their students against questionable facts and unsupported theories. As a result the usual Ph.D. thesis is a model of compulsive cautiousness, advancing only the most timid conclusions thoroughly hedged about with qualifications. But it is just the man capable of displaying such admirable caution who needs a touch of uncontrolled speculation. Possibly a generous exposure to psychological science fiction would help. . . .

One virtue in crackpot ideas is that they breed rapidly and their progeny show extraordinary mutations. Everyone is talking about teaching machines nowadays, but Sidney Pressey can tell you what it was like to have a crackpot idea in that field 40 years ago. His self-testing devices and self-scoring test forms now need no defense, and psychomotor training devices have also achieved a substantial respectability. This did not, however, prepare the way for devices to be used in verbal instruction—that is, in the kinds of teaching which are the principal concern of our schools and colleges. Even five short years ago that kind of instruction by machine was still in the crackpot category. . . .[70]

Even men of talent and creativity need encouragement, especially in their youth. Walter V. Bingham, the psychologist, approached the end of high school with no thought of entering college, until one day a teacher took him aside and planted the idea that led him to enroll at the University of Kansas the following fall. Bingham might or might not have attended college had his teacher not encouraged him, though it is possible that he would have, for even as a youth he revealed a character already marked by determination and self-confidence.[71]

One summarizing statement characterizes the creative scientist as being distinguished by both objectivity and a passion or zeal to find the truth and to shun error, recognizing that the extremes of passive objectivity and burning zeal are frequently present in scientific work, rather than some middle position.

If we piece together the different characteristics commonly ascribed to a creative scientist by the general public, and by some scientists, too, we produce the portrait of a person apparently suffering from a split personality. On the one hand, we are told that the creative scientist is distinguished by his objectivity. He is unfeeling, unmoved in his work, busy only with passive observation of phenomena. On the other hand, we are told that the creative scientist is a creature of great passion, a passion for proving his own favorite theories, or a passion for insuring, when the outcome of an experiment bears on public policy, that the outcome supports the policy he considers proper.

[70] Quoted from B. F. Skinner, "Pigeons in a Pelican." *American Psychologist* 15: 28–37; January 1960.

[71] Dael Wolfle, "Diversity of Talent." *American Psychologist* 15: 535–45; August 1960.

These opposing characteristics arise in part out of efforts at mutual correction. Each view is something of an exaggeration offered in an effort to correct the misconceptions promulgated by the opposing view. But a resolution of these apparently conflicting accounts does not consist in saying that a more accurate picture must lie somewhere between the two extremes. The extremes are there. Assuming that the scientific attitude, at least as an ideal, is not one of disharmony, a more accurate picture may be found by showing how scientists can fulfill both descriptions without contradiction.

How this may be done was nicely expressed some years ago by the philosopher and psychologist William James. In his essay "The Will To Believe," first published just before the turn of the century, James sees objectivity in science not as something impersonal and passive, but, like partisanship in behalf of a pet hypothesis, as a kind of passion, the passion not to be deceived. The scientific attitude as an ideal then emerges as the possession of two passions, as zeal in obedience to two commands, the command to gain the truth and the command to shun error.

The two commands, as James goes on to point out, are, in general, independent. Rarely is one confronted with the demand: if you do not believe this, then you must believe that. To deny that there is a pot of gold at the end of the rainbow does not commit you to the hypothesis that the pot contains silver. Occasionally, to be sure, belief in one hypothesis rules out the acceptance of another hypothesis. If you believe that the pot contains only gold, you cannot believe it contains silver. The two rules, then, are independent, and which you choose will determine the flavor of your intellectual life. You may, James continues, devote yourself to guessing the truth, paying little attention to avoiding errors. Or you may be so dedicated to avoiding error that you are prepared to let truth fend for itself.

Any attempt to sum up the scientific attitude in a few tidy phrases may justly be regarded with suspicion. After all, science is diverse both in its subject matter and in its approaches to that subject matter. But some summations are better than others, and the characterization of science as embracing simultaneously both rules strikes close to the mark. In the matter of making discoveries, unconcern is not a promising trait. But the desire to gain the truth must be balanced by an equally strong desire not to be played false.[72]

The Popular Image of the Scientist

An executive in industry has commented on the negative image of the scientist among a sampling of high-school pupils. He goes on to refute this false impression by data from approximately half the 2,400 technically trained specialists engaged in research for the du Pont Company. These scientists received their education in 258 colleges and universities in the United States and 34 foreign institutions, 68 per cent with doctoral degrees, with specialization chiefly in chemistry, physics, bacteriology,

[72] Quoted from Joseph Turner, "On Being Fair Though One-Sided." *Science* 134: 585; September 1, 1961. Reprinted from *Science* by permission.

and biochemistry. The data from these specialists refute the negative image of the scientist among high-school pupils, as reported by a well known anthropologist.[73]

1. "A scientist should not marry. No one wants to be such a scientist or to marry him." For the sample, 88 per cent of the scientists are married, with an average of two children per family.

2. "His work may be dangerous. Chemicals may explode. He may be hurt by radiation, or may die." The injury frequency rate for the scientists was lower than the over-all company rate during the same period.

3. "He may not believe in God, or may lose his religion." 75 per cent of the research workers mentioned church in listing their activities.

4. "He is a brain; he is so involved in his work that he doesn't know what is going on in the world. He has no other interests and neglects his body for his mind. . . . He has no social life, no other intellectual interests, no hobbies or relaxations." Among 37 per cent of the scientists there was a range of 64 different civic activities.

5. "His work is uninteresting, dull, monotonous, tedious, time-consuming, and, though he works for years, he may see no results or may fail, and he is likely to receive neither adequate recompense nor recognition. He may live in a cold-water flat; his laboratory may be dingy." Only a few scientists found research dull. One out of four of these scientists decided upon his career before reaching the age of fifteen, and most of these specialists had a strong personal interest in the field of research represented.

6. "If he works by himself, he is alone and has heavy expenses. If he works for a big company, he has to do as he is told, and his discoveries must be turned over to the company and may not be used; he is just a cog in a machine." It is common for the scientist to share through a bonus system in the rewards resulting from his discoveries. Although scientists are different from ordinary people, in terms of creativity, it is this difference that contributes to the understanding of our world.

A partly erroneous image of the scientist among college students resembles in many ways the image held by high-school pupils, especially with respect to the personality of the scientist and the mode of life associated with a career in science. This image may leave the effect of recruiting to science careers a certain type of person and discouraging others. The strong features of the image of the scientist are his high intelligence, driving concern to discover and extend knowledge, service to mankind, sense of satisfaction in achievement, and a fair measure of success. The weaknesses of the image are disturbing: indifference to

[73] Margaret Mead and Rhoda Metraux, "Image of the Scientist among High-School Students: A Pilot Study." *Science* 126: 348–90; August 30, 1957.

Samuel Lenher, *The Scientist as a Person.* Tenth Annual Management Conference, Graduate School of Business and Public Administration, Cornell University, Ithaca, N.Y., April 18, 1958. E. I. du Pont de Nemours and Co., 1958. 15 p.

people and no success in dealing with them, indifference to art and the life of the spirit so vital to the life of the mind, noncomformist and radical attitudes, and only moderate control of impulses.[74]

Summarized in other language, a definite personality pattern, including a wide range of traits, characterizes the creative scientist, as reported by a psychologist.

How do these personality characteristics relate to the creative process in science as I have discussed it? An open attitude toward experience makes possible accumulation of experience with relatively little compartmentalization; independence of perception, cognition, and behavior permit greater than average reordering of this accumulated experience (the behavioral eccentricities so often noted are consistent with this). The strong liking for turning disorder into order carries such individuals through the searching period which their tolerance for ambiguity permits them to enter. The strong egos, as noted, permit regression to prelogical forms of thought without serious fear of failure to get back to logical ones. Preoccupation with things and ideas rather than with people is obviously characteristic of natural scientists, and even of some social scientists. This characteristic is not directly related to creativity, I think, but rather to the content of it.

I need not add that such statements as these are generalizations and that any individual case may be an exception. We may go farther, however, and generalize differences among men who follow different branches of science. That a man chooses to become a scientist and succeeds means that he has the temperament and personality as well as the ability and opportunity to do so. The branch of science he chooses, even the specific problems he chooses and the way he works on them, are intimately related to what he is and to his deepest needs. The more deeply engaged he is, the more profoundly is this true. To understand what he does, one must try to know what his work means to him. The chances are that he does not know or care to know. Indeed, he does not need to know. We do.[75]

Attitudes in Educational Research

The practical approach, informal language (probably unacceptable to many scientists), and human (even sentimental) qualities represented in a description of the research worker's attitudes toward attacking curriculum problems may prove appealing to many beginning graduate students and field workers of limited experience. The concrete suggestions, as abbreviated and summarized below, will help answer two major questions: "What sorts of attitudes do I want to guide me as I do research?" and "What sorts of problems do I want to work on?" The list

[74] David C. Beardslee and Donald D. O'Dowd, "The College-Student Image of the Scientist." *Science* 133: 997–1001; March 31, 1961.

[75] Quoted from Anne Roe, "The Psychology of the Scientist." *Science* 134: 456–59; August 18, 1961.

is presented with full recognition of the possibility that arch critics of education may object to both the language and the sentiment.[76]

1. In doing research, I do not have to act like somebody who isn't "me"; I can do research so that what I do is more and more clearly mine.

2. Research is an operation by which I am trying to become a better self-teacher so that my experience can say more things to me, give me more to think about and feel.

3. I can do research just for myself if I want to. However, I can have more fun if, on some things at least, I can share my experiences with others.

4. A man doesn't have to publish to do research; he can communicate the shape of his experience in a lot of ways, and often the best way is right on the job with those with whom he associates daily.

5. There is very little to differentiate a good teacher from a researcher since both are avid inquirers.

6. It is no disgrace not to know a particular skill; I need not apologize for that. What would embarrass me in my own eyes would be to forget that my authority has to come from my own handling of myself.

7. A good place to think about doing research is in the middle of some activity where I am trying to do something that is important to me. My research is then my attempt to improve my actions in getting the values I want out of my experience.

8. My research will require a clarification of what I want just as much as it will require a clarification of how to get what I want in the most effective ways.

9. Teaching is at the very heart of life's most cogent situations. Human behavior is then as complex as it ever gets. Research depends on a willingness to accept the complexity and work within it.

10. The curriculum can be thought of in a number of different ways.

11. Proof is not a sledge hammer which can drive things into other people's heads. Proof is an "illustration," a "suggestion," an "offering"—not a bludgeon.

12. When I hit the "intangibles," as I most certainly will, I will consider them as useful constructions of mine which I can make more useful by (a) specifying what is meant in concrete situations and (b) showing how the constructions fit into a larger system of constructions. To run from engagement with the intangibles is to run from the problem of organizing one's experience.

13. In curriculum building, I cannot stop with a naming of "activities" I feel are valuable for children to do; I have to know what the children are actually experiencing while they are acting.

14. The critical unit is the experience of an experiencer. This means I am not down to basic data until I know what's going on in an individual child's experiencing.

[76] Quoted from Ross L. Mooney, "The Researcher Himself," *Research for Curriculum Improvement*. 1957 Yearbook. Washington: Association for Supervision and Curriculum Development, a Department of the National Education Association, 1957. p. 179–81.

15. Studying behavior is not the same as studying experience. I can watch a child's behavior without relating the action I see to what I think the child is experiencing.

16. To be sensitive to the experiencing of a child, I have to be able to posit myself as if I were in the center of experiencing of the child.

17. I can never be the child, of course, nor can I ever know what the full inclusion of his experience may be, but there is no escape for me—my primary data are my "as if" projections.

18. These projections are, of course, within my experience. I do not get outside my experience. Projections are a function of myself.

19. The more "as if" selves I can differentiate in myself, the richer my humanity and the greater the resources for projecting reliable data in the next "as if" case.

20. What is important in "objectifying" is the capacity to hold a form in the center of attention while differentiating it from as many other forms as possible. This makes a form stand out for easy and reliable grasping.

21. Objectivity can be fostered by the way I give my attention to the field in which the form is taken to appear, i.e., by looking at the whole with the intention of seeing the whole while, at the same time, noting as many differentiations as possible within the whole. When this happens, I have a maximum of relations by which to structure forms in the field. My judgments are then more reliable.

22. Scientists who deal with inanimate material use the same basic methods I do; it is only that they can check their "as if" position in their on-going experience with greater ease than I. My compensation is that I am already nearer what I value in life at the point where I get my data. The physical scientist has a long way to go to make wisdom out of his knowledge.

23. I will know I'm off the track if, at any time, my getting of data seems to require that I treat others in ways I would not treat myself.

24. I will not be a failure in research as long as I'm learning better how to make good use of me. I am my own final judge in this matter.

25. When I seek criticism of what I'm doing in research, I'm asking my critics to tell me how they organize their experience in situations similar to those I present. This is a good sharp way of challenging a sharing right at the point where communication can be most poignant.

FREEDOM AND RESPONSIBILITY FOR RESEARCH

Freedom in Science

Freedom is important in research to the extent that it contributes to the wise choice of problems and to the enthusiastic and successful pursuit of solutions to problems. Like food, we need enough freedom, but should not be guilty of gluttony. The research worker must be free to work on a problem that challenges him, yet is within his capabilities, rather than a problem that is dull or beyond the worker's abilities. The investigator must be free to equip himself adequately with any necessary physical apparatus, and also to equip himself intellectually, through study or through contact with other specialists.

Freedom in research does not necessarily require that a man work on his own ideas. First-rate scientists have traveled great distances to work under a particular person or with a group of specialists, and have gladly pursued problems suggested by the person or pursued by the group. The idea may come from a colleague near or far, or from an older or wiser associate. It may be that even good research workers suffer more frequently from lack of help than from lack of freedom. They need help in choosing problems wisely, in overcoming difficulties, in judging the merit of their work, in getting rid of old projects that are finished, and in starting new investigations that will prove important and attractive. Investigators also need encouragement and recognition for work well done.[77]

It should be pointed out that freedom in research is curtailed by certain forms of behavior, particularly by "snobbishness":

A college president once described to me a sort of pecking order of the sciences. According to him, the mathematicians look down on the physicists, the physicists on the chemists, the chemists on the biologists, and the biologists on the psychologists.

One sure and utterly frivolous and destructive way for a man to lose his freedom is for him to feel overwhelmingly impelled to choose his work, not on the basis of its suitability to his talents, not on the basis of its interest to him, not on the basis of its urgency or importance, but rather on the basis of its status in the eyes of some person, group, society, journal, or what not.[78]

The history of science includes many instances of resistance by scientists themselves to scientific discovery, with the sources of resistance varied in character: substantive concepts and theories currently prevailing, methodological conceptions currently entertained, religious ideas of scientists themselves, relative professional standing of the discoverer, pattern of specialization prevailing in science, attitudes of professional organizations and societies, rivalries of "schools" of theory or research, and relative seniority of the investigator.[79]

All over the world today people are comparing the institutions designed to assure the freedom of science with those agencies that maintain science under some form of dictatorship. It is significant, however, that at the time of the apparent triumph of Russian technology, the prestige of communism among scientists throughout the world seemed lower than in the days when Soviet science was still being discussed in largely

[77] J. R. Pierce, "Freedom in Research." *Science* 130: 540–42; September 4, 1959.
[78] Quoted from *ibid.* Reprinted from *Science* by permission.
[79] Bernard Barber, "Resistance by Scientists to Scientific Discovery." *Science* 134: 596–602; September 1, 1961.

theoretical terms. It is true that varying national patterns for support of science result from basic constitutional differences.

Among free nations we will doubtless continue to manage our affairs and support our science in different ways. In the United States, it seems to me, our best hope is for a science which will grow, not as a guild under the patronage of a traditional sovereignity, but as a most important element in a highly diversified and free system. In this system the scientist gets his influence not from a complete detachment from politics but from sharing in the political obligations of society. And in this system, too, politics may get its strength not by meddling with the processes of research, and not by strait-jacketing science in an ideology, but by freeing science to question and improve all aspects of policy, all forms of social organization.

The economic and political system that Marx attacked is almost as obsolete as the one he envisaged. We have created something new in the United States through the influence that science has had on our society, and we are only beginning dimly to understand it. But we need to learn how to use it better if we are to continue to promote the general welfare as well as provide for the common defense. And we need to learn rapidly—to learn political wisdom and administrative competence as well as scientific ability—or there will not be any posterity to inherit the blessings of the liberty that we find so enjoyable.[80]

Freedom in Social Science

Certain inhibiting conditions restrict research in the various social fields. Chapin points out that application of social-science knowledge to the solution of problems of human relations is hampered by existing habits of thought and action, with at least eight social obstacles to the acceptance of current knowledge or evidence in the social-science field:[81]

1. The subject matter of social science is emotion-arousing.
2. The normative set and value-judgment approach tend to attach "praise" and "blame" to natural situations in human relationships.
3. The scientific social observer is himself a part of the social process he tries to observe.
4. The confidential and privileged character of much sociological information makes scientific or objective formulation of knowledge a difficult process.
5. "Conspiracies of silence" involve conventions that often block social research or implementation of evidence.
6. There may be unpleasant consequences to minority groups when social-science knowledge is applied.

[80] Quoted from Don K. Price, "Organization of Science Here and Abroad." *Science* 129: 759–65; March 20, 1959. Reprinted from *Science* by permission.

[81] Francis S. Chapin, *Experimental Designs in Sociological Research*. Revised Edition. New York: Harper & Brothers, 1955. p. 250–66.

7. Much of the subject matter of social science consists of verbal behavior, which frequently is intangible and trite.

8. Concentrated and continuous mental effort is required to know that such concepts as intangibility, relativity, and probability are basic to social understanding.

On the other hand, college social scientists have reported relatively good conditions by way of freedom of inquiry and teaching:

Consider the following statistics: 85 percent of the social scientists interviewed denied that they had toned down anything they had written in recent years in order to avoid controversy; 85 percent denied that they were now more careful about assigning reference materials to students; 71 percent said they never went out of their way to make it clear that they had no extreme political opinions; 78 percent denied that they felt their academic freedom had been threatened in any way during the preceding few years.

One may argue that these data simply demonstrate how orthodox and noncontroversial most college professors are, and there is evidence that this is in fact a partial explanation, especially so far as the denominational colleges are concerned. The fact remains, however, that social scientists generally, and especially those in secular colleges (where most social scientists are), are far more "liberal" than the general public in their views on political issues. No doubt many professors were unmoved by the investigations of subversion, either because they sympathized with them or because they could not imagine themselves being affected by them; other professors were threatened and drew back in the face of threat; others, including what would appear to be a substantial majority of the more distinguished members of the profession, perceived the threat clearly enough and were disturbed by it but did not yield to it. It would be regrettable indeed if this final fact were lost in the concentration which this book gives to its documentation of weakness and retreat on the campus.[82]

External Factors Inhibiting Freedom

Certain conditions external to the investigator himself may inhibit freedom for research:[83]

1. Tradition in the school or community may prove a powerful retarding influence.

2. Lack of time, energy, and resources has been a block for most teachers and administrators.

---

[82] Quoted from review by Angus Campbell, Science 129: 34–35; January 2, 1959, of Paul Lazarsfeld and Wagner Thielens, Jr., The Academic Mind: Social Scientists in a Time of Crisis. Glencoe, Illinois: Free Press, 1958. xiii + 460 p. Reprinted from Science by permission.

[83] Ronald C. Doll, "Freedom for Research," Research for Curriculum Improvement. 1957 Yearbook. Washington: Association for Supervision and Curriculum Development, a Department of the National Education Association, 1957. p. 249–68.

3. A climate of cooperative group work is lacking in many schools.
4. Research activity has failed significantly in one or more instances, and it has been deemed unworthy of further expenditure of time and money.
5. A particular research project is believed to have endangered the educational welfare of children.
6. Research looks so much like John Dewey's "experimentalism" that it is out of step with the prevailing educational philosophy.
7. Research procedures have been found difficult—even incomprehensible.
8. Research is considered to be the business of a few administrators.
9. Research has threatened the strongly held but vaguely supported opinions of certain supersensitive and influential teachers and administrators.

Internal Factors Inhibiting Freedom

Internal factors, such as feelings of fear, threat, and uncertainty, may inhibit freedom for research on the part of school people and others:

1. They are afraid to experiment with public money and with other people's children.
2. They fear starting research activity in the wrong situation or in the wrong way.
3. They feel threatened when they are urged to do research concerning matters about which they are already insecure.
4. They believe they lack the necessary understanding and skill to make the end result satisfactory in their own and other people's eyes.
5. They are wanting in the adventuresome spirit that would impel them to take calculated risks in solving their problems.

Ways to Promote Freedom in Research

Specific ways in which school personnel can overcome obstacles to freedom in research, especially in the curriculum field, have been simply phrased, in terms of the language, principles, and procedures of action research:[84]

1. Building a feeling among potential researchers that it is all right to have problems.
2. Design researches that will satisfy the needs people feel.
3. Start gently, perhaps on a modified-voluntary basis.
4. Talk often about the importance of getting evidence.
5. Help people find security in groups, and help them work together successfully as group members.
6. Provide safety valves through which to "blow off steam" when things do not go well.

[84] Ronald C. Doll, *op. cit.*

7. Allow for the lone researcher as well as for the researcher who wishes to work with only one or two other persons.
8. Use every legitimate means to build understanding of the research process.
9. Involve in research activities those teachers, parents, and other persons who are high in the power structure of school and community.
10. Provide all the time, resources, and help you can.
11. Attend to the climate of the school as a whole, as a valuable stimulus to research.
12. Be realistic about the limits, internal and external.
13. Resolve to press against the limits that actually exist.
14. Capitalize on growing expertness by urging its use in additional research.

Research and University or College Teaching

The university staff member is generally expected to engage in research and to communicate the results to others, since it has been commonly accepted that this is a basic duty of the university to society. The faculty adviser who supervises the theses and dissertations of graduate candidates must be alive to the current problems of research in his field of specialization. Certainly the graduate faculty member must progress beyond his own dissertation stage in the intellectual adventure of scholarship. How often we hear the statement from professors many years out of the graduate school: "Now in my dissertation, I . . ." Participation in research on the part of the professor should make for an intellectually alert person and a better teacher.[85]

The obligation of the well-equipped professor to conduct the needed basic research is all the more apparent when we realize that most master's theses or projects are minor studies with local applications, while the doctor's dissertation is frequently a "one-shot" investigation to meet a degree requirement. Therefore, much of the leadership and coordination for research in a particular area remains for the university specialist, as in science education, even though he is busy with teaching and advisory duties.[86]

To the view that stresses the primacy of teaching, we must add, I think, that a professor is a good teacher only if he stimulates his students to engage lovingly, vigorously, and seriously in the process of learning.

Yet no professor can stimulate his students in this way if he himself

[85] Everett Walters, "On the Results of Research." *Graduate School Record* 8: 1, 3; March 1955.
[86] Fletcher G. Watson and William W. Cooley, "Needed Research in Science Education," *Rethinking Science Education*. Fifty-ninth Yearbook of the National Society for the Study of Education, Part 1. Chicago: University Press, 1960. p. 297–312.

does not engage lovingly, vigorously, and seriously in the process of learning. That is, he cannot be a good teacher if he is not also an eager researcher whom his students can respect for his scholarly or scientific achievements.

If the viewpoint on the importance of teaching is incomplete, the other viewpoint—that service to students is an incidental function of the college—is both unrealistic and terrifying. It is unrealistic because, first, it does not recognize that, in many scientific fields, the universities have already begun to play second fiddle to government and industry in matters of vigorous and functioning research. The universities no longer have a corner, or even a principal share, in scientific research. Their function, more and more every year, is to train researchers for government and industry. That is, they are being forced, willy-nilly, to become teaching agencies.

In the humanities and in certain nonutilitarian branches of certain sciences, the universities may continue to be the nation's primary intellectual centers. But the fact remains that unless professors can impart their intellectual spirit to others and stimulate appreciation of it in steadily growing numbers of citizens, the spirit must eventually perish.

Certainly a major responsibility of the university, quite as important as keeping "a life of mind vigorous and functioning" within its own walls, is to communicate—to teach, to pass on to the nation at large the respect for pure learning that comes to the typical citizen only after he himself has been a student and a learner.[87]

Although the place of research in the small or independent liberal-arts college is not so clearly defined as in the university, the contribution of research to education seems so clear that we wonder why research is opposed or played down in some liberal-arts colleges. While there probably are competent scientists engaged in research who are not good teachers, the competence of effective teachers certainly is increased by sound scholarship. Therefore, there is no basis for the attitude of some instructors in small colleges that research and teaching are incompatible. It is true that the overly conscientious teacher or the overworked teacher may find no time for the activities of research and scholarship. It may be that some instructors play down the importance of research and scholarship because encouragement of such activities by the college causes sharper competition for positions and promotions.[88]

Research and Education of Graduate Students

Reference has been made to the importance of research on the part of the staff member in the university and even in the small college, with particular emphasis placed on the scholarly pursuits of the university

[87] Quoted from George Williams, "Teaching and Research in the University." *NEA Journal* 48: 13–14; May 1959.

[88] Joseph Turner, "Small Colleges and Small Minds." *Science* 131: 71; January 8, 1960.

professor who supervises the work of graduate students. Research and its encouragement constitute the domain and commitment of every graduate school that is fulfilling its purpose.[89] While we have understandably depended in the past on European research in certain fields, American graduate schools must depend much more upon themselves, at present and in the future. The modern graduate school serves at least two major purposes or provides two types of opportunity for the student: extending his range of knowledge and understanding in a field of special interest, and engaging in creative research. Expressed in another way, the satisfactions in graduate education may be identified in the form of its possible and desirable accomplishments as follows:

The years in the graduate school constitute the educational period when self-responsibility asserts itself, the processes of inquiry and research in particular are learned, a subject-matter area is staked out and explored, ability to express thoughts and to write creatively is acquired, an intellectual career is anticipated, and professional responsibilities and behavior are understood.[90]

Graduate education ought eventually to take the student back to the simple; that is, graduate education, whatever else it accomplishes, should lead to knowledge of the fundamental processes and concepts which give root to a discipline or a profession. And since root concepts and processes adhering to a discipline or a profession must be subjected to modification and at times revision, the graduate school needs to keep open the avenue of basic research. Stagnant theory leads not to knowledge but to dogma. Research is perhaps the only assurance we have that a discipline or a profession will not decay into meaningless scraps of dogmatic utterances.[91]

With respect to the interrelationships between scientific progress, the universities, graduate education, and the federal government, the President's Science Advisory Committee has reached the following specific conclusions:[92]

1. Excellence deserves strong support.
2. Additional centers of excellence are urgently needed.
3. Graduate education needs expansion.
4. It is important to attract a larger number of talented students to science as a career.
5. Graduate education in science needs constant modernization.

[89] Theodore C. Blegen, "Graduate Education and Research: Problems and Prospects." *Graduate School Record* 11: 3–7; December 1957.

[90] Quoted from N. P. Hudson, "On Satisfactions in Graduate Education." *Graduate School Record* 9: 1, 3; December 1955.

[91] Quoted from Bernard Mehl, "Graduate Education and the Teaching Profession." *Graduate School Record* 9: 3–4; July 1956.

[92] President's Science Advisory Committee, *Scientific Progress, the Universities, and the Federal Government.* Washington: Government Printing Office, 1960. x + 33 p.

6. The financing of graduate education needs continued and flexible reinforcement.

7. The need for improved facilities is urgent.

8. New fields of research and education need particular encouragement.

9. Separate research installations should be avoided whenever possible.

10. New research laboratories for special fields should be attached to universities whenever it is practicable, and universities should make full educational use of such facilities.

11. Scientists outside universities can be fruitfully connected to graduate education.

12. Postdoctoral studies should be encouraged and their legitimate costs recognized.

13. University faculties must be strengthened.

14. Universities must attend to these matters and especially to their relations with the government.

15. The government must strengthen its ability to make policy in this area.

16. Increased government activity is not a good ground for lessened efforts by others.

Research by Workers in Elementary or Secondary Schools

After traveling in the United States, Canada, England, Scotland, and France, inquiring into the organization and structure of educational research (especially in the United States), an Australian investigator has reported favorably, even highly optimistically, on the possibilities for research by workers in elementary and secondary schools. In determining whether teachers and other staff members in the public schools could reasonably undertake research, he asked questions as to whether the staff had the ability, time, interest, and power to participate in educational investigation. In each instance he answered in the affirmative, with the conviction that teachers in every country have the opportunity and the capacity to undertake some research, usually carried out in day-to-day work of the school and concerned directly with the problems of the particular school.[93]

A more critical survey concludes that many useful activities conducted under the name of educational research are incorrectly labeled research in the accepted meaning of the term, particularly in the research offices of large city school systems, state departments of education, and state education associations. It has been suggested that progress may be made toward meeting the need for basic research, if persons trained and

[93] W. C. Radford, "The Function of the School, Department of Education, University, National Centre and Independent Body in Educational Research," *Report of the First International Conference on Educational Research*. Educational Studies and Documents, No. 20. Paris: UNESCO, 1956. p. 36–40.

experienced in investigation, such as the members of the American Educational Research Association, will increase their efforts to help teachers and administrators in the public schools realize the essential nature of research and its contribution to school practice and to education in general.[94]

SCIENTIFIC PROGRESS AND SOCIAL RESPONSIBILITY

Research in the physical sciences developed much earlier than in the social fields because of certain favorable factors and conditions: greater freedom of inquiry, seemingly more urgent problems, financial support, objectivity of problem and procedure, invention of instruments for recording and measuring, standardization of terminology, collection of specimens such as in museums, emphasis on scientific training, and publication of scientific materials.

A number of factors, however, have favored educational research in the United States: a democratic philosophy, decentralized schools, financial support, research departments and bureaus, teacher training and graduate work, and publication facilities.

Science and Moral-Social Responsibility

In general, the accomplishments of science in our time are almost miraculous, with the rate of progress still accelerating. Research can continue to expand as long as society is friendly toward this form of progress. There is evidence of stress and strain, however, between the great accomplishments of the physical sciences and the much slower development of the social sciences (which provide the controls for human behavior). At times an impossible course of action has been suggested, to the effect that physical research should take a holiday until social science catches up, since certain discoveries (as in the domain of atomic energy) involve the potential for great harm to, or even destruction of, society when wrongly applied. Scholars and scientists have a grave social obligation to see that scientific and technological (and social) discoveries are used for the benefit of society and that appropriate controls of human behavior are developed, with the aid of knowledge in social science, psychology, education, and religion.

Specific examples of advances in science that also generate new hazards of unprecented magnitude include certain dangers to life from widely disseminated radiation, the burden of man-made chemicals, fumes, and smogs of unknown biological effect which we now absorb, large-

[94] David G. Ryans, "Are Educational Research Offices Conducting Research?" *Journal of Educational Research* 51: 173–83; November 1957.

scale deterioration of our natural resources, and the potential of totally destructive war.

The determination that scientific knowledge is to be used for human good or for purposes of destruction is in the control of social agencies. For such decisions, these agencies and ultimately the people themselves must be aware of the facts and the probable consequences of action. Here scientists can play a decisive role: they can bring the facts and their estimates of the results of proposed actions before the people.[95]

Counts asks whether the nations can learn to "live together on this vastly shrunken planet before they all go down in final catastrophe,"[96] and quotes a 1937 gloomy diagnosis of the condition of Western man: "Whenever his practical inventiveness ran ahead of his moral conscious-ness and social organization, then man has equally faced destruction. Perhaps today we are in this stage."[97]

Benjamin Franklin long ago recognized the importance of social and moral responsibility in a 1780 letter to Joseph Priestley of England, who was a famous clergyman, chemist, and physicist:

We may perhaps learn to deprive large Masses of their Gravity, and give them absolute Levity, for the sake of easy Transport. Agriculture may diminish its Labour and double its Produce; all Diseases may by sure means be pre-vented or cured, not excepting even that of Old Age, and our Lives lengthened at pleasure even beyond the antediluvian Standard. O that moral Science were in as fair a way of Improvement, that men would cease to be *wolves* to one another and that human Beings would at length learn what they now im-properly call Humanity!

A graduate student, after considering this same problem in class and in study, expressed her conclusion in verse:

Sonnet

THE NATIONS—ANNO DOMINI, 1961

Our intellectual pride has brought us grief,
Has been a cancer on our days; the power
We blindly trusted in was not Belief
But Bombs to detonate the darkening hour.

[95] Quoted from Ward Pigman and Others, "Association Affairs: Preliminary Report of AAAS Interim Committee on the Social Aspects of Science." *Scientific Monthly* 84: 146–51; March 1957.

[96] George S. Counts, "The Closing of the Great Cycle." *Phi Delta Kappan* 42: 329; April 1961.

[97] Stanley Casson, *Progress and Catastrophe*. New York: Harper & Brothers, 1937. 264 p.

The finite mind of man has dared to probe
The atom; has outstripped his infinite soul.
Without the wise humility of Job,
Man fancies he is master of the Whole.
Eden will come again when Abram's words
To Lot, "I pray thee let there be no strife
Twixt me and thee or those who keep our herds,
For we are brethren," become Man's way of life.
Nor would the nations fear the Geiger count
Had they but learned the Sermon on the Mount.

By Emilie W. Bullock, Cincinnati, Ohio

Scientists and Ethical Neutrality. Scientists occasionally have adopted the doctrine of the ethical neutrality of science, based on invention of comfortable categories of specialization, which would assign responsibility for discovery to the research worker and for implementation to others (for example, the politician):

It consists of the invention of categories—or, if you like, of the division of moral labor. That is, the scientists who want to contract out say, *we* produce the tools. *We* stop there. It is for *you*—the rest of the world, the politicians— to say how the tools are used. The tools may be used for purposes which most of us would regard as bad. If so, we are sorry. But as scientists, that is no concern of ours.

. . . Scientists [have] a direct and personal responsibility. It is not enough to say that scientists have a responsibility as citizens. They have a much greater one than that, and one different in kind. For scientists have a moral imperative to say what they know. It is going to make them unpopular in their own nation- states. It may do worse than make them unpopular. That doesn't matter. Or at least, it does matter to you and me, but it must not count in the face of the risks.

. . . For all these reasons, I believe the world community of scientists has a final responsibility upon it—a greater responsibility than is pressing on any other body of men. I do not pretend to know how they will bear this respon- sibility. These may be famous last words, but I have an inextinguishable hope. For, as I have said, there is no doubt that the scientific activity is both beauti- ful and truthful. I cannot prove it, but I believe that, simply because scientists cannot escape their own knowledge, they also won't be able to avoid showing themselves disposed to good.[98]

Probably any doctrine of the ethical neutrality of science will dimin- ish and disappear when all natural scientists come to agree completely with Wordsworth that ultimately science belongs to all mankind:

[98] Quoted from Charles P. Snow, "The Moral Un-Neutrality of Science." *Science* 133: 256–59; January 27, 1961. Reprinted from *Science* by permission.

> ... For I have learned
> To look on nature, not as in the hour
> Of thoughtless youth; but hearing oftentimes
> The still, sad music of humanity,
> Nor harsh nor grating, though of ample power
> To chasten and subdue. And I have felt
> A presence that disturbs me with the joy
> Of elevated thoughts; a sense sublime,
> Of something far more deeply interfused,
> Whose dwelling is the light of setting suns,
> And the round ocean and the living air,
> And the blue sky, and in the mind of man. ...."

Scientists and Military Technology. Since science supports an ever expanding military technology and, therefore, acquires moral properties, many people wonder to what extent American scientists should assume responsibility for the uses to which the government puts their discoveries and talents. There are three positions relating to the social obligations of the scientists, with the preferred position probably somewhere between too little and too much responsibility for the social consequences of research.[99]

One view of the scientist's responsibility for the social consequences of scientific truths is that this responsibility ends with the scientist's willingness to do work directly or indirectly for the government, including work on weapons. According to this view, being a good scientist no more gives one special privileges in determining national policy than being a good information clerk at an airport entitles one to select destinations for travelers. The area of special competence of scientists lies in the discovery of technical facts; decisions of public policy rest with elected or appointed public officials.

An opposite opinion concerning the obligations of scientists holds that scientists should consider the possible consequences of any piece of research before it is begun, and if the research is judged more a threat to the country, or humanity at large, than a benefit, they should refuse their services. A man cannot delegate to a superior the responsibility for the moral consequences of his acts, the second view claims. To be sure, to predict future applications of new discoveries calls more for the talents of a prophet than for those of a scientist. No one now knows to what uses, or abuses, the fall of parity in physics may some day prove amenable. But somewhere along the line, basic research becomes applied research, and forecasts about the uses of discoveries become something more than anybody's guess.

Between the two opposing positions lies a third position which holds that at least some scientists, although they fear the dangers posed by a further increase in military power, have the duty to work on projects that the govern-

---

[99] Quoted from Joseph Turner, "Between Two Extremes." *Science* 131: 1013; April 8, 1960. Reprinted from *Science* by permission.

ment deems necessary, but that scientists also have the duty to state their opinions on matters lying outside science. If this is the age of specialization, so this argument runs, it is also the age of specialists working together on teams. Public officials should have the final word, but any attempt to understand the full range of consequences—military, political, economic, and moral—of new advances in research, requires the views of the men who understand those advances best.

It is this third position that expresses our own convictions, and that seems to express the convictions of most of the persons in this country who are presently concerned with these problems—although, admittedly, agreement on general principles does not necessarily imply agreement on particular cases. The first position errs because, pushed to its conclusion, it turns the citizen's obligations to the state into despotism; while the second position errs because, if pushed, it turns the moral integrity of the individual into anarchy. The third position seeks the mean between the scientist's assuming too little responsibility for the consequences of his research and his assuming too much responsibility.

Science and National Policy. One view emphasizes that science should cooperate with other disciplines and professions in meeting the great responsibility which rests upon science today in the light of its extraordinary opportunities to participate in the formulation of national policy. The increasingly strong linkage of science and technology with government requires of science a new order of poise, steadiness, and statesmanship, and demands of scientists who serve in advisory capacities a deep understanding of the role and the limitation of the adviser.

The current emphasis on science, if it is not to cause reactions adverse to science, also requires of the scientific community humility and a sense of proportion. It requires of scientists a recognition that science is but one of the great disciplines vital to our society and worthy of first-rate minds—a recognition that science is a partner, sharing and shouldering equally the responsibilities which rest in the great array of professions which provide the intellectual and cultural strength of our society.[100]

Another parallel view of the social responsibility of science points out that science from its beginning has had important effects outside the realm of pure science itself, although scientists have differed as to their own responsibility for such effects. The view that the function of the scientist is to supply knowledge, without concern for the use made of such knowledge, is no longer tenable in our time. The scientist also is a citizen with an obligation to use his skill in the public interest. More specifically: "What is the social responsibilty of science?" This question rephrased is: "What contribution can scientists make to the social and political process of our society?"

[100] Quoted from James R. Killian, Jr., "Science and Public Policy." *Science* 129: 129–36; January 16, 1959. Reprinted from *Science* by permission.

In a democratic society like the United States, of course, each individual scientist must choose for himself just what kind of responsibility he will assume as a result of his membership in the scientific group. It is of the very basic character of our society that social responsibility is largely a matter of moral obligation voluntarily assumed. This holds for all of us, scientists and others alike. Our democratic values permit a great deal of exhortation to responsibility, but only a little compulsion. Now some individual scientists, like some other members of the society, do not feel morally obligated to participate actively in the political process. In such a choice they are subject, to be sure, to the moral judgment of their fellow citizens. This does not mean, however, that democratic moral judgment should, or will, always condemn the socially inactive scientist. For, over quite a wide range of behavior, we do acknowledge that some of our fellows may be called by other compelling interests, by other values, than direct political or social participation. We do grant a great deal, that is, to the man who cares overwhelmingly for his work, particularly when we admire what he is doing. It would certainly be unfair not to grant this privilege to some, at least, of our scientists, since we grant it to other kinds of experts and specialists. We admit that the scientist has no peculiar or exclusive social responsibility.

Furthermore, even when he does wish to participate actively in social affairs other than his scientific ones, the scientist may justifiably claim the democratic privilege of choosing those activities most congenial to him and in which he thinks he can be most effective. Only a few scientists, for example, as a result of the restrictions imposed by their occupational specialization, can make a large contribution to direct political and social action. Yet some have done just this, at least for a little while in times of social crisis. During World War II, scientist-statesmen like James B. Conant and Vannevar Bush took on a great deal of responsibility in the Government's use of science. In such direct political participation, the scientist deals with social problems directly and helps to form social decisions, bringing to the process his expert view of science as a body of substantive theory and his wise familiarity with it as a certain kind of social activity. Such direct political responsibility by scientists, however few can assume it, is of the first importance to society.[101]

There may even be a form of hypocrisy when laymen ask of scientists special things by way of social responsibility, beyond the obligations necessarily required of any human being today, scientist or not:

Here . . . persons who do not follow a certain pursuit have the chance to indulge themselves by expecting special things of persons who do. Laymen can persuade one another that it is a simple matter to be a scientist and, from the vantage point of no personal involvement, expect scientists to be more selfless and lofty of purpose than they themselves are. Scientists and former scientists, it is true, sometimes encourage such expectations by saying that such virtues play an essential role in the scientific enterprise. There is the claim,

[101] Quoted from Bernard Barber, "An Ignorance We Take for Granted." *Teachers College Record* 60: 297–305; March 1959.

for example, that there is something moral in the very grain of science. Scientists rarely fake experiments, and the reason, so the argument runs, is not that they are afraid of being caught in a lie by other scientists who try to repeat their experiments, but that scientists cannot tell lies and still achieve their objective of getting answers to the questions they put to nature.

There is an opportunity, then, to regard scientists as just a bit more saintly than other men, and so to make special demands of them. At the same time, interestingly enough, there is also an opportunity to regard scientists as just slightly greater sinners than other men, and so to make the same demands again. Men who are not scientists expect special atonement by scientists for the role they have played in the creation of many of the ills that now beset us. They demand atonement especially for the creation of that Sword of Damocles that hangs over us all, the atom bomb and the missile to deliver it. And again scientists have encouraged such demands.

But let us not give one another opportunities to indulge in hypocrisy. On the one hand, scientists may practice truthfulness in their work as a welcome necessity, but this does not mean that they embrace truth with equal fervor when it comes to seeking funds and recognition. And, on the other hand, in the application of science to military technology, it was not scientists who invented the occupation to which their talents have been applied with such stunning effectiveness. Any group, it is granted, has the prerogative to hold itself accountable in special ways. . . . If there is anyone who can make demands of the scientist, it is the scientist himself. But what can laymen ask of scientists? . . . There are obligations laymen can require of scientists, but these can only be the obligations necessarily required of any human being today, scientist or not.[102]

Science, International Relations, and Human Welfare. Looking beyond our own borders, we see that science and technology have had a dramatic effect on international relations and foreign policy in four ways:

1. The political importance to a nation of having the appearance of world scientific leadership
2. The effect of international scientific activities on the relations between nations
3. The importance of the technical component of some prospective arms-control measures
4. The relation of science to technical aid for less-developed countries.

Perhaps science and engineering graduates should be attracted for regular careers in the foreign service and in our other overseas programs. I believe we must also provide a better scientific background for nonscientists in the international affairs field, and that this, perhaps, is the most important measure of all. Essential to these efforts is the development of an academic field of teaching and research in the interrelationship of science and foreign affairs, in order

[102] Quoted from Joseph Turner, "What Laymen Can Ask of Scientists." *Science* 133: 1195; April 21, 1961. Reprinted from *Science* by permission.

to provide education in and better understanding of the underlying significance and opportunities of this relationship.

These are not easy tasks or tasks that can be accomplished overnight. We cannot push a button and mass-produce diplomats in striped pants and laboratory coats, in the way that we produce toasters, automobiles, and television sets.

In discussing international relations, the American historian Julius Pratt states: "Neither the tools of diplomacy nor the tools of force can be suddenly improvised for use in crisis. They must be kept in a state of readiness for use. The success of a nation's foreign policy will depend, in part, upon the efficiency and the readiness of the instruments with which that policy is pursued." We, as scientists, must do all we can to help keep the tools of our diplomacy and the tools of our force in efficient readiness.

We have entered a new era, an era of scientific revolution, as C. P. Snow terms it, in which science and technology are transforming our way of life and the relations between nations. As practicing scientists, we cannot stand aside and simply watch this process, regardless of where it takes us; we must and we can use science and technology to achieve the humanistic goals of our free society. Let us learn to take greater advantage of the opportunities science offers us to contribute to the striving for peace in international relations and to improve the lot of man throughout the world.[103]

Another international view of science agrees that it is impossible in the modern world for a man of science to say with any honesty, "My business is to provide knowledge, and what use is made of the knowledge is not my responsibility," because knowledge that a scientist provides may fall into the hands of men or institutions devoted to utterly unworthy objects. It is not suggested that a man of science, or even a large body of scientists, can altogether prevent this, but they can diminish the magnitude of the evil.

There is another direction in which men of science can attempt to provide leadership. They can suggest and urge in many ways the value of those branches of science of which the important practical uses are beneficial and not harmful. Consider what might be done if the money at present spent on armaments were spent on increasing and distributing the food supply of the world and diminishing the population pressure. In a few decades, poverty and malnutrition, which now afflict more than half the population of the globe, could be ended. But at present almost all the governments of great states consider that it is better to spend money on killing foreigners than on keeping their own subjects alive. Possibilities of a hopeful sort in whatever field can best be worked out and stated authoritatively by men of science; and, since they can do this work better than others, it is part of their duty to do it.

As the world becomes more technically unified, life in an ivory tower becomes increasingly impossible. Not only so; the man who stands out against the powerful organizations which control most of human activity is apt to find

[103] Quoted from G. B. Kistiakowsky, "Science and Foreign Affairs." *Science* 131: 1019–24; April 8, 1960. Reprinted from *Science* by permission.

himself no longer in the ivory tower, with a wide outlook over a sunny land-
scape, but in the dark and subterranean dungeon upon which the ivory tower
was erected. To risk such a habitation demands courage. It will not be necessary to inhabit the dungeon if there are many who are willing to risk it, for
everybody knows that the modern world depends upon scientists, and, if they
are insistent, they must be listened to. We have it in our power to make a
good world; and, therefore, with whatever labor and risk, we must make it.[104]

As Russell says, now life for the scholar and scientist in an ivory
tower becomes increasingly impossible, and many authorities argue for
popularization of science, based on the belief that any distinction between
the man of science and the ordinary man is no longer admissible, any
more than a form of segregation based on an inequality of knowledge:

Whether we like it or not, the laboratory henceforward opens right onto
the street. Science not only affects us at any given moment of our day-to-day
existence, it dogs us, it pursues us. Have we not, all of us, been transformed
into involuntary guinea pigs ever since atomic fission, without asking our opinion, began to plant harmful particles in our bones?
    The obligation to endure gives us the right to know.
    The time is clearly coming when the man in the street will have his say
with regard to the great social, national, international and moral issues latterly
raised by certain applications of science; and it may be that the specialist himself, weary of bearing on his own the weight of his too-heavy responsibilities,
will rejoice at finding understanding and support in public awareness.[105]

To summarize, scientists concerned about the interaction between
science and society have a responsibility to deal as effectively as possible
with the following problems, as outlined by the A.A.A.S. Committee on
Science in the Promotion of Human Welfare:[106]

1. *The social consequences of technological progress.* It is characteristic
of the present situation that scientific advances lead to a very profound level of
control over our environment and to widespread effects on nature. Often the
benefits which are the original aim of a particular application of science are
accompanied by secondary effects that cause unanticipated harm. The application of new scientific advances calls for social decisions which weigh the benefits against the disadvantages, and the public needs to have the facts relevant
to such a decision. The scientific community faces an immediate need for
developing the necessary educational programs. Important examples of such
problems include: (i) the general effects of technological advances, such as
that of automation on industrial development, or of rapid social changes on

[104] Quoted from Bertrand Russell, "The Social Responsibilities of Scientists."
Science 131: 391–92; February 12, 1960. Reprinted from *Science* by permission.
    [105] Quoted from Jean Rostand, "Popularization of Science." *Science* 131: 1491;
May 20, 1960. Reprinted from *Science* by permission.
    [106] Quoted from Barry Commoner and Others, "Science and Human Welfare."
Science 132: 68–73; July 8, 1960. Reprinted from *Science* by permission.

health; (ii) the effects of radiation from military and peaceful applications of nuclear energy; (iii) the effects of new organic insecticides, food additives, and food colors on animals and man; (iv) artificial control of the weather; and (v) population control.

2. *The association of scientific research and military activities.* Military usefulness is, at present, a dominant motivation in the social support of scientific research and has a profound effect on the development of our scientific establishment. Any significant change in the pattern of military activities—disarmament, for example—is likely to cause serious changes in research opportunities. The close association of science with recent military advances tends to foster a public image of science and the scientist which is not in keeping with the inherent goals of the discipline. The secrecy associated with military applications may restrict the development of science. Some observers regard the problem of preventing the catastrophic application of the power of science in war as a matter which overshadows all others.

There is an obvious need for the scientific community to give attention to the wide range of problems arising from the close linkage of science and military activity. The role of science in possible efforts toward disarmament and the practical impact of disarmament on scientific research are of immediate concern.

3. *International aspects of science.* Science figures prominently in the intense political rivalry among the major nations of the world. This use of science tends to conflict with its basic international character, and means must be found to resolve this difficulty. A useful innovation has been the development of collaborative international scientific programs, such as those associated with UNESCO, the World Health Organization, CERN, and the IGY. A number of proposals for similar programs in medicine, space research, and oceanography have been made. This area is a fruitful field for developing new ways to foster a sound development of collaborative science. Of particular importance are international programs to provide scientific and technological assistance to underdeveloped nations.

4. *Government support for scientific research.* The basic difficulties seem to be the absence of any over-all rationale in the support of science and the overemphasis on projects that give promise of immediate practical results. We find, as a consequence of this emphasis, that the major part of governmental research support is in the military area, that basic research is inadequately supported, that the pattern of support is not conducive to the development of free inquiry into nature and that the narrow base of support is distorting the development of science as a whole, in our universities in particular.

5. *How can scientists best meet their social responsibilities?* From what has been said above it is clear that the scientific community has not yet developed a widely accepted means of performing its function in connection with public issues related to science. It would be useful, therefore, to stimulate discussion among scientists on how such activity can best be developed and to encourage efforts which seem to promise success.

6. *The integrity of science.* As science becomes more deeply involved in the frequently discordant affairs of public life and in highly competitive

social endeavors, we may expect a growing pressure toward relaxation of the traditional rules for the conduct of science: objective, open communication of results; rigorous distinction between fact and hypothesis; candid recognition of assumptions and sources of error. It is these rules which permit science to progressively increase our understanding of and control over nature. Without them science becomes useless, and even dangerous to the social order. If the scientific community is to accept the obligation to participate in public affairs, means must be found to strengthen the discipline's rules of conduct. Some observers favor the adoption of a code of ethics; others propose less direct means of maintaining scientific objectivity.

Science Organizations and Responsibility

The annals and other statements of national associations covering the various fields of science recognize that all scholars and scientists must share the burden of solving our social, economic, and political problems:

Public issues, and especially those of world-wide portent, are the concern of all of us, and scientists of every kind (as well as nonscientists) must learn to think constructively about them, to speak out, and to make their voices heard. For this, we need to find efficient organizational patterns through which scientists may effectively express their views on vital issues. The annals, brief though they are, of such an organization as the Federation of American Scientists demonstrate, I think, that vigilant action groups of this type are indispensable in our society.

But we must not forget that the American Association for the Advancement of Science itself is constitutionally committed "to improve the effectiveness of science in the promotion of human welfare" as well as "to increase public understanding of the importance and promise of the methods of science in human progress." It is my firm hope that the Association will quickly find ways for an increasingly effective implementation of these mandates.

It has recently been said that the record of the past decade amply justifies the statement that the scientific community has a social conscience as well as a newly heightened social role. I am certain that the social consciences of the scientists will insure that they will find the way to fulfill the solemn obligations of that role.[107]

The Parliament of Science, sponsored by the American Association for the Advancement of Science, illustrates a way whereby scientists may appropriately consider the social consequence of their findings or explore the problems of science and public policy. The general principles (which underlie a larger number of specific conclusions) are as follows:[108]

[107] Quoted from Laurence H. Snyder, "What We Most Need to Know." *Scientific Monthly* 84: 17–23; January 1957.

[108] Quoted from American Association for the Advancement of Science, "1958 Parliament of Science." *Science* 127: 852–58; April 18, 1958. Reprinted from *Science* by permission.

1. Scientific endeavor is one phase of human intellectual effort; the degree to which it flourishes depends largely upon the extent to which intellectual effort generally is supported and encouraged.

2. Optimal progress in science requires increased support for basic research.

3. As funds for the support of science increase, it becomes increasingly necessary to formulate appropriate plans and procedures for the administration and correlation of the total scientific effort and to give closer scrutiny to national scientific policy.

4. In order that science may progress most effectively, and in order that science may be wisely used for the improvement of human welfare, scientists must have the maximum possible freedom to communicate with each other, both in person and by publication, and to communicate with the public.

5. Scientists are dedicated to the finding of new knowledge. As citizens, they have the responsibility to concern themselves with the social consequences of their scientific findings and to inform the public of the consequences they foresee.

6. The primary goal of education is the intellectual development of the individual. The primary need of education is to employ quality and to raise standards—of teachers, of curricula, and of what is expected of students.

7. In the assignment of funds to the improvement of education, first priority should go to improvements in curricula, teaching, and the status and salaries of teachers.

The hope has been expressed that the National Science Foundation can help the national government realize the need for greatly increased federal support of research outside the military field:

Outside the field of military research, government support of research is only a small fraction of the amount that would yield enormous returns to the community. Indeed, it is safe to say that there is no field where larger government expenditures would produce as rich a return as greater outlays on research—and also on the necessary foundations for research, the education of talented people. Perhaps it is unreasonable to expect the members of Congress and the members of legislatures to see this fact clearly without assistance from the scientists themselves. To help the government policy-makers appreciate the nation's need for greatly enlarged government research outlays outside the military field is one of the responsibilities of the National Science Foundation. It is a great national asset that the country has this Foundation to help the country make wise use of its resources.[109]

On the other hand, in view of increasingly larger government appropriations for scientific and technological projects during recent years, some scientists are coming to wonder whether success will spoil basic research. It is argued that scientists become involved in projects that

[109] Quoted from Sumner H. Slichter, "The Industry of Discovery." *Science* 128: 1610–13; December 26, 1958. Reprinted from *Science* by permission.

have little to do with basic research, however important these projects may be in terms of military security or international good will. It is further argued that many scientists involved in these projects spend their time in administrative duties rather than creative efforts. It should be noted, however, that further progress in some of our most fundamental and interesting scientific investigations involves the construction of extraordinarily expensive and complicated equipment, which makes government support essential. Therefore, our defense of bigness is that in some areas of research it may be a necessary condition for further progress. One reason for the large role of the government in support of science is that science is playing such a large role in the prestige and power of nations. Possibly scientists will come to say of some of our huge projects that the resulting gains in our understanding of nature fully warranted the effort, even though hope of such gains was not the only reason for supporting particular projects.[110]

Social Science and Responsibility

Scientists can help overcome the uncertainty, confusion, and fear generated by the war crisis by presenting objectively and calmly the necessary facts to the public. The same call of duty that has placed science at the command of warfare now requires scientists to serve with equal devotion the social need for peace and find a means of protecting society that does not run the risk of destroying it.

The importance of peaceful means of resolving social conflicts has, of course, long been recognized. Students of human behavior and of social, economic, political, international, and legal processes and many research organizations and foundations have made important contributions to the understanding of social conflicts and have investigated possible methods of resolving them. But these efforts, valuable as they are, do not measure up to the urgency of the need.

Separate analyses of the different aspects of the problem of peaceful resolution of national conflicts are inadequate to the task. These problems are inherently complex, and a scientific attack on them, if it is to succeed, must acknowledge and deal with this complexity. For example, the negotiations on a nuclear test ban treaty—such a treaty represents only a rather small part of the total problem—involve a wide array of questions in the natural sciences, sociology, and economics.

We believe that if the complexity of the problem is not only recognized but accepted in advance as inescapable, it can be solved. For this purpose we will need to marshal the full resources of *all* the sciences. We shall need to use the special experimental skills of the natural sciences and the knowledge

[110] Joseph Turner, "Bigness Has Its Place." *Science* 129: 1709; June 26, 1959.

of man accumulated by the social sciences of anthropology, human biology, psychology, sociology, political science, economics, and history.[111]

We are reminded that in the past man's basic problems were concerned with the complexities of his physical environment, but now in our time the focus of the basic problem has changed from the external to the internal environment. Our primary need is now to learn rapidly how to cope with ourselves and with each other, particularly with regard to intergroup and international conflicts, so that we can preserve freedom in peace. Toward this end significant beginnings have been made.[112]

Useful work has been done in studying such problems as the relationship between personality variables and foreign policy attitudes; the structuring and changing of attitudes; and the structure and interaction of certain segments of the government decision-making apparatus. Multidisciplinary centers for the study of peace and war have recently been established in a number of universities and a new journal, the *Journal of Conflict Resolution*, which is devoted to such research, has appeared. A substantial effort at defining specific researchable questions, numbering in the hundreds, has been accomplished by a series of task groups working under the auspices of the Institute for International Order. Yet the relative meagerness of the present effort is astounding in view of the urgency of the problem. No comprehensive study of the extent of the research effort currently mounted in this area is available, but best current estimates indicate that in the entire nation there are less than 100 individuals working full time at projects which might be thought of as aimed at the development of a social and behavioral science of peace.

Governmental agencies are now placing more reliance on social science in determining public policy and in improving communication between social scientists and public officials:

As an illustration of the aid social scientists might render public officials, consider the following problem. In a fast-growing suburb, the land needed for schools, libraries, playgrounds, and parks must be acquired while such land is still readily available, for as the region fills in, prices may rise prohibitively. But how does one know that a housing trend will continue? Suburban growth may slacken because of changes in, say, construction costs and family income. Accordingly, one use of the social sciences may be in examining the elements that govern housing trends. Further, housing trends do not only affect public policy, but are, in part, affected by such policy—or the lack of it. Thus, a second use of the social sciences may be evaluating the effects of such measures as revising the building codes to permit more economical methods of construc-

111 Quoted from A.A.A.S. Committee on Science in the Promotion of Human Welfare, "Science and Human Survival." *Science* 134: 2080–83; December 29, 1961. Reprinted from *Science* by permission.
112 Quoted from review by William Pollin, *Science* 135: 305–306; January 26, 1962, of Erich Fromm, *May Man Prevail.* Garden City, New York: Doubleday, 1961. 236 p. Reprinted from *Science* by permission.

tion. The social sciences may also have something to say about such factors influencing the housing scene as the increase in leisure time resulting from shorter working hours. . . .

Use of the social sciences in setting public policy is similar to use of the natural sciences for this purpose, but there are differences. For one thing, results in the social sciences are likely to provide a considerably less firm basis for decisions than are results in the natural sciences. Selecting the best route for a new expressway through a city is not quite the same thing as selecting the best route for a road across a mountain range. For another, use of the social sciences can pose its own special paradoxes. If research reveals that people who throw stones should not build glass houses, it may also reveal that such people like glass houses. Nevertheless, to act on the basis of knowledge, whatever its limits, is better than acting blindly, provided one is aware of those limits.[113]

Sears maintains that, among the practical problems of humanity to-day, our relation to the immediate space in which we live is of greater critical importance than man's dramatic invasion of outer space. Our concern with the technological applications of mathematics, physics, and chemistry may have beclouded the fact that we need biology in general and ecology in particular to illuminate man's relation to his environment. It is not enough that the biological sciences are supported primarily in the fields of medicine and agriculture, and that social sciences are used for dealing with the immediate ills of society; we need general encouragement and utilization of all science to guide the cultural and physical aspects of future evolution. We need more and better science teaching, not merely to produce scientists, but also to develop scientific literacy among our citizens in general, in order that society may support a science whose results are applied for the welfare of mankind. From this point of view, "our future security may depend less upon priority in exploring outer space than upon our wisdom in managing the space in which we live."[114]

The preceding paragraphs of this section indicate that much has been said about the social responsibility of the scientist, frequently meaning the physical scientist. The rapid increase of knowledge about the control of the physical world, as illustrated in the preceding paragraphs, has posed the question of whether society will be able to direct this knowledge, applying it for the benefit of mankind rather than for the destruction of man and his civilization. The social responsibility of the social scientist is equally great in the sense of discovering enough knowledge about society so that society can, if it wishes to employ this information, control the use of physical knowledge. The next question

[113] Quoted from Joseph Turner, "Towards More Reliance on Social Science." *Science* 131: 577; February 26, 1960. Reprinted from *Science* by permission.
[114] Paul B. Sears, "The Inexorable Problem of Space." *Science* 127: 9–16; January 3, 1958.

logically follows: Once the social scientists gain the social knowledge that is needed to control physical knowledge and society, how will this social evidence be controlled and what is to prevent a social scientist from taking advantage of such social knowledge to expedite the enslavement or the destruction of society? What is there to prevent one group in society from exploiting this social knowledge for the purpose of controlling another group? Examples of this problem may be found in the fields of market research, public opinion, industrial relations, and economic control (as in price and monetary controls). The social scientist's activities should be an asset to democratic society.[115]

The view just expressed means that the social scientist must be continually conscious of his obligation as a member of society:

> He may not, any more than anyone else, violate the law or general moral understandings. It is no defense to say that he has techniques that enable him to do so—so does the gangster. Nor may the social scientist feel any special pride in the fact that the indirect nature of his techniques makes detection unlikely. He cannot conceive of himself as an observer only, as one who stands off and surveys the world as a kind of curious drama. If it is a drama, then he is on-stage himself. The social scientist tries to keep values out of his research; they are felt to interfere with objectivity. A favorite way of putting the matter is this: "We all have many roles. I have a role as a citizen and with it go certain faiths and beliefs. But when I enter my laboratory, I am a scientist, and I leave my values at the door, along with my galoshes." This sort of schizophrenia may be possible for the physicist, but it is not for the social scientist. For it is as a social scientist that he is a citizen. This is his position in society, just as others are blacksmiths, physicians, or newsdealers, and society pays him for it because he makes a contribution it values. But society will not long pay a man who violates its laws, its mores, or its tacit understandings. And if the man claims that his work demands it, society is likely to put an end to his work. Nor is the social scientist abroad immune from the controls of our society. He is still a member of our society, nay more, a representative of our society, and he has the same obligations that we enjoin on any visitor to a foreign land.
>
> The question remains of how these controls are to be enforced. I doubt that legal protections alone would be sufficient. Even in the case where a subject's legal rights may have been violated, he may not, in practice, be able to protect himself. He may not have the money to fight a difficult case through court, and even if he has, a court case is likely to force him to reveal, for all the world to hear, the very secret things he did not want even the social scientist to know. He may prefer to salvage some solace from the fact that few people read professional social science journals.
>
> In order to have controls that work, they must come from within the profession itself, just as the strongest controls on any professional come from

---

[115] Arnold M. Rose, "The Social Responsibility of the Social Scientist," *Theory and Method in the Social Sciences, op. cit.*, p. 179–92.

his own colleagues. Now I am well aware of the fact that many, perhaps most, social scientists feel no need for controls. In practice, although they might do so, they do not lie to their subjects or ever violate a confidence. They are extremely careful of a subject's personal or private life and accord him complete respect for any rights that he claims. But they do so not because they have been formally trained to do so as researchers, but because of their own upbringing as individuals. From this point of view, the social scientist learned more at his mother's breast than he did at his professor's feet. It is no contradiction to point out that in research courses the student is told that he should not violate confidences and should respect a subject's rights. These suggestions are justified, not in moral terms, not in terms of the understandings that a member of our society should respect, but as being, simply, good for research. It seems to me that the responsibility of graduate schools of social research extends further than this, for the university, the social scientist it produces, and the subjects he studies are united as members of the same moral community.[116]

Psychology and Responsibility

Physicists, by releasing the might of the atom, were forced to face the ethical issues concerning use and control of this potentially destructive force, while lacking both training and temperament to deal with such problems of ethics. Psychologists, particularly applied and clinical psychologists, also inevitably meet ethical issues because of the nature of their subject matter and techniques.

In addition to psychotherapy, psychologists in making recommendations to the public are usually making implicit ethical judgments. In giving information on methods of child rearing, for example, the psychologist usually assumes that the methods advocated should produce certain kinds of behavior and potentially certain kinds of adults. He usually assumes, furthermore, that these kinds of behavior and these kinds of adults are desirable.

It seems obvious that ethical issues are often involved in applying psychology to industry, e.g., in giving personal information to management concerning employees, in using depth motivational methods in advertising, and in dealing with certain problems in management-labor disputes. Recently many psychologists have become concerned over the ethical implications involved in the use of subliminal stimulation in advertising.

However, just as ethical problems were increased for the physicists upon unlocking nature's power in the atom, so will psychologists' ethical problems be increased as they gain the capacity to control human behavior. With limited control over human behavior the psychologist is also limited in his power to either benefit or harm mankind. However, with extreme capacity for controlling man (and our knowledge seems to be growing in geometric proportions) psychologists may unleash power far greater than that held in the atom.

[116] Quoted from Edward Gross, "Social Science Techniques: A Problem of Power and Responsibility." *Scientific Monthly* 83: 242–47; November 1956.

Psychologists should not be caught unprepared for dealing with the ethical problems involved in controlling power, as were the physicists. However, as a profession we are much more likely to be influential in helping determine the use and control of the power potentially contained in psychological knowledge if we think through the ethical issues now which may face us more forcibly in the future. What is perhaps more important, we need to think through the ethical issues as a profession in order to bring these issues to the attention of the public and thus place fair and adequate choices before society at large.[117]

Developing psychological knowledge presents the same conjunction of good and evil that we have all felt so keenly in the development of atomic energy. Atomic energy can ease man of drudgery and disease, and it can also annihilate him. Psychological knowledge can bring man increased certitude, dignity, and joy, and it can also enslave him. These antinomies are among the most exciting and demanding developments of our time. They have within them the seeds of ultimate tragedy or triumph. The stakes seem to be getting even higher, and the rules of the game, embodied in ethics, ever more important.[118]

A sharp comment on the "social indifference" of psychology maintains that workers in such disciplines as sociology, anthropology, political science, and economics are too often disappointed when they turn to psychology for help, following the admonition "to see the psychologist, he deals with people." The reason cited is that the major areas of social activity are commonly the *place* where psychologists study interesting problems, rather than the *focus of inquiry*.

If someone is interested in social behavior he ought not to rely upon or even trust the analysis that a psychologist makes of most of it. I am impressed with how naive and conventional my colleagues and I are when confronted with most social phenomena. We are ignorant of the historical dimensions of most social activity, we do not see the complex interweaving of institutions and arrangements, when we think of social meanings and facts we tend to deal with them in terms of their possessors, we substitute fancy for fact, preference for actuality—not, to be sure, that political scientists and sociologists do not do this too often, too. In general, psychologists tend to be like laymen when they confront social phenomena, particularly those that involve large scale patterns. And the reason for all of this is that the main areas of social activity are only the *place* where psychologists study interesting sorts of things, rather than being the *focus of inquiry*.[119]

[117] Quoted from David B. Lynn, "A Model Man for Applied Psychology." *American Psychologist* 14: 630–32; October 1959.
[118] Quoted from Nicholas Hobbs, "Science and Ethical Behavior." *American Psychologist* 14: 217–25; May 1959.
[119] Richard A. Littman, "Psychology: The Socially Indifferent Science." *American Psychologist* 16: 232–36; May 1961.

To cite a specific positive example in the field of psychology, Edward Tolman, following his death in November, 1959, was characterized as one who led a life of both scientific and social purpose. He was described as a gentle and humane teacher of psychology, capable of instilling permanent scientific enthusiasms in his students. Beyond his major contributions as a respected scientist and rare teacher, Tolman was a citizen with a social conscience who sought in many ways to understand the psychological sources of warlike behavior, to protect civil rights and academic freedom, and to promote individual justice.[120]

CONCLUDING STATEMENT

It is both logical and functional to discuss research in terms of the characteristics and sequence of scientific method. It has been well said that the greatest invention of the nineteenth century was the invention of the method of invention and that the most important instrument or element in research is the mind of man.

Interdisciplinary research and professional collaboration in the social and behavioral fields of inquiry have led to the development of certain theoretical concepts and propositions that are regarded as the common property of education, psychology, sociology, and anthropology. We need a broad base of mutual understanding between all physical scientists and all social scientists, with education playing the key role in achieving this understanding.

Values are inescapably present in research, in the form of such factors as purpose, motive, aspiration, interest, need, attitude, feeling, emotion, and sentiment, with a proper place for the great humanities, the spiritual ends of life, and faith. Without such a philosophy of values, science is blind or lacks direction.

The hallmarks of the scientist are typically problem awareness, appropriate specialization, intellectual curiosity and drive, willingness to encounter hazards in research, and creativity and ingenuity. Great scholars and scientists have been compared with torches shining at long intervals, to guide the advance of science.

Although certain external and internal factors may inhibit freedom for research, there are definite ways in which the investigator, including school personnel, may overcome obstacles to freedom in research. Like food, we need enough freedom in research, but should not be guilty of gluttony. Development of self-responsibility and freedom of inquiry in graduate education may well serve the two purposes of broadening and

[120] Richard S. Crutchfield, David Krech, and Robert C. Tryon, "Edward Chace Tolman: A Life of Scientific and Social Purpose." *Science* 131: 714–16; March 11, 1960.

deepening the student's knowledge in a particular field, and of creative investigation.

It is not enough to emphasize the social responsibility of the physical scientist. Social scientists, psychologists, and educators have equally great obligations (and inevitably meet ethical issues) as they seek to use their knowledge for the benefit of democratic society.

SELECTED REFERENCES

ACKOFF, Russell L. *Scientific Method:* Optimizing Applied Research Decisions. New York: John Wiley & Sons, 1962. xii + 464 p.

ALTICK, Richard D. *Scholar Adventures.* New York: The Macmillan Co., 1960. 338 p.

ANDREWS, F. Emerson. *Philanthropic Foundations.* New York: Russell Sage Foundation, 1956. 459 p.

BARBER, Bernard. *Science and the Social Order.* Glencoe, Ill.: Free Press, 1952. xxiii + 288 p.

BARR, A. S. "Research Methods," *Encyclopedia of Educational Research.* Edited by Chester W. Harris. Third Edition. New York: The Macmillan Co., 1960. p. 1160-65.

BATES, Ralph S. *Scientific Societies in the United States.* Second Edition. New York: Technology Press and Columbia University Press, 1959. 308 p.

BECK, William S. *Modern Science and the Nature of Life.* New York: Harcourt, Brace and Co., 1957. 319 p.

BECKER, Howard, and Others. *For a Science of Social Man.* New York: The Macmillan Co., 1954. 289 p.

BENNE, Kenneth D., and Others. "The Philosophical and Social Framework of Education." *Review of Educational Research.* 31: 1-113; February 1961.

BERELSON, Bernard. *Graduate Education in the United States.* New York: McGraw-Hill Book Co., 1960. vi + 346 p. (Comprehensive study, including short history of graduate education in America, analysis of current programs and problems based in part on survey data, and recommendations for future changes.)

BERGMANN, Gustav. *Philosophy of Science.* Madison: University of Wisconsin Press, 1957. xiii + 181 p.

BLANK, David M., and STIGLER, George J. *The Demand and Supply of Scientific Personnel.* New York: National Bureau of Economic Research, 1957. xiv + 200 p.

BLESSING, James H. *Graduate Education:* An Annotated Bibliography. Office of Education Bulletin 1961, No. 26. Washington: Government Printing Office, 1961. vi + 151 p.

BOGARDUS, Emory S. *The Development of Social Thought.* Fourth Edition. New York: Longmans, Green and Co., 1960. x + 689 p.

BONNEY, Merl E. "Sociometric Methods," *Encyclopedia of Educational Research.* Edited by Chester W. Harris. Third Edition. New York: The Macmillan Co., 1960. p. 1319-23.

BORING, E. G. *A History of Experimental Psychology.* Second Edition. New York: Appleton-Century-Crofts, 1950. xxi + 777 p.

BRAITHWAITE, Richard B. *Scientific Explanation.* Cambridge, England: Cambridge University Press, 1953. 376 p.

BRODBECK, May. "Logic and Scientific Method in Research on Training," *Handbook of Research on Teaching.* Edited by N. L. Gage. Chicago: Rand McNally, 1963. Chapter 2.

BRODBECK, May. "The Philosophy of Science and Educational Research," in "Methodology of Educational Research." *Review of Educational Research* 27: 427-40; December 1957.

BRONOWSKI, Jacob. *The Common Sense of Science.* Cambridge: Harvard University Press, 1953. 154 p.

BROWN, Clarence W., and GHISELLI, Edwin E. *Scientific Method in Psychology.* New York: McGraw-Hill Book Co., 1955. xii + 368 p.

BROWN, Harcourt, Editor. *Science and the Creative Spirit:* Essays on Humanistic Aspects of Science. Toronto: University of Toronto Press, 1958. xxvii + 165 p.

BROWN, Harrison, BONNER, James, and WEIR, John. *The Next Hundred Years:* Man's Natural and Technological Resources. New York: Viking Press, 1957. xi + 193 p.

BROWN, Laurence D., and SLATER, J. Marlowe. *The Doctorate in Education:* An Inquiry into Conditions Affecting Pursuit of the Doctoral Degree in the Field of Education. Vol. 1, The Graduates. Washington: American Association of Colleges for Teacher Education, 1960. ix + 110 p.

BURCHARD, John E., Editor. *Mid-Century:* The Social Implications of Scientific Progress. Cambridge: Massachusetts Institute of Technology Press, 1950. xx + 549 p.

BURTON, William H. "Scientific Criticism Aids Education." *Bulletin of the National Association of Secondary-School Principals* 42: 172-79; December 1958.

BUSH, George P., and HATTERY, Lowell H., Editors. *Teamwork in Research.* Washington: American University Press, 1953. xii + 191 p.

CAPLOW, Theodore, and McGEE, Reece J. *The Academic Marketplace.* New York: Basic Books, 1958. x + 262 p. (Anatomy of the academic profession—its mores, morale, machinations.)

CARMICHAEL, Oliver C. *Graduate Education:* A Critique and a Program. New York: Harper & Brothers, 1961. ix + 213 p.

A Century of Progress in the Natural Sciences, 1853–1953. Published in celebration of the centennial of the California Academy of Sciences. San Francisco: California Academy of Sciences, 1955. 807 p.

CHAMBLISS, Rollin. *Social Thought:* From Hammurabi to Comte. New York: Dryden Press, 1954. ix + 469 p.

CLARK, Kenneth E. *America's Psychologists:* A Survey of a Growing Profession. Washington: American Psychological Association, 1957. ix + 247 p.

CLOUGH, Shepard B. *Basic Values of Western Civilization.* New York: Columbia University Press, 1960. x + 132 p.

Committee on Institutional Research Policy. *Sponsored Research Policy of*

Colleges and Universities. Washington: American Council on Education, 1955. vii + 93 p.

CONANT, James B. *Science and Common Sense.* New Haven: Yale University Press, 1951. xii + 371 p.

COOLEY, William W. "Attributes of Potential Scientists." *Harvard Educational Review* 28:1-18; Winter 1958.

COREY, Stephen M. *Action Research to Improve School Practices.* New York: Bureau of Publications, Teachers College, Columbia University, 1953. xii + 161 p.

CURTI, Merle, Editor. *American Scholarship in the Twentieth Century.* Library of Congress Series in American Civilization. Cambridge: Harvard University Press, 1953. vii + 252 p.

DANTO, Arthur, and MORGENBESSER, Sidney, Editors. *Philosophy of Science.* New York: Meridian Books, 1960. 477 p.

DINGLE, Herbert, Editor. *A Century of Science: 1851-1951.* New York: Roy Publishing Co., 1951. ix + 338 p.

DOBY, John T., Editor. *An Introduction to Social Research.* Harrisburg: The Stackpole Co., 1954. x + 275 p.

The Doctorate in Education. Vol. 3, Conference Report. Washington: American Association of Colleges for Teacher Education, 1961. v + 150 p.

DUNSHEATH, Percy, Editor. *Century of Technology: 1851-1951.* New York: Roy Publishing Co., 1951. ix + 346 p.

EHLERS, Henry, Editor. *Crucial Issues in Education.* New York: Henry Holt and Co., 1955. 277 p.

EIDUSON, Bernice T. *Scientists:* Their Psychological World. New York: Basic Books, 1962. xvi + 299 p.

ELMER, M. C. *Contemporary Social Thought:* Contributors and Trends. Pittsburgh: University of Pittsburgh Press, 1956. viii + 256 p.

FANGE, Von Eugene. *Professional Creativity.* Englewood Cliffs, N. J.: Prentice-Hall, 1959. 260 p.

FEIGL, Herbert, and BRODBECK, May, Editors. *Readings in the Philosophy of Science.* New York: Appleton-Century-Crofts, 1953. ix + 811 p.

FESTINGER, Leon, and KATZ, Daniel, Editors. *Research Methods in the Behavioral Sciences.* New York: Dryden Press, 1953. xi + 660 p.

FLUGEL, J. C. *A Hundred Years of Psychology.* Revised Edition. New York: The Macmillan Co., 1951. 424 p.

FOSHAY, Arthur W., and Others. *Research for Curriculum Improvement.* 1957 Yearbook. Washington: Association for Supervision and Curriculum Development, National Education Association, 1957. x + 348 p.

FRANK, P. *Philosophy of Science.* Englewood Cliffs, N. J.: Prentice-Hall, 1957. xxii + 394 p.

FREEDMAN, Paul. *The Principles of Scientific Research.* Second Edition. New York: Pergamon, 1960. 245 p.

FULLER, B. A. G. *A History of Philosophy.* Third Edition. Revised by Sterling M. McMurrin. New York: Henry Holt and Co., 1955. 618 p.

FULTON, James S. *Science and Man's Hope.* New York: Bookman Associates, 1955. 179 p.

GAGE, N. L. "Paradigms for Research on Teaching," *Handbook of Research on Teaching.* Chicago: Rand McNally, 1963. Chapter 3.

GOOD, Carter V., and SCATES, Douglas E. *Methods of Research:* Educational, Psychological, Sociological. New York: Appleton-Century-Crofts, 1954. xx + 920 p.

GREENWOOD, David C. *Solving the Scientist Shortage.* Washington: Public Affairs Press, 1958. 77 p.

HALL, Everett W. *Modern Science and Human Values:* A Study in the History of Ideas. Princeton: D. Van Nostrand Co., 1956. 483 p.

HILLWAY, Tyrus. *Introduction to Research.* Boston: Houghton Mifflin Co., 1956. p. 3-53.

HOROWITZ, Irving L. *Philosophy, Science, and the Sociology of Knowledge.* Springfield, Illinois: Charles C Thomas, 1961. 192 p.

HULLFISH, H. G., and SMITH, P. G. *Reflective Thinking:* The Method of Education. New York: Dodd, Mead, 1961. xii + 273 p.

HUTCHINGS, Edward, Jr., Editor. *Frontiers in Science:* A Survey. New York: Basic Books, 1958. 362 p.

IRVING, John A. *Science and Values:* Exploration in Philosophy and the Social Sciences. Toronto: Ryerson Press, 1952. xi + 148 p.

JACOB, Philip E. *Changing Values in College:* An Exploratory Study of the Impact of College Teaching. New York: Harper & Brothers, 1957. x + 178 p.

JEFFREYS, H. *Scientific Inference.* Second Edition. Cambridge, England: Cambridge University Press, 1957. 236 p.

KANTOR, J. R. *The Logic of Modern Science.* Bloomington, Ind.: Principia Press, 1953. xvi + 359 p.

KOMAROVSKY, Mirra, Editor. *Common Frontiers of the Social Sciences.* Glencoe, Ill.: Free Press, 1957. viii + 439 p.

LANGFELD, Herbert S., and Others, Editors. *A History of Psychology in Autobiography.* Vol. 4. Worcester, Mass.: Clark University Press, 1952. xii + 356 p.

LAZARSFELD, Paul F., and ROSENBERG, Morris, Editors. *The Language of Social Research:* A Reader in the Methodology of Social Research. Glencoe, Ill.: Free Press, 1955. xiii + 590 p.

LAZARSFELD, Paul F., and THIELENS, Wagner, Jr. *The Academic Mind:* Social Scientists in a Time of Crisis. Glencoe, Illinois: Free Press, 1958. xiii + 460 p.

LIKERT, Rensis, and HAYES, Samuel P., Jr., Editors. *Some Applications of Behavioural Research.* UNESCO Publication. New York: Columbia University Press, 1957. 333 p.

LITTLE, J. Kenneth. "Graduate Education," *Encyclopedia of Educational Research.* Edited by Chester W. Harris. Third Edition. New York: The Macmillan Co., 1960. p. 593-602.

LUNDBERG, George A. *Can Science Save Us?* Second Edition. New York: Longmans, Green and Co., 1961. 150 p.

LUSZKI, Margaret B. *Interdisciplinary Team Research:* Methods and Problems. No. 3 of the Research Training Series. New York: New York University Press (for the National Training Laboratories), 1958. xvii + 355 p.

MASLOW, Abraham H., Editor. *New Knowledge in Human Values.* New York: Harper & Brothers, 1959. xiv + 268 p.

MASON, S. F. *Main Currents of Scientific Thought:* A History of the Sciences. New York: Abelard-Schuman, 1954. viii + 520 p.

McCAMY, James L. *Science and Public Administration.* University, Alabama: University of Alabama Press, 1961. viii + 218 p.

McCORMICK, Thomas C., and FRANCIS, Roy G. *Methods of Research in the Behavioral Sciences.* New York: Harper & Brothers, 1958. Chapter 1.

McGRATH, E. J. *The Graduate School and the Decline of Liberal Education.* New York: Bureau of Publications, Teachers College, Columbia University, for the Institute of Higher Education, 1959. xii + 65 p.

MISIAK, Henryk. *The Philosophical Roots of Scientific Psychology.* New York: Fordham University Press, 1961. xiv + 142 p.

NAGEL, Ernest. *The Structure of Science:* Problems in the Logic of Scientific Explanation. New York: Harcourt, Brace, and World, 1961. xiii + 618 p. (Philosophy of science, a separate discipline, meets philosophy proper on the question, "What exists?")

NESS, Frederic W., Editor. *A Guide to Graduate Study.* Washington: American Council on Education, 1958. xi + 335 p.

New Frontiers of Knowledge: A Symposium. Washington: Public Affairs Press, 1957. 125 p.

ODUM, H. W. *American Sociology:* The Story of Sociology in the United States through 1950. New York: Longmans, Green and Co., 1951. vi + 501 p.

PERRY, Ralph B. *Realms of Value:* A Critique of Human Civilization. Cambridge: Harvard University Press, 1954. xii + 497 p.

POOLE, Lynn. *Frontiers of Science.* New York: McGraw-Hill Book Co., 1958. 173 p.

ROBACK, A. A. *History of American Psychology.* New York: Library Publishers, 1952. xiv + 426 p.

ROBACK, A. A. Editor. *Present-Day Psychology:* An Original Survey of Departments, Branches, Methods, and Phases, including Clinical and Dynamic Psychology. New York: Philosophical Library, 1955. 993 p.

ROE, Anne. *The Making of a Scientist.* New York: Dodd, Mead and Co., 1953. ix + 244 p.

ROSE, Arnold M. *Theory and Method in the Social Sciences.* Minneapolis: University of Minnesota Press, 1954. xii + 351 p.

RUSSELL, Bertrand. *The Impact of Science on Society.* New York: Simon and Schuster, 1953. 114 p.

SARTON, George. *A Guide to the History of Science.* Waltham, Mass.: Chronica Botanica Co., 1952. xvii + 316 p.

Scientific and Technical Societies of the United States and Canada. Sixth Edition. Washington: National Academy of Sciences-National Research Council, 1955. 441 p.

SCOTT, William A., and WERTHEIMER, Michael. *Introduction to Psychological Research.* New York: John Wiley & Sons, 1962. 445 p.

SEARLES, Herbert L. *Logic and Scientific Methods:* An Introductory Course. Second Edition. New York: Ronald Press, 1956. 378 p.

SELLTIZ, Claire, and Others. "The Research Process," and "Research and Theory," *Research Methods in Social Relations.* Revised One-Volume Edition. New York: Henry Holt and Co., 1959. Chapters 1, 14.

STARK, Werner. *The Sociology of Knowledge:* An Essay in Aid of a Deeper Understanding of the History of Ideas. London: Routledge and Kegan Paul, 1958. xi + 356 p.

STORR, Richard J. *The Beginning of Graduate Education in America.* Chicago: The University of Chicago Press, 1953. x + 196 p.

TATON, R. *Reason and Chance in Scientific Discovery.* New York: Philosophical Library, 1957. 171 p.

THOMPSON, Laura. *Toward a Science of Mankind.* New York: McGraw-Hill Book Co., 1961. xxviii + 276 p.

TOULMIN, Stephen. *The Philosophy of Science:* An Introduction. New York: Longmans, Green and Co., 1953. xiii + 176 p.

TRAVERS, R. M. W. *An Introduction to Educational Research.* New York: The Macmillan Co., 1958. Chapters 1-3.

TRYTTEN, M. H., and HARMON, L. R. *Doctorate Production in United States Universities, 1936-1956:* With Baccalaureate Origins of Doctorates in the Sciences, Arts, and Humanities. Publication 582. Washington: National Academy of Sciences—National Research Council, 1958. vii + 155 p.

TYLER, R. W., and Others. *Graduate Study in Education.* Fiftieth Yearbook, National Society for the Study of Education. Chicago: The University of Chicago Press, 1951. xix + 369 p.

UNDERWOOD, Benton J. *Psychological Research.* New York: Appleton-Century-Crofts, 1957. ix + 298 p.

VAN DALEN, Deobold B. *Understanding Educational Research:* An Introduction. New York: McGraw-Hill Book Co., 1962. p. 1-63.

WATSON, Robert I. *Psychology as a Profession.* Garden City, N. Y.: Doubleday & Co., 1954. x + 65 p.

WHITE, Lynn, Jr., Editor. *Frontiers of Knowledge in the Study of Man.* New York: Harper & Brothers, 1956. xii + 330 p.

WIENER, Philip P., and NOLAND, Aaron, Editors. *Roots of Scientific Thought:* A Cultural Perspective. New York: Basic Books, 1957. x + 677 p.

WINTHROP, Henry. "Some Neglected Considerations Concerning the Problem of Value in Psychology." *Journal of General Psychology* 64: 37-59; January 1961.

WOLFLE, Dael. *America's Resources of Specialized Talent.* The Report of the Commission on Human Resources and Advanced Training. New York: Harper & Brothers, 1954. xviii + 332 p.

WOLFLE, Dael. *Science and Public Policy.* Lincoln: University of Nebraska Press, 1959. 81 p.

YOUNG, Pauline V. *Scientific Social Surveys and Research.* Third Edition. Englewood Cliffs, N. J.: Prentice-Hall, 1956. xx + 540 p.

CHAPTER TWO

Development of the Problem and Hypothesis

This chapter discusses problem awareness or sensitivity to problem situations; identification of problems through advanced study and critical reading, analysis of trends and needs, and repetition or extension of investigations; factors important in selection of the problem—novelty and importance, curiosity and drive or motivation, background of scholarship and personal traits or characteristics, technique and working facilities, sponsorship and cooperation, risks and costs, and time requirements; initial statement and fuller definition of the problem; and development and testing of hypotheses.

AWARENESS OR IDENTIFICATION OF PROBLEMS

Many beginners in research and graduate students are prone to conclude that most of our educational problems have been solved. They may be overawed by the large number of research studies in print. At the time the first edition of the *Encyclopedia of Educational Research* was published in 1941 it was estimated that if research was liberally interpreted and unpublished studies were included, the total number of studies was near 100,000. Since that time, an estimate based on the bibliographies appearing in the *Review of Educational Research* indicates that by 1965 the total will reach approximately 175,000. The number of doctoral dissertations and studies per year in education was about 2,000 at the beginning of the 1960's. To these figures should be added a considerable number of master's theses and projects, although many master's degrees are awarded without a thesis requirement.

Sensitivity to Problems

The difficulty for many beginners in research lies in an insensitivity to problems or "problem blindness." Later chapters of this book will present many examples of studies essential to future progress in education. Historical sources accumulate with each passing event, making necessary the extension of earlier historical narratives and sometimes a reinterpretation of older accounts. Descriptive-survey studies are soon out of date and must be repeated, as in the annual school census for a local system. Controlled experiments are repeated to test the validity of earlier investigations.

It may seem surprising that, early in the development of public schools in the United States, some educators mistakenly concluded that most of our educational problems had been solved, as expressed by the writer of more than a century ago in the *Ohio Journal of Education* (1856):

> The popular interest, which has, of late years, attached to everything connected with Education, has prompted inquiry into all the departments of the subject; and to such a degree has the general surface of the subject been examined and expounded, that it is difficult to find a point of space unoccupied, or at least unnoticed. We have abounded in lectures, on all the theories, and all the arts of teaching; we have had volumes of codes for the government of schools.

At times, even able scientists and scholars have overlooked problems and answers nearby. Moses G. Farmer said that the discovery of a telephone had flaunted itself before him a dozen times within ten years before release of the first description of Bell's telephone.

The poet at times has recognized the human tendency to overlook problems close at hand or even in one's "backyard." Lowell, in his "The Vision of Sir Launfal," tells of the young knight who scornfully tossed the leper a piece of gold as he left the castle gate to seek the Holy Grail. Later the knight, returning old and broken after a fruitless search, found in this same beggar and in the wooden bowl the object of his quest:

> In many climes, without avail,
> Thou hast spent thy life for the Holy Grail;
> Behold, it is here,—this cup which thou
> Didst fill at the streamlet for me but now.

It may be that the investigator who is sensitive to problems nearby understands rather well the meaning of the lines in Shakespeare's *Much Ado About Nothing:*

> Finds tongues in trees, books in the running brooks,
> Sermons in stones, and good in everything.

So great was Kettering's wish to know and so keen his awareness of how little we do know, that often he spoke after the following fashion: "We have great libraries all over the country which contain the books of things we know. But I want to build libraries . . . to hold the books that we don't know anything about—the unwritten books. That would be a great library as I see it. . . . Someday it is going to be filled."[1]

The insight essential to recognition of research problems differs from the background necessary for sensing and doing practical or routine tasks in the school. Frequently the answers to these practical questions are provided in terms of judgment or experience, without resort to an investigational approach. The beginner in research may have to reorient his thinking to achieve the research perspective or may even find it necessary to undertake a more difficult task, an intellectual reorganization so as to interpret his educational world in the form of problems to be solved. The graduate student or field worker may make his choice with respect to investigating problems close at hand or more distant in time or space.

SOURCES FOR IDENTIFICATION OF PROBLEMS

Advanced Study and Critical Reading

The background of scholarship resulting from thorough training in a particular field of specialization and research should identify both the available evidence and the unsolved problems. Helpful related activities may include instruction, administration, reading, writing, and investigation. It has been typical for the graduate student to select a thesis problem in his major field of concentration and quite common for the more mature research worker to follow up the area of interest represented in his doctoral dissertation. As a caution against too narrow specialization, however, we are reminded of the current interest in interdisciplinary training and research, as described in Chapter 1.

The Senior Scholar and the Younger Worker. Stimulating contacts between professor and student inside and outside the classroom or seminar, or between the senior scholar and younger worker, frequently have been profitable in selection and development of problems for investigation. Well-known examples are the influence of William James on Dewey, Thorndike, and Woodworth; Wundt on Cattell, Stanley Hall, Judd, and Titchener; and Dewey, Thorndike, and Judd on many educational and

---

[1] Quoted from T. A. Boyd, *Professional Amateur:* The Biography of Charles Franklin Kettering. New York: E. P. Dutton and Co., 1957. p. 214.

psychological investigators active in the mid-twentieth century and later.

In tracing the influence of the senior scholar or teacher on his students, we find Dewey's case to be an interesting one. Some persons have thought that Dewey derived his educational ideas from Rousseau and Froebel, although Dewey told Kilpatrick explicitly that he had not read the works of either man until after he had formed his educational outlook. Dewey said that he got help in his educational thinking from Francis W. Parker and his psychology from William James; both Dewey and James were greatly indebted to Darwin's *Origin of Species*. As to Dewey's comparative place in the history of philosophy, Kilpatrick places him next to Plato and Aristotle; first in the history of philosophy of education; and in his current influence on education, in the company of William James, Francis W. Parker, and Edward L. Thorndike.[2]

Dewey is an example of a scholar whose great influence on his students far exceeded his skill as a teacher and lecturer. Many dozens of his students became pivotal figures in the intellectual life of our country, yet by all the usual criteria of effective instruction Dewey was a poor teacher. Many of these students tell tales of Dewey's dullness as a lecturer and in the next breath say that Dewey's teaching fundamentally changed their thinking. His appearance was farmer-like, weather-beaten, and unpretentious. He remained seated throughout the hour, seldom seemed to be looking directly at his audience, often would turn in his chair and glance sideways, as if half-looking out the window and half-absorbed in his private thoughts. There is the standard legend of Dewey's lecture on "Interest in Education," which put many of his hearers to sleep. An inspired understatement concerning his style is to the effect that "Professor Dewey was a quiet talker."[3] Dewey's quiet temperament was apparent as early as completion of his doctoral program at Johns Hopkins in 1884, when President Gilman called him to the office and, after warning him not to remain so "seclusive and bookish," offered a loan for study in Europe.

Kilpatrick says that he got little from his first personal contact with John Dewey through an 1898 summer course in education at the University of Chicago, chiefly because he was not ready for Dewey's thinking and method of teaching. Dewey's practice was to come to the class with a problem on his mind and sit before the class thinking out loud as he sought a solution. Two years later Kilpatrick studied Dewey's monograph, *Interest as Related to Will*, under Charles DeGarmo, which did have a deep and lasting effect. In 1907 Kilpatrick received a scholarship which

[2] William H. Kilpatrick, "Personal Reminiscences of Dewey and My Judgment of His Present Influence." *School and Society* 87: 374–75; October 10, 1959.

[3] Harold A. Larrabee, "John Dewey as Teacher." *School and Society* 87: 378–81; October 10, 1959.

permitted him to study at Columbia University under Dewey for the next three years. Later Dewey read and approved Kilpatrick's manuscript for the 1912 book, *The Montessori System Examined.* In turn Kilpatrick suggested problems for inclusion as chapters in Dewey's book, *Democracy and Education.*[4]

James R. Angell had studied with Dewey at Michigan (and also with James and Royce at Harvard), and later became a colleague at Chicago. Angell, a psychologist, became one of the most influential proponents of a functional psychology, a carrier of the thinking of James and Dewey conjoined.[5]

The relationship between Binet and Simon is a striking example of the influence of a senior scholar on a younger associate. Terman guaranteed that Alfred Binet would be remembered by calling his revision of the scale Stanford-Binet, but Théodore Simon (trained as a physician) became almost a forgotten figure. While Binet died in 1911, Simon was found active as late as 1959-60 in Paris, serving as long-time president (since 1912) of the Société Alfred Binet, housed in Simon's study. In his eighty-seventh year, the slight old man, bearded and bent, walked with shuffling steps. Originally Binet was slow to accept Simon's offer of assistance by way of subjects and advice, but later Simon did provide some needed subjects for testing and proved an intelligent, professionally oriented, loyal research associate, with a mixture of admiration and hero worship for Binet. Shortly before his death, Binet is reported to have said:

I have had many students and collaborators, but I have never had any as sincere and as loyal as Simon. And another thing, never would he say "yes" to me when he thought "no." How I regret going so soon! Now I shall never see Simon at the height of the scale.[6]

It is interesting to summarize in further detail the training and influence of a number of psychologists. John B. Watson, self-styled "the behaviorist," died September 25, 1958, at the age of 80, although his scientific life as such had come to a close a third of a century earlier, and he was unknown personally to a whole generation of younger men in psychology.

In dispensing with mentalistic explanations of behavior, Watson cleared the way for a scientific analysis. In doing so he acknowledged his debt both to Lloyd Morgan and to Thorndike, who, though he remained a mentalist, sup-

[4] William H. Kilpatrick, "Personal Reminiscences of Dewey and My Judgment of His Present Influence." *School and Society* 87: 374–75; October 10, 1959.

[5] Maxine Greene, "Dewey and American Education, 1894–1920." *School and Society* 87: 381–86; October 10, 1959.

[6] Quoted from Theta H. Wolf, "An Individual Who Made a Difference." *American Psychologist* 16: 245–48; May 1961.

plied a classical alternative explanation of "reasoning" in his experiments on trial-and-error learning. The epistemological issue was also in the air. Watson never took to philosophy (though, as he later said, his "milk teeth were cut on metaphysics"), but it was George Herbert Mead's great personal interest in Watson's animal experiments which supplied an immediate and crucial contact with relevant philosophical issues. A behavioristic interpretation of mental processes was later adopted by operationists and logical positivists, but the issue was to remain primarily empirical rather than logical.

Born in Greenville, South Carolina, Watson was to remember himself as a below-average and troublesome schoolboy with little to show for his early education except a love for manual skills. (He later built a ten-room house with his own hands.) His five years at Furman University, where he received an A.M. instead of an A.B., were also remembered as a bitter disappointment. But his educational luck suddenly improved when an interest in philosophy took him to the University of Chicago. Few men have made as many fortunate contacts during their graduate careers: with John Dewey (though Watson later complained "I never knew what he was talking about and, unfortunately, still don't"); with Angell (who taught him to write); with Jacques Loeb (whom Angell thought "unsafe" as Watson's thesis advisor); and, particularly, with Mead. Under the Chicago influence his interests turned to biology, and he always regretted that, in addition to his Ph.D., he was not able to finish work for the M.D. degree at Chicago. At the age of 29 he went to Johns Hopkins University as professor of psychology, where he came into even closer contact with biologists and medical men, particularly Jennings and Adolph Meyer. Among psychologists he worked with Knight Dunlap and Robert Yerkes (who were later to formulate their own variety of "psychobiology") and with Curt Richter and Lashley, the latter fresh from Jennings' laboratory.

From all this exceptional stimulation, Watson emerged with a burning recognition of the need for a science of behavior.[7]

In 1904 Herbert Sidney Langfeld resigned his position as Secretary to the Naval Attache of the American Embassy in Berlin, in favor of graduate study in psychology at the University of Berlin. While this decision was a loss to American foreign service, at the same time it was an important gain for American education in general and psychology in particular.

Langfeld was the last American to study under the first generation of German psychologists, and revealed during his long career in this country, both as teacher and administrator, a serene wisdom and detachment together with a breadth of outlook which may have resulted in part from his experiences in the German universities. The psychologists with whom he studied in Germany were also philosophers with imposing ideas and a sweep of imagination which often made up for their lack of knowledge regarding the experi-

---

[7] Quoted from B. F. Skinner, "John Broadus Watson, Behaviorist." *Science* 129: 197–98; January 23, 1959. Reprinted from *Science* by permission.

mental techniques and statistical analyses in which our students today are so carefully trained. . . .

Langfeld was a good lecturer, skilled in clear exposition and in the use of language "understanded of the people." He was not dramatic, nor did he ever lose his natural dignity by trying to be popular or obvious. The duller students were not impressed, but he had the teacher's reward of knowing that those who took the pains to follow and grasp his ideas retained an enduring and favorable impression. . . .

Langfeld's eclectic interests in psychology and his respect for good writing made him an ideal editor. As the years went on, he spent an ever increasing amount of time in going over manuscripts with painstaking care for professional journals and for a publishing house. . . .

Throughout his long professional career Langfeld provided a valuable link between psychology in America and psychology in other countries. . . .[8]

In his autobiography Wallin cites a number of examples of the influence of able psychologists on their students. He characterizes J. Mark Baldwin of Princeton as debonair, companionable, popular, fluent, brilliant, resourceful, and creative, with great charm as a classroom lecturer, in spite of a slight lisp or speech mannerism. Wallin speaks of Henry H. Goddard as personable, kindly, a good social mixer, a productive worker with a flair for popular presentations of scientific data, and as a practical worker who was the trail blazer for the Binet-Simon scale in the United States. Wallin describes Stanley Hall as a genial, stimulating, and helpful teacher, but one who knew how to "put the heat" on graduate fellows if they appeared to be loafing on the job or if they failed to produce research results. This may explain in part why the Clark fellows majoring under Hall were so productive, although an important cause was also the fact that Hall was an inspiring teacher and writer with a brilliant, retentive, and encyclopedic mind. Wallin speaks of Hall as having enormous breadth of erudition, fertile imagination, catholicity of view, effective presentation, untiring industry, and prodigious productivity.[9]

The following is a rather dramatic example of instruction in sociology. When Lester F. Ward began a summer class in 1909 at the University of Wisconsin, he reached into his pocket and pulled out two peach stones. He threw one of them out of the window and said: "That peach stone may fall upon responsive soil and may grow into a peach tree. This other peach stone will be planted in soil which has been discovered to be suitable for peach trees. The young seedling will be grafted upon

[8] Quoted from Carroll C. Pratt, "Herbert Sidney Langfeld." *Psychological Review* 65: 321–24; November 1958.

[9] J. E. Wallace Wallin, *The Odyssey of a Psychologist:* Pioneering Experiences in Special Education, Clinical Psychology, and Mental Hygiene with a Comprehensive Bibliography of the Author's Publications. Wilmington, Del.: The Author, 1955. p. 19, 24, 39.

a sturdy root stock. It will be protected from disease, San Jose scale, and insect pests. As all the established knowledge of peach culture will be applied to aid the growth and protection of this tree, we are more certain of having a satisfactory peach tree." Ward concluded his remarks with the assertion that those students who understood what he had said already knew everything that would be presented to the class group, and persons who wished further discussion on this problem might find some profit in remaining in the class.[10]

On the other hand, great men have sometimes been dull in their class-lecture presentation. Albion W. Small's lectures in sociology were occasionally very monotonous. At times his graduate students developed a plan to break the monotony of these presentations. A student was assigned each day to ask questions for the purpose of interrupting the lecture. The questions would stimulate Small to lay down his sheaf of papers, step forward, and launch into an interesting discussion of the point concerning which he had written rather ponderous notes in preparation for the lecture. In general, Small was an able teacher and author, with a dynamic personality.

Franklin H. Giddings of Columbia University (1855-1931) found time to encourage younger workers in sociology. When a young teacher in a small western community reported a local study in the village newspaper, with some wider publicity, he received a long-hand letter from Giddings, suggesting continuation of the study, some advice about publication, and ideas for future investigations. For several years, whenever this young teacher published anything, Giddings wrote to him, giving advice and suggestions. A long list of Ph. D. candidates completed their work under Giddings' guidance, and scattered throughout the United States and to foreign lands.[11] In most fields the influence of the senior scholar is reflected in the work of his doctoral graduates.

During his senior year at Indiana University, 1890-91, Ellwood P. Cubberley had an unusual opportunity to become well acquainted with David Starr Jordan, the president of Indiana University. Jordan had gained wide recognition as a speaker and was accustomed to traveling and speaking on a variety of subjects, illustrating his lectures at times with slides projected by a stereopticon lantern. Cubberley accompanied Jordan on these tours and operated the lantern. The long hours together on slow trains, the prolonged stay at stations between trains, and occupancy of the same hotel room provided opportunities for conversation

---

[10] M. C. Elmer, *Contemporary Social Thought:* Contributors and Trends. Pittsburgh: University of Pittsburgh Press, 1956. p. 12, 25.

[11] *Ibid.*, p. 16–17.

Emory S. Bogardus, *The Development of Social Thought.* Fourth Edition. New York: Longmans, Green and Co., 1960. p. 451–61.

and exchange of ideas that influenced the younger man throughout his long career in education.[12]

Harold Rugg speaks of his long association with John Dewey as his "credentials" for appraising Dewey and his contemporaries from the perspective provided by the centennial of Dewey's birth and by a common interest in certain phases of educational philosophy.

A brief personal note on my credentials may not be out of order. I was born the year Dewey's first book was published (1886). This was *Psychology,* a very un-Dewey-like book if judged by his creative library after 1896. I was ten (1896) when he and his University of Chicago colleagues opened the Laboratory School. I entered college (1904) the year he abruptly left Chicago and retired permanently from educational experimentation to the philosophic cloisters of Columbia. In 1909-1910 I was witness to the chief indoor sport of my colleagues in a small Illinois college telling jokes about Dewey's crazy theories of educating his and other people's children—all of which, by the way, were based on total ignorance of both his theories and his practices. I worked with Judd, in Dewey's former School of Education at the University of Chicago, from 1915 to 1920. (Judd continued the tradition that Dewey's work was a joke, publicly "getting Dewey's goat" by deriding the School's pet); I was there in 1916 when Dewey published *Democracy and Education* (which Kilpatrick dragged out of him, piece by piece, for Monroe's new series on education). I was a colleague of Dewey at Columbia for twenty years, had close fellowship with him in the Teachers College Discussion Group for two winters in the 1930's, went to the Union of South Africa with him for the New Education Fellowship in 1934, and in the middle '30's was a fellow editor of the *Social Frontier* for which he wrote his monthly "John Dewey's Page." Throughout this thirty-year period, I learned much from Dewey about the psychology of verification, but not about the psychology of discovery, and I have been an admirer of his ability to think a problem through to its roots (he told me once that he thought that was his best capacity). But since my *Culture and Education in America* (1930), I have been a critic of the curious blind spots and lopsidedness of his pragmatic experimentalism.[13]

Extensive and Critical Reading. With respect to wide reading, in all scientific endeavor the interdependence of research workers is recognized in the identification and solution of problems. In spite of difficulties in securing the works of other scholars, even such early investigators as Roger Bacon and Leonardo da Vinci relied on extensive knowledge of the writings of others in their special fields of interest. The inspiration for many of Bacon's experiments may be found in the work of other

[12] Jesse B. Sears and Adin D. Henderson, *Cubberley of Stanford: And His Contribution to American Education.* Stanford, Calif.: Stanford University Press, 1957. p. 15–16.

[13] Quoted from Harold Rugg, "Dewey and His Contemporaries," *John Dewey in Perspective.* Bulletin of the School of Education, Indiana University, Vol. 36, No. 1. Bloomington, Indiana: Indiana University, January, 1960. 42 p.

scholars. The 5,000 manuscript pages of Leonardo's notebooks disclose his indebtedness to other workers and his wide reading (he quotes from 72 medieval and classical authors).

Charles H. Judd had exceptional opportunities for extensive reading in his undergraduate training in the United States and in his graduate work in Germany; his advice to beginning students is that they select teachers with broad interests and read widely. Although Edward L. Thorndike considered himself an investigator or experimenter rather than a scholar, in the sense of devoting his time to books and the literature, he estimated in 1936 that he had spent well over 20,000 hours reading and studying scientific books and journals. The extensive reading, erudition, and range of information of William James may well explain his success in bringing together the work of the Scottish, English, French, and German schools of psychology.

As an example of wide reading, Dewey's early book on psychology (written in 1887, when he was only twenty-eight years of age) was based largely upon his extensive reading, including the American, British, French, German, and Italian authors. For example, in his chapter of fifty-three pages on "Elements of Knowledge," Dewey refers to seventy-eight sources, and in his chapter, "Processes of Knowledge," of seventy-three pages he cites fifty-four sources.[14]

Cubberley's meticulous habits of work and extensive reading are illustrated by the manner in which he prepared for the teaching of a new course.[15] He began immediately to develop syllabus outlines with references for reading. For his history of education course, the syllabus developed in the direction of a history of culture. For his first course in school administration he drew upon collections of documents. A typical scene was that of Cubberley leaving his office after class in the evening with an armful of school laws and reports. Next morning he would lug them back to their shelves in the library. Night after night he read, made notes, and kept his syllabus growing. Sometimes when he had left the campus for lectures at institutes, his notes were not far ahead of the class. Even after retirement in 1933, Cubberley did a great deal of reading on a wide variety of subjects. After each title he placed a rating such as he was accustomed to do in his entries of stocks or bonds—double "A" if excellent, etc. He left notes on 25 books read in 1934 and 46 in 1935.

As background for his major contributions to philosophy, Whitehead had the benefit of extensive reading in the classics (Latin and Greek), mathematics, science, theology over a period of some eight years, and philosophy. His varied experience and teaching at Cambridge University, London University, and Harvard University profoundly affected the

[14] Junius L. Meriam, "John Dewey in History." *School and Society* 87: 376–78; October 10, 1959.

[15] Jesse B. Sears and Adin D. Henderson, *op. cit.*, p. 69, 83.

development of his philosophy. In view of the size of Whitehead's library, his remark to a friend about not having read a great quantity of books should be taken relatively:

"I read very slowly," said Whitehead. "Sometimes I see myself referred to as 'a well-read man.' As a matter of fact, I have not read a great quantity of books; but I think about what I read, and it sticks."

"Speed is not for me. On the other hand, some of my reading is 'skippy.' Last night, for example, I was reading that book in your lap on the Jesuits, but finding, at the beginnings of successive chapters that he was still on the same aspect of a subject whose point I had already grasped, I did not hesitate to skip."[16]

The youthful reading of Thomas Huxley, the scientist, foreshadowed his later interests:

He consumed popular novels, histories of Europe, works on science, philosophy, and religion, idling away the hours thumbing through a large, illustrated Bible that delighted him. Although he had no formal schooling for 10 years, like Herbert Spencer and others of the self-educated greater Victorians, he occupied himself advantageously in his spare time, speculating on the causes of sunset colors and inventing what he fondly thought was a perpetual-motion machine. After explaining the latter to Michael Faraday, who received him kindly but the machine rather unfavorably, the young boy vowed that some day he would have something of much import to show Faraday.[17]

It should be pointed out, however, that some scholars and scientists have not been interested in making a study of the earlier writings or related literature in their fields of specialization and research. Agassiz found the study of things themselves more attractive than what was printed in books about the particular subject; he usually was satisfied with paging through the volumes of natural history, so that he might later identify the objects he examined in nature. Comte, in the latter part of his life, practiced what he called "cerebral hygiene," that is, he refrained from reading the books of other social thinkers, which meant that he was not always abreast of the times, although in his synthetic thinking and encyclopedic work Comte borrowed ideas from many predecessors. W. G. Sumner, the sociologist, paid little attention to the work of other writers in his field, not even mentioning in bibliography or index the names of Comte, Ward, and Giddings, although he did draw upon the ideas of other scholars.

Some of these scientists and scholars have considered it undesirable or even unwise to study closely the related literature, fearing that the

---

[16] Quoted from *Dialogues of Alfred North Whitehead*. As Recorded by Lucien Price. New York: New American Library of World Literature, 1954. p. 140, 320.

[17] Quoted from Charles S. Blinderman, "Thomas Henry Huxley." *Scientific Monthly* 84: 171–82; April 1957.

research worker's mind might be conditioned to see the problem in the same way or in a traditional manner and thus overlook a new or more fruitful approach. Charles Kettering, a research specialist in industry, believed that, as a result of studying conventional textbooks, we fall into a rut, escape from which may take as much effort as the solution of the specific problem. He chided men of science who "create obstacles to their progress by referring to theories which say certain matters cannot be accomplished." Kettering's unorthodox advice to specialists is "to throw away the books and work toward the objective," based on his opinion that "the smaller the library the less chance to find excuses that it can't be done."

We know that there is no absolute knowledge, that there are only theories; but we forget this. The better educated we are, the harder we believe in axioms. I asked Einstein in Berlin once how he, a trained, drilled, teaching scientist of the worst sort, a mathematician, physicist, astronomer, had been able to make his discoveries. "How did you ever do it," I exclaimed, and he, understanding and smiling, gave the answer: "By challenging an axiom!"[18]

The poet, Byron, has aptly expressed the dilemma of creative workers: "To be perfectly original one should think much and read little, and this is impossible, for one must have read before one has learnt to think." It would seem that for most graduate students and research workers the solution of this dilemma does depend on critical reading as a stimulus to thinking.

Analysis of Evidence, Practices, Trends, or Needs in a Particular Area

When a field of knowledge is being analyzed to identify problems for study, the particular research area should be sufficiently limited to serve effectively as sources of specific problems for investigation; for example, physical growth, mental development, or reading readiness rather than child psychology or abnormal psychology. On the other hand, the research area under analysis should be large enough to permit development of meaningful, integrating concepts of interpretation; for example, language development rather than the phonetic range of the one-year-old. Much of the background for separating a subject into its constituent parts and for identifying the research problems in each subarea is derived from the programs of reading and instruction described in the preceding section of this chapter.

Beginners in research frequently are not sensitive to problems, practices, trends, and needs close at hand, as illustrated earlier in this chapter. To cite another example, even as early as 1915, when a young sociologist

---

[18] Lincoln Steffens, Quoted in *Contemporary Psychology* 5: 105; March 1960.

went to teach at the University of Kansas, Frank W. Blackmar asked, "Young man, what do you know about the people of Kansas?" When the new staff member admitted his ignorance, Blackmar said, "You can't teach young people without knowing something about their background." He handed the new teacher a copy of the *Kansas City Star*, with the question, "Do you see anything about Kansas that interests you?" When the young man replied that he saw the name of a city, Beloit, Kansas, Blackmar answered: "All right, I have arranged for a fund of $900. You will teach five hours a week this semester. Next week, you go to Beloit, spend a couple of days there, talk with anyone and everyone until you have an idea of what people around Beloit do and think."[19]

An illustration in the field of education identifies fifteen trends and areas of needed curriculum research:[20]

1. We have developed more effective research techniques for studying social and economic trends than we have research techniques for the derivation and validation of values.

2. We have clearer analyses of the social and economic trends in our society than we have of our value systems.

3. We have more analyses of aspects of our society from specific disciplines than we have interdisciplinary studies exploring the implications of such findings for human living.

4. We know more about trends in our society than we do about the implications of these trends in terms of children and youth growing up in that society.

5. We know more about norms for separate aspects of development than we do about the interrelationships among these aspects of development in the growing organism.

6. We have more techniques for studying the learner in the light of norms and averages than we have techniques for studying him in the light of his goals and his concept of himself.

7. We know more about learners as individuals than we do about the interrelationships among learners in groups.

8. We know more about learners' interests than we do about day-by-day problems of living they are trying to handle.

9. We know more about general processes of maturation than we do about the developmental tasks which each new stage of maturity brings.

10. We know more about how to organize a classroom or school for effective learning than we do about how to decide what should be taught.

11. We know more about how to develop skills such as reading and handwriting, and about how to teach facts, than we do about how to develop concepts or attitudes.

[19] M. C. Elmer, *op. cit.*, p. 48.

[20] Quoted from Margaret G. McKim, "Curriculum Research in Historical Perspective," *Research for Curriculum Improvement.* 1957 Yearbook. Washington: Association for Supervision and Curriculum Development, a Department of the National Education Association, 1957. p. 34–35.

12. We know more about how to study the outcomes of a child's work than we do about how to study the processes by which he works—the steps he takes in solving an arithmetic problem, the way he reasons in drawing conclusions.

13. We have more techniques for evaluating growth in skills and knowledge than we have techniques for evaluating growth in such areas as attitudes and feelings.

14. We know more about planning for the effective learning of children and youth than we do about planning for the effective learning of those who are to teach them.

15. We know more about achieving effective interpersonal relations in the classroom than we do about achieving effective interpersonal relations in the faculty of a whole school system.

As another example in education, nine types of problems for research in the classroom setting indicate urgent needs that have developed over a half century.[21]

1. We accept the general assumption that the role of the school is to prepare the learner for effective living in our society, but we have little evidence regarding the type of curriculum design most likely to achieve this goal.

2. We are in substantial agreement that it is important to develop ability to think creatively, to be self-directing, to work cooperatively, but we are just beginning to learn what classroom practices will best achieve these goals.

3. We assume that the most effective motivation is intrinsic, but we have much to learn about the respective roles of teacher and pupils in the determination of goals; about the respective roles of pupil interest, need and purpose in the establishment of goals; and about the most effective functioning of pupil-teacher planning. We have much to learn, also, about how to study the learner in order correctly to identify his goals.

4. We accept the concept of maturation, but we have much to learn regarding the degree to which physiological growth patterns actually affect learning.

5. We accept the concept of readiness, but we have meager evidence regarding the role of classroom experiences in developing readiness, and much to discover regarding the appropriateness of various methods for pupils of different maturity levels.

6. We accept the concept of individual differences, but we do not yet have the evidence we need to plan the most effective program for gifted children; we do not yet have much research as a guide to the developmental tasks faced by slow learners; neither have we tested thoroughly in practice the range of possibilities for the effective grouping of learners.

7. We operate on the general assumption that learning comes through experience, but we need more evidence regarding the types of experiences most effective for different maturity levels, backgrounds and levels of intellectual ability. We also need more help in determining how the goals, needs

[21] Quoted from *ibid.*, p. 35–36.

and background of the particular learner influence the structure of an experience for him.

8. We accept the concept that we are teaching the "whole" child, but we have much to discover regarding the influences upon learning of the affective tone of the classroom, of the child's feeling of security and of his personality patterns.

9. We are in substantial agreement that evaluation should be a continuous process, but we do not yet possess the techniques we need to measure progress toward all our goals, nor do we know much about the effect of various methods of evaluation upon the learning process.

Repetition, Extension, or "Budding Out" of Problems

In this chapter we have already indicated that history is never complete, that descriptive-survey studies are accurate only for the time and sample represented, and that many experiments should be repeated under the same or different conditions for purposes of verification. The scientist favors duplication of experiments under various conditions, lest some uncontrolled factor be present in the original experiment. At times, however, even the experienced investigator has failed to follow up a discovery in the direction of even more important conclusions or applications, as illustrated by the discovery and development of penicillin.

In 1928 a spore of a green mold drifted into the laboratory of Alexander Fleming, a Scottish scientist, and "spoiled" a culture of bacteria. When Fleming returned from a short vacation he noticed the mold growing in the culture dish of bacteria and was ready to discard the "spoiled" culture when he saw a transparent ring around the mold. Outside the ring bacteria thrived, but there was none inside it, for something was killing the germs. Fleming then began his research leading to the discovery of penicillin, following up what has been termed a "chance" discovery. Although the discovery was a fortunate "accident," it should be remembered that Fleming had the training and ability to recognize the significance of the accident. It should be added that, although Fleming described crude preparations of penicillin in 1929, he left this work, after a time, without developing a therapeutic agent, and it remained for Florey to complete this task.

To comment further on so-called "chance" discovery in science and research, we know that Roentgen was already a scientist of some repute before he made his "accidental" discovery of x-rays:

The reader will be quite impressed with Roentgen's experimental ability and logical mind, particularly in his three papers on x-rays (December 28, 1895, March 9, 1896 and March 10, 1897). . . . The x-ray expert and the lay reader both will be amazed at the wide scope, completeness, carefulness and significance of his measurements. He practically "cleaned out the field," there being very few further important advances in x-rays until 1912 when x-ray diffraction was discovered. He was not famous by a chance discovery, he was a superior scientist. Not only was Roentgen great in science but he was great in humility for he refused to accept nobility.[22]

In 1912, nearly a decade before the discovery of insulin by Banting and Best, one of Anton J. Carlson's graduate students isolated a crude extract of insulin which mitigated the effect of diabetes in dogs. Carlson freely admitted to what he called his "stupidity" in not following up this promising line of investigation.

In many instances an "offshoot" of a problem under study or of a technique in use leads to more fruitful results than the original problem or approach; for example, the idea of the delayed-reaction experiment, as a method of studying animal mentality, came to Edward L. Thorndike after two years of work with animals. Willis R. Whitney's apt statement concerning the "budding out" of problems is: "We found nature easy to follow and difficult to drive. We usually wanted what she gave for our seeking, but we could seldom get exactly what we thought we wanted at the time. We wanted light. She gave us rectifiers."[23] Sometimes the term "serendipity" is used: "the gift of finding valuable or agreeable things not sought for."

Sometimes the "bypath" in an investigation proves to be a blind alley, but careful reporting of this fact may prevent other research workers from wasting time on the same project. By way of illustration, when an enthusiastic but immature student proposed a research project dealing with attempts to standardize an aspect of social research, he first sought assistance from two professors in sociology, without success. As a last resort, the graduate student went to a third sociologist, Albion W. Small, and received the following reaction:[24]

> Young man, I believe you are on the wrong track. I believe that you will find your search for research methods leading you into a blind alley. That, however, is perfectly satisfactory. Do your job so well that no one need ever waste any time on that project again. I spent three years of hard work on a study of the Cameralists. I think it was largely futile. But I covered the ground completely enough that no one needs to go over it again. Therefore, I consider it three years well spent.

FACTORS IN SELECTION OF THE PROBLEM

The investigator usually considers a number of external factors in choosing a problem for study: novelty, significance, sources, technique,

---

[22] Quoted from review by Leonard Muldawer, *American Scientist* 47: 86A; March 1959, of Otto Glasser, *Dr. W. C. Roentgen*. Second Edition. Springfield, Ill.: Charles C Thomas, 1958. 169 p.

[23] T. A. Boyd, *Research*. New York: Appleton-Century-Crofts, 1935. p. 270.

[24] Quoted from M. C. Elmer, *op. cit.*, p. 24.

equipment, working conditions, sponsorship, and cooperative relationships. He also evaluates such internal or personal factors as interest, motivation, intellectual curiosity, background of scholarship and training, temperament and personal characteristics, costs, risks, and timing.

Novelty, Cooperative Studies, and Significance

The next chapter describes the library guides or keys for determining the research completed in a particular sphere of investigation. As pointed out earlier in the present chapter, when it seems desirable to repeat or extend earlier experiments or investigations, what is implied is deliberate and systematic planning rather than accidental or random duplication of earlier studies through ignorance of the research literature. We have already noted that even able scientists and scholars sometimes have been negligent or indifferent to the literature in their particular fields of specialization.

In view of the number and complexity of problems in education, and of the relatively recent application of research methods to such problems, the question of uniqueness may be less important than the ways in which studies are comparable or related, or fit into a pattern of investigation and results.

The question of overlapping of dissertation problems or novelty sometimes arises when two or more graduate students engage in a cooperative program of research, which is a type of investigation that has come into increasing use on the part of commissions, survey teams, and research agencies (often with the assistance of graduate students). Many teams of scholars or inventors have found it profitable to work cooperatively in seeking answers to their problems.

To cite a specific example of cooperation in the graduate field at the University of Texas, team studies have been undertaken, in order that broader research problems may be studied than is usually possible when the responsibility is carried by one person. Four doctoral candidates have cooperated in attacking the problem of class size, two such candidates have worked together to discover what happens to children whose parents insist that they enter the first grade below the age of six, and four students have been investigating methods of reporting to parents at the elementary-school level.

Two graduate students at the University of Cincinnati worked together on a two-part master's study, "Simplified Versions of the *Constitution* and the *Declaration of Independence* for Use in the Junior High School, Parts I and II."

While recognizing the value of team work, Kettering did not want to suppress originality in any way. When another man who was doing much to support research on cancer suggested to Kettering that, in order to get better coordination in cancer research and to avoid duplication of effort, the two of them go together and try to organize all the cancer studies in the nation and get them under one common head or guidance, Kettering said he would not favor the proposal:

> I'm afraid of a single direction in such things. It is too likely to steer the endeavor down one road, which may turn out to be the wrong road. I'm not worried about the duplication of effort in research. Such duplication is sometimes a good thing. It is not what two groups do alike that matters. It's what they do differently that is liable to count.[25]

The trend toward teamwork and cooperation in education, psychology, and other fields is resulting in multiple authorship, especially when working with the sponsorship or support of large research organizations:

> More and more psychologists may be expected to become accustomed to work as members of research groups and to have the assistance of large research organizations in bringing their efforts to successful conclusion. The trend toward multiple authorship in psychology and in the totality of the sciences may also accelerate as more and more funds become available to conduct research on the larger and more difficult problems that now demand attention and as group research extends in nonpsychological as well as psychological fields.[26]

It should be recognized that some contributions to the literature are valuable for purposes other than novelty or creativity; for example, Charles A. Ellwood (1873-1946) did not produce particularly new ideas in especially brilliant style, but he wrote in such a clear, logical manner that his work was readily understood and easily translated. Ellwood's discussion of methods in sociology vigorously criticized the tendency to overemphasize objective and statistical methods, and did much to revive interest in nonstatistical procedures.[27]

The criterion of significance or importance for the field represented and for the individual involves the realm of values. The discussions of the role of values in research and of the social responsibility of the scientist in Chapter 1, as well as certain topics of the present chapter, deal with values that frequently play a prominent part in the selection of problems for study. The literature includes a large number of analyses of

---

[25] Quoted from T. A. Boyd, *Professional Amateur:* The Biography of Charles Franklin Kettering. New York: E. P. Dutton and Co., 1957. p. 184–85.

[26] Quoted from Mapheus Smith, "The Trend Toward Multiple Authorship in Psychology." *American Psychologist* 13: 569–99; October 1958.

Also see Mildred B. Mitchell, "Trends Toward Multiple Authorship in Scientific Publications." *Journal of Psychology* 52: 125–31; July 1961.

[27] M. C. Elmer, *op. cit.,* p. 35.

Emory S. Bogardus, *op. cit.,* p. 590–604.

problems for research, frequently with an indication of the importance or significance for the field represented (as listed in the chapter bibliography).

Curiosity and Drive

Many scientists and scholars have been urged forward by an insatiable curiosity, driving interest, or other powerful motivation, sometimes to extremes in concentration, withdrawal from social contacts, or neglect of health. One scientist has suggested that our ideas need to be jostled about so that we do not become intellectually sluggish, or that we need a certain amount of "dither" in our mental mechanisms:

When working, early in World War II, on antiaircraft computing and gun-laying devices, I learned from British colleagues a new use of an old word. When building such devices, they often included a small eccentric or vibrating member which kept the whole mechanism in a constant state of minor but rapid vibration. This they called the "dither."

The purpose, once one thinks a moment, is perfectly clear. Kinetic friction is less than static friction. If the parts are constantly in slight motion, then the whole device is alert, is on the jump, is ready to respond promptly to the earliest beginnings of forces seeking to move the gun, the little dither gimmick preventing any sluggish delay caused by static friction. The same phenomenon arises in other connections. For example, the types of flight instruments which are dependably responsive in an aircraft with reciprocating engines and a good deal of resulting general vibration might tend to stick or respond tardily in jet aircraft with their almost vibrationless flight.

We need a certain amount of dither in our mental mechanisms. We need to have our ideas jostled about a bit so that we do not become intellectually sluggish. The British are good at this, too, and use Hyde Park corner, His Majesty's Loyal Opposition, and a variety of other techniques to make sure that mental static friction does not dominate.

It is a wonderful thing to have in science fresh, unorthodox, nimble, and vibrating minds. The recent phenomenon of Edwin Land's essentially 17th-century type of discovery in the field of color vision is an excellent case in point. This really shakes every scientist, and in so doing it benefits him.

The same consideration, I think, furnishes an extremely powerful argument for carrying out as much basic research as possible under circumstances which involve eager young persons. My scientific godfather, Dean Charles Sumner Slichter of the University of Wisconsin, used to say that every laboratory ought to have "one damn fool who doesn't know yet what you can't do." When a professor who does research also has the marvelous opportunity of teaching elementary courses he finds that the contacts with the youngsters constantly jostle his own mind. It may at times put him in a dither, but that is good for him.[28]

[28] Quoted from Warren Weaver, "Dither." *Science* 130: 301; August 7, 1959. Reprinted from *Science* by permission.

Intellectual Curiosity, Drive, and the Scientist. As a youth, Agassiz was
a model of industry; he led in his studies and soon mastered the classical
learning that was available to him in the Collège de Bienne in his native
Switzerland, but this was not enough:

> He wanted to become a naturalist, and without the entire approval of his
> family, he extended his studies and his field researches. Even as a boy he
> revealed both his ambition and his determination. He decided to become the
> greatest naturalist of his generation, and he determined that no person, no
> hardship, and no obstacle should deter him.
>   He was remarkably well equipped for his chosen career. He learned easily
> and quickly, and he retained great masses of facts almost automatically and
> without effort. He also understood what he learned and he could organize his
> knowledge and recognize the underlying principles in his accumulated data,
> as he showed when he classified the fishes of the world and when he devised
> his theory of continental glaciers.[29]

An example of early assumption of responsibility for a heavy load
of teaching and editing, and of a compelling drive to achieve, is found
in the life and work of Charles J. Herrick, the neurologist, who died at
the age of 91, before he had completed all he had planned to do:[30]

> In 1893 his brother had to resign his professorship at Denison University
> and hasten to Arizona because of tuberculosis. "C.J.," two years out of college,
> undertook to conduct, single-handed, all of the scheduled courses in biology.
> He assumed an even heavier burden in saving the *Journal of Comparative
> Neurology,* which his brother had founded, "because its suspension would
> break my brother's heart and retard his recovery." He became editor, business
> manager without a secretary, proofreader, and supervisor of the printing of
> engravings. Until 1908 he paid the inevitable deficits of the journal from his
> own salary. On one occasion he felt called upon to decipher a manuscript in
> longhand which had been charred black in the fire which destroyed his
> laboratory. Many a robust man would have been overwhelmed by these labors.
> They did not keep C. J. Herrick from continuing his research. . . .
>   The reputation established by these studies resulted in an invitation to
> Herrick to become professor of neurology at the University of Chicago when
> H. H. Donaldson resigned to go to the Wistar Institute in 1907. Herrick hesi-
> tated to make so radical a change because of his health. The matter was
> decided by his wife's question, "Would you rather go to Chicago and burn out
> or stay here and rust out?". . .
>   Ten years after his retirement to Grand Rapids, Michigan, he found it
> necessary to give up the long hours of observation at the microscope. He de-

[29] Quoted from review by Conway Zirkle, *Science* 132: 1655–56; December 2,
1960, of Edward Lurie, *Louis Agassiz: A Life in Science.* Chicago: University of
Chicago Press, 1960. 449 p. Reprinted from *Science* by permission.
[30] Quoted from George W. Bartelmez, "Charles Judson Herrick, Neurologist."
Science 131: 1654–55; June 3, 1960. Reprinted from *Science* by permission.

voted himself to meditation, reading, and writing on the philosophy of science. In his last book, *The Evolution of Human Nature* (1956), he brought sociology into the field of psychobiology. He died at the age of 91 on 29 January 1960, before he had completed all he had planned to do.

In a long and active life, Charles Singer (1876-1960) found time for virtually three careers. As a young man he qualified in medicine in 1905, traveled extensively as a medical officer, and later engaged in pathological research and a consulting practice in London. In a second career he turned to full-time study of the history of science and medicine. After retirement he continued with these historical interests, broadened to include the history of technology. At the time of Singer's death in his 84th year, his mind was still full of plans for new works.[31]

Charles Oberling (1895-1960) was constantly active in cancer research, medical administration and organization, and teaching in France, the United States, and Iran, in spite of repeated cardiac episodes which harassed him during the last seventeen years of his life. It was ironical that, at the age of 65, an emergency operation disclosed an unsuspected widely distributed cancer, and he died within a few hours.[32]

Alvin Seale was an adventurer, explorer, field naturalist, ichthyologist and aquarium expert, soldier of fortune, and one of the last of David Starr Jordan's personal disciples, and lived to the age of 87 with the drive and tenacity to follow through extensive field work, even to the extent of delaying college graduation until 13 years after admission:

This Indiana Quaker farm boy rode his bicycle across the country to enter Stanford in 1892. He was an outstanding zoology student and in the usual course of events should have graduated in 1896. But he was an unusual student, and his field trips often caused great gaps in classroom work. In 1896 Jordan selected Seale and Norman B. Scofield to go to the mouth of the Mackenzie River, British America, to see if there were salmon there. . . .

He went back to Stanford in the fall of 1899, only to leave for Honolulu when appointed field naturalist for the Bishop Museum. In 1900 he made the first zoological survey of Guam, returning via Manila, Hong Kong, China, and Japan. From then until September 1903 he collected all over Polynesia. . . .

He returned again to Stanford in the fall of 1904 and graduated the following May, 13 years after matriculating. During those 13 years he had come to know more about Polynesia and about its fishes and fisheries than anyone else in the United States and had published a creditable number of important papers.[33]

[31] Trevor I. Williams, "Charles Singer, Historian of Medicine, Science, Technology." *Science* 132: 1296–97; November 4, 1960.

[32] Peyton Rous, "Charles Oberling, Research Worker on the Nature of Cancer." *Science* 132: 1534–35; November 25, 1960.

[33] Quoted from Albert W. C. T. Herre, "Alvin Seale, Naturalist and Ichthyologist." *Science* 129: 313–14; February 6, 1959. Reprinted from *Science* by permission.

Motivation and the Historian. The accomplishments of Douglas Southall Freeman in his 67 years as editor, historian and biographer, educator, and broadcaster and lecturer are attributed to discipline and hard work through almost incredible hours. In his own words, "Outside writing by a newspaperman is primarily a matter of forgetting other things. He cannot do his day's work, share all the social activities that others enjoy, and still have time for historical research or literary work. If he wants the leisure that unhurried composition and painstaking revision demand, he must pay the price." With iron discipline, Freeman cheerfully paid the price through a daily working schedule that stretched over 17 hours, usually rising at 3:15 A.M. and retiring at 8:00 P.M.[34]

Historians frequently have been prodigious workers with remarkable powers of concentration. Ranke continued incessantly busy at work until the age of ninety-one, driving his assistants to the point of exhaustion. He lived a long life, during which he produced some 50 volumes of history. Lord Acton tells of his last meeting with Ranke, who at that time, in 1876, was past eighty. Acton says of him: "He was feeble, sunken, and almost blind, scarcely able to read or write. He uttered his farewell with a kindly emotion, and I feared that the next I should hear of him would be the news of his death."[35] However, Ranke produced another group of volumes before his death in 1886, including a *World History,* which was broken off somewhere in the late Middle Ages.

Compelling Drive and the Psychologist. It is not strange that strong motivation should play a prominent role in the life and work of psychologists. Edwin G. Boring attributes his achievements in research and writing to certain irresistible compulsions, to a capacity for hard work, and to a persistent sense of insecurity during the earlier decades of his life. He says that his compulsive temperament drove him hard, especially during the 1920's, on an eighty-hour week, fifty-week year, which he found near his physiological limit. Somehow Boring had persuaded himself that he was not as bright as most of his colleagues and could make up for the deficiency by working harder. This decade produced his *History of Experimental Psychology,* a major work, although Boring feared for a time that psychologists would regard history as less important than laboratory experimentation. In 1934-35 Boring spent 168 sessions, $1680 at the special reduced rate, in psychoanalysis with Hanns Sachs, because he felt himself insecure, unhappy, frustrated, afraid, and unproductive, and for many years thereafter continued his search for maturity, although

[34] Charles H. Hamilton, "The Most Unforgettable Character I've Met." *Reader's Digest* 77: 149–54; July 1960.

[35] Pieter Geyl, *From Ranke to Toynbee:* Five Lectures on Historians and Historiographical Problems. Northampton, Mass.: Smith College Studies in History, 1952. p. 3.

most psychologists have envied Boring for his achievements as experimentalist, teacher, critic, theorist, administrator, popular expositor, and editor.

Lewis M. Terman had tremendous drive and persistence that lasted in his pursuit of knowledge all through his life, in spite of setbacks with tuberculosis, being burned in a fire, breaking a hip, and other disabilities.

When Lewis M. Terman died, near the end of his 80th year, he was working on the manuscript of volume 5 of *Genetic Studies of Genius* and was simultaneously planning the next 3 years' research on his group of 1500 "gifted children." No other facts could mark the man so well. From 1903, when he arrived at Clark University to begin graduate work, until his death, his career was a continuous sequence of research and writing, broken now and then by illness and accident but never interrupted in its main course.[36]

Motivation and the Sociologist. Illustrations of the driving force of intellectual curiosity and of related types of motivation are available in the field of sociology. The sociologist, Lester F. Ward (1841-1913), was the youngest of ten children, whose mechanic father had a tendency to drift from place to place in his work. When Ward was sixteen his father died, and the boy went to Pennsylvania to live with a brother, where he worked on a farm and in a sawmill for his board and room. In his spare time he made wagon hubs, which were traded for books, articles of clothing, and other things that he needed. Ward picked up a scattered education, largely undirected, although he attained some proficiency in French, German, Greek, and Latin. Later in Washington, while an employee of the government, he was able to earn the A.B., LL.B., M.A., and LL.D. degrees. When Ward left government service in 1906 and went to teach sociology at Brown University at the age of sixty-five, he had achieved a full lifetime of outstanding work in botany, geology, and paleontology, and was regarded as the leading sociologist in America. Ward was characterized by an impressive command of his subject and by a "terrific mental drive."[37]

Another example of delay in beginning collegiate academic work is found in the life of the sociologist Howard Becker (1899-1960), who left school at the age of 14, worked as a laborer in the West, later became an industrial engineer, and then in 1922 turned to academic pursuits, receiving the A.B. degree in 1925, the A.M. in 1926, and the Ph.D. in 1930.[38]

[36] Quoted from Robert R. Sears, "L. M. Terman, Pioneer in Mental Measurement." *Science* 125: 978–79; May 17, 1957. Reprinted from *Science* by permission.

[37] Emory S. Bogardus, *op. cit.*, p. 305–23.

M. C. Elmer, *op. cit.*, p. 11, 127–28.

[38] Hans H. Gerth, "Howard Becker, 1899–1960." *American Sociological Review* 25: 743–44; October 1960.

A rugged physique and dogged determination helped George Lundberg accomplish tasks that others thought very difficult. One night in Wisconsin, when driving with another professor, the car stopped because of carburetor trouble. Lundberg walked eight miles to the next town, found a place to buy repair parts, then walked back to the car and put it in running order. His philosophy of work was: "When anything needs to be done—do it." Lundberg considered large-scale studies and quantitative methods important, but said, "I sometimes wonder whether the most important research done in the world is not what people steal time from the regular employment to do, rather than what they are paid and honored for doing."

Other Examples of Compelling Motivation. Strong motivation impelled Ellwood P. Cubberley to draw up careful plans for retirement, with his projects scheduled by years and the achievements checked against the calendar. He expected his program of writing to continue after retirement, including the editing of his series of professional textbooks in education. As early as 1913, Cubberley estimated what his income would be that year, at the age of forty-five, again for 1915, and at five-year intervals to the age of seventy-five.[39]

The years as Commissioner of Education in Rhode Island were probably the happiest and most successful in Henry Barnard's career. His educational statesmanship and prodigious work were reflected in numerous reforms, almost countless addresses and visitations, and his famous annual reports. A trait that became habitual was to outline carefully in advance whatever he planned to do.[40]

A psychologist-psychiatrist said of the drive behind W. K. Kellogg:[41]

Dominated as he was by an older brother for many years, Will Kellogg developed what is known today as an inferiority complex. In overcompensating for this complex, Mr. Kellogg went to limitless bounds and it is likely this was the greatest driving force behind the success. He was going to show his brother, himself, and the world that he, too, had superior qualities and that only an unfortunate set of circumstances had prevented him from being as eminent as the Doctor. Those circumstances he eliminated.

Alexandre Dumas wrote day and night, working with and without collaborators. On one occasion, when he returned to Paris by night train after a long absence, his son was waiting to take him home. However, the father demanded to be taken at once to the home of a friend, where

[39] Jesse B. Sears and Adin D. Henderson, *op. cit.*, p. 229–30.

[40] Richard K. Morris, "Parnassus on Wheels: A Biographical Sketch of Henry Barnard, 1811–1900." *Teacher Education Quarterly* 18: 45–57; Winter 1960–61.

[41] Quoted from Horace B. Powell, *The Original Has This Signature—W. K. Kellogg.* Englewood Cliffs, N. J.: Prentice-Hall, 1956. p. 182.

they gossiped until four o'clock, finally reaching home at six. The elder Dumas immediately demanded a lamp. "A lamp? But why?" asked his son. "To see by, of course. I am going to get to work." Forthwith the elder Dumas began work on another novel.

Seeking to explain these extraordinary manifestations of concentration and intensity in the form of powerful driving impulses or compulsions, we enter the realm of depth psychology:

> What is the significance of this extraordinary concentration and intensity? What powerful impulses are driving their way at such moments? For there is every reason to suppose that men of genius are characterized by possessing exceptionally strong emotions and usually a correspondingly strong capacity for containing them. The tension induced by the preceding efforts to find a solution gradually mounts until it reaches a climax. The great mathematician of genius, Henri Poincaré, in describing how he made his own discoveries, said: "One is struck by these appearances of sudden illumination, obvious indications of a long course of previous unconscious work. . . . These sudden inspirations are never produced except after some days of voluntary efforts which appeared absolutely fruitless." Einstein has given a very similar description, and in the Fliess correspondence there are numerous allusions to the exhausting stress and strain Freud experienced in the continuously hard work of attaining his various pieces of insight. Kretschmer speaks of the great scientists' "passionate emotions developing which drive their thought constantly in the same direction, producing the utmost tension until at last a short-circuit occurs: somewhere a spark leaps to a new spot where up till then no human thought had ever passed.[42]

Background of Scholarship and Personal Characteristics

The analysis of the hallmarks of the scientist and scholar in Chapter 1, and the earlier section of the present chapter dealing with advanced study and reading, are pertinent to a discussion of criteria for selection of the problem for investigation. Illustrations of the part played by training and certain personal or temperamental characteristics in choice and development of research problems will be drawn from such fields as psychology, sociology, history, education, and other areas of scholarship and research. Frequently, training or scholarship in other fields (for example, physics, mathematics, physiology, biology, medicine, philosophy) has provided important background for the early development of psychology and psychologists, and later through psychology for the field of education.

Scholarship in Education. Harold Rugg (1886-1960) was versatile and talented and was at the forefront of many significant movements in edu-

[42] Quoted from Ernest Jones, "Nature of Genius." *Scientific Monthly* 84: 75–83; February 1957.

cation. He first taught engineering, wrote one of the first books in educational statistics, did extensive work in test development during World War I, wrote social studies textbooks, pioneered in progressive education, played a major part in developing the "foundations" courses in education, and explored aesthetics and creativity in relation to education. The fact that he sometimes stammered in speaking did not lessen his effectiveness and influence in conveying a challenging message to his audience or class.[43]

William C. Bagley (1874-1946), characterized as a stalwart educator, had the advantage of graduate study in psychology under Joseph Jastrow at Wisconsin and E. B. Titchener at Cornell, and of early association with William T. Harris in St. Louis. In spite of his competence in the various professional activities of surveys, editing, writing, lecturing, and teaching, Bagley showed evident signs of nervousness before he entered a classroom or mounted a platform to speak, but once started, usually with a slight nervous cough, he went forward with clarity and conviction to the end. Bagley's claim to a prominent place in the history of American education is not based on a reputation as a reformer or innovator, but on his balanced point of view and steady sense of direction in the midst of a succession of innovations relating to educational aims, methods, and content.[44]

An example of productive activity is found in the life and work of Ellwood P. Cubberley, who made early contributions to educational history, administration and school surveys, and textbook editing. Early in his career Cubberley learned certain elementary but useful concepts of research, at a time during the first decade of the twentieth century when the field of education was just beginning to develop. Cubberley had studied some phases of the method of historical research while preparing his syllabus in the history of education. During his graduate work at Columbia University he secured what was then an acceptable introduction to statistical method, a new field being developed by Edward L. Thorndike. In the course of his doctor's dissertation he learned useful procedures of a descriptive-survey type, as he found his way factually into the then unexplored field of school administration.[45]

Cubberley's long and busy life was spent in building a small department of education into a school of wide reputation, developing his own field of work, carrying a full-time schedule of teaching, writing and editing books, and serving as consultant and adviser. Of the 106 books in the professional series that Cubberley edited, he wrote ten, fifteen others

[43] B. O. Smith, "Harold Rugg: A Memoir." *Educational Theory* 10:176–78; July, 1960.

[44] I. L. Kandel, *William Chandler Bagley:* Stalwart Educator. New York: Bureau of Publications, Teachers College, Columbia University, 1961. ix + 131 p.

[45] Jesse B. Sears and Adin D. Henderson, *op. cit.*, p. 87–88, 97–98.

bore the names of his colleagues, and a number of others were prepared by his former students. Cubberley's ten books in this series sold to the number of 341,000 copies, and the figures for the entire series of 106 books amounted to "approximately 3,070,000 copies."

In summary, Cubberley contributed to five areas of activity: as teacher, educational historian, writer in school administration, investigator and consultant, and editor and author of textbooks. His insight in developing and editing the series of professional textbooks in education is significant, especially as viewed against the background of the undeveloped status of education when plans were first made for the series in 1911:

> School administration was scarcely recognized as a field of study. The curriculum, as a field, had hardly been thought of. The psychology was at most only partly applicable and parts of it were being questioned as to their validity. The literature on methods and management and on supervision was little more than armchair opinion. Educational theory was vague and general at best. There were books promoting special systems of arithmetic or of reading but the systems had been conjured from successful experience, not from careful observation and experiment.[46]

Scholarship in Psychology. Terman's long lifetime of research and writing followed up the pioneer area of his doctoral dissertation:

> The half-century since Terman finished his doctoral training is almost coincident with the history of mental testing. So is Lewis Terman. From the first, there was something provocative and exciting to him in the very idea of measuring complex psychological qualities. His doctoral dissertation was a comparison of seven bright and seven dull schoolboys. He gave each child a battery of more than 40 hours of individual tests, probably the most overwhelming test-assault inflicted on any child up to that time. Nothing much came of the study, but it did give Terman a chance to try his hand at making up tests. He loved it, and he went right on loving it to the end of his life. He built test after test for 40 years, all of them good (technically) and nearly all of them useful.[47]

Terman and Merrill—that means, since Terman has gone, Maud Merrill James—have now come out with the 1960 revision of the Stanford-Binet Intelligence Scale, in lovely blue cloth by Houghton-Mifflin and three bright gold normal distribution curves on the outside. It is a thread through Terman's lifetime, with a prenatal phase fixed in the Binet-Simon scale of 1908 and now this postmortem by Maud Merrill.

In a way Stanley Hall was the godfather, much as he disapproved of tests. His Clark Ph.D.'s, when he was being so deeply concerned with psychology in education, tended to turn up teaching at normal schools. Stanford wanted an

---

[46] Quoted from *ibid.*, p. 191–94.
[47] Quoted from Robert R. Sears, *op. cit.*

educational psychologist. It got Bergström, a Hall man, who unexpectedly died in 1910. Then Stanford invited Huey, another Hall man, who refused in order to stay at Hopkins, and who recommended Terman, a third Hallian, then at the Los Angeles State Normal School, at the same time advising Terman to take the job and to make the development of Binet-Simon intelligence testing his main endeavor in his new post. The result presently was the Stanford Revision of the Binet scale in 1916, introducing the IQ as a practical concept. Then ten years of testing the tests, in association with Maud Merrill, and the Terman-Merrill revision of 1937, improved, extended at the ends, with two forms. Then more years of criticism and now the third distillate, carried through to completion by Dr. Merrill after Terman's death in 1956. It is a single form that keeps the "best" items and continues to push the concept measured, "intelligence," over toward the Binet type of general functioning, "mental adaptability to new problems," "intelligence in action," away from the more manipulative abilities.

So that is one strand in psychology's warp, 57 years long if you start with Binet's *L'étude expérimentale de l'intelligence* of 1903 and come right on up to now. For 46 of those years Lewis Terman was weaving the weft on the warp, and for 30 of them Maud Merrill.[48]

We have a better understanding of the broad interests and abilities of Harold E. Jones (1894-1960) in child-development research when they are viewed against the background of his undergraduate major in biology and graduate study and early teaching in physiological, experimental, and general psychology.[49]

Arnold Gesell (1880-1961), in a remarkably single-minded effort, concentrated his life on scientific investigation and guidance of child behavior, serving from time to time as school teacher and principal, graduate student in psychology, professor of psychology, medical student, clinical psychologist, physician, investigator, author, and teacher.[50]

To cite specific instances of the contributions of other fields of scholarship to the background of psychologists, Wundt, physician and physiologist, accepted a chair of philosophy at Leipzig in 1875, although his place is that of a founder in the history of psychology. Stanley Hall came into psychology with a diversified background of theological preparation, European study, college teaching, and physiology. The broad training and experience of Edward B. Titchener covered music, collection of coins, classical languages, half a dozen modern languages, linguistics and philology, biology, physiology, and anthropology.

---

[48] Quoted from E. G. Boring, "Revised Revision Revised." *Contemporary Psychology* 5: 187; June 1960.

[49] R. N. Sanford and Others, "Harold Ellis Jones, 1894-1960." *Child Development* 31: 593-608; December 1960.

[50] Louise B. Ames, "Arnold L. Gesell: 'Behavior Has Shape'." *Science* 134: 266-67; July 28, 1961.

Although many of the founders of modern psychology came from philosophy or other disciplines, it is also true that a number of modern psychologists have entered the field as graduates of other areas of specilization: Edwin G. Boring, L. L. Thurstone, and Edward C. Tolman from engineering, Godfrey Thomson from physics, Jean Piaget from natural science. Tolman speaks of a number of sources that influenced his psychological points of view: the Gestalt psychologists, a year's stay in Vienna (involving both the academic and psychoanalytical traditions of European psychology), war experiences that developed points of view relating to personality psychology, and contacts with a group of workers interested in sociology, anthropology, personality, and social psychology. Walter Bingham's interest in music as a hobby led to a topic for his doctoral dissertation dealing with the nature of melody.

Scholarship in History. Many historians have drawn on an exceptional background of training and scholarship. Barthold Niebuhr at the age of eighteen knew 18 European languages, as well as Hebrew, Persian, and Arabic. His phenomenal memory was an enormous asset as he went on to master philosophy, mathematics, physics, chemistry, natural history, history, Roman law, and practical politics and administration. The great German scholar, Theodore Mommsen, published 1,513 different titles, and was a scholar in at least six fields of knowledge: epigraphy, numismatics, history, law, archaeology, and early Italian philology. Adolf von Harnack published at least 1,800 titles of books and articles, a record that invites comparison with Mommsen.

Scholarship in Sociology. Examples from sociology indicate the varied training, broad scholarship, and wide reading of the pioneers in this field. Lester F. Ward studied and read philosophy, medicine, law, botany, geology, and anthropology. William G. Sumner had at his command a dozen languages in studying cultural-anthropological problems, and did extensive reading in history, theology, metaphysics, and general literature. Franklin H. Giddings read extensively in European philosophy and sociology, and had six years of experience in journalism and six years of teaching in experimental school situations.

Although officially classified as a sociologist, William F. Ogburn (1886-1959) had far-reaching interests that carried him through all the social sciences for almost 50 years of research and teaching. He wrote in 1932 about the death of the great German psychologist:

> When Wilhelm Wundt died in 1920 it was remarked that the last of the great men who knew it all had passed away. Seventeen years earlier when Herbert Spencer died he took with him a greater range of knowledge than Wundt had possessed. . . . Previous to Spencer there were many great in-

tellects that covered the whole field of human knowledge. . . . Wundt was the last of the old men of our modern civilized tribes.[51]

Ogburn, in his interests and works, must be called the last of the great social scientists who wished to know it all. It is a tribute both to the man who was able to foresee events and to the social sciences that the field has become so diversified and the total volume of knowledge so large that no one man can any longer expect to know all the social sciences.[52]

In his wide travels, Ogburn revealed his interests in the arts and natural history, as well as social life, with special knowledge of the dances of Indonesia, the music of India, the bird life of Burma, the vegetation of the Alps, the textiles of Guatemala, and the marine life of the Florida Coast:

What kind of man was responsible for so many achievements? He was a physically sturdy man, who played tennis and squash with regularity even at 72, his age when he died. He was an intellectually versatile man with profound curiosity, who would seek out informed persons from a wide variety of disciplines for conversation and questioning. From 1910 to 1918 he taught economics, politics, and history, as well as sociology. Intrigued by the revolutionary concepts of psychoanalysis, he submitted to analysis himself and later served as Chairman of the Psychoanalytic Institute in Chicago. A man with regular, dependable habits of work, he could be counted on to deliver on his commitments.[53]

Robert Redfield was trained for law and practiced briefly, but during the course of a short trip to Mexico he became interested in anthropology, later took a doctorate in anthropology, and contributed a series of important books to this field.[54]

Personal Traits, Special Talents, and Achievement. The earlier discussions of advanced study, critical reading, and creative scholarship, as well as the illustrations just presented, remind us that classroom instruction and the library are only part of the background for the accomplishments of scientists and scholars. Able scientists sometimes have not appeared to good advantage in meeting formal examination requirements. The examiners recognized the special talents of Paul Ehrlich, and somewhat reluctantly passed him on his final medical examinations. History records

[51] Quoted from W. F. Ogburn, "Volume of Knowledge." *Journal of Adult Education* 4: 26–29; January 1932.

[52] Quoted from A. J. Jaffe, "William Fielding Ogburn, Social Scientist." *Science* 130: 319–20; August 7, 1959. Reprinted from *Science* by permission.

[53] Quoted from M. F. Nimkoff, "William Fielding Ogburn, 1886–1959." *American Sociological Review* 24: 563–65; August 1959.

[54] Milton Singer, "Robert Redfield, Anthropologist." *Science* 130: 609–10; September 11, 1959.

that Einstein failed at the entrance examinations to the Polytechnic School. It is possible that the inventive scientist or creative scholar may even be at a disadvantage in accumulating the factual information frequently tested on formal examinations, in contrast to the bright student with a good memory who accepts uncritically what he is told or what he reads. Graduate students sometimes quote with appreciation the reply of George Lyman Kittredge, American philologist and author, when he was asked why he did not qualify for a Ph.D. degree: "Who would give me the examination?"

A high grade record may be evidence of high intelligence, but it may also be evidence of a tendency to social conformity which may be undesirable for research. Indeed, many types of deviant behavior may be assets in a research man. For example, rejection of authority, perseveration on "pet" ideas, unwillingness to commit energy in subject areas of low interest, and general independence of thinking are all probably desirable characteristics for research. These same characteristics, however, may result in an appearance of undesirable deviation from the norm—for example, in a spotty grade record. Evidence of high intelligence is important, but this need not be in the form of a high grade average. Even more important, evidence must be sought of those characteristics such as independence of thought and creativity without which high intelligence is of little use in research.[55]

The greatness of George Washington is not obscured by the fact that he possessed quite human and personal characteristics: a strong vocabulary (although he once issued an order that banned any swearing throughout the U. S. Army), a poor speller, difficulty in getting the names of even close friends right, something of a hypochondriac, unsmiling, solemn, moody, sensitive, and easily hurt by criticism.

For some scientists and scholars certain traits of personality or temperament have helped at times; others have been hindered in their work and influence on advanced students. The personal factor manifests itself in the very structure of science:

Polanyi discovers it wherever there is an act of appraisal, choice, or accreditation. Each science operates within a conceptual framework which it regards as the "most fruitful" for those facts which it "wishes" to study because they are "important," and thereby it chooses to ignore other facts which are "unimportant," "misleading," and "of no consequence." In short, the framework *selects* out of a chaos of phenomena those circumstances which are susceptible of "fruitful" investigation and formulation. But the framework itself is not selectable by any formalizable process; it represents a passionate commitment by the person of the scientist, a commitment which then proceeds to make itself good, but always to a degree only. The framework itself is never

[55] Quoted from Donald W. Taylor and Others, "Education for Research in Psychology." *American Psychologist* 14: 167–79; April 1959.

logically decidable by the simple, uninterpreted facts themselves. Further, the conceptual framework itself can never be exhaustively understood by the scientist using it; it has implications beyond what can at any time be foreseen, and the skillful use of it demands a faith in it which can never be adequately grounded by explicit thought. Finally, science in any significant sense is never the work of a single man. The thought of any one scientist would be impossibly trivial unless that man had faith in the skill, reliability, and veracity of a continuing community of investigators.

Scientific knowledge, then, from mathematics through astronomy, physics, chemistry, and biology, is an activity of men who seriously investigate nature from the standpoint of changing conceptual frameworks passionately believed in, within a trusted community of scientists, professionally accredited, using methods which are better described as "skills," "arts," or a kind of connoisseurship than as an impersonal calculus.[56]

Personal Traits and Psychology. Psychologists have been cautioned that overemphasis on factual materials and formal requirements in graduate work may actually inhibit development of creativity and scholarship:

A knowledge of the facts of psychology is important for research. How much of this is to be imparted during graduate study, however, is not easy to determine. Much of the factual knowledge of the mature scientist has been accumulated during the course of his career and probably cannot be duplicated by explicit instruction. Moreover, substantive courses inevitably compete for the student's time with practical experience in the methods and art of research. For all these reasons, we urge caution against the overloading of an individual's graduate program with substantive courses, either as the result of department requirements or as the result of choice by the student.

The kind of scholarship is probably more important than the amount. More attention needs to be given to the development of methods of teaching subject matter and of methods of individual study, such that the student acquires knowledge in ways which make it most available for use and such that he can readily acquire whatever additional knowledge he may need. . . .

In general, we question the assumption that the more formal preparation the individual has for research, the more productive and creative he will be in research. Specifically, we doubt that the more complete the individual's mastery of statistical and other tools, the more effective he will be in research; we doubt that the greater his scholarly knowledge of the literature, the more likely he will be to contribute to that knowledge; we doubt that the value of theory in research increases continuously as it becomes more formalized and detailed, or (for the student) as the theories of others are more intimately and closely studied.

However, the reader should not misunderstand us: statistical competence, scholarship, and theoretical sophistication are all important in research. The

---

[56] Quoted from review by William Earle, *Science* 129: 831–32; March 27, 1959, of Michael Polanyi, *Personal Knowledge:* Towards a Postcritical Philosophy. Chicago: University of Chicago Press, 1958. xiv + 428 p. Reprinted from *Science* by permission.

point is that each of these should be means toward the end of contribution to knowledge, not ends in themselves. The danger is that the individual may become so enamoured of statistical techniques that they largely determine his research decisions, so identified with particular theories that he cannot see problems beyond them. The danger also is that so much time will be devoted to the mastery of these means that too little time will be left for the other experiences crucial to the development of the creative researcher.[57]

From a long life of direct contacts with psychologists, Wallin sketches many interesting pictures of personalities. For example, Wallin speaks of Howard C. Warren of Princeton as lacking the glamour or capacity for social contacts of J. Mark Baldwin, and as reserved and somewhat inhibited (possibly because of a physical blemish). Warren was a rather uninspiring classroom lecturer, unable to arouse much enthusiasm among his undergraduates; yet he possessed a keenly critical and orderly mind and business acumen, with far more ability than appeared on the surface. He slavishly followed his lecture notes, with few interest-provoking asides.[58]

Wallin characterizes W. B. Pillsbury as somewhat reticent and uncommunicative, rather fidgety, nervous, and apparently inhibited. Pillsbury's lectures were well organized and effectively documented, but with the presentation somewhat marred by a rather halting and jerky manner of speaking. Nevertheless, Pillsbury made substantial contributions to the literature of experimental and theoretical psychology, and was a solid scientist. Edward W. Scripture was said to be somewhat nervously unstable but very approachable, helpful, and sympathetic, with energetic, inventive, and imaginative traits, as well as great capacity for original research in psychology and something of a popularizer in his writings.

Ladd is described by Wallin as a scholar of profound erudition, an indefatigable worker, and an amazingly productive author. Wallin draws a picture of Ladd as a somewhat aloof person, with a coldly analytical mind, endowed with the rare power of systematically pursuing a sustained line of thought in his class lectures without recourse to, or with very little dependence on, notes, and with the same inexorable logic, precision of verbal expression, and freedom from rambling that characterized his textbooks. Ladd's sentence structure was so exact that it gave the impression that he was reading chapters verbatim from one of his books. He was the author of some 33 books, including revisions but exclusive of articles, at least 28 of which were in the fields of psychology, philosophy, ethics, religion, and education. Unfortunately, his style of writing was ponderous and involved, which robbed him of the recog-

[57] Quoted from Donald W. Taylor and Others, *op. cit.*
[58] J. E. Wallace Wallin, *op. cit.*, p. 12–24.

nition from his colleagues he so richly deserved, and he was not accorded the acclaim by psychologists at large that was his just due by virtue of outstanding ability and accomplishments. One of Ladd's anecdotes was to the effect that one day on the campus a former student accosted him and said about one of Ladd's most recent books: "Professor, that was a corking book you issued recently, but it is way above my head." Ladd's quick retort was: "The book may be above your head, but God understands it, and so does Ladd, and possibly President Hadley [of Yale] also."

Willam James' work reveals both his early exposure to his father's therapeutic Swedenborgianism and his incipient awareness of psychoanalysis, with the latter culminating in the walk he took with Sigmund Freud in 1909, when Freud made his only visit to America:

> Commenting on that visit in one of his letters, William James noted the intellectual tenacity of his companion—"a man obsessed with fixed ideas" but insisted characteristically that no impediment be placed in the way of his working out the full implications. Freud in a corresponding comment recalled James' remarkable courage in the face of an attack of angina pectoris which he suffered during the walk; the victim asked his companion to walk ahead and leave him to his recovery. James did recover and continued the walk, but the following year he was dead.[59]

Personal Traits and Anthropology and Sociology. We have been reminded that anthropology, as a scholarly profession, has drawn more than its share of nonconformists who are comforted by its findings that each culture has its own values and standards of behavior, and that the demands of our own society are no more right in an absolute sense than those of any other culture:

> Ruth Benedict, however, seemed to be an exception. Her outward calm, mild demeanor, and Mona Lisa smile seemed to indicate a good adjustment to her world. The error of this inference is startlingly disclosed by the materials published for the first time in Dr. Mead's book. These materials reveal a tortured, nonconformist individual who finally found a creative outlet, and we hope relief, in anthropology. From this point of view the book might well have been entitled "The Making of an Anthropologist."
>
> Dr. Mead does not present the life of Ruth Benedict as an ordered, direct, biographical narrative. Instead, she has assembled what might be called case history materials which can be read in any order. . . .
>
> Ruth Benedict's diaries and an unfinished autobiographical sketch, "The Story of My Life. . . ," expose with surprising candor the black depressions and self-doubts that made her early life almost insupportable. These feelings, however, were so carefully concealed that Ruth Benedict was in effect two per-

[59] Quoted from review by Saul Rosenzweig, "The Jameses' Stream of Consciousness." *Contemporary Psychology* 3: 250–57; September 1958, of Frederick W. Dupee, Editor, *Henry James*: Autobiography. New York: Criterion Books, 1956. xiv + 622 p.

sons, a private self and a social self. The double pattern began in her earliest childhood, when Ruth Benedict shut part of herself off from her friends and family and lived in a secret world of imagination. This imagination later found expression in poetry which, however, was written under a nom de plume. It was not until she was well established in anthropology that Ruth Benedict's somewhat secret literary endeavors were abandoned and her private and public selves merged in creative professional work.[60]

Although Gillin's interest in sociological theory and history of social thought was active and productive, his reputation rested mainly on his critically constructive work and extensive writings in criminology and penology, and on his equally important role as adviser, consultant, and administrator in Wisconsin:

> Within Wisconsin, Professor Gillin was known to many people who were relatively unfamiliar with his scholarly achievements; what he meant to them was immediate, direct, and personal. It was mainly his interest in social reforms which touched their lives closely. Many a prisoner was grateful that Professor Gillin not only launched programs looking toward his betterment but also took a warm and friendly interest in him as a human being.
>
> In the community, throughout the State, and among his colleagues at Wisconsin the qualities of his personality made a deep impression on all who knew him. Honesty and simplicity sometimes go with a lack of warmth, but in Professor Gillin's case there was no such lack. Students and colleagues in need of friendly counsel did not hesitate to take him into their confidence, for they could count on his warmly human attitude. His relaxed and easy manner of meeting with people who were troubled or perhaps even obsessed by their problems did not mean any lack of firm principle. He consistently applied in his intimate relations with those who sought his counsel his favorite maxim, "You must love the sinner, but you must also hate his sin."
>
> It may well be that this combination of honesty, simplicity, warmth, and firm principle accounts for his remarkable influence in advancing many social reforms in Wisconsin. It would be a stubborn legislator or administrator who could not be brought to see the wisdom of the proposals that Professor Gillin took the trouble to recommend.[61]

At times, traits of personality or temperament (or a feeling of self-sufficiency) have influenced able scholars to disregard the work of their fellows or to disagree sharply among themselves. Lester F. Ward had a feeling of self-sufficiency and finality about his own views and statements, and was outspoken in his rejection of other points of view. Another sociologist once commented on certain of Ward's conclusions as

[60] Quoted from review by Julian H. Steward, *Science* 129: 322–23; February 6, 1959, of Margaret Mead, *An Anthropologist at Work:* Writings of Ruth Benedict. Boston: Houghton Mifflin, 1959. xxii + 583 p. Reprinted from *Science* by permission.
[61] Quoted from Howard Becker and Neal B. DeNood, "John Lewis Gillin, 1871–1958." *American Sociological Review* 24: 562–63; August 1959.

follows: "It appears to me that Ward's conclusions are not correct. However, I may not be a competent critic since Ward has stated that, because of my different point of view, I am not a sociologist."[62]

William G. Sumner (1840-1910) was one of the first teachers of sociology in the United States. He was never quite accepted by Small, Ward, or Giddings as a sociologist, but neither did Sumner accept them. Small expressed surprise when Sumner was elected president of the American Sociological Society: "It came to me consequently as a surprise and a shock that he was thought of as second president of the American Sociological Society. At that time (1907) he was not within my field of vision as even nominally a sociologist."

Personal Traits and Other Fields of Science.

Newton had a markedly irritable and suspicious temperament, and much of the controversy that disfigured his life arose from his credulous belief in the statements of overcandid friends. In later life these qualities deteriorated for a while into paranoic delusions of persecution; perhaps in this connection it is not irrelevant to remark that Newton never fell in love and never married.

Faraday, the supreme physicist of the 19th century, had also his vein of credulousness. He said: "In early life I was a very imaginative lively person who could believe in the *Arabian Nights* as easily as in the *Encyclopedia*, but facts were important to me and saved me." Throughout his life he was an adherent of the obscure sect of Sandemanians, followers of the religious prophet Robert Sandeman, and for 3 years regularly preached sermons before them. One must place this in contrast with Faraday's exceptional intelligence in other spheres, since it would be commonplace otherwise.

Darwin was a man of far more placid temperament, and it is probable that any turmoil of emotions found their expression in the psychosomatic afflictions to which he was a martyr. But his skepticism was tempered by a credulous attitude toward other authorities. Even after his great discovery of the operation of evolution through natural selection he still believed in Lamarck's doctrine of evolution through the inheritance of acquired characters, a doctrine his own work had rendered superfluous and indeed erroneous.

His friend and contemporary Huxley offers a very interesting contrast to the genius Darwin. Although possessing a wider knowledge than Darwin, and gifted with more originality and a greater intellectual daring, Huxley's actual achievements are of a different order. On first reading Darwin's theory he exclaimed: "How extremely stupid of me not to have thought of that." Now, Huxley was endowed with any amount of skepticism, of indeed a rather pugnacious brand. It has been said of him: "He allowed himself no prejudice, no sentimentalities, no illusions." But there is no record in his life of any evidence of credulousness to match it and, according to my view, to enable him to make really great discoveries.[63]

[62] M. C. Elmer, *op. cit.*, p. 16, 21–22.
Emory S. Bogardus, *op. cit.*, p. 305–51.
[63] Quoted from Ernest Jones, *op. cit.*

On the other hand, many scientists have been extremely modest people. Stating that the number of men widely recognized as possessing the attributes of genius is very small (Newton, Darwin, and Einstein), Jones speaks of Freud's disclaimer:[64]

"The genius of Freud" is a phrase that has been used so widely that I think we must subscribe to a truth contained in it. Characteristically enough, Freud himself vehemently dissented from its being applied to him. Even as far back as 1886, when he was 29, he wrote to his betrothed: "There was a time when I grieved that Nature had not, in one of her gracious moods, impressed on me that stamp of genius as she sometimes does. Since then I have long known that I am no genius, and I no longer understand how I could have wished to be one. I am not even very talented; my whole capacity for work probably lies in my character attributes." On one occasion in later life when it was applied to him he burst out with the protest: "Geniuses are unbearable people. You have only to ask my family to know how easy a person I am to live with. So I cannot be a genius." This disclaimer, however, was based on a very partial definition of genius, so we need not take it too seriously.

Pavlov has provided an inspiring statement that seems an apt partial summary of the requirements for sound scholarship: sound basic training, thorough acquaintance with the factual evidence, and devotion to the scientific approach.

What shall I wish for the young students of my country? First of all, sequence, consequence and again consequence. In gaining knowledge you must accustom yourself to the strictest sequence. You must be familiar with the very groundwork of science before you try to climb the heights. Never start on the "next" before you have mastered the "previous." Do not try to conceal the shortcomings of your knowledge by guesses and hypotheses. Accustom yourself to the roughest and simplest scientific tools. Perfect as the wing of a bird may be, it will never enable the bird to fly if unsupported by the air. Facts are the air of science. Without them the man of science can never rise. Without them your theories are vain surmises. But while you are studying, observing, experimenting, do not remain content with the surface of things. Do not become a mere recorder of facts, but try to penetrate the mystery of their origin. Seek obstinately for the laws that govern them. And then—modesty. Never think you know it all. Though others may flatter you, retain the courage to say, "I am ignorant." Never be proud. And lastly, science must be your passion.[65]

Sources, Technique, Equipment, and Working Conditions

Procedure and Equipment. The problems in selection of sources and method are closely related to the scholar's background of training and

[64] Quoted from Ernest Jones, *op. cit.*
[65] Quoted from Ivan Pavlov, *Scientific Monthly* 81: 129; September 1955.

personal characteristics. The several methodological chapters of this book provide appropriate orientation for selection of a suitable technique for the problem at hand, although we should remember that investigators vary in their degree of devotion to highly formalized methods. When a group of young sociologists, over-impressed by the rigors of formalized approaches in gathering data, quizzed Edward A. Ross about his methods of research, he smiled and replied:[66]

I am not a research man, I just write what I think best explains a process or a situation. For example, a number of years ago I decided to spend some time in China. I told everybody I was going to China and asked if they knew anybody there. By the time I left for China I had three thousand names and addresses of people: Chinese officials, Chinese scholars, coolie brothers of laundry men, beach combers, missionaries, teachers, relatives. I made up a list of five things I would like to know about changes taking place in China. I contacted, wherever possible, the names I had and countless others. When I talked with them at first our general conversation might lead to the person expressing himself on one or more of these five questions. If the answer did not come up naturally, I asked him questions. After the interview I would sit down on the side of the road on a stone or back in my room and write up, as nearly as possible, an exact account of what had been said to me. I returned to Wisconsin with many boxes full of notes and with the aid of some intelligent assistants classified these notes and put them in the form of a little book, *The Changing Chinese.* Nothing scientific about it, it was just what I had gathered from hundreds of sources.

Ross traveled widely in the United States and abroad; he was a keen observer and recorder of social life.

As illustrated in the later chapters on research methods, special equipment or tools must be devised or adapted for certain types of investigation. Favorable working conditions are usually helpful, but not an absolute prerequisite to successful research or productive scholarship. The quality of scientific work depends much less on the complexity of the equipment or instruments than on the soundness of the thinking and the validity of the evidence, since the most important instrument or element in research is the mind of man. Work in improvised laboratories sometimes has produced remarkable results. There are many examples of great discoveries outside the laboratory or study.

With John MacGillivray, son of the famous ornithologist, Huxley improvised dredging nets, often finding his specimens kicked off the deck by sailors; nevertheless, the lack of scientific instruments, the necessity of lashing his microscope to the mast, the paucity of scientific literature, and the presence of unsympathetic mates merely threw him upon his own resources.[67]

[66] Quoted from M. C. Elmer, *op. cit.*, p. 33–34.
Emory S. Bogardus, *op. cit.*, p. 523–39.
[67] Quoted from Charles S. Blinderman, *op. cit.*

Appropriate illustrations may be drawn from the field of psychology. William James contended that he began instruction in experimental psychology at Harvard either in 1874-75 or 1876 with equipment described by Stanley Hall as a "tiny room under the stairway of Agassiz Museum . . . with a metronome, a device for whirling a frog, a horopter chart, and one or two bits of apparatus." However, as early as 1879 Stanley Hall exposed the fallacy of theatrical methods and "brass-instrument" psychology, insisting that curves, instruments, and flashing charts of themselves would not insure the accuracy of a doubtful generalization, and objecting to the fad of reducing everything to mechanics and motion (a movement that was spreading even in the 1870's). Lewis M. Terman was inept with apparatus just when American psychology was becoming brass-instrument conscious, but he found in Stanley Hall (not an apparatus man) an erudite interpreter of the mind, fitted himself into the Hall pattern, took his doctor's degree at Clark, and went on to the top in psychology, with specialization in mental testing and the gifted child.

Edward L. Thorndike modestly underrates his background in mentioning an extreme ineptitude and distaste on his part for using machinery and physical instruments. He regrets the absence in his training of a systematic course in the use of standard physiological and psychological apparatus for exposing, timing, and registering, and of extended preparation in mathematics. Yet William James once said of his pupil Thorndike that, more than any other contemporary, Thorndike had the quality most essential to a scientific man—the ability to see things apart from acquired perspective and personal reference. Thorndike, together with Charles H. Judd of the University of Chicago, revolutionized the techniques of educational investigation through emphasis on fact-finding, statistical, and experimental procedures.[68]

The work of many other psychologists has benefited from their considerable ingenuity in devising equipment or apparatus. Clark L. Hull conceived the idea of building a machine that would do nearly all of his correlation work automatically. Although Hull could not make mechanical drawings and his assistant could not read such drawings, they achieved their purpose by making marks free-hand on bits of paper at the mechanic's work bench; both had an idea of how the wheels should go around to do certain things.

An experimental geologist began graduate study with an extraordinary range of techniques and skills:

Skilled in observation, both by eye and with a camera; possessed of unusual ability to visualize lines, planes, and curved surfaces in three dimensions, thanks to superb training in geometry; master of the slide rule and

[68] Merle Curti, *The Social Ideas of American Educators.* Revised Edition. Paterson, N.J.: Littlefield, Adams and Co., 1959. p. 459–60.

possessing the engineer's knowledge of the mechanics of solids; of original bent and adept in the use of machine tools; and keenly interested in determining the how and why of natural phenomena and in developing ways and means of demonstrating and applying these phenomena, Warren Mead was exceptionally well equipped to attack both quantitatively and experimentally the whole broad front of physical geology as he entered Wisconsin's graduate school in 1906.[69]

Important as apparatus is, we are warned that too great dependence on expensive or elaborate equipment may actually restrict freedom in research if the investigator proves reluctant or unwilling to leave his apparatus for research in other important fields:

Another thing that we can't do without is apparatus. Some ideas, some projects call for lots of expensive equipment. If a man has acquired a large-scale accelerator, a big radio telescope, or a large-scale computer, or if he has set to work on a large-scale experimental system of some sort, he is not likely to walk out on it because an attractive idea in some other field occurs to him. If a systems experiment is shackling him, he can abandon it if it is bad or complete it if it is good, but if he has an accelerator, a radio telescope, or a computer around his neck, he may be stuck in a field for life. This isn't fatal, of course; he can direct his thoughts to the field in question and have and pursue ideas in that field only. But he has lost freedom in that there is little chance that he will actually do something else, however much he may daydream about it. If he wants to recover his freedom, he can perhaps find a substitute, put him in charge, and leave him holding the bag.[70]

Working Conditions and Environment. Varied conditions of work and environment have contributed to the solution of important problems, depending in part on the temperament of the scientist or scholar. Helmholtz has said that, after working on a problem for some time, happy ideas for a solution frequently came to him at some place other than his working table. Some scientists have claimed that an unexpected insight or intuition, at times in sleep, produces the answer to a problem, although these solutions probably do not take place spontaneously; rather, such "insights" come from a mind with a rich background of knowledge. Scientists and scholars have reported certain conditions or environmental setting as favorable to the emergence of solutions to problems: freedom from competing problems or worries, periods of relaxation or sleep, and recovery from fatigue. In so far as Helmholtz offers an explanatory theory, it is based on fatigue and recovery from fatigue. In 1896, at a dinner in

[69] Quoted from Robert R. Shrock, "W. J. Mead, Experimental Geologist." *Science* 132: 1235–6; October 28, 1960. Reprinted from *Science* by permission.

[70] Quoted from J. R. Pierce, "Freedom in Research." *Science* 130: 540–42; September 4, 1959. Reprinted from *Science* by permission.

honor of his seventieth birthday, Helmholtz spoke of his methods of work on original problems as follows:[71]

I must say that those fields of work have become ever more agreeable to me in which one need not depend on lucky accidents and "happy thoughts." But as I have found myself pretty often in the uncomfortable position of [waiting for thoughts my story is useful to others]; . . . they never came to a fatigued brain and never at the writing desk. It was always necessary, first of all, that I should have turned my problem over on all sides to such an extent that I had all its angles and complexities "in my head" and could run through them freely without writing. To bring the matter to that point is usually impossible without long preliminary labor. Then, after the fatigue resulting from this labor had passed away, there must come an hour of complete physical freshness and quiet well-being, before the good ideas arrived. Often they were there in the morning when I awoke, just according to Goethe's oft-cited verses, and as Gauss also once noted. But they liked specially to make their appearance while I was taking an easy walk over wooded hills in sunny weather. The smallest amount of alcohol seemed to frighten them away.

A characterization or analysis of the nature of genius takes cognizance of examples of intuition or spontaneity in problem-solving, but recognizes that this feature is not always present in research and scholarly activity:

This seems to accord with the frequency with which geniuses often receive their inspiration in a sudden flash that startles the recipient himself. It is a feature that has always been recognized. Both Plato and Aristotle commented on it, and they associated it with the divine source of the inspiration. The description of Apollo in the third book of *Hyperion* seemed to Keats to have come by chance or magic—to be, as it were, something given to him. He said also that he had often not been aware of the beauty of some thought or expression until after he had composed and written it down. It had then struck him with astonishment and seemed rather the production of another person than his own. Alfred Russell Wallace wrote: "Finally both Darwin and myself, at the critical period, had our attention directed to the system of *positive checks* as expounded by Malthus in his *Principles of Population*. The effect was analogous to that of friction upon the specially prepared match, producing that flash of insight which led us immediately to the simple but universal law of the 'survival of the fittest.'" This is, however, a feature by no means always present. The flash of insight which Wallace described did presumably happen to him, but Darwin himself seems to have reflected on the suggestion more calmly. No one can have accepted revelation more tardily and gradually, even cautiously and very timidly, than Darwin, whose dawning vision came only as the result of many years of hard work.[72]

[71] Quoted from Robert S. Woodworth and Harold Schlosberg, *Experimental Psychology*. Revised Edition. New York: Henry Holt and Co., 1954. p. 838.
[72] Quoted from Ernest Jones, *op. cit.*

Although the diverse and powerful forces of the Chicago environment contributed greatly to ten productive years in creating Dewey's philosophic system, with a metaphysics, a logic, an ethics, and a psychology, the accompanying stresses eventually led to his move to Columbia University. Here was a mild, diffident philosopher who confessed that "administrative work is not just in my line." Although possessed of great inner strength and a superior mind, he did not have the physical and temperamental attributes of leadership for a complex administrative position. Dewey and President Harper became estranged, his faculty split into hostile factions, and his wife was dropped from her school post. In 1904 Dewey went to Columbia University as professor of philosophy, where he spent the remainder of his long and eminent career. It is possible that, had Dewey remained at Chicago to work out more fully his theory in an empirical setting of experience, such a mature educational theory and methodology might have prevented much of the bickering and controversy that hampered educational progress during the first half of the twentieth century.[73]

In contrast to the notion that we need a certain amount of "dither" in our mental mechanisms in order to avoid intellectual sluggishness, the autobiography of Mark Van Doren is the story of a man who worked almost all his life under favorable and tranquil conditions. Van Doren has expressed a theory about teaching which suggests that the more abundant a man's life is, the better he will teach, and the story of his own life of nearly forty years of teaching at Columbia University deals everywhere with abundance. The autobiography is a record of the many-sided life of a distinguished professor and poet, and the tale of a happy man. Mark's life on his father's farm in Illinois during his childhood at the turn of the century reads a little like a Victorian tale, one of innocence and enchantment, yet oddly real in spite of the fact that he is unable to recall any unhappy memories. In the family there were a devoted mother, a country doctor father who never punished, and five affectionate sons, reared in a world of security and love. Mark particularly liked some of his instruction at the University of Illinois, and also liked the teachings of Thoreau, whom he read for many months and about whom he eventually wrote a master's essay that became his first published book. Thoreau may have been Mark's greatest teacher, for Mark seemed to understand the wisdom of Thoreau's advice, "Do what you love," and followed this advice for the rest of his life. After service in Army camps in 1917-18, Mark faced with some uncertainty the question, "Would I teach or would I write? Or both?" The answer was to be "both," and he gladly accepted an instructorship at Columbia College. He writes of people with affection

[73] Robert L. McCaul, "Dewey's Chicago." *School Review* 67: 258–80; Summer 1959.

and of experiences with a certainty that they were worth having. His students listened to him and he to them, and Mark came to believe more and more in teaching that is personal, patient, and alive. His academic story is that of the poet as teacher and of the teacher as poet. One reason for his contentment with life might be that when faced with a choice of alternatives he simply chose both. He is a man of conversation, always ready to talk, yet he says, "I can do with long silences." He loves both country and town. So it may be that the choices all became one choice of an abundant life that he lived greatly, with a wife and two sons, with courses to teach and books to write, and with many friends. (Some sadness came with the participation of one son in the investigations of television quiz programs during 1959-62.) Although the story sounds like a leisurely and reflective life, the fact is that Van Doren taught uninterruptedly through the years until his retirement, and he wrote and edited more than forty volumes. Certainly he worked long and hard at his poetry, which in the end reveals only the harmony in his life and something of the secret of his quiet serenity and content.[74]

Sponsorship and Cooperation

In selection of a thesis or research adviser, it is essential to reflect carefully on the availability and personality characteristics of the particular professor or staff member under consideration; among the important factors are leave of absence, a heavy teaching schedule, a large number of advisees, concentration on writing or research, numerous speaking engagements, ill health, or temperamental difficulties. For certain types of studies sponsorship, cooperation, or special permission from responsible school officers may be necessary; for example, to administer tests to pupils, to interview employees, to distribute questionnaires, to observe pupils and teachers at work, to evaluate buildings or equipment, to try out innovations in curriculum or method, or to make case studies of pupils.

The present chapter and other sections of this book identify directly or indirectly many instances of helpful cooperation between professor and student. It is only honest to say that graduate students and others sometimes have suffered from lack of intelligent advising, appropriate sponsorship, or administrative cooperation. To cite an example, Wallin believes that the dissension caused by the ouster of certain psychologists from Yale University in the first decade of this century proved especially disastrous for Yale psychology graduates over a number of years, with respect to securing major positions in philosophy or psychology. He

[74] Condensed from review by Helen Bevington, *AAUP Bulletin* 45: 295–97; June 1959, of Mark Van Doren, *The Autobiography of Mark Van Doren*. New York: Harcourt, Brace and Co., 1958. 371 p.

speaks of the young Yale graduates in psychology of those early days as a "lost generation," in terms of finding or being recommended for attractive positions in psychology.[75]

Scripture's sudden severance from Yale University made it impossible for him to do the editorial work on Wallin's thesis, which had been accepted for publication in the Studies from the Yale Psychological Laboratory (Scripture was the editor). Wallin himself had to do all the editorial work at a time when he had no experience in scientific publication. The one suggestion Scripture had made was that the copy for publication should be boiled down about 50 per cent, not by eliminations but by condensing the sentences and by packing them brim full of content. (Scripture said that he scarcely recognized his own thesis when Wundt, the great German psychologist and founder of the world's first psychological laboratory in 1879, got through with it.)

To cite an example of either extreme independence in working out the dissertation or of an authoritarian adviser (possibly both), E. G. Boring says that in his thesis research at Cornell he conferred with Titchener only twice, once when the problem was planned and once eighteen months later when Titchener had gone over the finished manuscript.

Risks and Costs

In the selection and development of certain types of problems there are sometimes special risks, penalties, handicaps, or costs of a physical, financial, personal, social, or professional character. Fortunately the costs of graduate study and research have been considerably eased during recent years through a variety of financial resources.

Risks and Ethics. The risks in educational research, where human relationships usually are involved, may include problems of professional ethics:

To what extent is the investigator free to tamper with complex organisms and their relationships to one another?

To what extent is he free to set up conditions which are strictly his—conditions with which the subjects of research may not even be familiar and which are not of their making?

Are the proposed risks in research legitimate? For example, to what extent does one have the right to use an untried method of instruction? On the other hand, to what extent is one obligated to try out new methods of instruction in order that progress might be made?

Do the child and his parents have the right to expect that the school will make use in its instructional program of those methods and procedures which have been found somewhat productive, or is the child's school experience to be a testing ground for untried, albeit promising hypotheses?

75 J. E. Wallace Wallin, *op. cit.*, p. 12, 15–16.

What is the effect on the learner whose opportunity to learn has been impeded by the research process (the process to produce the information that the procedure in question was not efficacious)? Would the deprived learner have legitimate grounds for complaint, and would his parents?

To what extent does the learner bear a part of the burden of extending knowledge as to how learning takes place?

To what extent is the research worker free to disregard the expectations of the learner in a given situation?

If a deficiency discovered in a survey has been corrected, should the results of the survey be published?

Should we be as assiduous in trying to find external factors which might cause substantially better performance than was anticipated, as we are in seeking such explanations for performances which are not up to our expectations?

If the unfortunate personal traits of a staff member in a school system have created a barrier to research, to what extent should he be informed of the effects of his own personal idiosyncrasies?

To what extent are we justified in using students and faculty members as unwitting guinea pigs? Can we excuse this type of procedure on the grounds that their awareness of the nature of the research would invalidate the findings and make these less generally applicable? Or can we justify giving full information with the general conclusion that people will do better and behave more intelligently if they know what they are doing and why they are doing it?[76]

Physical Hazards and Costs. The hazards of research in the field of medicine and health are well known to the doctors, scientists, interns, medical students, research workers, patients, and others who test new treatments for disease, new drugs, or new scientific equipment. Selected research volunteers for service in this field have formed the Walter Reed Society, named after Major Walter Reed of Spanish-American War fame, who dramatized the use of human volunteers in medical experience and helped to solve the riddle of yellow fever.

Men of high achievement have often accomplished their work in spite of physical or health handicaps. Sir Walter Scott was lame as a result of a childhood attack of polio and was ill for much of his life. At times he dictated while racked by pain from gallstone and stomach cramps.

Samuel Johnson achieved greatness in spite of lifelong suffering from a compulsive neurosis, the distorting convulsions of his severe tic, and his attacks of depression. It has been suggested that, had Johnson lived at a later date, science would have been able at least to name his oddities, if not to cure them. His habits with respect to eating, drinking, and personal

[76] Quoted from James A. Hall, "Some Ethical Problems," *Research for Curriculum Improvement.* 1957 Yearbook. Washington: Association for Supervision and Curriculum Development, a Department of the National Education Association, 1957. p. 269–77.

cleanliness should be viewed in the perspective of the eighteenth century rather than in terms of standards or customs two hundred years later.[77]

Although George Washington had great physical strength and endurance, he was subjected to a number of diseases in his lifetime, including at least ten serious illnesses that on several occasions brought him near the brink of death. These ailments included malaria (at that time called ague), smallpox, acute pleurisy, a febrile disease (apparently of the influenza type), dysentery, what was probably typhoid fever, and his last fatal illness, probably a streptococcic laryngitis. The great man's cheeks were sunken because of ill-fitting dentures, his complexion was sallow and pock marked (as the result of smallpox), and he was flat-chested and somewhat hollow in the center of the chest (probably from rickets).

John Lubbock paid a high price for his contributions to zoology. The boy John went to a private school when he was eight and on to Eton at 11, but was removed by his father before the age of 15, from motives which seem to have been mixed:

> Ostensibly and probably quite genuinely Sir John disapproved of the education given at Eton at that time, which consisted of Latin and Greek undiluted by science, mathematics, a modern language, or even English, though history (ancient) and geography (classical) entered into it to a limited extent. But also, he had two ailing partners in the family bank and found that banking was getting in the way of his mathematics. Young John was made a partner forthwith, and with increasing frequency he was left to hold the fort while his father got on with the tides. So he had to face loneliness and responsibility very young, and, with a self-discipline almost incredible today, he set himself to remedy the defects of his education. He organized his day of 17½ hours minutely, beginning with mathematics shown up to his father before breakfast and ending with German from 11 to midnight, because, as he said, nothing else kept him awake so well. It is true that the timetable admitted three-quarters of an hour of whist after dinner and a walk in the afternoon and made ample provision for prayer, meditation, and the reading of sermons. Even so, it is hardly surprising that John's health was at this time thought to be uncertain. It is clear that he had already acquired the faculty of economizing time and of turning from one subject to another without pause or hesitancy which was the marvel of his contemporaries to the end of his life.[78]

A number of psychologists have been confronted with physical and health problems. A nervous disorder William James had during his twenties may have contributed indirectly to his intellectual development, since it gave him psychological insight into abnormal conditions and took him

[77] Edward Hitschmann, *Great Men:* Psychoanalytic Studies. New York: International Universities Press, 1956. p. 176.

[78] Quoted from R. J. Pumphrey, "The Forgotten Man: Sir John Lubbock." *Science* 129: 1087–92; April 24, 1959. Reprinted from *Science* by permission.

abroad in search of a cure, with profitable visits to the intellectual and artistic centers of Europe. Eminent specialists and the cures at expensive watering places on the Continent gave James little help. Finally, by disciplined reading and by speculation, in which there was an element of mysticism, he whipped himself into shape for an active career at Harvard University.[79]

The tic (blinking) of Edward B. Titchener may have struck the young student as a strange flaw in a famous psychologist, but Titchener's personality was so natural and spontaneous that in the course of the seminar or lecture the tic was disregarded and forgotten. Clark L. Hull was handicapped by a severe attack of typhoid fever that left him with a generalized bad memory for names; an attack of polio left one leg badly paralyzed and crippled; and his earlier years of psychological study were made much more difficult because of his weak eyes. James R. Angell, near the end of his college course, considered medicine as a career, but weak eyes caused him to believe that he could not do the exacting microscopic work required as part of the medical program.

For sixteen years at Cambridge University, Whitehead had a constant struggle with insomnia, and each September, after a summer's vacation in the country or by the sea, he would wonder whether he could endure another year of teaching. However, the insomnia never seemed to affect his work, and when he moved to London University it diminished and finally ceased.[80]

The sociologist, Charles H. Cooley (1864-1929), spent seven years as an undergraduate student at the University of Michigan because of ill health. We do not know how much effect his ill health, and the influence of his able jurist father, may have had on his quiet, effective thinking and writing. Most of his work assumed the form of digesting and interpreting the writings of others, and in applying the conclusions to life around him.[81]

When Clyde Kluckhohn (1905-1960) was forced, because of ill health, to delay his college education, he retired to a ranch in New Mexico to recuperate. This event played a large part in shaping his subsequent career in anthropology. From the ranch he made pack trips through the adjacent Navaho country and, after recovery of his health, frequently revisited the Southwest during the summers. As an ethnographer Kluckhohn devoted most of his life to the Navaho Indian. He spoke fluent French and Spanish, as well as German and Navaho, and traveled

[79] Merle Curti, *The Social Ideas of American Educators.* Revised Edition. Paterson, New Jersey: Littlefield, Adams and Co., 1959. p. 430–31.

[80] *Dialogues of Alfred North Whitehead.* As Recorded by Lucien Price. New York: New American Library of World Literature, 1954. 320 p.

[81] M. C. Elmer, *op. cit.,* p. 36.
Emory S. Bogardus, *op. cit.,* p. 492–504.

in Mexico, Australia, Japan, and India in following his wide-ranging interests.[82]

Ellwood P. Cubberley produced a large volume of published material and edited works, in spite of colds, stomach ulcers, and sinus disturbances that caused him frequent discomfort for many years. His notebooks record the symptoms and the treatment, often including a record of temperature and blood pressure together with the physician's diagnosis. Later he was hospitalized a number of times, and underwent several serious operations, the details of which he set down in his notebooks. His major illnesses included surgery for an ulcer in 1918, removal of his appendix in 1934 and of a kidney in 1935, and the handicap of a serious heart ailment.

Graduate students of the latter part of the past century, including those at Johns Hopkins in the 1880's, voiced complaints all too familiar today about cramming for examinations, long hours, too little recreation, loss of sleep, eyestrain, and the drudgery of copying materials for reports and dissertations.[83]

Worse than cramming was the unavoidable drudgery of copying. Cyrus Adler's transcribing of his dissertation of over six hundred pages in two weeks was herculean. Excepting the Sabbaths, his daily regimen allowed time for meals, an hour's walk, and two hours' sleep; the rest of each day he spent copying. Students paid a physical price for their intellectual excesses in headaches, strained eyes, and nervous dyspepsia.

Financial Risks, Costs, and Resources. Scientists and scholars frequently have encountered financial difficulties or have sacrificed their personal resources. Sir Walter Scott's badly managed ventures in printing and publishing failed, with debts of 130,000 pounds charged against him. Refusing bankruptcy, during the last six years of his life Scott produced a nine-volume life of Napoleon and in two years turned over 40,000 pounds to his creditors. He continued writing best sellers until his frail health cracked, and he died at the age of sixty-one. Later, the sale of Scott's works settled the last of the debts that helped kill him.

Herbert Spencer was an invalid most of his life, with an uncertain income. He invested more in his early books than he received from them, since he usually employed an amanuensis. In the early days of the *American Journal of Psychology*, Stanley Hall had to spend $8,000 of his own money on the publication, in order to keep it going.

Henry Barnard devoted a considerable part of his long life, 1811-1900, to the thirty-one volumes of the *Journal of Education*, not merely

[82] George P. Murdock, "Clyde Kluckhohn (1905–1960)." *Behavioral Science* 6: 2–4; January 1961.

[83] Quoted from Hugh Hawkins, *Pioneer:* A History of the Johns Hopkins University, 1874–1889. Ithaca, New York: Cornell University Press, 1960. p. 283–84.

as editor, but later as promoter and publisher.[84] His financial sacrifices for the *Journal* included the mortgaging of his home, personal savings, and generous gifts of copies to persons who could not afford the purchase price. At one time the financial status of the *Journal* was so shaky that Barnard considered the melting of the plates in order to sell the metal to meet his indebtedness. In reply to this proposal, the English educator Robert H. Quick said, "I would as soon hear that there was talk of pulling down one of our cathedrals and selling the stones for building material."[85] These financial difficulties probably were due in part to mismanagement and poor record-keeping, which were a matter of concern to Barnard's wife, who closed her letter written to him in 1856, "I am lonesome and cross at being left so much alone, the evenings are too dismal to live through. Love to all but the Journal to whom (*sic*) I have sworn eternal enmity."[86]

In many instances scientists have disregarded monetary costs and returns, particularly when their work was supported by educational institutions and agencies. Pasteur declared, "I could never work for money, but I would always work for science," and Agassiz said, "I have no time to make money." On the other hand, early in life Agassiz exhibited a characteristic that we are only now beginning to appreciate fully—he was always able to raise money:

When his father's resources for financing his extended education in Germany proved insufficient, he found a maternal uncle whom he persuaded to take over. His teachers were also uniformly helpful. Later, in France, Cuvier did his part and made it possible for Agassiz to remain a while in Paris. Baron Alexander von Humbolt contributed to Agassiz from his personal funds and used his political influence to get Agassiz grants from the Prussian state. Later, at Harvard, Agassiz routinely and conscientiously ignored all budget limitations and overspent his funds almost as a matter of principle, but he was always able to raise enough money to cover the deficits. He could always rehabilitate his own personal finances by giving a few public lectures. Such talents we can appreciate.[87]

In some instances the scientist may even have religious or moral scruples about accepting money for research or consultation:

Faraday was an active member of a very strict sect of the Nonconformist Church. His lofty religious ideals and his urge to pursue as far as possible the

[84] Richard K. Morris, "Parnassus on Wheels: A Biographical Sketch of Henry Barnard, 1811–1900." *Teacher Education Quarterly* 18: 45–57; Winter 1960–61.

[85] Reprinted in the *Journal of Education* 14: 7; August 25, 1881.

[86] Quoted in R. E. Thursfield, *Henry Barnard's American Journal of Education*, p. 47. From a letter in the Monroe Collection, New York University, dated June 8, 1856.

[87] Quoted from review by Conway Zirkle, *Science* 132: 1655–56; December 2, 1960, of Edward Lurie, *Louis Agassiz: A Life in Science*. Chicago: University of Chicago Press, 1960. 449 p. Reprinted from *Science* by permission.

spiritual implications of his scientific work led him to abandon all industrial consultation work and to renounce the monetary and social advantages that he could have derived from his immense fame. Yet, while he properly emphasized the usefulness of science in the practical affairs of man, he rarely voiced his inner conviction that science is an attempt to understand the universe as much as it is a technique to exploit nature; that—to use an expression of which he was fond—science is above and beyond everything else, "natural philosophy."[88]

Some scientists have had the benefit of large personal resources for conducting their research. Roger Bacon was a member of a wealthy family and probably earned substantial fees for lecturing. He spent 10,000 pounds, in modern money, on the purchase of books, experiments and instruments, journeys to meet scholars, and secretaries. Charles Darwin was an English gentleman of wealth and leisure, with favorable conditions for making his scientific studies.

The grandfather of William and Henry James had left a fortune of three million, a huge sum for pre-Civil War America. This wealth profoundly influenced the lives of his grandsons through rich cultural opportunities in the form of special schools, foreign travel, and favorable living conditions. William James was able to spend ten years in higher studies as preparation for his life work, trying his hand at painting, science, philosophy, and medicine. He could comment to his banker about his lack of anxiety concerning money, "beyond wishing not to live on capital."[89]

Occasionally a professional risk and related financial costs are involved in a disagreement between graduate student and professor. Hugo Münsterberg disagreed with Wundt in setting up a dissertation problem in the Leipzig laboratory and was shifted to another (less important) problem which was accepted. Although Münsterberg later adapted the rejected dissertation for another purpose, he lost the favor of Wundt and as a result was handicapped in securing a position. On the other hand, Wundt's treatment of Münsterberg won James' sympathy for the young psychologist and led to a Harvard appointment for Münsterberg.

When John Dewey was offered a head professorship in 1894 by President Harper of the University of Chicago, the philosopher asked for $5,000 a year, $2,000 more than his salary at the University of Michigan. Dewey said that the proposed salary of $4,000 per year was inadequate to meet the needs of his family in a city like Chicago, but he finally accepted the offer, expressing the hope that in due time an increase would be provided. Thus it appears that problems of cost of living in relation to salary have been with us for a long time. Possibly Dewey left

[88] Quoted from René Dubos, "Scientist and Public." *Science* 133: 1207–11; April 21, 1961. Reprinted from *Science* by permission.

[89] Merle Curti, *The Social Ideas of American Educators*. Revised Edition. Paterson, New Jersey: Littlefield, Adams and Co., 1959. p. 430–31.

his well established position at the University of Michigan at a salary less than he thought adequate in order to work in the stimulating atmosphere of a large city.[90]

Occasionally a specialist in psychology or education has made himself financially independent. Edward L. Thorndike made it a rule early in his career to spend so little and earn so much that he would be free from financial worry, and in so doing became a person of considerable means. Ellwood P. Cubberley was able to accumulate a fortune, derived chiefly from royalties on books and fees for editorial services, with smaller sums from services as consultant, investigator, and lecturer. These sums were increased greatly through investments that proved sound. The gifts by Cubberley and his wife to Stanford University totaled more than three quarters of a million dollars, including more than a half million dollars for a new School of Education building.[91]

When that academic dynamo J. McKeen Cattell at the age of 31 was head of Columbia's Department of Psychology, many of his colleagues confidently expected him to leap to first place in the new and characteristically American science of pragmatic psychology. Instead, Cattell chose to divert some of his remarkable energies to founding a publishing and business empire, which eventually included seven scholarly periodicals (each edited on a different day of the week from the Cattell home, with the entire family at work), as well as *American Men of Science* and the Psychological Corporation.[92] Cattell apparently had a nonacademic gift for both psychology and financial management, and thus he began his tenure as publisher of *Science* in January, 1895.

Time Requirements for Research

The variables of worker, problem, technique, adviser, sponsorship, and working conditions are such that it is extremely hazardous to predict the length of time required to complete a specific investigation. Beyond a certain point additional money, equipment, and personnel resources will not shorten the period of development and maturation essential for successful research. Charles F. Kettering once estimated that a certain project would require a year for completion. When urged to double his force and reduce the time to six months, he made a characteristic, homely reply:

Pressure for development of the drawer-operated cash register was made stronger by the circumstance that President Patterson was soon to leave on a

[90] Robert L. McCaul, "Dewey's Chicago." *School Review* 67: 258–80; Summer 1959.

[91] Jesse B. Sears and Adin D. Henderson, *op. cit.,* p. 267, 280.

[92] "Our 81-Year-Old Weekly." *AAAS Bulletin:* 1–4; July 1961.

trip to Europe. Kettering was asked whether he thought the development could be finished before the date of his departure. Yes, he thought it could.

"We ought really to have the job completed sooner," said Patterson. So he directed that Kettering be given more help. "Give him twice as many men," he said, "so he can finish it up in half the time."

At that, Kettering protested that he could not use so many helpers to advantage.

"Why can't you?" Patterson asked. "If ten men can dig a rod of ditch in an hour, then surely twenty men can dig two rods."

"This is more a job of hatching eggs than digging ditches, Mr. Patterson," was the reply. "Do you think that if two hens were put on a nest a setting of eggs could be hatched out in less than three weeks?"[93]

Adequate preparation, patience, thorough investigation, and sufficient time are emphasized in a letter written by Pavlov in the eighty-eighth year of his life:

What can I wish to the youth of my country who devote themselves to science?

Firstly, gradualness. About this most important condition of fruitful scientific work I never can speak without emotion. Gradualness, gradualness, and gradualness. From the very beginning of your work, school yourselves to severe gradualness in the accumulation of knowledge.

Learn the ABC of science before you try to ascend to its summit. Never begin the subsequent without mastering the preceding. Never attempt to screen an insufficiency of knowledge even by the most audacious surmise and hypothesis. Howsoever this soap-bubble will rejoice your eyes by its play, it inevitably will burst and you will have nothing except shame.

School yourselves to demureness and patience. Learn to inure yourselves to drudgery in science. Learn, compare, collect the facts!

But learning, experimenting, observing, try not to stay on the surface of the facts. Do not become the archivists of facts. Try to penetrate to the secret of their occurrence, persistently search for the laws which govern them.[94]

A neurophysiologist and philanthropic foundation adviser expresses the hope that science may pursue its course free from pressure for quick results:[95]

Finally it should be said that it makes no sense to criticize a science for not knowing more than it does. This would seem to be particularly true of psychology. Everybody else, prophets, priests, philosophers, doctors, lawyers, the man in the street—ever since the time when there were no streets—has tried to understand the behavior of man. And it is now more true than it ever

[93] Quoted from T. A. Boyd, *Professional Amateur:* The Biography of Charles Franklin Kettering. New York: E. P. Dutton and Co., 1957. p. 57–58.

[94] As quoted by Robert S. Morison, "Gradualness, Gradualness, Gradualness." *American Psychologist* 15: 187–97; March 1960.

[95] Quoted from *ibid.*

was that man's greatest mystery is man himself. Why should not science have its chance? May it pursue it free from pressure for quick results.

And just in case you feel like brushing off these comments as those of a philanthropoid who should never have been allowed out of his Ivory Tower, let me quote a practical politician, Theodore Heuss, President of the German Republic: "We have the obligation to free the scientist from the nervousness of this era and to put the gift of time again at his disposal."

With painstaking German thoroughness, Paul Ehrlich made his great discovery of a syphilis cure by wading without success through 605 organic arsenic compounds in search of a chemical that could destroy a disease-producing organism without harming the victim of the disease; he finally was dramatically successful with the next drug, named "606."

In 1807 Noah Webster wrote of the painstaking effort and time required to produce a dictionary:

I hope to be able to finish my Complete Dictionary. . . . It will require the incessant labor of from three to five years." In 1812 he moved to Amherst, Massachusetts, where for ten years he labored from point to point about the large circular table that held the dictionaries and grammars of twenty languages. In 1824 he sailed to spend a year in the libraries of Paris, London, and Cambridge in order to consult books that could not be had in America. In 1828, at the age of seventy, he at length published the *American Dictionary of the English Language* in an edition of 2500 copies. . . .

Webster brought out a revised edition of the Dictionary in 1841, just before his death.[96]

The need for relatively long periods of sustained effort in research is aptly expressed by Cannon:[97]

An investigator may be given a palace to live in, a perfect laboratory to work in, he may be surrounded by all the conveniences money can provide; but if his time is taken from him he will remain sterile. On the other hand, as the history of science abundantly shows, an investigator may be poverty-stricken, he may be ill-clothed, he may live in a garret and have only meager appliances for his use; but given time he can be productive.

It is unusual to have as exact (and surprisingly short) a time schedule for completion of a dissertation as that left on record by Ellwood P. Cubberley, who made a study of state school laws on finance under the title, "School Funds and Their Apportionment." This dissertation was the beginning of many years of study by Cubberley of the financing of public-education administration. He began the research for his dis-

[96] Quoted from *Webster's Third New International Dictionary of the English Language, Unabridged*. Springfield, Mass.: G. and C. Merriam Co., 1961.

[97] Quoted from Walter B. Cannon, *The Way of an Investigator*. New York: W. W. Norton and Co., 1945. p. 87.

sertation on January 24, 1905; Mrs. Cubberley began the typing on March 17, and Cubberley presented the dissertation to his adviser on April 14. In his diary he entered the comment: "Handed it to Dr. Perry, returned borrowed sections of Teachers College Library, and breathed a sigh of relief—Done!" He took his oral examination on May 19 and received the Ph.D. degree on June 14, 1905, at Columbia University.[98]

William James was relatively slow in his development and program of writing; he required considerable persuasion to complete a textbook in psychology, his famous *Principles of Psychology* (1890), after twelve years of hard work. On the other hand, John Dewey was only 26 years of age when he produced his *Psychology*, which means that he was engaged in writing this book at the age of 24 or 25 (an unusual accomplishment for so young a man).

One aspect of timing involves historical or research perspective—the ability to evaluate one's work or the efforts of others in the contemporary setting and also in relation to changed conditions or new evidence after a period of time. For example, Edward A. Ross (1866-1952) was outspoken in criticism, even of his own works, when conditions changed or new evidence appeared:[99]

> In the thirty-five years since the book left my anvil, I have scrutinized society in many countries and a society which "controls" does not look so global to me now as it did to me in 1900. . . . I doubt if "lessons from history" will have much to do with shaping humanity's future. Basic conditions are changing so rapidly that most of the old techniques of control are junk. . . . Science and invention—together with applied psychology open vistas into a wondrous new age with its own problems of control, in which control devices will be employed that the past never heard of.

Ross, speaking of his 1920 book on *Principles of Sociology*, stated that when published he thought it sound, but "even then sensed that certain parts were labored and foggy." He said that almost every month fresh shortcomings had appeared and that, if by 1960 it should prove forty to fifty parts sound, he would be content.

INITIAL STATEMENT OF THE PROBLEM

Focusing Topics for Research

After the title of a thesis or investigation has been phrased within one or two lines, the next step is to provide an adequate statement of the

[98] Jesse B. Sears and Adin D. Henderson, *op. cit.*, p. 81.
[99] Quoted from M. C. Elmer, *op. cit.*, p. 29–30.
Emory S. Bogardus, *op. cit.*, p. 523–39.

problem in one or more paragraphs in the introductory chapter. Certain errors in the phrasing of thesis or research topics should be avoided:

1. Naming a broad field or area of study instead of a specific problem for investigation; for example, "the effect of various factors on learning," which might be delimited as "the effect of three thirty-minute periods of practice versus five eighteen-minute periods on learning silent reading in the fifth grade"; or the history of music the world over for all time, which was delimited by one student to present a history of a particular conservatory of music.

2. Narrowing or localizing a topic to such an extent that it may prove a "pinpoint" problem; for example, a proposed history of a one-room school might be broadened to deal with the history of the school district or even the history of the county school system in which the one-room school is located.

3. Wording of a hortatory or biased character, or citing undigested data without identifying a problem; for example, "an argument for free textbooks in the public schools" might better be phrased as "the practices of public schools in a particular area in providing free textbooks." "Fifty tape recordings of home room programs" might become "an analysis of the content of home room programs, based on tape recordings."

Brief Statement of the Problem

The problem may be stated in the form of a question (or series of questions) or as a declarative statement (or series of statements). The question form may have an advantage in sharpening or focusing the issue, but the declarative statement probably is more common. The following example combines the two ways (question and declarative statement) of phrasing the problem:[100]

The purpose of this study, broadly stated, was to investigate the effectiveness of a method of teaching arithmetic in which children's immature procedures in dealing with number are accepted as normal and valuable steps toward their achievement of competent, mature behavior with reference to number. More narrowly, the objective of the investigation was to determine the effect upon the arithmetical development of children of their temporary use of certain immature procedures, when careful guidance is given by teachers. These procedures are designated as "intermediate," since they occur between the initial awareness of number and the achievement of mature modes of dealing with number relationships. The study was limited to the development of understanding in the four fundamental processes, on the part of the second-grade children.

[100] Quoted from Edwina Deans, "The Effect of Certain Immature Procedures on the Learning of Arithmetical Processes by Second-Grade Children," *Abstracts of Graduate Theses in Education*, 1944–54, Vol. 5. Cincinnati: Teachers College, University of Cincinnati, 1955. p. 129–47.

Preliminary problems.—Two preliminary problems which were basic to the major purpose of the study may be stated as follows:

1. The discovery of the intermediate procedures that were being used by children at the beginning of the study.
2. The selection of those intermediate procedures which showed promise as aids to more mature understanding of number ideas by pupils.

Sub-problems.—In the evaluation of a teaching technique in which the immature or intermediate procedures of children are regarded as of central importance, a number of pertinent questions arise. Such questions, which may be regarded as sub-problems, include the following:

1. In what ways can experience be provided for all children on the selected intermediate procedures?
2. Is it possible for some children to bypass some intermediate procedures without jeopardizing understanding?
3. Do some children tend to move to more advanced procedures before understanding is present?
4. How can readiness for a more advanced intermediate procedure be determined?
5. Do children willingly discontinue the use of immature procedures?
6. Under what circumstances are less mature methods dropped and replaced by more mature methods?
7. What steps can be taken by the teacher to encourage children to discontinue the use of immature methods?
8. As children are taught intermediate procedures, to what extent is their later thinking characterized by increasingly higher levels of maturity in dealing with number situations?
9. What problems do teachers encounter as they attempt to guide children through succeeding maturity levels in dealing with number situations?

To cite a briefer illustration, the general purpose of a study of school dropouts was to determine the characteristics of the early leaver in the Cincinnati Public Schools who returned to formal schooling in the Cincinnati Public Evening Schools; that is, the student who withdrew before graduation and who came back to evening classes. The more specific purposes[101] were concerned with a characterization of the school leaver and with reasons for withdrawal and return.

1. To characterize the early school leaver as revealed through interviews and school records
2. To discover the reason or reasons for his withdrawal from day school
3. To discover the reason or reasons for his return to evening classes.

[101] Charles E. Reigel, "Early School Leavers Who Return to Cincinnati Public Evening Schools." Doctor's dissertation. Cincinnati: University of Cincinnati, 1960. xii + 353 p.

An investigation of individualized teaching in elementary psychology involved three questions:[102]

1. Was the special elementary tutorial instruction more effective than conventional instruction?
2. What types of students volunteer to participate in a tutorial program?
3. What types of students benefit or lose by participation in a tutorial program?

FULLER DEFINITION OF THE PROBLEM

The brief introductory statement of the problem usually is followed by a fuller definition and development of background concerning sub-problems, scope, related literature, sources of data, method, significance, terminology, assumptions, and hypotheses. Of course it may not be appropriate for a particular study to include all of these items of background as part of the fuller development of the problem, which means that the candidate has certain options.

Constituent Elements and Scope

The preceding illustrative study of arithmetical processes by Deans also shows how the major problem is divided into subproblems, constituent elements, or questions to answer. A statement of the limits or scope of the investigation well may provide information concerning "who, what, when, where, and how many."

Thoughtful analysis of problems for action research involves answers to such questions as the following:[103]

1. What conditions need to prevail both to allow and to invite teachers to state problems of importance to them?
2. In what context do problem identification and analysis produce the maximum of identification, allow for varied levels of involvement depending on the capacity and the insight of individuals, and permit significant problems to emerge?
3. What is the sequence in opening up a problem for research with teachers?
4. What is the timing factor? How is one to gauge how fast or how slowly to proceed, at which point to introduce which considerations?
5. What is a team pattern in guiding action research which yields the greatest possible combined competence? What is the role of the research consultants? of the supervisor? of teachers?

[102] W. J. McKeachie and Others, "Individualized Teaching in Elementary Psychology." *Journal of Educational Psychology* 51: 285–91; October 1960.
[103] Hilda Taba, "Problem Identification," *Research for Curriculum Improvement*. 1957 Yearbook. Washington: Association for Supervision and Curriculum Development, a Department of the National Education Association, 1957. p. 42–71.

The analysis of action-research problems should proceed in an atmosphere that provides for at least three conditions:[104]

1. It is necessary to provide a climate which facilitates an analysis of the factors which those who propose a "problem" may not be quite ready to see.

2. It is necessary to proceed so as to maintain an optimum identification with the problem. It is easy to "detach" a teacher from his concern by suggesting a greater complexity or a greater change in approach than the teacher can take for the time being. This means that the levels of analysis or of investigation need to be gauged to each individual's ability and insight, so as to maintain his self-respect, while challenging some assumptions and cherished concepts.

3. This in turn means that the steps in the analysis need to be broken down to provide an "easy road in." One needs to gauge the speed with which to proceed with each individual.

Related Literature and Terminology

We have already noted the importance of the literature in the selection of problems for investigation. The next chapter presents the keys to the related literature, from which may come explanatory hypotheses, techniques for gathering evidence, and comparative data for purposes of interpretation. The orientation provided by a survey of the related research is helpful in making a straightforward statement of the need for the investigation, avoiding the two extremes of an apologetic attitude and exaggerated claims or boastfulness. Chapters of the *Encyclopedia of Educational Research, Review of Educational Research,* and the *Annual Review of Psychology* may serve as useful examples of summaries of the research literature on specific topics.

Certain specialized terms in the technical report or in the related studies may require definition. Comprehensive dictionaries[105] are available for the fields of education, psychology, and sociology.

Sources of Data and Method

An introductory section of the technical report should include appropriate information concerning sources of evidence and techniques of data-gathering, including a frank admission of any weaknesses or short-

---

[104] *Ibid.,* p. 53–54.

[105] Carter V. Good, Editor, *Dictionary of Education.* Second Edition. New York: McGraw-Hill Book Co., 1959. xxx + 676 p.

Horace B. English and Ava C. English, *Comprehensive Dictionary of Psychological and Psychoanalytical Terms.* New York: Longmans, Green and Co., 1958. xiv + 594 p.

H. P. Fairchild, Editor, *Dictionary of Sociology.* New York: Philosophical Library, 1944. viii + 342 p.

comings. Detailed discussions of sources and methods are found later in this book in the several chapters on research methodology. The following illustrative statement of sources and method involves a case-study procedure:[106]

The fifty-five subjects represented consecutive cases seen in the psychological clinic of the Juvenile Court of Hamilton County, Ohio, from November 1, 1947, to May 1, 1948, who had attended public schools for one month or more of this period. Every subject was given Form L of the Stanford Binet Intelligence Test, Form D of the Stanford Achievement Tests, and a structured interview. Probation officers checked questionnaires which provided pertinent social history material about each child. All thirty-two schools attended by subjects were visited and the principals or assistant principals, counselors, homeroom teachers, and classroom teachers of each child were interviewed by a structured procedure. Cumulative and other available records in the schools and the work of the court and clinic were used as research data.

Basic Assumptions

In social investigations and in school and community life, certain premises or assumptions are generally accepted, frequently without identification in the technical or research reports; for example, in a democracy we assume that cooperation rather than strife and respect for the individual rather than rigid regimentation are desirable. We accept the premise that schools and education are necessary, and that transportation of pupils in rural areas is desirable.

The scientist typically accepts two basic assumptions:[107]

1. That there is lawfulness in the events of nature as opposed to capricious, chaotic, or spontaneous occurrences (in other words, determinism)
2. That every natural event or phenomenon has a discoverable and limited number of conditions or factors which are responsible for it (an assumption of finite causation).

To the extent that basic assumptions are open to question, the results of the particular investigation are subject to challenge. Even great scientists have encountered difficulties in understanding the basic assumptions of other scientists or in defending their own postulates:

That Agassiz failed to become the greatest naturalist of his time was due to a development he could never quite understand. He was equipped with almost unlimited industriousness and ambition. He was exceptionally intelligent

---

[106] Quoted from Vera C. Edwards, "A Study of the School Adjustment of Fifty-Five Delinquent Children," *Abstracts of Graduate Theses in Education, 1944–54,* Vol. 5. Cincinnati: Teachers College, University of Cincinnati, 1955. p. 266–76.

[107] Benton J. Underwood, *Psychological Research.* New York: Appleton-Century-Crofts, 1957. p. 3–6.

and attractive. As a youth, he worked with the leading scientists of his time, and they one and all liked him, admired him, and advanced his fortunes in every way they could. He had also prepared himself in the best possible ways. He had mastered *Naturphilosophie* in Germany but had also learned, by studying in France with the hard-headed and practical Cuvier, to prefer the factual to the speculative aspects of science. He had mastered and practically dominated ichthyology and was credited with establishing the glacial theory. For a time he dominated biology in America, all the while remaining a very potent force in Europe. He and his work were universally respected, but something went wrong.

In 1859, Charles Darwin hit him in his postulates, and he found his basic assumptions under attack. That Agassiz did not know at first what had happened to him is clear from his reactions. Later on, when he began to suspect, he was dazed and puzzled. He made an honest effort to understand the newer developments and to evaluate the evidence on which the theory of evolution was based, but he failed completely, as he showed by a paper he wrote just before his death.[108]

Many assumptions or premises in the social areas involve the realm of values and are not subject at present to validation through any known scientific procedure. Underlying assumptions should be stated as part of the definition and development of the problem, and also in connection with the conclusions of the investigation.

DEVELOPMENT AND TESTING OF HYPOTHESES

Characteristics and Functions of Hypotheses

A hypothesis is an informed or shrewd guess or inference, with a reasonable chance of being right, formulated and tentatively adopted to explain observed facts or conditions and to guide in further investigation, in other words, to serve as the investigator's "eyes" in seeking answers to questions. The scientist's hypothesis parallels the common man's personal opinion or hunch.

Expressed in other language, Charles Darwin said in an 1857 letter to his contemporary Alfred R. Wallace, "Without speculation there is no good and original observation." Speculation, or intuitive contemplation guided by past discoveries, led Darwin to his famous observations, as set forth in *Origin of Species*.

Hypotheses may serve the following functions: [109] They may contribute as explanations, stimuli to research, sources of methodology,

[108] Quoted from review by Conway Zirkle, *Science* 132: 1655–56; December 2, 1960, of Edward Lurie, *Louis Agassiz: A Life in Science*. Chicago: University of Chicago Press, 1960. 449 p. Reprinted from *Science* by permission.

[109] Clarence W. Brown and Edwin E. Ghiselli, *Scientific Method in Psychology*. New York: McGraw-Hill Book Co., 1955. p. 157–59.

criteria for evaluating experimental and other techniques, and as organizing principles. In thus limiting the area of investigation, sensitizing the worker to pertinent data and relationships, and providing a unifying concept, the single hypothesis should not blind the research worker's observation of all pertinent data, even though some facts may not contribute to validation of the chosen hypothesis. As emphasized later, it is common for a particular study to involve formulation and testing of more than one hypothesis.

Factors that contribute to the emergence of hypotheses[110] include generalizing beyond the results of previous investigations, analyzing factual conditions requiring explanation, intellectual equipment and resources of the scientist, and inspiration. Expressed otherwise, hypotheses originate from substantially the same background as that which serves to identify problems: the insight and imagination that should result from a sound instructional program, extensive and critical reading, knowledge of existing practices and needs, and meaningful contact with pertinent data.

There is no sharp line of demarcation between hypothesis and theory, since the basic difference is one of complexity and the extent of testing against the evidence. In its early stages of testing, a theory usually has been called a hypothesis but, as the hypothesis is checked against the data and their logical implications toward a successful conclusion, it may become known as a theory. A law represents an order or relation of phenomena that is invariable under the given conditions and permits of no exception in its operation.

The working hypothesis, when checked against the data, may emerge as a central explanatory theme for purposes of interpretation, although the hypothesis, as a tentative supposition, shrewd guess, conjecture, inference, or "if-then" statement, is not always stated explicitly in the graduate thesis, particularly the descriptive-survey study. In many investigations of status or current conditions, a formal expression of the hypothesis is omitted in favor of a direct question or declarative statement of purpose, as illustrated earlier in this chapter.

Testing Hypotheses and Reporting False Hypotheses

The hypothesis may be evaluated in terms of agreement with and explanation of the evidence, absence of conflict with satisfactorily proved generalizations, success for purposes of prediction, simplicity and clarity of statement, and logical consistency.[111] Although a specific investigation usually involves the development and testing of more than one hypothesis,

110 *Ibid.*, p. 162–63.
111 Morris R. Cohen and Ernest Nagel, *An Introduction to Logic and Scientific Method*. New York: Harcourt, Brace and Co., 1934. p. 207–15.

many scientists and scholars have been reluctant to describe their rejected hypotheses or failures. This means that it is frequently impossible to learn about the blind alleys traveled by earlier investigators. Since the technical report is usually prepared at the conclusion of the study, the author commonly tells a simple story of "smooth sailing." If research workers are overly cautious about making and reporting mistakes, they are not likely to make either errors or discoveries. As Whitehead says, "Panic of error is the death of progress." According to Humphrey Davy, "The most important of my discoveries have been suggested to me by my failures." It may be surprising that so able a scientist as Charles Darwin could not recall a single first-formed hypothesis, with the exception of the Coral Reefs, which had not after a time been given up or greatly modified.[112]

This reluctance to describe the scientist's mistakes to the reader is aptly described by Helmholtz, in commenting on his work during 1891, including the solution of certain problems in mathematics and physics over which great mathematicians had puzzled in vain:[113]

But any pride I might have felt in my conclusions was perceptibly lessened by the fact that I knew that the solution of these problems had almost always come to me as the gradual generalization of favourable examples, by a series of fortunate conjectures, after many errors. I am fain to compare myself with a wanderer on the mountains, who, not knowing the path, climbs slowly and painfully upwards, and often has to retrace his steps because he can go no farther—then, whether by taking thought or from luck, discovers a new track that leads him on a little, till at length when he reaches the summit he finds to his shame that there is a royal road, by which he might have ascended, had he only had the wits to find the right approach to it. In my works I naturally said nothing about my mistakes to the reader, but only described the made track by which he may now reach the same heights without difficulty.

A similar view concerning the development and testing of hypotheses has been expressed by Cannon, a research worker in medicine and physiology:[114]

Investigators do not march straight to their goal with ease and directness. In their imagination they see a possible fact and they set forth to learn whether their foresight can be realized. Or they come upon something which is puzzling and challenging and which they wish to explain; then they try in various ways to relate it to other phenomena that would solve the riddle. Obstacles and difficulties are sure to be encountered. The search for understanding is an adventure or, more commonly, a series of adventures. If an attempt in one direction fails, the failure is not discouraging to an eager explorer. There are

[112] Allen Johnson, *The Historian and Historical Evidence*. New York: Charles Scribner's Sons, 1926. p. 166–67.
[113] Quoted in William H. George, *The Scientist in Action:* A Scientific Study of His Methods. London: Williams and Norgate, 1936. p. 229–30.
[114] Quoted from Walter B. Cannon, *op. cit.*, p. 22.

other possible approaches to the end in view and relentlessly, one after another, these are tried.

Kettering expressed the opinion that he could teach young men to be inventors, provided they could overcome fear of failure:

I can take any group of young people and teach them to be inventors, if I can get them to throw off the hazard of being afraid to fail. . . . A study made a number of years ago, said the more education a man has the less likely he is to be an inventor. Now the reason for that is quite simple.

It is because throughout his life he has been taught the danger of failure. From the time he enters the first grade until he graduates from the university he is examined three or four times each year, and if he fails he is out and in many cases disgraced; while in research and inventions work you fail hundreds and even thousands of times; and, if you succeed once, you are in.

It therefore seems that the only factor which needs to be corrected is to teach the highly educated person that it is not a disgrace to fail and that he must analyze every failure to find its cause. We paraphrase this by saying, "You must learn how to fail intelligently!" . . . For failing is one of the greatest arts in the world. . . . Once you've failed, analyze the problem and find out why, because each failure is one more step leading up to the cathedral of success. The only time you don't want to fail is the last time you try.[115]

The wisdom of the ancient Persian proverb applies equally to the scholar's recognition of false hypotheses and to identification of sound conclusions:

He who knows not
And knows not that he knows not
Is a fool. Shun him.
He who knows not
And knows that he knows not
Is a child. Teach him.
He who knows
And knows not that he knows
Is asleep. Waken him.
He who knows
And knows that he knows
Is wise. Follow him.

It has even been suggested that a journal should be established for publication of negative results:

The usual first step in an experimental study is a search of the literature for previous work relevant to the proposed research. Certainly no problem exists if the researcher finds the work has been done. Unfortunately, the only

---

[115] Quoted from T. A. Boyd, *Professional Amateur:* The Biography of Charles Franklin Kettering. New York: E. P. Dutton and Co., 1957. p. 209–10.

studies that are likely to appear in any journal are those which come up with "publishable results" (i.e., results that are statistically significant). If an experiment yields "negative results" (i.e., results which fail to confirm the tested hypothesis), the findings are usually relegated to the experimenter's filing cabinet and are likely to remain there. This approach can hardly be thought of as extending scientific communication.

It is suggested that the value of negative results has been underestimated. Negative findings can add to our knowledge by indicating unfruitful aspects of a given problem, thereby eliminating wasted research time and energy. In building up the empirical foundation of a science, it is important to know not only what *does* exist, but what does *not* exist as well.

A way of coping with this problem would be to have a place to publish these findings. This could be done by establishing a *Journal of Negative Results*. Considering the costs and limited space of present-day publications, such a journal could follow the format of the *Psychological Abstracts;* investigators could obtain detailed descriptions of the studies from the authors. Investigators would then be able to make more adequate surveys of the work done in their areas. One risk might be the inclusion of studies whose findings were due to methodological inadequacies; but in this area where communication is practically nil, errors of commission are more desirable than errors of omission.[116]

Examples of Hypotheses

To cite an example of the working hypothesis, an investigation of the correlates of daydreaming expresses its general hypothesis as follows:

The general hypothesis of this study is that subjects who indicate a greater frequency of daydream behavior are also characterized by greater reported frequency of night dreams, social introversion, and creativity in their spontaneous reports of daydreams or storytelling activity. They are, in addition, more likely to be identified with their mothers (on the basis of measures of assumed similarity of interests); those who report less daydreaming, on the other hand, are expected to show greater evidence of repression or denial of problems and a lesser tendency toward identification with their mothers.[117]

To use another example, a dynamic hypothesis in social psychology may be formulated by restating Hamilton's principle of physics, to the effect that, "In a system of particles subject only to their own gravitational forces, any particle will move, over a period of time, on a path such that the difference between the kinetic and potential energies of the system

---

[116] Quoted from Marvin R. Goldfried and Gary C. Walters, "Needed: Publication of Negative Results." *American Psychologist* 14: 598; September 1959.

[117] Quoted from Jerome L. Singer and Rosalea A. Schonbar, "Correlates of Daydreaming: A Dimension of Self-Awareness." *Journal of Consulting Psychology* 25: 1–6; February 1961.

will be minimized." The restatement of Hamilton's principle for investigation in social psychology[118] would be:

An individual S in a social group G behaves, over a period of time, in such a way as to minimize the difference between
A. the ability of G to accomplish its work by virtue of its position, prestige, status or reputation among other groups; and
B. the ability of G to do its work by virtue of its interaction, conflict, etc., with other groups.

Many predictions of what S will do in G, if the restatement be true, are obvious. For example, if $A < B$, the members S_i should then behave, on the average, in such ways as either to raise A or lower B or both. Or if $A = B$, the S_i will behave in such ways as to preserve the balance within certain limits, etc.

Other illustrations of hypotheses may be found in the chapter on history and historiography. In summary and by way of further example, thinking analytically involves not only thinking in terms of what is actual, as illustrated by the data of many descriptive-survey studies, but also thinking in terms of what is possible:

Thinking what is possible is hypothetical thinking. Such thinking is characterized in part by the employment of conditional propositions which are of the form, "if p then q." A proposition of this form is suppositional.

In the sciences conditional statements are often about inferred entities—e.g., statements about molecules or atoms or electrons. Consider the following statement: "If the kinetic energy of a gas is increased then molecules travel at a higher rate of velocity." The inferred entity, molecule, which is talked about in the preceding statement differs from an actual entity. It is derived, not observed. Thus, the statement is suppositional rather than actual.

Hypothetical thinking also employs the contrary-to-fact statement which differs from the conditional statement in being expressed in the subjunctive mood. For example, the chemist states: "If the temperature were to fall to $-273\,°C$ there would be zero volume." This statement does not relate directly to what is actual. All known substances solidify at a temperature above $-273\,°C$, thereby fixing observable volume at some definite value greater than zero. Every schoolboy and every physical scientist uses the concept of Absolute Zero, a concept which is derived from the proposition just stated. Although the schoolboy may be, the scientist is not disturbed by the obvious discrepancy between his thinking and his experience of the actual. The scientist knows that he can describe the actual with greater certainty by considering what is possible, rather than by solely considering what is actual.[119]

[118] Quoted from Harold Webster, "Dynamic Hypotheses in Psychology." *Psychological Review* 59: 168–71; March 1952.
[119] Quoted from George S. Maccia, "Hypothetical Thinking in Education." *Educational Theory* 10: 182–86; July 1960.

CONCLUDING STATEMENT

The investigator is aided in identifying significant problems through advanced study and critical reading, analysis of practices and needs, and repetition or extension of earlier studies. For most scholars and scientists, criticial reading of the related literature serves as a stimulus to thinking and creativity. The chapter bibliography includes references dealing with surveys of progress and critiques of research, trends, prophecies, and needed research.

Important factors in selection of the problem include: novelty and significance, intellectual curiosity and drive, scholarship and personal characteristics, sources and technique, sponsorship and cooperation, risks and costs, and timing. A famous inventor said that he was more interested in what investigators do differently than what they do alike, and did not worry about duplication of effort in research. A scientist has suggested that our ideas need to be jostled about to prevent intellectual stagnation. Overemphasis on factual materials and formal requirements in the training of research workers may actually inhibit development of creativity. We are warned that too great dependence on elaborate equipment may even restrict freedom in research. It has been said that we have an obligation to "free the scientist from the nervousness of this era and to put the gift of time again at his disposal."

The initial statement and fuller definition of the problem involve appropriate focusing of the topic, constituent elements and scope, related literature and terminology, sources of evidence and methodology, and basic assumptions. As a rule the graduate student avoids both "global" and "pinpoint" problems.

The hypothesis may serve the purposes of explanations, stimuli to research, sources of methodology, criteria for evaluating research techniques, and organizing principles. In other words, speculation, or intuitive contemplation guided by past discoveries, should lead to careful observations as a basis for testing hypotheses. Great scientists and inventors have urged beginners in research to overcome fear of failure and to analyze their mistakes, since the overly cautious investigator is not likely to make either errors or discoveries.

SELECTED REFERENCES

AARONS, Z. Alexander. "Some Problems of Delinquency and Their Treatment." *Social Casework* 40: 254-62; May 1959.

ALEXANDER, Franz. "Unexplored Areas in Psychoanalytic Theory and Treatment." *Behavioral Science* 3: 293-316; October 1958.

ARENSBERG, Conrad M., and Others. *Research in Industrial Human Relations: A Critical Appraisal.* New York: Harper & Brothers, 1957. x + 213 p.

AUSUBEL, David P. "Relationships between Psychology and Psychiatry: The Hidden Issues." *American Psychologist* 11: 99-105; February 1956.

BAIL, Milo. "Six Decades of Progress." *North Central Association Quarterly* 30: 193-207; October 1955.

BAITSELL, George A., Editor. *Science in Progress*. Ninth Series. New Haven: Yale University Press, 1956. 482 p.

BARR, Arvil S., DAVIS, Robert A., and JOHNSON, Palmer O. *Educational Research and Appraisal*. Philadelphia: J. B. Lippincott Co., 1953. p. 5-13, 308-13, 335-39.

BARZUN, Jacques, and GRAFF, Henry F. *The Modern Researcher*. New York: Harcourt, Brace and Co., 1957. p. 18-27.

BELSON, William A. "New Developments in Audience Research Methods." *American Journal of Sociology* 64: 174-79; September 1958.

BERDIE, Ralph F. "A Program of Counseling Interview Research." *Educational and Psychological Measurement* 18: 255-74; Summer 1958.

BERTHOFF, Rowland. "The American Social Order: A Conservative Hypothesis." *American Historical Review* 65: 495-553; April 1960.

BIGELOW, Karl W. "New Directions in Teacher Education Appraised." *Teachers College Record* 59: 350-56; March 1958.

BOGARDUS, Emory S. *The Development of Social Thought*. Fourth Edition. New York: Longmans, Green and Co., 1960. x + 689 p.

BOGARDUS, Emory S. "Forty Years of 'Sociology and Social Research.'" *Sociology and Social Research* 40: 426-32; July-August 1956.

BORGATTA, Edgar F., and COTTRELL, Leonard S., Jr. "Directions for Research in Group Behavior." *American Journal of Sociology* 63: 42-48; July 1957.

BORING, E. G. *A History of Experimental Psychology*. Second Edition. New York: Appleton-Century-Crofts, 1950. xxi + 777 p.

BOROW, Henry, PEPINSKY, Harold B., and DRESSEL, Paul L. "Frontiers of Personnel Research in Education," *Personnel Services in Education*. Fifty-eighth Yearbook of the National Society for the Study of Education, Part 2. Chicago: University of Chicago Press, 1959. p. 210-58.

BOWEN, Howard R. *The Business Enterprise as a Subject for Research*. Social Science Research Council Pamphlet 11. New York: The Council, 1955. viii + 103 p.

BOWMAN, Claude C. "Research in Family Dynamics: A Criticism and a Proposal." *Social Forces* 34: 201-7; March 1956.

BREEN, Leonard Z. "Some Problems of Research in the Field of Aging." *Sociology and Social Research* 41: 412-16; July-August 1957.

BROWN, Clarence W., and GHISELLI, Edwin E. *Scientific Method in Psychology*. New York: McGraw-Hill Book Co., 1955. p. 133-76.

BROWN, Harrison, BONNER, James, and WEIR, John. *The Next Hundred Years: Man's Natural and Technological Resources*. New York: Viking Press, 1957. xi + 193 p.

BRUNO, Frank J. *Trends in Social Work, 1874-1956*. New York: Columbia University Press, 1957. xv + 462 p.

BURGESS, Ernest W. "Seven Significant Changes in Sociology." *Sociology and Social Research* 40: 385-86; July-August 1956.

BURGESS, Ernest W., and Others. "Symposium: Important Changes in Sociology During the Past Forty Years." *Sociology and Social Research* 40: 383-432; July-August 1956.

CARLE, Wayne M. "Needed Research in School Broadcasting." *Educational Research Bulletin* 38: 120-30; May 13, 1959.

CARMICHAEL, Leonard, and Others. "Child Development Research: The Next Twenty-Five Years." *Child Development* 31: 191-208; March 1960.

CARROLL, John B. "Neglected Areas in Educational Research." *Phi Delta Kappan* 42: 339-46; May 1961.

CARTER, G. S. *A Hundred Years of Evolution.* New York: The Macmillan Co., 1957. x + 206 p.

CASWELL, Hollis L. "Great Challenges for Education." *Teachers College Record* 59: 69-75; November 1957.

A Century of Progress in the Natural Sciences, 1853-1953. Published in celebration of the centennial of the California Academy of Sciences. San Francisco: California Academy of Sciences, 1955. 807 p.

CHAMBERLAIN, N. W., and Others. *A Decade of Industrial Relations Research, 1946-1956.* New York: Harper & Brothers, 1958. 212 p.

CHAMPLIN, Nathaniel L. "Some Neglected Philosophic Problems of Education." *Educational Theory* 7: 122-27; April 1957.

CHASE, FRANCIS S. "The Next 50 Years in Public Education." *Ohio School Boards Journal* 3: 12-14, 27-28; October 1959.

CHENG, C. K., and YAMAMURA, Douglas S. "A Proposal for Research in Delinquency Causation." *Social Forces* 39: 346-52; May 1961.

COHEN, Morris R., and NAGEL, Ernest. *An Introduction to Logic and Scientific Method.* New York: Harcourt, Brace and Co., 1934. p. 207-15.

COHEN, Wilbur J. "Current and Future Trends in Public Welfare." *Social Service Review* 29: 247-59; September 1955.

COTTRELL, W. Fred. "Research to Establish the Conditions for Peace." *Journal of Social Issues* 11, No. 1: 13-20; 1955.

CRANDALL, Vaughan J. "Some Problems of Personality Development Research." *Child Development* 27: 197-203; June 1956.

CRISWELL, Joan H. "Sociometric Measurement: Some Practical Advantages and New Developments." *Sociometry* 18: 383-91; December 1955.

CRONBACH, Lee J., Editor. *Text Materials in Modern Education:* A Comprehensive Theory and Platform for Research. Urbana: University of Illinois Press, 1955. 216 p.

CRUMMEL, Robert A. "The Development of Higher Education in the United States, 1900-1955." *Educational Record* 38: 320-28; October 1957.

DANE, Chase. "The Need for a Research Program in Library Problems." *College and Research Libraries* 16: 20-23; January 1955.

DANIEL, Glyn E. *A Hundred Years of Archaeology.* New York: The Macmillan Co., 1950. 343 p.

DINGLE, Herbert, Editor. *A Century of Science: 1851-1951.* New York: Roy Publishing Co., 1951. ix + 338 p.

DUNSHEATH, Percy, Editor. *A Century of Technology: 1851-1951.* New York: Roy Publishing Co., 1951. ix + 346 p.

DYER, Henry S. "The Need for Do-It-Yourself Prediction Research in High School Guidance." *Personnel and Guidance Journal* 36: 162-67; November 1957.

Educational Television: The Next Ten Years. Stanford, Calif.: Institute for Communication Research, Stanford University, 1962. xi + 375 p.

EHLERS, Henry, Editor. *Crucial Issues in Education.* New York: Henry Holt and Co., 1955. 277 p.

ELMER, M. C. *Contemporary Social Thought:* Contributors and Trends. Pittsburgh: University of Pittsburgh Press, 1956. viii + 256 p.

FARBER, Maurice L. "New Directions in the Study of National Character." *Journal of Social Issues* 11: 3-56; 1955.

FARBER, Maurice L. "Psychoanalytic Hypotheses in the Study of War." *Journal of Social Issues* 11, No. 1: 29-35; 1955.

FAUNCE, William A., and FULTON, Robert L. "The Sociology of Death: A Neglected Area of Research." *Social Forces* 36: 205-9; March 1958.

FAURI, Fedele F., and COHEN, Wilbur J. "Twenty Years of Progress in Social Security." *Public Welfare* 13: 143-51; October 1955.

FELIX, R. H. "New Scientific Developments in the Mental Health Field." *Social Service Review* 31: 123-34; June 1957.

FINCH, James K. "A Century of Engineering Progress: 1852-1952." *Scientific Monthly* 75: 99-108; August 1952.

FLUGEL, J. C. A *Hundred Years of Psychology.* Revised Edition. New York: The Macmillan Co., 1951. 424 p.

FOOTE, Nelson N., and COTTRELL, Leonard S., Jr. *Identity and Interpersonal Competence:* A New Direction in Family Research. Chicago: The University of Chicago Press, 1955. ix + 305 p.

FOSHAY, Arthur W., and Others. *Research for Curriculum Improvement.* 1957 Yearbook. Washington: Association for Supervision and Curriculum Development, National Education Association, 1957. p. 42-71.

FREEMAN, Howard E., and KASSEBAUM, Gene G. "The Illiterate in American Society: Some General Hypotheses." *Social Forces* 34: 371-75; May 1956.

FREUDENTHAL, Kurt. "Need for Research in the Area of Treatment Relationships." *Social Casework* 36: 369-71; October 1955.

FURFEY, Paul H. "The Humanitarian Philosophy and the Acceptance of Sociological Generalizations." *American Catholic Sociological Review* 16: 117-22; June 1955.

GANS, Herbert J. "The Sociology of New Towns: Opportunities for Research." *Sociology and Social Research* 40: 231-39; March-April 1956.

GARRETT, Henry E. *Great Experiments in Psychology.* Third Edition. New York: Appleton-Century-Crofts, 1951. 400 p.

GERARD, R. W. "Problems in the Institutionalization of Higher Education; An Analysis Based on Historical Materials." *Behavioral Science* 2: 134-46; April 1957.

GEWIRTZ, Jacob L. "A Program of Research on the Dimensions and Antecedents of Emotional Dependence." *Child Development* 27: 205-21; June 1956.

GOETHALS, George W. "A Framework for Educational Research." *Harvard Educational Review* 28: 29-43; Winter 1958.

GOLDSCHMIDT, Richard. "Fifty Years of Zoology." *Scientific Monthly* 71: 359-69; December 1950.

GOLDSMITH, Maurice. "One Hundred Years of British Science." *Scientific Monthly* 74: 170-79; March 1952.

GOLLIN, Eugene S. "Some Research Problems for Developmental Psychology." *Child Development* 27: 223-35; June 1956.

GOOD, Carter V. "Educational Research After Fifty Years." *Phi Delta Kappan* 37: 145-52; January 1956.

GOOD, Carter V., and SCATES, Douglas E. *Methods of Research:* Educational, Psychological, Sociological. New York: Appleton-Century-Crofts, 1954. p. 33-132.

GOODE, Cecil E. *Personnel Research Frontiers.* Chicago: Public Personnel Association, 1958. viii + 176 p.

GOODE, William J., and HATT, Paul K. *Methods in Social Research.* New York: McGraw-Hill Book Co., 1952. Chapters 6, 7.

GUILFORD, J. P., Editor. *Fields of Psychology.* Second Edition. New York: D. Van Nostrand Co., 1950. 779 p.

HAIRE, Mason. "Psychological Problems Relevant to Business and Industry." *Psychological Bulletin* 56: 169-94; May 1959.

HALPERN, Ben. "History, Sociology, and Contemporary Area Studies." *American Journal of Sociology* 63: 1-10; July 1957.

HANSON, Robert C. "Evidence and Procedure Characteristics of 'Reliable' Propositions in Social Science." *American Journal of Sociology* 63: 357-70; January 1958.

HARLOW, Harry F. "Current and Future Advances in Physiological and Comparative Psychology." *American Psychologist* 11: 273-77; June 1956.

HARRIS, Chester W., Editor. *Encyclopedia of Educational Research.* Third Edition. New York: The Macmillan Co., 1960. xxix + 1564 p.

HASKEW, L. D. "Teacher Education in the Years Ahead." *Educational Research Bulletin* 36: 189-98; September 11, 1957.

HERRICK, Virgil E. "Our Future in Teacher Education." *Teachers College Record* 57: 323-32; February 1956.

HILLWAY, Tyrus. *Introduction to Research.* Boston: Houghton Mifflin Co., 1956. p. 95-119.

HODNETT, Edward. *The Art of Problem Solving:* How to Improve Your Methods. New York: Harper & Brothers, 1955. ix + 202 p.

HORN, Francis H. "Problems Facing Higher Education." *Teachers College Record* 57: 360-70; March 1956.

HOSELITZ, Bert F. "The Social Sciences in the Last Two Hundred Years." *Journal of General Education* 4: 85-103; January 1950.

HUTCHINGS, Edward, Jr., Editor. *Frontiers in Science:* A Survey. New York: Basic Books, 1958. 362 p.

JOHNSON, Leighton H. "Education Needs Historical Studies." *Phi Delta Kappan* 36: 157-59; January 1955.

JONES, G. P., and POOL, A. G. *A Hundred Years of Economic Development.* New York: The Macmillan Co., 1950. 420 p.

KANDEL, I. L. "Problems of Comparative Education." *International Review of Education* 2: 1-15; 1956.

KANDEL, I. L. "Some Unsolved Issues in American Education." *Educational Forum* 20: 269-78; March 1956.

KOMAROVSKY, Mirra, Editor. *Common Frontiers of the Social Sciences.* Glencoe, Ill.: Free Press, 1957. viii + 439 p.

KONOPKA, Gisela, and VINTER, Robert R. "Group Work with Children and Youth: Unanswered Questions and Research Problems and Possibilities." *Social Service Review* 30: 300-21; September 1956.

LANGFELD, Herbert S., Editor. *A History of Psychology in Autobiography.* Vol. 4. Worcester, Mass.: Clark University Press, 1952. xii + 356 p.

LIEBERMAN, Myron. "Education for Tomorrow: 67 Theses." *School and Society* 88: 34-38; January 16, 1960.

LORD, Frederic M. "Further Problems in the Measurement of Growth." *Educational and Psychological Measurement* 18: 437-51; Autumn 1958.

LUCK, J. Murray. "Man against His Environment: The Next Hundred Years." *Science* 126: 903-8; November 1, 1957.

LUSZKI, Margaret B. "Some Social Problems of Social Research." *American Sociological Review* 22: 333-35; June 1957.

MAAS, Henry S., and GOULD, Ramond F. "Psychiatric Clinic Services for Children: Unanswered Questions and Research Strategy and Possibilities." *Social Service Review* 30: 276-99; September 1956.

MAAS, Henry S., and Others. "Proceedings of the Conference on Research in the Children's Field." *Social Service Review* 30: 237-357; September 1956. (Research problems and techniques in the areas of foster-care and adoption, residential treatment, psychiatric clinic services, and group work.)

MAASKE, Roben J., and Others. *Needed Research in Teacher Education.* Washington: American Association of Colleges for Teacher Education, 1954. 62 p.

MACCIA, George S. "Hypothetical Thinking in Education." *Educational Theory* 10: 182-86; July 1960.

MARCUSE, F. L., Editor. *Areas of Psychology.* New York: Harper & Brothers, 1954. viii + 532 p.

McCONNELL, T. R. "The Diversification of American Higher Education: A Research Program." *Educational Record* 38: 300-15; October 1957.

McCORMICK, Thomas C., and FRANCIS, Roy G. *Methods of Research in the Behavioral Sciences.* New York: Harper & Brothers, 1958. Chapters 2, 3.

McGUIGAN, F. J. "A Crash Research Program for Peace." *American Psychologist* 13: 224-28; May 1958.

MEISELS, Joseph F., LOEB, Martin B., and BRIELAND, Donald. "Foster-Care and Adoption: Unanswered Questions About Foster-Care and Current Research on Adoption." *Social Service Review* 30: 239-59; September 1956.

MELTON, Arthur W. "Present Accomplishment and Future Trends in Problem-Solving and Learning Theory." *American Psychologist* 11: 278-81; June 1956.

MERTON, Robert K. "The Role-Set: Problems in Sociological Theory." *British Journal of Sociology* 8: 106-20; June 1957.

MILLS, Theodore M. "Some Hypotheses on Small Groups from Simmel." *American Journal of Sociology* 63: 642-50; May 1958.

MOEHLMAN, Arthur H. "Fifty Years of Educational Thought." *Phi Delta Kappan* 37: 131-40; January 1956.

MORRISON, J. Cayce, and Others. "Twenty-five Years of Educational Research." *Review of Educational Research* 26: 199-344; June 1956.

MOWRER, O. Hobart. "Some Philosophical Problems in Psychological Counseling." *Journal of Counseling Psychology* 4: 103-11; Summer 1957.

MURPHY, Gardner. *An Historical Introduction to Modern Psychology.* Revised Edition. New York: Harcourt, Brace and Co., 1949. xiv + 466 p.

NEHNEVAJSA, Jiri. "Sociometry: Decades of Growth." *Sociometry* 18: 48-95; December 1955.

ODUM, Howard W. *American Sociology: The Story of Sociology in the United States through 1950.* New York: Longmans, Green and Co., 1951. vi + 501 p.

OGBURN, William F. "Social Trends." *Sociology and Social Research* 42: 3-9; September-October 1957.

PARSONS, Talcott. "Some Problems Confronting Sociology as a Profession." *American Sociological Review* 24: 547-59; August 1959.

PAULSEN, F. Robert. "Basic Assumptions of Educational Administration." *Peabody Journal of Education* 34: 270-82; March 1957.

PENNIMAN, T. K. *A Hundred Years of Anthropology.* Revised Edition. London: Duckworth and Co., 1952. 512 p.

POLLACK, Otto, and ORMSBY, Ralph. "Design of a Model of Healthy Family Relationships as a Basis for Evaluative Research." *Social Service Review* 31: 369-76; December 1957.

POOLE, Lynn. *Frontiers of Science.* New York: McGraw-Hill Book Co., 1958. 173 p.

POWELL, F. De Sales. "Recent Trends in Industrial Sociology." *American Catholic Sociological Review* 18: 194-204; October 1957.

REED, Glenn A. "Fifty Years of Conflict in the Graduate School." *Educational Record* 33: 5-23; January 1952.

REISS, Albert J., Jr. "Research Problems in Metropolitan Population Redistribution." *American Sociological Review* 21: 571-77; October 1956.

Research Needs in Traffic Safety Education: A Questionnaire Survey Prepared by the N.E.A. Research Division for the National Commission on Safety Education, N.E.A. Washington: National Education Association, 1956. 20 p.

RIEMER, Svend. "Prehypothetical Studies in Sociology." *Sociology and Social Research* 42: 37-43; September-October 1957.

ROBACK, A. *A History of American Psychology.* New York: Library Publishers, 1952. xiv + 426 p.

ROGERS, Carl R., and SKINNER, B. F. "Some Issues Concerning the Control of Human Behavior." *Science* 124: 1057-66; November 30, 1956.

RUMMEL, J. Francis. *An Introduction to Research Procedures in Education.* New York: Harper & Brothers, 1958. p. 20-56.

RUSSELL, Roger W. "Contemporary Issues of Concern to Psychologists." *American Psychologist* 13: 199-216; May 1958.

"The School of the Future—1985." *Educational Leadership* 17: 470-508; May 1960.

SCOTT, M. Gladys, Editor. "Selection and Definition of a Problem," *Research Methods in Health, Physical Education, Recreation.* Second Edition. Washington: American Association for Health, Physical Education, and Recreation, 1959. Chapter 3.

SELLTIZ, Claire, and Others. "Selection and Formulation of a Research Problem," *Research Methods in Social Relations.* Revised One-Volume Edition. New York: Henry Holt and Co., 1959. Chapter 2.

SHEPS, Cecil G., and TAYLOR, Eugene E. *Needed Research in Health and Medical Care: A Biosocial Approach.* Chapel Hill: University of North Carolina Press, 1954. ix + 216 p.

SIEGEL, Bernard J. "High Anxiety Levels and Cultural Integration: Notes on a Psycho-Cultural Hypothesis." *Social Forces* 34: 42-48; October 1955.

SILBERMAN, Leo. "Problems of Evaluation Research." *Rural Sociology* 20: 229-41; September-December 1955.

SIMEY, T. S. "Social Investigation: Past Achievements and Present Difficulties." *British Journal of Sociology* 8: 121-29; June 1957.

SIMMONS, Ozzie G., and DAVIS, James A. "Interdisciplinary Collaboration in Mental Illness Research." *American Journal of Sociology* 63: 297-303; November 1957.

SIMON, Abraham J., and GERSHENSON, Charles P. "Residential Treatment of Children: Unanswered Questions and Research Problems and Possibilities." *Social Service Review* 30: 260-75; September 1956.

SINGLETON, W. Ralph. "Some High Lights of the First Half Century of Genetics." *Scientific Monthly* 71: 401-7; December 1950.

SMITH, M. Brewster. "Cross-Cultural Education as a Research Area." *Journal of Social Issues* 12: 3-8; 1956.

SMITH, M. Brewster. "A Perspective for Further Research on Cross-Cultural Education." *Journal of Social Issues* 12: 56-58; 1956.

SNYDER, Laurence H. "Fifty Years of Medical Genetics." *Science* 129: 7-13; January 2, 1959. (The union of biochemistry and genetics offers a rational approach to diagnosis, prevention, and therapy.)

SNYDER, Laurence H. "What We Most Need to Know." *Scientific Monthly* 84: 17-23; January 1957.

SPALDING, Eugenia K. "Current Problems of Nurse Educators." *Teachers College Record* 57: 38-46; October 1955.

STEPHENS, J. M. *Educational Psychology:* The Study of Educational Growth. New York: Henry Holt and Co., 1951. Chapter 4.

STEWART, Lawrence H. "Some Needed Research on Problems of Retirement." *Educational Administration and Supervision* 42: 68-71; February 1956.

STONE, Donald C. "Some Research and Action Needs in International Educational Exchange." *Educational Record* 39: 374-81; October 1958.

STROUP, Herbert. "Some Unexplored Problem Areas in Student Activities." *Teacher College Record* 57: 469-74; April 1956.

SUPER, Donald E., and Others. *Vocational Development: A Framework for Research.* New York: Bureau of Publications, Teachers College, Columbia University, 1957. xiv + 142 p.

TAYLOR, Griffith, Editor. *Geography in the Twentieth Century: A Study of Growth, Fields, Techniques, Aims, and Trends.* New York: Philosophical Library, 1951. x + 630 p.

TEAD, Ordway. "A Ten-Year Look Ahead at the Liberal Arts College." *Educational Record* 40: 22-36; July 1959.

THOMAS, John L. "Theory and Research in Family Sociology." *American Catholic Sociological Review* 16: 104-16; June 1955.

THOMAS, Lawrence G., and Others. "Prospects of Scientific Research into Values." *Educational Theory* 6: 193-214; October 1956.

TRAVERS, R. M. W. *An Introduction to Educational Research.* New York: The Macmillan Co., 1958. Chapter 4.

VAN DALEN, Deobold B. *Understanding Educational Research:* An Introduction. New York: McGraw-Hill Book Co., 1962. p. 108-58, 392-419.

VINACKE, W. Edgar. *The Psychology of Thinking.* New York: McGraw-Hill Book Co., 1952. 369 p.

WALLACE, Anthony F. C. *Human Behavior in Extreme Situations:* A Survey of the Literature and Suggestions for Further Research. Disaster Study No. 1, Publication No. 390. Washington: Committee on Disaster Studies, National Academy of Sciences-National Research Council, 1956. v + 35 p.

WATSON, Fletcher G., and COOLEY, William W. "Needed Research in Science Education," *Rethinking Science Education.* Fifty-ninth Yearbook of the National Society for the Study of Education, Part 1. Chicago: University of Chicago Press, 1960. p. 297-312.

WATSON, Robert I. "The History of Psychology: A Neglected Area." *American Psychologist* 15: 251-55; April 1960.

WEBB, Wilse B. "The Choice of the Problem." *American Psychologist* 16: 223-27; May 1961.

WEBER, Eugen. "The Right in France: A Working Hypothesis." *American Historical Review* 65: 554-68; April 1960.

WEST, S. S. "The Hypothesis of Slow Cyclical Variation of Creativity." *American Journal of Sociology* 63: 143-51; September 1957.

WEY, Herbert. "The South Calls for Research." *Phi Delta Kappan* 38: 19-24; October 1956.

WHITE, Lynn, Jr., Editor. *Frontiers of Knowledge in the Study of Man.* New York: Harper & Brothers, 1956. xii + 330 p.

WILLIAMS, C. B., and STEVENSON, A. H. *A Research Manual.* Revised Edition. New York: Harper & Brothers, 1951. p. 62-75.

WILLIAMS, Robin M., Jr., FISHER, Burton R., and JANIS, Irving L. "Educational Desegregation as a Context for Basic Social Science Research." *American Sociological Review* 21: 577-83; October 1956.

WILSON, J. T., and Others. *Current Trends in Psychology and the Behavioral Sciences.* Pittsburgh: University of Pittsburgh Press, 1954. xvi + 142 p.

WISEMAN, Stephen. "Trends in Educational Psychology." *British Journal of Educational Psychology* 29: 128-35; June 1959.

WRIGHT, Quincy. "The Peaceful Adjustment of International Relations: Problems and Research Approaches." *Journal of Social Issues* 11, No. 1: 3-12; 1955.

YOUNG, Pauline V. *Scientific Social Surveys and Research.* Third Edition. Englewood Cliffs, N.J.: Prentice-Hall, 1956. p. 115-27.

CHAPTER THREE

Keys to the Literature and Library Usage

The importance of the related literature as background for problem-solving has already been emphasized in Chapter 2. The present chapter describes the guides or keys to the vast storehouse of research (books, periodicals, and theses) now available in education, psychology, sociology, and cognate social fields. This chapter also presents certain problems closely related to library technique, such as note-taking and synthesis of pubished findings, although the topic of documentation and bibliographical form is reserved for the last chapter, dealing with the technical report. The present chapter can do no more than mention briefly a few of the most generally used library tools (including extensive bibliographies, exhaustive summaries of research, and research handbooks), leaving for the guides to reference works the detailed information concerning several hundred helpful titles of reference books.[1] In the description later in this chapter of the guides to the literature, it will be helpful to identify major subdivisions or the larger subheadings in education, psychology, and sociology, under which the related studies usually are classified or indexed.

---

[1] Carter Alexander and Arvid J. Burke, *How to Locate Educational Information and Data*. Fourth Edition. New York: Bureau of Publications, Teachers College, Columbia University, 1958. xvii + 419 p.

I. G. Mudge, *Guide to Reference Books*. Sixth Edition. Chicago: American Library Association, 1936. xii + 504 p. Also see earlier editions and the informal supplements.

Constance M. Winchell, *Guide to Reference Books*. Seventh Edition. Chicago: American Library Association, 1951. xvii + 645 p.

Constance M. Winchell and O. A. Johnson, *Guide to Reference Books*. Seventh Edition Supplement, 1950–52. Second Supplement, 1953–55. Third Supplement, 1956–58. Chicago: American Library Association, 1954, 1956, 1960. 140 p., 134 p., 145 p.

Louis Shores, *Basic Reference Sources*. Chicago: American Library Association, 1954. ix + 378 p.

The comprehensiveness of one major handbook for searching the educational literature and of the library resources is indicated by the following chapter topics:[2]

General Suggestions for Library Searching
Procedures in Library Searching
Selecting Headings before Searching for References
Locating Books through the Library Card Catalog
Locating Books Outside the Library Used
Locating Periodicals and Other Serials
Making the Most of the Education Index
Making a Bibliography
Securing a Guide to the Professional Literature of One's Field
Library Reading
Note-Taking in Work with Library Materials
Reference Books
Evaluations of Books and Other References
Publications of Educational Associations
United States Office of Education Publications
Government Documents
Instructional Materials and Aids
History of an Educational Problem or Topic
Legal Aspects of Education
Biographical Information
Names and Addresses
News Items
Quotations and Proverbs
Educational Researches
Statistics and Statistical Methodology.

INTEGRATION OF PUBLISHED FINDINGS

It is generally recognized that a field of knowledge makes progress as a scientific discipline through the activities of the worker who is engaged in conducting and interpreting research. There is another function, however, that involves important activities of integration and assimilation of the bodies of data and published findings in the many sub-areas of such fields as education and psychology. Unless the research findings from many thousands of individual studies are incorporated within appropriate theories, it is virtually impossible for graduate students and others to assimilate the knowledge in a particular field of specialization. It is possible that data and published studies are accumulating more rapidly than they can be integrated or summarized effectively, as witnessed by recent difficulties in securing qualified persons to prepare sum-

[2] Carter Alexander and Arvid J. Burke, *op. cit.*

marizing articles for the *Review of Educational Research, Encyclopedia of Educational Research,* and *Annual Review of Psychology.* Therefore, it seems appropriate to give due recognition to the scholar who does his work in the library, sorting research findings according to an integrating scheme, summarizing sound empirical findings, noting contradictory results, identifying needed research, and noting the status of explanatory efforts. This type of assimilating or integrating work may prove more valuable to the profession as a summary of several hundred research reports than for a scholar to spend the same amount of time in collecting original data on a single limited problem.[3]

It is estimated that in 1960 alone, 212 core psychological journals published 1,500 articles, mostly in English, representing a floodtide of materials for colleagues in many lands. "While there has been growing concern about communication across language barriers, psychologists have given relatively little attention to new techniques of selective electronic dissemination of scientific papers, micropublication, and mechanized retrieval of stored information."[4]

To cite an illustration, the problem of reporting and disseminating evidence is especially urgent in medical research, which has moved so rapidly into new fields that doctors are faced by an ever-growing mountain of new facts, theories, and procedures, as reported in some 900 medical journals published in the United States alone. For example, among the few truly effective drugs early in this century were morphine and digitalis, but by 1960 there were some 500 pure and potent therapeutic substances, marketed in at least 20,000 forms and combinations.

The survey of the related literature may provide guiding hypotheses, suggestive methods of investigation, and comparative data for interpretative purposes. Sometimes textbooks and subjective critiques of a problem area provide important insights and hypotheses that may well have a place in the summary of the related literature. The summarizer of research always has before him the problem of striking a balance between tedious detail and superficial sketchiness. One technique is to group similar studies, with a representative investigation analyzed in some detail. The weaknesses of unsound studies and the merits of outstanding investigations should be indicated in a constructive manner, but without the ordinary adjectives of denunciation or praise as such.

The review of related research should be an integral part of the total report rather than an appendage or a loosely related supplement.

[3] Benton J. Underwood, *Psychological Research.* New York: Appleton-Century-Crofts, 1957. p. 290–91.

Carter V. Good and Douglas E. Scates, *Methods of Research:* Educational, Psychological, Sociological. New York: Appleton-Century-Crofts, 1954. p. 84–86.

[4] Henry P. David and William M. Swartley, "Toward More Effective International Communication in Psychology." *American Psychologist* 16: 696–98; November 1961.

The purpose of this review is not primarily to produce a relatively complete annotated bibliography. A number of existing agencies have much better facilities than the graduate student for exhaustive bibliographical work; for example, the *Encyclopedia of Educational Research, Review of Educational Research, Psychological Abstracts, Annual Review of Psychology,* and *Sociological Abstracts.*

Another, and perhaps even more common, misconception is the idea that the review is presented to show that the candidate's research has not been done previously by someone else. But any necessarily limited review cannot provide this proof of originality. At best it can only show that no piece of research reviewed by the candidate is exactly the same as his study. With educational research being carried on at a multitude of educational institutions and by numerous other agencies, it is extremely doubtful that any candidate can even discover references to any considerable portion of the studies that have been carried out in his area of interest. Also, in an area such as education where problems are so numerous and so complex and where the application of scientific methods is relatively new, it is doubtful that the question of the uniqueness of research is nearly as important as many other questions. It might be suggested that finding the ways in which studies are comparable and in which they are related to one another is a more important problem. . . .

. . . It is this fitting of a particular project into a broader scheme, enabling one to see its importance and to relate it to many other studies, that is the real purpose of the review of related research. Through this study of existing research, the candidate locates and defines his exact problem. Then in writing up this review, he so organizes these previous findings that the reader can see just why the problem is important and how it is going to fit into a wider pattern of research results.

This purpose of the review of research may also be viewed in another manner. It may be considered as a small contribution to the building of research theory.[5]

Careful handling of references is imperative in relation to effective summarizing. In the matter of bibliographical work, even as experienced and prolific an author as Ellwood P. Cubberley encountered criticisms that seemed merited. A reviewer of Cubberley's *Syllabus of Lectures on the History of Education* thought the bibliographies were useful but complained of the defective or incomplete references, having found 39 on a single page. The number of such faulty references throughout the book caused the reviewer to wonder whether much of the bibliographical work had not been done by students. For the careless reference work, Cubberley could have no excuse, except that he had only a master's degree

[5] Quoted from C. M. Lindvall, "The Review of Related Research." *Phi Delta Kappan* 40: 179–80; January 1959.

at that time, with no record of bibliographical training. His later reference work evidenced improvement.[6]

LANGUAGE SKILLS

Although the traditional acceptance of the basic position of foreign languages in the qualifications for the doctoral degree has been considerably modified since the 1930's, especially for professional degrees, a reading knowledge of one or more modern foreign languages should prove helpful in canvassing the related literature on a problem for investigation. It has been typical to stress the "tool" aspect of the foreign language, supporting the view that a doctoral candidate should be able to read German or French, so that he can translate the most recent technical articles relating to his special field or problem. This use of a foreign language is similar to the study of statistics in psychology, education, sociology, or economics, as a necessary or practical tool or technique. On the other hand, many graduate students and some professors maintain that all the important literature has been translated into English or is being translated, so that there is no longer a need for the foreign-language requirement in the doctoral program. One answer to this view is that it smacks of provincialism, and that something usually is lost in translation. Many scientists and scholars still take pride in the ability to translate for themselves, supporting the adage, "Never read a book about a book, read the book."

Another important advantage of foreign-language facility as a tool is its practical employment by the scholar or scientist who travels abroad. With an increasing number of overseas fellowships and scholarships available, and more American specialists in demand as technical advisers to foreign governments and American overseas financial enterprises, more academic people now are enabled to travel abroad. When such persons have been able to converse directly with men in their own fields, the value of a foreign language has been demonstrated, not only on the practical grounds of communication, but also as a means of better understanding of another nationality, with some lessening of the narrow provincialism of which our nation and our higher institutions have sometimes been guilty.[7]

Lest we become too unrealistic about expectations for mastery of a foreign language, it is wise to remember the plaint of the undergraduate:

[6] Jesse B. Sears and Adin D. Henderson, *Cubberley of Stanford: And His Contribution to American Education.* Stanford, Calif.: Stanford University Press, 1957. p. 119–20.

[7] Everett Walters, "Foreign Languages: Benefit or Barrier?" *Graduate School Record* 9: 1, 3; January 1956.

> *What's pat in the Latin*
> *Or chic in the Greek*
> *I always distinguish*
> *More clearly in English.*

To use the field of psychology as an example, the "language require-ment" too frequently has been perfunctory rather than functional in terms of the particular field or problem for specialization or research:[8]

If knowledge of one or more foreign languages is important to an indi-vidual's field of research, then he will need to achieve much higher proficiency than is presently typically attained; and such proficiency should be required in those fields where language competence is critical. However, for some fields of research endeavor, knowledge of other tool subjects may be far more critical than knowledge of a foreign language. For example, thorough com-petence in mathematics is of vital importance to those attempting to con-tribute to statistical behavior theory. Similarly, new developments in research in learning, taking place largely in the United States, place a high premium on competence in electronics and relay engineering.

Given the development of adequate translation services, as well as the somewhat unpredictable shifts in major research activity in some specialties from one language area to another, substantial foreign language proficiency, as any other tool competence, should be required selectively for those indi-viduals to whose interests and plans it is relevant, and not as a *rite de passage* for all.

NOTE-TAKING[9]

It is essential, especially in summarizing the literature and in historical studies, to collect the material systematically, with a well-arranged plan of note-taking. A note system should be flexible, to permit addition of new material, without disarranging the older notes, and with the possi-bility of rearranging the notes as desired. To make this possible, it is necessary that the notes be taken on separate sheets of paper, slips, or cards.

[8] Quoted from Donald W. Taylor and Others, "Education for Research in Psy-chology." *American Psychologist* 14: 167–79; April 1959.

[9] Carter Alexander and Arvid J. Burke, *op. cit.*, p. 52–56, 168–80.

Jacques Barzun and Henry F. Graff, *The Modern Researcher*. New York: Har-court, Brace and Co., 1957. p. 18–39.

William W. Brickman, *Guide to Research in Educational History*. New York: New York University Bookstore, 1949. p. 191–200.

E. W. Dow, *Principles of a Note-System for Historical Studies*. New York: Century Co., 1924. vi + 124 p. plus numerous illustrations.

Homer C. Hockett, *The Critical Method in Historical Research and Writing*. New York: The Macmillan Co., 1955. p. 89–142.

Robert E. Tuttle and C. A. Brown, *Writing Useful Reports:* Principles and Applications. New York: Appleton-Century-Crofts, 1956. p. 263–76.

Three kinds of notes are regularly made by historical workers and are also appropriate, with some adaptations, for summarizing studies. The bibliographical note includes the standard data, author, title, pages, place and date of publication, and other formal facts about the document or study. The subject note contains one item of information about a specific topic, with the source indicated; most notes collected by the summarizer or historian usually are of this type. The "method" notes include suggestions or ideas useful in interpreting the facts.

Some preliminary reading and note-taking probably have taken place before the major topics of the outline begin to stand out in relief, and in turn the tentative outline and its headings serve as a guide for further reading, study, and note-taking. Expansion of the bibliography, analysis of content, and gathering of notes probably continue until the actual writing of the report begins and even later.

Although able historians like George Bancroft, J. B. McMaster, James Ford Rhodes, and Edward Gibbon used bound notebooks instead of a flexible system, it can only be said that they succeeded in spite of their notebooks in calendar form. During the 1840's Bancroft had a number of quarto-size blank books, in which one or more pages were allocated to the successive days of the years, and the data were entered on the page corresponding to the day and year when the event occurred. Even as late as the 1890's, Rhodes used blank books for his notes, since the card system at that time was something of a novelty.

William G. Sumner, the sociologist, had no financial assistance for research and little help, yet his files of notes compared favorably with many later research workers supported by relatively large financial grants. Sumner filled 52 drawers and boxes of notes, averaging 3,000 sheets each.

Soon after Clark Hull, the psychologist, began graduate study, he initiated a permanent notebook system of the original ideas on psychological subjects that came to him on reading a new book, agreements or disagreements with the author, and views on subjects discussed in class or seminar. Near the end of his career, this series of notebooks totaled 27 volumes. To his surprise Hull discovered that the notes were valuable not so much as aids to memory, but as stimuli to systematic thinking. Hull confesses that he had little success in persuading promising graduate students in his seminars to keep similar notebooks, even when he presented notebooks to the students.[10]

Throughout his life Ellwood P. Cubberley kept notes on a wide variety of subjects which interested him, particularly matters revealing significant trends (by studying data in series). Cubberley left an unusual record for his biographer: a long series of pocket calendar notebooks

[10] Herbert S. Langfeld, Editor, *A History of Psychology in Autobiography.* Vol. 4. Worcester, Mass.: Clark University Press, 1952. xii + 356 p.

which he kept with regularity through the years from 1905 to 1940. These booklets were filled with facts about home, work, travel, accounts, attendance at operas and concerts and dinner meetings, illnesses, books he was working on as author or editor, trips for business or pleasure, expenses for clothes, lecture dates and topics, life-insurance policies with dates when premiums were due, library interests, his college program of study and reading, notes on the weather, and other memoranda of items he liked or wanted to remember or think about. Although Cubberley said that he did not want to be run by a card catalogue and seemed to dislike the thought of a system of formal records, in his notebooks there is evidence of care and considerable labor in recording a mass of detail, but detail dictated by his own personal interests and tastes rather than by any scheme of logic or plan of systematic accounting.[11]

CLASSIFICATION SYSTEMS

The reader who uses such documentary materials as books is indebted to the workers who have given their attention to classification for the purpose of affording order and system, without which library work would be virtually impossible. The two principal systems of library classification in the United States are that worked out by Melvil Dewey and published in 1876, commonly referred to as the "Dewey decimal" system, and the Library of Congress system (devised because developments in certain fields seriously crowded the older Dewey scheme). In addition to the basic systems, many special rules are necessary to cover detailed questions that arise, and some libraries have issued their own rule publications.

These classification schemes or systems are supplemented from time to time by efforts toward classification in special fields, as in education,[12] psychology, and sociology. The first extensive list of subject headings in education was prepared by Voegelein, *List of Educational Subject Headings*, 1928, which influenced the *Education Index*, first published in 1929. A latter list by Pettus, *Subject Headings in Education*, 1938, was arranged in classified rather than dictionary (alphabetical) form, and included definitions of various heads and subheads. Other sources that indicate the scope of a particular field or discipline are the *Review of Educational Research, Encyclopedia of Educational Research, Dictionary of Education, Psychological Abstracts, Annual Review of Psychology*, and *Sociological Abstracts*, as illustrated by the lists of subtopics later in this chap-

[11] Jesse B. Sears and Adin D. Henderson, *op. cit.*, p. 82.

[12] L. Belle Voegelein, *List of Educational Subject Headings*. Columbus: Ohio State University Press, 1928. xiv + 338 p.

Clyde Pettus, *Subject Headings in Education: A Systematic List for Use in a Dictionary Catalogue*. New York: H. W. Wilson Co., 1938. 188 p.

ter. If librarians, professors, and graduate students will learn to think outside the limitations of the Dewey decimal system and the Library of Congress system, there is opportunity for a much closer relationship between bibliographical organization in the social fields and its physical implementation in libraries, thus furthering an interdisciplinary approach to problems in the behavioral and human sciences.

THE CARD CATALOG

The card catalog of the library is of major importance, as illustrated by a description of this tool in a particular university library:[13]

Judged by almost any standard the card catalog in the main library is the most valuable single possession of the University of Cincinnati. What other tool, machine, computer or instrument is insured for one and a third million dollars, or costs, in annual maintenance, over $75,000? What other instrument is comprised of nearly two million pieces, each precision-made by skilled craftsmen? If, as most educators claim, the library is the heart or center of the university, certainly the catalog is the heart *and* center of the library. Those who have been using it merely as a means of getting the call number of main library books are missing a great deal. It performs many services for those who are sufficiently sophisticated to use them. In analogy, some of us would have difficulty in using the university's computer to add two and two, while our more knowledgeable colleagues use it to compute orbits. So it is with the catalog which must be both an abacus and an electronic brain, equally useful to the most naive freshman and the senior scholar. There are not more than a handful here, or on any other campus, sufficiently sophisticated to utilize the card catalog to its maximum potential.

Coverage: In theory any main catalog records the book and manuscript holdings of a university. Actually, it seldom does all this, and it does not do so here. It records most of these, but not all. It also records much that is not owned by the University of Cincinnati.

Most, but by no means all, American university library catalogs are dictionary catalogs, so-called because author, title, subject, and other entries are filed in one alphabet. So it is at Cincinnati. We depart from this only when the sheer bulk requires further breakdown. Thus U.S. History is subdivided by periods and George Washington precedes John Adams in this file in spite of alphabet. As most users are aware, cards called "added entries" are often made for translators, joint authors, illustrators, and other individuals or corporate bodies which have played important roles in the preparation of a publication.

If the card catalog is the heart of the library, there are a number of important related organs which are just as vital to the body corporate as the liver, the lungs, or the stomach to the human body, and very, very useful to faculty and students as well as to librarians.

[13] Quoted from Arthur Hamlin, *News Notes from the Library* (University of Cincinnati) 6: 1-5; May 1961.

The Shelf-list: In simplest terms, the shelf list is a record of the university library holdings by call number, regardless of physical location. The mathematician can easily look in the card catalog for a subject such as Permutations or Vector Analysis, but he would never find, under mathematics, or journals, or anything else, a list of the serials in mathematics. This the shelf list provides.

A few American research libraries no longer make subject cards and require all subject approach to the collection to be made through a very much expanded shelf-list. Scholars who have become experienced with this approach generally approve of it. This, combined with an index on cards, is called a "classed catalog."

The shelf list is extremely valuable for many needs of readers as well as librarians. It is easily available for public use.

The Serial record: Another key file is the list of our holdings of periodicals or journals. The card catalog merely tells when our file of a serial began and does not attempt to state how complete the holdings are. Instead it states "See Serial Record." Many of us assume, quite rightly, that holdings of a standard periodical, like *Harpers,* will be complete, and send for the volume needed with confidence. But the situation is different under a heading like *Royal Society of London.* The brief moment it takes to consult the adjacent Serial Record is well spent. The reasons for maintaining this separate record are complex and involved. Suffice it to say that an official of the Library of Congress spent several days here this very month in a search for certain material they did not have, and wanted. Our Serial Record caused an admiring comment that this was one library which "had everything listed—no more, and no less."

Contents file: This is a minor and possibly unique organ of the body corporate. It is not essential to existence, but serves a worthy purpose. There are many numbered series, like the *Publications* of the Harvard Graduate School of Engineering, which are kept as a series but must include, under that entry, the author and title of each number. Some of these series run into many hundred separate numbers and monographs and therefore take several score cards to list all the parts. In such cases the main catalog includes a single card for the series and refers the occasional student, who wishes to look over the various monographs included, to the Contents File.

Each departmental library catalog contains the same author, subject and some title cards, but of course only for the books in that collection.

Let us now look at the catalog for its function in providing an approach by subject. Obviously we must use indexes and bibliographies to dig out periodical articles. No library makes subject cards for issues of the *New Yorker* or even the *Transactions of the American Philosophical Society.* A Festschrift may contain many really significant contributions, but libraries cannot and should not spend ten times the purchase price in preparing 50-100 subject cards for an individual issue or volume. On the other hand there are hundreds of series in which each volume consists of several scholarly monographs. For each of these individual contributions a full set of author and subject cards should be made. These are called "analytics." Every library must decide for itself which series it will analyze. The limitation is, of course, the expense.

The Cincinnati catalog has gone extensively into "analytics." We are now cautiously revising this policy. For example the *Bulletin of the U. S. Geological Survey* was analyzed until very recently. This one series is represented in the main and geology library catalogs by well over five thousand cards. Important as this series is, the advanced student has subject access to the individual numbers through the *Bibliography of North American Geology*. Similar economies are regularly considered.

Returning now to the catalog as a whole, what does it attempt to do? First, it is a record of ownership, an inventory of what we have. Then it is a record of location, the key which tells where or how to get any item. It is also a subject bibliography which tells the student what material is available on his subject. Finally, it provides some physical description of every book as well as very scholarly, detailed description of selected material.

EDUCATIONAL AND GENERAL GUIDES

Earlier in this chapter we emphasized that the need for rapid communication of messages to other research workers concerned with the same problem area has always been with us, but it becomes ever more important as the rate of acquisition of scientific knowledge increases, as illustrated by the field of psychology.

There is also need for opportunities for discussion and comparison of findings among scientists of common interests. Face-to-face meetings of scientists permit rapid identification of sources of conflict in empirical results or theoretical notions and the generation of a common base of technical information. They also provide for special-interest groups the opportunity to establish formal or informal channels of communication within the area of their interest. . . .

A fundamental need, in any science, is an efficient method for storage and selective retrieval of the results of scientific research, whether such be in the form of theoretical ideas and integrations of knowledge or in the form of reports of observations and the conditions under which the observations were obtained. During the history of scientific psychology it has been generally assumed that the need for storage of information is satisfied by printed archives in the form of journals, monographs, or books and that the technique of retrieval is the responsibility, and skill, of the individual scientist with such aid as can be given by abstract journals, bibliographies, and bibliographies of bibliographies. Psychology should be alert to the possibility of developments in information storage and retrieval which make more efficient use of printed archives, as well as those which might replace or at least supplement printed archives.

In psychology the traditional emphasis continues to be more on the storage function served by journals and books than upon the retrieval function served by abstract journals, encyclopedic compendia of archival materials, and integrated (even inventive) summaries of the literature in special areas. However, the efficiency of retrieval should be an important consideration in determining what and how material gets into the archives. In spite of efforts to solve the problem of retrieval through publication of abstracts and improvements of indexing and cataloging techniques, it is often said that there has been a decline in "scholarship" among our scientists. It may, in fact, sometimes be true that it is more economical to produce new data in the laboratory than to search for studies in the literature that would provide the needed data. Certainly, the psychologist today cannot read all of the principal journals and books in psychology, and it is an uncommon specialist who reads all of the literature in his area of specialization. . . .

The techniques of scientific communication now employed by psychologists have evolved from past experiences, conditions, and needs, without much self-conscious analysis or deliberate planning. We are now facing a crisis with repercussions throughout our whole scientific enterprise. Some symptoms of the crisis are: (a) an overloading of the various channels of publication; (b) a stereotyping of publications so as to fit a standardized mold of reporting; (c) an excessive amount of reporting in archival journals of fragmentary findings, of "first steps" of research which are often never followed up, and too little integrative reporting of "firm" conclusions; (d) an overloading of the programs of regional and national conventions with "bit-by-bit" reports of research; and (e) a failure to use the conventions as an occasion for the exchange of important ideas and information or for the stimulation of quality and originality in psychological research.

Any effort to deal constructively with the present crisis should be guided by an understanding of the factors which have brought it about. The following factors may be suggested, though systematic effort should be devoted to analyzing them: a rapid growth in the number of psychologists, a great increase in the scope of psychological research, a reluctance to apply qualitative rather than quantitative criteria in evaluating scholarship and research productivity, an increase in research financed by agencies demanding project reports, the practice of paying travel costs to conventions only for those who read papers, a reluctance to impose qualitative distinctions in the selection of papers for publication or for conventions, a lack of adequate values inculcated by graduate training concerning quality of publications, and a failure, so far, to achieve an accepted taxonomy of behavior or of environmental contexts in which behavior occurs or with which it interacts. . . .

There are as yet few signs of inventive solutions to the basic problems, either in the organization of annual meetings or in the publication policies of our journals. But the crisis cannot be met effectively by a single remedy. It requires a concerted attack by many agencies within psychology. Editorial policies, convention policies, graduate training, policies of research sponsors, criteria for professional advancement all need to be examined separately and together in order to discover ways in which to deal effectively with the problem.[14]

[14] Quoted from Board of Scientific Affairs, "Technical Communication in Psychology: A Statement of the Problem." *American Psychologist* 14: 267–71; June 1959.

Before beginning a systematic examination of the titles in the library guides, it may prove desirable to secure certain background concerning the problem by reading the kind of overview treatment commonly found in textbooks and general reference works. From this more general reading should come at least an initial list of subtopics for use in examining the library guides.

The beginner in research or graduate student probably will start with the *Education Index,* which lists virtually all the educational materials in published form in the United States, except elementary and high-school textbooks. For research materials the summaries in the *Encyclopedia of Educational Research*[15] (published in 1941, and revised in the 1950 and 1960 editions) are useful. For current research studies and to supplement the *Encyclopedia of Educational Research,* the *Review of Educational Research* is the chief summarizing guide (beginning in January, 1931). The *Review* originally planned to cover fifteen major subdivisions of education within a three-year cycle, but as the years passed the number of topics increased and the appearance of a particular topic once in three years was not always possible or desirable. It is of interest to examine the following list of selected topics covered in the *Review,* noting the appearance of a particular subject at three-year intervals during recent years.

REVIEW OF EDUCATIONAL RESEARCH

ADMINISTRATION: XXII:4 (October 1952); XXV:4 (October 1955); XXVIII:4 (October 1958); XXXI:4 (October 1961).

EDUCATIONAL MEASUREMENT: XX:1 (February 1950); XXIII:1 (February 1953); XXVI:1 (February 1956); XXIX:1 (February 1959); XXXII:1 (February 1962).

GUIDANCE AND COUNSELING: XXI:2 (April 1951); XXIV:2 (April 1954); XXVII:2 (April 1957); XXX:2 (April 1960).

MENTAL AND PHYSICAL DEVELOPMENT: XXII:5 (December 1952); XXV:5 (December 1955); XXVIII:5 (December 1958); XXXI:5 (December 1961).

TEACHER PERSONNEL: XXII:3 (June 1952); XXV:3 (June 1955); XXVIII:3 (June 1958).

The *Bibliographic Index* is really a cumulative bibliography of bibliographies dealing with a wide range of subjects. The first number, published in 1938, includes 4,400 references.

The monthly *Book Review Digest* takes the form of a specialized periodical index, in the sense that it provides excerpts from the reviews

15 Douglas E. Scates, "Unlocking for the Profession a Wealth of Educational Research." *Journal of Teacher Education* 11: 558–62; December 1960. Describes the *Encyclopedia of Educational Research.*

that appear in some eighty book-review periodicals. In the course of a year it lists approximately 4,000 books, and cumulates at intervals.

The inclusive term *serials* has been defined as any publication issued serially or in successive parts more or less regularly. The Ayer list[16] is a bibliography of newspapers and periodicals, but it includes much additional information. The Gregory union list[17] of serials indicates the extent to which more than 75,000 different serials are found in the more important libraries in the United States and Canada. Ulrich's directory of periodicals[18] lists the titles published in the United States and in foreign countries that have proved most useful in American collections.

The *United States Catalogue* lists virtually all books in print in this country on a specific subject. It is kept up to date by the monthly *Cumulative Book Index,* which cumulates at irregular intervals during the year, annually into a supplement, and after several years into a large supplement. The *Publishers' Weekly* is regarded as a supplement to the *Cumulative Book Index,* in the sense that it describes and indexes new books in a convenient reference and buying list.

Guides are available for current graduate theses[19] and dissertations in education, although a research master's study is no longer generally required for the awarding of the first graduate degree. Since many graduate institutions publish abstract volumes or lists of their graduate theses, it is helpful that we have available an older basic guide[20] to such summaries.

Starting with 1952, Phi Delta Kappa has sponsored an annual list of doctoral dissertations completed in education and a list of doctoral dissertations under way of education, classified under the following headings for current numbers:[21]

[16] *Directory of Newspapers and Periodicals.* Philadelphia: N. W. Ayer and Sons, 1880–.

[17] Winifred Gregory, Editor, *Union List of Serials in Libraries of the United States and Canada.* Second Edition. New York: H. W. Wilson Co., 1943. 3,065 p. Also see supplements.

Also see *New Serial Titles:* A Union List of Serials Commencing Publication After December 31, 1949. Washington: Library of Congress, 1959. vii + 1275 p.

[18] Eileen C. Graves, Editor, *Ulrich's Periodicals Directory:* A Classified Guide to a Selected List of Current Periodicals, Foreign and Domestic. Ninth Edition. New York: R. R. Bowker Co., 1959. xvi + 825 p.

[19] Herbert M. Silvey, Editor, *Master's Theses in Education, 1960–61.* No. 10. Cedar Falls, Iowa: Research Publications, 1961. Also see later numbers.

[20] Thomas R. Palfrey and Henry E. Coleman, *Guide to Bibliographies of Theses —United States and Canada.* Second Edition. Chicago: American Library Association, 1940. 54 p.

Also see Willard Brehaut, "An Analysis of Dissertations (English) in Education Accepted by Canadian Universities, 1930–1955." *Ontario Journal of Educational Research* 2: 109-222; April 1960.

[21] Mary L. Lyda, Harold Anderson, and Carter V. Good, *Research Studies in Education, 1960:* A Subject-Author Index and Research Methods Bibliography. Bloomington, Indiana: Phi Delta Kappa, 1961. vi + 133 p. Also see later numbers.

Areas of Education

Philosophy of Education; Educational Principles and Trends
International Education; Intercultural Education; United Nations
Religious Education; Religion and the Schools
Educational Administration—General
Educational Administration—Local
Educational Administration—School Boards; Trustees; Regents;
    Reorganization
Supervision
Public Relations; School and Community Relations
Recruitment
Finance
School Plant (Construction; Space Allotment; Maintenance); Pupil
    Transportation
Educational Legislation; School Laws; Court Decisions
Educational History; Biography
Child Study; Child Psychology
Educational Psychology; General Psychology
Studies in Adolescence; Youth Groups and Problems
Measurement and Evaluation; Research
Teacher Education; In-Service Training
Audio-Visual Education
Curriculum; Co-Curriculum Activities; Camping
Methods of Teaching; Teaching Aids; Libraries
Desegregation
Pre-School; Kindergarten; Elementary Education
Secondary Education; Junior High School; High School
Language Arts (Speech, Writing, Communications)
Reading; Literature
Foreign Language Instruction
English in High School
English in the University
Science; Aviation
Arithmetic; Mathematics
Social Studies
Art; Music
Vocational Education; Industrial Arts Education
Business Education
Vocational Agriculture
Guidance and Counseling
Student Problems—General
Student Problems—Kindergarten to Twelfth Grade
Student Problems Beyond the High School
Health
Physical Education

Safety Education; Driver Education
Recreation; Athletics; Sports
Special Education
Juvenile Delinquency; Rehabilitation
Home Economics; Family Life Education; Consumer Education
Rural Education; Conservation
Teachers' Problems—Personal and Personnel
Teachers' Problems—Professional
Undergraduate Education—College and University
Graduate Education—College and University
Junior College; Extension; Continuation
Adult Education; Veteran Education
Accreditation; Certification; Professional Education.

It usually is possible to borrow typewritten graduate theses or dissertations by interlibrary loan, although occasionally it is difficult or even impossible to secure one of the older studies. John Dewey's doctoral dissertation (1884) at Johns Hopkins University, dealing with the psychology of Kant, was never published and no copy is available, since the Johns Hopkins Library apparently did not preserve the manuscript.[22]

The *List of American Doctoral Dissertations* (covering 1912 through 1938, Library of Congress) and *Doctoral Dissertations Accepted by American Universities* (1933-34 through 1954-55, sponsored by the Association of Research Libraries) overlapped some 5½ years. The successor to these two series of dissertation lists appears under the title *Index to American Doctoral Dissertations*, published annually by University Microfilms, beginning in 1957. The same publisher also issues *Dissertation Abstracts* monthly and for each abstract makes available a microfilm of the entire manuscript.[23]

EDUCATIONAL LITERATURE IN RELATION TO NATIONAL AND INTERNATIONAL AGENCIES

It is informative to note the major contributions to the literature made by selected organizations or agencies in education.

[22] A. A. Roback, *History of American Psychology*. New York: Library Publishers, 1952. p. 98.

[23] Douglas E. Scates, "Changing Sources of Information about Thesis Research." *Journal of Teacher Education* 8: 210–13; June 1957.

Index to American Doctoral Dissertations, 1959–1960. Ann Arbor, Mich.: University Microfilms, 1960. 218 p.

Also see Bert Kaplan, "Dissemination of Primary Research Data in Psychology." *American Psychologist* 13: 53–55; February 1958. With the development of microcopy as a medium of scholarly publication, the financial barriers to publication are partly eliminated, although the cost of a good microcard reader still presents a problem. On a 3 × 5-inch microcard, up to 60 pages of material can be reproduced.

U. S. Office of Education[24]

In performing its three major functions, the United States Office of Education has an extensive program of publication in the fields of educational research, educational services, and administration of grants. The Office carries on its work through publishing its research studies and survey reports, participating in conferences, speaking and writing, consultation and field work, contracting with higher institutions and state departments of education to conduct research, and administering grant funds as stipulated by the Congress. Through its publications and otherwise, the Office interprets the educational needs of the nation and promotes a general understanding of educational objectives, collects and disseminates information on education in the states and territories to make possible intelligent comparison and wise decisions on programs and operations, presents proposals for improving practices and the adoption of educational standards (arrived at by cooperative planning and research), and with the aid of authentic information seeks to stimulate improvement in educational leadership.

The Office is organized in three Bureaus:

1. Educational Research and Development, with Divisions of Educational Statistics, Educational Research, Higher Education, Elementary and Secondary Education, and Continuing Education and Cultural Affairs

2. International Education, with Divisions of International Education Studies and Technical Assistance and Exchange Programs

3. Educational Assistance Programs, with Divisions of Vocational and Technical Education, School Assistance in Federally Affected Areas, State Grants, and Institutional Grants.

Through its statistical services, the Office of Education:

Collects, verifies, analyzes, and publishes educational statistics of wide interest and national significance.

Provides technical statistical services to the divisions of the Office, including consultation and advice on research methods, as well as operational assistance in data collection, tabulation, calculation, and analysis.

Responds to requests for information in the field of educational statistics.

Maintains liaison with other departments or agencies, especially the Office of Statistical Standards of the Bureau of the Budget.

Through its publications services, the Office of Education:

Plans and directs its over-all program of publications and information.

Maintains liaison with educational and information groups and individuals outside the Office.

---

[24] *Handbook, Office of Education.* Washington: Government Printing Office, 1960. 49 p. Also see later numbers.

Assists authors in planning individual publications, and edits, designs, and
handles the technical production and distribution of all the professional publications issued by the Office.

Plans, edits, and distributes the *Education Fact Sheet* and the monthly
magazine *School Life*, and produces and distributes an annual report
and other reports.

Prepares official statements, messages, articles, scripts, speeches, and news
releases, and acts as a clearing house for information requested by the
Congress, the White House, other government agencies, communications media, the educational profession, and the public.

N. E. A.

Since 1922 the Research Division of the National Education Association has performed the two functions of providing information required
currently, and of undertaking long-time investigations in anticipation of
future needs. The two major fields of study have been in the areas of
(1) teacher personnel, particularly economic status and welfare, and
(2) school finance and support, plus a wide range of investigations
relating to curriculum, instruction, and administration. Since 1922 the
Division has answered more than 200,000 letters of inquiry with the current average about 1000 a month, issued 172 numbers of the *Research
Bulletin* (more than 4,000,000 copies printed and distributed), and prepared 73 yearbooks for the departments of classroom teachers, elementary-
school principals, school administrators, and other groups (with more
than 700,000 copies distributed). Other surveys and studies have dealt
with tenure conditions and laws, academic freedom, teaching procedures,
economic status of teachers, teacher retirement, and other special
problems.[25]

American Council on Education

The American Council on Education has served as a clearing house
for the exchange of information and opinion, has conducted numerous
inquiries into specific educational problems, and has secured the cooperation of appropriate agencies (especially higher institutions) for the
solution of such problems.

The Educational Record, the quarterly journal of the American Council
on Education, has been issued regularly since 1920. It is a general educational
periodical of considerable circulation, and numbers among its contributors
many well-known college administrators, teachers, public officials, and
writers. . . .

[25] *N.E.A. Handbook, 1961–1962*. Washington: National Education Association,
1961. p. 79–80. See also later numbers.

A second periodical, widely distributed, is the occasional bulletin, *Higher Education and National Affairs*, which aims to report and interpret significant federal developments and other activities of concern to educational institutions and organizations.

As the end result of its research, special studies, conferences, and surveys, the Council publishes from 15 to 20 books a year. About 200 titles are currently in print and on sale.

Two standard directories inaugurated by the Council are the only directories composed exclusively of *accredited* institutions of higher education. They are: *American Universities and Colleges*, first issued in 1928, and the companion volume *American Junior Colleges*, first issued in 1940. These volumes are issued every four years.[26]

UNESCO[27]

In collaboration with the Education Press of America, UNESCO has produced the *International List of Educational Periodicals* as an accurate and up-to-date list representing all systems of education. The volume is divided into two parts totaling more than 3,400 periodicals from 79 countries and territories, in three languages (English, French, and Spanish).

UNESCO publishes an extensive list of periodicals and monographs in the educational and social areas. *Fundamental and Adult Education* is a quarterly technical journal, mainly for specialists. *Education Abstracts*, published 10 times a year, includes bibliographical details relating to documents, publications, and textbooks on education, with each issue devoted to a single subject. Another serial, usually with 10 numbers each year, is *Educational Studies and Documents*. A valuable number in this series describes education clearing houses and documentation centers. Major studies have appeared as volumes of three important series. *Studies in Compulsory Education* have been made for a number of countries; these constitute major sources of information on such topics as attendance and legal provisions for education. The *Monographs on Fundamental Education* deal with such problems as literacy, the use of vernacular languages in education, and the program of fundamental education. *Problems in Education* is a series of volumes devoted to issues of international interest, such as teacher preparation and mental hygiene

---

[26] Quoted from *A Brief Statement of the History and Activities of the American Council on Education, 1918–1961*. Washington: The Council, 1961. 48 p. Also see later numbers.

[27] *An International List of Educational Periodicals*. Educational Studies and Documents, No. 23. New York: UNESCO Publications Center, 1957. 212 p.

Colin D. Ewers, "The Education Clearing House of UNESCO." *School and Society* 82: 114–18; October 15, 1955.

Carter V. Good, "Bibliographic Sources," *Encyclopedia of Educational Research*. Third Edition. New York: The Macmillan Co., 1960. p. 143–45.

in the schools. UNESCO also publishes the *World Survey of Education*, a handbook of educational organization and statistics.

PSYCHOLOGICAL GUIDES

For the field of psychology, the major guides to the literature are *Psychological Abstracts*, founded in 1927, and the *Annual Review of Psychology*, initiated in 1950, with the references classified under the following headings for current numbers:

Psychological Abstracts

General
> Theory and Systems, Methods and Apparatus, New Tests, Statistics, Reference Works, Organizations, History and Biography, Professional Problems of Psychology, Films

Physiological Psychology
> Nervous System

Receptive and Perceptual Processes
> Vision, Audition, Other Modalities

Response Processes

Complex Processes and Organizations
> Learning and Memory, Thinking and Imagination, Intelligence, Personality, Aesthetics

Developmental Psychology
> Childhood and Adolescence, Maturity and Old Age

Social Psychology
> Methods and Measurements, Cultures and Cultural Relations, Social Institutions, Language and Communication

Clinical Psychology, Guidance, Counseling
> Methodology, Techniques, Diagnosis and Evaluation, Treatment Methods, Child Guidance, Vocational Guidance

Behavior Deviations
> Mental Deficiency, Behavior Problems, Speech Disorders, Crime and Delinquency, Psychoses, Psychoneuroses, Psychosomatics, Clinical Neurology, Physically Handicapped

Educational Psychology
> School Learning, Interests, Attitudes and Habits, Special Education, Educational Guidance, Educational Measurement, Education Staff Personnel

Personnel Psychology
> Selection and Placement, Labor-Management Relations

Industrial and Other Applications
> Industry, Business and Commerce, Professions, Military.

Annual Review of Psychology

Developmental Psychology
Comparative Psychology
Scaling and Test Theory
Aesthetics
Personality Structure
Group Dynamics
Psychotherapy
Classification of the Behavior Disorders
Motivation and Performance
Motor-Skills Learning
Brain Functions
Visual Sensitivity
Hearing
The Chemical Senses
Personnel Selection
Industrial Social Psychology
Concept Formation
Behavioral Decision Theory.

SOCIAL SCIENCE GUIDES

For the social fields the fifteen-volume *Encyclopedia of the Social Sciences*[28] covers the fields of anthropology, economics, education, history, law, philosophy, political science, psychology, social work, sociology, and statistics. In order to include the numerous advances and most recent development in the social sciences, a new work rather than a revision of the original encyclopedia is tentatively scheduled for simultaneous publication of the twelve to fifteen volumes in 1965. The contents will be distributed fairly evenly among the various social sciences: anthropology, economics, political science, psychology, and sociology.

Other useful guides in the social sciences include the *Dictionary of American Biography*,[29] *Dictionary of American History*,[30] *Guide to Historical Literature*;[31] and the periodicals *Biography Index* and *Sociological Abstracts*, with the following headings for current numbers of the latter:

[28] Edwin R. A. Seligman and Alvin Johnson, Editors, *Encyclopedia of the Social Sciences*. New York: The Macmillan Co., 1930–34. 15 vols.

[29] Allen Johnson and Dumas Malone, Editors, *Dictionary of American Biography*. New York: Charles Scribner's Sons, 1928–37. 20 vols. and index, plus supplements.

Also see *Biography Index:* A Cumulative Index to Biographical Material in Books and Magazines. New York: H. W. Wilson Co., 1946–.

[30] James T. Adams and R. V. Coleman, Editors, *Dictionary of American History*. New York: Charles Scribner's Sons, 1940. 5 vols. and index.

[31] George F. Howe and Others, *Guide to Historical Literature*. New York: The Macmillan Co., 1961. xxxv + 962 p.

Sociological Abstracts

General
Theory
Methodology-Statistics
Social Structure (Organization)
Personality
Interaction within Groups
Interaction between Groups
Social Movements
Rural and Urban Sociology
Sociology of Occupations and Professions
Social Stratification
Political Sociology
Communication and Public Opinion
Sociology of Knowledge, Education, Language, Literature, Religion, Art,
    and Science
Demography and Ecology
Social Change and Control
Marriage and Family
Social Disorganization (Criminology)
Social Anthropology
Industrial Sociology
Social Biology and Medicine
Applied Sociology (Social Work)
Bureaucratic Structure.

Historical Abstracts summarizes articles on political, diplomatic, economic, social, cultural, and intellectual history relating to the period 1775-1945, published in the periodical literature (some 800 journals) the world over. The publication also includes general articles on historiography, bibliography, and research methods.

CONCLUDING STATEMENT

In educational research the question of uniqueness or originality may prove less important than the ways in which studies are comparable, or related, or fit into a pattern of investigation and results. We now recognize the importance of the efforts of the scholar engaged in assimilating and integrating the results of research as reported in numerous and varied sources.

In addition to the bibliographic and summarizing guides, important tools or aids are foreign languages, note-taking systems, and classification schemes. If a foreign language is essential for a particular field of research, the "language requirement" should be in functional terms rather than perfunctory. Careful notes may prove valuable not only as aids to memory, but also as stimuli to systematic thinking, just as extensive and critical reading serves as a stimulus to thinking. Improved and expanded classification systems for the literature may identify closer relationships between the social, educational, and psychological areas and may further an interdisciplinary approach to problems in the behavioral and human sciences.

The keys to the vast storehouse of published literature may open doors to sources of significant problems and explanatory hypotheses, and provide helpful orientation for definition of the problem, background for selection of procedure, and comparative data for interpretation of results. The major reference works and guides since the late 1920's have greatly simplified the canvass of related literature and have appeared just in time to help the graduate student and investigator explore the greatly increased volume of research published during this period. The numerous bibliographic and documentary guides and sources suggest that there has been a trend toward such aids as an ally of the scientific and experimental movements.

SELECTED REFERENCES

ALEXANDER, Carter, and BURKE, Arvid J. *How to Locate Educational Information and Data.* Fourth Edition. New York: Bureau of Publications, Teachers College, Columbia University, 1958. xvii + 419 p.

BARTON, Mary N., Compiler. *Reference Books:* A Brief Guide for Students and Other Users of the Library. Fourth Edition. Baltimore: Enoch Pratt Library, 1959. 117 p.

BARZUN, Jacques, and GRAFF, Henry F. *The Modern Researcher.* New York: Harcourt, Brace and Co., 1957. p. 61-87.

BATES, Ralph S. *Scientific Societies in the United States.* Second Edition. New York: Technology Press and Columbia University Press, 1958. 308 p.

BREHAUT, Willard. "An Analysis of Dissertations (English) in Education Accepted by Canadian Universities, 1930-1955." *Ontario Journal of Educational Research* 2: 109-222; April 1960.

BRYAN, Roy C. *Keys to Professional Information for Teachers.* Kalamazoo: Western Michigan University, 1957. 28 p.

BUROS, Oscar K., Editor. *The Fourth Mental Measurements Yearbook.* Highland Park, N. J.: Gryphon Press, 1953. 1,189 p.

BUROS, Oscar K., Editor. *The Fifth Mental Measurements Yearbook.* Highland Park, N. J.: Gryphon Press, 1959. 1,292 p.

BUROS, Oscar K., Editor. *Tests in Print:* A Comprehensive Bibliography of Tests for Use in Education, Psychology, and Industry. Highland Park, N.J.: Gryphon Press, 1962. xxix + 479 p.

CERTAIN, Julia L., and Others. "Educational Books of 1960." *Educational Horizons* 39: 86-112; Spring 1961. Also see later numbers.

CERTAIN, Julia L., and Others. "Outstanding Education Books of 1961." *NEA Journal* 51: 66-67; May 1962. Also see later numbers.

DELAVENAY, Emile. *An Introduction to Machine Translation*. New York: Frederick A. Praeger, 1960. 144 p.

"Doctoral Dissertations in Progress, 1960." *American Journal of Sociology* 67: 75-85; July 1961. Also see later numbers.

ENGLISH, Horace B., and ENGLISH, Ava C. *Comprehensive Dictionary of Psychological and Psychoanalytical Terms*. New York: Longmans, Green and Co., 1958. xiv + 594 p.

FAIRCHILD, H. P., Editor. *Dictionary of Sociology*. New York: Philosophical Library, 1944. viii + 342 p.

FARNSWORTH, P. R., and MCNEMAR, Quinn, Editors. *Annual Review of Psychology*. Vol. 11. Palto Alto, Calif.: Annual Reviews, 1960. x + 544 p.

FARNSWORTH, P. R., MCNEMAR, Olga, and MCNEMAR, Quinn, Editors. *Annual Review of Psychology*. Vol. 12. Palo Alto, Calif.: Annual Reviews, 1961. x + 533 p. Also see later issues.

FARNSWORTH, P. R., MCNEMAR, Olga, and MCNEMAR, Quinn, Editors. *Annual Review of Psychology*. Vol. 13. Palo Alto, Calif.: Annual Reviews, 1962. ix + 602 p. Also see later issues.

FERM, Vergilius. *A Dictionary of Pastoral Psychology*. New York: Philosophical Library, 1955. xi + 336 p.

FROEHLICH, Gustav J. "Research Bureaus," *Encyclopedia of Educational Research*. Edited by Chester W. Harris. Third Edition. New York: The Macmillan Co., 1960. p. 1155-59.

GITTLER, Joseph B., Editor. *Review of Sociology: Analysis of a Decade*. New York: John Wiley & Sons, 1957. 588 p.

GOOD, Carter V. "Bibliographic Sources," *Encyclopedia of Educational Research*. Edited by Chester W. Harris. Third Edition. New York: The Macmillan Co., 1960. p. 143-45.

GOOD, Carter V., Editor. *Dictionary of Education*. Second Edition. New York: McGraw-Hill Book Co., 1959. xxx + 676 p.

GOOD, Carter V., and SCATES, Douglas E. *Methods of Research: Educational, Psychological, Sociological*. New York: Appleton-Century-Crofts, 1954. p. 133-69.

HALL, V. E., FUHRMAN, F. A., and GIESE, A. C., Editors. *Annual Review of Physiology*. Vol. 22. Palo Alto, Calif.: Annual Reviews and the American Physiological Society, 1960. x + 725 p.

HARRIS, Chester W., Editor. *Encyclopedia of Educational Research*. Third Edition. New York: The Macmillan Co., 1960. xxix + 1,564 p.

HARRIS, Theodore L. "Summary of Investigations Relating to Reading, July 1, 1960 to June 30, 1961." *Journal of Educational Research* 55: 197-220; February 1962. Also see later reports, as well as the earlier summaries by William S. Gray.

"Higher Degrees in Sociology, 1960." *American Journal of Sociology* 67: 61-74; July 1961. Also see later numbers.

HILLWAY, Tyrus. *Introduction to Research*. Boston: Houghton Mifflin Co., 1956. p. 72-86.

HINSIE, L. E., and CAMPBELL, R. J. *Psychiatric Dictionary.* Third Edition. New York: Oxford University Press, 1960. x + 788 p.

HOLLIS, Ernest V. "Foundations," *Encyclopedia of Educational Research.* Edited by Chester W. Harris. Third Edition. New York: The Macmillan Co., 1960. p. 565-69.

HOWE, George F., and Others. *Guide to Historical Literature.* New York: The Macmillan Co., 1961. xxxv + 962 p.

LEVY, Leon H. "Anxiety and Behavior Scientists' Behavior." *American Psychologist* 16: 66-68; February 1961. (Topical analysis of *Psychological Abstracts* and *Child Development Abstracts,* 1945-1958.)

LIEBERMAN, Irving. "Libraries and Museums," *Encyclopedia of Educational Research.* Edited by Chester W. Harris. Third Edition. New York: The Macmillan Co., 1960. p. 770-76.

LOUTTIT, C. M. "Publication Trends in Psychology: 1894-1954." *American Psychologist* 12: 14-21; January 1957.

LYDA, Mary L., ANDERSON, Harold, and GOOD, Carter V. *Research Studies in Education,* 1960: A Subject-Author Index and Research Methods Bibliography. Bloomington, Ind.: Phi Delta Kappa, 1961. vi + 133 p. Also see later numbers.

LYDA, Mary L., and BROWN, Stanley B. *Research Studies in Education:* A Subject Index of Doctoral Dissertations, Reports, and Field Studies, 1941-1951. Boulder, Col.: The Authors, 1953.

MARTIN, Michael, and GELBER, Leonard. *The New Dictionary of American History.* New York: Philosophical Library, 1952. vi + 695 p.

McCORMICK, Thomas C., and FRANCIS, Roy G. *Methods of Research in the Behavioral Sciences.* New York: Harper & Brothers, 1958. Chapter 4.

MORRIS, R. B., Editor. *Encyclopedia of American History.* New York: Harper & Brothers, 1953. xv + 776 p.

MORRISON, J. Cayce, and Others. "Twenty-five Years of Educational Research." *Review of Educational Research* 26: 199-344; June 1956.

MURPHEY, Robert W. *How and Where To Look It Up:* A Guide to Standard Sources of Information. New York: McGraw-Hill Book Co., 1958. 721 p.

PIERSTORFF, Lola R. "Research Tools: Library Resources," in "Methodology of Educational Research." *Review of Educational Research* 27: 471-75; December 1957.

SARTON, George. "Notes on the Reviewing of Learned Books." *Science* 131: 1182-87; April 22, 1960. (Good books, bad books, scholarly books, popular books, all pose problems for the conscientious reviewer.)

SCATES, Douglas E. "Changing Sources of Information about Thesis Research." *Journal of Teacher Education* 8: 210-13; June 1957.

SCHMECKEBIER, Laurence F., and EASTIN, Roy B. *Government Publications and Their Use.* Revised Edition. Washington: Brookings Institution, 1961. xi + 476 p.

SCOTT, M. Gladys, Editor. "Library Techniques," *Research Methods in Health, Physical Education, Recreation.* Second Edition. Washington: American Association for Health, Physical Education, and Recreation, 1959. Chapter 2.

SEEGER, Ruth E. *Library Resources in Educational Research*. Columbus: Bureau of Educational Research, Ohio State University, 1957. v + 26 p.

SHERA, J. H., KENT, Allen, and PERRY, James W., Editors. *Information Systems in Documentation*. Vol. 2. New York: Interscience Publishers, 1957. 639 p.

SHEVIAK, Margaret R., and McMULLEN, Haynes. "Research Tools: Access to the Literature of Education," in "The Methodology of Educational Research." *Review of Educational Research* 30: 487-95; December 1960.

SHORES, Louis. *Basic Reference Sources*. Chicago: American Library Association, 1954. ix + 378 p.

SILVEY, Herbert M., Editor. *Master's Theses in Education, 1960-61*. No. 10. Cedar Falls, Iowa: Research Publications, 1961. Also see later numbers.

SIEGEL, Bernard J., Editor. *Biennial Review of Anthropology, 1959*. Stanford, Calif.: Stanford University Press, 1959. iv + 273 p.

SWANSON, Don R. "Searching Natural Language Text by Computer." *Science* 132: 1099-1104; October 21, 1960. (Machine indexing and text searching offer an approach to the basic problems of library automation.)

TROTIER, Arnold H., and HARMAN, Marian, Editor. *Doctoral Dissertations Accepted by American Universities 1954-1955*. No. 22. Compiled for the Association of Research Libraries. New York: H. W. Wilson Co., 1955. 298 p. Also see earlier numbers.

TRYTTEN, M. H., and HARMON, L. R. *Doctorate Production in United States Universities 1936-1956:* With Baccalaureate Origins of Doctorates in the Sciences, Arts, and Humanities. Publication 582. Washington: National Academy of Science-National Research Council, 1958. vii + 155 p.

VAN DALEN, Deobold B. *Understanding Educational Research:* An Introduction. New York: McGraw-Hill Book Co., 1962. p. 64-107.

WALFORD, Arthur J. *A Guide to Reference Material*. London: Library Association, 1959. 543 p.

WILLIAMS, C. B., and STEVENSON, A. H. *A Research Manual for College Studies and Papers*. Revised Edition. New York: Harper & Brothers, 1951. p. 16-61.

WINCHELL, Constance M. *Guide to Reference Books*. Seventh Edition. Chicago: American Library Association, 1951. xvii + 645 p. Also see later supplements.

WINCHELL, Constance M., and JOHNSON, O. A. *Guide to Reference Books.* Seventh Edition Supplement, 1950-52. Second Supplement, 1953-55. Third Supplement, 1956-58. Chicago: American Library Association, 1954, 140 p.; 1956, 134 p.; 1960, 145 p.

WINICK, Charles. *Dictionary of Anthropology*. New York: Philosophical Library, 1956. vii + 579 p.

YOUNG, Pauline V. *Scientific Social Surveys and Research*. Third Edition. Englewood Cliffs, N. J.: Prentice-Hall, 1956. p. 127-36.

YOUNG, Raymond J., Compiler. *A Directory of Educational Research Agencies and Studies*. First Revision. Bloomington, Ind.: Phi Delta Kappa, 1959. 92 p. Second revision scheduled for 1962.

CHAPTER FOUR

Historical Method and Historiography

This chapter considers history as a field of knowledge and then presents the major steps, processes, or aspects of historical research and historiography: collection of data, with consideration of sources as documents and remains, and as primary and secondary; evaluation of data, including external and internal criticism; and presentation of the facts in readable narrative form, including problems of organization, composition, and interpretation.

HISTORY AS A FIELD OF KNOWLEDGE AND RESEARCH

Definition and Scope of History[1]

Viewed as research, history may be defined as an integrated narrative or description of past events or facts, written in the spirit of critical inquiry, to find the whole truth and report it.[2] A newspaper or journalistic report of some current event, or a debate in Congress or a state legislature, is not history, because it is not typically an inquiry into the *whole*

---

[1] Herman Ausubel, *Historians and Their Craft:* A Study of the Presidential Addresses of the American Historical Association, 1884–1945. New York: Columbia University Press, 1950. p. 300–358.

Jacques Barzun and Henry F. Graff, *The Modern Researcher.* New York: Harcourt, Brace and Co., 1957. p. 3–17, 43–56.

Gilbert J. Garraghan, *A Guide to Historical Method.* Edited by Jean Delanglez. New York: Fordham University Press, 1946. p. 1–32.

Louis R. Gottschalk, *Understanding History:* A Primer of Historical Method. New York: Alfred A. Knopf, 1950. p. 26–37.

Homer C. Hockett, *The Critical Method in Historical Research and Writing.* New York: The Macmillan Co., 1955. p. 237–54.

[2] Allan Nevins, *The Gateway to History.* Boston: D. C. Heath and Co., 1938. p. 22–23.

truth. The campaign book of a political party summarizing the events and activities of the party for the four years preceding the election is not history, since it was not written as a *critical* inquiry into the truth. The historical novel is not history, even though incorporating certain events and threads of historical truth, but rather it seeks to entertain the reader. Biography or autobiography becomes history when adequate historical perspective enables the author to see the individual in relation to the society and events of his time, but is not history when the account is limited to a single life in isolation. Antiquarian research or writing does not become history merely through the process of preserving material or records in almanac or museum-like fashion.

As to scope, history embraces the entire field of the human past and is as broad as life itself. Our human past includes many areas of social experience and activities that frequently have proved more significant than political history or military campaigns; for example, culture, ideals, institutions, law, religion, literature, art, travel, engineering, industry, technology, medicine, science, philosophy, economics, education, psychology, anthropology, and sociology. There is general agreement among modern historians concerning the richness of the content of history, including social, cultural, economic, and intellectual developments, and on a broad view of past events, extending far beyond the study of politics, diplomatics, constitutions, and "drum and trumpet" war materials.

Interrelationships of History and Science

It is without profit to argue the question of whether history is science or art. History qualifies as science in the sense that its methods of inquiry are critical and objective, and that the results are accepted as organized knowledge by a consensus of trained investigators. The research aspects of history in dealing with sources are scientific in approach, while narration and historiography commonly involve the art of expression and philosophy of the author. The historian thinks of the method of investigation as scientific, and of the manner of presentation as belonging to the realm of art.

Until recent years the natural sciences and the cultural sciences were generally regarded as far apart, yet these two fields of research are parts of a meaningful whole when we think of scientific knowledge not merely as a finished product but as a historical development, with a dimension of historic depth. On the other hand, the unique or disparate events of human history may fit into a unified, integrated pattern or process, if we view the gradual advance of man's knowledge as a central theme of historical development. These interrelationships of history and science make it important that the modern historian be well grounded in the natural sciences:

A glance at the present era suffices to convince us that science makes history, that the growth of our knowledge is a compelling force in historical events—and here I am far from thinking of atom bombs alone, for the past teaches the same lesson. The historic changes in the life of man are an expression and consequence of intellectual development; a new manner of thinking, a new way of seeing the world, inevitably brings about changes in man's activity, even in his everyday life. True, it seems to many of us today that our century is dominated, to a terrifying degree, by ruthless brute force; that an unrestrained lust for pleasure or profit or power has triumphed over all spiritual forces. But even these manifestations are conditioned by the spiritual and intellectual state of our world: our own day-to-day life is shaped by what the philosophers and scientists of the last two centuries have thought and expounded.

Thus it is to be expected that the ideas which are taking form today, the knowledge which is being acquired in our time, will be the crucial factors in tomorrow's decisions. And an awareness of the headlong intellectual transformations taking place today will give us an idea of the momentous changes that the future has in store for us.[3]

The history of society and ideas now has joined the history of kings and generals as part of the study of the past in what has been called the new history of science and technology.

A study of the history of science and technology does not prove that the progress of mankind is necessarily guaranteed, but it does show us that the possibility of progress is always present in human affairs. In the darkness which surrounds us, some ray of hope for the future is necessary. Granted that science and technology have now made it possible to obliterate mankind, and that these can be used for evil and destructive ends as well as for good and constructive purposes, the fact remains that while nearly all indices of the level of culture and civilization seem to have advanced not one whit in our century—and some of them seem to have retrogressed—in one field we can point indisputably to progress: in science and technology. If the history of science and technology can provide us with some hope for the future, if it can show us how man can transcend petty national rivalries and how the human mind can employ its reason for the solution of complex and disturbing problems which have long defied the human intellect and imagination—that is reason enough for turning to its study. This is not escapism from the realities of the present. Rather, by realistic appraisal of the road which man has trod in developing science and technology to their present eminence, we may gather faith and hope that the other problems which beset us may be conquered by the use of human reason, ingenuity, and imagination. And nowhere do these human traits show more clearly than in the study of the "newest" history: science and technology.[4]

[3] Quoted from Pascual Jordan, *Science and the Course of History*. Translated by Ralph Manheim. New Haven: Yale University Press, 1955. p. vii–viii, 3–4.

[4] Quoted from Melvin Kranzberg, "The Newest History: Science and Technology." *Science* 136: 46–68; May 11, 1962. Reprinted from *Science* by permission.

Also see Thomas S. Kuhn, "Historical Structure of Scientific Discovery." *Science* 136: 760–64; June 1, 1962.

History differs in method from the natural sciences, since it is not a discipline of direct observation or experimentation, but utilizes reports of observations that cannot be repeated; the historian cannot recall the actors of the past to reproduce the famous scenes of history on the stage of today. Instead of the direct observations used in science, the historian usually must depend on the observations of others (often untrained observers). Therefore, the historical method involves a procedure supplementary to observation, a process by which the historian seeks to test the truthfulness of the reports of observations made by others. Both historian and scientist examine data, formulate hypotheses, and test the hypotheses against the evidence until acceptable conclusions are reached. A number of historians, in emphasizing the interpretation and meaning of facts, have sought to identify tendencies, themes, patterns, and laws of history, while some of these investigators have dealt with such philosophical or theoretical problems in history as discovery of laws, unity and continuity, possibility or impossibility of prediction, and oversimplification growing out of the search for clues or keys.

History in Relation to Other Social Fields

History and Economics. History has close interrelationships with other social fields. The economists have introduced a quantitative emphasis into modern history; for example, citing numerical data such as the United States census for a given year, or basing certain computations upon such data, in calculating by decades the rate of increase of the population of the United States. Handling of quantitative material is important in economic history, in sound social history (with its dependence on knowledge of population movement, inheritance, and social mobility), and sometimes in military history.

History and Sociology. As another example of close interrelationships between the social fields, history and sociology are complementary, in the sense that both areas seek to explain the past, although the sociologist is interested primarily in generalized descriptions and in types of societal evolution, without the historian's concern with time-and-place relationships and unique events. It is true that American sociologists by choice ignore the bulk of historical findings by restricting themselves to a single culture and to the short time span they consider relevant to contemporary conditions. Even within the present, the interests of sociologists are normally narrower than those of historians, who deal with the contemporary national scene in relation to foreign, political, legal, and economic issues, as well as the rise and decline of communities, corporations, families, ideologies, and the fortunes of ethnic groups. When it serves its purpose, to clarify an argument or exposition, the historian does introduce new elements of explicit theory (economic, social, political, or legal). Specific ways in which history and sociology can learn from each other involve questions of the observation, selection, and organization of factual evidence or data:

> Does first hand observation, the overwhelming detail of the living scene, give an unqualified advantage, or are there compensating advantages in the severity of the criticism that the historian has to apply to his more limited sources? To him, every personal record is a psychological document, the shades of validity in its testimony to be checked by other kinds of evidence. Should the interview report, said now to be the key tool in the sociologist's kit, be similarly handled? Can the historian's techniques of criticism help the sociologist to counteract the bias of his interview work, which excludes those important classes of people who resent the interviewer's intrusion? In return, can the sociologist help the historian counteract the bias of his written sources, which too often reveal the lowest classes only in their economic relations or in their tangles with the law? How far is the sociologist's fuller observation of short-run change colored by his own effect upon the situation? Is any community quite the same after an interpersonal rating survey?[5]

History and Literature. History may serve to link literature with social science, whereas it once linked philosophy with poetry:

> History has always thought of itself as an inclusive, a mediating discipline. Once it linked philosophy with poetry. Now it is linking literature with social science. History's new consciousness of its debt to social science need not mean a weakening of its artistic ties. Indeed, the contrary is the case. For it is history that can lead social science itself along the path of imagination and bold hypothesis toward literature—back to the realms in which it dwelt and prospered in the century and three quarters of great achievement that began with Montesquieu and ended with Weber.[6]

Comparative Education and Educational History. Comparative education is an aspect of educational history—an extension of the past into the present and the substance of tomorrow's history of education. While the historian must reach the elusive past through documents and relics, the student of comparative education has the advantage of coming in direct touch with the subject under scrutiny, as in tracing the movement of a current educational idea or practice from one culture to another, although the literature is soon out of date. Many things done by historians are cross-cultural and comparative, and comparative studies of movement of ideas or practices from one country to another reach into the past, which means there is no sharp line drawn between historical and

---

[5] Quoted from Sylvia L. Thrupp, "What History and Sociology Can Learn from Each Other." *Sociology and Social Research* 41: 434–38; July-August 1957.

[6] Quoted from H. Stuart Hughes, "The Historian and the Social Scientist." *American Historical Review* 66: 20–46; October 1960.

comparative investigations. Better research in comparative education may discourage the casual commentator, the returning tourist with a manuscript or speech, and others who feel that their opinions on problems of comparative education are as good as those of the specialist. The problem of evaluation in comparative education is difficult, since there are at present no comparable standards by which the quality of an educational system can be measured, and such evaluative criteria will not be available until comparative standards are developed for assessing the quality of a culture in general.[7]

Uses and Functional Nature of History

Historians of the twentieth century have commonly emphasized the immediate usefulness of history in dealing with contemporary problems. They have stressed the importance of a social consciousness for the historian, use of history to throw light on the present, inquiry into the past for solutions to contemporary problems, and avoidance of the charge of antiquarianism. Modern historians, like economists, political scientists, sociologists, and psychologists, have maintained that they too have answers to contemporary social problems. History may enable communities to grasp their relationship with the past and to plan more intelligently for the future; it may give to people a sense of continuity and a consciousness of unity in their efforts and achievements. "Seated at the roaring loom of time, for six thousand years man has woven a seamless garment. But that garment is invisible and intangible save where the dyes of written history fall upon it, and forever preserve it as a possession of generations to come."[8]

The wide-ranging mind of Charles A. Beard grasped the significance of Lord Acton's precept: "Study problems, not periods." In Collingwood's language, "Scissors-and-paste historians study periods; they collect all the extant testimony about a certain limited group of events, and hope in vain that something will come of it. Scientific historians study problems; they ask questions, and if they are good historians they ask questions which they see their way to answering." Beard was forever asking questions, and, following in the train of European scholars (notably Croce) who were more than a generation in advance of Americans in this matter, he and Carl Becker asked fellow historians to consider the meaning of their research and their writing. Beard

[7] George F. Kneller, "Comparative Education," *Encyclopedia of Educational Research*. Edited by Chester W. Harris. Third Edition. New York: The Macmillan Co., 1960. p. 316–22.

C. Arnold Anderson, "Methodology of Comparative Education." *International Review of Education* 7: 1–23; 1961.

Roy M. Hall and Others, "Educational Research in Countries Other than the United States." *Review of Educational Research* 32: 213–362; June 1962.

[8] Allan Nevins, *op. cit.*, p. 3, 5.

reminded them that in every era contestants had used the writing of history to capture the human mind. Catholics and Protestants had done so, and Voltaire had made history "a dynamic force for the French Revolution." At a later time, "under the guise of romanticism, history had served the reaction." Every history, it was maintained, was "a selection of facts made by some person or persons and is ordered or organized under the influence of some scheme of reference, interest or emphases—avowed or unavowed—in the thought of the author or the authors." As Collingwood expressed it, "history is nothing but the re-enactment of past thought in the historian's mind." Modern historians, said Beard, "working in the scientific spirit, seeking emancipation from the tyranny of old assumptions" should legitimately use their discipline to illuminate "all divisions of contemporary thought and all formulations of public policy." Historical writing, he believed, was to be an instrument for the advancement of social reform.

More than anyone else, Beard stimulated scholars to recognize frankly the functional nature of historical knowledge and to make them aware of what they were doing. "Just what intellectual operations does the historian perform in studying and writing history?" he asked. "For what reason . . . are particular aspects of history chosen for emphasis and other aspects excluded?"[9]

To comment further on the concept of a historical period, it is characterized as inherently fluid and slippery:

One of the more common and successful ways for a young historian to make a reputation is to juggle this essential symbol. He may create a new period, or demonstrate that an old one has no validity. The "Renaissance" happened much earlier than is usually thought, these promising scholars will write; or they may undertake to prove that there "really" was no "Renaissance" at all. What a historian does when he consciously concerns himself with periods is to look for the existence or absence of certain common characteristics that reappear a certain number of times. What these are and how often they must reappear in order to justify the use of the symbol are matters to be determined by the writer's expert opinion. To conclude because it is opinion that the concept of a historical age has no validity, or to say that one opinion of this kind is as good as another, is a common error. It is not so common but even more of an error to conclude that something exists in nature that divides the past up into sections like those of a bamboo pole.[10]

History of Education. To cite another example, in order to understand education as a social process with a long history, and to evaluate school theories and plans, we need to know the historical evidence or approach in the form of origins that have influenced the present state of educa-

---

[9] Quoted from Michael Kraus, *The Writing of American History.* Norman: University of Oklahoma Press, 1953. p. 372–73.

[10] Quoted from H. Stuart Hughes, Editor, *Teachers of History:* Essays in Honor of Laurence Bradford Packard. Ithaca, N. Y.: Cornell University Press for Amherst College, 1954. p. 314–17.

tion and of the schools, serial or temporal data for identification of significant causal factors, and the insights of educational thinkers in appraising panaceas, half-truths, and fads or frills. Specific competencies to be developed through instruction in the history of education have been listed as follows:[11]

1. Understanding the dynamics of educational change
2. Increased understanding of the relationship between education and the culture in which it operates
3. Increased understanding of contemporary educational problems
4. Understanding the functions and limitations of historical evidence in analyzing educational problems
5. Development of elementary ability in locating, analyzing, and appraising historical evidence
6. Development of a sense of the dignity and responsibility of the teaching profession.

Among the modern problem areas of functional value in educational history are the non-school educational agencies and their influence on man's behavior, including newspapers, popular journals, novels, drama, radio, and television, which will give clues about what the image of child, school, or teacher has been through the years. Other problems relate to the school as the moulder or "container" of national and regional character, academic freedom (especially at elementary and secondary levels), pupil dropout, relation between political and educational patterns, shifts in educational leadership, and purgation of vague and confusing concepts commonly found in education.[12] Certain problem areas of educational sociology frequently involve historical sources and approaches: longitudinal analysis of the socialization process in educational institutions, changes in student and faculty value systems, emergence of educational institutions, and the impact of social-class background upon educational motivation and achievement.[13]

Specific applications of the historical approach extended beyond the general field of educational history to comparative education; to legal

[11] Committee on Historical Foundations of the National Society of College Teachers of Education, R. Freeman Butts, Chairman, *The Role of the History of Education in the Professional Preparation of Teachers.* Ann Arbor, Mich.: The Society, 1957. p. 19–29, 65–66, 84–98, 123–29.

[12] Bernard Mehl, "History of Education," in "The Philosophical and Social Frame Work of Education." *Review of Educational Research* 31: 7–19; February 1961.

Wilson Smith, "The New Historian of American Education." *Harvard Educational Review* 31: 136–43; Spring 1961.

Richard Starr, "The Education of History: Some Impressions." *Harvard Educational Review* 31: 124–35; Spring 1961.

[13] Wilbur B. Brookover and David Gottlieb, "Sociology of Education," in "The Philosophical and Social Framework of Education." *Review of Educational Research* 31: 38–56; February 1961.

research in education, with the statutory law and the case or common law as the sources; to thorough bibliographical and summarizing studies, as illustrated by the *Encyclopedia of Educational Research* and *Review of Educational Research;* to psychology, as illustrated by biographical and autobiographical narratives, general histories of psychology, and the *Annual Review of Psychology;* and to the biographical, case-history, and life-history materials and other historical approaches of sociology and certain related social disciplines.

History of Psychology. Especially during the second quarter of the present century and later, historical studies have made important contributions to psychology, as illustrated in a five-fold classification:[14]

1. Topical surveys, dealing with specific psychological concepts, such as Greek theories of cognition
2. Surveys of periods, and expositions of the views of particular men or groups, such as the history of Greek psychology
3. Source books, sometimes making available important materials in foreign languages
4. Biography, providing accounts of the lives of men who have made significant contributions to psychology
5. General histories of psychology, some devoted to the late modern period, and others purporting to cover the entire scope of psychological history.

In the field of psychology many genetic, biographical, autobiographical, case, and clinic studies are essentially historical in approach. One of the areas for further development in psychology is the training of specialists to do research and to give instruction in the history of psychology:

If psychologists are determined to remain ignorant of our history, are we not, at best, determined to have some of our labors take the form of discoveries which are truisms found independently and, at worst, to repeat the errors of the past? To embody a past of which they are ignorant is, at best, to be subject passively to it, at worst, to be distorted by a false conception of it. Ignorance does not necessarily mean lack of influence upon human conduct, including the human conduct of psychologists. Ignoring the study of the history of one's field through formal sources and published accounts does not result in lack of opinions about the past. Like the traditional man in the street who, too, refuses to read history, such psychologists inevitably have a picture of the past, by and large one which deprecates its importance. This inevitably influences their views just as does any other aspect of the "unverbalized." However little their ahis-

[14] Knight Dunlap, "The Historical Method in Psychology." *Journal of General Psychology* 24: 49–62; January 1941.
    Also see A. A. Roback, Editor, *Present-Day Psychology.* New York: Philosophical Library, 1955. xiv + 995 p. Chapter 20 lists and reviews contemporary histories of psychology.

torical view of the past may correspond to reality, it still helps to determine their views of the present. To neglect history does not mean to escape its influence.

This has been a plea for greater attention on the part of psychologists to their history. With assumption of some knowledge and experience in contemporary psychology, the first stage of development of attention to history would be an interest in it and a conviction that it is a worthwhile field of endeavor. But knowledge, interest, and conviction are not enough for competence. It is not merely a matter of deciding to work in historical aspects of our field. With justice, professional historians have been indignant about the bland assumption, all too often made by scientists, that, because one knows something about a scientific field, the essential equipment for historical research automatically is available. Historical work does not consist of finding a few old books and copying this and that. Trained as he is in his own exacting techniques, the psychologist does not always realize that the technique of establishing the truth of the maximum probability of past events, in other words historical research, has its own complicated rules and methods.

There is a variety of areas with which more than a passing acquaintance is necessary if historical study is planned. Knowledge of the methodology of history—historiography—is essential for more than anecdotal familiarity with any area capable of being aproached historically. Knowledge of the philosophy of history is also needed by the psychological historian as a defense against errors of procedure and of content. In psychology, as in similar disciplines, acquaintance with the history of science in general is demanded. Moreover, some appreciation of the influence of social and cultural factors in history is important if the findings are to be seen in broad context. I, for one, think it would be worth the trouble and time to secure this background in order to carry on the task of understanding and interpreting our past in the perspective of today.[15]

PROBLEM AND PROCESS

The selection and development of the problem for study, and the chief library guides, have been discussed in earlier chapters. As in other fields, the beginner in historical research frequently chooses too broad a topic. As examples of delimitation of an overly large topic, a history of political parties in the United States became a treatment of a presidential campaign in one state, and a study of Negro land-grant colleges in the United States became the story of a particular land-grant college. Less frequently the historical problem is broadened as a study progresses, as when the history of a small church-related college became a history of the program of higher education supported by the specific church denomination. In the background program of reading for development of the problem, the investigator may proceed from the best general

---

[15] Quoted from Robert I. Watson, "The History of Psychology: A Neglected Area." *American Psychologist* 15: 251–55; April 1960.

treatises to specialized volumes and printed collections of sources, then to calendars of documents, expert bibliographies, and reviews in historical and other appropriate journals. Specialized and detailed advice for selection and development of the historical problem is available.[16]

Historical research and historiography involve three major steps, processes, or aspects:

Collection of data, with consideration of sources as documents and remains or relics, and as primary and secondary

Criticism of the data, including the process of external criticism (questions of authorship, time, place, genuineness, and actual language or text of the original document) and the process of internal criticism (questions of accuracy and value of the statements made)

Presentation of the facts in readable narrative form, including problems of organization, composition, exposition, and interpretation.

HISTORICAL SOURCES

A classification of sources appropriate for history, as well as other social fields, is as follows:[17]

1. Physical remains: historic sites, roads, aqueducts, pyramids, fortifications, buildings ruined or whole, furniture, human remains, clothing, food, utensils, pottery, implements, weapons, machinery, industrial processes, and fine arts and museum pieces of many kinds

2. Orally transmitted material (sometimes in writing), such as folklore, legends, ballads, tales, anecdotes, sagas, traditions, customs, manners, burials, ceremonials, social institutions, and language

3. More elementary and durable kinds of representative or artistic materials, not written in the ordinary sense, such as inscriptions baked upon clay, chiselled stones, monuments, stamped coins, woven tapestries, vases, scenic or portrait sculptures, historical paintings, and portraits

[16] Carter Alexander and Arvid J. Burke, *How to Locate Educational Information and Data.* Fourth Edition. New York: Bureau of Publications, Teachers College, Columbia University, 1958. p. 298–303.

Jacques Barzun and Henry F. Graff, *op. cit.*, p. 18–27.

William W. Brickman, *Guide to Research in Educational History.* New York: New York University Bookstore, 1949. p. 1–8.

Louis R. Gottschalk, *op. cit.*, p. 62–70, 174–78.

Homer C. Hockett, *op. cit.*, p. 86–89, 184–86.

[17] Jacques Barzun and Henry F. Graff, *op. cit.*, p. 4–15.

Gilbert J. Garraghan, *op. cit.*, p. 103–23.

Louis R. Gottschalk, *op. cit.*, p. 41–61, 70–73, 86–117, 179–80.

Allan Nevins, *op. cit.*, Chapters 3, 4.

Thomas Woody, "Of History and Its Method." *Journal of Experimental Education* 15: 175–201; March 1947.

Pauline V. Young, *Scientific Social Surveys and Research.* Third Edition. Englewood Cliffs, N. J.: Prentice-Hall, 1956. p. 127–33.

4. Hand-written materials (sometimes in print), including papyri, bricks bearing cuneiform writing, vellum or parchment manuscripts, and such more recent documents as chronicles, annals, biographies, memoirs, diaries, and genealogies

5. Printed books, papers, and literature

6. Motion-picture film, microfilm, and recordings, including radio and television

7. Personal observation (by the writer or by people whom he interviews).

A simplified and practical classification of sources for our contemporary history includes the accounts of participants, reports of observers, publications of government agencies, research reports by scholars, and the writings of popularizers.[18]

Documents and Remains

The preceding longer classification of sources suggests that certain of the earlier simple categories have become more complex and probably will continue to expand in the future. In illustrating the varied sources in educational history, it is reasonably satisfactory to use two broad divisions: documents and remains or relics. Documents are reports of events, consisting of impressions made on some human brain by past events and consciously or deliberately recorded for the purpose of transmitting information. The observer's or eye-witness's impression of the event is illustrated by such documents as the opinion of a judge, minutes prepared by the secretary of a board of education, a superintendent's annual report, the director's report of a school survey, a college catalogue prepared by a dean, or a course of study transmitted to the superintendent by the chairman of the particular curriculum committee. Relics are physical objects (sometimes written materials of historical value) produced without the conscious intention of imparting connected information. Through documentary sources one sees not the event of the past, but what the eye-witness thought the act was. In remains or relics one sees the actual objects as handed down from the past. Sometimes man more nearly reveals the truth unconsciously through these physical objects or remains than through the documents that he deliberately records. For example, a schoolmaster may write in his annual report or diary (documentary source) of the humane and kindly methods of discipline employed, whereas the remains in the form of his devices for physical punishment (bundle of switches, iron-bound ruler, and whipping post) may reveal the truth and the inaccuracy of the documentary source.

[18] Walter C. Langsam, "Truth in History." *Bulletin of the Historical and Philosophical Society of Ohio* 16: 95–103; April 1958.

A useful list of sources in educational history is especially appropriate for modern materials in the form of documents or remains:[19]

Documents
1. Legislative acts such as constitutions, laws, charters
2. Court decisions
3. Executive and other official records
   a. Proceedings of administrative officers and bodies
      (1) Minutes of boards of education
      (2) Reports and orders of principals, superintendents, presidents
      (3) Reports of committees, including recommendations for executive action
      (4) Systems of student records and salary lists
   b. Proceedings of deliberate bodies, such as the National Education Association and the North Central Association
   c. Reports of commissions; for example, the Educational Policies Commission
   d. Reports of school surveys and of official observers; for example, the report of Victor Cousin
   e. Courses of study
   f. Catalogues, prospectuses, advertisements
4. Newspapers and periodicals
   a. Articles
   b. News notices
   c. Advertisements
5. Personal materials
   a. Autobiographies, memoirs, reminiscences, and biographies
   b. Annals and histories written by actors in the events narrated
   c. Letters
   d. Legal instruments executed by individuals in a personal capacity, contracts, wills, and deeds
   e. Legal instruments conferring powers upon individuals; for example, certificates
   f. Lecture notes
6. Literary materials, as the novels of Charles Dickens or Edward Eggleston. (All literature has a potential use in the history of education. A great amount of such material is found in the publications of the Early English Text Society and similar bodies.)

Remains
1. School buildings and their furnishings
2. Photographs of buildings or furnishings, or of children, teachers, and parents engaged in educational activities
3. Forms of diplomas, attendance, and certificates; and record blanks

---

[19] H. G. Good, "Historical Research in Education." *Educational Research Bulletin* 9: 7–18, 39–47, 74–78; January 8, January 22, and February 5, 1930.

4. Various physical devices of the school for teaching, punishment, exercise, or health

5. Textbooks, manuscript exercise-books made by pupils, and pupils' maps and drawings (The collection of more than 8,000 textbooks at the University of Pittsburgh, between 60 and 400 years old, provides sources for a reasonably clear picture of what was actually taught in the schools. Thus, the results of textbook analysis [including the author's preface] take the form of a history of the content of education with respect to trends and changes in aims, content, presentation of material, and teaching and learning aids.[20])

6. Under certain conditions all kinds of written materials, if the problem is to observe what people unconsciously reveal about themselves rather than to determine what they consciously or deliberately say about themselves.

As sources, government publications cover almost every field of human knowledge and endeavor and have become increasingly important tools for investigators and educators; these publications include: catalogs and indexes, bibliographies, congressional publications, federal and state constitutions, federal laws, state laws, court decisions, administrative regulations and departmental rulings, presidential papers, foreign affairs, reports on operations, organization and personnel, maps, technical and other department publications, periodicals, and microfacsimile editions of government publications.[21]

The preceding classifications of historical sources suggest that many types of materials have not been fully utilized, especially remains or relics. In the writing of history, physical remains usually have been considered more valuable for social and economic history than for political history, and more useful for descriptive than analytical phases of history. Some remains or relics are called "memorials," with the characteristics of both remains and documents. A gravestone including only a name is a relic, but with the addition of dates of birth and death, and possibly other information, it becomes a "memorial." The cornerstone or dedication plaque of a school building, including identifying dates, architect, or school board, has the characteristics of both remains and documents. The significance of educational remains has not been fully recognized, and space for housing bulky collections of remains has not been so commonly provided as for documents.

As an indication of recent interest in relics or remains, an Associated Press report, quite appropriately on July 4, 1961, announced that the Fine Arts Committee had collected for the White House a tufted chair

[20] John A. Nietz, "A Gift of Old School Textbooks." *School and Society* 87: 340–41; September 12, 1959.

[21] Laurence F. Schmeckebier and Roy B. Eastin, *Government Publications and Their Use*. Revised Edition. Washington: Brookings Institution, 1961. 476 p.

from Lincoln's bedroom, Dolley Madison's empire sofa, James Madison's medicine chest, James Monroe's bellange armchair and piertable, a bust of Martin Van Buren, a sheraton sofa on which Daniel Webster once rested, and an early nineteenth century sofa owned by Nellie Custis.

The same source at different times may be classified as either a document or a remain, when used for different purposes; for example, when letters written by George Washington and others (before Noah Webster's efforts toward standardization of spelling) are studied to determine variations in spelling, rather than the messages deliberately recorded in the letters, these sources would serve the purposes of remains and would be so classified. If the historian searches the same letters to identify attitudes toward education, his interest is in the recorded messages, which means that the source serves the purposes of a document and is so classified. A printed diploma or report card in blank is a remain, but when the name of a pupil and his attainments are entered in the proper blanks, the source presents a message and becomes a document. School textbooks are remains, since they do not deliberately or consciously record information concerning school practice or teaching procedure, although they do throw considerable light on such problems for a particular period of time. As a rule, the author's preface in a textbook comments on certain curricular, teaching, or learning problems and as such is a documentary source. The school textbook in some instances illustrates the relative values of documents and remains in the search for truth; in the preface the author may deliberately or consciously lay claim to modern curriculum materials and methods, but the discussion and exercises in the body of the textbook, serving as a silent witness, may testify that the materials and methods are obsolete.

Primary and Secondary Sources

An earlier section of this chapter has characterized sources as documents and as remains or relics. Another possible classification of sources[22] is as primary or secondary, and even tertiary or a greater number of times removed from the eye witness or direct observer of the event. Primary sources are the original documents or remains, the first witnesses to the event, with only the mind of the observer or eye witness coming between the original event and the user of the source. The preceding lists of documents and remains provide numerous examples of primary sources. The secretary's minutes of a school-board meeting are primary, but the newspaper editor's comment on the meeting of the board, even though based

[22] Jacques Barzun and Henry F. Graff, *op. cit.*, Chapters 1, 3–5.
William W. Brickman, *op. cit.*, p. 91–116.
H. G. Good, *op. cit.*, p. 43–47, 74–76.

on the minutes of the meeting, is secondary, since both the secretary and the editor have come between the event and the person who reads the newspaper comment. If the editor is present in person at the meeting of the school board, then his comments are primary.

The primary sources for writing the history of equipment in the science laboratories of secondary schools would include the equipment itself as preserved in storerooms or museums, pictures of apparatus, state or local manuals specifying laboratory equipment, written records by science teachers describing their laboratory apparatus or procedures, order blanks for requisitioning science materials, and the oral testimony of pupils and teachers who worked in the science laboratories of the past. Secondary sources for the same topic would include such materials as portions of histories of education, special bibliographies, and parts of books on the teaching of science, which usually are several times removed from the original event or have several minds between the laboratory equipment described and the user of the source.

The official registration cards for students in a school are a primary source for analyzing age, sex, and geographical distribution, but a newspaper report based on this analysis is a secondary source.

The nature of the problem and its purpose sometimes determine whether a particular source is primary or secondary. For most purposes, textbooks in the history of education are secondary sources, with most chapters and sections of the book many times removed from the original event; the author actually witnessed only a few of the events during the modern period in writing a history of education in the United States. If the problem and purpose of the historical study should change to the organization of materials, philosophy of interpretation, and style of writing employed by certain authors, then their books become primary sources; the author's book is as close as one can come to his philosophy of interpretation and style of writing. In the initial stage of a particular problem, a secondary source (such as a history of education) may prove more helpful and even more accurate than a primary source, if the educational historian has been successful in evaluating primary sources, interpreting meaning, and writing the narrative. As a first step in writing a history of reading instruction in the elementary school for a stipulated period of time, it probably is desirable to begin with such secondary sources as historical chapters in books on the teaching of reading.

The vitality of history is enhanced not only through reading the original sources but also through visitation of place of origin of events. Aristotle says that a Libyan, when asked to name the best manure, replied: "The land-owner's footprints." When asked about the best feed to fatten a horse, a Persian answered: "His master's eye." If Livy had paid more attention to factors of geography and topography, and had he

visited Lake Trasimenus, only some thirty miles from his birthplace, he
would have written differently about that famous battlefield.[23]

Preservation of Sources. An interesting example of modern literary scholarship and extensive travel in the recovery of a large quantity of manuscripts involves the papers of James Boswell, the biographer of Samuel
Johnson. Through painstaking efforts an American professor became
acquainted with Boswell's descendants and located the Boswell manuscripts in Ireland, after which the papers were purchased and brought
to the United States.

Without papers and documents from the past, the historian of science
would be helpless. Unfortunately, these valuable source materials are being
destroyed at a startling rate in present-day America. Children today do not
carry on a long family tradition, and heirlooms and papers kept for decades
are being disposed of summarily.

Professor W——, for example, was a key figure in American science at the
turn of the century. He carried out impressive research at one of our leading
universities, founded an important journal, and organized one of our great research laboratories. His ideas were provocative and influential, and his pupils
rose to eminent positions in the world of science. Yet today there exist no
primary source materials relating to his work. His correspondence, notebooks,
photograph albums, and manuscripts have disappeared.

What is needed to correct the situation is a Commission to Preserve the
Private Papers of American Scientists. Whether the commission is set up as a
private or government agency, its members would represent such institutions as
the National Academy of Sciences, the Library of Congress, and the National
Archives and such organizations as the Society of American Archivists and the
History of Science Society. The commission would have a twofold task. It
would be a central agency carrying on a systematic and comprehensive search
for source materials for the history of science, and, in this regard, it ought to
be empowered to establish a national history of science archives in Washington.

It is doubtful whether any single collection, however grand, can do the job
on the comprehensive scale required. As its second, and more important task,
the commission should take action to stimulate and coordinate the archival work
of the present scientific institutions and organizations. It is not enough that we
have the papers of an Einstein. We need material concerning the *hundreds* of
top-notch men doing important creative work in theoretical science and in the
applied fields—medicine, engineering, industry, and so on. And we cannot predict which of these men will be of greatest interest to the future. Each scientific
and educational institution—be it a university, museum, library, or research
laboratory—has a part to play in finding and storing papers of potential historical value. And every scientific organization should have collections of
relevant data at the national, regional, and local levels.

[23] Thomas Woody, *op. cit.,* p. 175–201.

The heroic age of American science began shortly after the Civil War and reached its climax just after World War II. These years, during which we won a position of world leadership, will be of unique interest to future historians of science. Already we have let much of this rich heritage slip through our fingers. A strong and active commission of the kind proposed can still repair some of the damage. But time is running out.[24]

Scientists and scholars themselves need a more general awareness of the importance of preserving personal and professional records for our future historians:

When Samuel Henshaw succeeded Alexander Agassiz as director of the Museum of Comparative Zoology at Harvard University, he wrote to E. S. Morse, director of the Peabody Museum of Salem, as follows: "It is strange that Mr. Agassiz kept so few mementos of the M.C.Z. I have been getting together such data as I can find as to early workers in the museum—I want to leave a good lot of M.C.Z. data for someone if I do not get a chance to use it myself."
. . . Over 40 years ago T. D. A. Cockerell at the University of Colorado wrote to Morse as follows: "I wish we had some systematic way of preserving data on American Science. At the New York Botanical Garden they have a good plan. For each American Botanist they have a large, open envelope or folder into which can be stuffed any letter, Ms., portrait or whatnot. Thus all sorts of data accumulate and will some day be very handy for the historian of American Botany—what a blessing it would be if naturalists habitually filed somewhere, brief accounts of all their collecting expeditions."[25]

A professional historian urges the preservation of historical materials in the field of psychology:[26]

Sometime in the decades between 1890 and World War II the United States won a position of world leadership in the field of psychology. Now records of this heroic age of American psychology are fast disappearing, and the future worker in history who attempts to chronicle and assess the course of the science and its role in civilization will have little with which to work except for surviving published writings. Personal papers, the chief sources of a rich history, are scarce and neglected. The situation is not unique to psychology.
Some few psychologists' correspondence and notes have been preserved, and they afford an excellent example of what others might do. The William James papers are safe in the Houghton Library of Harvard University. The J. McKeen Cattell papers rest now in the Library of Congress. The University of Wisconsin received a few items out of the last years of Joseph Jastrow.

[24] Quoted from Gerald J. Gruman, "Preserving the Stuff of History." *Science* 127: 1471; June 27, 1958. Reprinted from *Science* by permission.
[25] Quoted from Ralph W. Dexter, "Records for Future Historians." *Science* 133: 209; January 20, 1961. Reprinted from *Science* by permission.
[26] Quoted from John C. Burnham, "Preservation of Historical Materials." *American Psychologist* 14: 655–56; October 1959.

Regrettably, these three sentences come close to being a catalog of the manuscript resources available for the writing of the history of psychology. The list of scientists such as John B. Watson who left no personal papers is a much longer one.

This, then, is a call for all American psychologists to contribute to the heritage of the discipline. It is a plea to preserve—and ultimately to deposit in a responsible archive—the following types of materials:

1. Letters from major and secondary figures in psychology and other sciences

2. Notes on unpublished lectures of such figures

3. Personal recollections of historical occurrences, such as the founding of SPSSI and of the American Psychological Association itself

4. One's own personal files of correspondence, private memoranda, unpublished lectures

While modesty is in general a desirable trait, an undue amount can be fatal to historical materials. The man who in the 1920's transformed one of the other social sciences recently destroyed all of his files when he retired because he did not think that he was important enough to have a library interested in *his* stuff. Archivists and historians are finding much of the exciting material of the past in legacies from individuals who were on only the sidelines of important developments.

It is a common misapprehension that family letters and other personal documents have no place in a collection of historical papers. Actually some of the most important information comes from such sources: detailed descriptions of activities and associates, impressions of movements and men. Who could forget, for example, the frank letter in which William James wrote to his novelist brother, Henry James:

"Harvard must lead in psychology; and I, having founded her laboratory, am not the man to carry on the practical work. I have *almost* succeeded, however, in clinching a bargain whereby Münsterberg, the ablest experimental psychologist in Germany, allowance made for his being only 28 years old—he is in fact the Rudyard Kipling of psychology—is to come here. When he does he will scoop out all the other universities as far as that line of work goes."

Not everyone, of course, wrote with the charm of William James, but even routine letters throw light on such matters as crucial appointments. When the University of California inquired of psychiatrist Adolf Meyer in 1913 for a teacher in abnormal psychology, for example, his reply suggested why he did not recommend calling a young psychoanalyst. Still another letter, written by G. Stanley Hall just before his death to a man who was only a modest worker in the profession, illustrates the complex factors of personal loyalty in essentially scientific differences. (Copies of these letters are in the possession of the writer.) The uses of otherwise unpretentious personal documents are difficult to foretell: it may be that such materials will have a psychological as well as purely historical interest.

Most individuals feel that no collection of correspondence should be turned over to anyone else without going through it. In general it is better to turn over a collection intact to a trained archivist who can, if necessary, sort out the useful items. Should there be any doubts as to confidential or indiscreet items contained in a collection, it would be better not to destroy such material but simply deposit it with the formal understanding that it cannot be opened for a given number of years. Most archives have definite procedures providing for the legal protection of donors and their heirs.

Psychologists usually are either employees or alumni of academic institutions that maintain manuscript collections suitable for the deposit of personal papers.

The manuscripts of social welfare present special questions about the preservation and use of the files of social agencies. These working files are among the most valuable sources of information on modern social welfare, but they involve complex problems of preservation, availability, and confidentiality. Even though social agencies are considered "hard for the outsider to reach," careful protection of the individual is essential:

Archivists should not be deluded into thinking that adoption or aid files from the 19th century can be accepted for deposit and research use without trepidation. Who in this audience would like to read in a footnoted treatise that his mother was left on a doorstep in 1889? . . .

Social workers have stood implacably opposed to the revelation of such entirely personal material, and statutory laws or the common law appear normally to protect it (as they should). Whatever one may think of publicizing naked relief roll lists (as was done in Indiana amid much controversy), one can only hope that archivists will be vigilant to avoid *needless* opening of the private lives of obscure people. And researchers will want to follow the criterion that *to count* is one thing; *to name*, another.

If our archives one day come to contain casework files on the individuals and families, those in charge will have to assume the burden of indoctrinating every researcher on his responsibilities. Archivists must also weed out divorce-oriented private detectives up to no good. Since the ultimate goal of the social worker is *rehabilitation of individuals and families,* that noble goal will only be made more difficult of permanent accomplishment if archivists innocently facilitate the work of even one careless researcher.[27]

Importance of Nonofficial Documents. Both historians and sociologists are agreed on the importance of such nonofficial documents as personal letters, autobiographies, diaries, life histories, and similar records. Especially of late, a keen public interest in such historical sources has developed, as witnessed by accounts in popular magazines of collections relating to Lincoln, the Lewis and Clark explorations, Boswell, and works of art.

Collections of private letters have certain limitations when published

[27] Quoted from Vaughn D. Bornet, "The Manuscripts of Social Welfare." *Social Service Review* 33: 452–53; December 1959.

by the writer himself or by a literary executor, since damaging passages or even entire letters may be omitted; an editor without personal relations with the author of the letters is much more likely to present an unbiased treatment. Diaries and autobiographies edited and published by the author are subject to the same limitations mentioned for letters. It is only natural that many self-centered persons who write letters, diaries, and autobiographies will describe themselves and their motives, and edit their collections, as they wish to appear to the public rather than as they actually are. An exception to this characterization is Samuel Pepys, who presumably wrote with candor and honesty in his diary, since he probably did not expect anyone to decode his special system of shorthand. Although James Boswell was almost ideally qualified to write the *Life of Johnson,* in view of his close relationships with his subject, Boswell omitted interesting details in following what he considered the dictates of good taste in biography.

Essentially similar views are expressed in the discussion between Whitehead, his wife, and Lucien Price:[28]

"I think you get a truer picture of a period from intimate letters written spontaneously and without a thought of publication than you do from its fiction and often better than from its historians."

"And women write better than men in that vein," said his wife.

"Certainly better than authors writing letters to each other with an eye to future publications," he agreed.

"Edmund Gosse used to complain that while the letters Robert Louis Stevenson wrote him were works of art and literature they didn't tell him what he wanted to know about his friend—which touched off Carolyn Wells to write that ballade with the refrain, 'They must look well in print!' "

EXTERNAL CRITICISM: AUTHENTICITY[29]

The historian is obligated to determine the authenticity and meaning of sources. Many writers on the historical method and on historiography have labeled these processes of criticism and evaluation as external criticism and internal criticism, while other historiographers have avoided the formality or logic of such a classification of the aspects of criticism.

[28] Quoted from *Dialogues of Alfred North Whitehead.* As Recorded by Lucien Price. New York: New American Library of World Literature, 1954. p. 43.

[29] William W. Brickman, *op. cit.,* p. 116–60.
Gilbert J. Garraghan, *op. cit.,* p. 168–231.
H. G. Good, *op. cit.,* p. 17–18.
Louis R. Gottschalk, *op. cit.,* p. 118–38.
Homer C. Hockett, *op. cit.,* p. 13–82.
Allan Nevins, *op. cit.,* Chapters 5, 6.
Chauncey Sanders, *An Introduction to Research in English Literary History.* New York: The Macmillan Co., 1952. p. 95–124, 142–206.

For present purposes it seems helpful to employ the terms *external* and *internal criticism.*

External criticism deals with the genuineness of the document, whether it is what it seems to be and reads true to the original. It is concerned with form and appearance of the document rather than meaning of the contents, although external criticism at times may employ internal evidence from the document through a study of its contents, in an attempt to establish questions of authorship. Problems of external criticism, in testing the genuineness of a document or remain, involve questions about the characteristics of the author and his qualifications as a reporter; factors or conditions that may have influenced the production of the document, such as time, place, purpose, and circumstances of composition; and the extent to which the document and its parts read true to the original.

The work of external criticism has been greatly facilitated through the development of a number of auxiliary sciences, and of printing and photography, especially in dealing with older sources. A partial list of the important auxiliary aids or fields includes: anthropology, archaeology, astronomy, cartography, chemistry, chronology, diplomatics, economics, education, epigraphy, exact sciences, genealogy, geography, geology, heraldry, historical method and philosophies, languages, law, literature, military affairs, natural history, numismatics, paleontology, paleography, philately, philology, philosophy, politics, prehistory, and psychology.

The Problem of Error

Before the invention of printing, when manuscripts were copied by hand, there were frequently inadvertent errors in the form of unintentional omissions or insertions, and sometimes deliberate changes in the text. During recent years microphotography has made it possible to reproduce and transmit entire books, bulky records, newspapers, and other manuscripts for projection in some distant library or research center, thus obviating the type of error that arises in copying.

Even today, however, the problem of error in transmitting messages is still with us. There are differences in wording with respect to the cable of October 29, 1918, sent by Woodrow Wilson to Colonel House in Paris, when the text written on the President's own typewriter is compared with the cable or message actually received by House:

According to a common practice when code is used, words are often transposed or slightly different words are used in order to protect the security of the code. In this instance it is not known whether the changes were made deliberately when encoding in America or decoding in Europe or whether they resulted from carelessness. Most of the minor variations are of no consequence: "which will prevent" is the same as "which will not permit"; "within those limits" is equivalent to "within that condition"; "because it is certain" means approximately the same as "because lately I am certain"; and "Foresight is wiser than" equals "Foresight is better than."

The other change is, however, really important. The meaning of Wilson's words "too much success or security on the part of the Allies" is significantly different from the meaning of the message House received saying "too much severity on the part of the Allies." The latter thought is on the character of the terms to be imposed on the Germans. It does not contain some of the elements in the mind of Wilson. His thinking was focused on the Allies, on their security and his desire for some insecurity so that they could be coerced by an American threat of a separate peace.

The words "too much severity" could support an interpretation of Wilson as a Lincolnian character who wishes to make peace with malice toward none and with charity for all. The words "too much success or security" support the view that Wilson was not the naive innocent which he came to be regarded but was a hard-boiled practitioner of balance-of-power politics. The pictures are quite different.

Both versions of the message are, of course, correct depending on the purpose for which they are to be used. If the scholar is primarily concerned with House and his negotiations with the Allies in Paris, the words he actually received are what matter. If the scholar is trying to state the policy of the United States as formulated by Wilson or to understand his mind and character, the message he composed is what counts.

Inevitably one wonders if there were other changes in thought resulting from the coding of messages between the two men and if they might have contributed to the misunderstanding that developed. At least it is clear that scholars should add alterations through coding to the long list of pitfalls they must avoid.[30]

It may be added that Wilson personally typed many historic documents now on file in the Library of Congress. The precision of his mind and his effectiveness in typing and shorthand were such that he seldom made a mistake in either wording or typing. Before Wilson became ill in 1919 he did not use "ghost" writers and frequently composed declarations and diplomatic communications at his typewriter, recently placed on exhibition at the White House along with facsimiles of historic documents typed on it. It is probable that some of Wilson's state documents contained technical material prepared for him by Cabinet officers and after 1919 his messages to Congress were prepared by various members of the Cabinet.

[30] Quoted from W. Stull Holt, "What Wilson Sent and What House Received: Or Scholars Need to Check Carefully." *American Historical Review* 65: 569–71; April 1960.

Honesty of Scientists and Scholars

As a group, scientists have an outstanding record for morality and honesty in seeking and reporting the truth, with only a few exceptions deviating from the search for truth:[31]

Anyway, truth in their own straightforward sense is what the scientists are trying to find. They want to find what is *there*. Without that desire, there is no science. It is the driving force of the whole activity. It compels the scientist to have an overriding respect for truth, every stretch of the way. That is, if you're going to find what is *there*, you mustn't deceive yourself or anyone else. You mustn't lie to yourself. At the crudest level, you mustn't fake your experiments.

Curiously enough, scientists do try to behave like that. A short time ago, I wrote a novel in which the story hinged on a case of scientific fraud. But I made one of my characters, who was himself a very good scientist, say that, considering the opportunities and temptations, it is astonishing how few such cases there are. We have all heard of perhaps half a dozen open and notorious ones, which are on the record for anyone to read—ranging from the "discovery" of the L radiation to the singular episode of the Piltdown man.

We have all, if we have lived any time in the scientific world, heard private talk of something like another dozen cases which for various reasons are not yet public property. In some cases, we know the motives for the cheating —sometimes, but not always, sheer personal advantage, such as getting money or a job. But not always. A special kind of vanity has led more than one man into scientific faking. At a lower level of research, there are presumably some more cases. There must have been occasional Ph.D. students who scraped by with the help of a bit of fraud.

But the total number of all these men is vanishingly small by the side of the total number of scientists. Incidentally, the effect on science of such frauds is also vanishingly small. Science is a self-correcting system. That is, no fraud (or honest mistake) is going to stay undetected for long. There is no need for an extrinsic scientific criticism, because criticism is inherent in the process itself. So that all that a fraud can do is waste the time of the scientists who have to clear it up.

The remarkable thing is not the handful of scientists who deviate from the search for truth but the overwhelming numbers who keep to it. That is a demonstration, absolutely clear for anyone to see, of moral behavior on a very large scale.

It is true that students in education and other social fields do not often encounter problems of actual genuineness in dealing with modern documents, especially printed sources. There is little temptation to forge

[31] Quoted from Charles P. Snow, "The Moral Un-Neutrality of Science." *Science* 133: 256–59; January 27, 1961. Reprinted from *Science* by permission.

a modern arithmetic textbook, a course of study, or school-board minutes. Even though there may not be any great incentive to perpetrate frauds or forgeries in the modern literature of the social fields, there is still the question of authorship (external criticism) in determining the extent to which a city superintendent has written his annual report rather than his assistant superintendents and supervisors, and the part played by a university president in preparing his annual report as compared with contributions by the deans of his several component colleges.

Typical motives for deception in the preparation of older documents were: use of a well-known name to increase the sales or prestige of a manuscript, enhancement of the reputation of prominent persons through employment of "ghost" writers, and use of pseudonyms to stimulate the curiosity of the public.[32] Types of invention or forgery that have appeared in the past include: witty sayings of famous persons, invented speeches placed in the mouths of famous personages by the older historians, insertion of applause in the written record of legislative speeches never delivered, genealogies and family trees, interpolations or insertions for deceptive purposes by copyists or others, and business documents, works of art, and antiques.

Merton presents a sociological interpretation[33] of the frequently puzzling aspects of conflicts over priority or originality in scientific discovery. His interpretation is that, like other social institutions, science has its characteristic values, norms, and organization, including emphasis on the value of originality. As emphasis upon originality and its recognition is stepped up, the greater becomes the involvement of the scientist in the successful outcome of inquiry and his emotional vulnerability to failure. This cultural and social background can lead scientists to develop an extreme concern for recognition, which is in turn the validation by peers of their work, and can lead to reprehensible conduct on the part of individual scientists. The history of science reports many instances of deviant behavior in the form of contentiousness, self-assertive claims, secretiveness lest one be forestalled, reporting only the data that support a hypothesis, false charges of plagiarism, even the occasional theft of ideas and, in rare cases, the fabrication of data. This misbehavior is in response to a discrepancy between the great emphasis in the culture of science upon original discovery and the actual difficulty many scientists experience in making an original discovery, with the result that, in a situation of stress and strain, various forms of questionable adaptive behavior are adopted.

[32] Gilbert J. Garraghan, *op. cit.*, p. 81–99.
H. G. Good, *op. cit.*, p. 13–14.
Chauncey Sanders, *op. cit.*, p. 408–11.
Thomas Woody, *op. cit.*, p. 175–201.
[33] Robert K. Merton, "Priorities in Scientific Discovery: A Chapter in the Sociology of Science." *American Sociological Review* 22: 635–59; December 1957.

Illustrations of Frauds and Forgeries[34]

Interesting examples of hoaxes, frauds, and forgeries from a number of fields may be cited to illustrate the range and complexity of problems of genuineness in external criticism. For example, a painting is brought to the United States labeled as a self-portrait done by a great Dutch artist. The authenticity of the painting is challenged by the artist's nephew, and a battle develops between art experts in the United States, in Europe, and the U. S. Treasury Department. The customs officers are interested because original works of art are duty-free, whereas copies and reproductions are not. One group of experts on art, handwriting, pigment, and language decides that the picture is genuine, so it is admitted to this country duty-free, but another group of specialists is unwilling to accept the painting as an original work by the Dutch artist.

The newspapers and magazines in 1961 told of some thirty fake paintings attributed to Maurice Utrillo, which were confiscated by Paris police, who supervised a bonfire of them (in the widow's presence) in Montmartre where the artist had painted many of his real ones.

In 1961 the Metropolitan Museum of Art in New York sadly reported that the three sculptures of Etruscan warriors, supposedly dating from 500 B.C., were twentieth century forgeries. One of the museum's experts had discovered that the black glaze on the statues was produced by the modern dyeing agent, manganese dioxide, and not by the ancient Greek oxidizing method. The credentials of the three sculptures had seemed impressive when they came to the museum in fragments, seemingly worn by the centuries and with a glaze like the ancient Greek black, but a retired art expert living in Rome later became suspicious of the statues stylistically. He discovered that three men, specialists in mending ancient pottery for Italian antique dealers, decided they could create as well as mend ancient works of art. In 1914 they began work on the three Etruscan figures and on completion painted the unfired creations in the Etruscan manner, broke them into pieces, fired the fragments, smeared them with mud, and turned over the pieces to a dealer. In 1961, when the museum sent an art expert to Rome with a plaster cast of one of the warrior's hands from which the thumb was missing, the chief forger

[34] Jacques Barzun and Henry F. Graff, op. cit., p. 88–114.
William W. Brickman, op. cit., p. 156–57.
Gilbert J. Garraghan, op. cit., p. 184–85.
Tyrus Hillway, Introduction to Research. Boston: Houghton Mifflin Co., 1956. p. 138.
Homer C. Hockett, op. cit., p. 26–28.
Allan Nevins, op. cit., p. 124–25, 131–37.
James W. Thompson and Bernard J. Holm, A History of Historical Writing. Vol. 1. New York: The Macmillan Co., 1942. p. 6.

produced a thumb of baked pottery that he had been keeping for years. When placed together, thumb and hand fitted perfectly.

Although Abraham Lincoln has proved to be the greatest figure of his period, he was not appreciated in his own time and no engravings of him were made in his lifetime. Suddenly, after his assassination in 1865, there was an enormous public demand for such engravings, and to meet it, the hasty expedient was adopted of creating "grafted" or "hybrid" engravings by placing photographs of Lincoln's head on the bodies of other statesmen (for example, John C. Calhoun and Martin Van Buren) whose plates were already available in stock. Recently, years of detective work have revealed these century-old deceptions or frauds.

Forgery was practiced even thousands of years ago. The Egyptian pharaohs often claimed for themselves the deeds of their ancestors by erasing the name of the hero on the wall and by chiseling in their own names. Sometimes the pharaohs reproduced on another slab or monument the record of the hero's achievements, with their own names inserted to receive credit.

The public interest of recent years in antique furniture has made the manufacture of fakes a profitable business. Tests of genuineness are based on certain facts and conditions. A new pine table may have been smoked (with a resulting odor) to give it a smudgy color or aged effect, or may even have been left in the hot sun to let it "mellow." The "joiners" or carpenters of the early American period did not make four-poster double beds. Circular saw markings on the bottom of cabinet drawers cannot date back to Queen Anne's days of 1710. The old joiners chose their wood with care; pine and oak furniture was made of carefully matched boards and rarely had knots. The early carpenters made dowels or pegs by hand which were never perfectly round like the later machine-made pegs. Hand-made chair legs are not perfectly round, and diameter varies slightly on the length of the leg. If the glass in the doors of a cupboard is perfectly smooth, flat, and transparent, the claim of antiquity is open to serious question.

In modern times the forger has little chance of deceiving the handwriting expert or "questioned document examiner." The forger must attempt to disguise or suppress every revealing characteristic of his own handwriting, and at the same time must include all the telltale traits of the handwriting he is trying to imitate. It may be that the ink or paper used actually was not available on the purported date of the forged instrument. Typewriters develop idiosyncrasies, in that type may be knocked askew or tiny bits of letters are chipped off. Design or size of type sometimes varies with the model of the machine, which may mean that the type used for the forged document was not even in existence on the purported date.

News agencies have reported a secret forgery factory of world importance in an obscure corner of a run-down district of East Berlin, established for the purpose of producing faked documents calculated to embarrass the West. Ingenious techniques of criticism have been employed to expose the forgeries. A faked letter with State Department engraving was addressed to "Dear Clare," whereas this Ambassador has been called "Tim" since boyhood. One purported United States document, supposedly a highly secret paper, used the British spelling, "defence," instead of "defense." A glaring linguistic error in a forged memorandum was a reference to the "National Safety Agency," whereas in American usage the phrasing is "National Defense Agency."

Ultraviolet rays and fluorescence photography have been developed as new methods of examining documents, especially in detecting alterations and erasures. Through such techniques it has been discovered that numerous changes were made in the personal journals of Nathaniel Hawthorne by Mrs. Hawthorne after her husband's death. By reading even heavily blacked out portions of Hawthorne's journals, the scholar has found him a man of real vigor and some bluntness of expression, although Hawthorne's widow had toned down his writing to sound more genteel or inoffensive.

It is difficult to believe that a standard encyclopedia of American biography included at least 47 sketches of the lives of men who never existed. The author (paid according to amount of space) sought to increase his remuneration by creating characters out of his imagination, including a scientist who supposedly won fame by combating the Asiatic cholera in South America, in 1783, 52 years before the disease first appeared there.

In a letter under an 1834 date, attributed to Lincoln, is an expression "that North East quarter of Section 40" of which Lincoln as an experienced surveyor could hardly have been guilty, since he knew quite well that a Congressional township was made up of 36 sections. The same letter included the geographical term *Kansas;* the territory of Kansas was not organized and open for settlement until 1854, and the term probably was not in use as early as 1834. The fact that the handwriting bore no resemblance to Lincoln's authenticated style helped establish the letters as forgeries. One of the spurious letters attributed to Ann Rutledge mentions a Spencerian copybook not in use until 1848; Ann died in 1835.

A striking example of a hoax or fraud is *The Diary of James Gallatin, Secretary to Albert Gallatin, A Great Peacemaker, 1813-1827,* edited by Count Gallatin and published in London and New York late in 1914:

In the preface, Count Gallatin explained that thirty-nine years before, in 1875, his grandfather had handed him "a large sealed packet, telling me it contained his Diary . . . also many important documents. I was not in any case to publish any part of it until 1900. . . . It lay unopened and nearly forgotten until last year. On reading it, I found it of the deepest interest. This decided me (after weeding out large portions and suppressing anything that might offend) to offer it to the public."[35]

The authenticity of the *Diary* has been questioned for the following reasons:

1. Critics observed that the text of the *Diary* is not "pure" and contains a number of "aberrations."
2. Among the entries in the *Diary* are many expressions that seem to throw doubt on its authenticity as a whole, including expressions that were not in use at the time the *Diary* was supposed to have been written.
3. Many of the persons described in the *Diary* as having been at a particular place on a given date are known, on the basis of standard sources, to have been elsewhere at the time.
4. Members of the family and others were unable to find any trace of the original manuscript of the *Diary* or of anyone who had ever seen it.
5. The *Diary* does not check with other sources; for example, it includes many obvious inaccuracies about the French political and social scene.
6. Neither the literary style of the *Diary* nor the personality it displays of its supposed author jibes with the style or personality of James Gallatin exhibited elsewhere.
7. It is unlikely that the *Diary* was written earlier than 1879, at least three years after James Gallatin died, because much of the material is obviously drawn from two works published in that year by Henry Adams, dealing with the life and writings of Albert Gallatin. Of the twenty-nine letters and documents reproduced in the *Diary*, all but three appeared in one or both of Adams' works. Numerous entries in the *Diary* simply paraphrase passages found in Adams.
8. There are many discrepancies in matters of dates and events. The author of the hoax or fraud probably is the "Count Gallatin" who is listed as the editor of the *Diary* and signed its Preface. This man is James Francis Gallatin, grandson of the ostensible keeper of the *Diary*. This grandson was born in New York City in 1853, and had sufficient motivation and background for perpetrating the hoax.

In its crudest form, falsification of personal documents is conscious, deliberate deceit, with the possible motives of material gain or malice, or as a practical joke or literary exercise. An impressive example in the psychological literature is a very skillful forgery of the diary of an adolescent girl, which deceived even Freud. After several years the critics discovered the falsification, concluding that the style was too mature for a girl between 11 and 14 years, that erroneous references were made

---

[35] Quoted from Raymond Walters, Jr., "The James Gallatin Diary: A Fraud?" *American Historical Review* 62: 876–85; July 1957.

to the weather on particular days, and that a place mentioned was non-existent at the date on which the entry appeared in the diary.[36]

An instance of forgery in the 1930's came to light when two young English book dealers were exposed as having printed certain rare and expensive books by well-known British authors, books presumed to have been published in limited or small editions about the middle of the nineteenth century. The temptation for a clever printer to issue these forged editions was the high price of the original editions in the rare-book market.

Piltdown Man, the so-called "Eoanthropus dawsoni," was generally (although not universally) accepted for approximately 40 years as an important fossil link in the chain of human evolution. His exposure as a fraud—as a synthetic monster compounded of the brain-case of a relatively recent, modern type of man and the doctored lower jaw of a recent anthropoid ape—rocked paleontological and anthropological circles in 1953.

The story of the hoax, as now revealed, is presented in detail by J. S. Weiner, the Oxford anthropologist who first suspected that the Sussex "fossil" was a concatenated chimera, and at whose insistence the anatomical and chemical investigations were undertaken which proved beyond doubt that the "earliest Englishman" was a diabolically clever forgery. The discovery of the skull, the ensuing scientific controversies, the problems that acceptance of the skull as an actual fossil entailed, and the events leading to the exposure of its true nature, are set forth by Weiner in an absorbing manner. No detective story or fiction could be more engrossing or more challenging. The personalities involved receive considerable attention.[37]

Inventions and Distortions[38]

Thucydides, the Greek historian, created elaborate speeches or orations for his leading characters, intended not merely for rhetorical effect but also to set forth the politics and diplomacy of his philosophy of history. The Roman dictator, Sulla, after his retirement from public life wrote a fabulous autobiography, pointing to a series of miraculous occurrences coincident with his public work, for the purpose of showing that the hand of the Goddess Tyche was visible throughout his activities. In marked contrast, Caesar's Commentaries present at least an external illu-

[36] Claire Selltiz and Others, *Research Methods in Social Relations.* Revised One-Volume Edition. New York: Henry Holt and Co., 1959. p. 325–26.

[37] Quoted from review by William L. Straus, Jr., *Scientific Monthly* 83: 209–10; October 1956, of J. S. Weiner, *The Piltdown Forgery.* New York: Oxford University Press, 1955. xii + 214 p.

[38] Gilbert J. Garraghan, *op. cit.,* p. 228, 265.
Michael Kraus, *op. cit.,* p. 14–18, 39, 51, 80, 305.
Allan Nevins, *op. cit.,* p. 134, 139–40, 162–63.
J. T. Shotwell, *The History of History.* Vol. 1. New York: Columbia University Press, 1939. p. 210, 284–86.

sion of impartiality and self-restraint, although we should remember that Caesar wrote primarily to justify himself before the Roman people. When Alexander the Great was listening to an account of how he slew his opponent's elephant with a single blow of his spear, the young conqueror's sense of historical accuracy could not condone such exaggerated hero worship, and he snatched the book and threw it into the water with the comment that the author of such untruth also should be ducked.

In the writing of Thucydides, rhetorical speeches had served a genuinely dramatic purpose, but many of his successors made these inventions occasions for dramatic flourishes and illustrations of their command of style.

In most humanist historical writing of the fifteenth century the device of imaginary direct discourse was used not only to conform to rhetorical rules but also to construct idealized portraits. In this way individual historical characters came to exemplify abstract virtues and vices and thus serve as material for moral instruction. A great gulf separated the purpose of this use of direct discourse from that of a realist like Guicciardini, who in his masterpiece which covered the years of Erasmus' mature life used the same rhetorical device to underline the ironic difference between what men said and what they did. Erasmus' position in the *De copia* is that of traditional humanism.[39]

Parson Weems' rhetorical *Life of George Washington* includes many inventions in the form of dialogues, speeches, and anecdotes. The pioneer historian, Jared Sparks, edited the everyday language of George Washington and corrected his spelling, in order to picture Washington as a character of almost superhuman traits. Sparks has been accused of omitting materials that did not support his purpose of exalting some individual, and even of manufacturing a source or narrative as needed.

Belated appearance of a tradition, especially after the death of the person involved, may give rise to doubt. Captain John Smith's second version of his adventures in Virginia describes dramatically how Pocahontas saved his life, whereas she was barely mentioned in the first version. The story of Ann Rutledge and Abraham Lincoln is thought to be mainly legendary, since no mention of the episode appeared until 31 years after her death.

Authorship and Borrowing[40]

Problems of external criticism are much less those of forgery or invention than of authorship, time, dependence of documents upon each

[39] Quoted from H. Stuart Hughes, *op. cit.*, p. 14–15.
[40] H. G. Good, *op. cit.*, p. 16.
Homer C. Hockett, *op. cit.*, p. 23–24.
Michael Kraus, *op. cit.*, p. 4, 13, 93–99, 105–14, 123–27, 140–47, 164, 316.
Allan Nevins, *op. cit.*, p. 153–56.
Thomas Woody, *op. cit.*, p. 175–201.

other, and borrowing. It has already been pointed out in this chapter that annual reports of university presidents and school superintendents pose a problem of determining authorship in relation to the contribution of their assistants. A difference in style or language in the several parts of such an annual report is not so important as whether the president's or superintendent's ideas are accurately presented in the phrasing of a dean or assistant superintendent. Washington's "Farewell Address" raises the question of what contribution Madison and Hamilton made to it. A similar question of authorship is present in identifying the numbers of *The Federalist* written by Madison, Hamilton, and Jay.[41] Prominent persons in governmental positions and in other walks of public life frequently have employed "ghost" writers. It is believed that Bancroft, the historian, wrote the message that Andrew Johnson sent to Congress in December 1865, although the discovery was not made until some forty years later.

Borrowing has been common, especially during earlier periods when authors copied freely from a variety of sources without acknowledgment of the borrowing. For more than a century John Marshall's *Life of George Washington,* published in 1804, was considered a great original work and a classic in its defense of federalism. The work has now been pronounced a mosaic of borrowings, carelessly pieced together, with unacknowledged instances of copying found on 268 of the 488 pages in one volume.

INTERNAL CRITICISM: CREDIBILITY[42]

Internal criticism deals with the meaning and trustworthiness of statements remaining within the document after any spurious or interpolated matter has been removed from the text; in other words, it weighs the testimony of the document in relation to the truth. These questions of accuracy and value of the statements made (credibility) normally come in sequence after questions of authorship, genuineness, time, place, and actual language or text of the original document have been answered through the processes of external criticism. The shift of emphasis in internal criticism is from the document as such to statements within the document. Many authentic or genuine documents (so determined by

[41] Irving Brant, "Settling the Authorship of *The Federalist.*" *American Historical Review* 67: 71–75; October 1961.

[42] William W. Brickman, *op. cit.,* p. 161–79.
Gilbert J. Garraghan, *op. cit.,* p. 232–317.
H. G. Good, *op. cit.,* p. 39–47, 74–76.
Homer C. Hockett, *op. cit.,* p. 41–82.
Louis R. Gottschalk, *op. cit.,* p. 139–71.
Allan Nevins, *op. cit.,* Chapter 7.
Chauncey Sanders, *op. cit.,* p. 207–52.

external criticism) may not be completely accurate or truthful, and require the processes of internal criticism in the form of textual criticism, as well as investigation of such factors as the competence, good faith, position, and bias of the author of the document.

There is no sharp dividing line between the external and internal phases of historical criticism, and the two processes may progress simultaneously, with a considerable amount of overlapping. Internal criticism may use external evidence concerning authorship, or time and place of writing, in determining the truthfulness and accuracy of the statements made in the document. The terms *external* and *internal* refer to the purpose of the criticism and not to a specific method of dealing with sources, or whether one looks within or without the document for evidence to accomplish the particular purpose.

Before proceeding with specific illustrations, it is helpful to summarize basic principles of internal criticism:[43]

1. Do not read into earlier documents the conceptions of later times.

2. Do not judge an author ignorant of certain events, necessarily, because he fails to mention them (the argument *ex silentio*), or that they did not occur, for the same reason.

3. Underestimating a source is no less an error than overestimating it in the same degree, and there is no more virtue in placing an event too late than in dating it too early by the same number of years or centuries.

4. A single true source may establish the existence of an idea, but other direct, competent, independent witnesses are required to prove the reality of events or objective facts.

5. Identical errors prove the dependence of sources on each other, or a common source.

6. If witnesses contradict each other on a certain point, one or the other may be true, but both may be in error.

7. Direct, competent, independent witnesses who report the same central fact and also many peripheral matters in a casual way may be accepted for the points of their agreement.

8. Official testimony, oral or written, must be compared with unofficial testimony whenever possible, for neither one nor the other is alone sufficient.

9. A document may provide competent and dependable evidence on certain points, yet carry no weight in respect to others it mentions.

Literal Meaning and Real Meaning

Internal criticism is concerned with questions of the real meaning as distinguished from the literal meaning, the competence of the observer for careful and accurate reporting, and the good faith of the observer in making statements without bias or prejudice. The virtues of the his-

[43] Thomas Woody, *op. cit.*, p. 175–201.

torian include accuracy, love of order, logic, honesty, self-awareness, and imagination.[44]

The attempt to discover the literal meaning and the real meaning of the document is a positive aspect of internal criticism. While the literal meaning and the real meaning are usually the same in modern documents, except for rhetorical figures of speech and ambiguities in political speeches and platforms, many of the older sources present a difficult task of determining the real meaning, because of unfamiliar or obsolete terms and reference to strange institutions or customs. The language of Cotton Mather must be interpreted, to understand what he is saying about certain events in the lives of the colonists that might seem trivial to the outside world: "If a war between us and a handful of Indians do appear no more than a Batrachomyomachie [battle of frogs and mice] to the world abroad, yet unto us at home it hath been considerable enough to make a history." Even in modern history we find rhetorical figures and literary artifices such as allegory, symbolism, irony, satire, jests, hoaxes, allusions, implications, metaphors, and hyperboles. George Bancroft's high-flown rhetoric needs tempering in determining an appropriate shade of meaning: "History has ever celebrated the heroes who have won laurels in scenes of carnage. Has it no place for the founders of states; the wise legislators, who struck the rock in the wilderness, so that the waters of liberty gushed forth in copious and perennial fountains?"[45]

There is an ever-present inclination of the uneducated to transform an allegorical allusion into a literal reality, to bring a metaphor clumsily and inappropriately to earth. Once a history student, presented with the statement that Napoleon "cut" the Austrian lines of communication in the Italian campaign of 1796, pictured the operation in its most literal sense. There had to be something physical if one was to cut as with a pair of shears. Hence he imagined railway, telephone, and telegraph lines—snip, snip, snip, snip. When, pushed to further investigation, he discovered that humanity was blessed with none of these conveniences at the time, his picture disintegrated, leaving only a blank canvas and the conviction, which still prevailed, that something had been cut. And it is likely that he was unusual only in making further investigation. Most students never come to a position where they can hear with comfort an argument to show that there was no "Renaissance," or that the "fall" of Rome was not noticeable at the time.[46]

Competence and Accuracy of the Observer

To question either the competence and accuracy or the truthfulness and honesty of the observer is a negative aspect of internal criticism, in

[44] Jacques Barzun and Henry F. Graff, *op. cit.*, p. 56–60.
[45] Michael Kraus, *op. cit.*, p. 14, 115–27.
[46] Quoted from H. Stuart Hughes, *op. cit.*, p. 312.

that every possible reason for disbelieving is sought and every statement is questioned as long as any reasonable doubt remains. An observer's competence is evaluated in relation to his status as a trained eye witness, presence of emotional stress or pressure that might affect observation, extent to which the position for observing was favorable, and extent to which memory was used after a lapse of time.

Even the secretary of a professional organization is not always an accurate observer and reporter. A history[47] of the American Psychological Association indicates that the minutes of a recording secretary cannot always be trusted as evidence of what actually happened at a particular meeting. The published facts of the founding of the A.P.A. indicate that seven psychologists (Hall, Fullerton, James, Jastrow, Ladd, Cattell, and Baldwin) met at Clark University on July 8, 1892, to discuss the advisability and possibility of forming an association of psychologists. At the time the history was prepared Cattell and Jastrow were still living, but when asked to recall any important events concerning this founding meeting both replied that they had been unable to attend the meeting of July 8, 1892. It is true that sometimes a secretary lists in full the committee members in reporting the minutes, not noting absences, especially if the absent members have made recommendations by mail in advance of the meeting.

As an example of the problem of accuracy in determining a date of birth, when institutions were celebrating in 1944 the one hundredth anniversary of the birth of G. Stanley Hall, it was found that different sources gave three birth dates for him. A biography of Hall, written by a man who had worked closely with him, included the date of February 1, 1846. Another investigator found that the vital records of Ashfield, Massachusetts, Hall's apparent birthplace, did not contain the name of G. Stanley Hall, that Hall himself did not refer to his birth date in a biographical article, that different editions of *Who's Who in America* mention different dates, and that Hall's monument in Ashfield carried the inscription, "Born, February 1, 1844," which was accepted by the second investigator. A third author communicated with all the institutions with which Hall had been affiliated, with Hall's son, and with the General Land Office, and concluded that the most probable month and day of Hall's birth appeared to be February 1, although he was not certain about the year. Despite certain evidence favoring 1844, this third investigator (a scholar and research specialist in educational history) concluded that Hall was evidently confused about his own birth

[47] Samuel W. Fernberger, "The American Psychological Association, 1892–1942." *Psychological Review* 50: 33–60; January 1943.

Wayne Dennis and Edwin G. Boring, "The Founding of the APA." *American Psychologist* 7: 95–97; March 1952.

date and that no final answer can be reached until some indisputably authentic record of his birth date is discovered.[48]

Another illustration of internal criticism relates to determining the first American work in the field of education:

> Many writings on American educational history refer to Samuel R. Hall's *Lectures on School-Keeping* (1829) as the first American work in the field of education. Knight and Monroe, for example, make this statement in their respective textbooks. J. P. Gordy describes Hall's volume as "the first book on the subject ever written in this country" (*Rise and Growth of the Normal-School Idea in the United States*, p. 12). In their foreword to their Hall's *Lectures on School-Keeping*, Arthur D. Wright and George E. Gardiner refer to it as the "first book on education published in the United States in the English Language." This leaves out of account Christopher Dock's *Schulordnung* (1770), and Joseph Neef's *Sketch of a Plan and Method of Education* (1808) and *Method of Instructing Children* (1813), all three published in Philadelphia. Of course, the claim may be made that Dock's book was written in German and that Dock and Neef were born abroad. In that event, the statement should read, "the first book on education written by an American."[49]

When Ellwood P. Cubberley, in 1898, started to teach at Stanford University, he had never studied the history of education, as such, although his undergraduate specialization in science may have thrown some light upon the history of science. If Cubberley had had the benefit of graduate work in history, he would have read and heard much about scientific procedure, historical method, analysis of documents for evidence, and in some universities might have heard criticism of the older concepts of history, including hints concerning a new outlook. Highly desirable as this preparation for his new position might have been, Cubberley had to face the task with the equipment he had, and he developed his course in the history of education as time, energy, and insight made possible.[50]

Critics of Cubberley's publications in the history of education have questioned the quality of his books as historical works. The criticisms have been concerned with the method of writing history, erroneous views of history, wrong interpretations, easy generalizations, and errors in fact. Certain of these defects may have been due to Cubberley's rapid methods of work. When reading history or studying documents, he quickly perceived a major trend, and became less concerned with minor considerations, at times appearing too quick in drawing conclusions.

---

[48] William W. Brickman, *op. cit.*, p. 121–22.

[49] Quoted from *ibid.*, p. 129.

[50] Jesse B. Sears and Adin D. Henderson, *Cubberley of Stanford: And His Contribution to American Education*. Stanford, Calif.: Stanford University Press, 1957. p. 104–5.

Although Cubberley never overcame completely his lack of technical training in historical method and based much of his writing upon secondary sources, he had extensive acquaintance with a wide range of original papers, records, and documents. His contribution to the history of education has been evaluated by an enthusiastic colleague as follows:[51]

To have begun with no technical preparation and to have written so much and to so many different purposes; to have written in terms of an essentially new idea of the task in hand; to have chosen as the aims of his major works two ultimate values that could scarcely fail to glorify as well as increase the efficiency of teaching; to have organized so massive an amount of fact in a clear and simple manner; to have depicted education as going hand in hand with politics, religion, industry, recreation, and family life—all building themselves separately and yet together and moving forward in terms of their great common values of freedom and democracy; all this is an achievement of high order. In contrast to this the shortcomings of his writings seem small and one cannot be surprised that his work was well received and that it was and is widely influential.

To cite other examples of the methods of different observers, Major William Jackson was the official secretary of the Federal Convention of 1787, but his minutes were little more than brief, disorderly notes. James Madison was an unofficial reporter, but he was an intelligent and careful eye witness. The conditions were therefore almost ideal for observation, note-taking, and transcription of his complete notes, with the result that posterity has depended on Madison's reporting of the Convention. Francis Parkman, in writing the narrative of the Anglo-French conflict for control of North America, during his vacations went on long walks through the woods to trace the battle lines and took trips to the West to gather information concerning the Indians. Because of the fallibility of memory, an entry in a careful diary or similar source by a reputable person probably is more accurate than recollection. John Quincy Adams in 1844 based on his notable diary the assertion that Andrew Jackson, a quarter of a century earlier, had approved relinquishment of the claim of the United States to Texas, whereas Jackson's denial was based only on memory.

Bias and Prejudice

A competent observer may know the truth, but for reasons of bias or prejudice may report the evidence only in part or in distorted form. The tests of truthfulness and honesty include evaluation of the observer's characteristics and statements in relation to personal or vested interest, race, nation, party, region, sect, social level, economic group, profession, conventional formulas rather than true sentiments, vanity or boasting,

[51] Quoted from *ibid.*, p. 123–26.

attempt to please some individual or group, exaggerations, and embellishments.

An example[52] of bias may be found in the writing of an author opposed to current tendencies in American higher education, especially at the graduate level. Flexner criticized the theses and dissertations accepted at certain institutions, confining himself to mention of the titles, without attempting to analyze the content of a sampling of such graduate studies. Flexner made certain comparisons with the dissertations completed in Germany, and apparently was still under the impression that German universities are superior institutions where trivial subjects are never accepted as doctoral dissertations and where these graduate investigations are models of scientific writing. Available evidence has indicated that many German dissertations reveal immature thinking, a superficial grasp of the problem, amateurish method of research, and other inadequacies. Flexner's approach discloses his bias in favor of German higher education and his lack of impartiality in analyzing American higher education.

As an example of the influence of family loyalty, readers of the *Education* will recall that Henry Adams' treatment of his distinguished ancestors is both favorable and respectful:

> To be sure the ironic questions are present in these earlier chapters of the *Education* but the edges are blunted by his willingness to admit the greatness of his grandfather—overpowering as it was to a mere boy. To Adams, the family heritage was symbolized in the "law of Resistance; of Truth, of Duty, and of Freedom" and, if these represented an eighteenth-century system of order no longer applicable to the nineteenth and twentieth centuries, they had made for a distinguished family tradition of political responsibility. Evidence for this respect and regard for his family can be abundantly confirmed in the letters of Henry Adams. Family loyalty, whether Adams was willing to admit it or not, was a personal solution that he always clung to in the face of his "problem" of finding direction through space, of running order through chaos.

> But family tradition was more than a mere legend for Adams; it was an intellectual experience as well. From his boyhood, he had lived under the spell of his grandfather's and great-grandfather's writings. As a boy, he had helped his father with the proofs of an edition of the work of John Adams. By constant use of the magnificent Adams family library he became familiar with the papers of John Quincy Adams. At one time, when trying to find some occupation for himself after graduation from Harvard, he toyed with the idea of editing the works of J. Q. Adams, but he abandoned the project because he thought "it is not in me to do them justice"—a judgment which betrays respect and reverence as well as his own insecurity and indecision at the time. Nevertheless, it is important to remember that Henry Adams' first

[52] William W. Brickman, *op. cit.*, p. 177–78.
Abraham Flexner, *Universities: American, English, German.* New York: Oxford University Press, 1930. ix + 381 p.

significant publication in the field of American history, *Documents Relating to New England Federalism, 1800-1815,* was prepared in order to defend the reputation of his grandfather and to provide documentary evidence for the high motives of John Quincy Adams in his desertion of the Federalist party in 1807. The publication of the *Documents* in 1877 began the painstaking spadework of investigation that was to result in the publication of the nine-volume *History* more than a decade later.[53]

A number of specific historical works may be cited as illustrations of the effect of bias, even in the writing and interpretation of able historians:

Livy, in his patriotic ardor, does less than justice to the enemies of Rome. Matthew Paris, a leading medieval chronicler, is influenced by anti-papal prejudice. Macaulay is notoriously unfair to the anti-Whigs. From his ultra-democratic viewpoint, Grote could see no good in the Greek "tyrants." A recent reissue of his *History of Greece,* admittedly a work of value, omits the chapter on the "Tyrants" as a distortion of the facts. Froude's *History of England* is saturated with anti-Catholic feeling. Gardiner's *History of the Commonwealth* has not escaped the imputation of bias in favor of the Cromwellians. Bancroft's exaggerated nationalism often results in one-sided presentation of the facts. Parkman's stirring narratives of the French-English conflict in North America are out of focus as a result of his preoccupation with Anglo-Saxon "superiority." Mommsen's *History of Rome* has its patent prejudices, in regard to Cicero. Motley's *Rise of the Dutch Republic* is unfair to the Spanish actors in the drama. Rhodes' *History of the United States* betrays animus against certain political figures, against Douglas, for instance, while the accuracy of the picture he draws of slavery has been called into question. Osgood's *American Colonies* has been charged with prejudice against the Quakers. Von Holst, in his *Constitutional and Political History of the United States,* is against the South.[54]

Other illustrations of bias or prejudice in historical writing may be summarized briefly. Thomas Carlyle was essentially a moralist, who sometimes was tempted to suppress evidence in favor of artistic effect. Francis Bacon altered both literary and documentary sources, in keeping with his purpose, although his intentions were not deliberately to deceive but to clarify and interpret by including his own opinions. The bias of Thomas Macaulay assumed the form of a great pride in England and a theme of English superiority that appealed to national patriotism. Cotton Mather's superstition is revealed when he says, "Molestations from evil spirits have so abounded in this country, that I question whether any one town has been free from sad examples of them.[55]

[53] Quoted from H. Stuart Hughes, *op. cit.,* p. 50.
[54] Quoted from Gilbert J. Garraghan, *op. cit.,* p. 50.
[55] Michael Kraus, *op. cit.,* p. 35.

Brave man though he was, John Smith's vanity and boastfulness led him to write glowing accounts of his own achievements, picturing himself always a match for the Indians, except where great odds overcame him. Parson Weems glorified the name of George Washington by assigning to a great but quite human character the traits of almost superhuman nobility. The bias or prejudice of John Quincy Adams, in accusing Thomas Jefferson of loose morals, of being a free thinker (irreligious and probably atheistic), of displaying selfishness in trying to gratify ambition, of duplicity, of treachery to superiors and friends, and of deliberate falsehood, was occasioned by Adams' faulty memory at the age of sixty-three, by political differences, and by his New England attitude toward cards, horse racing, and mere amusement. George Bancroft's bias was in the form of an exaggerated patriotism; he characterized the American Revolution as a crusade of virtuous and disinterested patriots on behalf of the liberties of civilization, and described the Constitution as the product of a group of unique mental giants, never before equaled and not to be matched in the future.

Even the great German historian, Leopold von Ranke, was prejudiced in his enthusiasm for Luther, the Hohenzollerns, and Prussia, although he is customarily considered the founder of the objective school. Ranke said in his first book, when he was not yet thirty years of age, that he did not presume, as did most historians, to sit in judgment on the past, and only wished to show "what had really happened." Although Ranke is representative of the period that instituted the modern study of history, and sought to be critical, colorless, and new, we do meet the mind of Ranke, or his mind is revealed, in his works. Ranke was not successful in achieving his goal—that of repressing the poet, the patriot, the religious or political partisan—of sustaining no cause, of banishing himself from his books, and of writing nothing that would gratify his own feelings or disclose his private convictions. Among other things, there was the effect of the mystical religious faith that he drew from his Lutheran family tradition; he experienced not merely an aesthetic enjoyment of the ever-varying scene, but a view of God's government as well.[56]

Macaulay's style and method of conducting an argument were those of the orator who enjoys the clash and thrust of debate. Sometimes in the heat of debate, while remaining master of his argumentative powers, Macaulay was inclined to be swept along by antagonism and to lose respect for the personality of his opponent. At times certain characteristics of his mind or temperament seemed to be projected into his style in the form of straight, unhesitating phrasing, of surprising effect, and of

[56] Pieter Geyl, *From Ranke to Toynbee:* Five Lectures on Historians and Historiographical Problems. Northampton, Mass.: Smith College Studies in History, 1952. p. 3–10.

sharp, dramatic contrasts. Macaulay "viewed with the eye of the zealot for public virtues and for progress and for the cause of liberty"; he could approve and admire, as well as detest and denounce, but seemed incapable of establishing "disinterested" contact with a human being in historic or even literary personages.[57]

A fascinating account of "detective" work to check the story concerning Amala and Kamala, supposedly nurtured by wolves in India, is given by an American sociologist and a Calcutta anthropologist, with the setting for their application of the techniques of criticism in India and with grave doubts as to the credibility of the document written by the eyewitness.[58]

In summary, the historian's values and activities may be influenced by professional standards, the institutional needs of his employer and departmental or college jurisdiction over course content for teaching purposes, availability of archives and collections of documents, attitudes and interests of the great public audience, which in one way or another pays the bills, and the culture in which the historian lives, together with the psychological and institutional purposes served by history in this social setting. Pertinent questions of objectivity need to be answered through careful study. Are personal and environmental influences almost entirely offset by rigorous professional training? On the other hand, are biases indeed inevitable and even desirable?[59]

HISTORICAL WRITING: COMPOSITION[60]

The writing of history or historical composition is the work of synthesis that follows the evaluation and criticism of sources, including the mechanical problem of documentation, the logical problem of relative importance and arrangement of topics, and the theoretical or philosophical problem of interpretation. Since documentation is discussed in another chapter of this book, such details need not be repeated here, and we will turn to problems of organization and interpretation.

[57] *Ibid.*, p. 28–30.
[58] William F. Ogburn and Nirmal K. Bose, "On the Trail of the Wolf-Children." *Genetic Psychology Monographs* 60: 117–93; August 1959.
A. L. Gesell, *Wolf-Child and Human Child*. New York: Harper & Brothers, 1941. xvi + 107 p.
J. A. L. Singh and R. M. Zingg, *Wolf-Children and Feral Man*. New York: Harper & Brothers, 1943. 365 + xii p.
[59] Corinne L. Gilb, "Should We Learn More About Ourselves?" *American Historical Review* 66: 987–93; July 1961.
[60] Herman Ausubel, *op. cit.*, p. 148–88.
Jacques Barzun and Henry F. Graff, *op. cit.*, 115–354.
William W. Brickman, *op. cit.*, p. 161–90, 201–15.
Homer C. Hockett, *op. cit.*, p. 143–80, 189–254.
Gilbert J. Garraghan, *op. cit.*, p. 321–49, 381–95.
Allan Nevins, *op. cit.*, p. 355.

Although general principles of organization and presentation of materials in the technical report have been outlined in another chapter, it is appropriate at this time to make specific applications to historiography. Older types of historical writing and history textbooks usually followed a chronological arrangement of materials in the form of an almanac or calendar of dates, facts, events, and names, with the chapters covering a relatively short time span, sometimes a period of several years or even a few months. A common arrangement was to mark off the chapters in terms of presidential administrations.

A topical or thematic grouping of historical materials has been recommended as a functional organization to meet the criticism that older histories of education and courses in this field were a mass of comparatively unrelated facts, with little consideration of the pertinent social forces and of the activities and problems of schools and professional workers. Good history of education observes the conditions of good storytelling, shows purpose and meaning, and provides background for better understanding of current educational problems. A history of education that adopts a functional basis of organization, in the form of major problems or areas of contemporary education, includes such chapters as: the aim, method, and curriculum of education; elementary, secondary, and higher education; and the political, psychological, and philosophical bases of education.[61] Many historians of today regard overemphasis on facts as a major obstacle to good history and are convinced that facts must be selected for the sake of clarity and conciseness, with the needs of the present serving as an important criterion in the selection or omission of facts. Macaulay regarded facts in isolation as the dross of history (worthless matter when separated from meaning).

Philosophies and Schools of Interpretation

History is rewritten whenever discovery of new sources and helpful reinterpretation of old data make it possible to correct the errors and inadequacies of existing history. In applying new social theory or evidence, it is essential to give appropriate emphasis to all causal factors or forces in a synthetic or eclectic treatment of data, rather than to follow narrowly a single school of interpretation that might exclude some part of the evidence. As an example of historical reinterpretation, during the latter part of the past century social and economic conditions began to receive the attention of historians, as compared with earlier preoccupation with political and military affairs.

[61] John S. Brubacher, *A History of the Problems of Education*. New York: McGraw-Hill Book Co., 1947. 688 p.

Three new fields of historical reinterpretation have been suggested, as occasioned by certain developments:[62]

1. The end of the age of free and effective security in America
2. The end of an age of mass warfare
3. The end of the age of European hegemony or preponderant authority, sometimes referred to as the political collapse of Europe.

Illustrative general theories or philosophies of historical interpretation may be summarized briefly. These philosophies of history are broader in scope than the specific schools of interpretation, do not lend themselves readily to pragmatic tests of their workability, and have not often touched the larger or more comprehensive works in history:[63]

1. The Greek and Roman historians viewed Fate as controlling human destiny.
2. The Christian philosophy of history was based on the dominant ideas of divine concern for mankind and of changes in history as slowly tending toward the progress and universality of the true religion.
3. According to Voltaire's rationalistic theory, the events of history were attributable not to design but to chance or fortuity.
4. Hegel's doctrine was that every epoch in history was inspired and dominated by some specific idea.
5. The Darwinian theory of evolution, as applied to history, means that in social institutions, as well as in the animal kingdom, the rule of the survival of the fittest applies and that acquired characteristics of society are passed on to succeeding generations.
6. The Marxian philosophy applied to history is that the mode of production in economic life primarily determines the general character of the social, political, and cultural processes of life, which shift as the economic foundation changes.
7. Since the World War of 1914-18 a rhythm-philosophy explains history as a series of pulsations, the swing and counter-swing of the pendulum, a series of cycles of summer-fall-winter-spring seasons, with the present period representing a very bleak season.

Both the reader and the writer of history are interested more in the special interpretations or schools of history, as illustrated below, than in the broad philosophies of history. The more limited scope of a specific interpretation of historical evidence permits a pragmatic test of the explanatory concept, whereas it requires many centuries to test such a broad theory as the cycle or evolutionary philosophy of history. It should be recognized that the specific schools of interpretation are not mutually

[62] C. V. Woodward, "The Age of Reinterpretation." *American Historical Review* 66: 1–19; October 1960.
[63] Allan Nevins, *op. cit.*, p. 240–50.
Harry E. Barnes, *A History of Historical Writing*. Norman: University of Oklahoma Press, 1937. p. 42–43, 147–206, 330–35.

exclusive, but serve supplementary purposes, and that many of our best historical works are eclectic or synthetic in interpretation rather than directly related to any special interpretation or school of thought:[64]

1. The personal, biographical, or "great-man" theory is the best known and has been emphasized most by the conventional historians. It holds that the great personalities of history are the main causative factors in historical development, and that history is collective biography.

2. The spiritual or idealistic interpretation of history is found in the discovery of spiritual forces cooperating with geographic and economic factors to produce truly personal conditions, and in human activities finding expression in social relations for the more complete subjection of physical nature to human welfare.

3. The scientific and technological theory views human progress as directly correlated with the advances in natural science and technology, emphasizing that the prevailing state of scientific knowledge and its technical interpretation will determine the existing modes of economic life and activities.

4. The economic school of historical interpretation contends that the prevailing type of economic institutions and processes in society will, in a large measure, determine the nature of the resulting social institutions and culture.

5. The geographical theory holds that the actions of man cannot be fully understood or adequately described when divorced from their physical setting.

6. Sociological interpretation of history draws from sociology (the science of the life and activities of men in groups) a knowledge of both the causes and the results of group life as the basis for a generalized view of the social process and of social causation.

7. The relatively recent synthetic, eclectic, pluralistic, or "collective psychological" theory is considered the most inclusive and most important type of historical interpretation, holding that no single category of causes is sufficient to explain all phases and periods of historical development, and that only the collective psychology of any period is strong enough to dominate the attendant historical development. Therefore, the new history is necessarily eclectic in approach and interpretation in contrast to the older, conventional history which overstresses political causation or holds that historical development is entirely arbitrary.

To cite examples[65] of how certain schools of history interpret historical development, Charles A. Beard rewrote, in terms of economic forces, the history of American colonization, American expansion, the

---

[64] Harry E. Barnes, *op. cit.*, p. 337–60.
Allan Nevins, *op. cit.*, p. 265–71.
[65] Herman Ausubel, *op. cit.*, 373 p.
Herman Ausubel, J. Bartlet Brebner, and Erling M. Hunt, Editors, *Some Modern Historians of Britain:* Essays in Honor of R. L. Schuyler. New York: Dryden Press, 1952. 385 p.
Louis R. Gottschalk, *op. cit.*, p. 193–250.
Michael Kraus, *op. cit.*, p. 38–376.
Allan Nevins, *op. cit.*, Chapters 1, 2, 9.

Revolutionary and Civil Wars, and party conflicts, although later he recognized the effects of the heritage, politics, culture, economics, and international filiations of any civilization as interrelated factors in historical causation and interpretation. Ellsworth Huntington developed a geographical theory, stressing the stimulating effect of certain climates, together with rich natural resources and other factors, to explain the rise of great civilizations in such favored countries as the western part of Europe, the British Isles, and eastern North America. If an eclectic or synthetic point of view prevails in historical interpretation, the historian should be familiar with the literature and concepts in many fields of knowledge.

Agatha Christie, in one of her books, *The Moving Finger,* introduces a girl fresh from school and lets her run on about what she thinks of it. "Such a lot of things seem to me such rot. History for instance. Why, it's quite different out of different books!" To which the sensible elderly confidant replies: "That is its real interest."

Let me remind you of this before everything else. History is infinite. It is unfixable. We are trying all the time to reduce past reality to terms of certainty, but all that we can do is to render our own impression of it. No book can reproduce more than a part of that reality, even within the confines of its particular subject; and each book contains something else, which gets mixed up with historical truth in an almost untraceable manner, which does not necessarily turn it into falsehood, but which nevertheless transforms it into something different from the simple truth—I mean the opinion, or the sentiment, or the philosophy of life, of the narrator; or in other words, the personality of the historian.[66]

To cite an example from the field of education, many current writings in the history of education follow a pragmatic philosophy of history in an attempt to prove that many specific proposals of progressive education are in step with history and that the pragmatic temper is in keeping with the American pattern, even as early as colonial days. This new history of education is functional in focusing on the practical concerns of school policies and larger social issues (for example, educational opportunity, control, and policy), frequently drawing methodological models from anthropology, sociology, psychology, and political theory.[67]

Hypothesis, Theme, Causation, Perspective[68]

Examples of Hypotheses. Since an earlier chapter has dealt with the formulation and testing of hypotheses, only a few examples from history

[66] Quoted from Pieter Geyl, *op. cit.,* p. 3.
[67] Bernard Mehl, "History of Education," in "The Philosophical and Social Framework of Education." *Review of Educational Research* 31: 7–19; February 1961.
[68] Gilbert J. Garraghan, *op. cit.,* p. 350–67.
Louis R. Gottschalk, *op. cit.,* p. 209–50.
Allan Nevins, *op. cit.,* p. 214–36, 271–75, 352–53.

will be given at this time. Channing formulated and tested several hypotheses in seeking to determine why the Confederacy collapsed in April, 1865, with unexpected speed and completeness. He asked whether the breakdown was the result of military defeat, dearth of military supplies, starving conditions of the soldiers and people, or disintegration of southern morale and the despair of the people. Channing accepted the last hypothesis, although it is not satisfactory, since it does not tell us why morale collapsed. Multiple causation probably is the correct explanation, and Channing's interpretation would have been stronger and sounder had he assigned to each causal factor its proportionate weight. Carlyle's theory or hypothesis of historical interpretation was that great men are the major causal factors in important events, but he overlooked the effect of challenging times or crises in producing the powerful leader or hero. The hypotheses explaining the fall of the Roman Empire range from that of Gibbon on the refusal of the Roman soldiers to wear armour, to moral corruption, overtaxation, overpopulation, disintegration of the Roman army through staffing with barbarian officers, soil exhaustion, and "climatic pulsations."

Central Theme or Thesis. Once the hypothesis has been tested satisfactorily against the evidence, it may become a central thesis, unifying theme, or principle of interpretation. Such a central theme may prove helpful in gathering evidence and in interpretation, although we must be on guard against forcing the data into some particular frame of reference. Charles A. Beard advanced a thesis of economic determinism, showing in his interpretation of the United States Constitution a direct relationship between the holders of the government debt and a strong central government that would pay it off, although later he recognized the influence of other causal factors.

Frederick J. Turner's thesis concerning the effect of the frontier upon American life and character has influenced historical interpretation, as well as literary, social, and political thought, although needed correctives later were applied to his explanatory thesis. When an author writes of the West and the frontier, the question naturally arises as to his relation to Turner. It is often said that Webb belongs to the Turner school, but Webb himself speaks otherwise:

No one respects Turner more than I, and no one is less patient with the critics who take exception to some detail in Turner and argue from this small base that his thesis is wrong. There are few so foolish as to say that the existence of a vast body of free land would not have some effects on the habits, customs, and institutions of those who had access to it. That is essentially what Turner said in his essay about the United States, and that is what I said in *The Great Frontier* about Western European civilization. Though my canvas was bigger than Turner's, and my span of time a century longer, the thesis is the same. Turner looked at a fragment of the frontier; I tried to look at the whole thing. If Turner's thesis is true, then mine is true; if his is a fallacy, then mine is also fallacious. Since Turner was first in time and I a generation later, I will probably always be counted as a part of the Turner school. And this I accept as an honor.

The question that may arise is this: Am I in the frontier school because Turner led me there or because I stumbled into it independently? I think I stumbled in. I cannot prove this, but I would like to submit the evidence of my assumption.

As already stated, I never had a course in western history. I never saw Turner. At the time I began writing *The Great Plains* I had never read the Turner essay and I refrained from reading it until I had completed the study. There is little in Turner's writing to suggest that he anticipated the idea developed in *The Great Plains*. The frontier that he knew was east of the Mississippi.[69]

Toynbee cites the history of the settlement of the North American continent to support his central thesis, namely, that it is difficulties or obstacles which lead to the flowering out of a civilization. He has labeled this notion by the striking phrase, Challenge and Response:

Challenge and Response is indeed the central theme of Toynbee's philosophy of history. To him the interest of the study of humanity lies in the indomitable quality of the spirit of man. The significance, the motive forces, the causation—to him it must all be spiritual. The lot of man is cast in a material world, but Toynbee sees his relations with the material as a struggle. Man's *significant* relations at least—his emergence into civilization, his adventures and his triumphs as a civilized being, everything that distinguishes him from the animals and from the barbarians and makes him the protagonist of what we call History—all this can never be *deduced from* the material world; it can be related to the material world only in terms of opposition, and of victory.

A striking idea! And often an illuminating one. But the point that I want to make is that Toynbee has driven it to extremes, and that the system with which he has tried to bolster it up obscures the process of history as much as the idea can occasionally illumine it.[70]

To comment further on the historical conception of a trend or central theme, it is regarded by historians as one of the most characteristic and basic of all the concepts of history:

The discernment of temporal patterns of change is what the historian regards as his main business. He observes and describes unique events, and at the same time he endeavors to establish their relation to one another. If we

[69] Quoted from Walter P. Webb, "History as High Adventure." *American Historical Review* 64: 265–81; January 1959.

[70] Quoted from Pieter Geyl, *op. cit.*, p. 68–69.

took from him such ideas as growth and decay, change and persistence, increase and decrease, rise and fall, he would be left with little to say.

There is no question but that the concept of a trend is highly abstract. One must conceptualize concrete actuality in order to perceive a trend. It is not the kind of thing that can be kicked or pointed at. When one speaks of a trend in temperature, there is nothing one can hold in one's hand and examine. Instead one must first create some measuring device, then read it at particular moments in time, and finally make a comparison of a number of readings over a given period of time. In the field of physics the meaning of a trend can be defined only in terms of some such set of operations.

In history, however, the operations are often forgotten, and trends seem to take on a separate existence of their own above and beyond the particular events which go to make them up. Thus, students in history courses are encouraged to recognize trends. They are sometimes told that factual materials are relatively unimportant; instead of memorizing these, they are instructed to concentrate on the larger currents in human affairs and tendencies of society. Trends are spoken of as "inevitable" and "irresistible." They sweep individuals along willy-nilly, and determine the course of their lives. Personalities like Napoleon's or Hitler's are said to be shaded by the trends of the age. Ultimately one approaches the conclusion (acceptable to Plato, but absurd to modern science) that the abstract determines the concrete, that the Form or the Idea is the only reality.

Few historians consciously subscribe to this conclusion. If you do not accept it (if, that is, you have some doubt that a trend belongs to a higher order of existence, a kind of supernature with an independent being of its own), then the meaning of a trend is to be determined by what a historian does. And he may do one of two things. Either he performs the sorts of operations that a physicist does in dealing with temperature trends, or he is making a literary, metaphorical, comparison.[71]

Causation. The earlier historians frequently associated trivial causes or supernatural explanations with major events and important social changes. It was said that the cackling of geese and the bite of an asp enabled Rome to develop unhindered her great power and influence. The older historians believed that the cause of the Trojan War was a quarrel over a beautiful woman, Helen of Troy. It has been said that, after the Norsemen had settled somewhere near the New England coast in 1003-4, the bellowing of a bull frightened the natives, causing them to give battle. The Norsemen returned to their own country, and therefore the bellowing of a Norse bull delayed the settlement of America for 500 years.

To cite another example of causation, on the morning of June 28, 1914, Europe was still enjoying the longest reign of peace she had known in modern times, with no major war for 43 years. At noon that day, in Sarajevo, an undersized high-school student, Gavrilo Princip, assassinated

[71] Quoted from H. Stuart Hughes, *op. cit.*, p. 314–17.

Archduke Franz Ferdinand, heir to the Austrian throne, and his morganatic wife. These two shots resulted in one of history's most consequential murders and set in motion a train of events that started World War I a few weeks later, with millions of men engaged. If the two shots themselves are considered only as "sparks" that ignited the world-wide holocaust, there remains the question of the part played by a number of other factors: immediate diplomatic events, imperial rivalries of longer standing, intensification of nationalism, or development of capitalism to a culminating stage.

It is argued by some scholars that important, crucial events in history are often determined by chance, by unpredictable events that may seem trivial in themselves:

> To those who are interested in the psychology of the history of science, culture, and thought, Handlin's *Chance or Destiny* provides the occasion to reread the similar discussion in Tolstoy's *War and Peace* (1869), for the two discussions, if you take the trouble to read them both on the same afternoon, are surprisingly alike. It is true that Tolstoy makes more of the inscrutable forces of History that enslave uncomprehending kings and that promote the trivial royal intentions into the service of History's indiscernible designs, but Handlin too recognizes the existence of great trends like industrialization and democratization, trends that advance themselves—perhaps by some kind of positive feedback—and are insusceptible to influence by the individual person.
>
> The main undertaking of Handlin's book is to show that important crucial events in history are often determined by chance, by unpredictable events that are apt to seem trivial in themselves. Cornwallis surrendered because his attempt to withdraw his army from Yorktown was ruined by a sudden storm that wrecked many of his boats and left his army divided across the York River. But for the storm, would the U. S. A. now be a Dominion? Handlin does not say that, yet the course of American history in 1781 would have been greatly changed but for the storm. The Revolution could have failed. Not all revolutions succeed. . . .
>
> Lieutenant Commander Schweiger, commanding the German submarine U-20, was returning to his home port on May 7, 1915, discouraged at his lack of successes, when he saw through his periscope a large vessel in British waters which the Germans had proscribed. He let go a torpedo, and, as the vessel went down stern-first, he could just make out the name on the bow: *Lusitania.* And so—is or isn't *so* the right word here?—the United States came into that war.
>
> The United States Navy thought Pearl Harbor impregnable. They were prepared for attack anywhere else in the Pacific. And the Japanese, following out Admiral Tojo's perilous plan on December 7, 1941, were anything but confident. Their slim chance succeeded and the United States then was in another war. What if the majority opinion about Pearl Harbor's being impregnable, an opinion widely held in Japan too, had been right? . . .

You can find chance operating in scientific discovery and in the happy insight that leads to an important discovery, and one argument for basic research is founded on the unpredictability of the useful applications of fundamental laws; nevertheless, given motivation, there is a rational orderedness to scientific discovery that introduces into the historical process a predictability that is hindered or sped up by chance events but is not ordinarily completely stalled. This is why we speak of the Zeitgeist when we seek a concept to explain synchronous independent identical discoveries, inventions, and insights. History lords it over the scientist because history—Tolstoy's History, Handlin's Destiny —is the culture, the total accumulation of fact and value available to the individual scholar. By them is he influenced without his knowing how or how much. Because of them his contribution becomes a "next step," and often it is in spite of them that the "next step" is the unpredictable one of creative originality. So is originality necessarily chance? It can be. Remember Fermat's theorem that no one else ever proved, the theorem with the lost proof? But what about an originality's happening twice in the same year? What about Alfred Russell Wallace's and Charles Darwin's formulating the theory of natural selection independently by 1858? Adams' and Leverrier's independent discoveries of the planet Neptune in 1845? Gray's and Bell's invention of the telephone in 1876? . . .

It is a good thing to have the case for the operation of chance in history, for unpredictability, made so clearly and irrefutably. The notion of a Zeitgeist as imperative Destiny ought to be scotched. Progress is what happens, usually what has happened, as Handlin says; its direction is never certain or clear until it has entered the past. But after—with Handlin's help—you have got rid of superstitions about the inevitability of history and have fully accepted the fact that unpredictable chance may in important ways intervene in the causal nexus, there still remain the various problems as to how the total mass of available fact and value, too complex ever to be specified, influences and determines human conduct and thought, discovery and originality, governed, it seems at times, by some positive feedback that makes their course appear purposive because it is consistent and not wholly unpredictable.[72]

Perspective. Sound historical perspective in using evidence and in interpretation enables us to evaluate events and personages, distant in time or space, in terms of the contemporaneous standards and conditions then prevailing rather than in comparison with our present-day time and culture. The cruelties of the Inquisition, for example, when compared with the practices of the Middle Ages, are believed milder than the provisions of the contemporaneous civil law, although such excesses seem inhuman in the perspective of twentieth century standards. Accurate evaluation and interpretation of the personal hygiene of a people, community, or

[72] Quoted from review by E. G. Boring, *Contemporary Psychology* 2: 234–35; September 1957, of Oscar Handlin, *Chance or Destiny:* Turning Points in American History. Boston: Little, Brown & Co., 1955. 220 p.

individual of a century ago must be done in relation to the general absence of central plumbing and heating at that time. Children in the elementary school gradually gain space and time perspective through early experience with home geography and with relatively recent historical materials of the home community.

The judgments of educational historians are often summary, sometimes contradictory, and change with time. Thomas Davidson, who knew John Dewey, did not mention him in *A History of Education* (1900), while Paul Monroe in 1905 and Ellwood P. Cubberley in 1920 emphasized the great contribution of Dewey to education.[73]

Whitehead has commented on the importance of historical perspective in understanding the contributions of philosophers:[74]

> The few first-rate philosophic minds need to be understood in relation to the times in which they lived and thought, and this is precisely what is not done. A philosopher of imposing stature doesn't think in a vacuum. Even his most abstract ideas are, to some extent, conditioned by what is or is not known in the time when he lives. What are the social habits around him, what are the emotional responses, what do people consider important, what are the leading ideas in religion and statesmanship?

Whitehead has been critical of historians who lack historical perspective:[75]

> The more history I read, the less I think of historians. Most of them strike me as men who presume to write authoritatively about events which they are not qualified to understand. Or else they accept the official documents of an epoch at their full value, omitting to reflect that its real significance lay in the emotional atmosphere which activated its people and the general ideas under whose sway they lived. I make two exceptions: Gibbon is one and the other is Thucydides. Gibbon had had some practical experience of managing men in that regiment of his, the Hampshire Volunteers; he had had experience in politics; he had known an interesting set of literary men in London; and then just at the right moment, he emigrated to Geneva where he came into contact with the point of view of traveled and cultivated people on the Continent. These, with his other qualifications, gave him an equipment for the writing of history which is unique among modern historians. As for the ancient one, Thucydides was a general who had been a part of the life and times which he depicts.

[73] Maxine Greene, "Dewey and American Education, 1894–1920." *School and Society* 87: 381–86; October 10, 1959.
[74] Quoted from *Dialogues of Alfred North Whitehead, op. cit.*, p. 186.
[75] Quoted from *ibid.*, p. 225.

Mastery of Materials, Synthesis, Style[76]

Although the writing of the technical report is treated at some length in another chapter, certain principles of presentation and literary or style aspects of historical writing may be summarized briefly at this time.

Mastery and Synthesis. Effective historical writing shows evidence of scholarship and mastery of materials. Thackeray said of Macaulay that he read twenty books to write a sentence and traveled a hundred miles to produce a line of description. Mastery of sources is always a challenge and frequently has been a burden to able historians. Livy worked with such large masses of data that he was sometimes overwhelmed and not able to synthesize or organize his materials effectively, with consequent contradictions and chronological errors. Leopold von Ranke had great respect for facts and accuracy, and found genuine history more attractive and interesting than romantic fiction, which explains in part the drive that kept him actively at work until the age of ninety-one. Failure to digest and master materials may be due to a false vanity that seeks to impress by including discarded materials and long quotations, a timidity that causes the inclusion of unnecessary data as a protection against possible attack, and lack of literary judgment, which causes some authors to believe that a patchwork of quotations and crude summaries is satisfactory history in contrast to an integrated narrative of events. With the materials carefully digested and classified in a good note system, the working outline emerges as a guide to a chronological or topical arrangement of evidence, or possibly a combination of the two.

Effective Style. Good history applies the principle of progression or moves forward with the story, frequently presenting an explanatory thesis or principle of synthesis as a theory of causation, as discussed earlier in this chapter. The major elements in historical writing should stand out in bold relief, as do the main parts in other technical reports. This means that some data usually must be discarded to attain condensation and to prevent minor details from obscuring the major elements of the narrative. William Douglass, a physician, in his closing chapter on the history of Virginia included a discussion of smallpox; in writing up other colonies also, he sometimes digressed to discuss problems of medicine. In the writing and

[76] Gilbert J. Garraghan, *op. cit.*, p. 396–407.
Michael Kraus, *op. cit.*, p. 147–49.
Allan Nevins, *op. cit.*, Chapter 13.
Chauncey Sanders, *op. cit.*, p. 125–41.
James W. Thompson and Bernard J. Holm, *op. cit.*, Vol. 1, p. 53, 76–77, 83, 120, 539–40, 613, 615, 623; Vol. 2, p. 71, 170, 253, 299, 306–7, 492–93, 633.

editing of biography it is a major problem to deal judiciously with sensational stories about the private life of the subject. Many of these stories are not true, and others are not major elements in the historical narrative; for example, the quite human foibles of George Washington should not be permitted to obscure his greatness of character.

There is every reason for history to possess literary excellence and effective style,[77] although the historian will not fill in missing details through exercise of his imagination, merely for the sake of completeness and a connected story. Good history can be written simply and clearly, without emotional dramatization or exaggerated rhetoric. Modern historians interested in the practical uses of history have emphasized the desirability of effective literary style as a means of commanding the attention of the layman and general reader. Certainly good modern history would not be properly characterized by the ditty written on the fly leaf of a history textbook by a bored pupil more than a century ago:

> If there should be another flood,
> Then to this book I'd fly;
> If all the earth should be submerged
> This book would still be dry.

As to literary style and communication of a message to the democratic public, a recent president of the American Historical Association reminds us that a century ago the literary historians (romantic, unscientific, and eloquent) were widely read, including Prescott, Motley, Bancroft, Parkman, Hallam, Macaulay, Carlyle, and Froude. With the rise of "scientific" history, the subject ceased to be literature and lost much of its influence on democracy. History, however, should continue to reach the general public, since it faces no such communication difficulties as science (with its esoteric discoveries) and painting, poetry, or music (with its conflicts between innovation and conservatism). A good democratic audience expects history to be available in plentiful supply, to a considerable extent written with gusto, largely applicable to current needs, and humanized in interpretation. General readers and writers have said of the academic historian that he overemphasizes fullness of research and accuracy and undervalues insight and imagination. The academic scholar may

[77] Herman Ausubel, *op. cit.*, p. 120–47.
Jacques Barzun and Henry F. Graff, *op. cit.*, p. 229–354.
Louis R. Gottschalk, *op. cit.*, p. 13–19, 181–190.
Homer C. Hockett, *op. cit.*, p. 164–73.
W. T. Hutchinson and Others, *Marcus W. Jernegan Essays in American Historiography.* Chicago: The University of Chicago Press, 1937. p. 21, 35–36, 342, 352–54, 393–94.
Michael Kraus, *op. cit.*, p. 118.
James W. Thompson and Bernard J. Holm, *op. cit.*, Vol. 1, p. 25–26, 32–33, 70–71, 76–77, 86–88, 118; Vol. 2, p. 220–23.

have to teach the lay writer something about precision and depth, while the able lay author teaches the guild historian a great deal about human warmth and literary form. The professional historian has the greater obligation to facilitate this communication and cooperation, since he has the greater resources in the way of academic and professional organizations, libraries and manuscripts, grants, favorable arrangements for work and leisure, basic security, and professional and institutional prestige.[78]

In spite of limitations in the work of the earlier historians, many could express their thoughts with simplicity and power, as quoted below:

Thucydides: "The whole earth is the sepulchre of famous men."

Byron's description of Livy's writing: "Livy's pictured page."

Tacitus: "No hatred is so bitter as that of near relations." "The more corrupt the state, the more numerous the laws."

Augustus: "I found Rome of clay; I leave it to you of marble."

Bancroft, in speaking of the failure of Raleigh to plant a colony: "If America had no English town, it soon had English graves."

On the other hand, Bancroft's rhetoric is extreme in describing the effect of the battles of Lexington and Concord: "With one impulse, the colonies sprung to arms; with one spirit, they pledged themselves to each other 'to be ready for the extreme event.' With one heart, the continent cried: 'Liberty or Death.'"

Hildreth did not often indulge himself in the flowery style in which he described Hamilton, Washington, and Jay: "We have a trio not to be matched, in fact, not to be approached in our history, if indeed, in any other. Of earth-born Titans, as terrible as great, now angels, and now toads and serpents, there are everywhere enough. Of the serene and benign sons of the celestial gods, how few at any time have walked the earth!"

CONCLUDING STATEMENT

Viewed as research, history is an integrated narrative of past events, written in the spirit of critical inquiry. History differs in method from the natural sciences, since it is not a discipline of direct observation or experimentation, but uses reports of observation that cannot be repeated. Good history is both science and art in that sound research is characteristic of all science and effective narration is a form of art. History has close interrelationships with other social fields, including economics, political science, sociology, psychology, comparative education, and educational history in general. Historians of the present century have emphasized that they, too, have answers to current social problems.

[78] Allan Nevins, "Not Capulets, Not Montagus." *American Historical Review* 65: 253–70; January 1960.

The earlier simple categories of sources (including documents and remains or relics) have become more complex and probably will continue to expand in the future. Documents and remains are the most common primary sources, the first witnesses to a fact, although it has been difficult to preserve adequate collections of the physical objects known as relics or remains.

The historian determines the authenticity and meaning of sources through the processes of external and internal criticism. External criticism is concerned with the genuineness of the document as such, while internal criticism determines the meaning and trustworthiness of statements within the document.

Historical composition or synthesis includes the mechanical problem of documentation, the logical problem of relative importance and arrangement of topics, and the theoretical or philosophical problem of interpretation. In regard to style and impartation of message, the increasing use of scientific methods has decreased the influence of history on the public. History should continue to be available and appealing to the general public, incorporating the best of the academic scholar and the lay writer.

As to meaning, since history is a reenactment of the past in the historian's mind, with a continuous process of interaction between the historian and his facts, interpretations necessarily change. The historian is an individual who lives in a society during a particular time, which means that to judge his history it is necessary to study him, as well as his historical and social environment.[79]

With respect to the literature of the history of education, the middle of this century has proved fruitful, including textbooks, guides to historiography, biography, and treatments of geographical or regional areas, school levels, and particular movements or problems in education. Major historical contributions have been made to psychology and related social disciplines. Sharp criticisms, however, have appeared with an underlying assumption that somewhere education took the wrong turn, thus centering the great educational debate in part on America's educational history. As in other periods of crises, when people have turned to their history for guidance and a sense of direction, educational historians are challenged to a sober reappraisal of our educational tradition.[80]

SELECTED REFERENCES

ADAMS, James T., and COLEMAN, R. V., Editors. *Dictionary of American History*. New York: Charles Scribner's Sons, 1940. 5 vols. and index.

[79] Edward H. Carr, *What Is History?* New York: Alfred A. Knopf, 1962. iii + 209 p.

[80] Merle L. Borrowman, "History of Education," *Encyclopedia of Educational Research*. Edited by Chester W. Harris. Third Edition. New York: The Macmillan Co., 1960. p. 661–66.

AUSUBEL, Herman. *Historians and Their Craft:* A Study of the Presidential Addresses of the American Historical Association, 1884-1945. New York: Columbia University Press, 1950. 373 p.

AUSUBEL, Herman, BREBNER, J. Bartlet, and HUNT, Erling M., Editors. *Some Modern Historians of Britain:* Essays in Honor of R. L. Schuyler. New York: Dryden Press, 1952. 385 p.

BAGBY, Philip. *Culture and History:* Prolegomena to the Comparative Study of Civilizations. Berkeley: University of California Press, 1959. ix + 244 p.

BARNES, Harry E. *Historical Sociology:* Its Origins and Development. New York: Philosophical Library, 1948. x + 186 p.

BARNES, Harry E. *A History of Historical Writing.* Norman: University of Oklahoma Press, 1937. xiii + 434 p.

BARNES, Harry E. *An Introduction to the History of Sociology.* Chicago: The University of Chicago Press, 1948. xvi + 960 p.

BARNES, Harry E., and BECKER, Howard. *Social Thought from Lore to Science.* Vols. I and II. Revised Edition. Washington: Harren Press, 1952. 790 + cx p.; viii + 1178 + cxxxv p.

BARRACLOUGH, Geoffrey. *History in a Changing World.* Norman: University of Oklahoma Press, 1956. viii + 246 p.

BECKER, Howard. "Culture Case Study and Greek History: Comparison Viewed Sociologically." *American Sociological Review* 23: 489-504; October 1958.

BELLOT, H. Hale. *American History and American Historians.* Norman: University of Oklahoma Press, 1952. x + 336 p.

BENSON, Lee. "Research Problems in American Political Historiography," in *Common Frontiers of the Social Sciences.* Edited by Mirra Komarovsky. Glencoe, Ill.: Free Press, 1957. p. 113-83.

BENSON, Lee. *Turner and Beard:* American Historical Writing Reconsidered. Glencoe, Ill.: Free Press, 1960. xiii + 241 p.

BLOCH, M. L. B. *Historian's Craft.* New York: Alfred A. Knopf, 1953. 197 p.

BOCK, Kenneth E. *The Acceptance of Histories:* Toward a Perspective for Social Science. Berkeley: University of California Press, 1956. 132 p.

BOGARDUS, Emory S. *The Development of Social Thought.* Fourth Edition. New York: Longmans, Green and Co., 1960. x + 689 p.

BORING, E. G. *A History of Experimental Psychology.* Second Edition. New York: Appleton-Century-Crofts, 1950. xxi + 777 p.

BORROWMAN, Merle L. "History of Education," *Encyclopedia of Educational Research.* Edited by Chester W. Harris. Third Edition. New York: Macmillan Co., 1960. p. 661-66.

BRADFORD, S. C. *Documentation.* Washington: Public Affairs Press, 1948. 146 p.

BRAIDWOOD, Robert J. "Near Eastern Prehistory." *Science* 127: 1419-30; June 20, 1958. (The swing from food-collecting cultures to village-farming communities is still imperfectly understood.)

BRICKMAN, William W. *Guide to Research in Educational History.* New York: New York University Bookstore, 1949. ix + 220 p.

BRUBACHER, John S. *A History of the Problems of Education.* New York: McGraw-Hill Book Co., 1947. 688 p.

BUTTERFIELD, Herbert. *Man on His Past:* The Study of the History of Historical Scholarship. New York: Cambridge University Press, 1955. xvii + 238 p.

CHALLENER, Richard D., and LEE, Maurice, Jr. "History and the Social Sciences: The Problem of Communications." *American Historical Review* 61: 331-38; January 1956.

COHEN, Robert S. "Alternative Interpretations of the History of Science." *Scientific Monthly* 80: 111-16; February 1955.

CURTI, Merle. "Intellectuals and Other People." *American Historical Review* 60: 259-82; January 1955.

CURTI, Merle, Editor. *American Scholarship in the Twentieth Century.* Library of Congress Series in American Civilization. Cambridge: Harvard University Press, 1953. vii + 252 p.

CURTI, Merle, Editor. *Theory and Practice in Historical Study:* A Report of the Committee on Historiography. Social Science Research Council Bulletin No. 54. New York: The Council, 1946. xi + 177 p.

CURTIN, Philip D. "The British Empire and Commonwealth in Recent Historiography." *American Historical Review* 65: 72-91; October 1959.

DAWSON, Christopher. *The Dynamics of World History.* Edited by John J. Mulloy. New York: Sheed and Ward, 1956. xiv + 489 p.

DENNIS, Wayne, Editor. *Readings in the History of Psychology.* New York: Appleton-Century-Crofts, 1948. 598 p.

DIAMOND, Stanley, Editor. *Culture in History.* New York: Columbia University Press for Brandeis University Press, 1960. 1038 p. (Essays in honor of Paul Radin.)

DODSON, Dan W. "Educational Sociology," *Encyclopedia of Educational Research.* Edited by Chester W. Harris. Third Edition. New York: Macmillan Co., 1960. p. 408-11.

DOW, E. W. *Principles of a Note-System for Historical Studies.* New York: Appleton-Century-Crofts, 1924. vi + 124 p.

EDWARDS, Newton. *The Courts and the Public Schools.* Revised Edition. Chicago: The University of Chicago Press, 1955. 622 p.

FELDMAN, A. B. *The Unconscious in History.* New York: Philosophical Library, 1959. 269 p.

FESTINGER, Leon, and KATZ, Daniel, Editors. *Research Methods in the Behavioral Sciences.* New York: Dryden Press, 1953. p. 300-326.

FLUGEL, J. C. *A Hundred Years of Psychology.* Second Edition. London: Gerald Duckworth and Co., 1951. 424 p.

FULLER, B. A. G. *A History of Philosophy.* Third Edition. Revised by Sterling M. McMurrin. New York: Henry Holt and Co., 1955. 618 p.

GARBER, Lee O. *The Yearbook of School Law 1961.* Danville, Ill.: The Interstate, 1961. 249 p.

GARDINER, Patrick, Editor. *Theories of History.* Glencoe, Ill.: Free Press, 1959. 558 p.

GARRAGHAN, Gilbert J. *A Guide to Historical Method.* Edited by Jean Delanglez. New York: Fordham University Press, 1946. xv + 482 + 30 p.

GARRATY, John A. *The Nature of Biography.* New York: Alfred A. Knopf, 1957. xi + 289 + xii p.

GEE, Wilson P. *Social Science Research Methods.* New York: Appleton-Century-Crofts, 1950. p. 280-99.

GEYL, Pieter. *Debates with Historians.* The Hague: Martinus Nijhoff, 1955. vii + 241 p.

GEYL, Pieter. *From Ranke to Toynbee:* Five Lectures on Historians and Historiographical Problems. Northampton, Mass.: Smith College Studies in History, 1952. 80 p.

GEYL, Pieter. *Use and Abuse of History.* New Haven: Yale University Press, 1955. vi + 97 p.

GOOD, Carter V. "Bibliographic Sources," *Encyclopedia of Educational Research.* Third Edition. New York: The Macmillan Co., 1960. p. 143-46.

GOTTSCHALK, Louis R. *Understanding History:* A Primer of Historical Method. New York: Alfred A. Knopf, 1950. 290 p.

GOTTSCHALK, Louis R., KLUCKHOHN, Clyde, and ANGELL, Robert. *The Use of Personal Documents in History, Anthropology, and Sociology.* Social Science Research Council Bulletin No. 53. New York: The Council, 1945. xiv + 243 p.

GUERLAC, Henry E. "Teaching and Research in the History of Science." *North Central Association Quarterly* 33: 242-47; January 1959.

HALPERN, Ben. "History, Sociology, and Contemporary Area Studies." *American Journal of Sociology* 63: 1-10; July 1957.

HANDLIN, Oscar, Compiler. *Harvard Guide to American History.* Cambridge: Harvard University Press, 1954. xxiv + 689 p.

HANS, Nicholas. "The Historical Approach to Comparative Education." *International Review of Education* 5: 299-309; 1959.

HARRIS, Chester W., Editor. *Encyclopedia of Educational Research.* Third Edition. New York: The Macmillan Co., 1960. xxix + 1564 p.

HARTE, Thomas J. "The Use of Parish Records in Social Research." *American Catholic Sociological Review* 19: 113-23; June 1958.

HILLWAY, Tyrus. *Introduction to Research.* Boston: Houghton Mifflin Co., 1956. p. 129-52.

HITSCHMANN, Edward. *Great Men:* Psychoanalytic Studies. New York: International Universities Press, 1956. xiii + 278 p.

HOCKETT, Homer C. *The Critical Method in Historical Research and Writing.* New York: The Macmillan Co., 1955. 368 p.

HOWE, George F., and Others. *Guide to Historical Literature.* New York: The Macmillan Co., 1961. xxxv + 962 p.

HUGHES, H. Stuart, Editor. *Teachers of History:* Essays in Honor of Laurence Bradford Packard. Ithaca, N. Y.: Cornell University Press for Amherst College, 1954. vi + 372 p.

HUGHES, H. Stuart. "The Historian and the Social Scientist." *American Historical Review* 66: 20-46; October 1960.

HULL, L. W. H. *History and Philosophy of Science:* An Introduction. New York: Longmans, Green and Co., 1959. 339 p.

HUNT, Erling M. "Historians and the Teaching of History: A Study in Leadership and Responsibility." *Teachers College Record* 61: 290-300; March 1960.

HUTCHINSON, W. T., and Others. *Marcus W. Jernegan Essays in American Historiography.* Chicago: The University of Chicago Press, 1937. x + 417 p.

IHDE, Aaron J. "Are There Rules for Writing History of Chemistry?" *Scientific Monthly* 81: 183-86; October 1955.

International Bibliography of Historical Sciences, 1926–. New York: H. W. Wilson Co., 1930–. Published annually.

JAMESON, J. Franklin. "The Future Uses of History." *American Historical Review* 65: 61-71; October 1959.

JASPERS, Karl. *Origin and Goal of History.* London: Routledge and Kegan Paul, 1953. 294 p.

JOHNSON, Allen, and MALONE, Dumas, Editors. *Dictionary of American Biography.* New York: Charles Scribner's Sons, 1928-37. 20 vols. and index, plus supplements. Also see *Biography Index:* A Cumulative Index to Biographical Material in Books and Magazines. New York: H. W. Wilson Co., 1946–.

JORDAN, Pascual. *Science and the Course of History.* Translated by Ralph Manheim. New Haven: Yale University Press, 1955. x + 139 p.

KANDEL, I. L. "The Methodology of Comparative Education." *International Review of Education* 5: 270-80; 1959.

KANDEL, I. L. *William Chandler Bagley:* Stalwart Educator. New York: Bureau of Publications, Teachers College, Columbia University, 1961. xii + 131 p.

KAPLAN, Louis, Compiler. *A Bibliography of American Autobiographies.* Madison, Wis.: University of Wisconsin Press, 1961. xii + 372 p.

KRAUS, Michael. *The Writing of American History.* Norman: University of Oklahoma Press, 1953. 387 p.

KRIEGER, Leonard. "The Horizons of History." *American Historical Review* 63: 62-74; October 1957.

LAMPARD, Eric E. "American Historians and the Study of Urbanization." *American Historical Review* 67: 49-61; October 1961.

LANGFELD, Herbert S., and Others, Editors. *A History of Psychology in Autobiography.* Vol. 4. Worcester, Mass.: Clark University Press, 1952. xii + 356 p.

LANGSAM, Walter C. "Truth in History." *Bulletin of the Historical and Philosophical Society of Ohio* 16: 95-103; April 1958.

LAUWERYS, Joseph A. "The Philosophical Approach to Comparative Education." *International Review of Education* 5: 281-98; 1959.

LAZARSFELD, Paul F., STRAYER, Joseph R., and DAVID, Henry. "History and Public Opinion Research: A Debate," in *Common Frontiers of the Social Sciences.* Edited by Mirra Komarovsky. Glencoe, Ill.: Free Press, 1957. p. 242-78.

LONDON, Ivan D., and POLTORATZKY, Nikolai P. "The Problem of Contemporary Analysis in History and Psychology." *Behavioral Science* 3: 269-77; July 1958.

LOWITH, Karl. *Meaning in History:* The Theological Implications of the

Philosophy of History. Chicago: The University of Chicago Press, 1949. ix + 257 p.

MADGE, John. *The Tools of Social Science.* New York: Longmans, Green and Co., 1953. p. 80-116.

MALIN, James C. *On the Nature of History.* Ann Arbor, Mich.: Edwards Brothers, 1954. vii + 290 p.

MASON, S. F. *Main Currents of Scientific Thought:* A History of the Sciences. New York: Abelard-Schuman, 1954. viii + 520 p.

MERTON, Robert K. "Priorities in Scientific Discovery: A Chapter in the Sociology of Science." *American Sociological Review* 22: 635-59; December 1957.

MONTAGU, M. F. Ashley, Editor. *Toynbee and History:* Critical Essays and Reviews. Boston: Porter Sargent, Extending Horizons Books, 1956. xvi + 385 p.

MORRISON, J. Cayce, and Others. "Twenty-five Years of Educational Research." *Review of Educational Research* 26: 199-344; June 1956.

MULTHAUF, Robert P. "European Science Museums." *Science* 128: 512-19; September 5, 1958. (Problems of displaying famous apparatus.)

MURPHY, Gardner. *An Historical Introduction to Modern Psychology.* Revised Edition. New York: Harcourt, Brace and Co., 1949. xiv + 466 p.

NEVINS, Allan. *The Gateway to History.* Boston: D. C. Heath and Co., 1938. vii + 412 p.

NEVINS, Allan. "Not Capulets, Not Montagus." *American Historical Review* 65: 253-70; January 1960.

ODUM, H. W. *American Sociology:* The Story of Sociology in the United States through 1950. New York: Longmans, Green and Co., 1951. vi + 501 p.

RANDALL, John H., Jr. *Nature and Historical Experience:* Essays in Naturalism and in the Theory of History. New York: Columbia University Press, 1958. viii + 326 p.

RATNER, Sidney. "Facts and Values in History." *Teachers College Record* 56: 429-34; May 1955.

REMMLEIN, Madaline K. *The Law of Local Public School Administration.* New York: McGraw-Hill Book Co., 1953. xi + 271 p.

REMMLEIN, Madaline K. *School Law.* New York: McGraw-Hill Book Co., 1950. xxi + 376 p.

REMMLEIN, Madaline K. "Tools and Procedures in School Law Research," *Growing Points in Educational Research.* Washington: American Educational Research Association, 1949. p. 166-75.

RICHEY, Herman G., and Others. "The Philosophical and Social Framework of Education." *Review of Educational Research* 28: 1-76; February 1958. (Urges preparation of scholarly biographies of important educational figures, and historical studies of the development of higher education and of public education in cities.)

ROBACK, A. A. *History of American Psychology.* New York: Library Publishers, 1952. xiv + 426 p.

ROBACK, A. A. *History of Psychology and Psychiatry.* New York: Philosophical Library, 1961. xiii + 422 p.

ROSE, Edward, and FELTON, William. "Experimental Histories of Culture." *American Sociological Review* 20: 383-92; August 1955.

SANDERS, Chauncey. *An Introduction to Research in English Literary History.* New York: The Macmillan Co., 1952. vi + 423 p.

SARTON, George. *A Guide to the History of Science.* Waltham, Mass.: Chronica Botanica Co., 1952. xvii + 316 p.

SCHEVILL, Ferdinand. *Six Historians.* Chicago: The University of Chicago Press, 1956. xv + 200 p.

SCHWEINITZ, Karl De. "Social Values and Social Action—The Intellectual Base as Illustrated in the Study of History." *Social Service Review* 30: 119-31; June 1956.

SCOTT, M. Gladys, Editor. "The Historical Method," *Research Methods in Health, Physical Education, Recreation.* Second Edition. Washington: American Association for Health, Physical Education, and Recreation, 1959. Chapter 14.

SEARS, Jesse B., and HENDERSON, Adin D. *Cubberley of Stanford: And His Contribution to American Education.* Stanford, Calif.: Stanford University Press, 1957. xii + 301 p.

SELIGMAN, Edwin R. A., and JOHNSON, Alvin, Editors. *Encyclopedia of the Social Sciences.* New York: The Macmillan Co., 1930-34. 15 vols.

SHERA, J. H. *Historians, Books, and Libraries.* Cleveland: Western Reserve University Press, 1953. 126 p.

SHINN, R. L. *Christianity and the Problem of History.* New York: Charles Scribner's Sons, 1953. 302 p.

SHOTWELL, J. T. *The History of History.* Vol. 1. New York: Columbia University Press, 1939. xiv + 407 p.

SMITH, B. Othanel. "Philosophy of Education," *Encyclopedia of Educational Research.* Edited by Chester W. Harris. Third Edition. New York: Macmillan Co., 1960. p. 957-63.

The Social Sciences in Historical Study: A Report of the Committee on Historiography. Bulletin 64. New York: Social Science Research Council, 1954. x + 181 p.

SPIELMAN, William C. *Introduction to Sources of American History.* New York: Exposition Press, 1951. 175 p.

STRAUS, William L. "The Great Piltdown Hoax." *Science* 119: 265-69; February 26, 1954.

STRAYER, Joseph R., Editor. *The Interpretation of History.* Princeton: Princeton University Press, 1943. vi + 186 p.

SWABEY, Marie C. *The Judgment of History.* New York: Philosophical Library, 1954. x + 257 p.

THOMPSON, James W., and HOLM, Bernard J. *A History of Historical Writing.* New York: The Macmillan Co., 1942. xvi + 676, x + 674 p. 2 vols.

THORNDIKE, Lynn. "Whatever Was, Was Right." *American Historical Review* 61: 265-83; January 1956.

THRUPP, Syvlia L. "History and Sociology: New Opportunities for Co-operation." *American Journal of Sociology* 63: 11-16; July 1957.

THRUPP, Sylvia L. "What History and Sociology Can Learn from Each Other." *Sociology and Social Research* 41:434-38; July-August 1957.

TOYNBEE, Arnold J. *A Study of History.* London: Oxford University Press, 1934-39. Abridgment by D. C. Somervell, 1947. 6 vols.

VAN DALEN, Deobold B. *Understanding Educational Research:* An Introduction. New York: McGraw-Hill Book Co., 1962. p. 159-83.

WALLIN, J. E. Wallace. *The Odyssey of a Psychologist:* Pioneering Experiences in Special Education, Clinical Psychology, and Mental Hygiene with a Comprehensive Bibliography of the Author's Publications. Wilmington, Del.: The Author, 1955. xvii + 243 p.

WALTERS, Raymond, Jr. "The James Gallatin Diary: A Fraud?" *American Historical Review* 62:878-85; July 1957.

WATSON, ROBERT I. *The Great Psychologists:* From Aristotle to Freud. Philadelphia: J. B. Lippincott Co., 1963. 592 p.

WEBB, Walter P. "History as High Adventure." *American Historical Review* 64: 265-81; January 1959.

WIENER, J. S. *The Piltdown Forgery.* New York: Oxford University Press, 1955, 214 p.

WILKINS, Burleigh T. "Pragmatism as a Theory of Historical Knowledge: John Dewey on the Nature of Historical Inquiry." *American Historical Review* 64: 878-90; July 1959.

WILLEY, Gordon R. "New World Prehistory." *Science* 131: 73-86; January 8, 1960. (The main outlines of the pre-Columbian past are only beginning to emerge.)

WILLIAMS, William A. "A Note on Charles Austin Beard's Search for a General Theory of Causation." *American Historical Review* 62: 59-80; October 1956.

WISH, Harvey. *The American Historian:* A Social-Intellectual History of the Writing of the American Past. New York: Oxford University Press, 1960. ix + 366 p. (A history of historiography in the United States, from colonial times to the present.)

WOLFF, Kurt H. "Sociology and History; Theory and Practice." *American Journal of Sociology* 65: 32-38; July 1959. (A few of the discussions of the relation between sociology and history consider historiography not as science but as practice, and history as the schoolmaster of mankind.)

WOODY, Thomas. "Of History and Its Method." *Journal of Experimental Education* 15: 175-201; March 1947.

YOUNG, Pauline V. *Scientific Social Surveys and Research.* Third Edition. Englewood Cliffs, N.J.: Prentice-Hall, 1956. p. 139-53.

CHAPTER FIVE

Descriptive-Survey, Normative, and Status Studies

This chapter presents a variety of descriptive-survey studies and techniques:[1] investigations emphasizing general description, analysis, or classification; social, community, and school surveys; questionnaire inquiries; interview studies; observational investigations; small-group study or group-behavior analysis; critical-incident technique; action or co-operative research; content analysis of documentary materials; and such survey-appraisal procedures as rating scales, score cards, check list, and index numbers. By delimitation of scope and purpose this book leaves to the numerous specialized volumes the various types of mental measurements and tests of achievement, intelligence, aptitude, and personality, with full recognition that many of these instruments serve data-gathering purposes in descriptive-survey investigations and in experimental, case-clinical, and developmental studies. Under each section the plan of presentation is to identify areas appropriate for descriptive-survey investigation, to characterize the research procedure or data-gathering technique, and to summarize illustrative studies. Many details must remain for treatment in the voluminous survey literature, where it is common for a book of several hundred pages to be devoted to a single data-gathering technique or procedure. In general the processes of enumeration, measurement, and evaluation are left for the textbooks on quantitative methods that deal with statistical methods, measurement, and appraisal.[2]

[1] Carter V. Good and Douglas E. Scates, *Methods of Research:* Educational, Psychological, Sociological. New York: Appleton-Century-Crofts, 1954. p. 255–688.

Claire Selltiz and Others, "Exploratory and Descriptive Studies," *Research Methods in Social Relations.* Revised One-Volume Edition. New York: Henry Holt and Co., 1959. Chapter 3.

Stephen B. Withey, "Survey Research Methods," *Encyclopedia of Educational Research.* Edited by Chester W. Harris. Third Edition. New York: The Macmillan Co., 1960. p. 1447–51.

[2] Oscar K. Buros, *The Fifth Mental Measurements Yearbook.* Highland Park, N.J.: Gryphon Press, 1959. 1292 p.

EDUCATION AND STATUS STUDIES

Although the theory and practice of sample surveys developed in other fields, education has come to make extensive use of this research approach. The large foundation grants of recent years usually require status studies to determine the present position of education in our culture and thus provide a basis for comparison and future evaluation. The major impetus for status studies, utilizing the techniques of sample surveys, has been the need for vital statistics that can be used for social research and determination of public policy; for example, the evaluation of Salk polio vaccine, the Kinsey reports, and the election straw polls. Status studies may be artificially classified into two divisions according to goals.[3]

One type is represented by the operations of the United States Government agencies in conducting status studies on many national social and economic characteristics for the purpose of collecting and publishing vital statistics, with the results made available to government, industry, labor, and educational groups as aids in policy-making. Other specific examples of application of sample-survey techniques to status studies in education include the work of the United States Bureau of the Census, school enrollment, employment of students, summary of government finances, and school districts in the United States, all representing the collection of vital statistics rather than single studies motivated by specific educational problems.

The evaluation trials of the Salk vaccine consitute a specific goal before experimentation and technically should be classified as controlled experimentation, with difficult and technical problems of sampling. Other examples of sample surveys to explore specific educational issues include a survey of college freshmen and sophomores to assess their perceptions of the instructor, the influence of sociocultural characteristics on educational opportunities in public-school instrumental music for eighth-graders, achievement of objectives of elementary-school science by fifth-grade teachers, impact of social stratification on occupational expectations of twelfth-grade boys, attitudes of public-school teachers in a large city toward school and living conditions, and the effect of exposure to mass media of communication on readiness for desegregation among white males eighteen years of age and older.

Another example relates to the performance of our soldiers. *The Lost Divisions* gives a sympathetic account of the difficulties involved in the sudden creation of a mass army and the near chaos that resulted from manpower policies that were considered unrealistic, vacillating, and mis-

[3] Rosedith Sitgreaves and Herbert Solomon, "Research Methods: Status Studies and Sample Surveys," in "Methodology of Educational Research." *Review of Educational Research* 27: 460–70; December 1957.

understood; and includes an analysis of the relation to performance of such background factors as age, marital status, educational level, and race.[4] *Patterns of Performance* integrates the mass statistical data and the clinical materials, and brings in some new approaches to readjustment by interpreting the follow-up data obtained through the Veterans Administration; a chapter on the management of men attempts to spell out the lessons applicable to civilian industry.[5]

CHARACTERISTICS OF DESCRIPTIVE-SURVEY STUDIES

Terminology

The literature and terminology of descriptive-survey investigations include such expressions as descriptive, survey, normative, status, and trend. Descriptive studies may include present facts or current conditions concerning the nature of a group of persons, a number of objects, or a class of events, and may involve the procedures of induction, analysis, classification, enumeration, or measurement. The terms *survey* and *status* suggest the gathering of evidence relating to current conditions. The expression "normative" sometimes is applied to descriptive investigations, because the purpose is to determine the normal or typical condition or practice, as in comparing local test results with a city, state, or national norm (central tendency).[6] In certain other disciplines, such as ethics, philosophy, and religion, norm has another meaning (an ideal or desirable goal). For some studies "normative-survey" is an appropriate label, as illustrated by many investigations involving standardized tests. The expression "comparative method" is too limited for our purposes, since comparison is a part of description, in interpreting survey data as well as evidence gathered by other research techniques. For present purposes the more inclusive term *descriptive-survey studies* seems appropriate.

Purposes and Uses

The purposes of descriptive-survey investigations may be:

1. To secure evidence concerning an existing situation or current condition
2. To identify standards or norms with which to compare present conditions, in order to plan the next step

[4] Eli Ginzberg and Others, *The Ineffective Soldier*. Vol. 1, *The Lost Divisions*. New York: Columbia University Press, 1959. xx + 225 p.

[5] Eli Ginzberg and Others, *Patterns of Performance*. Vol. 3. New York: Columbia University Press, 1959. xix + 340 p.

[6] William B. Schrader, "Norms," *Encyclopedia of Educational Research*. Edited by Chester W. Harris. Third Edition. New York: The Macmillan Co., 1960. p. 922–26.

3. To determine how to take the next step (having determined where we are and where we wish to go).

To cite an example, the more analytical school surveys of recent years tell us not only where we are in a particular school system, but also recommend next steps by way of progress and suggest the methods of reaching the goal of an improved instructional program. This view is one answer to critics of the descriptive-survey method who sometimes say that it is not a forward-looking approach to the solution of educational problems. Certainly adequate survey data in the hands of an investigator of insight can be used for forward-looking purposes.

Another criticism of the descriptive-survey method has been that it is superficial and not worthy of recognition as a research approach to important problems. It should be pointed out that descriptive studies provide essential knowledge about the nature of objects, events, and persons. Descriptive-survey specialists have devised many tools and techniques for gathering evidence, including standard tests and norms, score cards and rating scales, inventories and schedules, and public-opinion polls.

Contributions to Other Types of Research

Descriptive-survey studies have been helpful in contributing to other types of investigation. Survey investigations of present conditions are concerned essentially with history in the making. When survey studies are repeated annually or at other intervals, such cross-section pictures of conditions at different time periods provide the data for historical studies; for example, the annual school census and the United States census make possible historical studies of school enrollment and of the growth of population in the United States. The annual reports of the school superintendent and of the university president furnish material for writing the history of the school system and higher institution.

As in many historical studies, there are occasions in descriptive-survey investigations when it is necessary to rely on verbal data or verbal statements of facts. An example of use of nonquantitative data would be a study of comparative education, involving the educational conditions and practices in another country.[7] A survey of compulsory education in the forty-eight states would require verbal or nonquantitative data concerning the administrative machinery for enforcing the laws, the varying provisions under the state laws, and the different social and

[7] Carter V. Good and Douglas E. Scates, *op. cit.*, p. 583–96.
George F. Kneller, "Comparative Education," and William Van Til, "Intercultural Education," *Encyclopedia of Educational Research.* Edited by Chester W. Harris. Third Edition. New York: The Macmillan Co., 1960. p. 316–22, 718–24.

educational philosophies underlying the state legislation for compulsory education.

For some types of descriptive-survey studies data are available in the files of state departments of education, regional accrediting organizations, and national professional associations, gathered through annual reports and in other ways. If the investigator has recourse to such sources of data, it is important for his questions and the major divisions of his inquiry to correspond with the report blanks that provide the data for state departments of education, regional groups, and national organizations. Use of documentary sources for historical purposes has been discussed in an earlier chapter. Many of the library guides to the published sources are listed in the chapters on library technique and on the historical method. The basic principles of historical criticism apply in dealing with documents for descriptive-survey purposes.

Genetic or growth studies secure measurements of the individual or group at different stages of development and thus may be considered a series of cross sections of growth or a sequence of survey studies separated by time intervals. It is true that genetic or developmental studies usually follow an individual or a group in terms of one or only a few aspects of growth, whereas descriptive-survey investigations usually cover a larger number of traits or characteristics of the group.

In group experimentation, the testing usually done at the beginning to determine current status or to provide the evidence for equating groups, as well as the end testing, may be regarded as forms of survey-testing or measurement, but so used as to serve as an important part of the total experimental procedure.

Analysis and Classification[8]

Many descriptive investigations are highly analytical in character and sometimes have been characterized as "analytical studies," although analysis as a process is present in all types of research. The varieties of analysis in descriptive-survey studies may be illustrated by the buildings of a city school system. The investigator may be interested in a general aspect of the school buildings such as architectural style or in the component parts of the building (classrooms, laboratories, libraries, cafeterias, and other parts of the building). For purposes of an analytical study the interest may be in matters of form, pattern, or organization; for example,

[8] Carter V. Good and Douglas E. Scates, *op. cit.*, p. 277–547.

Claire Selltiz and Others, "Analysis and Interpretation," *Research Methods in Social Relations.* Revised One-Volume Edition. New York: Henry Holt and Co., 1959. Chapter 11.

Nicholas A. Fattu, "Processing of Data," *Encyclopedia of Educational Research.* Edited by Chester W. Harris. Third Edition. New York: The Macmillan Co., 1960. p. 1047–54.

the grouping of the classrooms in relation to fire escapes, cafeteria, or library, or even the seating arrangement of the pupils in particular classrooms. Another type of analytical study in the descriptive-survey area concerns itself with the dynamics of the school, as illustrated by pupil-teacher relationships or teacher-principal relationships.

Classification, the recognition of similarities and differences among experiences, is a basic process in all research, including descriptive-survey studies. Grouping or the forming of categories is conducive to economy of thought. Examples of major classification plans or schemes are the Dewey decimal and Library of Congress systems for cataloguing books, the taxonomy or classification system for animals and plants in the biological sciences, and the periodic table of elements in chemistry and physics.

The primary uses of classification are as follows:

1. To provide codified data, as in dividing the data of the United States census or school census according to sex, age, place of residence, nationality, and the like

2. To form useful classes according to kind, as in classifying and reporting frequencies for the reasons high-school pupils give for leaving school before graduation

3. To afford logical order and system, as in cataloguing books in the library according to a system

4. To develop the meaning of class concepts, as in examining court decisions to determine the meaning of the category "discretionary powers of school boards"

5. To create cases through delimitation, as in studying parent-child relationships by taking different cultures (probably in different parts of the world) as representing varying categories of parental behavior

6. To standardize observations that describe, as in studying the behavior of mothers during their visits to pediatricians working in clinics

7. To select and categorize scale indicators, as in determining that the manner of a particular pediatrician is positive and reassuring (rather than negative, disturbing, and offensive) by counting the number of instances of detailed behavior classified under these different categories.

Criteria for Survey Research

This introductory discussion has not attempted to answer specifically whether the descriptive-survey method is a superior or an inferior approach to problem-solving. The important consideration is whether a particular technique provides answers to significant questions, which means that the descriptive-survey method is best for certain purposes. Many of the illustrative survey studies in this chapter evidence ingenuity in planning, skill in devising techniques, and insight in interpretation of data, thus providing answers to important questions, as well as helpful illustrations of technique and high standards for research. The challenge is to produce survey studies of high quality, in keeping with the criteria[9] listed below:

1. The research report usually has a distinctive form, with definite attention given to describing the methodology, the sources, the population, the trait being studied, and other appropriate methodological or technical details.

2. Presumably original observations are taken.

3. Each step in the work proceeds with meticulous care and with due consideration for the large plan and purpose of the work. The data are verified and evaluated.

4. The data are resolved, or organized into certain more general terms, and are sometimes related to a single, over-all thesis. Certainly the data will be summarized in some form or other, as systematic as possible. What is done with the data is a definite part of the contribution of the study.

5. The background, sensitivity, and general competence of the investigator, as well as the spirit with which he works, are vital elements. As to whether a study must have more or less than the qualities in this list, probably no definite rule can be stated. These qualities vary in degree; various types of research have their own criteria. One should aim, in doing his own research, not at the minimum requirements of research, but at a fairly full-bodied attack.

Limitations of Survey Studies[10]

Although the survey method is an important tool or instrument which has developed greatly during recent years and is valuable for many purposes, it has certain limitations which restrict its use in gathering information on such a field as consumer behavior and its underlying causes:

1. Information that is not known to the respondents cannot be obtained in surveys; for example, annual increases in the value of life insurance reserves (on policies owned by individual families) and amounts of depreciation on houses or automobiles owned would be needed for the sake of an exact determination of amounts saved by individual families. As a general rule, such information is not available to individual policy holders or owners of homes and automobiles.

2. Information that is not salient to the respondents cannot be obtained in a reliable way; for example, most people have not given much thought to the amount of money spent on food or clothing, or on most individual food and clothing items, over a year. Therefore, annual surveys are not reliable or suitable for determining such amounts of expenditures.

3. A request for information that is considered secret should be avoided, as should questioning that appears to check upon the honesty of the respondent.

[9] Quoted from Carter V. Good and Douglas E. Scates, *op. cit.*, p. 271.
[10] Lawrence R. Klein, Editor, *Contributions of Surety Methods to Economics.* New York: Columbia University Press, 1954. p. 60–64.

The success of the interview will be endangered if questions are asked about income from gambling, or about currency hidden in mattresses or locked in safety deposit boxes, or about tax returns already filed.

4. Information about activities shared by a very small proportion of the population cannot be obtained in a reliable way in cross-section surveys; for example, it has been found that over a period of years less than 3 per cent of the population purchased publicly traded common stock, while about 75 per cent of all families paid life-insurance premiums.

5. Data that can be obtained only with very great sampling error do not constitute proper topics of sample surveys; for example, it is impossible to determine through sample surveys what the highest income in a given year was. It is a matter of mere chance whether a small-sample survey finds one, two, several, or no families with an annual income of more than $100,000.

6. Information obtained from a single survey is less reliable than trend data derived from two or more consecutive surveys made by the same methods.

7. Surveys cannot be aimed at obtaining exact quantitative forecasts of things to come; for example, plans to purchase houses or automobiles during the next twelve months.

In survey studies there is real need for cooperation; for some twenty-five years or more public-opinion agencies have developed rather reliable techniques for describing the attitudes of people concerning public affairs. Historians should welcome this method of obtaining information, which heretofore was available only indirectly, if at all, but in reality there has been little collaboration between historians and "pollsters." The difficulty or problem appears to be one of significance, in that the pollsters ask questions for the newspaper headlines rather than to gather data of lasting or permanent significance. The result is that the historian in the main disregards public-opinion surveys, and the pollsters work without the broader view of the historian that would lead to more meaningful studies. This separateness of the two fields of research suggests that the historian and the pollster should cooperate to their mutual benefit and to aid the future historian in interpreting our times.[11]

THE SOCIAL SURVEY[12]

In presenting the types and data-gathering techniques of descriptive-survey studies, we could begin with the larger and more complex investi-

[11] Paul F. Lazarsfeld, Joseph R. Strayer, and Henry David, "History and Public Opinion Research: A Debate," in *Common Frontiers of the Social Sciences*. Edited by Mirra Komarovsky. Glencoe, Ill.: Free Press, 1957. p. 242–78.

[12] Mark Abrams, *Social Surveys and Social Action*. London: William Heinemann, 1951. 153 p.

Leon Festinger and Daniel Katz, Editors, *Research Methods in the Behavioral Sciences*. New York: Dryden Press, 1953. p. 15–97.

Wilson Gee, *Social Research Methods*. New York: Appleton-Century-Crofts, 1950. p. 300–329.

gations (such as the social, community, and school surveys) or with the simpler types of studies. We have chosen to present first the more complex types of surveys, which usually employ a variety of research procedures and instruments (such as questionnaires, interviews, observation, and other techniques).

The social survey is usually a cooperative study of a current social problem, situation, or population within definite geographical limits, ordinarily with some concern for a constructive program of social reform and amelioration.

European Backgrounds

The background of the social-survey movement is found in the European studies of more than a century ago. Frederic Le Play, a French social reformer and economist, used social-survey methods in his monographs on family standards of living, and at the same time combined effectively case-study and statistical procedures:

It was the Revolution of 1848, once more plunging the capital into a bloodbath, that determined Le Play at last to publish the conclusions of his thought as to the true path of peaceable social reform. This initial work took the shape of a folio volume, entitled *Les Ouvriers Européens* and published at the expense of the government in 1855, comprising an introductory essay and detailed case studies of thirty-six families which Le Play had observed in the course of his travels. In the introduction, he set forth the outline of his thought. In brief, he argued that the ultimate unit in the consideration of social problems was not the individual, but the family, and that the key to human happiness was not the freedom of the individual to seek his own pleasure, but the well-being of the family, which alone could afford the individual a complete and secure happiness. The proper method of social reform, he further held, was not a speculative discussion of one or another series of principles dealing with the

---

Tyrus Hillway, *Introduction to Research*. Boston: Houghton Mifflin Co., 1956. p. 175–87.

D. Caradog Jones, *Social Surveys*. London: Hutchinson's University Library, 1949. 232 p.

George Katona, "The Function of Survey Research in Economics," in *Common Frontiers of the Social Sciences*. Edited by Mirra Komarovsky. Glencoe, Ill.: Free Press, 1957. p. 358–75.

John Madge, *The Tools of Social Science*. New York: Longmans, Green and Co., 1953. 332 p.

C. A. Moser, *Survey Methods in Social Investigation*. New York: The Macmillan Co., 1958. Chapters 1–4.

Mildred Parten, *Surveys, Polls, and Samples: Practical Procedures*. New York: Harper & Brothers, 1950. p. 1–23.

Claire Selltiz and Others, *op. cit.*, p. 50–78.

Rosedith Sitgreaves and Herbert Solomon, *op. cit.*,

Pauline V. Young, *Scientific Social Surveys and Research*. Third Edition. Englewood Cliffs, N. J.: Prentice-Hall, 1956. p. 3–81.

state and the citizen, but rather the scientific observation of particular families. Accordingly, he specified the procedure for the compilation of case studies, or family monographs, involving an examination of the background of the family, its sources of income, the conditions of its work, its habitation and diet, recreation, and moral and religious convictions and practices. As a means of rendering the observation more precise and objective, he urged a careful inventory of all its capital, including household furnishings and wardrobe, and a budget of its annual expenditures.[13]

The English statistician and reformer Charles Booth was interested primarily in the conditions of poverty in the East Side of London. He began his seventeen-volume investigation[14] in 1886, in an attempt to help social reformers find remedies for the existing evils. Among the factors affecting life and labor in London, Booth investigated income, hours and conditions of work, housing, standards of living, number of children, size of household in relation to size and type of dwelling, type and frequency of sickness, leisure activities, and club and union membership.

A later survey of London life and labor, published in 9 volumes,[15] 1930-35, was made to discover changes in the socioeconomic life of a new generation of London workers, for comparison with Booth's earlier survey. The second survey describes the habits of laboring people after the advent of the automobile, telephone, wireless, and cinema, which had greatly changed the life and work of the people of London.

Trends in the United States

A social survey[16] in the United States was begun in 1909 by Paul Kellogg and a group of social economists and professional social workers to study the forces that affected the lives of steel workers in Pittsburgh, to discover the underlying factors in the city's growth as they affected the wage earners, to secure an inventory of an urban industrial community, and to determine how far human or social engineering had kept pace with mechanical developments in a steel district. Completion of publication of the Pittsburgh survey in 1914 stimulated many American communities to make social surveys of their own complex and changing problems. The growth of the social-survey movement was so great that

[13] Quoted from H. Stuart Hughes, Editor, *Teachers of History:* Essays in Honor of Laurence Bradford Packard. Ithaca, N. Y.: Cornell University Press, 1954. p. 63–65.

[14] Charles Booth, *Life and Labour of the People in London.* London: Macmillan and Co., 1892–1903. 17 vols.

[15] Hubert L. Smith, *The New Survey of London Life and Labour.* London: King and Son, 1930–35. 9 vols.

[16] Paul U. Kellogg, Editor, *The Pittsburgh Survey.* New York: Russell Sage Foundation, 1909–14. 6 vols.

by 1928 a published bibliography included a total of 2,775 titles or projects.[17]

During the 1940's and later, relatively few social surveys were undertaken by individual investigators. The increasing interest of social agencies and of the federal and state governments in social problems in local communities is evidenced by the large masses of census data and other government reports on a variety of problems, such as social security, economic conditions, employment and unemployment, wages, income, health, housing, child-welfare services, and crime and delinquency. The complexity of the social survey and the variety of research methods are illustrated by a social study of Pittsburgh, which included statistical analyses; ecological studies of Pittsburgh and its satellite districts as "natural" areas; case study of agencies, families, and districts as units; group and personal interviews; and schedules and questionnaires.[18]

THE COMMUNITY SURVEY[19]

Social surveys and community studies are similar in many respects, with no sharp dividing line. The community survey, like many school

[17] Allen Eaton and Shelby M. Harrison, *A Bibliography of Social Surveys.* New York: Russell Sage Foundation, 1930. xlviii + 487 p.

[18] Philip Klein and Others, *A Social Study of Pittsburgh:* Community Problems and Social Services of Allegheny County. New York: Columbia University Press, 1938. xxvi + 958 p.

[19] Conrad M. Arensberg, "The Community-Study Method." *American Journal of Sociology* 60: 109–24; September 1954.

Leon Festinger and Daniel Katz, *op. cit.,* p. 15–97.

Bess Goodykoontz, "Selected Studies Relating to Community Schools," *The Community School.* Edited by Nelson B. Henry. Fifty-second Yearbook of the National Society for the Study of Education, Part 2. Chicago: The University of Chicago Press, 1953. p. 64–82.

Otto G. Hoiberg, *Exploring the Small Community.* Lincoln: University of Nebraska Press, 1955. xii + 199 p.

Robert Redfield, *The Little Community:* Viewpoints for the Study of a Human Whole. Chicago: The University of Chicago Press, 1955. 182 p.

Irwin T. Sanders, *Making Good Communities Better:* A Handbook for Civic-minded Men and Women. Lexington: University of Kentucky Press, 1950. 174 p.

H. Clay Tate, *Building a Better Home Town:* A Program of Community Self-Analysis and Self-Help. New York: Harper & Brothers, 1954. xvi + 236 p.

William A. Van Til and Others, "Research on Human Relations and Programs of Action." *Review of Educational Research* 23: 285–385; October 1953. Chapters 3, 5, 8 deal with community surveys and programs of action.

Arthur J. Vidich and Joseph Bensman, *Small Town in Mass Society:* Class, Power, and Religion in a Rural Community. Princeton: Princeton University Press, 1958. xvi + 329 p.

Roland L. Warren, *Studying Your Community.* New York: Russell Sage Foundation, 1955. xii + 385 p.

S. R. Wayland and Others, *Aids to Community Analysis for the School Administrator.* New York: Teachers College, Columbia University, 1956. 51 p.

Stephen B. Withey, "Survey-Research Methods for the Study of Communities surveys, is made to provide data for planning future developments, such as an adequate system of sewage disposal or new buildings for the school system, although the recommendations of the community study frequently are broader and more general than those found in the school survey.

Characteristics and Scope

In the literature of social research the term *community* sometimes refers to small and stable communities such as a peasant village, to a large and complex urban area such as a ghetto community, to large cities and small towns or villages, or to a small, temporary unit such as a trailer camp. The local community or "natural area" is characterized by sociologists as having a territorial area, common interests, common patterns of social and economic relations, a common bond of solidarity from the conditions of its abode, a constellation of social institutions, and some degree of group control.

A survey of community life in urban and rural natural areas usually deals with the historical setting, social influence of physical configuration, social isolation, social contacts, economic centers, demographic characteristics, and population mobility, with an interest in the problems of social disorganization, poverty and dependency, unemployment, child labor, health, and crime and delinquency, as well as the local government and the various social institutions and organizations (economic and industrial, labor, health, religious, social welfare, delinquency control, police and criminal, educational, and recreational).[20]

The numerous studies of community schools, chiefly descriptive in character, are not as broad in scope as community surveys, but do provide answers for a number of significant questions: How can schools learn the community's needs and resources so as to serve it effectively? How have schools and communities worked together to improve the school program and the community? In what ways are community-school programs effective?[21]

Techniques and Examples

Many examples of community surveys may be found in the chapter bibliography, in the illustrations of case studies of communities in a later chapter on case and clinical techniques, and in succeeding paragraphs. It is pertinent at this time to characterize certain manuals or guides for

---

and Community Problems," in "Research on Human Relations and Programs of Action." *Review of Educational Research* 23: 329–36; October 1953.

Pauline V. Young, *op. cit.*, p. 470–506.

[20] Pauline V. Young, *op. cit.*, p. 470–506.

[21] Bess Goodykoontz, *op. cit.*, p. 64–82.

studying the community and to summarize illustrative community surveys drawn chiefly from the disciplines of sociology and anthropology.

Fifteen chapters of *Studying Your Community* are devoted to specific phases of community living, such as housing, education, recreation, religious activities, social insurance and public assistance, aids to family living and child welfare, health, and intergroup relations, with each chapter serving as a guide to a study or survey of that particular aspect and including provocative questions for the survey group to ask itself in order to define and sharpen the focus of the inquiry:

> These fifteen chapters are supplemented by five additional ones which deal with the larger, basic issues of survey-making, and with the "how" of community studies. This portion of the book contains some valuable pointers on such questions as the choice of the geographic area to be studied, the use of census data and other reference materials, hints about interviewers and the interviewing process, the use of the survey committee or sponsoring group, designing and compiling questionnaires and schedules, and many others. This section of the book also contains some useful observations on the general background and setting of the modern community, its economic life, its governmental structure, its social and class organizations, its primary and other interrelationships, and its readiness and ability to change.[22]

In another manual or guide, Redfield views the "little community" as an ecological system, social structure, typical biography, kind of person, outlook on life, history, community within communities, combination of opposites, and a whole and its parts, with these themes constituting ways to study the small community, or methods designed to view the object of study as a whole. Redfield illustrates the various approaches with concrete cases drawn from anthropological science, including British and American works, as well as his own adventures in Mexico, in order to understand the premises on which a scientific description of a human whole (in this case the little community) can be adequately based.[23]

Example: Greenbelt Co-operative Community[24]

The author lived in Greenbelt, served on several committees, and became its mayor. His book is dedicated, "To all who confidently struggle toward a more perfect democracy." He describes in detail, as an understanding insider, the founding of this democratically functioning community. He describes its

---

[22] Quoted from review by C. William Chilman, *Social Service Review* 29: 432–33; December 1955, of Roland L. Warren, *op. cit.*

[23] Review by Paul Nyberg, *Harvard Educational Review* 25: 196–98; Summer 1955, of Robert Redfield, *op. cit.*

[24] Quoted from review by Emory S. Bogardus, *Sociology and Social Research* 41:70; September-October 1956, of George A. Warner, *Greenbelt—The Cooperative Community:* An Experience in Democratic Living. New York: Exposition Press, 1956. 232 p.

problems carefully and answers its unsympathetic critics. He traces its growth from its beginnings in 1935-37 as a community for government employees in need of housing to its achievement of an independent community functioning under the auspices of the Greenbelt Veterans Housing Corporation on December 30, 1952. On that date its former tenants (of the government) became homeowners and crossed "the threshold to a new and challenging future of complete self-reliance," a thriving community of 3,000 individuals.

This community was founded to a large extent on the Rochdale Principles of cooperation. It established its businesses on the basis of cooperative principles, "which make capitalists of all their members" and which lead to "the exact antithesis of state socialism." These cooperatives have achieved a remarkable success. The *Cooperator*, the city's newspaper, has made an unusual record. Only the health association has not succeeded, for reasons which are explained. The author thinks that the voluntary health-group plan will come into its own some day when the "people get fed up with our present antiquated method of dispensing medical care," and will see its superiority over federalized or state medicine. He believes that the achievements in cooperative living in Greenbelt are remarkable in view of the strong individualistic backgrounds of its members. Mr. Warner has rendered an important service to all who believe in what independent people working together can accomplish.

Example: Community Political Systems[25]

Janowitz brings together five case studies, from the United States, on different aspects and approaches to urban community political systems and one study of an electoral contest held in a Norwegian province. The American urban communities studies include a small trading center or town, a satellite city, a suburban community, a larger industrial city, and a giant metropolis. The methods used in these studies include historical analysis, survey techniques, statistical analysis, the ecological approach, and case study. Since these studies use different hypotheses, different methods, and different definitions, it is hard to compare them. Among the significant findings are the decline of the influence of large businessmen in community affairs, the survival of the old patronage system in an industrial satellite city, and the lack of priorities among business leaders as to their self-interests.

Example: Community Health[26]

This book provides a good example of the type of role that the social scientist can play in the fields of health. Written by an anthropologist, it is based on a project which was designed to introduce to professional health

[25] Quoted from review by Harold F. Gosnell, *Science* 134: 186–87; July 21, 1961, of Morris Janowitz, Editor, *Community Political Systems*. Vol. I, International Yearbook of Political Behavior Research. Glencoe, Ill.: Free Press, 1961. 259 p. Reprinted from *Science* by permission.

[26] Quoted from review by Arthur J. Rubel, *Social Forces* 38: 274–75; March 1960, of Margaret Clark, *Health in the Mexican-American Culture:* A Community Study. Berkeley: University of California Press, 1959. 253 p.

workers the culture and society of Americans of Mexican descent. In order to gather the materials a small unincorporated community on the outskirts of San Jose, California was chosen to be the subject of the study. During the investigation Clark and her associate, Thomas McCorkle, utilized standard ethnographic techniques which included participant observation of community life and intensive interviewing of 20 percent of the families.

On the assumption that "medical systems are integral parts of the cultures in which they occur," Clark devotes the first six chapters to a description of various aspects of life in the Mexican-American community. In chapters seven and eight a number of the Mexican-American's concepts of health and disease are introduced as well as a very illuminating discussion of what kind of role behavior he expects of the medical technician.

Example: Mental Illness in a Community[27]

Basing their study on the New Haven community, they sought out as many as possible of the mentally disordered persons in that community. Since the sampling bias in hospitalized patients is well known, they threw a wider net which covered not only all hospitals and clinics in Connecticut and such neighboring areas as might contain New Haven persons, but also all psychiatrists in a like region who might have New Haven persons under treatment. Data were furnished by all 28 of the institutions, and by 46 of the 66 psychiatrists. The sample lost cases from the 20 non-cooperating psychiatrists, and lacked all untreated cases, but still it may be one of the best samples of mentally abnormal patients ever obtained.

Example: Personality Study of a Community[28]

This book is an important landmark, for it is the first modern personality study of a Saharan community yet published. It deals with the sedentary Arabic-speakers of Sidi Khaled (a small oasis in the northwestern desert), including those who have remained and others who have become economic refugees in Algiers.

An excellent historical sketch and a detailed anthropological study by Miner are followed by a searching analysis of personality made by De Vos in consultation with Miner. The analysis is based mainly on Rorschach protocols of a random sample of 64 adult males.

Two main objectives were to test Kardiner's theory that institutions can be predicted from knowledge of basic personality and to discover at about what age personality really becomes set. "Blind" Rorschach analysis proved valid for

[27] Quoted from review by Robert E. L. Faris, Contemporary Psychology 4: 33–35; February 1959, of August B. Hollingshead and Fredrick C. Redlich, Social Class and Mental Illness: A Community Study. New York: John Wiley & Sons, 1958. xi + 442 p.

[28] Quoted from review by Lloyd C. Briggs, Science 132: 1390; November 11, 1960, of Horace M. Miner and George DeVos, Oasis and Casbah: Algerian Culture and Personality in Change. Anthropological Papers, Museum of Anthropology, University of Michigan, No. 15. Ann Arbor: University of Michigan, 1960. vi + 236 p.

cross-cultural personality rating, even with the intervention of interpreters, but inadequate for predicting relationships between psychological and cultural variables. . . .

To sum up, *Oasis and Casbah* is an enormously important book, even though it is too technical to be entertaining reading for any except specialists. Its importance lies in the fact that it is a searching "soil analysis," so to speak, of the ground in which the Algerian rebellion has its roots. Anyone interested in the march of events in North Africa today should read it without delay, as should anyone interested in the much broader problem of why Western governments so often fail to "make friends and influence people."

Example: A Mountain Community[29]

Tradition and change in a small segment of the southern Appalachians are expertly portrayed. Although names used are fictitious, Little Smoky Ridge, "more so than most neighborhoods . . . has suffered the abrasions of extreme poverty through several generations that prohibits any foreseeable improvement of conditions."

The reader will be fascinated by the colorful descriptions of the individuals and setting of this depressed remnant of an earlier American frontier. The researcher lived for several months in this remote area observing many facets of this cultural island. The author's absorbing account is supplemented by references to similar studies.

The geographical area is discussed also. Contrary to popular belief, the Great Smoky National Park has not brought the desired benefits to this particular, isolated neighborhood. This thorough presentation of a small segment of cultural anthropology vividly reveals a contemporary illustration of a frontier type of social organization and a value system in an environment no longer helpful to either. Historical explanations add authenticity to the descriptions. Family life is reported in its physical and social dimensions. Supernatural sanctions and religious phenomena are significantly related to the life of mountain folk. Dr. Pearsall's objective account nowhere reveals any biases, and generalizations for the total area are absent.

"The final foreseeable future for Little Smoky Ridge as a neighborhood is disintegration, which has already begun, and finally death."

Example: Regeneration of a City Neighborhood[30]

This book tells the proud story of the regeneration, over a ten-year period, of the Hyde Park-Kenwood community on the south side of Chicago. Beneath the account of who did what, when, and how, a universal human

[29] Quoted from review by Henry Shissler, *Rural Sociology* 24: 398–99; December 1959, of Marion Pearsall, *Little Smoky Ridge*. Tuscaloosa, Ala.: University of Alabama Press, 1959. xii + 205 p.

[30] Quoted from review by Herbert A. Thelen, *School Review* 67: 469–73; Winter 1959, of Julia Abrahamson, *A Neighborhood Finds Itself*. New York: Harper & Brothers, 1959. xiv + 370 p.

theme is evident: the struggle between aspiration and doubt, activity and passivity, courage and despair. The conflict is resolved through the conscious rediscovery of the values of co-operative action, compassion for all persons, and the insistence that communal action respect, protect, and enhance the rights of individuals. The book tells of the exciting and, at times, terrifying confrontation of these values by the social, physical, and psychological crises of a community that is rapidly becoming a slum.

Julia Abrahamson deals with these matters objectively. She tells what the community was like and what caused its deterioration. What she says about this decline could be said about many urban communities. Then we are shown how an action group—the Hyde Park-Kenwood Community Conference —came into existence, how it formulated and tested its goals, how it set up its programs. . . .

In more mundane and practical terms, the story is the account of what people did, how it came out, and what they did next. It is a considerable story, involving just about everyone, from a Pullman porter who became a block leader, to the President of the United States. We have ministers, rabbis, housewives, businessmen, union members, teachers, scientists, policemen, legislators, high-school students, PTA members, building inspectors, aldermen, two mayors, organization officials, grandmothers, bankers, and the whole gamut of city, state, and federal officials. Each of these has his place in the movement because he lives in the community or because his job impinges on the community. We become aware of the racial, philosophical, social, and educational differences that separate these people, and we see how they are brought together in quasi-autonomous working committees and block organizations that eventually blanket 85 per cent of the community of seventy-two thousand people. We see the first "budget" of $127.50, collected by passing the hat at a meeting, grow into an annual budget of sixty thousand dollars, two-thirds of which is raised in the community. We see the office staff grow from nobody at all to eleven full-time workers, and we are shown how literally hundreds of volunteers were helped to find intense reward and satisfaction through working in the Conference. We see the conflicts and frictions among organizations, the emergence of a powerful new organization that reaches people the Conference cannot reach, and the painful efforts of the two organizations to find a way of co-existing and complementing each other's resources, skills, and clientele. We pause to contemplate why there were two organizations—one for the grass roots and the other for the power people—and to wonder if, under other conditions, one organization could have reached both. Finally, we are astonished at the changes that are already achieved or clearly promised, involving one hundred and fifteen million dollars of private capital, thirty-eight million from federal funds, and ten million from the city of Chicago. The task is the rebuilding of 47.3 acres of blighted housing and the repair of the remaining 80 per cent of the dwelling units in the community—with all construction to follow an over-all community-approved plan for the neighborhood.

Examples: Puerto Rican Migrants to New York[31]

These are books about Puerto Rican migrants to New York City by an anthropologist, Padilla; a physician, Berle; and a journalist, Wakefield. The anthropologist and the physician were closely associated in the field, since Dr. Berle and her team opened their small office in the very neighborhood that was being studied by Elena Padilla and her team, and meanwhile, Wakefield was doing his research only a few blocks away.

Each of these three books is characteristically different, and all do a job different from the sociologist's. What they have in common is an emphasis on case studies—portraits of real people who suggest and illustrate the author's impressionistic observations. Padilla and Berle's cases tend to be presented as "typical"; and Wakefield's to be rather more newsworthy, such as politicians, or union organizers, or drug addicts. All the authors and their respondents are agreed that the neighborhood is "bad": housing conditions are insufferable, and little is being done about it. Wakefield's book is especially full of indignation.

Example: A Village in Japan[32]

Village Japan is the principal report of an extraordinary research project carried out by the University of Michigan's Center for Japanese Studies. A rural settlement of only 24 households was observed over a span of 7 years by members of an interdisciplinary research team composed of both Americans and Japanese representing anthropology, history, economics, political science, and geography, to name only the major fields. In studies basically concerned with cultural anthropology, seldom has so much been devoted for so long to so few.

Example: A Pineapple Town in Hawaii[33]

This volume is a case study of a pineapple plantation community, village-like in its physical structure, though far more industrial than rural in a number of ways. For five years the author was employed by the mainland company which operates this plantation, lived there over a year, and has returned twice since the end of World War II. The volume describes the plantation, the

[31] Elena Padilla, *Up from Puerto Rico.* New York: Columbia University Press, 1958. xiii + 317 p.

Beatrice B. Berle, *80 Puerto Rican Families in New York City.* New York: Columbia University Press, 1958. xii + 331 p.

Dan Wakefield, *Island in the City:* The World of Spanish Harlem. Boston: Houghton Mifflin Co., 1959. 278 p.

Quoted from review by Elihu Katz, *American Journal of Sociology* 65: 536–37; March, 1960.

[32] Quoted from review by John C. Pelzel, *Science* 130:1104–5; October 23, 1959, of Richard K. Beardsley, John W. Hall, and Robert E. Ward, *Village Japan.* Chicago: University of Chicago Press, 1959. 498 p. Reprinted from *Science* by permission.

[33] Quoted from review by Edmund DeS. Brunner, *Rural Sociology* 24: 398; December 1959, of Edward Norbeck, *Pineapple Town, Hawaii.* Berkeley, California: University of California Press, 1959. xii + 159 p.

community, and the three main ethnic groups—Filipinos, Japanese, and Caucasians—and then discusses community social relationships and the social changes produced largely, though not entirely, by changing technology.

While the study is largely descriptive, there are significant data on the attitudes and ways of living of the various groups and on the changing interactions among them. Kinship is decreasing in importance. Social classes are based upon both occupational status and race, with increasing emphasis on the former and attendant decline in social separation based on ethnic groups, since all groups are becoming more culturally alike.

Example: A Village after a Century and a Quarter[34]

A colonial surgeon named Coates made some observation of a village, Lonikand, near Poona, in 1819. Professor Ghurye in 1954 sent two of his research assistants, Drs. Chapakar and Kulkarni, to the same village. This book compares the state of the village at the two dates. The results are published in this book, which is one of the very few—perhaps the only—thorough reports of a century and more of change in an Indian village.

In a long introduction, "Perspectives," the author reviews some of the etymological and other evidence of village life in India from early time. He then turns to a point-by-point comparison of Coates's findings with his own. The layout of the houses of the village, the land and its cultivation, the families, castes, and households, the religious, economic, and social life of the village, the public institutions and activities—all are described in some detail. In a final chapter the changes are appraised.

It is obvious that the land of the village is much more congested now, but much of the increase has resulted from immigration. Irrigation pumps and a diesel-powered machine to grind grain have eased life somewhat, as has also the bicycle. The iron plow has made better cultivation possible. There is now a school, and arrangements have been made for teaching modern sewing and other arts to girls and women. The teacher acts as an innovator.

Yet, one gathers that the villages do not show any great ability to organize themselves for decisive improvements that they could afford.

Ghurye has given us a model which might well be followed in a study of social change. Of course, there is not always an earlier study to fall back on.

Example: Restudy of a Community in the Pacific[35]

The tiny Pacific island of Tikopia is already well known to anthropologists, thanks to Raymond Firth, who studied this isolated Polynesian community in 1929 and whose books, *We, the Tikopia* (1936), *A Primitive*

[34] Quoted from review by Everett C. Hughes, *American Journal of Sociology* 66: 535; March 1961, of G. S. Ghurye, *After a Century and a Quarter: Lonikand Then and Now.* Bombay: Popular Book Depot, 1960. xi + 126 p.

[35] Quoted from review by Ward H. Goodenough, *Science* 131: 1434; May 13, 1960, of Raymond Firth, *Social Change in Tikopia:* Re-study of a Polynesian Community after a Generation. New York: The Macmillan Co., 1960. 360 p. Reprinted from *Science* by permission.

Polynesian Economy (1939), and *Work of the Gods in Tikopia* (1940), are models of the highest standards in ethnographic reporting. *Social Change in Tikopia* represents a restudy of the island undertaken in 1952 with the assistance of James Spillius. It is a record of social change in Tikopia and, at the same time, of Firth's own growth as one of the leading anthropologists of our time. His account of political organization and social control, for example, is as sophisticated for the present as was his account of economic organization for two decades ago.

The book is more than a study of social change in other respects, also. Just before Firth's arrival in 1952 a serious hurricane had swept the island and destroyed most of its food resources. Firth provides an unusual account of the society's response to sudden crisis and of its operation during a famine. Rarely do anthropologists have such an opportunity to study isolated and economically self-sufficient communities trying to cope with disaster, largely through their own efforts and cultural resources; it is especially rare when such a study can be made of a community whose operation under normal circumstances has already been recorded.

Firth reviews in detail changes in economic outlook which have resulted from increased outside contact and population growth. Of interest is his analysis of how money has come to fit into the native economy. From economic change, he proceeds to a discussion of changes in land rights and calls attention to the greater individualization of holdings; this is not a result of Western influence, as might be supposed, but a response to internal pressures on subsistence resulting from the abandonment of traditional practices of population control. Analyses of patterns of residence and marriage, the system of lineages and clans, the political structure, and the system of social control are also presented in detail with an assessment of the amount and nature of change in each. Religious changes are not included in this volume.

Examples: Two Thailand Villages[36]

Each of these volumes constitutes a valuable addition to our increasing knowledge of South Asian community life and structure. Although both studies are laid in Thailand, they are of sharply contrasting ecological and cultural regions. Also contrasting are the styles of the respective authors and their approaches to community analysis. Both are anthropologists, and each spent about a year in field study.

Rusembilan deals with a Muslim coastal village in southern, peninsular Thailand. There, Malay Thai nationals have developed a seasonally balanced economy based chiefly upon fishing and rice cultivation. Fishing is the predominating concern. About a third of the book is devoted to various facets

[36] Thomas M. Fraser, Jr., *Rusembilan: A Malay Fishing Village in Southern Thailand.* Ithaca, N. Y.: Cornell University Press, 1960. xviii + 281 p.
Howard K. Kaufman, *Bangkhuad: A Community Study in Thailand.* Association for Asian Studies Monographs, Vol. 10. Locust Valley, N. Y.: J. J. Augustin (for the Association for Asian Studies), 1960. ix + 235 p.
Quoted from review by Bryce Ryan, *America Journal of Sociology* 66: 193; September 1960.

of economic life. In other chapters Fraser discusses community organization, including family structure; religious life and supernaturalism, both Muslim and folk; and "Rusembilan as part of the Thai Nation." In the last-named chapter and elsewhere, sensitivity to the minority position of the Malays is demonstrated, especially as Thai language and Buddhism impinge upon the Malays through the schools. The life-cycle is also treated as a chapter. Socio-cultural change is given some explicit treatment in two brief chapters and also in numerous topical contexts throughout the book.

Bangkhuad is a study of an exclusively Buddhist community in the great rice-producing delta near Bangkok. The general coverage is much the same as in *Rusembilan*, with chapters on economy, community structure, life-cycles, and the various institutions. A short summary chapter deals with changes in village life. Especially detailed treatment is given to temple structure and organiza-tion. In addition to a chapter on "The Life Cycle," Kaufman also treats the daily life of villagers and here draws in material on recreation, diet, and health.

Example: Changes in a Village in Mexico[37]

The first sociological study of Tepoztlan was made by Robert Redfield and published in 1930. The second study was made in 1943 and the third in 1956-57, both by Oscar Lewis. This document devotes seven chapters to Tepoztlan, as it appeared to the author in his earlier visits. "Chapter 8 of this book describes the village as of 1956" and notes some changes that have occurred since the earlier studies were made.

The list of changes includes: more varied and colorful clothes for the younger people, a shortage of house sites and houses, more health care includ-ing vaccinations, increase in nonagricultural occupations, a rise in the number of moneylenders, expansion of educational facilities, establishment of a movie theater, increase in number of radios, a greater child-orientedness, more per-missiveness in dealing with children, a more friendly attitude of the villagers toward outsiders. The *bracero* movement, or employment of the younger men in the United States for periods of time, is noteworthy and has played a role in creating changes. This study throws light on social change in general in Mexico.

THE SCHOOL SURVEY[38]

Historical Background

As indicated earlier in this chapter, the social surveys of the early years of the present century studied such problems as municipal organiza-

---

[37] Quoted from review by Emory S. Bogardus, *Sociology and Social Research* 44: 364; May–June 1960, of Oscar Lewis, *Tepoztlan, Village in Mexico*. New York: Henry Holt and Co., 1960. viii + 104.

[38] A. S. Barr, Robert A. Davis, and Palmer O. Johnson, *Educational Research and Appraisal*. Philadelphia: J. B. Lippincott Co., 1953. p. 124–57.

Harold H. Church and Others, *The Local School Facilities Survey*. Bulletin of the School of Education, Indiana University, Vol. 29, Nos. 1 and 2. Bloomington: Division of Research and Field Services, Indiana University, 1953. vii + 96 p.

tion, housing, recreation, and sometimes education. Therefore, it is a natural sequence that the beginning of the school-survey movement dates back to approximately 1910. Before that date, investigations of school systems had been made either by the school officers as part of their regular duties or by persons interested in some particular educational problem rather than in a comprehensive survey of the school system.

During the period from 1910 to 1915 there was a tendency in school systems to invite visiting experts for a relatively short period of time, sometimes a few weeks, to make recommendations concerning such problems as buildings, teachers, curriculum, organization, educational standards and achievement, financial management, and community attitude toward the schools. The early surveys include Boise, Idaho; Montclair and East Orange, New Jersey; Baltimore; New York City; and Cleveland.

Among others, Ellwood P. Cubberley was ready to play a part as investigator and consultant in the early days of the school-survey movement by reason of his school program and interests, professional experience, and methods of work:

Thus it happened that Cubberley grew to maturity and entered university work at a time when the scientific movement was taking hold of the country, but when such study of education was very new; when the country was greatly enthusiastic about its public schools, but also when it was beginning to find fault with them; when scientific studies were beginning to cast doubts upon the foundation of the traditional programs, but when tradition was still firmly in control; when the nature of our way of life was changing rapidly and bringing to light educational needs hitherto not recognized by the school, but when few men were scholastically equipped to enter upon a scientific study of education.[39]

After 1915 there was a trend toward more specialized surveys of limited aspects or problems of education, since the large number of

---

Carter V. Good and Douglas E. Scates, *op. cit.*, p. 567–76.

Calvin Grieder, "School Surveys." *Review of Educational Research* 19: 322-33; October 1949.

Virgil Rogers and Others, *Gary, Indiana:* A Study of Some Aspects and Outcomes of a General School Survey. Washington: National Commission for the Defense of Democracy Through Education, N.E.A., June 1957. 40 p.

Jesse B. Sears, "School Surveys," *Encyclopedia of Educational Research.* Revised Edition. Edited by Walter S. Monroe. New York: The Macmillan Co., 1950. p. 1126–33.

George D. Strayer, Jr., *Planning for School Surveys.* Bulletin of the School of Education, Indiana University, Vol. 24, No. 2. Bloomington: Division of Research and Field Services, Indiana University, 1948. 36 p.

A Survey of Surveys. Nashville, Tenn.: Division of Surveys and Field Services, George Peabody College for Teachers, 1952. 56 p.

[39] Quoted from Jesse B. Sears and Adin D. Henderson, *Cubberley of Stanford: And His Contribution to American Education.* Stanford, Calif.: Stanford University Press, 1957. p. 166.

recommendations in comprehensive surveys sometimes had proved confusing to the school staff and to the public. It was also thought desirable to add to the administrative staff of the local school system one or more specialists trained in methods of research, measurement, and survey techniques, who could assume leadership in conducting school-survey studies, rather than to depend entirely on the leadership of visiting experts. Frequently local staff members and consulting experts cooperated in conducting school surveys. As the movement spread widely through the local and state school systems, staff members of university departments of education were not able to meet the requests for leadership in surveys, with the result that a considerable part of this leadership was carried by the United States Office of Education, the educational division of the Russell Sage Foundation, and certain bureaus of municipal and governmental research. During the second quarter of the present century and later, the research and survey divisions of certain state universities, Teachers College of Columbia University, and George Peabody College for Teachers have made a large number of school surveys.

Types and Scope of School Surveys

In terms of purpose, modern school surveys may be divided into three types.[40] The *comprehensive survey* usually covers the following aspects of the school system:

1. Aims, outcomes, pupil achievement, curriculum, method, and instructional aids
2. Administrative problems and procedures of the schools
3. Financial policies and procedures
4. Operation and maintenance of the physical plant
5. Pupil transportation
6. Staff and personnel
7. School plant and related factors.

The *educational survey* deals with the instructional program and the related policies and procedures that affect the educational program. The *building survey* has been the most common type during recent years, because of the pressure of the greatly increased pupil population. The educational and building surveys together constitute a comprehensive survey.

Another classification of surveys,[41] in terms of purposes or objectives, is as follows:

1. Investigative, evaluative, or status, intended primarily to appraise existing conditions

[40] Harold H. Church and Others, *op. cit.*
[41] Dan H. Cooper, "School Surveys," *Encyclopedia of Educational Research.* Edited by Chester W. Harris. Third Edition. New York: The Macmillan Co., 1960.

2. Deliberative, developmental, or planning, serving chiefly to make proposals for development and improvement, with a minimum of criticism of present circumstances

3. Implementation or application, going beyond developmental recommendations to create conditions in the survey procedures that will promote achievement of the survey recommendations.

It is possible to classify surveys in other ways:

1. The major aspect of the school system: school plant, educational program, comprehensive

2. Geographical area: local, state, regional, national

3. Level of instruction: elementary, secondary, higher

4. Type of preparation: junior college, teacher education, engineering, medicine, law, social work

5. Purpose or problem: to follow up youth out of school, to describe the membership of a professional organization, to describe the characteristics of a group of institutions, to poll the opinion of a group of parents, to identify trends, to engage in survey testing

6. Data-gathering technique or procedure: questionnaire, interview, observation, group-behavior analysis, content analysis, survey-appraisal. (In the interest of emphasizing research methodology, this is the classification scheme adopted for succeeding sections of the present chapter.)

For illustrative purposes, the scope and procedures of the plant survey may be summarized briefly. The school-building survey usually includes the community and the setting of the schools, an estimate of future school enrollment, school-plant planning, the pupil-transportation system, and the available financial resources to provide the school buildings. The cooperative building survey by members of the local staff and by a team of visiting specialists combines the advantages of the "expert" survey and self-survey, in that it costs less than the survey conducted entirely by experts, safeguards the objectivity of survey procedures and conclusions, and through cooperation between the local staff and visiting experts, furthers acceptance and implementation of the survey recommendations.

The visiting survey specialist has an important role in developing procedures for setting up and conducting the survey, interpreting the findings, formulating recommendations, stimulating the local staff in answering important questions, and cooperating with the local administrator in his role of leadership.

There are some disadvantages when a single survey seeks to accomplish two separate purposes, such as administrative planning for a building program and evaluation of the efficiency of the educational program and personnel. Evaluation of the educational program and personnel (and working *with* persons for their own improvement) may prove incompatible with the purposes of a survey concerned with administrative planning.

Procedures and Results of Surveys

The following summary[42] of the procedures and practical results of survey studies is drawn from an evaluation of the school surveys sponsored by George Peabody College for Teachers and from many surveys made by other agencies. A primary purpose of the evaluation of the Peabody school surveys was to study the activities in the local school system following a survey, by way of implementing the recommendations, with the evaluative data based on interviews, conferences, and documentary sources.

1. The formal request for a local survey usually came from the board of education, upon the recommendation of the superintendent, although frequently the initiative came from such groups as a citizens' committee, an education association, or a chamber of commerce. (School surveys have been sponsored by the United States Office of Education, regional accrediting associations, national professional organizations, state legislatures, state departments of education, and private philanthropic foundations.)

2. As a general rule the Division of Surveys and Field Services had complete charge of plans and procedures for making the investigation.

3. Comprehensive reports and illustrated digests were prepared by the survey staff and printed, with oral reports always made to the boards of education or survey commissions and to other interested groups invited to attend the meetings.

4. As a rule the survey reports were enthusiastically received by the public and by the press, with community groups and citizens' committees actively supporting the recommendations.

5. The superintendent of schools, more than any other individual or group, was responsible for implementing the survey recommendations, with new superintendents particularly appreciative of the guidance of the report in winning public support for school policies.

6. Members of state survey commissions played an important part in formulating survey recommendations, and assumed the responsibility for drafting bills embodying the recommendations for presentation to the legislature. It proved difficult to implement changes that depended on action by the legislative bodies of the city, county, or state, and especially when constitutional changes were necessary. Political strategy in bringing about legislative action on survey recommendations varied, with the unity of the forces supporting public education an important factor in success.

7. When survey proposals involved as a major consideration the consolidation of schools, there was always opposition in the small communities, which

[42] *A Survey of Surveys.* Nashville, Tenn.: Division of Surveys and Field Services, George Peabody College for Teachers, 1952. 56 p.

sometimes led to compromise or even failure in implementing the survey recommendations.

8. Almost one-half of the survey recommendations were adopted. More immediate results were brought about in city schools than in county or state systems. Differences in favor of the city over the county systems were especially significant in the areas of administration, business management, and physical plant. (In many of our school systems the survey has been the initial stage of an educational advance, through challenging the attention of the school people and the public, even though immediate results have not always followed survey investigations.)

9. The superintendents of county and city school systems reacted favorably to recommendations for reorganization of their administrative and supervisory staffs, not only adding new members but also organizing them into a few clearly defined divisions or departments under the leadership of assistant superintendents.

10. Improvement of instruction followed slowly after a survey, although the majority of the school systems reported the adoption of many significant recommendations. (The direction of survey recommendations has been toward a positive emphasis, by way of search for and encouragement of desirable educational practices, rather than a negative emphasis in the form of a search for malpractices.)

11. The quick adoption of survey recommendations for schoolhousing reflected the critical shortage of buildings following the war years; bond issues for new school buildings were generally approved in the counties and cities.

12. Recommendations for the improvement of pupil transportation were readily adopted, with state and county systems carrying out most of the concrete proposals for a complete system of school-bus operation.

13. Proposed programs for financing the schools were frequently delayed by a variety of restrictions, although state systems made some progress in financing public education.

14. Gains in revenue receipts were only moderate in county systems, whereas the compactness and well-developed channels of communication in city schools secured relatively prompt action in increasing school funds. Recommendations concerning the business affairs of the schools were well received in both cities and counties.

15. The administrative officers in four school systems thought that the survey staff should have continuing follow-up contacts by way of consultative services in the system investigated, and suggested that survey specialists should spend more time in the classroom, as background for more accurate evaluation of the quality of teaching. Many school systems now maintain a continuing survey or study, sometimes known as an evaluation or an inventory, with a cooperative planning survey at intervals of approximately ten years, and financial and personnel provisions between surveys for securing the assistance of special consultants. (The stages of implementation of survey recommendations involve the processes of group interaction or group dynamics. Certain related techniques of group-behavior analysis and action research are summarized in other sections of this chapter.)

16. It is now recognized that many of the recommendations of school surveys are subjective (according to one specialist, 80 per cent subjective).[43] To the extent that direct observation, score cards, check lists, and rating scales are used in school surveys, there is a considerable element of subjectivity or personal reaction on the part of the investigator. Survey conclusions depend largely on committee deliberations or interpretations, with the recommendations based largely on the opinion of committee members, or the impact of opinion on facts. To cite an example, a state school survey may recommend an expanded plan of state aid for local school districts, which is a committee recommendation rather than a factual statement, although coming from or based on facts. The recommendation involves subjectivity in the frame of reference or philosophy of the survey committee: agreement on the general goal of a good school system, acceptance of the social philosophy that a good school system is desired for all, and agreement that a particular plan of equalization of support is best for the state and the local school districts.

Indiana University, as one of the pioneers in the school-survey movement, offered instruction on the survey as early as 1915, began making surveys of Indiana schools about 1936, and between 1949 and 1958 conducted 56 school surveys. Based on an appraisal of 43 of these investigations, involving the opinions of school officers concerning the value of such surveys, the conclusions and recommendations for making school surveys are as follows:

1. That school survey staffs plan a periodic follow-up study of all school surveys within three years following the survey and make the cost of such a study a part of a continuing contract.

2. That, in school surveys, greater emphasis and time be given to the study of the curriculum and the improvement of learning and, further, that the survey staff be augmented by the addition of specialists in education in so far as a school corporation can afford such services.

3. That, whenever a school corporation has fewer than 400 pupils enrolled in its high school (grades 9 through 12), it should seek an opportunity to join with one or more school corporations until the new school corporation has at least 400 resident high-school pupils.

4. That a school survey be conducted whenever the local school authorities have insufficient or unreliable data upon which to project their future plans and/or whenever it is expected that strong local opposition may defeat the plans of the board because the public is uninformed.

5. That a survey be made of the administrative staff, its duties and responsibilities, following a period of reorganization or unusual growth.

[43] Dan H. Cooper, "Contributions of School Surveys to Educational Administration," *Educational Administration: A Survey of Progress, Problems, and Needs*, p. 46–59. Edited by William C. Reavis. Proceedings of the Fifteenth Annual Conference for Administrative Officers of Public and Private Schools, 1946. Vol. 9. Chicago: The University of Chicago Press, 1946. 216 p.

6. That boards of education annually reserve for research in education an appropriation of funds which can be used periodically as needed for some form of school survey.[44]

Safeguards for School Surveys

An excellent statement of safeguards for school surveys (applying to consultant, school system, and survey agency) is based on an evaluation of the Gary, Indiana, survey and its outcomes, by the National Commission for the Defense of Democracy through Education of the National Education Association. After pointing out that the survey has been one of the most valuable procedures for the improvement of American school systems, the Commission emphasizes that the ultimate success of a survey depends on the interest, cooperation, good will, and confidence of the staff of the school system under study, and on the dignity and sincerity with which the survey is conducted and reported.[45]

Safeguards for the school system to be surveyed are as follows:

1. Before selecting an agency to conduct the survey, the board of education and administrative staff should make a careful study of the experience and philosophy of the agencies with respect to public education.

2. An agreement should be prepared that will indicate in detail the scope of the survey, including the areas with which the recommendations will be concerned.

3. All discussion between the board of education and the survey agency should be reported in detail in official minutes of the board.

4. The number of individuals to be employed as survey staff members and consultants should be clearly noted.

5. There should be a clear commitment that, in seeking information and in studying the school system, initial approaches should be made to persons in charge of areas under study, with free access to anyone who may have information concerning agreed-on phases of the study.

6. No factual data should be presented in the report unless they have been checked for accuracy with the person in the school system responsible for such data.

7. When the report is released, it should go simultaneously to all directly concerned (preferably, prior to its public release).

8. A plan should be developed for careful study and implementation of the survey report.

[44] Harold H. Church and Melvin S. Lewis, *An Appraisal of the School Surveys Conducted by the School of Education, Indiana University.* Bulletin of the School of Education, Indiana University, Vol. 35, No. 5. Bloomington, Indiana: Indiana University, September, 1959. x + 66 p.

[45] Virgil Rogers and Others, *op. cit.*

THE QUESTIONNAIRE[46]

Characteristics and Uses

By the turn of the past century many psychologists were convinced that experimental and laboratory methods did not answer many of the questions about childhood and youth. G. Stanley Hall and his students especially promoted wide use of the questionnaire, which more recently has appeared in the form of the history blank, clinical syllabus, and personality inventory or questionnaire. The terms *questionnaire* and *schedule* may be considered equivalent for present purposes, although sometimes a technical distinction is made. The questionnaire is generally regarded as a form distributed through the mail or filled out by the respondent under the supervision of the investigator or interviewer, whereas the schedule is a form filled out by the investigator or completed in his presence.

Many beginners in research turn almost automatically to the questionnaire as a device for securing answers to problems, even before the problem and technique are fully formulated, rather than to evaluate the merits of the various data-gathering methods in relation to the particular problem. A carefully devised questionnaire technique is not a simple, quick method of investigation, but requires time, patience, ingenuity, and skill. Many of these abilities and skills are important in interview studies,

---

[46] John T. Doby, Editor, *An Introduction to Social Research.* Harrisburg, Penn.: The Stackpole Co., 1954. p. 207–19.

Sol L. Garfield, *Introductory Clinical Psychology.* New York: The Macmillan Co., 1957. p. 115–30.

Carter V. Good and Douglas E. Scates, *op. cit.,* p. 604–34.

William J. Goode and Paul K. Hatt, *Methods in Social Research.* New York: McGraw-Hill Book Co., 1952. p. 132–83.

Robert L. Kahn and Charles F. Cannell, *The Dynamics of Interviewing:* Theory, Technique, and Cases. New York: John Wiley & Sons, 1957. p. 106–65.

C. A. Moser, *op. cit.,* Chapters 10, 12, 14.

Mildred Parten, *op. cit., p.* 157–218, 383–484.

Stanley L. Payne, *The Art of Asking Questions.* Princeton: Princeton University Press, 1951. xiv + 249 p.

J. Francis Rummel, *An Introduction to Research Procedures in Education.* New York: Harper & Brothers, 1958. p. 87–110, 361–403.

Douglas E. Scates and Alice V. Yeomans, *Developing a Depth Essay Questionnaire to Assess the Market for Further Education Among Employed Scientists and Engineers.* Washington: American Council on Education, 1950. 128 p.

Douglas E. Scates and Alice V. Yeomans, *Developing an Objective Item Questionnaire to Assess the Market for Further Education Among Employed Adults.* Washington: American Council on Education, 1950. 48 p.

Claire Selltiz and Others, "Questionnaire Construction and Interview Procedure," "Questionnaires and Interviews," *Research Methods in Social Relations.* Revised One-Volume Edition. New York: Henry Holt and Co., 1959. p. 546-87, Chapter 7.

Herbert A. Toops, "Questionnaires," *Encyclopedia of Educational Research.* Revised Edition. New York: The Macmillan Co., 1950. p. 948–51.

Pauline V. Young, *op. cit.,* p. 176–204.

and in certain other descriptive-survey techniques. Therefore, cross references are appropriate in the interest of economy of space, especially between the questionnaire and interview sections of this chapter.

As to uses and applications, the questionnaire extends the investigator's powers and techniques of observation by reminding the respondent of each item, helping insure response to the same item from all respondents, and tending to standardize and objectify the observations of different enumerators (by singling out particular aspects of the situation and by specifying the units and terminology for describing the observations). While many questionnaires seek factual information, others are concerned with opinions, attitudes, and interests. National, state, and local organizations frequently have been interested in questionnaire surveys of the status of the school personnel and current practices in school systems, including school finance. In frequency of use, the questionnaire may be outranked by the survey test; if all the practical questionnaire and testing studies are included, the two techniques probably involve more than one-half the total studies in education.

To cite a specific example,[47] the personality questionnaire or inventory attempts to measure a variety of personality attributes: rather broad categories such as emotional adjustment, social adjustment, neurotic tendency; more specific personality traits, such as introversion, extroversion, self-sufficiency, and ascendancy or dominance; and in terms of specific theoretical conceptions of personality or different psychiatric categories. The personality questionnaire or inventory usually includes a specific number of questions or test items (approximately 100–500 in number) to be answered by the subject by checking one of three possible responses—"yes," "no," and a third category designated either as a question mark or as "cannot say." Among the better known examples are the Bernreuter Personality Inventory and the Minnesota Multiphasic Personality Inventory (MMPI).

Appropriateness as an Instrument

Beginners in research and many others frequently overlook the cooperative nature of the questionnaire and lack perspective concerning what may reasonably be asked of busy respondents. The questionnaire study should be important not only to the investigator and to the particular field of knowledge, but also to the respondent, whose psychology of motivation involves his attention, sympathy, interest, cooperation, and honesty in answering questions. Better motivation for respondents is likely to prevail if they can see the investigator's side of the problem and procedure, and can see the end-results in the form of a

[47] Sol L. Garfield, op. cit., p. 115–27.

concise summary of the study and possibly in the implementation of the findings.[48]

One of the first questions the investigator should ask concerning the questionnaire is whether it is as appropriate as some other data-gathering instrument, or whether the answers may even be available in documentary sources or in the literature. Would the questionnaire be as effective as the interview in investigating the job opportunities available in the printing and tailoring trades of a large city for members of certain racial and minority groups, in studying the policy of city newspapers with respect to publication of school news, in canvassing the leisure-time activities of adolescent boys in an underprivileged area of a large city, and in asking highly personal questions such as those covered in the Kinsey reports?

The question under consideration involves an important rule of evidence, to the effect that only the "best evidence," the most valid and credible, should be used. To cite an example, a particular study of certain components of the programs in Ohio high schools was based on an elaborate questionnaire, with the data reported in some 70 tables. The material in half of the tables could have been secured from the annual reports of high-school principals on file in the State Department of Education. Instead of examining these official reports, the investigator took the easy way, probably less accurate, of mailing a questionnaire. He violated the principle of using the best evidence.[49]

A sociologist's comment on a student's questionnaire is not intended to be sharp, but to emphasize the desirability and necessity of considering the appropriateness of the questionnaire in relation to other available means of gathering evidence:

First of all, you are asking in the questionnaire certain questions you could easily answer for yourself by consulting *Who's Who in America* or the university catalogues.

More serious is the objection which I have to the rest of your questions; you are asking me for my opinions on very complex questions, and you formulate your questions in a way that indicates you expect a dogmatic answer. To do real justice to these questions, which concern the objectives and methods of . . . sociology, I would have to write you an essay, or several papers. It is hard to imagine that you really expect me to do this for you; if you do not, then why ask me these questions? Furthermore, it so happens that I have expressed my ideas on these matters in several publications; I admit that my opinions are in some cases not stated explicitly but by implication. Now there

48 Douglas E. Scates and Alice Yeomans Scates, "Developing a Depth Questionnaire to Explore Motivation and Likelihood of Action." *Educational and Psychological Measurement* 12: 620–31; Winter 1952.

49 R. H. Eckelberry, "We Should Use the Best Evidence." *Educational Research Bulletin* 39: 44, 56; February 10, 1960.

is an old and well established way of getting information about other scholars' opinions and theories; that is, by reading and by critical interpretation. There is no substitute for this. My advice to you is to forget about the questionnaire and to study the literature.[50]

Does the recipient of the questionnaire have the information requested, and is he free and willing to respond? Would a state survey of local administrative positions early in April find that the respondents know where they will be the following September and are willing to declare their positions vacant so early in the spring? Would a local school survey of the attitudes of parents toward curriculum and method find these citizens informed about the school program and willing to comment freely when their children are still attending school? A form of questionnaire without the signature of the respondent may encourage frank and truthful answers.

Stages and Administrative Aspects

A check list of certain requirements, stages, and administrative aspects of questionnaire surveys is especially appropriate for large-scale studies, and also is useful in planning smaller questionnaire studies:[51]

1. Purpose of the survey
2. Relation to other surveys or programs
3. Development of the survey plan
   a. Respondents
   b. Extent of coverage
   c. Frequency and timing
   d. Method of collection
   e. Consideration of nonsampling errors
   f. Standard definitions and classifications
   g. Processing and interpretation of the data
   h. Allowance for pretests and follow-ups
   i. Comparison with data from other sources
   j. Proposed calendar
   k. Cost estimates
4. Questionnaire and accompanying instructions
5. Pretests
6. Follow-ups
7. Development of the sampling plan for partial coverage surveys
8. Supervision of field enumeration

[50] Quoted from Rudolf Heberle, "On the Use of Questionnaires in Research: Open Letter to a Graduate Student." *American Sociological Review* 16: 549; August 1951.

[51] *Standards for Statistical Surveys*. Exhibit A, Circular No. A-46. Washington: Executive Office of the President, Bureau of the Budget, March 28, 1952. 10 p.

9. Manuals and other instructions for the conduct of the survey
10. Progress and cost reporting
11. Preparation and publication of the final report.

The graduate student also must consider certain administrative aspects in choosing his problem and procedure, including sponsorship, cost, space, time requirements, clerical aid, and tabulating or calculating machine work.

Sampling and Survey Design

Sampling is a technical and statistical problem of importance in most questionnaire investigations and in many other descriptive-survey studies. The literature on application of sampling theory to practical survey problems has appeared primarily since 1940, with leadership provided in the areas of opinion-polling, market research, and census operations. Although the methodology of statistics lies outside the scope of this book, it seems appropriate to summarize the characteristics of probability samples and the limitations of "unplanned," "nonprobability," or "judgment" samples, and to refer to the literature of sample surveys in education.[52]

Probability samples have these characteristics:

1. Each individual (or primary unit) in the sample has some known probability of entering the sample.
2. The process of sampling is automatic in one or more steps of the selection of elements or units in the sample.
3. Weights appropriate to the probabilities in (1) are used in the analysis of the sample.

The limitations of unplanned, nonprobability, or judgment sampling are represented in the following items:

1. The sample of convenience (e.g., the superintendent's office is housed in the high school; the high-school teachers being convenient, he asks some of them their opinions on a matter)
2. The canvass of experts (e.g., a questionnaire to several "informed" persons for judgment on teacher shortage or school construction needs in the United States)
3. The sample based on an obsolete list or *frame* which does not adequately cover the population (e.g., using a city directory or telephone book as a basis for sampling the adult population of a community)

---

[52] Francis G. Cornell, "Sample Surveys in Education," in "Statistical Methodology in Educational Research." *Review of Educational Research* 24: 359–74; December 1954.
  Francis G. Cornell, "Sampling Methods," *Encyclopedia of Educational Research.* Edited by Chester W. Harris. Third Edition. New York: Macmillan Co., 1960. p. 1181–83.

4. The sample with a high proportion of nonresponse (e.g., the common questionnaire study in education)

5. The pinpoint or representative-area sample (e.g., purposive selection of typical individuals, or a typical school, typical classroom, or typical community)

6. The *quota* sample, by which there is some system of selection of primary sampling units (such as communities), and assigning interviewers *quotas* for subsampling (e.g., an interviewer is asked to select for interview 10 females who are high-school graduates between the ages of 18 and 25 living in the northeast section of a city).

To cite specific examples of design, Hyman bases much of his discussion of survey design and analysis on seven published surveys, dealing with: industrial absenteeism, public opinion and the atom bomb, American opinion on commercial radio, prejudice and personality, American sexual behavior, class consciousness, and war-bond redemption. These inquiries include certain common features, particularly with respect to the consequences of size of inquiry, organizational form, sponsorship and subsidization, and controversial subject matter. Some of these surveys present a sheer description of some phenomenon and are known as descriptive surveys, whereas other inquiries seek an explanation and are known as explanatory surveys.

Although reasonable attention has been given to problems of sampling design and theory in survey research, there has been considerable neglect of certain prior questions of the location within which the phenomenon ought to be studied, including temporal location, location in some human population, relevant units, and differentiation of the description.

Certain factors affect the quality of research findings or may lead to error in surveys:[53]

1. Variability in response
2. Differences between different kinds and degrees of canvass
   a. Mail, telephone, telegraph, direct interview
   b. Intensive vs. extensive interviews
   c. Long vs. short schedules
   d. Check block plan vs. response
   e. Correspondence panel and key reporters
3. Bias and variation arising from the interviewer
4. Bias of the auspices

[53] W. E. Deming, "On Errors in Surveys." *American Sociological Review* 9: 359–69; August 1944.

Herbert H. Hyman, *Survey Design and Analysis.* Glencoe, Ill.: Free Press, 1955. p. 143–45.

5. Imperfections in the design of the questionnaire and tabulation plans
   a. Lack of clarity in definitions; ambiguity; varying meanings of same word to different groups of people; eliciting an answer liable to misinterpretation
   b. Omitting questions that would be illuminating to the interpretation of other questions
   c. Emotionally toned words; leading questions; limiting response to a pattern
   d. Failing to perceive what tabulations would be most significant
   e. Encouraging nonresponse through formidable appearance
6. Changes that take place in the universe before tabulations are available
7. Bias arising from nonresponse (including omissions)
8. Bias arising from late reports
9. Bias arising from an unrepresentative selection of data for the survey, or of the period covered
10. Bias arising from an unrepresentative selection of respondents
11. Sampling errors and biases
12. Processing errors (coding, editing, calculating, tabulating, tallying, posting, and consolidating)
13. Errors in interpretation
    a. Bias arising from bad curve fitting; wrong weighting; incorrect adjusting
    b. Misunderstanding the questionnaire; failure to take account of the respondents' difficulties (often through inadequate presentation of data); misunderstanding the method of collection and the nature of the data
    c. Personal bias in interpretation.

Some estimation of residual errors that remain despite all pretesting may be secured through two general classes of methods available for treating this problem, namely, methods involving internal and external checks. The internal check is predicated on the logic that the meaning and quality of a given reply can be inferred from its relation to some other datum or reply. The most direct internal check involves the use of questions that require the respondent to elaborate an initial reply. Through another method, dependent variables may be arrayed for given factual categories.

The most obvious external check is the comparison of the datum under study with findings on the same or related problems collected by other agencies or individuals, on equivalent samples of the same population. Among the types of external checks in a German bombing survey were: interviewer ratings, criterion data from official records, use of other samples as informants, split-ballot procedures, comparison with earlier survey data, and "captured-mail" check.[54]

[54] Herbert H. Hyman, *op. cit.*, p. 151–72.

Questionnaire Construction

In questionnaire construction important decisions relate to motivation of the respondent, significance of questions, simplicity of responses, avoidance of unnecessary specifications or details, pertinence to the situation of the respondent, clarity of purpose and questions, phrasing of items to facilitate summarization of responses, and possible precoding of the questionnaire in the interest of using tabulating machine cards for summarization. Questionnaires that go to local and state school systems, or to similar educational agencies, may well formulate questions in keeping with the items of official or regular reports.

As to form,[55] the structured questionnaire is definite, concrete, preordained in terms of items, with additional questions limited to those necessary to clarify inadequate answers or to elicit more detailed responses. The form of questions may be closed (categorical) or open-end (inviting free response). The check list (usually a closed form of questionnaire) is a set of categories for the respondent to check, as in listing frequency of performance of certain duties by school officers. The completeness of the original list is especially important, since the respondent is likely to consider it all-inclusive and may depend on the list so completely that he does not write in additional items. The check responses or similar answers in the closed form of questionnaire commonly provide categorized data that greatly facilitate tabulating and summarizing processes.

The open-end or free-response questionnaire frequently goes beyond statistical data or factual material into the area of hidden motivations that lie behind attitudes, interests, preferences, and decisions. Such questions are used extensively in depth and focused questionnaires and interviews, although the work of tabulating and summarizing is time-consuming and expensive.

The choice between open and closed questions in both questionnaire and interview surveys depends on the following criteria:[56] the objective or purpose, the respondent's level of information on the particular topic, the degree of structure that characterizes respondent opinions on the topic, ease with which the material can be communicated, and the investigator's knowledge and insight into the respondent's situation. The closed question is most appropriate when the investigator's objective is to classify the respondent, when there is little question as to the adequacy of respondent information, when the respondent's opinions on the specific topic are well structured, when there are no major barriers to communication, and when the investigator is well informed about the respondent.

[55] Pauline V. Young, *op. cit.*, Chapters 8, 9.
[56] Robert L. Kahn and Charles F. Cannell, *op. cit.*, p. 164–165.

Conversely, when the opposite of the foregoing conditions prevails, the open question is preferable.

The nonstructured questionnaire commonly serves as an interview guide, especially for focused, depth, or nondirective interviews. It includes definite subject-matter areas, but the interviewer is largely free to arrange the form and timing of the questions.

A helpful summary of criteria for constructing questionnaires includes nine items:[57]

1. It must be short enough so as not to take too much time and so that the respondent will not reject it completely.

2. It must be of sufficient interest and have enough face appeal so that the respondent will be inclined to respond to it and to complete it.

3. The questionnaire should obtain some depth to the response in order to avoid superficial replies.

4. The ideal questionnaire must not be too suggestive or too unstimulating, particularly with reference to choices.

5. The questionnaire should elicit responses that are definite but not mechanically forced.

6. Questions must be asked in such a way that the responses will not be embarrassing to the individual.

7. Questions must be asked in such a manner as to allay suspicion on the part of the respondent concerning hidden purposes in the questionnaire.

8. The questionnaire must not be too narrow, restrictive, or limited in its scope or philosophy.

9. The responses to the questionnaire must be valid, and the entire body of data taken as a whole must answer the basic question for which the questionnaire was designed.

Certain errors[58] in construction and pretesting of the questionnaire should be avoided, including questionnaires used for interview purposes:

1. Irrelevance of the research problem to respondents. If the study involves the social and psychological problems of aging, with emphasis on retirement from employment, the sample would include only respondents past sixty years of age.

2. Irrelevance or insufficiency of questionnaire items for the variable being investigated. In studying membership activity in a local union, the investigator cannot assume that what represents high activity to him will also represent high activity to his potential respondents; for example, regularity of attendance at union meetings might be an insufficient index of union activity for construction workers whose jobs frequently take them miles away from the town where the meetings are held.

    [57] Douglas E. Scates and Alice V. Yeomans, *The Effect of Questionnaire Form on Course Requests of Employed Adults.* Washington: American Council on Educaiton, 1950. p. 2–4.
    [58] John T. Doby, Editor, *op. cit.,* p. 207–10.

3. Ambiguous or inappropriate item wording. Some people misunderstood the following question: "Which of the following groups do you think your family belongs in—upper class, middle class, working class, lower class?" Some people thought that the phrase "belongs in" meant "deserves to be in." The question was reworded to read, "If you were asked to put yourself (your family) in one of these groups—the upper class, middle class, working class, lower class—how would you answer?" Ambiguous questions result in equally confusing responses. A newspaper printed a questionnaire concerning the items read by its subscribers, without indicating for a family whether the checking should be done by one member, by the head of the family, or by each member of the family.

4. Inadequate categories for responses. Acceptable standard forms are: "Often—sometimes—hardly ever," "more—some—less," "very happy—fairly happy —not so happy." A dichotomous questionnaire on the administrative policy of a college, with provision for answering "for" or "against," would not represent adequately the college faculty as respondents. A third alternative for each item, such as "no definite feeling or conviction," is needed, because it is as important to know that a faculty member is neutral toward a particular policy as to know that he has a strong conviction for or against the policy.

When a question involves a number of categories for checking (sometimes a dozen or more), they should be reasonably complete and detailed, and as a rule nonoverlapping and co-ordinate. The young investigator who studied teacher turnover in a county school system included in his questionnaire a classification of eight reasons for leaving a teaching position. In summarizing the results, he found that thirty-one additional reasons had been written in by the respondents. A tryout of the questionnaire would have revealed a more complete set of classes or categories.

5. Inappropriate item sequence; overlengthiness; insensitivity to the emotional impact on the respondent of an item or series of items. These sources of difficulty can be greatly minimized by careful pretesting.

In preparing directions for answering questions, there is the challenge of keeping between one extreme of completeness and detail that seems overwhelming to the respondent and the other extreme of incompleteness and vagueness that would brand the investigator as careless and superficial. Usually the investigator must work back and forth, shuttle-like, between the questions and directions, as he constructs a questionnaire satisfactory for his purpose, with necessary adjustments as work proceeds on all parts of the questionnaire pattern.

Some questions are for purposes other than obtaining information; for example, warming up or getting the respondent's mind on the subject or area, meeting the respondent's expectation that certain questions normally will be included, and catharsis or release of possible tensions.

There is a human tendency to answer "yes" when the respondent thinks that this is the expected answer. This tendency can be partially offset by inclusion of the opposite question, so as to have a number of such pairs of questions.

In many instances the questionnaire includes two or more questions, in order to make clear the answer to a single question; for example, "the number of college courses completed" would serve as a check on an item relating to "semester hours completed."

A device in questionnaire construction for placement of detailed lists of items or subjects is to print them at the end of the questionnaire, especially when such lists do not apply to every respondent. To cite an example, a questionnaire for the field of psychology, in the interest of gathering data for the National Register of Scientific and Technical Personnel, covers two pages, with one question referring to a four-page list of specialties covering all the major fields of scholarship and research, with comprehensive coverage in the mathematical, physical and life sciences, and engineering, and less detailed coverage for social sciences and other professional areas. The item in the questionnaire proper that refers to the four-page specialties list reads as follows: "From the accompanying complete Specialties List, regardless of your current employment, please select and give below in order of decreasing competence up to six of these specialties in which you have had professional experience and/or training."

Certain decisions about questions, with respect to content, wording, and form of response, may be summarized as follows:[59]

I. Decisions About Question Content
   1. Is this question necessary? Just how will it be useful?
   2. Are several questions needed on the subject matter of this question?
   3. Do respondents have the information necessary to answer the question?
   4. Does the question need to be more concrete, specific, and closely related to the respondent's personal experience?
   5. Is the question content sufficiently general and free from spurious concreteness and specificity?
   6. Do the replies express general attitudes and only seem to be as specific as they sound?
   7. Is the question content biased or loaded in one direction, without accompanying questions to balance the emphasis?
   8. Will the respondents give the information that is asked for?

II. Decisions About Question Wording
   1. Can the question be misunderstood? Does it contain difficult or unclear phraseology?

[59] Claire Selltiz and Others, *Research Methods in Social Relations.* Revised One-Volume Edition. New York: Henry Holt and Co., 1959. p. 552–73.

2. Does the question adequately express the alternatives with respect to the point?
3. Is the wording biased? Is it emotionally loaded or slanted toward a particular kind of answer?
4. Is the question wording likely to be objectionable to the respondent in any way?
5. Would a more personalized or less personalized wording of the question produce better results?

III. Decisions About Form of Response to the Question
1. If a check list is used, does it cover adequately all the significant alternatives without overlapping and in a defensible order? Is it of reasonable length? Is the wording of items impartial and balanced?
2. Is the form of response easy, definite, uniform, and adequate for the purpose?
3. Is the answer to the question likely to be influenced by the content of preceding questions?
4. Is the question led up to in a natural way? Is it in correct psychological order?
5. Does the question come too early or too late from the point of view of arousing interest and receiving sufficient attention, avoiding resistance, etc.?

Tryout

Before the final form is prepared and distributed to the respondents, tryout or pretesting of the questionnaire is essential, for the purpose of validation in terms of practical use. This tryout probably will lead to revision of certain questions, deletion of useless questions, and addition of other items. Tabulation of the tryout responses in rough tables will indicate whether the answers can be tabulated satisfactorily and whether answers to the major questions are forthcoming. The manual of the United States Bureau of the Budget emphasizes that it is desirable to test the feasibility of the questionnaire survey in advance, with pretests designed and conducted to secure answers to such problems as the following:

Relative effectiveness and costs of alternative questionnaires, instructions, and operating procedures
Acceptability and intelligibility of the questions from the respondent's point of view
Possible misunderstandings of questions and procedure on the part of the interviewers
Clarity and applicability of definitions and classifications
Completeness of questions for correct coding and interpretation
Defects in the forms, maps, lists, instructions, etc.
Estimates of strata means and variances
Response rates.

Validity

The validity of a questionnaire and of its parts may be judged by the following types of evidence:[60]

1. Is the question on the subject?
2. Is the question perfectly clear and unambiguous?
3. Does the question get at something stable, which is typical of the individual or of the situation?
4. Does the question pull or have extractive power? Will it be answered by a large enough proportion of respondents to have validity?
5. Do the responses show a reasonable range of variation?
6. Is the information consistent, in agreement with what is known, and in agreement with expectancy?
7. Is the item sufficiently inclusive?
8. Is there a possibility of obtaining an external criterion to evaluate the questionnaire?

Follow-up

Follow-up usually is necessary in reaching the goal of a high percentage of questionnaire returns (above 95 per cent). The following ingenious and persistent techniques of follow-up in a questionnaire analysis of a professional organization resulted in a return of 99 per cent from a membership list of 600:[61]

A card or letter calling attention to the questionnaire, one to two weeks after sending the blank.

Possibly a second reminder, probably only a post card.

Without waiting too long, a second mailing of the entire questionnaire, with a new cover page or accompanying letter; persons may have misplaced the first questionnaire, or it may have become buried on a desk.

Possibly a personal letter at this point, individually written and signed, as a special appeal for cooperation, with a return stamped envelope.

A short form of the questionnaire was mailed, asking for just a few questions or items of information (perhaps sent by airmail or special delivery), phrased so as to cover the items most essential to the study.

A second mailing of the short questionnaire was sent to a relatively small number by special delivery, with an encouraging personal letter. (It may be necessary to scratch off the list at intervals persons unduly irritated or those

[60] Douglas E. Scates and Alice V. Yeomans, *The Effect of Questionnaire Form on Course Requests of Employed Adults.* Washington: American Council on Education, 1950. p. 4–7.

[61] Douglas E. Scates, "Analysis of a Professional Organization: The American Educational Research Association in 1948," *Growing Points in Educational Research.* 1949 Official Report of the A.E.R.A. Washington: The Association, 1949. p. 111–42.

who have good reason for not responding; however, these names must be included in the count in calculating percentages.)

Supplementary material went to all those who had returned the abbreviated questionnaire, including a few more essential items of information, and informing them that this is the last round.

Other special means and techniques included mailing of a questionnaire to the member, partially filled out in advance with answers deemed likely for him, together with a personal letter, suggesting that the information would not be used without his approval and asking that he go the rest of the way to complete the questionnaire; forwarding of liberal postage, transportation, or communication expenses; long distance telephone; and telegraph.

Percentage of Returns

Although the goal of 90 to 100 per cent returns has not been achieved generally in questionnaire surveys, definite progress in this direction is being made through improved plans for sponsorship, formulation of questions, follow-up, checking results, and studying nonresponse. The mean percentages (rounded to the nearest whole number) of questionnaire returns from a large number of survey investigations were as follows: 170 master's theses at Indiana State Teachers College, 72 per cent; 204 doctoral dissertations at Teachers College, Columbia University, 71 per cent; and 59 research studies reported in the *Journal of Educational Research*, 81 per cent.[62]

As an example of bias or incompleteness of returns for mail questionnaires, during World War II a selected list of farmers was canvassed for the purpose of determining the need for farm laborers. Most of the large farm operators listed their shortages, but most of the small farmers were too busy doing their own work to take time to reply, with the result that a fantastic estimate of 3 or 4 laborers was indicated to meet the needs of the average farm.[63]

Editing, Tabulating, Summarizing

The investigator may need to check the returns to determine whether different parts of the questionnaire response are consistent, to correct plain errors, and to revise the summarizing categories as indicated by the responses. One respondent checked all possible answers, revealing later in an interview that a check mark was his way of showing that he had read or checked off every item in the questionnaire. Sometimes written notes on the margins must be read and interpreted, figures rearranged or

[62] J. R. Shannon, "Percentages of Returns of Questionnaires in Reputable Educational Research." *Journal of Educational Research* 42: 138–41; October 1948.
[63] George W. Snedecor, "On the Design of Sampling Investigations." *American Statistician* 2: 6–9, 13; December 1948.

moved to the correct column, or other details checked that go beyond mechanical and routine clerical operations. After tabulation of questionnaire returns, further re-examination of the data and editing of the returns may be necessary. In a job classification of the members of a research organization, when the 600 returns had been tabulated, two general categories were relatively high: "administrators not otherwise described," 26 cases; "none of the following descriptions fits me," 18 cases. The cards for these 44 cases were re-examined and, on the basis of position, title, and institution reported, most of the 44 were reclassified into more specific and meaningful categories of jobs. In the same questionnaire survey of membership, an editorial decision was made to the effect that persons who listed "Teachers College" and "Columbia University" as having granted their degrees were referring to the same institution (Teachers College of Columbia University), with the result that the two categories were combined (accompanied by an explanatory footnote).

In dealing with questionnaire returns for purposes of tabulation, there are three choices:

1. Sometimes the questionnaire can be used directly, without copying off the material before tabulation. This is likely to be true when the questionnaire is a single page, which permits the questionnaire to be handled much like a data card.

2. In an initial list table the responses for each questionnaire (or other case) may be put on a single line, which permits a preliminary overview of the results, by way of showing (perhaps better than data cards will) what the range is likely to be.

3. Data cards have their chief advantage for purposes of cross classification or tabulation, because they can be sorted once for a trait, and then sorted again on one or more secondary traits. Data cards also can be checked readily when tabulations are made. There is the physical advantage of allowing a subgroup of cards to be removed from the main pack for use at some other place.[64]

When tabulating machines are used to summarize questionnaire returns, the investigator probably will check back many times against original data, as in identifying the individuals at the extremes of a distribution, or listing by name in the report the individual cases at the extremes (or at the median) of a distribution. A discussion of computers and data processing is beyond the scope of this book, except as mentioned briefly under the topic of instrumentation in the chapter on experimental designs.[65]

We have already noted in this chapter the value of descriptive-survey studies in providing perspective concerning present status or current

[64] Quoted from Carter V. Good and Douglas E. Scates, op. cit., p. 630.
[65] "The Computer and Educational Research: A Symposium." Harvard Educational Review 31: 235–63; Summer 1961.

conditions, including novel or promising practices. In interpreting questionnaire results, perplexing questions concerning frequency of practice
are present. Can cruciality or importance be inferred from frequency?
Can the significance of an event or an activity for an individual be inferred from the frequency for the majority of the sample represented?

Literature on the Questionnaire

The procedures of the questionnaire survey, outlined only briefly
in this section, are treated fully in the literature, including such details
of technique as: classification and categories, enumeration, gathering data
from documentary sources and records, analysis, coding, hand and
machine tabulation, and evaluation and interpretation of data. Especially
helpful are Payne's recommendations and examples with respect to major
types of questions (free-answer, dichotomous, multiple-choice, and
others), treatment of respondents, selection and use of appropriate words
and language, and readability, as well as a summary list of 100 items at
the end of the book;[66] and Parten's detailed treatment[67] of construction
of schedules and questionnaires, procedures for the mail questionnaire,
sources of bias, editing the schedule data, and coding and tabulating
the data. Many additional references on the questionnaire are listed in
the bibliographies at the beginning of this section and at the end of the
chapter.

THE INTERVIEW[68]

In a treatment of interviewing, it is essential to consider the social
and psychological meaning of the interview for the two parties involved,

[66] Stanley L. Payne, *op. cit.*
[67] Mildred Parten, *op. cit.*, Chapters 6, 11–15.
[68] E. Anstey and E. O. Mercer, *Interviewing for the Selection of Staff*. London:
George Allen and Unwin, for the Royal Institute of Public Administration, 1956.
xiv + 111 p.
  W. V. Bingham, B. V. Moore, and J. W. Gustad, *How to Interview*. Fourth
Revised Edition. New York: Harper & Brothers, 1959. 277 p.
  Clifford E. Erickson, *The Counseling Interview*. New York: Prentice-Hall, 1950.
174 p.
  R. A. Fear, *The Education Interview:* Predicting Job Performance in Business
and Industry. New York: McGraw-Hill Book Co., 1958. xii + 288 p.
  Anne F. Fenlason, *Essentials in Interviewing:* For the Interivewer Offering Pro-
fessional Services. New York: Harper & Brothers, 1952. xi + 352 p. Revised, 1962.
  Leon Festinger and Daniel Katz, Editors, *op. cit.*, p. 327–80.
  John F. Fraser, *A Handbook of Employment Interviewing*. Revised Edition. Lon-
don: MacDonald and Evans, 1951. 214 p.
  Merton Gill, Richard Newman, and Fredrick C. Redlich, *The Initial Interview
in Psychiatric Practice*. New York: International Universities Press, 1954. 423 p.
  Carter V. Good and Douglas E. Scates, *op. cit.*, p. 635–45.
  William J. Goode and Paul K. Hatt, *op. cit.*, p. 184–208.

the cognitive and motivational processes affecting the behavior of the interviewer, the reactions of the respondent, and the relation of errors in the data to the behavior of the persons in interviewing situations of various types.[69]

Interviewing as Communication and Motivation[70]

The dynamics of interviewing begin with the concept that the interview is a process of communication or interaction. If the interviewer and the respondent share a common language and terminology that permit easy communication, there remains the challenge to the interviewer of motivating frank and complete answers from the respondent. The interviewer must be able to identify and, so far as possible, control the psychological forces present in the interview, which affect both the respondent and himself. The stimulus-response episodes of the interview involve the purposes, motives, attitudes, and beliefs of both the interviewer and the respondent. Of late, social scientists have gathered evidence concerning the process of communication between people and concerning

---

Herbert H. Hyman and Others, *Interviewing in Social Research.* Chicago: The University of Chicago Press, 1954. xvi + 415 p.

Robert L. Kahn and Charles F. Cannell, *The Dynamics of Interviewing:* Theory, Technique, and Cases. New York: John Wiley & Sons, 1957. x + 386 p.

Grace Langdon and Irving Stout, *Teacher-Parent Interviews.* New York: Prentice-Hall, 1954. 336 p.

Stanley G. Law, *Therapy Through Interview.* New York: McGraw-Hill Book Co., 1948. xiii + 313 p.

John Madge, *op. cit.,* p. 144–253.

Thomas C. McCormick and Roy G. Francis, *Methods of Research in the Behavioral Sciences.* New York: Harper & Brothers, 1958. Chapter 6.

Robert K. Merton, Marjorie Fiske, and Patrician L. Kendall, *The Focused Interview:* A Manual of Problems and Procedures. Glencoe, Ill.: Free Press, 1956. 186 p.

C. A. Moser, *op. cit.,* Chapters 11, 13.

Mildred Parten, *op. cit.,* p. 331–82.

Stanley L. Payne, *op. cit.*

R. E. Pittenger, C. F. Hockett, and J. J. Danehy, *The First Five Minutes:* A Sample of Microscopic Interview Analysis. Ithaca, N.Y.: Paul Martineau, 1960. xii + 264 p.

Claire Selltiz and Others, *op. cit.,* p. 236–78, 546–87.

Harry S. Sullivan, *The Psychiatric Interview.* New York: W. W. Norton and Co., 1954. 246 p.

James D. Weinland and Margaret V. Gross, *Personnel Interviewing.* New York: Ronald Press, 1952. vii + 416 p.

Helen L. Witmer, Editor, *Psychiatric Interviews with Children.* New York: Commonwealth Fund, 1946. viii + 444 p.

Leon J. Yarrow, "Interviewing Children," *Handbook of Research Methods in Child Development.* Edited by Paul H. Mussen. New York: John Wiley and Sons, 1960. Chapter 14.

Pauline V. Young, *op. cit.,* p. 205–28.

[69] Herbert H. Hyman and Others, *Interviewing in Social Research.* Chicago: The University of Chicago Press, 1954. p. 3.

[70] Robert L. Kahn and Charles F. Cannell, *op. cit.,* p. 3–21, 65–91.

sources of bias in the interview; social psychologists have observed how people communicate with each other in small groups; and clinical psychologists have studied the interaction between the therapist and the patient in the psychotherapeutic interview.

One major form of motivation for the respondent is the psychological reward of talking to an understanding, permissive interviewer. A second type of motivation is that of accomplishing certain practical ends or purposes, as in giving information to the physician to improve one's health, to the personnel interviewer to secure a job, and to the social worker to secure advice or economic assistance. At the beginning of the interview the respondent may be motivated almost entirely by his own needs and purposes, but as the process of interaction progresses the respondent may find motivation in the psychological climate of the interview itself.

Values and Uses of the Interview[71]

Practical use of the interview in simple form is as old as face-to-face communication between two persons. In Hamlet, Polonius checked on his son by surreptitiously sending a friend to interview people in the strange town as to his son's reputation. The interviewer began by saying, "He's a gay young blade!" This opening encouraged the interviewee to comment on any escapades.

Although the interview belongs to a class of methods that yield primarily subjective data, that is, direct descriptions of the world of experience, the interests of many social scientists call for such data, however crude the method of data-gathering may of necessity be. For example, the interview technique has certain advantages for collection of data relating to three of the most prominent emphases in social psychology, all implying subjective data: the emphasis on desires, goals, and values by students of personality; the current interest in social perception; and emphasis on the concept of attitude.

It is true that certain methods utilizing other personal documents (such as diaries, life histories, or letters) do yield an elaborate picture of the individual's world of desires and attitudes, but such techniques are relatively inflexible or inefficient for certain types of problems, in that they may not exist for the particular population of individuals to be studied, or these sources may be available only for some self-selected and possibly biased subsample of the particular population. Such life-history documents may not contain information relating to specific significant variables, since they are usually spontaneous in origin.

Many of the concepts and techniques of the questionnaire survey

[71] Herbert H. Hyman and Others, *Interviewing in Social Research*. Chicago: The University of Chicago Press, 1954. p. 15–19.

are useful in interviewing. The dynamics of interviewing, however, involve much more than an "oral questionnaire." Many types of information can be secured only through face-to-face contacts with people, especially data relating to personal history, family life, opinions, and attitudes. The interview has certain unique values, as compared with the questionnaire:

1. The interviewees may require the stimulus and confidential relationships of the interview in order to provide personal and confidential information which they would not ordinarily place on paper.

2. The interviewer may follow up leads and clues in a manner that is not possible by means of an instrument prepared in advance.

3. The interviewer may form some impression of the interviewee, in relation to the truth of the answers and the things that may have been left unsaid.

4. The interviewer may give information and develop attitudes on the part of the respondent, especially in a therapeutic relationship, sometimes encouraging exchange of ideas and information.

The self-administered questionnaire may provide subjective data from the respondent and has the advantages of cheapness because of the reduction of interviewer costs and the possibility of group administration, plus applicability on a systematic sampling basis, but has certain limitations not characteristic of the personal-interview technique:

1. The interview permits study of illiterates or near-illiterates for whom the written questionnaire is not applicable, which may be an important problem for investigations involving the national population, as in studies of recruits in the military forces with very limited education.

2. Since it is always possible for the respondent to read through the entire questionnaire first, or to edit earlier answers in the light of later questions, the advantages of saliency questions become dubious, and it is difficult to control the contextual effects of other questions upon a given answer. In the interview, later questions can be hidden from the knowledge of the respondent and, therefore, can have no effect on the results of an earlier question.

3. A resourceful interviewer with insight may produce certain favorable results not possible in the self-administering situation of the questionnaire, where the mistakes of the respondent have a quality of finality. For example, the interviewer may make ratings of given characteristics of the respondent, explain or amplify a given question, probe for clarification of an ambiguous answer or elaboration of a cryptic report, or even persuade the respondent to answer a question that he would otherwise skip.

Informal observation of behavior under natural conditions usually is not a flexible method, in that the environment may not provide any avenue for the expression of the behavior relevant to the particular problem. To discover a person's thoughts may require a question, as in the case of studies concerned with the past; for example, investigations of the reactions of certain populations to strategic bombing were not undertaken until after the end of hostilities, when the natural setting of the postwar world was not appropriate to observing the reaction to the bombing of three years earlier; hence it was necessary to reconstruct the past either through the memories of the respondent as reported in the course of interviewing or through historical records.

Sometimes an observational approach to attitudes is attempted by placing the subject in a specially contrived experimental or laboratory situation in which the behavior relevant to a given inference appears. However, the behavior exhibited in this laboratory situation is as much bound by the unstated conventions of the contrived situation, and by the explicit instructions characteristic of all experiments on humans, as is the verbal report restricted or limited by the nature of the formal interview. Observation under natural conditions or in real life deals with behavior conditioned by a host of unknown momentary factors operating in environment, just as the verbal report of an individual is bound or limited by the formal interview situation. One is always playing some role in relation to some situation—laboratory, everyday life, or the interview— and the real issue is the kind of situation in which the attitudinal findings are liberated, as well as the ability to relate the findings to the particular situation.

Many research problems merely require data that, by definition, are objective and consequently would not require interviewing. Even in many such instances, however, the interview technique has been applied extensively because of certain practical advantages; for example, the decennial census of the United States, governmental surveys of household possessions and the job record of the individual, insurance company surveys, and the political preference of the voter. The interview enables the investigator to relate the given datum to other characteristics of that same individual as measured simultaneously. For example, the records of an insurance company include a considerable amount of objective data on a health insurance policy covering a certain member of the population, but do not permit analysis of such coverage in relation to health needs and experiences, medical expenses, family income, and other significant variables. Voting records reveal the political behavior or preference of an individual, but do not indicate the social and psychological characteristics of the voter.

Often, the interview is used for practical purposes rather than to gather data for research. The following represent the variety of situations in which interviewing is appropriate, although in many instances it serves to accomplish the practical task at hand: student counseling, a variety of teacher and pupil-personnel contacts, occupational adjustment, applying for a position, employment offices, civil-service agencies, employer-employee relationships, public-opinion polls, radio and TV programs, commercial surveys and market studies, industrial surveys, advertising, censuses, social case work, psychiatric work, mental clinics, psychology, anthropology, sociology, journalism, and law. The interview is frequently employed in historical, experimental, and case-clinical studies.

Outline of Types of Interviews[72]

A working classification of interviews is as follows:

1. According to function (diagnostic, treatment, or research)
2. Number of persons participating (individual or group)
3. Length of contact (short or prolonged)
4. According to the roles assumed by the interviewer and interviewee, in relation to the sociopsychological process of interaction
Nondirective (uncontrolled, unguided, or unstructured)
Focused
Depth
Repeated, in order to trace change or development.

The Clinical Interview[73]

In clinical work some form of the interview or personal contact has been used in many kinds of situations to secure information about the client and to understand his problems. The two major purposes of the interview in clinical work are diagnosis and treatment. Social workers employ the interview to secure information about the client's problem, his past history, family relations, and job adjustment. Other persons than the client frequently are interviewed when the client is a child, a mental defective, or a psychotic, or when there are unusual discrepancies in the client's presentation of data about himself. The psychiatric examination and even the standardized individual psychological examination are interviewing procedures.

During the clinical interview, certain nonverbal behavior on the part of the patient has useful diagnostic value, including gait, expression, posture, rate of speech, topics avoided, digressions, and word choice. In addition to the general techniques that apply to any interview situation, special procedures may be needed to deal effectively with the problems that arise in the several types of clinical interviews: the intake or admission interview, concerned chiefly with the patient's complaints;

[72] Pauline V. Young, *op. cit.*, p. 210–13.

[73] Sol L. Garfield, *op. cit.*, p. 192–94.

L. A. Pennington and Irwin A. Berg, Editors, *An Introduction to Clinical Psychology*. Second Edition. New York: Ronald Press, 1954. p. 125.

the personal and social-history interview, to gather background data with a bearing on the complaints; the screening or diagnostic interview, to arrive at a judgment concerning the patient's condition; interviews before and after psychological test administration, and as a means of introducing the patient to therapy; the interview to assist friends and relatives in their dealings with the patient; and the exit or termination interview to facilitate the patient's discharge or transition from hospital to home.

Group and Individual Interviews[74]

Although there is little evidence concerning distinctive merits of group and individual interviews, certain relative advantages and disadvantages may be summarized briefly, with an introductory comment on the setting for the group interview. The size of the group should not be so large that it is unwieldy or inhibits participation by most members, and should not be so small that it lacks substantially greater coverage than in the individual interview. The optimum size is approximately 10 to 12 persons. Social, intellectual, and educational homogeneity are important for effective participation of all group members. A circular seating arrangement, with the interviewer as one of the group, is conducive to full and spontaneous reporting and participation.

The advantages of the group interview are as follows:

1. Release of inhibitions through personal comments and responses, with expressions of interest by the interviewer

2. A wider range of response as the result of a wider range of experience on the part of the group

3. Recall of forgotten details of experience through the process of group interaction.

Possible disadvantages of the group interview are as follows:

1. Group interaction may result in controversies or discussions unrelated to the stimulus situation or topic. The interviewer should redirect attention to the initial problem.

2. Articulate members may be accorded the status of "leader," with the result that others may look to the leader for guidance, or one or more leaders may monopolize the discussion.

3. Continuity of group discussion sometimes is interrupted by an informant or respondent, with the result that the topic is not explored in detail.

4. The group may have an inhibiting effect of two kinds, in that interviewees may hesitate to reveal certain attitudes or experiences in the quasi-public situation of the group interview, and articulate subjects may withhold significant responses on the assumption that others in the group want to express themselves.

[74] Robert K. Merton, Marjorie Fiske, and Patricia L. Kendall, *op. cit.*, p. 136–53.

Focused, Depth, and Nondirective Interviews

Nonstructured interviews and interview guides usually are labeled by the terminology "focused," "depth," "nondirective." Although definite subject-matter areas are involved, the interviewer is largely free to arrange the form and timing of the question. The focused interview concentrates attention on some particular event or experience rather than on general lines of inquiry about the event. The depth interview is intensive and searching, with emphasis on such psychological and social factors as attitudes, convictions, or emotions. The nondirective approach as an uncontrolled or unstructured technique permits much freedom on the part of the respondent to "talk about" the problems under study.[75]

The focused interview is a method for collection of data developed to determine the responses of individuals to specific communication situations such as a movie or a speech. The procedural and technical aspects of focused interviewing may well be considered in terms of its relationship to other methods for collection of data, namely, observational, interview and questionnaire, and projective methods. Although focused interviewing places primary emphasis on the subject's verbal report of his definition of a specific situation and response to it, the method also possesses certain characteristics resembling closely the techniques found in projective and observational studies. During the course of the interview, the interviewer may utilize certain projective techniques to evaluate and interpret discrepancies occurring between the investigator's appraisal and the subject's report of the stimulus situation. The interviewer's objective evaluation of the particular situation to which subjects are to be exposed resembles observational procedures, in that the investigator is enabled: (1) to develop an hypothesis regarding expected and appropriate subject responses, (2) to focus the interview upon the subject's definition of and his responses to a particular situation, and (3) to appraise and interpret discrepancies occurring between his objective definition and the subject's subjective definition of the situation. An inherent disadvantage of focused interviewing is its limitation to occasions or settings where the investigator is able to secure an objective measurement of the specific social situation to which all subjects will be exposed. This limitation is relatively serious in the social sciences where there has been only limited success in objectively defining any simple or complex social situation. Focused interviewing involves an unstructured form, nondirective orientation, and artistic and empathic skills.[76]

[75] Pauline V. Young, *op. cit.*, p. 205–28.
[76] Review by Charles G. McClintock, *Contemporary Psychology* 2: 220–21; August 1957, of Robert K. Merton, Marjorie Fiske, and Patricia L. Kendall, *op. cit.*, xx + 186 p.

In general the focused interview employs nondirective procedures in encouraging the respondent to structure the stimulus situation by indicating aspects of the situation most significant and by progressively exploring his responses. Nondirection in the focused interview means reliance on unstructured questions, but varying degrees of structure may be present:

1. *Unstructured question (stimulus and response-free)*
   For example, "What impressed you most in this film?" or "What stood out especially in this conference?"
2. *Semi-structured question*
   Type *A: Response-structured, stimulus-free.* For example, "What did you learn from this pamphlet that you hadn't known before?
   Type *B: Stimulus-structured, response-free.* For example, "How did you feel about the episode of Joe's discharge from the army as a psychoneurotic?"
3. *Structured question (stimulus- and response-structured)*
   For example, "Judging from the film, do you think that the German fighting equipment was better, as good as, or poorer than the equipment used by Americans" or "As you listened to Chamberlain's speech, did you feel it was propagandistic or informative?"
   Although especially useful in opening stages, relatively unstructured questions can be profitably used throughout the interview.[77]

Depth procedures in focused interviews enable the investigator through depth responses to determine the respondent's degree of detachment or personal involvement in the experience, and the peripheral or salient character of the responses. The procedures of such depth interviewing are as follows:[78]

Flexibility of Interview Situation

Flexible interviews encourage orientation to stimulus situation, rather than to interviewer, thus facilitating depth and curbing stereotyped reports.

Retrospective Focus

Focus on past experience, through reinstatement of stimulus situation, promotes elaboration of reported responses.

Focus on Feelings

Questions explicitly referring to affective aspects (e.g., "How did you feel when. . . ?" encourage reports of depth responses.

Restatement of Implied or Expressed Feelings

Occasional restatements of implied or expressed feelings prove effective by (1) inviting progressive elaboration of response, and (2) establishing com-

[77] Quoted from Robert K. Merton, Marjorie Fiske, and Patricia L. Kendall, *op. cit.,* p. 12–17.
[78] Quoted from *ibid.,* p. 96–113.

mon ground for mutual understanding. When interviewee indicates that he is not yet ready to admit these feelings, restatements can be extensive (in group interview) or projective (in individual interview).

Comparative Situations

Suggested comparisons between stimulus situation and significant experiences that subjects have known or can be presumed to have had often aid verbalization of effect.

Guiding the Course of an Interview: Overview[79]

A check list of recommendations for conducting the interview is as follows:

1. An interviewer generally should open an interview by asking factual nonthreatening questions.
2. The interviewer should locate the major data by unstructured "lead" questions.
3. The interviewer should make use of occasional guide questions.
4. The interviewer should make an effort to pick up leads.
5. The interviewer should cut through generalities with well-formulated probes.
6. The interviewer should stick with the fruitful areas once they open up.
7. The interviewer should reflect on the meaning of emerging data and ask questions that clarify or amplify their meaning for the research problem.
8. The interviewer should be especially alert to follow up only areas where the respondent shows emotional involvement.
9. The interviewer should try to redirect the interview to more fruitful topics when useful data are not emerging.
10. The interviewer should be alert to "touchy" subject matters and not just blunder in.
11. The interviewer should try to turn back respondent's direct questions.
12. The interviewer should wind up the interview before the respondent becomes tired.
13. Whether an interviewer should take notes depends on the situation.

Ways of Opening the Interview

Methods of beginning the interview include the following procedures:

An indirect social approach, as when a teacher calls on the parents of one of her pupils

Spontaneous reaction to controlled stimuli, as in administering an intelligence test to a child who has not learned to read

[79] John T. Doby, Editor, *op. cit.*, p. 240–48.

Distribution of forms prior to the interview, especially for the purpose of collecting statistical data

A direct frank approach, usually employed for research interviews, especially when factual data are involved.

Questions and Responses

Interviewing is an art which requires appropriate training and guided experience as essential background. Careful preparation of questions for the interview is fully as important as has been emphasized in preparing the questionnaire. A well-conducted interview is not just a haphazard series of questions and answers of a pleasant conversation. The interviewer has a set of carefully prepared questions to serve as a thread of conversation, although he may vary the order of the questions to adapt to special circumstances. These characterizations apply especially to data-gathering studies; nondirective or client-centered counseling permits greater freedom by way of an unstructured interview.

Inadequate responses which call for probing or secondary questions may be partial response, nonresponse, irrelevant response, inaccurate response, or verbalized response. In addition to problems of motivation and conflict of motives, other causes of inadequate response include the following:[80]

1. The respondent may fail to understand the purpose of the question or the kind of answer needed.
2. The language or concepts may go beyond the respondent's comprehension.
3. The respondent may lack the information or background necessary to answer the question.
4. The respondent may not remember the information requested.
5. The respondent may not be able to verbalize his feelings, as in the case of intimate "depth" questions or materials.
6. The respondent may feel that the question does not fit the purpose of the interview.
7. The respondent may regard a question as going beyond the limits of what he is willing to confide in the interviewer.
8. The respondent may feel that the interviewer is unable to understand his true feelings.

Sources of Error and Bias

Factors conducive to successful interviews (neglect of which may lead to failure) include the following:

An adequate number and length of interviews
Rapport and sensitivity to the interviewee

[80] Robert L. Kahn and Charles F. Cannel, *op. cit.*, p. 203–32.

A comfortable and relaxing physical setting

A favorable reputation on the part of the interviewer, in terms of integrity and knowledge of the subject under study.

The reliability of the information obtained through the interview is affected by such factors as the following:

The desire of many interviewees to make a good impression, particularly in answering questions relating to generally accepted standards of behavior

The reluctance of many subjects to reveal highly personal information that might appear damaging to the interviewee

An attitude of confidence in and respect for the interviewer, on the part of the interviewee.

In addition to basic psychological factors or processes (intellectual, perceptual, cognitive, or motivational) affecting the interviewer and the respondent's interaction within the context of social relations with the interviewer, there are other possible sources of error or bias:[81] content and form of questions, procedures established for the interview, physical setting, mode of recording, accidental distractions, and temporary state of the parties involved. Variation and bias are likely to result when interviewers have complete freedom to interview respondents of their choice, to ask any questions desired (in any form), to make comments as they choose, and to record answers as they prefer (particularly after the close of the interview). Standardized interview procedures, however, may at times break down under the pressure of a specific situation. The history of election-forecasting reveals that the successful forecasts of a dozen years did not preclude a failure in 1948.

Potential sources of error and bias in the interview include firmly fixed attitudes, personality characteristics, motives, and goals that frequently are related to group memberships and loyalties (age, sex, race, religion, income, and education). Although these psychological and social characteristics or factors are potentially biasing, it is only through behavior that bias can become operative. This behavior, on the part of the interviewer, includes asking questions, probing for additional information, recording responses, and motivating the respondent to communicate. Helpful investigations of these behavioral sources of error and bias have been made, especially in social psychology and sociology. To function effectively and without bias, the interviewer needs techniques for formulation of questions, for motivation of the respondent, and for focusing communication on the content objectives of the interview; he also needs a deep understanding of the dynamics of interaction and of the psychological forces that affect the processes of the interview.[82]

[81] Herbert H. Hyman and Others, *Interviewing in Social Research*. Chicago: The University of Chicago Press, 1954. p. 171–72, 275.

[82] Robert L. Kahn and Charles F. Cannell, *op. cit.*, p. 166–202.

Rapport, Interpersonal Relations, and Subjectivity[83]

It is generally accepted that a friendly atmosphere of rapport and skillful probing for meaningful answers are essential to a good interview. We question the skill of an interviewer who obtains numerous "don't know" responses. In attempting to establish favorable rapport, however, the interviewer should not err in the direction of extreme chumminess with the respondent. In depth-probing, to secure meaningful responses, the investigator should not pursue the question to the extreme of distorting the situation, since some people have no hidden depths and only superficial attitudes on certain issues. At such times, repeated probing may suggest inaccurate responses and may "salt the mine."

Both interviewer and respondent contribute to the effects of interpersonal relationships. While the interviewer enters the situation with certain attitudes and beliefs that operate to affect his perception of the respondent, his judgment of the response, and other relevant aspects of his behavior, the respondent also entertains beliefs and attitudes which influence the response he makes and are at least in part a product of the personal-interview procedure. Certain respondent reactions are independent of any act or conduct on the part of the individual interviewer, and are merely a function of the interpersonal nature of the interview situation. The involvement of any respondent in an interview situation includes two major components: "task involvement" (involvement with the questions and answers) and "social involvement" (involvement with the interviewer as a personality). Validity should increase in proportion to the extent of task involvement on the part of the respondent. So far as the respondent's action derives from social or interpersonal involvement, bias will result, since the response is primarily a function of the relation between the respondent and the interviewer rather than a response to the particular task (the questions and answers).

Removal of the interviewer from the physical environment, as in the case of self-administered questionnaires, is not a complete answer to the problem of interviewer effect. Subjects filling out questionnaires may take account of the prospective readers of their replies, and thus involve an "interviewer effect," even when no interviewer is present. It is true that the social component of involvement is increased as the interviewer looms larger in the psychological field of the respondent, which means that the respondent usually will be more sensitized to the "interviewer" when the latter is physically present.

Much of the criticism of the interview technique rests on the fact that the data are derived from interpersonal situations. We should remem-

[83] Herbert H. Hyman and Others, *Interviewing in Social Research*. Chicago: The University of Chicago Press, 1954. p. 8, 12–14, 24, 83, 138–39.

ber, however, that even in experimentation with animals in physiology and psychology, certain "interpersonal" relationships or effects may be present, as illustrated by research on conditioning in animals, although criticism of such experiments is rarely in terms of peculiar interpersonal relations between animal subject and human experimenter.

Although interviewer effect is a difficult problem in the social sciences, there are parallel errors of observation and measurement or interpretation in other sciences; for example, observer differences in reading chest x-ray films, in interpreting the results of laboratory tests, in appraising the malnutrition of children from medical examinations, or in noting the transit of stars in a telescope. We may be willing to pay the price of some crudity in the interview technique to secure the gains of essential information.

Examples of subjective or qualitative effects in the interview are numerous in the fields of clinical psychology and counseling. Differences between psychiatrists in the subtle dynamics of their interviewing behavior, differences which are possibly relevant to the variations in results reported, have been demonstrated through the application of instruments previously developed to describe social interaction processes; for example, significant differences in the degree of "activity" (ratio of talk to silence) of two psychiatrists, and similar differences in two psychiatrists with respect to an index of "tempo," another formal dimension of verbal behavior. Frequently there is interaction between the psychiatrist's previous experience and the experience of the patient under consideration. The psychiatrist, like any other human being, tends to associate unconsciously his own experiences and problems with what his patient is telling him, a reaction known as countertransference. In clinical psychology and counseling there are similar problems. In counseling, the great concern with the actual nature of the therapeutic procedure has led to a series of studies in which an accurate description of the entire content of the interview is available from electrical recordings. Comparison of the counselor's written report of interviews with an electrical transcription demonstrates that there are large and significant omissions of content in the written record, alterations in the time sequence of remarks, and lack of precision in the notes, leading to ambiguity. Presumptive evidence of differences in counseling behavior is available from studies of the attitudes of counselors toward given interviewing practices. Therefore, a basic issue is the magnitude of errors in the collection of data by interview, efficient ways of estimating the presence of such errors, and the safeguards or checks upon such errors.

Hyman found that skilled interviewers frequently have certain beliefs about their respondents and expectations as to answers, but that the existence of such role expectations, attitude-structure expectations, and probability expectations did not materially affect the behavior of interviewers so as to alter survey results. The skillful interviewer's expectations may have a foundation in truth and consequently may enhance validity.

Records and Recording

Clinical interview findings, together with other related material, usually are filed in a folder or case record, including four types of information: (1) historical or background data concerning the patient's past life; (2) quantitative, or test and measurement results; (3) impressionistic or nonverbal behavior, such as gestures and posture; and (4) the treatment record, or data on medical treatment and psychiatric interview notes.[84]

Helpful extracts from interviews and illustrative records of interviews are as follows:

Clinical interviews under such catchy topics as the envious man, beaten man, weak feet, bad conscience, struggle within, sacrifice, overburdened mouth, and color barrier[85]

The dynamics of interviewing, including the problems of cardiac symptoms and neurotic manifestations, experienced and inexperienced applicants for a clerical job, a production bottleneck and an office feud, and family and job adjustments of a discharged psychiatric patient[86]

Psychiatric interviews with children[87]

Therapy through interviews[88]

Interviews in the general area of professional services.[89]

Example: Role of the Superintendent[90]

. . . A report of findings from a systematic survey of role perceptions among public-school superintendents and school-board members. Since the hypotheses and findings are not unusual, the chief value of the book is its methodological orderliness and its thoroughness of exploitation of interview data in an area deserving of continued exploration.

The authors are concerned mainly with the concepts of *role consensus* and *role conflict* and their correlates. Role consensus is agreement concerning role

---

[84] L. A. Pennington and Irwin A. Berg, Editors, *op. cit.*, p. 125.

[85] Felix Deutsch and William F. Murphy, *The Clinical Interview*, Vol. 2: Therapy. New York: International Universities Press, 1955. 335 p.

[86] Robert L. Kahn and Charles F. Cannell, *op. cit.*, p. 253–351.

[87] Helen L. Witmer, *op. cit.*

[88] Stanley G. Law, *op. cit.*

[89] Anne E. Fenlason, *op. cit.*

[90] Quoted from review by David W. Lewit, *Contemporary Psychology* 4: 106–7; April 1959, of Neal Gross, Ward S. Mason, and Alexander W. McEachern, *Explorations in Role Analysis:* Studies of the School Superintendency Role. New York: John Wiley and Sons, 1958. xiv + 379 p.

definition. It was measured by the consistency among respondents of what they expect of a person in a given position, viz., the school superintendent's position or the school-board member's position. The respondents were incumbents of these positions. Their expectations were recorded as degrees of agreement or disagreement with lists of hypothetical obligations of superintendents or boards. The items appearing on these lists were constructed after lengthy preliminary interviews with persons similar to the respondents.

Role consensus is noted at two levels—the *macroscopic* or sociological level at which sample variance is used as the measure, and the *microscopic* or psychological level at which variance among face-to-face group members is used as the measure. *Intraposition consensus* is within the sample (or within local-board) variance; *interposition consensus* is between samples (or between superintendent and the mean of his local-board) variance.

Interviewers have made increasing use of instrumentation and forms of recording, including tape recording, the telephone,[91] radio, and television. Among the activities where tape recordings[92] may be used effectively are the following:

1. Exploratory interviewing, as when using an unstructured or nondirective technique

2. Pretest interviewing, permitting the interviewer to subject the record to objective and intensive analysis

3. Intensive unstructured or nondirective interviewing, freeing the investigator from the mechanics of note-taking and enabling him to devote full attention to meanings

4. Interdisciplinary research, permitting the representatives of each discipline to select the data most pertinent to their own problems and interests.

Some of the questions most frequently raised about the effect of tape recording on interview data are as follows:[93]

1. Will the use of tape recorders increase resistance to the interview and thereby raise the refusal rate? The answer to this question—based upon our own experience and that of other investigators—would appear to be a clear "no."

2. Will the presence of the tape recorder decrease or destroy interviewer-respondent rapport? Our experience also suggests a negative answer to this question.

3. Will the presence of the tape recorder alter the responses of the respondent? No unequivocal answer to this question can be given without further systematic research. However, our impression—based upon a general

[91] Paul Widen, "The Telephone Intake Interview in a Child Guidance Clinic." *Social Casework* 38: 485–89; November 1957.

[92] Rue Bucher, Charles E. Fritz, and E. L. Quarantelli, "Tape Recorded Interviews in Social Research." *American Sociological Review* 21: 359–64; June 1956.

[93] Quoted from *ibid*.

evaluation and the contrast of about 300 written interviews with the approximately 700 tape recorded interviews gathered in the course of our work —is that there is no noticeable or significant effect on interview data that can be attributed to the introduction of the tape recorder.

The basic advantages of tape recording over various forms of note-taking and memory reconstruction are as follows:[94]

1. Apart from the operational problems of obtaining proper audibility and voice fidelity, no verbal productions are lost in a tape recorded interview.

2. The tape recorded interview eliminates a major source of interviewer bias—the conscious and unconscious selection on the part of the interviewer of the material to note down.

3. The tape recorded interview not only eliminates the omissions, distortions, elaborations, condensations, and other modifications of data usually found in written interviews, but it also provides an objective basis for evaluating the adequacy of the interview data in relation to the performance of the interviewer.

4. The tape recorded interview is a liberating influence on the interviewer, because it permits him to devote full attention to the respondent.

5. Other things being equal, the interviewer who uses a tape recorder is able to obtain more interviews during a given time period than an interviewer who takes notes or attempts to reconstruct the interview from memory after the interview has been completed.

Interview transcriptions and commentaries, and records of the practice interviews of trainees, are valuable devices for training the beginner. Other techniques for acquiring the essential skills of interviewing include role-playing, with the trainee acting in turn as interviewer, respondent, and observer. Rating scales also are used in helping the interviewer evaluate the effectiveness of his techniques of probing for information.

OBSERVATIONAL STUDIES[95]

Observation, as a general rule, is concerned neither with what a respondent places on paper nor with what he says in an interview, but deals

[94] Quoted from *ibid.*

[95] Russell L. Ackoff, *The Design of Social Research.* Chicago: The University of Chicago Press, 1953. Chapter 9.

Robert F. Bales, *Interaction Process Analysis.* Cambridge, Mass.: Addison-Wesley Publishing Co., 1950. 203 p.

Roger G. Barker and Herbert F. Wright, *Midwest and Its Children:* The Psychological Ecology of an American Town. Evanston, Ill.: Row, Peterson and Co., 1955. vii + 532 p.

Roger G. Barker and Herbert F. Wright, *One Boy's Day:* A Specimen Record of Behavior. New York: Harper & Brothers, 1951. x + 435 p.

Clarence W. Brown and Edwin E. Ghiselli, *Scientific Method in Psychology.* New York: McGraw-Hill Book Co., 1955. p. 193–202.

with the overt behavior of persons in appropriate situations, sometimes under conditions of normal living and at other times with some special set of factors operating. In a questionnaire or interview, the respondent may tell what he thinks he does, but human beings are not generally accurate or reliable observers of themselves. Only direct observation of overt behavior can reveal what the subject actually does. It is sometimes desirable to observe the behavior of persons when completing a questionnaire, participating in an interview, or taking a standardized test, since significant aspects of behavior or personality may be revealed under such conditions.

Direct observation as a systematic research approach in the psychological and social areas has developed during the present century, with marked progress in educational studies during the second quarter of the century. Among the factors favorable to wider use of observation as an investigational procedure were the following: establishment of centers for research in child development; the demands of the newer or

Leon Festinger and Daniel Katz, Editors, *op. cit.*, p. 243–99, 381–417.

Elizabeth Gellert, "Systematic Observation: A Method in Child Study." *Harvard Educational Review* 25: 179–95; Summer 1955.

Carter V. Good and Douglas E. Scates, *op. cit.*, p. 646–62.

William J. Goode and Paul K. Hatt, *op. cit.*, p. 119–31.

Arthur T. Jersild and Margaret F. Meigs, "Direct Observation as a Research Method." *Review of Educational Research* 9: 472–82, 597–99; December 1939.

John Madge, *op. cit.*, p. 117–43.

Donald Medley and Harold E. Mitzel, "Measuring Classroom Behavior by Systematic Observation," *Handbook of Research on Teaching.* Edited by N. L. Gage. Chicago: Rand McNally, 1963. Chapter 6.

C. A. Moser, *op. cit.*, Chapter 9.

Morris S. Schwartz and Charlotte G. Schwartz, "Problems in Participant Observation." *American Journal of Sociology* 60: 343–53; January 1955.

Saul B. Sells, "Observational Methods of Research." *Review of Educational Research* 18: 424–47; December 1948.

Saul B. Sells and Robert W. Ellis, "Observational Procedures Used in Research." *Review of Educational Research* 21: 432–49; December 1951.

Claire Selltiz and Others, "Observational Methods," *Research Methods in Social Relations.* Revised One-Volume Edition. New York: Henry Holt and Co., 1959. Chapter 6.

R. M. W. Travers, *An Introduction to Educational Research.* New York: The Macmillan Co., 1958. Chapter 8.

Lovisa C. Wagoner and J. M. Castellanos, *Observation of Young Children: Their Behavior and Their Teaching.* Revised Edition. Oakland, Calif.: L. C. Wagoner, Mills College, 1951. xii + 142 p.

Robert I. Watson, *The Clinical Method in Psychology.* New York: Harper & Brothers, 1951. p. 64–82.

Herbert F. Wright, "Observational Child Study," *Handbook of Research Methods in Child Development.* Edited by Paul H. Mussen. New York: John Wiley and Sons, 1960. Chapter 3.

J. Wayne Wrightstone, "Observational Techniques," *Encyclopedia of Educational Research.* Edited by Chester W. Harris. Third Edition. New York: Macmillan Co., 1960. p. 927–33.

Pauline V. Young, *op. cit.*, p. 154–75.

progressive education; a desire to probe aspects of behavior not accessible to the conventional paper-and-pencil test, interview, or laboratory technique; a wish to obviate certain of the judgmental errors likely to enter into the customary rating procedures; and emphasis on the need for studying children in natural or social situations, and for observing the functioning child (including his social and emotional behavior), rather than relying exclusively on cross-sectional measurements of mental and physical growth.[96]

Planning the Design of Observational Studies

The following list of factors that affect reliability of observation may serve as a check list or summary of problems in planning the design of observational investigations. Poor reliability may be a function of one or more of these factors:[97]

1. Inadequate sampling
2. Lack of precision in defining behavior
3. Complexity of method of recording
4. Rapid, complex interaction
5. Difference in perspective of observers
6. Individual differences in degree of decisiveness of activities of subjects observed
7. Constant errors due to observer bias (overweighting, timing, "halo" effects, etc.)
8. Requiring high-order inferences in classifying behavior
9. Demanding the simultaneous observation of too many variables
10. Excessively long periods of observation without interspersed rest periods
11. Inadequate training of observers
12. The effect of individual observers upon the behavior of the subjects
13. Degree of acquaintance with the subjects.

Another classification of factors important in planning and conducting observations was prepared originally for the field of psychology, but applies also to education and other social areas:[98]

1. Nature of the observing process
   a. Mechanisms involved in observing
   b. Active nature of observing
   c. "Mental sets" in observing
2. Scientist as observer
   a. Distinguishing facts and inference

[96] Arthur T. Jersild and Margaret F. Meigs, *op. cit.*
[97] Elizabeth Gellert, *op. cit.*
[98] Clarence W. Brown and Edwin E. Ghiselli, *op. cit.*

      b. Safeguards in attitude
      c. Adequate training in observational techniques
      d. Mechanical supplements to observation
   3. Temporal course of the observations
      a. Necessity for constant conditions of observation
      b. Temporal variations in subjects
      c. Temporal variations in apparatus
   4. Number of observations
      a. Variability of behavior
      b. Replication of observations to achieve representativeness
      c. Statistical compared with practical significance
      d. Designing the study in order to increase the number of observations
   5. Recording the observations
      a. Need for records
      b. Records to be comprehensive
      c. Accuracy of records varying with degree of conceptualization
      d. Limitations of apparatus recording
      e. Keeping a daily record.

To summarize briefly, the aspects of planning for observation include the following factors that affect the success of the investigation:[99]

An appropriate group of subjects to observe
Selection and arrangement of any special conditions for the group
Length of each observation period, interval between periods, and number of periods
Physical position of the observer and possible effect on the subject or subjects
Definition of specific actiivties or units of behavior to be observed
Entry of frequencies or tallies in the record, as a total for the entire observation period or by subdivisions of time within the observation period
Scope of observation, whether for an individual child or for a group
Form of recording, including consideration of mechanical techniques and such quantitative factors as number, time, distance, and spatial relationships
Training of the observer in terms of expertness
Interpretation of observations.

Participant Observation

Participant observation is a dynamic process of interaction, involving registering, interpreting, and recording:

The process and the kinds of data are influenced by continuing observed-observer transactions. The role of the observer may be passive or active. In either case affective involvement with the observed develops inevitably and

[99] Carter V. Good and Douglas E. Scates, *op. cit.*

may range from sympathetic identification to projective distortion. The form it takes is a function primarily of the observer's experience, awareness, and personality. Anxiety and bias are sources of distortion, and their adequate handling is a major problem in refining the human instrument for gathering data.[100]

We are cautioned that participant observation needs better systematization of procedure and recording, and is something more than "having insights":

I have tried to describe the analytic field work characteristic of participant observation, first, in order to bring out the fact that the technique consists of something more than merely immersing oneself in data and "having insights." The discussion may also serve to stimulate those who work with this and similar techniques to attempt greater formalization and systematization of the various operations they use, in order that qualitative research may become more a "scientific" and less an "artistic" kind of endeavor. Finally, I have proposed that new modes of reporting results be introduced, so that the reader is given greater access to the data and procedures on which conclusions are based.[101]

The investigator may play any one of several roles in observation of social situations, with varying degrees of participation,[102] as a visiting stranger, an attentive listener, an eager learner, or a more complete role as participant-observer. As indicated, participation or role-playing is not necessarily complete, since it is possible to take part in many of the activities of the group, as an accepted member, and at the same time act in the role of observer and interviewer. Quasi-participation is illustrated by a study of "corner boys" in an Italian slum.[103] The observer or investigator came in as the local historian under the auspices of a key member of a gang. In other words, the investigator may be disguised in such a manner as to be accepted as a member of the group, although he may not carry out exactly the same activities as the other members, in order to be accepted as a participant-observer. Obviously, if the group has accepted the observer as a participant, their behavior is least likely to be affected by the presence of the participant-observer.

[100] Quoted from Morris S. Schwartz and Charlotte G. Schwartz, op. cit.

[101] Quoted from Howard S. Becker, "Problems of Inference and Proof in Participant Observation." American Sociological Review 23: 652–60; December 1958.

[102] Raymond L. Gold, "Roles in Sociological Field Observations." Social Forces 36: 217–23; March 1958.

William J. Goode and Paul K. Hatt, op. cit., p. 120–24.

Claire Selltiz, op. cit., p. 200–34.

Pauline V. Young, Scientific Social Surveys and Research, op. cit., p. 157–64.

[103] William F. Whyte, Street Corner Society: The Social Structure of an Italian Slum. Enlarged Edition. Chicago: The University of Chicago Press, 1955. xxii + 336 p.

The participant-observer commonly lives in the community or social setting under study, as he takes part in the activities and functions of the particular group or groups. In this way he gets the "feel" of what the various activities and processes mean to the regular participants. The participant-observer also plays a dual role, in that he must take an objective position after performing as a participant; otherwise his subjective reactions might distort his findings. Classic examples[104] are *Middletown* and *Middletown in Transition*.

Example: Blackways of Kent[105]

In research method, the book shows a happy combination of anthropological field work technique and sociological participant-observational technique. Approaching the study of the Negro subculture in the manner of an anthropologist and sociologist, Hylan Lewis, in Part One, not only places solidly the *Blackways of Kent* in their geographic, ecological, and demographic contexts but also in the broader cultural situation. In Part Two, he deals with contents of the subculture in terms of the institutions of courtship, marriage, and the family; the economics of Negro life; religion and salvation; teaching the children; government and social control; orientations and values; and social organization. He concludes the book by touching upon the consistency and coordination of ways of life, and briefly relates the Negro subculture to the dominant or "foreign" culture of Kent.

Example: When Prophecy Fails[106]

At the approach of midnight one December 20 not long ago, fifteen persons maintained anxious vigil in a "Lake City" living room. For all of them the occasion was momentous, but the reader of this remarkable book knows what a casual visitor to the gathering would not have guessed: for five members of the company the occasion had entirely different significance than for the other ten. Ostensibly, the entire group was awaiting spacemen who, at the appointed hour, were to rescue them in flying saucers from the worldwide cataclysm of earthquake and flood that they expected before dawn. In fact, five persons—a third of those present—were participant observers who

[104] Robert S. Lynd and Helen M. Lynd, *Middletown: A Study in Contemporary Culture.* New York: Harcourt, Brace and Co., 1929. x + 550 p.

Robert S. Lynd and Helen M. Lynd, *Middletown in Transition: A Study in Cultural Conflicts.* New York: Harcourt, Brace and Co., 1937. xviii + 604 p.

[105] Quoted from review by Jitsuichi Masuoka, *American Sociological Review* 21: 111–12; February 1956, of Hylan Lewis, *Blackways of Kent.* Chapel Hill: University of North Carolina Press, 1955. xxiv + 337 p.

Also see John K. Morland, *Millways of Kent.* Third volume of "Field Studies in the Modern Culture of the South." Chapel Hill: University of North Carolina Press, 1958. xxii + 291 p.

[106] Quoted from review by M. Brewster Smith, *Contemporary Psychology* 2: 89–92; April 1957, of Leon Festinger, Henry W. Riecken, and Stanley Schachter, *When Prophecy Fails.* Minneapolis: University of Minnesota Press, 1956. vii + 256 p.

had been following the band of believers for more than a month, awaiting opportunity to test some theoretically-based predictions about what happens in social movements "when prophecy fails." Fortunately for the reader, the prophecy did fail; less predictably, the prophecy was explicit and remained so to the crucial hour; the disconfirmation was unequivocal.

Clearly this is no routine research report. The book, an eminently readable one, represents a noteworthy venture in at least four respects, around which subsequent comments will be focused. First, it is an examplary instance in which alert social psychologists with a theory to test were able to see the relevance of a passing event, and to respond to it in time and in sufficient force to capture the pertinent data. Incidental to testing their central hypothesis, secondly, the authors provide an inside account of a miniature apocalyptic movement, an account that is fascinating quite apart from its bearing on the authors' theory. Securing the necessary information from such a socially marginal group, in the third place, tested the resourcefulness of the observers. Their account of the unusual problems they encountered and how they attempted to solve them (given in a methodological appendix) will be of special interest to investigators not intimidated by the barrier between the laboratory and "real life." Finally, the authors' temerity and success in covertly penetrating others' privacy, essential as it was to the enterprise, raises some serious problems of research ethics, problems hardly encountered when psychologists confine themselves to the accustomed laboratory or clinic. The authors have elected to present their findings without discussing the ethical ambiguities that must have troubled them and their associates. The difficulties remain, however, and the rest of us would do well to face them more explicitly.

Example: A Military Training Program[107]

To accomplish this purpose [of studying a military training program] it was decided that a research officer should "enlist" as a basic trainee. He would be a full-fledged member of the group under study, his identity, mission, and role as a researcher unknown to every one (except the investigators), even to his own commanding officer. This then became one of the few cases of real participant observation.   .

In summary, participant observation has certain advantages over such survey techniques as the questionnaire:[108]

1. The participant observer is not basically limited by prejudgment, but can reformulate the problem as he goes along.

2. Because of his closer contact with the field situation, he is better able to avoid misleading or meaningless questions.

[107] Quoted from Mortimer A. Sullivan, Jr., Stuart A. Queen, and Ralph C. Patrick, Jr., "Participant Observation as Employed in the Study of a Military Training Program." *American Sociological Review* 23: 660–67; December 1958.

[108] John T. Doby, Editor, *op. cit.*, p. 227–29.

3. The impressions of a participant field worker are often more reliable in classifying respondents than a rigid index based on one or two questions in a questionnaire.

4. The most expert and highest paid persons are in direct contact with the data in the field.

5. He can ease himself into the field situation at the appropriate pace and thus avoid rebuff by blundering into delicate situations or subject matter.

6. He can constantly remodify his categories to provide more meaningful analysis of problems under study.

7. He can generally impute motives more validly on the basis of the interlocking of aspersions and actual behavior, supplemented by occasional "feedback" reactions.

8. He can select later informants in such a way as to throw additional light on emerging hypotheses.

9. He can generally get at depth material more satisfactorily.

10. He may absorb considerable information which seems at the time irrelevant, but later proves valuable for perspective.

11. He can make use of selected informants' skills and insights by giving them free rein to report the problem situation as they see it.

12. He usually can move more easily back and forth between data-gathering in the field and desk analysis.

13. Through free data-gathering he probably distorts less the difficult-to-quantify situations or aspects of a problem.

14. While ostensibly just participating, he can do covert research in delicate areas.

15. Participant observation usually involves less expense.

Nonparticipant Observation

The nonparticipant observer takes a position where his presence is not disturbing to the group, such as a kindergarten or a nursery school. He may follow in detail the behavior of only one child or may describe one or two behavior characteristics of a dozen or more children. This type of observation permits use of recording instruments and gathering of large quantities of data that may be treated statistically. Also observations of different investigators may be checked against each other in terms of relative accuracy. Variations in the observations of trained and reliable observers frequently are surprisingly large.[109] Nonparticipant observation is illustrated by observing and recording conditions in such settings as a nursery school, classroom, teachers' meeting, playground, home, Sunday school, summer camp, factories, retail stores, police station, or court.

[109] Emory S. Bogardus, *The Development of Social Thought.* Fourth Edition. New York: Longmans, Green and Co., 1960. p. 654–55.

Illustrative Observational Studies

Interest in the behavior of infants and young children stimulated development of the technique of direct observation, as did a desire for improved instructional and supervisory procedure. Many of the earlier observational investigations were "omnibus" reports of everything a child did or said over long periods of minute observation, but later observational studies have been concerned with more limited characteristics of behavior, sometimes measurements of one or two traits. The older omnibus or case-history types of data were not usually suitable for statistical treatment and often reflected the particular ability or attitude of the observer himself. The later studies of limited scope are more reliable, with less personal variation between observers, and compare favorably with the reliability of paper-and-pencil instruments. Examples of the more limited observational studies during recent years are as follows: interpersonal smiling responses in the preschool years over a two-year interval, including 150 recorded observations; the spontaneous remarks of 12 nursery-school children during a period of four weeks; the behavior and changes over a period of seven weeks induced in a seven-year-old girl who moved suddenly from a small city apartment to an elegant country estate; recorded speech sounds for "only" infants and for those with older siblings; and 1001 recorded remarks overheard in conversations among the population of Manhattan.[110]

To cite an example[111] of minute observation of behavior, a record of what a seven-year-old boy did in the situations confronting him in his home, school, and neighborhood from the time he awoke one morning until he went to sleep that night represents a minute-by-minute chronology, showing him interacting with parents, teachers, adults, and other children. Eight trained observers took turns in gathering the data throughout the day. Each observational period was approximately 30 minutes in length, with brief notes made during the period and the observations dictated into a sound recorder immediately after the end of the period.

Parents with small children recognize the realism and magnitude of the problems and procedures in the observational study just described. The mother of four little boys reported that on one day her four-year old did the following:

Built a newspaper bonfire in the basement, using the pilot light of the hot water heater. Dribbled a quart of furniture cream from one end of the house to the other. Poured a brand new bottle of cream shampoo in the toilet.

110 Saul B. Sells and Robert W. Ellis, *op. cit.*
111 Roger G. Barker and Herbert F. Wright, *One Boy's Day:* A Specimen Record of Behavior. New York: Harper & Brothers, 1951. x + 435 p.

Broke a dozen eggs, a bottle of sirup, and a jar of cooking oil. Tore up his father's cigarettes and put them in the oven. His doctor tells his mother "it's normal and it'll pass," but in the meantime, his mother says, "We just can't afford him."

Barker and Wright have provided a sharp contrast to observation of one child's behavior in a description of 585 community settings and 10,406 episodes of child behavior. These 585 settings as a major scource of data are described in 26 ways; for example, "occupany" describes the total man-hours spent in each setting, while "penetration" indicates how important and central a person is in a setting (from leader down to spectator). If each participation in a setting in the role of a responsible functionary is taken as a performance, then the 721 midwest citizens accomplished a total of 5,659 performances, an average of about 7 performances per person per year. The second main source of data is 11 "specimen records," each describing one day's behavior of one child. Each of the 10,406 episodes in the eleven specimen records is described in terms of 29 variables, with the findings presented in the form of frequency distributions; for example, the action of midwest children toward other children shows the following characteristics in decreasing frequency: domination, appeal, resistance, nurturance, aggression, submission, compliance, and avoidance.[112]

Recording Techniques and Instruments

Methods and devices for recording observations include time-sampling procedures, shorthand records of conversations and of teacher and pupil participation in classroom lessons, still and motion-picture photography for infants and young children and in sports and physical activities, a photographic dome with a one-way vision screen and tracks for movement of the camera, a clinical crib or isolation cabinet for infants, a one-way vision screen or mirror, sound-recording devices for studying language, an electric-eye ticker to count the number of autos or persons passing a given spot, a counting apparatus at the gate or door to keep a current record of attendance, an observer with a ticker device in his hand to count the number of persons passing a particular spot, mechanical recording devices attached to the radio or telephone, and an applause meter. Recording of behavior has an element of objectivity, in that the observer may look at or hear the same record as often as desired, and comparisons may be made between the judgments of different persons

[112] Roger G. Barker and Herbert F. Wright, *Midwest and Its Children:* The Psychological Ecology of an American Town. Evanston, Ill.: Row, Peterson and Co., 1955. vii + 532 p. Reviewed by Alfred L. Baldwin, *Contemporary Psychology* 1: 149–50; May 1956.

who use the same record. Motion pictures have the advantage of presenting the action in slow motion. With mechanical methods of recording, it is important to include enough elements of behavior to represent typical social situations rather than to be limited to characteristics so narrow and simple that they are not significant in understanding behavior in actual social settings.

Special forms or types of observation are represented by the anecdotal technique and by procedures for study of small groups or group-behavior analysis. Anecdotal records are discussed in the chapter on case and clinical studies, and small-group studies are presented in the next section of the present chapter. In many of these investigations of small groups, observation has provided all or part of the data.

Observation in Relation to Experimentation

The pressure of clinical problems during recent years has brought many psychologists to a realization that observation and description usually are necessary prior to experimentation. Psychology and biology are making mutual contributions to the technique of observation. Animal behaviorists with biological training have been doing the basic collecting of observational facts on animal species as a prerequisite to understanding details of behavior which can be subjected to experimentation. Intelligent planning of experiments on the effect of early experience requires a knowledge of normal behavioral events. The descriptive material throws new light on human development and suggests possibilities for research. Psychology has contributed to the technique of observation through use of duplicate observers, statistical techniques of reliability, studies of perception, and use of moving pictures in which behavioral situations may be exactly repeated and discrimination more easily taught than in most real-life situations. The training of psychology students may well include more emphasis on the technique of objective observation. Many of the important problems of human behavior lie in the area of social relationships and personality interaction where a paper-and-pencil test cannot duplicate real-life situations, which means that, as in clinical psychology, observation is the only satisfactory technique.[113]

Direct observation makes a contribution not usually present in controlled experimentation. Observational studies may deal with certain stimuli in a complex social setting to which the children react, with possible comparisons between different subjects. Such social settings are regarded as natural or normal, whereas many experimental situations and laboratory settings are considered artificial or unnatural in character. It

[113] J. P. Scott, "The Place of Observation in Biological and Psychological Science." *American Psychologist* 10: 61–64; February 1955.

is true that many of the conditions in carefully planned observational studies are similar to the requirements of controlled experimentation, with the exception of manipulating a variable factor, in that basic factors or conditions of observation are controlled by selection of the room, equipment, children, stimuli, and observers. Direct observation of learning in a regular classroom setting can provide us with running accounts of what happens from day to day in teaching a group of children some complex skill, generalization, or attitude, including errors and their origins, improvement and the causes, instructional difficulties and methods of correction, plateau periods in learning and remedial techniques, and levels of pupil progress from time to time or stage to stage.[114]

Objectivity and Preparation for Observation

Even the simplest observation in physics or in the more objective areas of psychology has in it the essence of a judgment or interpretation, and in the early days of psychology Helmholtz recognized that:

Observation depends upon the past experience of the observer, his unconscious inferences and the resulting modification of the sensory core. . . . There is the influence of a "laboratory atmosphere" upon observational results, which means that investigators are likely to observe what they are trained to observe, and there is also the contrary fact that good observers have to be trained.[115]

The uncertainties and difficulties of correct observation are illustrated by the "flying saucers" of the early 1950's, owing to indefinite concepts, exaggeration, error, imagination, and absence of essential facts.[116] Attempts at direct observation of earth satellites probably involve similar difficulties and uncertainties.

The difficulties of counting and estimating in observation have been expressed in poignant rhyme:[117]

How Many Leaves

By Jane Merchant

I do not know how many leaves I see.
Has anyone counted the leaves on a maple tree?

---

[114] William A. Brownell, "A Critique of Research on Learning and on Instruction in the School," *Graduate Study in Education.* Fiftieth Yearbook of the National Society for the Study of Education, Part 1. Chicago: The University of Chicago Press, 1951. p. 62–65.

[115] Quoted from Edwin G. Boring, *A History of Experimental Psychology.* Second Edition. New York: Appleton-Century-Crofts, 1950. p. 313.

[116] C. C. Wylie, "Those Flying Saucers." *Science* 118: 124–26; July 31, 1953.

Donald H. Menzel, *Flying Saucers.* Cambridge: Harvard University Press, 1953. 319 p.

[117] Quoted from *Saturday Evening Post* 232: 85; June 13, 1959.

> How does one estimate the green amount
> Of any summertime? And who can count
> How many thousand leaves may come—and go—
> Upon a single maple in four slow
> Unquiet years? Four years he has been gone,
> And now the flickering myriads upon
> Our maple bring again their green redress.
> Oh, I am thankful that I could not guess
> How many thousand green leaves it would take
> To ease my heart a little of its ache.

The problem of objectivity in observation has perplexed survey experts and other students of administrative questions in higher education (and secondary schools as well). By the accrediting standards and procedures of some years ago, a too narrow conception of research and survey technique centered the attention of visiting committees on matters that could be enumerated or counted (students, courses, faculty members, books, average teaching loads, unit expenditures, laboratory and classroom space per student, and duties of administrative officers), to the partial neglect of careful observation and logical analysis by observers of insight. Many aspects of secondary schools and higher institutions, as appraised by accrediting teams of observers, are now reported at least in part in qualitative rather than statistical terms (including administrative organization, objectives, curriculum, instructional methods, evaluative techniques, personnel and guidance policies, and student-faculty morale).[118]

The investigator who plans to use direct observation of behavior as a research approach should realize that careful preparation and training are necessary. In the earlier days of the child-study movement the observational method was popular, partly because it was thought that no special preparation or apparatus was needed; one simply watched the child and reported what he saw. As an illustration of the thoroughness of training recommended for observations of the introspective type, "it is said that no observer who had performed less than 10,000 of the instrospectively controlled reactions was suitable to provide data for published research from Wundt's laboratory. Some Americans, like Cattell, had the idea that the minds of untrained observers might also be of interest to psychology, and later a bitter little quarrel on this matter developed."[119]

---

[118] Norman Burns, "Higher Education." *Review of Educational Research* 22: 375–85; October 1952.

[119] Edwin G. Boring, "A History of Introspection." *Psychological Bulletin* 50: 169–89; May 1953.

SMALL-GROUP STUDY OR GROUP BEHAVIOR ANALYSIS[120]

In studying small groups or in group-behavior analysis, much of the discussion of the preceding section of this chapter is pertinent, including the topics of particular aspects of behavior observed and recorded, non-

---

[120] Michael Argyle, *The Scientific Study of Social Behavior*. New York: Philosophical Library, 1957. 239 p.

Robert F. Bales, *Interaction Process Analysis*. Cambridge, Mass.: Addison-Wesley Publishing Co., 1950. 203 p.

Joseph Berger and Others, *Types of Formalization in Small-Group Research*. Boston: Houghton Mifflin Co., 1962. 160 p.

Leland P. Bradford and Jack R. Gibb, "Developments in Group Behavior in Adult Education." *Review of Educational Research* 23: 233–47; June 1953.

Dorwin Cartwright and Alvin Zander, *Group Dynamics:* Research and Theory. Second Edition. Evanston, Ill.: Row, Peterson and Co., 1960. xii + 826 p.

W. W. Charters, Jr., and Others, "Human Relations in Education." *Review of Educational Research* 29: 313–90; October 1959.

Leon Festinger, Stanley Schachter, and Kurt Back, *Soical Pressures in Informal Groups*. New York: Harper & Brothers, 1950. 240 p.

Eric F. Gardner and George G. Thompson, *Social Relations and Morale in Small Groups*. New York: Appleton-Century-Crofts, 1956. ix + 312 p.

Harold Guetzkow, Editor, *Groups, Leadership, and Men:* Research in Human Relations. Pittsburgh: Carnegie Press, 1951. 293 p.

Paul Hare, *Handbook of Small-Group Research*. New York: Free Press of Glencoe, Macmillan Co., 1962. xiv + 512 p.

Paul Hare, Edgar F. Borgatta, and Robert F. Bales, *Small Groups:* Studies in Social Interaction. New York: Alfred A. Knopf, 1955. xv + 666 p.

George C. Homans, *The Human Group*. New York: Harcourt, Brace and Co., 1950. 484 p.

Gale E. Jensen and Others, *The Dynamics of Instructional Groups*. Fifty-ninth yearbook of the National Society for the Study of Education. Chicago: University of Chicago Press, 1960. xi + 286 p.

William W. Lambert, "Interpersonal Behavior," *Handbook of Research Methods in Child Development*. Edited by Paul H. Mussen. New York: John Wiley and Sons, 1960. Chapter 20.

Arnold M. Rose, *Human Behavior and Social Processes*. Boston: Houghton Mifflin Co., 1962. xv + 680 p.

Mary E. Roseborough, "Experimental Studies of Small Groups." *Psychological Bulletin* 50: 275–303; July 1953.

Muzafer Sherif and M. O. Wilson, *Group Relations at the Crossroads*. New York: Harper & Brothers, 1953. viii + 379 p.

F. L. Strodtbeck and A. P. Hare, "Bibliography of Small Group Research, from 1900 through 1953." *Sociometry* 17: 107–78; May 1954. Includes 1407 items.

F. L. Strodtbeck and Others, "Small Group Research." *American Sociological Review* 19: 651–781; December 1954.

Marvin Taylor and Harold E. Mitzel, "Research Tools: Observing and Recording Group Behavior," in "Methodology of Educational Research." *Review of Educational Research* 27: 476–86; December 1957.

Herbert A. Thelen, *Dynamics of Groups at Work*. Chicago: The University of Chicago Press, 1954. 379 p.

Herbert A. Thelen, "Educational Dynamics, Theory and Research." *Journal of Social Issues* 6: 1–96; 1950.

George C. Thompson, "Children's Groups," *Handbook of Research Methods in* participant and participant observation, instruments for observation, forms of recording, categories or units of behavior, time units for tallying responses, length of the observation period, scope in relation to number of subjects, training and reliability of the observer, and interpretation of observational data.[121]

It is more time-consuming to study group-member interaction by direct observation of a group in some artificial or natural setting, as described in the preceding section. Large amounts of time are required to train judges or raters, who usually are more numerous than is true for sociometric or peer-group ratings. Direct observation is especially effective, however, in investigations that deal with such areas as communications and problem-solving. Many of the studies of group dynamics include some combination of observational and paper-and-pencil techniques.

Procedures and Instruments

During the second half of the 1950's and the 1960's discussion and experimental activity concerned with group behavior (group processes or group dynamics) continued at a vigorous rate, with further refinement of useful observational methods and increased knowledge of variables operating to bias and distort the observations themselves. A number of investigations have been concerned with locating and studying variables affecting group-member interaction; for example, a conceptual framework for observing both the social structure and the interaction within classroom groups (problem-solving, authority-leadership, power, friendship, personal prestige, sex, and privileges). Other studies have dealt with administrative and leadership relationships within an established hierarchal organization, utilizing scales which produce sociometric data, and with peer- and self-ratings. These techniques are useful in obtaining intimate data about intragroup relations which are not easily accessible to the observer's eye or to other forms of paper-and-pencil tests.

The development and refinement of sociometric instruments are illustrated by a variety of studies: relationship between sociometric choices of preschool-age children and criteria of social behavior; a

---

Child Development. Edited by Paul H. Mussen. New York: John Wiley and Sons, 1960. Chapter 19.

William A. Van Til and Others, "Research on Human Relations and Programs of Action." *Review of Educational Research* 23: 285–385; October 1953.

John Withall and W. Lewis, "Social Interaction in the Classroom," *Handbook of Research on Teaching.* Edited by N. L. Gage. Chicago: Rand McNally, 1963. Chapter 13.

Alvin Zander, "Systematic Observation of Small Face-to-Face Groups," *Research Methods in Social Relations.* Edited by Marie Jahoda and Others. New York: Dryden Press, 1951. p. 515–38.

[121] Alvin Zander, *op. cit.,* p. 515–38.

picture sociometric test for use with preschool-age children, utilizing large photographs of children in the same group and several oral sociometric-type questions; relationship between choices of friends and such variables (observed by a group of sophisticated judges in two-minute segments) as associative play, friendly approach, conversation, hostile interaction, attention, and no response; and development of social-relations instruments or scales which provide indexes of an individual's social-relations status in a group and indexes of social-group structure. Some of the activity in this area has been concerned with problems other than the development of new sociometric instruments: reliability and invalidity of the sociometric-type test in a variety of military, industrial, and educational settings; relations between sociometric choice and perceived similarity and dissimilarity; measures of prestige as revealed by a sociometric-type questionnaire and an anthropological field-worker's ratings; number of choices to be allotted the subject, in the construction of sociometric tests; ways of analyzing and charting or mapping the results of sociometric tests; and social growth of a group over a period of time, as revealed by test-retest sociometric data.[122]

Illustrative Studies and Problem Areas

Varied illustrations[123] of group-behavior studies, as found in the literature, may be listed in outline form, classified according to the problem area represented:

Communications: direction of remarks between members of the group in leaderless and in trainer-dominated sessions; relationship between the type of participation in a small-group discussion and feelings of satisfaction; emotional responsiveness, as measured by a paper-and-pencil technique and by observation of the group

Group problem-solving: effectiveness of group versus individual problem-solving, development of criteria for measuring effectiveness, and the process of group problem-solving

Conformity behavior: amount of agreement between group participants in discussion, and effect of simulated group discussion or of a tape recording of a simulated group in producing conformity

Social-emotional climate: use of rating instruments and scales to assess the quality of social acceptance in a classroom, consistency of teacher behavior in the area of social-emotional climate, "esprit de corps" and "group effectiveness" components of morale, and group cohesiveness

Role behavior: structuring over a period of time of initially informal groups, role differentiation by the various members of a group, and relation between leadership, followership, and friendship in a group

[122] Marvin Taylor and Harold E. Mitzel, *op. cit.*
[123] *Ibid.*

Assessment and selection: use of group techniques in selection and training of candidates for critical jobs, primarily through development of situational tests that yield data relevant to prediction of individual performances
on a job; a functional observation room for studying small groups, including
comfort and space requirements, needs of research staff, visiting spectators,
and the design of the experimental room; utility of leaderless-group discussions
for evaluating leadership behavior; and factors affecting the validity of the
judgment of assessors, pointing to a consensus of judges' ratings for valid
results.

Another classification of the literature of group processes includes:
the objectives of groups; atmosphere, climate, and morale in relation
to autocratic versus democratic control, dominative versus integrative
control, cooperation and competition, responsibility and obligation,
and morale; group structure, in terms of membership, prestige hier-
archy, patterns, position and role, and cohesiveness; leadership, with
respect to characteristics, activities, group-related behavior, and training; dynamics of groups, in terms of influence, decision-making, communication, locomotion, and conformity; and group processes in education.[124]

To cite a special application of small-group study, an attempt has
been made to explore the relevance for political science of certain
theories developed by sociologists and social psychologists who have
been studying the behavior of small face-to-face groups. Verba shows
that in the political process important decisions are made by small
face-to-face groups, including courts, cabinet meetings, administrative
tribunals, and legislative committees as examples of important decision-making bodies.[125]

Bibliographical and Summarizing Reports

Fortunately, the background literature on group processes and
dynamics provides a theoretical frame of reference or guiding theory
for investigators in this area, and helpful bibliographical and summarizing tools for the subject of group behavior are available:

A bibliography of small-group research for the period from 1900 through
1953, including 1,407 items[126]

A summary and interpretation of 169 experimental studies of small groups,
covering the topics of contrasts and comparisons between the behavior of

[124] William C. Trow, "Group Processes," *Encyclopedia of Educational Research.*
Edited by Chester W. Harris. Third Edition. New York: The Macmillan Co., 1960.
p. 602–12.
[125] Sidney Verba, *Small Groups and Political Behavior:* A Study of Leadership.
Princeton, N. J.: Princeton University Press, 1961. xii + 273 p.
[126] F. L. Strodtbeck and A. P. Hare, *op. cit.*

groups and individuals, manipulation of social-structure variables important to group functioning (authority relationships), effect of cultural variables (sharing of values and goals in a group), manipulation of situational conditions (such as group task, size of group, communication networks), and personality variables affecting group behavior[127]

A 94-item bibliography and summary of the research literature on group behavior for the period of the early 1950's, covering the topics of trends in small-group research, development in methodology, leader style and group atmosphere, communication in small groups, interpersonal perceptions, the decision-making process, emotional factors in group interaction, group size and the large meeting, and leadership and human-relations training[128]

A bibliography of 62 items and summary, dealing with the research tools for observing and recording group behavior, under the topics of measurement of group-membership interaction, sociometric instruments, direct observational techniques, communications, group problem-solving, conformity, social-emotional climate, role behavior, and assessment and selection.[129]

Next Steps

During recent years improvements and refinements in small-group study have been marked by replication of earlier investigations, development of mathematical models, interdisciplinary research, and expenditure of large amounts of money for long-range studies in natural settings, as in the military services and in industry. Further progress in group theory and methodology will depend on continuous development of more rigorous techniques of locating and measuring variables connected with group characteristics and group structure, a closer relationship between theory and data-gathering, and greater uniformity in semantics or terminology.[130]

THE CRITICAL-INCIDENT TECHNIQUE[131]

The critical-incident technique is a set of procedures for collecting direct observations of human behavior in such a way as to facilitate their potential usefulness in solving practical problems and in developing broad

[127] Mary E. Roseborough, *op. cit.*

[128] Leland P. Bradford and Jack R. Gibb, *op. cit.*

[129] Marvin Taylor and Harold E. Mitzel, *op. cit.*

[130] *Ibid.*

[131] John E. Corbally, Jr., "The Critical Incident Technique and Educational Research." *Educational Research Bulletin* 35: 57–62; March 14, 1956.

John C. Flanagan, "The Critical Incident Technique." *Psychological Bulletin* 51: 327–58; July 1954.

D. Wells Goodrich and Donald S. Boomer, "Some Concepts about Therapeutic Interventions with Hyperaggressive Children: Part 1." *Social Casework* 39: 207–13; April 1958. Critical-incident technique.

Lewis B. Mayhew, "The Critical Incident Technique in Educational Evaluation." *Journal of Educational Research* 49: 591–98; April 1956.

psychological principles, with emphasis on observed incidents possessing special significance and meeting systematically defined criteria. An incident is any observable human activity sufficiently complete in itself to permit inferences and predictions about the person performing the act. To be considered critical, an incident must occur in a situation where the purpose or intent of the act seems fairly clear to the observer and where its consequences are sufficiently definite to leave little doubt concerning its effects.

Examples

The origin of the critical-incident technique may be found in time-sampling studies of recreational activities, controlled observation tests, and anecdotal records, although the method as such may be regarded as an outgrowth of studies in the Aviation Psychology Program of the United States Army Air Forces in World War II. Illustrations of these studies include an analysis of the specific reasons for failure in learning to fly, reasons for the failures of bombing missions, critical requirements of combat leadership, disorientation while flying, and factual incidents as a basis for research on the design of instruments and controls and the arrangement of these within the cockpit; other investigations have sought to determine critical requirements for the work of an officer in the United States Air Force, a commercial airline pilot, research personnel on a particular project, hourly wage employees in an industry, and for many other specific occupational groups or activities.

An example of the critical-incident technique is found in an analysis of approximately 2,000 responses revealing attitudes of students and adults in terms of excellent and poor citizenship, in that the study is a process of analyzing free responses to critical-incidents questions on citizenship, classified under 19 categories.[132]

A study of critical incidents in psychotherapy reveals the many and great differences among schools of psychotherapy, and even among individuals within the schools, as 28 experts comment on 23 different cases. This diversity of points of view and techniques regarding the handling of specific situations is great, and raises questions regarding our basic knowledge in this field when so many experts differ so widely.[133]

[132] Citizenship Education Project, *Content Analysis Manual: Classification System for Analysis of Responses to Four Questions on Citizenship.* Publication No. 9. New York: Teachers College, Columbia University, 1950. 52 p.

Citizenship Education Project, *Building Better Programs in Citizenship.* New York: Teachers College, Columbia University, 1958. 320 p. Describes the nature of the project and the techniques for planning and promoting the program at the local school level.

[133] Quoted from review by Starke R. Hathaway, *Contemporary Psychology* 5: 164–66; May 1960, of Stanley W. Standal and Raymond J. Corsini, Editors, *Critical Incidents in Psychotherapy.* Englewood Cliffs, N. J.: Prentice-Hall, 1959. xx + 396 p.

The problems or incidents are stated in a page or two with three headings: history, incident, and discussion. Discussion usually is follow-up information and the psychotherapist's own comment. After each incident is an alphabetically arranged trail of commentators' names, five to fourteen of them, with what they say. . . .

The 23 incidents could be considered separately or as a group to evaluate their appropriateness or representativeness among things that happen in psychotherapy, but anything said would be quite arbitrary. These incidents, or closely parallel ones, did happen to the narrators and might happen to other therapists. One could only object that the number of incidents is too small for a reliable sample. It is even less possible to review the comments. There are 166 of them! Each commentator says the kinds of things for which he can be known in his other publications. As a group, then, the collected comments by each person become a short course on his point of view.

Procedures and Applications

The five steps in the critical-incident procedure are as follows:[134]

1. Determination of the general aim of the activity, in the form of a brief statement from the authorities in the field that expresses in simple terms those objectives to which most people would agree

2. Development of plans and specifications for collecting factual incidents regarding the activity, with the instructions to the persons reporting their observations stated as specifically as possible with respect to the standards used in evaluating and classifying the observed behavior

3. Collection of data, with the incident reported in an interview or written up by the observer himself, so as to be objective and include all relevant details

4. Analysis of data, in the form of an effective summary and description which can be used for practical purposes

5. Interpretation and reporting of the statement of the requirements of the activity, indicating both limitations and values of the results.

The two basic principles of the critical-incident technique may be summarized concisely as follows:

1. Reporting of facts regarding behavior is preferable to the collection of interpretations, ratings, and opinions based on general impressions.
2. Reporting should be limited to those behaviors which, according to competent observers, make a significant contribution to the activity.

Applications of the critical-incident procedure have been made in the following areas:[135]

1. Measures of typical performance (criteria)
2. Measures of proficiency (standard samples)

[134] John C. Flanagan, *op. cit.*
[135] *Ibid.*

3. Training
4. Selection and classification
5. Job design and purification
6. Operating procedures
7. Equipment design
8. Motivation and leadership (attitudes)
9. Counseling and psychotherapy.

Use in Education

In applying the critical-incident technique to education, it is essential to include the following aspects: observation of on-the-job behavior, evaluation of significant success or lack of success in meeting the aims of the job, reporting incidents which led to marked success or failure in meeting the aims of the job, and treatment of the data in such incidents so as to isolate and categorize the critical elements of the job. It should also be kept in mind that the technique was originally intended to study men at work on machines (including airplanes, scientific instruments, and assembly lines), whereas in the field of education men are studied as they work with men, involving human interaction and a number of variables. Therefore, certain cautions are significant:[136]

1. The use of the critical-incident technique in educational research should be restricted to studies of situations with limited complexity.

2. In designing a research project in which the critical-incident technique is to be applied, great care must be taken to insure that the problem is one in which aims and outcomes can be recognized by various competent observers with both validity and reliability.

3. Reports of critical-incident studies must stress that the technique is not designed to discriminate between several types of behavior with regard to their criticalness, except to indicate that some behaviors are critical and others are noncritical.

4. Efforts should be made to improve the method, but its use should not be discouraged because it seems to possess elements of subjectivity.

5. In reporting research using this method, great care must be taken to make clear the meaning of such terms as *critical element, critical incident,* or *noncritical elements.*

6. In view of the problems arising from the choice of observers and the interpretation of observers' reports, it is likely that the team approach can provide more fruitful results than can the individual approach.

In the area of educational evaluation, the critical-incident technique is thought to have certain values not obtainable by other techniques of measurement:[137]

[136] John E. Corbally, Jr., *op. cit.*
[137] Lewis B. Mayhew, *op. cit.*

1. Adequate collection of critical incidents places categories of human behavior on an empirical base, thus providing for greater validity for any subsequent measuring instrument.

2. Collections of critical incidents provide realistic bases for any of a variety of evaluation techniques, although the incidents do not of themselves comprise a measurement instrument.

3. The critical incidents themselves can frequently serve as a source for the raw material out of which evaluation items are constructed, since incidents expressed in the words of the students may overcome the tendency either to over- or under-shoot the level of the prospective examinees.

ACTION OR COOPERATIVE RESEARCH[138]

Action research (or cooperative research or cooperative-action research), as comparatively new terminology, has appeared in the literature primarily since the midpoint of the present century, although teachers have been urged for many years to be more consistent consumers of research and to conduct appropriate studies as a means of improving instruction. The term *operational research* sometimes has appeared as a synonym for action research. Such research in the schools is an attempt to provide investigational procedures suitable for study and solution of school problems in relation to the total situation, and is a program to be conducted by teachers as part of their teaching activity, usually with the advice and cooperation of research specialists.

Long ago the basic philosophy of action research and of leadership was expressed in verse. Six hundred years before the birth of Christ

[138] Association for Supervision and Curriculum Development, *Research for Curriculum Improvement*. 1957 Yearbook. Washington: The Association, 1957. 350 p. Especially Matthew B. Miles, "Human Relations in Cooperative Research," p. 187–226.

Alphonse Chapanis, *Research Techniques in Human Engineering*. Baltimore: Johns Hopkins Press, 1959. Chapters 2, 3.

A Comprehensive Bibliography on Operations Research, through 1956 with Supplement for 1957. New York: John Wiley & Sons, 1958. 199 p.

Stephen M. Corey, *Action Research to Improve School Practices*. New York: Teachers College, Columbia University, 1953. xiii + 161 p.

Bernard R. Corman, "Action Research: A Teaching or a Research Method?" in "Methodology of Educational Research." *Review of Educational Research* 27: 544–47; December 1957.

Arthur W. Foshay and Others, *Children's Social Values: An Action Research Study*. New York: Teachers College, Columbia University, 1954. 323 p.

Harold L. Hodgkinson, "Action Research—A Critique." *Journal of Educational Sociology* 31: 137–53; December 1957.

Ernest J. McCormick, *Human Engineering*. New York: McGraw-Hill Book Co., 1957. 467 p.

Aaron H. Passow and Others, *Training Curriculum Leaders for Cooperative Research*. New York: Teachers College, Columbia University, 1955. 158 p.

Gladys M. Scott, "Action Research," *Research Methods in Health, Physical Education, Recreation*. Second Edition. Washington: American Association for Health, Physical Education, and Recreation, 1959. Chapter 13.

(604 B.C.) the Chinese philosopher and moralist Lao-tzu spoke of leadership:[139]

> A leader is best
> When people barely know that he exists,
> Not so good when people obey and acclaim him,
> Worse when they despise him.
>
> Fail to honor people
> They fail to honor you.
>
> But of a good leader, who talks little,
> When his work is done, his aim fulfilled,
> They will say,
> "We did this ourselves."

Characteristics and Procedures

The social psychology and group dynamics of action-research programs are based on the concept of bringing about desirable change step by step through group participation. In the early stage of a co-operative project, the role of participating observer separates study of the problem from possible fear of any change which might be required by the findings or recommendations. In later stages, participation as a member of the group identifies the individual with the project and develops attitudes favorable to support of the findings and recommendations.

Certain differences in emphasis have characterized basic or fundamental research (outlined below), as compared with action studies or programs:[140]

1. Formulation of new generalizations, explanatory principles, and scientific theories or laws that go beyond the populations and situations represented, with the expectation that some other person will bring about improvement in practice

2. High value placed on sampling procedures as a basis for generalizations

3. Careful planning in advance of the investigation and adherence to the design of the study throughout the project, with the reporting done in sufficient detail to permit repetition of the study

4. Desirability of technical training or equipment which frequently involves statistical, sampling, testing, or experimental procedures

[139] Witter Bynner, *The Way of Life According to Lao-tzu*. New York: John Day Co., 1944. p. 34–35.

[140] Carter V. Good and Douglas E. Scates, *op. cit.*, p. 883–84.

Stephen M. Corey, "Fundamental Research, Action Research and Educational Practices," *Growing Points in Educational Research*. Washington: American Educational Research Association, 1949. p. 261–65.

5. Judgment of the quality of the investigation based on the possibility of generalizing the methods and findings beyond the sample and situation studied, thus adding to the body of knowledge in the particular field.

The contrasting major emphases in action research are as follows:

1. Usually stemming from an urgent practical or felt need, with a goal of application of results and improvement of practice in the particular setting where the group or investigator works, through processes of group planning, execution, and evaluation (by both research specialists and volunteer or lay participants).

2. Interest in the particular subjects investigated rather than in the total theoretical population represented by the sample under study.

3. A developmental design, with the hypothesis and method subject to modification during the course of the action program, and with due consideration of all interdependent groups concerned in any changes to be made.

4. Desirability of training in concepts of group dynamics as background for cooperative study of practical problems, with the guiding theory that of human interaction by which change is either facilitated or resisted, and with frequent difficulties of interaction with the particular community by way of choice of problem areas, specific formulation of the problem, selection of procedures, presentation of findings, and application to practices. The scientists or scholars in their role of democratic leaders stimulate and develop the talents of the group, and train and supervise the participants in the project.

5. Determination of the value of the action project in terms of the extent to which methods and findings make possible improvement in practice in a particular situation and realization of social and educational purposes.

A Teaching or a Research Method?[141]

Questions have been raised as to whether action research is a new investigational method or a form of in-service training for school workers. Some writers contrast cooperative or action research with so-called traditional or fundamental research, as outlined above, while other persons make a distinction on the basis of the kinds of problems investigated, adaptability of the findings to real situations, motivation of the workers, kinds of generalizations sought, intrinsic value of the investigation to the practitioner, and the individual who does the research (as summarized above in part). It is doubtful that any of these distinctions, even though significant, provides the foundations for new methodology in terms of a new way of organizing or analyzing phenomena, so as to lead to the development and testing of new hypotheses (or to improved methods of testing old hypotheses). In other words, the major contribution of action or cooperative research is to in-service training and stimulation of teachers rather than as a basic research methodology paralleling the

[141] Bernard R. Corman, *op. cit.*

historical, descriptive-survey, experimental, case-clinical, and developmental techniques. All of these fundamental methods of investigation are available for cooperative research on the part of field workers, with the assistance of research specialists. Probably the descriptive-survey approaches are more common in action programs; to cite a specific example in a social field:

This is an account of an unusual social-action and sociological research project conducted in a community of 13,000 in the Piedmont region in Alabama, a project made possible by a grant to University of Alabama sociologists for the purposes of studying the processes of a community self-survey in health. The major part of the volume is devoted to description and explanation of the self-survey events, presented as an application of community status-structure analysis to a relatively specific action problem and as a demonstration of the advantages of studying social process through participation in action activities, specifically through participation in the community self-survey.[142]

Example: College Self Studies

Over a two-year period the Fund for the Advancement of Education made grants to thirty-eight colleges—seeking to analyze and reassess the aims and methods of liberal education. A committee of college presidents and deans was appointed to cooperate with the effort. Colleges themselves determined how best to accomplish the purposes of self study. Studies were intended to go deeper than the conventional "accreditation" survey of institutional strengths and weaknesses, and covered aspects of concern to both faculty and administration as they looked at current operations, histories and hopes of the colleges.

An evaluative report summarizes experiences in these projects and includes suggestions from participants as to how future programs can be strengthened. It is written for academic and lay people who are considering "self study" as a means of improving education. All of the participating colleges and universities prepared full reports on the studies. These documents, among others, were examined in preparing this report. Formal visits were made to seventeen of the colleges receiving grants, and informal visits to twelve colleges doing similar work under independent budgets. Field interviews included discussions with administrators, faculty members, students, trustees, alumni, and laymen.[143]

Contributions and Next Steps

Many of the reports of action studies include statements to the effect that teachers have found cherished prejudices challenged, leadership developed, lines of communication made clearer, interest in research

---

[142] Quoted from review by Warren A. Peterson, *American Journal of Sociology* 61: 393–94; January 1956, of Solon T. Kimball and Marion Pearsall, *The Talladega Story: A Study in Community Process*. University, Ala.: University of Alabama Press, 1954. xxxii + 259 p.

[143] Quoted from Robert S. Donaldson, *Fortifying Higher Education: A Story of College Self Studies*. New York: Fund for the Advancement of Education, 1959. 64 p.

engendered, curriculum change facilitated, and success in incorporating the action approach both in the training of teachers and in the teaching of public-school classes. These statements suggest an emphasis on problem-solving in teacher education and in instruction as an important contribution for cooperative or action research to make. The action-research movement developed as a result of the partial failure of educational research to play a significant role in changing practice and as a means of avoiding the separation of facts and values.

In too many instances experimenters have published data in spite of such poor rapport with the classroom setting that their findings were misleading. Research "imposed" upon the school by an outsider, with his own special purposes and no objective of immediate action or change by the school, may secure relatively rigorous results, but results not generally applicable to the classroom. The so-called "action" investigator, with the cooperation of teachers, may get results that are highly applicable, but probably not "true" because of extreme lack of rigor in the research. It would seem better for the school personnel to originate the ideas for classroom investigation, with the research designs developed cooperatively by specialists in research methodology, who will advise in the investigation itself, supervise the statistical analysis, and feed back the results through a supervisor or director of research in the school system.[144]

Certain problems or difficulties in conducting action or cooperative studies have included the reluctance of teachers to undertake research because of their concept of formal research, lack of time to conduct studies, difficulty of communication, and inadequate training for research activities. Suggestions for facilitating cooperative investigation have mentioned the need for a climate in the schools favorable to study and experimentation, ways to provide time for teachers to participate, and leadership and consultative help for the workers. In involving field workers more directly in programs of cooperative investigation, it will require time and effort to acquire the necessary tools and techniques of inquiry for sound research. The need for this training presents a real challenge to programs of teacher education. A second challenge relates to the amount and quality of cooperative research by teachers-college personnel themselves, which should be stimulated in several ways:[145]

1. To value and reward this type of study within the institution itself
2. To provide staff members with the research and professional literature, and with facilities for meeting together on their problems

[144] Donald T. Campbell and Julian C. Stanley, "Experimental Designs for Research on Teaching," *Handbook of Research on Teaching.* Edited by N. L. Gage. Chicago: Rand McNally, 1963. Chapter 5.

[145] Stephen M. Corey, "Implications of Cooperative-Action Research for Teacher Education," *op. cit.*

3. To provide expert assistance in research methodology
4. To recruit staff members with an experimental attitude towar〔 work and a willingness to conduct research to improve it
5. To provide appropriate experience in doctoral programs in the〔 cedures of co-operative-action research.

QUANTITATIVE OR CONTENT ANALYSIS OF DOCUMENTARY MATERIALS[146]

Like historical research, quantitative or content analysis of documentary materials uses as sources the collections of records already in existence. The survey type of documentary analysis expresses the results in quantitative terms, and in the studies of an earlier period was concerned with counting and frequencies rather than with the meaning or message within the documents analyzed. The investigator in this area

[146] William M. Alexander and Others, "The Curriculum: Organization and Development." *Review of Educational Research* 24: 191–261; June 1954.

Bernard Berelson, *Content Analysis in Communication Research*. Glencoe, Ill.: Free Press, 1952. 220 p.

Bernard Berelson and M. Janowitz, *Reader in Public Opinion and Communication*. Glencoe, Ill.: Free Press, 1953. xi + 611 p.

Citizenship Education Project, *Content Analysis Manual:* Classification System for Analysis of Responses to Four Questions on Citizenship. Publication No. 9. New York: Teachers College, Columbia University, 1950. 52 p.

Edgar Dale and Others, *Mass Media and Education.* Fifty-third Yearbook of the National Society for the Study of Education, Part 2. Chicago: The University of Chicago Press, 1954. x + 290 p.

Leonard W. Doob, *Public Opinion and Propaganda.* New York: Henry Holt and Co., 1948. vii + 600 p.

Leon Festinger and Daniel Katz, *op. cit.,* p. 419–70.

Carter V. Good and Douglas E. Scates, *op. cit.,* p. 665–77.

William J. Goode and Paul K. Hatt, *op. cit.,* p. 325–30.

Harold D. Lasswell, Nathan Leites, and Others, *Language of Politics.* New York: Stewart Co., 1949. vii + 398 p.

Donald V. McGranahan, "Content Analysis of the Mass Media of Communication," *Research Methods in Social Relations.* Edited by Marie Jahoda and Others. New York: Dryden Press, 1951. p. 539–60.

Nathaniel B. McMillian, *An Analysis of Regional Items in the Content of Southern State Education Association Journals,* 1935–49. Bulletin of the Bureau of School Service, Vol. 23, No. 4. Lexington: University of Kentucky, June 1951. 91 p.

Henry J. Otto and Donald McDonald, "Learning Materials." *Review of Educational Research* 21: 220–26; June 1951.

J. Galen Saylor and Others, "Curriculum Planning and Development." *Review of Educational Research* 27: 237–304; June 1957.

Claire Selltiz and Others, "The Use of Available Data as Source Material," *Research Methods in Social Relations.* Revised One-Volume Edition. New York: Henry Holt and Co., 1959. Chapter 9.

T. D. Weldon, *The Vocabulary of Politics.* Baltimore: Penguin Books, 1953. 199 p.

Ralph K. White, *Value-Analysis:* The Nature and Use of the Method. New York: Society for the Psychological Study of Social Issues, Columbia University, 1951. 87 p.

must deal with problems of locating or bringing together an appropriate collection of documents, of determining what characteristics to count or measure, and of defining the aspects selected for study.

Earlier Studies

An earlier form of quantitative or content analysis used textbooks as sources, dealing with such frequencies or measures as: sentence length, word difficulty, pictures, tables, exercises for pupils, content topics and space allotment, grade placement or difficulty of material, and vocabulary load. Although many of these earlier analyses of textbooks were regarded as mechanical, they proved valuable in textbook-writing and in instruction, as in using standard word lists to select the vocabulary appropriate for a certain age group or grade level.

Many of the earlier content analyses of documentary materials dealt with bodies of literature larger than a collection of a dozen or two textbooks. Such studies and textbook analyses were used extensively in curriculum development, based on the hypothesis that knowledge most frequently applied (or appearing in the literature) should be included in the instructional program. In the earlier analyses of relatively large bodies of literature, illustrative topics and sources are as follows: major fields of human concern, in terms of topics covered in periodical literature; column-inches of space devoted to topics in newspapers; distribution of space to topics in the volumes of a standard encyclopedia; topics covered in a weekly news magazine; duties and traits of a good citizen, as emphasized in newspaper editorials and magazine articles on citizenship; civic and social shortcomings, identified in the editorials of newspapers and magazines; shortcomings in the written English of adults, as revealed in letters written for newspaper publication; and mathematics used in popular science, based on analysis of magazines and books.

Other earlier content analyses have been based upon specimens of child or adult usage or performance, including children's compositions and test papers, social letters, and other specimens of usage or performance. Vocabulary analysis has made possible basic word lists helpful in textbook-writing and in grade placement of curriculum materials. Error studies in such areas as reading, language usage, arithmetic, spelling, and writing have been useful in remedial and developmental aspects of instruction.

In interpreting frequency analyses of documentary materials, important questions of permanent values and social significance arise. Frequency of appearance of a topic or interest in the current literature may reflect only the passing fancy of the average reader rather than an appropriate goal or aim in improving interests and activities. In any given year the name of the leading batter in baseball or the most popular

TV star probably will appear more frequently in the periodical literature than the names of George Washington or Thomas Jefferson. In interpreting error studies, as a basis for teaching the child, we need to know why he made certain mistakes and what objectives he should be able to attain, if we are to develop a sound psychology of learning. Studies of frequency of usage and errors may lead to overemphasis on very limited aspects of the child's activities and difficulties, and may fail to recognize even more important aspects of learning by way of purpose, interest, satisfaction, and emotional adjustment.

New Theory and Technique

The content analyses since approximately 1940 represent a more complex and subtle type of study, which should be differentiated from the rather mechanical and simple statistical studies of frequencies made during the 1920's and 1930's. As early as 1940, questions were being asked concerning a new type of content analysis; for example, analysis of propaganda in films, radio, and print in relation to responses elicited, and truth or falsity.

Especially since 1950, the complex content analyses have had little relation to the simple textbook analyses of the 1920's and 1930's, as illustrated by Berelson's survey of several hundred titles in the area of content analysis.[147] According to his findings, the content of communication includes that body of meanings through symbols (verbal, musical, pictorial, plastic, and gestural) which makes up the communication itself. Content analysis has been used to investigate such diverse topics as the following: the slogans of May Day propaganda in the U.S.S.R., dominant images in Shakespeare's plays, values in American plays as compared with German plays of the same period, treatment of minority ethnic groups in short stories published in popular magazines, comparison of newspapers and radio and their treatment of a sensational murder case, manner in which motion pictures reflect popular feelings and desires, similarities and differences in the political symbols that come to the attention of people in the major power states, and intelligence data secured from analysis of enemy propaganda.

A method for describing quantitatively and objectively any kind of verbal data (propaganda and public-opinion materials, autobiographies, clinical interviews, letters, conversational records, and other devices of personality study) includes appropriate consideration of emotional dynamics and certain psychological factors on which data can be obtained —hostility, self-approval, social perception (stereo-types), self-picture

---

[147] Bernard Berelson, *Content Analysis in Communication Research.* Glencoe, Ill.: Free Press, 1952. 220 p.

and ego-ideal, areas of frustration, and ability to take another's viewpoint.[148]

With the advent of sound recording of interviews, content-analysis studies of psychotherapy became quite common. These studies of psychotherapy may be divided into three general classes: methodological investigations, in which the aim was primarily to develop measures; descriptive studies of cases; and theoretically guided studies of therapy, that is, investigations of cause-and-effect relationships.[149]

Newspaper reading may be analyzed in terms of five types or classes of content: public affairs (delayed reward), human interest (immediate reward), comics, illustrations, and advertising. In relation to these five classes of content, *The Continuing Study of Newspaper Reading*, a series of leadership surveys made under the sponsorship of the Advertising Research Foundation, shows the following general patterns in newspaper reading.[150]

Comics, illustrations, and human interest are often read by more than half the readers.

Comics, illustrations, and human interest almost invariably have more readers for more items than public affairs or advertisements.

Most newspapers have fewer comics, illustrations, and human-interest items than public-affairs articles or advertisements. For example, many newspapers publish two to four times as many public-affairs articles as human-interest items.

Few public-affairs articles and few advertisements are read by more than half the readers. About 1 public-affairs article in 10 may be read by more than 50 per cent of a sample of readers.

Some newspapers are more successful than others in attracting readers to different classes of content. Family newspapers in small cities, for example, may have more readership of articles about local public affairs but less readership for comic strips than metropolitan dailies.

In analyzing the content of radio (and TV), common classifications[151] of programs are as follows:

Entertainment-type
   Music programs—popular and dance, semiclassical and classical, old familiar and western
   Drama programs—daytime serial or domestic, mystery, comedy
   Variety programs—quiz, sports, miscellaneous

[148] Ralph K. White, *op. cit.*
[149] Frank Auld, Jr., and Edward J. Murray, "Content-Analysis Studies of Psychotherapy." *Psychological Bulletin* 52: 377–95; September 1955.
[150] Edgar Dale and Others, *op. cit.*, p. 157–58.
[151] *Ibid.*, p. 195–204.

Information-type
  News and commentators
  Farm
  Homemaking
Orientation-type
  Religious
  Talks
  Forums and panels.

Illustrative Studies

To begin with TV, an analysis of television programs is classified under seventeen headings: news, weather, public issues, public events, institutional, information, religion, drama, dance, music, fine arts, variety, personalities, quiz-stunts-contest, sports, homemaking, and children's programs.[152]

The educator in movies: The description and analysis of the educator in movies is based upon the story synopses of 81 feature motion pictures produced in the United States which portray an educator as either a major or a minor character in the film. The story synopses were selected from 2692 movie reviews in *Variety* and/or *The Green Sheet*. Any motion picture review which mentioned the characterization of an educator at a public or private school devoted to a general curriculum of study was selected for analysis. Consequently, such roles as private tutors, members of the academic staffs of such specialized institutions as military school, missionaries, corrective, fireman-, policeman-, dancing-, modelling-, sports-, and scouting-schools are excluded here. This analysis of motion pictures, therefore, must be considered in terms of the limitations set by the method.[153]

Community structure as described through newspaper analysis: A standard form permits abstracting from reports in American newspapers certain information on familial and associational roles of members of the community other than the lowest-ranking social class. From these data a picture of the kinds of interpersonal and interrole activities which constitute a local social structure can be drawn. The interfamilial participation tends toward activities centering on marriage, death, and incidents of the birth or aging processes. Newspaper reports contain much information on events involving persons in associational roles. The number of associations in a community appear to be great, and the largest amount of associational life involves shared participation about common interests of the membership rather than concerns of the larger community. Fraternal, social-recreational, and religious organizations constitute the greatest bulk of associations. Newspaper mentions also supply information

[152] Dallas W. Smythe, "An Analysis of Television Programs." *Scientific American* 184: 15–17; June 1951.
[153] Quoted from Jack Schwartz, "The Portrayal of Educators in Motion Pictures 1950–58." *Journal of Educational Sociology* 34: 82–90; October 1960.

on certain social characteristics such as place of nativity and locality, endogamy-exogamy which are not easily available elsewhere. Certain considerations such as newspaper policy on reporting persons of various class groups, seasonal factors in associational and familial activities, and typical forms of reporting local activities must be accounted for with respect to the validity of the picture of local social structure drawn from newspaper items. There is evidence that newspapers drawn from a range of different-sized communities will give comparable data for drawing a picture of local social structure.[154]

Behavior characteristic of a social movement: Rural community development may be viewed as a social movement. Four features or traits of a behavior collectivity which have been posited as characteristic of a social movement were abstracted from existing literature. These concepts were then applied to the phenomenon of community development. Through the use of these four concepts—change, organization, geographical scope, and persistence in time—it has been possible to take the position that community development is not only a social movement in the South but that it is also a world-wide movement.[155]

Media of mass communication: Summarized, it appears that the media typically screen out such items as these: elite individuals or groups, usually business-based, gaining unfair advantage in a privileged, rather than democratic manner; shortcomings in religious behavior, such as lack of piety or respect by parishioners, discontent shown by the clergy, or "human weakness" in church relationships; doctors acting in selfish rather than professional fashion; anything calling into question national or community pride or integrity; shortcomings in mother, judge, or other institutions or unpleasant role deviations. This is a knotty list, making classification difficult. The list is not exhaustive and there are exceptions in the various media, and changes over time.[156]

Problems of married working women: Articles were drawn from the three leading magazines which appeal primarily to the working woman: *Mademoiselle, Glamour,* and *Charm.* Each monthly publication has a circulation of 550,000 or more, and all publish articles of interest to women who work. The leading articles are, in many cases, designed to help women in selection of careers, training for vocations, and solution of problems contingent upon their occupations. Over a period of a year, 1956-57, all issues of these three magazines were analyzed for articles dealing primarily with the problems of the married woman employed outside the home. Articles dealing with problems common to all working women, such as attitude toward employer, relationship to other workers, or problems of insurance and taxation were eliminated. Articles dealing with problems peculiar to the working widow or divorcee were also discarded.

[154] Quoted from Robert W. Janes, "A Technique for Describing Community Structure through Newspaper Analysis." *Social Forces* 37: 102–109; December 1958.
[155] Quoted from Selz C. Mayo, "An Approach to the Understanding of Rural Community Development." *Social Forces* 37: 95–101; December 1958.
[156] Quoted from Warren Breed, "Mass Communication and Socio-Cultural Integration." *Social Forces* 37: 109–16; December 1958.

Thirty-five articles were found which dealt primarily with the problems of the married working woman. The particular problem dealt with was recorded, together with the solution proposed by the author of the article. The problems were then classified in three general groups: problems involving conflict among objects of striving, problems involving vagueness of goals, and problems due to failure of the objects of striving. The general attitude of the writer of the article toward the possibility of achieving a satisfactory solution was also noted.[157]

Principles of executive action: Twenty-three principles of executive action in the college and university derived from the literature of higher education in the period from 1920 to 1955 cover the writings of educators on administrative problems, as concerned with the nature of executive responsibility, selection of the chief executive, organization of the executive department, and specific responsibilities of the president of a college or university.[158]

An analysis of 4,760 cartoons contained in six popular magazines for the years 1949 and 1959 reveals considerable overlap in public image between psychologists, psychiatrists, and other psychologically oriented personnel.[159]

An analysis of journals published by state education associations, for the purpose of locating materials contributing to regional improvement, in terms of criteria relating to: a point of view of regionalism instead of traditional sectionalism; awareness of the South as a region; ample natural and human resources; deficiency of technological skill, capital wealth, and institutional services; waste of resources; a plan or program for alleviating a problem or relieving a deficiency; and progress in the direction of regional improvement.[160]

An analysis of the acts of the Indiana General Assembly relating to formal education, classified under the following subject headings: township schools, county seminaries, Indiana College (Indiana University), private educational institutions, school lands, school funds, school officials, fines and license fees, school taxes, education of special groups, and libraries.[161]

[157] Quoted from Mary G. Hatch and David L. Hatch, "Problems of Married Working Women as Presented by Three Popular Working Women's Magazines." *Social Forces* 37: 148–53; December 1958.

[158] Donald Faulkner, "Principles of College Executive Action." *Journal of Higher Education* 30: 266–75; May 1959.

[159] Raymond A. Ehrle and Bob G. Johnson, "Psychologists and Cartoonists." *American Psychologist* 16: 693–95; November 1961.

[160] Nathaniel B. McMillian, *op. cit.*

[161] Velorus Martz and Stanley E. Ballinger, *A Guide to the Source Materials Relating to Education in the Laws of the State of Indiana, 1816–1851, Part I: 1816–1838.* Bulletin of the School of Education, Vol. 29, No. 4. Bloomington: Indiana University, July 1953. 96 p.

Textbook analyses in sociology: a content analysis of 12 widely used textbooks in beginning sociology, concerned with the treatment of race,[162] and a survey of 33 introductory texts in sociology, 28 social-problems texts, and 22 family texts published over the period 1926-45, in terms of treatment of personality, marriage and the family, social controls, social disorganization, and social change.[163]

An analysis of 266 textbooks in the light of their handling of materials pertaining to intergroup relations.[164]

A content analysis of humor, based on three anthologies of jokes concerning three American ethnic groups; 300 Negro jokes, 160 Jewish, and 274 Irish, a total of 734 jokes; divided into six categories—dialect, theme, proper names, sex composition, occupations, and intergroup or intragroup composition.[165]

An analysis of approximately 2,000 responses revealing attitudes of students and adults in terms of excellent and poor citizenship; a process of analyzing free responses to critical-incidents questions on citizenship, classified under nineteen categories.[166]

A study of 5,188 terms, having 4,294 different bases or stems, necessary to understanding and interpreting the business and economic news available through the mass media.[167]

SUMMARY OF USES OF CONTENT ANALYSIS[168]

Seventeen types of uses (applications, functions) of content analysis have been identified:

[162] Chester L. Hunt, "The Treatment of 'Race' in Beginning Sociology Textbooks." *Sociology and Social Research* 35: 277–84; March–April 1951.

[163] A. H. Hobbs, *The Claims of Sociology:* A Critique of Textbooks. Harrisburg, Penn.: The Stackpole Co., 1951. iv + 185 p.

[164] J. L. Hanley, *Intergroup Relations in Teaching Materials:* A Survey and Appraisal. Washington: American Council on Education, 1949. 231 p.

Maxwell S. Stewart, *Prejudice in Textbooks.* National Conference of Christians and Jews. Public Affairs Pamphlet No. 160. New York: Public Affairs Committee, 1950. 31 p.

[165] Milton L. Barron, "A Content Analysis of Intergroup Humor." *American Sociological Review* 15: 88–94; February 1953.

[166] Citizenship Education Project, *op. cit.*

Improving Citizenship Education: A Two-Year Progress Report of the Citizenship Education Project. Publication No. 29. New York: Teachers College, Columbia University, 1952. 44 p.

[167] Dean R. Malsbary, "A Study of the Terms That People Need to Understand in Order to Comprehend and Interpret the Business and Economic News Available Through the Mass Media." *Studies in Education,* 1952. Iowa City: State University of Iowa, January 1953. p. 199–204.

[168] Bernard Berelson, "Content Analysis," *Handbook of Social Psychology:* Theory and Method. Vol. 1. Edited by Gardner Lindzey. Cambridge, Mass.: Addison-Wesley Publishing Co., 1954. p. 488–522.

Characteristics of Content: Substance

1. To describe trends in communication content
2. To trace the development of scholarship by way of interests and activities
3. To disclose international differences in communication content
4. To compare media or levels of communication
5. To audit communication content against objectives
6. To construct and apply communication standards
7. To aid in technical-research operations

Characteristics of Content: Form

8. To expose propaganda techniques
9. To measure readability
10. To discover stylistic features

Producers of Content

11. To identify the intentions and other characteristics of the communicators
12. To determine the psychological state of persons and groups
13. To detect the existence of propaganda (primarily for legal purposes)
14. To secure political and military intelligence

Audience of Content

15. To reflect attitudes, interests, and values (cultural patterns) of population groups

Effects of Content

16. To reveal the focus of attention
17. To describe attitudinal and behavioral responses to communications.

The units of content analysis have been the word, theme, character, item, and space-and-time measures.

The categories of content analysis have been as follows:

"What is said" categories—subject matter, direction, standard, values, traits, actor, authority, origin, target

"How it is said" categories—form or type of communication, form of statement, intensity, device.

To summarize in another way applications and trends in using content-analysis techniques:[169]

[169] Quoted from review by Franklin Fearing, *Contemporary Psychology* 6: 152–53; May 1961, of Ithiel de Sola Pool, Editor, *Trends in Content Analysis*. Urbana: University of Illinois Press, 1959. 244 p.

A political scientist, Alexander George, compares quantitative and qualitative techniques as applied to the analysis of political propaganda in wartime. Charles Osgood, a psychologist, is concerned with certain techniques of quantitative analysis, especially with "evaluative assertion analysis," and the methods of discovering contingencies, that is to say, the co-occurrences of symbols, in the content of a message. George E. Mahl, a psychologist, considers the inferences which may be made from speech disturbances regarding the anxiety state of the speaker. Sol Saporta and Thomas A. Sebeok, linguists, apply the methods of content analysis, especially the contingency methods, to folklore texts. A folklorist, Robert Plant Armstrong, applies quantitative methods to the folk tales of the Bush Negroes of Paramaribo, Dutch Guiana, and the Dakota Indians of the United States. John A. Garraty, an historian, discusses the methods and uses of content analysis for the historian, particularly in the study of biography and autobiography. . . .

What is to be said about the future of content analysis as revealed in the *Trends*? The papers present a carefully reasoned case for certain types of approach to an exceedingly difficult problem. This reviewer has no difficulty in recognizing the important new avenues of research which are opened up, but it seems a pity that so little attention was given to nonquantitative methods. As the editor points out, quantitative and qualitative methods complement each other, but one cannot escape the impression that the writers, with the exception already noted, had so little or no interest in nonquantitative methods.

In quantitative content analysis *something* must be counted. The size of the "units of meaning"—a matter of some concern to the editor—may vary, but quantitative analysis is inevitably atomistic. Whether *atomistic* is a bad word depends, of course, on one's philosophy of science, or perhaps even on one's philosophy of life. One may wonder if all the enormously subtle and complex patterns of human discourse can be compressed into "units of meaning" regardless of size.

SURVEY-APPRAISAL TECHNIQUES[170]

The various survey-appraisal procedures, including index numbers, are beyond the scope and purpose of this book; they are treated extensively in the books on evaluation and measurement.[171] In some of these techniques, direct judgment rather than some more objective form of evaluation is employed. The several types of direct judgment or rating are as follows:

[170] William H. Angoff, "Measurement and Scaling," *Encyclopedia of Educational Research*. Edited by Chester W. Harris. Third Edition. New York: Macmillan Co., 1960. p. 807–16.

Robert L. Ebel and Dora E. Damrin, "Tests and Examinations," *ibid.*, p. 1502–14.

Elizabeth P. Hagen and Robert L. Thorndike, "Evaluation," *ibid.*, p. 482–85.

Claire Selltiz and Others, "Placing Individuals on Scales," *Research Methods in Social Relations*. Revised One-Volume Edition. New York: Henry Holt and Co., 1959. Chapter 10.

[171] Oscar K. Buros, Editor, *The Fifth Mental Measurements Yearbook*. Highland Park, N.J.: Gryphon Press, 1959. 1292 p.

Rating of specimens or items, as in pooling the judgments of a "jury" concerning the traits considered important for success as a teacher

Ranking of human beings, as in direct comparison of the pupils in a class with respect to some characteristic

Comparison with scaled specimens, as in a handwriting or composition scale

Check lists, with items to be marked "yes" or "no," "present" or "absent," as illustrated by check lists for school buildings, supervision of instruction, or characteristics of a successful teacher

Rating scales, with a scale of values for certain aspects or characteristics, as illustrated by a series of numbers, qualitative terms (excellent—strong—average—weak—poor), named attributes, verbal descriptions (applied to buildings, playgrounds, educational institutions, teachers, administrators, supervisors)

Score cards, usually somewhat more elaborate than rating scales, as illustrated by instruments for evaluating school plants and textbooks.

An index number is an average in the sense that it combines in one figure the average of a number of different factors or variable elements. This technique has been applied to certain phases of education and to many social and economic areas. The index numbers for the purpose of rating the state school systems usually have included such factors as: "per cent of school population attending school daily," "average number of days schools were kept open," "average expenditure per child in average attendance," "expenditure per teacher employed, for salaries," and so on. Other applications or forms of index numbers have included: changes in prices of commodities, cost of school supplies, interest rate for school bonds, cost of school buildings, cost of living (food, clothing, housing, fuel and light, house furnishings, and miscellaneous), wholesale prices, retail prices, increasing costs of education, and purchasing power of teachers' salaries.

For many educational, sociometric, and psychometric areas of appraisal, tests, rating scales, score cards, and check lists have been developed and used extensively, with applications to teachers, curriculum, home environment, social distance, socioeconomic status, attitudes, opinions, morale, social and personal behavior, personality and character, temperament, interests, and selection and evaluation of personnel. An extensive literature deals with the details of appraisal techniques.

CONCLUDING STATEMENT

The descriptive-survey investigations are too varied in type and technique to permit more than a summary of recent trends by way of challenging theoretical concepts, improved techniques, or standards of practice. The literature and terminology of descriptive-survey investigations include such expressions as descriptive, survey, normative, status, and trend.

1. Support of foundation grants for status studies to determine the present position of education in our culture and thus provide a basis for comparison and future evaluation.

2. Increased use of the processes of analysis and classification, especially in certain complex studies. Many descriptive investigations are highly analytical in character and sometimes have been characterized as "analytical studies," although analysis as a process is present in all types of research. Classification, the recognition of similarities and differences among experiences, is a basic process in all research, including descriptive-survey studies. Grouping or the forming of categories is conducive to economy of thought.

3. Increased interest of social agencies and of the federal and state governments in social problems of local communities, as illustrated by social surveys. The social survey is usually a cooperative study of a current social problem, situation, or population within definitive geographical limits, ordinarily with some concern for a constructive program of social reform and amelioration.

4. Studies of community schools to improve the school program and community. The community survey, like many school surveys, is made to provide data for planning future developments, such as an adequate system of sewage disposal or new buildings for the school system, although the recommendations of the community study frequently are broader and more general than those found in the school survey.

5. Trends in school surveys toward: the continuing survey (with a cooperative planning survey at appropriate intervals), recognition of the qualitative aspects of recommendations, and essential safeguards for consultants, school system, and survey agency. The *educational survey* deals with the instructional program and the related policies and procedures that affect the educational program. The *building survey* has been the most common type during recent years, because of the pressure of the greatly increased pupil population. The educational and building surveys together constitute a comprehensive survey.

6. New standards, depths, and uses for the questionnaire. The questionnaire is generally regarded as a form distributed through the mail or filled out by the respondent under the supervision of the investigator or interviewer, whereas the schedule is a form filled out by the investigator or completed in his presence. A carefully devised questionnaire technique is not a simple, quick method of investigation, but requires time, patience, ingenuity, and skill. Many of these abilities are important in interview studies and in certain other descriptive-survey techniques.

7. Recognition of the interview as a process of communication or interaction, and development of focused, depth, and nondirective interviewing. Although the interview belongs to a class of methods that yield primarily subjective data, that is, direct descriptions of the world of experience, the interests of many social scientists call for such data, however crude the method of data-

gathering may of necessity be. For example, the interview technique has certain advantages for collection of data relating to three of the most prominent emphases in social psychology, all implying subjective data: the emphasis on desires, goals, and values by students of personality; the current interest in social perception; and emphasis on the concept of attitude.

8. New skills and examples in both participant and nonparticipant observation. Observation, as a general rule, is concerned neither with what a respondent places on paper nor with what he says in an interview, but deals with the overt behavior of persons in appropriate situations, sometimes under conditions of normal living and at other times with some special set of factors operating. The participant-observer commonly lives in the community or social setting under study, as he takes part in the activities and functions of the particular group or groups, and gets the "feel" of what the various activities and processes mean to the regular participants.

9. Further refinement of observational methods for studying group behavior and increased knowledge of variables that serve to bias and distort observations, with future progress dependent on development of more rigorous techniques of locating and measuring variables, closer relationship between theory and data-gathering, and greater uniformity of terminology.

10. Invention of a critical-incident technique for collecting direct observations of human behavior, so as to facilitate their usefulness in solving practical problems and in developing broad psychological principles. In applying the critical-incident technique to education, it is essential to include the following aspects: observation of on-the-job behavior, evaluation of significant success or lack of success in meeting the aims of the job, reporting incidents which led to marked success or failure in meeting the aims of the job, and treatment of the data in such incidents so as to isolate and categorize the critical elements of the job.

11. Action or cooperative research, designed to involve field workers directly in programs of cooperative investigation, with future progress requiring time and effort on the part of teachers to acquire necessary tools and techniques of inquiry for sound research. Long ago the basic philosophy of action research and of leadership was expressed in the feeling of the participants in a task that "We did this ourselves."

12. New theory, technique, and use for content analysis of documentary materials. The content analyses since approximately 1940 represent a more complex and subtle type of study, which should be differentiated from the rather mechanical and simple statistical studies of frequencies made during the 1920's and 1930's.

13. Development and application of a variety of educational, psychometric, and sociometric instruments of appraisal, including tests, scales, score cards, check lists, and indexes. By delimitation of scope, this text has left to the many specialized graduate courses and books the quantitative details of testing and statistics (except as mentioned briefly from time to time for illustrative purposes): intelligence tests and measures of general mental ability, measurement and prediction of special abilities or aptitudes, personality and character tests, measures of attitudes and interests, projective methods and

other devices for the study of personality, psychometric and sociometric techniques with emphasis on standardized testing and statistics, and educational or accomplishment tests in schools and elsewhere.

SELECTED REFERENCES

ABRAHAMSON, Julia. *A Neighborhood Finds Itself.* New York: Harper & Brothers, 1959. xiv + 370 p.

ABRAMS, Mark. *Social Surveys and Social Action.* London: William Heinemann, 1951. 153 p.

ACKOFF, Russell L. *The Design of Social Research.* Chicago: The University of Chicago Press, 1953. Chapter 9.

ADAMS, J. S. *Interviewing Procedures:* A Manual for Survey Interviewers. Chapel Hill: University of North Carolina Press, 1958. viii + 56 p.

ANGELL, Robert C., and FREEDMAN, Ronald. "Use of Documents, Records, Census Materials, and Indices," *Research Methods in the Behavioral Sciences.* Edited by Leon Festinger and Daniel Katz. New York: Dryden Press, 1953. Chapter 7.

ANSTEY, E., and MERCER, E. O. *Interviewing for the Selection of Staff.* London: George Allen and Unwin, for the Royal Institute of Public Administration, 1956. xiv + 111 p.

ARGYLE, Michael. *The Scientific Study of Social Behavior.* New York: Philosophical Library, 1957. 239 p.

BAILEY, Helen M. *Santa Cruz of the Etla Hills.* Gainesville: University of Florida Press, 1958. ix + 292 p. (Anthropological study of a Mexican village.)

BALES, Robert F. *Interaction Process Analysis.* Cambridge, Mass.: Addison-Wesley Publishing Co., 1950. 203 p.

BANFIELD, Edward C. *The Moral Basis of a Backward Society.* Glencoe, Ill.: Free Press, 1958. 204 p. (Study of a village in southern Italy.)

BARKER, Roger G., and WRIGHT, Herbert F. *Midwest and Its Children:* The Psychological Ecology of an American Town. Evanston, Ill.: Row, Peterson and Co., 1955. vii + 532 p.

BARKER, Roger G., and WRIGHT, Herbert F. *One Boy's Day:* A Specimen Record of Behavior. New York: Harper & Brothers, 1951. x + 435 p.

BARR, A. S., DAVIS, Robert A., and JOHNSON, Palmer O. *Educational Research and Appraisal.* Philadelphia: J. B. Lippincott Co., 1953. p. 51-62, 124-57.

BEARDSLEY, Richard K., HALL, John W., and WARD, Robert E. *Village Japan.* Chicago: The University of Chicago Press, 1959. xv + 498 p. (Study of a Japanese village of 130 people.)

BECKER, Howard. "Problems of Inference and Proof in Participant Observation." *American Sociological Review* 23: 652-60; December 1958.

BERDIE, Ralph F. "A Program of Counseling Interview Research." *Educational and Psychological Measurement* 18: 255-74; Summer 1958.

BERELSON, Bernard. "Content Analysis," *Handbook of Social Psychology:* Theory and Method. Vol. 1. Edited by Gardner Lindzey. Cambridge, Mass.: Addison-Wesley Publishing Co., 1954. p. 488-522.

BERELSON, Bernard. *Content Analysis in Communication Research.* Glencoe, Ill.: Free Press, 1952. 220 p.

BERELSON, Bernard, and JANOWITZ, M. *Reader in Public Opinion and Communication.* Glencoe, Ill.: Free Press, 1953. xi + 611 p.

BERGER, Bennett M. *Working-Class Suburb:* A Study of Auto Workers in Suburbia. Berkeley: University of California Press, 1960. xiii + 143 p.

BINGHAM, Walter V. D., MOORE, Bruce V., and GUSTAD, John W. *How to Interview.* Fourth Edition. New York: Harper & Brothers, 1959. 277 p.

BIRCH, A. H. *Small-Town Politics:* A Study of Political Life in Glossop. New York: Oxford University Press, 1959. viii + 199 p. (Case study of the government and political behavior of a small English town.)

BUROS, Oscar K., Editor. *The Fourth Mental Measurements Yearbook.* Highland Park, N. J.: Gryphon Press, 1953. 1189 p.

BUROS, Oscar K., Editor. *The Fifth Mental Measurements Yearbook.* Highland Park, N. J.: Gryphon Press, 1959. 1292 p.

CARTWRIGHT, Dorwin, and ZANDER, Alvin, Editors. *Group Dynamics:* Research and Theory. Second Edition. Evanston, Ill.: Row, Peterson and Co., 1960. xii + 826 p.

CAUDILL, William. *The Psychiatric Hospital as a Small Society.* Cambridge, Mass.: Harvard University Press (for the Commonwealth Fund), 1958. xxii + 406 p. (A study of a small, private mental hospital.)

CHAMBERS, M. M. "Something Could be Added to the Self-Surveys." *North Central Association Quarterly* 33: 281-84; April 1959.

CHAPANIS, Alphonse. *Research Techniques in Human Engineering.* Baltimore: Johns Hopkins Press, 1959. xii + 316 p.

CHARTERS, W. W., Jr. "Beyond the Survey in School Board Research." *Educational Administration and Supervision* 41: 449-52; December 1955.

CHIVA, I. *Rural Communities:* Problems, Methods and Types of Research. Reports and Papers in the Social Sciences, No. 10. New York: UNESCO, Columbia University Press, 1959. 52 p.

CHURCH, Harold H., and LEWIS, Melvin S. *An Appraisal of the School Surveys Conducted by the School of Education, Indiana University.* Bulletin of the School of Education, Indiana University, Vol. 35, No. 5. Bloomington, Indiana: Indiana University, September 1959. x + 66 p.

CHURCH, Harold H., and Others. *The Local School Facilities Survey.* Bulletin of the School of Education, Indiana University, Vol. 29, Nos. 1 and 2. Bloomington: Division of Research and Field Services, Indiana University, 1953. vii + 96 p.

CHURCHMAN, C. W., ACKOFF, R. L., and ARNOFF, E. L. *Introduction to Operations Research.* New York: John Wiley & Sons, 1957. x + 645 p.

Citizenship Education Project, *Content Analysis Manual:* Classification System for Analysis of Responses to Four Questions on Citizenship. Publication No. 9. New York: Teachers College, Columbia University, 1950. 52 p.

CLARK, Margaret. *Health in the Mexican-American Culture:* A Community Study. Berkeley: University of California Press, 1959. xii + 253 p.

COHEN, Dorothy H., and STERN, Virginia. *Observing and Recording the Be-*

havior of Young Children. New York: Bureau of Publications, Teachers College, Columbia University, 1958. 86 p.

CORBALLY, John E., Jr. "The Critical Incident Technique and Educational Research." *Educational Research Bulletin* 35: 57-62; March 14, 1956.

CORBALLY, John E., Jr. "A Second Look at the Critical Incident Technique." *Phi Delta Kappan* 38: 141-42; January 1957.

COREY, Stephen M. *Action Research to Improve School Practices.* New York: Bureau of Publications, Teachers College, Columbia University, 1953. xii + 161 p.

CORNELL, Francis G., and Others. *The Index of Local Economic Ability in State School Finance Program:* A Review of the Theory and Practice in the Use of Measures of Local Taxpaying Ability Based upon Economic Indexes. Washington: National Education Association, October 1953. 63 p.

CROOK, Isabel, and CROOK, David. *Revolution in a Chinese Village:* Ten Mile Inn. New York: Humanities Press, 1960. xxiii + 190 p. (History of a Chinese village during the ten years immediately prior to establishment of the present regime.)

DALE, Edgar, and Others. *Mass Media and Education.* Fifty-third Yearbook of the National Society for the Study of Education, Part 2. Chicago: The University of Chicago Press, 1954. x + 290 p.

DAVIES, Elwyn, and REES, Alwyn D., Editors. *Welsh Rural Communities.* Cardiff: University of Wales Press, 1960. xi + 254 p.

DE SCHWEINITZ, Elizabeth, and DE SCHWEINITZ, Karl. *Interviewing in Social Security:* As Practiced in the Administration of Old-Age Survivor's and Disability Insurance. Baltimore: Bureau of Old-Age and Survivor's Insurance, 1961. 97 p.

DOBRINER, William M., Editor. *The Suburban Community.* New York: G. P. Putnam's Sons, 1958. xxviii + 416 p. (Twenty-four collected readings on that fashionable ecological area—the suburb.)

DONNISON, D. V. *Welfare Services in a Canadian Community:* A Study of Brockville, Ontario. Toronto: University of Toronto Press, 1958. vii + 200 p. (Community study of a town of 12,000 between Montreal and Toronto, its voluntary organizations and welfare services.)

DOOB, Leonard W. *Public Opinion and Propaganda.* New York: Henry Holt and Co., 1948. vii + 600 p.

EGLAR, Zekiye. *A Punjabi Village in Pakistan.* New York: Columbia University Press, 1960. xxv + 240 p. (Community study of a traditionalist village in Pakistan which is beginning to feel the impact of changes taking place in the world outside.)

ERICKSON, Clifford E. *The Counseling Interview.* New York: Prentice-Hall, 1950. 174 p.

FEAR, R. A. *The Evaluation Interview:* Predicting Job Performance in Business and Industry. New York: McGraw-Hill Book Co., 1958. xii + 288 p.

FENLASON, Anne. *Essentials in Interviewing:* For the Interviewer Offering Professional Services. New York: Harper & Brothers, 1952. xi + 352 p. Revised, 1962.

FESTINGER, Leon, and KATZ, Daniel, Editors. *Research Methods in the Be-*

havioral Sciences. New York: Dryden Press, 1953. p. 15-97, 243-99, 327-535.

FESTINGER, Leon, SCHACHTER, Stanley, and BLACK, Kurt. *Social Pressures in Informal Groups.* New York: Harper & Brothers, 1950. 240 p.

FIRTH, Raymond. *Social Change in Tikopia:* Re-Study of a Polynesian Community after a Generation. New York: The Macmillan Co., 1960. 360 p.

FLAGLE, C. D., HUGGINS, W. H., and ROY, R. H., Editors. *Operations Research and Systems Engineering.* Baltimore: Johns Hopkins Press, 1960. x + 889 p.

FLANAGAN, John C. "The Critical Incident Technique." *Psychological Bulletin* 51: 327-58; July 1954.

FORM, William H., and Nosow, Sigmund. *Community in Disaster.* New York: Harper & Brothers, 1958. xiv + 273 p.

FRASER, John F. *A Handbook of Employment Interviewing.* Revised Edition. London: MacDonald and Evans, 1951. 214 p.

FRIED, Jacob. "Forty Years of Change in a Hawaiian Homestead Community: Anahole." *Rural Sociology* 20: 51-57; March 1955.

GALLAHER, Art, Jr. *Plainville Fifteen Years Later.* New York: Columbia University Press, 1961. xvi + 301 p.

GARDNER, Eric F., and THOMPSON, George G. *Social Relations and Morale in Small Groups.* New York: Appleton-Century-Crofts, 1956. ix + 312 p.

GEE, Wilson. *Social Science Research Methods.* New York: Appleton-Century-Crofts, 1950. p. 198-204, 300-329.

GEIST, Joanne, and GERBER, Norman M. "Joint Interviewing: A Treatment Technique with Marital Partners." *Social Casework* 41: 76-83; February 1960.

GELLERT, Elizabeth. "Systematic Observation: A Method in Child Study." *Harvard Educational Review* 25: 179-95; Summer 1955.

GIBBS, Jack P., Editor. *Urban Research Methods.* New York: D. Van Nostrand Co., 1961. xxii + 625 p.

GIEDT, F. Harold. "Comparison of Visual, Content, and Auditory Cues in Interviewing." *Journal of Consulting Psychology* 19: 407-16; December 1955.

GILL, Merton, NEWMAN, Richard, and REDLICH, Fredrick C. *The Initial Interview in Psychiatric Practice.* New York: International Universities Press, 1954. 423 p.

GILLIN, John, and Others. *For a Science of Social Man:* Convergences in Anthropology, Sociology, and Psychology. New York: The Macmillan Co., 1954. 296 p.

GLICKMAN, Albert S., and VALLANCE, T. R. "Curriculum Assessment with Critical Incidents." *Journal of Applied Psychology* 42: 329-35; October 1958.

GOOD, Carter V., and SCATES, Douglas E. *Methods of Research:* Educational, Psychological, Sociological. New York: Appleton-Century-Crofts, 1954. p. 255-688.

GOODE, William J., and HATT, Paul K. *Methods in Social Research.* New York: McGraw-Hill Book Co., 1952. p. 119-208, 232-95, 375-430.

GOODYKOONTZ, Bess. "Selected Studies Relating to Community Schools," *The*

Community School. Edited by Nelson B. Henry. Fifty-second Yearbook of the National Society for the Study of Education, Part 2. Chicago: The University of Chicago Press, 1953. p. 64-82.

GORDEN, Raymond L. "Dimensions of the Depth Interview." *American Journal of Sociology* 62: 158-64; September 1956.

GRAHAM, Warren R. "An Experimental Comparison of Methods to Control Faking of Inventories." *Educational and Psychological Measurement* 18: 387-401; Summer 1958.

GUETZKOW, Harold, Editor. *Groups, Leadership, and Men:* Research in Human Relations. Pittsburgh: Carnegie Press, 1951. 293 p.

HALPERN, Joel M. *A Serbian Village.* New York: Columbia University Press, 1958. xxii + 325 p.

HANDLIN, Oscar. *The Newcomers:* Negroes and Puerto Ricans in a Changing Metropolis. Garden City, N.Y.: Doubleday, 1962. xvii + 177 p.

HARE, Paul, BORGATTA, Edgar F., and BALES, Robert F. *Small Groups:* Studies in Social Interaction. New York: Alfred A. Knopf, 1955. xv + 666 p.

HEYNS, Roger W., and LIPPITT, Ronald. "Systematic Observational Techniques," *Handbook of Social Psychology:* Theory and Method. Vol. 1. Edited by Gardner Lindzey. Cambridge, Mass.: Addison-Wesley Publishing Co., 1954. p. 370-404.

HODGKINSON, Harold L. "Action Research—A Critique." *Journal of Educational Sociology* 31: 137-53; December 1957.

HOIBERG, Otto G. *Exploring the Small Community.* Lincoln: University of Nebraska Press, 1955. xii + 199 p.

HOLLINGSHEAD, August B., and REDLICH, Fredrick C. *Social Class and Mental Illness:* A Community Study. New York: John Wiley & Sons, 1958. ix + 442 p.

HOMANS, George C. *The Human Group.* New York: Harcourt, Brace and Co., 1950. 484 p.

HONIGMANN, John J. *Three Pakistan Villages.* Chapel Hill: University of North Carolina Institute for Research in Social Science, 1958. iv + 95 p. (Anthropological field studies.)

HUGHES, Charles C. *An Eskimo Village in the Modern World.* With the collaboration of Jane M. Hughes. Ithaca, N.Y.: Cornell University Press, 1960. xiv + 419 p. (Anthropological study of an Eskimo village on St. Lawrence Island in the Bering Sea.)

HYMAN, Herbert H. *Survey Design and Analysis:* Principles, Cases and Procedures. Glencoe, Ill.: Free Press, 1955. xxviii + 425 p.

HYMAN, Herbert H., and Others. *Interviewing in Social Research.* Chicago: The University of Chicago Press, 1954. xvi + 415 p.

JAHODA, Marie, and Others. *Research Methods in Social Relations:* With Especial Reference to Prejudice. Part One: Basic Processes. New York: Dryden Press, 1951. p. 47-58, 91-208, 229-50, 423-513, 539-60, 569-75, 611-41, 681-711.

JAMRICH, John X. "Research Techniques in State Surveys of Higher Education." *College and University* 35: 195-203; Winter 1960.

JANES, Robert W. "A Technique for Describing Community Structure Through Newspaper Analysis." *Social Forces* 37: 102-109; December 1958.

JENNINGS, Helen H. *Sociometry in Group Relations:* A Manual for Teachers. Second Edition. Washington: American Council on Education, 1959. xii + 105 p.

JOHNSON, Palmer O. "Development of the Sample Survey as a Scientific Methodology." *Journal of Experimental Education* 27:167-76; March 1959.

JONES, D. Caradog. *Social Surveys.* London: Hutchinson's University Library, 1949. 232 p.

JONES, Maxwell. *The Therapeutic Community.* New York: Basic Books, 1953. 727 p.

KAHN, Robert L., and CANNELL, Charles F. *The Dynamics of Interviewing:* Theory, Technique, and Cases. New York: John Wiley & Sons, 1957. x + 368 p.

KAHN, Robert L., MARM, Floyd C., and SEASHORE, Stanley, Editors. "Human Relations Research in Large Organizations, II." *Journal of Social Issues* 12: 1-69; 1956.

KATONA, George. "The Function of Survey Research in Economics," in *Common Frontiers of the Social Sciences.* Edited by Mirra Komarovsky. Glencoe, Ill.: Free Press, 1957. p. 358-75.

KERR, Madeline. *The People of Ship Street.* New York: Humanities Press, 1958. vii + 215 p. (A study of psychological aspects of life in a matriarchical Liverpool slum, with reports on projective test data.)

KLEIN, Lawrence R., and Others. *Contributions of Survey Methods to Economics.* New York: Columbia University Press, 1954. viii + 269 p.

LANGDON, Grace, and STOUT, Irving. *Teacher-Parent Interviews.* New York: Prentice-Hall, 1954. 336 p.

LANTZ, Herman R. *People of Coal Town.* New York: Columbia University Press, 1958. 310 p.

LASSWELL, Harold D., LEITES, Nathan, and Others. *Language of Politics.* New York: Stewart Co., 1949. vii + 398 p.

LAW, Stanley G. *Therapy Through Interview.* New York: McGraw-Hill Book Co., 1948. viii + 313 p.

LENSKI, Gerhard E., and LEGGETT, John C. "Caste, Class, and Deference in the Research Interview." *American Journal of Sociology* 65: 463-67; March 1960.

LEWIS, Oscar. *Tepoztlan:* Village in Mexico. New York: Henry Holt and Co., 1960. viii + 104 p.

LIFTON, Walter M. *Working with Groups:* Group Process and Individual Growth. New York: John Wiley and Sons, 1961. x + 238 p. (Discussion of how groups can liberate the individual; for group workers.)

MACCOBY, Eleanor E., and MACCOBY, Nathan. "The Interview: A Tool of Social Science," *Handbook of Social Psychology:* Theory and Method. Vol. 1. Edited by Gardner Lindzey. Cambridge, Mass.: Addison-Wesley Publishing Co., 1954. p. 449-87.

MADGE, John. *The Tools of Social Science*. New York: Longmans, Green and Co., 1953. 332 p.

MAIER, N. R. F. *The Appraisal Interview:* Objectives, Methods, and Skills. New York: John Wiley & Sons, 1958. xiii + 246 p.

MANN, Richard D. "A Review of the Relationships Between Personality and Performance in Small Groups." *Psychological Bulletin* 56: 241-70; July 1959.

MARSHALL, Max S. "The Questionnaire Complex." *Educational Forum* 24: 173-79; January 1960.

MAYHEW, Lewis B. "The Critical Incident Technique in Educational Evaluation." *Journal of Educational Research* 49: 591-98; April 1956.

McCLOSKEY, J. F., and COPPINGER, J. M., Editors. *Operations Research for Management*. Vol. II: Case Histories, Methods, Information Handling. Baltimore: Johns Hopkins Press, 1956. xxxvi + 563 p.

McCORMICK, Ernest J. *Human Engineering*. New York: McGraw-Hill Book Co., 1957. 467 p.

McCORMICK, Thomas C., and FRANCIS, Roy G. *Methods of Research in the Behavioral Sciences*. New York: Harper & Brothers, 1958. ix + 244 p.

McGRANAHAN, Donald V. "Content Analysis of the Mass Media of Communication," *Research Methods in Social Relations*. Edited by Marie Jahoda and Others. New York: Dryden Press, 1951. p. 539-60.

MEARES, Ainslie. *The Medical Interview:* A Study of Clinically Significant Interpersonal Reactions. Springfield, Ill.: Charles C Thomas, 1957. x + 117 p.

MERTON, Robert K., FISKE, Marjorie, and KENDALL, Patricia L. *The Focused Interview:* A Manual of Problems and Procedures. Glencoe, Ill.: Free Press, 1956. 186 p.

MORLAND, John K. *Millways of Kent*. Third volume of "Field Studies in the Modern Culture of the South." Chapel Hill: University of North Carolina Press, 1958. xxii + 291 p.

MOSER, C. A. *Survey Methods in Social Investigation*. New York: The Macmillan Co., 1958. xiii + 352 p.

NAFZIGER, Ralph O., and WHITE, David M., Editors. *Introduction to Mass Communications Research*. Baton Rouge: Louisiana State University Press, 1958. ix + 244 p. (Collection of essays on elementary methods.)

NELSON, Lowry. *The Minnesota Community*. Minneapolis: University of Minnesota Press, 1960. 175 p.

NELSON, Lowry, RAMSEY, Charles E., and VERNER, Coolie. *Community Structure and Change*. New York: The Macmillan Co., 1960. xiii + 464 p.

NORBECK, Edward. *Pineapple Town:* Hawaii. Berkeley: University of California Press, 1959. xii + 159 p.

PACE, C. R., and BROWNE, Arthur D. "Trend and Survey Studies." *Review of Educational Research* 21: 337-49; December 1951.

PARTEN, Mildred. *Surveys, Polls, and Samples:* Practical Procedures. New York: Harper & Brothers, 1950. p. 1-23, 82-85, 157-228, 331-484.

PASCAL, G. R., and JENKINS, W. O. *Systematic Observation of Gross Human Behavior*. New York: Grune and Stratton, 1961. x + 126 p.

PAYNE, Stanley L. *The Art of Asking Questions.* Princeton: Princeton University Press, 1951. xiv + 249 p.

PITTENGER, Robert E., HOCKETT, Charles F., and DANEHY, John J. *The First Five Minutes:* A Sample of Microscopic Interview Analysis. Ithaca, N.Y.: Paul Martineau, 1960. xii + 264 p.

POOL, Ithiel De Sola, Editor. *Trends in Content Analysis.* Urbana: University of Illinois Press, 1959. 244 p.

REDFIELD, Robert. *The Little Community:* Viewpoints for the Study of a Human Whole. Chicago: The University of Chicago Press, 1955. 182 p.

REISS, Albert J., Jr. "The Sociological Study of Communities." *Rural Sociology* 24: 118-30; June 1959.

RIESMAN, David, and BENNEY, Mark, Editors. "The Interview in Social Research." *American Journal of Sociology* 62: 137-217; September 1956.

ROGERS, Virgil, and Others. *Gary, Indiana:* A Study of Some Aspects and Outcomes of a General School Survey. Washington: National Commission for the Defense of Democracy Through Education, N.E.A., June 1957. 40 p.

ROSEBOROUGH, Mary E. "Experimental Studies of Small Groups." *Psychological Bulletin* 50: 275-303; July 1953.

RUMMEL, J. Francis. *An Introduction to Research Procedures in Education.* New York: Harper & Brothers, 1958. p. 57-148, 225-77.

SANDERS, Irwin T. *Making Good Communities Better:* A Handbook for Civic-minded Men and Women. Lexington: University of Kentucky Press, 1950. 174 p.

SASAKI, Tom T. *Fruitland, New Mexico:* A Navaho Community in Transition. Ithaca, N.Y.: Cornell University Press, 1960. xvi + 217 p.

SAUNDERS, Irwin T. *The Community:* An Introduction to a Social System. New York: Ronald Press Co., 1958. xvi + 431 p.

SCHWARTZ, Morris S., and SCHWARTZ, Charlotte G. "Problems in Participant Observation." *American Journal of Sociology* 60: 343-53; January 1955.

SCOTT, J. P. "The Place of Observation in Biological and Psychological Science." *American Psychologist* 10: 61-64; February 1955.

SCOTT, M. Gladys, Editor. "Tools for Obtaining Data," *Research Methods in Health, Physical Education, Recreation.* Second Edition. Washington: American Association for Health, Physical Education, and Recreation, 1959. Chapter 5.

SEARS, Jesse B. "School Surveys," *Encyclopedia of Educational Research.* Second Edition. Edited by Walter S. Monroe. New York: The Macmillan Co., 1950. p. 1126-33.

SELLS, Saul B., and ELLIS, Robert W. "Observational Procedures Used in Research." *Review of Educational Research* 21: 432-49; December 1951.

SHERIF, Muzafer, and WILSON, M. O. *Group Relations at the Crossroads.* New York: Harper & Brothers, 1953. viii + 379 p.

SHUMSKY, Abraham. *The Action Research Way of Learning.* New York: Bureau of Publications, Teachers College, Columbia University, 1958. 210 p.

SMITH, Louis M. *Group Processes in Elementary and Secondary Schools.* What Research Says to the Teacher, No. 19. Washington: N.E.A., 1959. 29 p.

STACEY, Margaret. *Tradition and Change:* A Study of Banbury. New York: Oxford University Press, 1960. xii + 231 p.

STANDAL, S. W., and CORSINI, R. J., Editors. *Critical Incidents in Psychotherapy.* Englewood Cliffs, N. J.: Prentice-Hall, 1959. xx + 396 p. (Case materials.)

Standards for Statistical Surveys. Exhibit A, Circular No. A-46. Washington: Executive Office of the President, Bureau of the Budget, March 28, 1952. 10 p.

STANTON, Howard, BACK, Kurt W., and LITWAK, Eugene. "Role-Playing in Survey Research." *American Journal of Sociology* 62: 172-76; September 1956.

STEIN, Maurice R. *The Eclipse of Community:* An Interpretation of American Studies. Princeton, N.J.: Princeton University Press, 1960. xi + 354 p.

STEPHAN, F. F., and McCARTHY, P. J. *Sampling Opinions:* An Analysis of Survey Procedure. New York: John Wiley & Sons, 1958. 451 p.

STRANG, Ruth. *Group Work in Education.* New York: Harper & Brothers, 1958. x + 322 p.

STRAYER, George D., Jr. *Planning for School Surveys.* Bulletin of the School of Education, Indiana University, Vol. 24, No. 2. Bloomington: Division of Research and Field Services, Indiana University, 1948. 36 p.

STRODTBECK, F. L., and HARE, A. P. "Bibliography of Small Group Research, from 1900 through 1953." *Sociometry* 17: 107-78; May 1954. (Includes 1,407 items.)

STRODTBECK, F. L., and Others. "Small Group Research." *American Sociological Review* 19: 651-781; December 1954.

SUCHMAN, J. R. *Observation and Analysis in Child Development:* A Laboratory Manual. New York: Harcourt, Brace, 1959. x + 276 p.

SULLIVAN, Harry S. *The Psychiatric Interview.* New York: W. W. Norton and Co., 1954. 246 p.

SULLIVAN, Mortimer A., Jr., QUEEN, Stuart A., and PATRICK, Ralph C., Jr. "Participant Observation as Employed in the Study of a Military Training Program." *American Sociological Review* 23: 660-67; December 1958.

A Survey of Surveys. Nashville, Tenn.: Division of Surveys and Field Services, George Peabody College for Teachers, 1952. 56 p.

SUSSMAN, Marvin B., and WHITE, R. Clyde. *Hough, Cleveland, Ohio:* A Study of Social Life and Change. With the collaboration of Eleanor K. Caplan. Cleveland, Ohio: Western Reserve University Press, 1959. x + 95 p. (Description of social characteristics of a sub-community of Cleveland, based on a sample survey.)

SWEET, Louise E. *Tell Toqaan:* A Syrian Village. Anthropological Papers, Museum of Anthropology, University of Michigan, No. 14. Ann Arbor: University of Michigan, 1960. xiv + 280 p.

TATE, H. Clay. *Building a Better Home Town:* A Program of Community Self-Analysis and Self-Help. New York: Harper & Brothers, 1954. xvi + 236 p.

THELEN, Herbert A. *Dynamics of Groups at Work.* Chicago: The University of Chicago Press, 1954. 379 p.

TOOPS, Herbert A. "Questionnaires," *Encyclopedia of Educational Research.* Second Edition. Edited by Walter S. Monroe. New York: The Macmillan Co., 1950. p. 948-51.

TRAVERS, R. M. W. *An Introduction to Educational Research.* New York: The Macmillan Co., 1958. Chapters 5-11.

VAN DALEN, Deobold B. *Understanding Educational Research:* An Introduction. New York: McGraw-Hill Book Co., 1962. p. 184-220, 249-75.

VAN TIL, William A., and Others. "Research on Human Relations and Programs of Action." *Review of Educational Research* 23: 285-385; October 1953.

VICKERY, B. C. *Classification and Indexing in Science.* New York: Academic Press, 1958. 202 p.

VIDICH, Arthur J. "Participant Observation and the Collection and Interpretation of Data." *American Journal of Sociology* 60: 354-60; January 1955.

VIDICH, Arthur J., and BENSMAN, Joseph. *Small Town in Mass Society:* Class, Power, and Religion in a Rural Community. Garden City, N.Y.: Doubleday and Co., 1960. xviii + 337 p.

VIDICH, Arthur J., and SHAPIRO, Gilbert. "A Comparison of Participant Observation and Survey Data." *American Sociological Review* 20: 28-33; February 1955.

WAGONER, Lovisa C., and CASTELLANOS, J. M. *Observation of Young Children:* Their Behavior and Their Teaching. Revised Edition. Oakland, Calif.: L. C. Wagoner, Mills College, 1951. xxi + 142 p.

WARREN, Roland L. *Studying Your Community.* New York: Russel Sage Foundation, 1955. xii + 385 p.

WARRINER, Charles K. "Leadership in the Small Group." *American Journal of Sociology* 60: 361-69; January 1955.

WAYLAND, S. R., and Others. *Aids to Community Analysis for the School Administrator.* New York: Teachers College, Columbia University, 1956. 51 p.

WEINLAND, James D., and GROSS, Margaret V. *Personnel Interviewing.* New York: Ronald Press, 1952. vii + 416 p.

WHITE, Ralph K. *Value-Analysis:* The Nature and Use of the Method. New York: Society for the Psychological Study of Social Issues, Columbia University, 1951. 87 p.

WHYTE, William F. *Street Corner Society:* The Social Structure of an Italian Slum. Enlarged Edition. Chicago: The University of Chicago Press, 1955. xxii + 366 p.

WILL, Robert F. *The State Department of Education Report.* Washington: Office of Education, 1953. vii + 58 p.

WITHALL, John. "Research Tools: Observing and Recording Behavior," in "The Methodology of Educational Research." *Review of Educational Research* 30: 469-512; December 1960.

WITMER, Helen L., Editor. *Psychiatric Interviews With Children.* New York: Commonwealth Fund, 1946. viii + 444 p.

WRIGLEY, Charles. "Data Processing: Automation in Calculation," in "Methodology of Educational Research." *Review of Educational Research* 27: 528-43; December 1957.

YOUNG, Pauline V. *Scientific Social Surveys and Research.* Third Edition. Englewood Cliffs, N.J.: Prentice-Hall, 1956. xx + 540 p.

ZANDER, Alvin. "Systematic Observation of Small Face-to-Face Groups," *Research Methods in Social Relations.* Edited by Marie Jahoda and Others. New York: Dryden Press, 1951. p. 515-38.

CHAPTER SIX

Developmental, Genetic, and Growth Studies

This chapter discusses developmental and growth studies in terms of purposes and uses, sources for genetic research, cross-section and longitudinal techniques of investigation, longitudinal study of cultural growth, the cross-cultural method, developmental techniques in relation to other methods, principles for analysis and interpretation of growth data, stages of maturity and developmental tasks, and illustrative studies and applications in major areas of development (physical, mental, social, personality, and learning).

PURPOSES AND USES

The increased interest of the twentieth century in genetic and developmental psychology is related to the rapid progress of biology, which explains in part the early emphasis of genetic research on physical and anatomical development. Other early influences contributing to the genetic approach in psychology and education include: recognition of the importance of the child as an individual, formulation and development of evolutionary theories, observational and questionnaire studies of the growth of infants and young children, certain psychological movements, and the invention and use of measuring and recording instruments (especially mental tests) in growth studies. Before World War I the topic of mental growth and its measurement received little attention in the psychological and educational literature.

As indicated in the preceding paragraph, the concept of development is fundamentally biological and has been most commonly associated with the organization of living structures and life processes, although a developmental concept sometimes is applied to physical systems, cultures, social institutions, or systems of ideas. This concept has been applied to educational, psychological, sociological, anthropological, historical, economic, political, artistic, and aesthetic phenomena.[1]

The purpose of genetic or developmental studies is to discover origin, direction, trend, rate, pattern, limit, and decline of growth, with a somewhat more recent interest in causes and interrelationships as factors affecting growth. For example, the relationships and pattern of development for mentality, emotional stability, and physical growth are more meaningful than separate analysis of each aspect of growth. Adequate interpretation of behavior includes consideration of direction of growth, rate, and optimal development. Direction indicates whether the child is moving forward, is stationary, or regressing. Rate indicates whether progress is slow or rapid. It is particularly important in the instruction of gifted children to know whether the level attained represents optimal development in relation to ability.

Investigations of developmental problems have been extended beyond the classroom, laboratory, nursery school, and child clinic to the church school, home, child-care agency, camp, playground, and discussion group, with interests going beyond the earlier physical and anatomical studies to phases of mental, social, and personality development. The genetic approach could be applied more readily in tracing the development of the insane, criminal, and maladjusted, if suitable methods were available for identifying the several types of abnormality or maladjustment at an early age, as has been done for the gifted, so as to permit a forward movement of observation through the several stages of growth or development (the longitudinal approach). In most studies of abnormality or maladjustment, it has been necessary to work backwards to origins or causes through case and clinical methods or the life history, since these cases usually have reached some critical stage before coming to the attention of persons equipped to make appropriate studies.

SOURCES OF GENETIC DATA

Among the sources for study of child development are the following:[2]

1. The present behavior of the child, including verbal output, as based on observations, measurements, and records in test or experimental situations, or on direct observation of behavior in play and social settings

[1] Dale B. Harris, *The Concept of Development:* An Issue in the Study of Human Behavior. Minneapolis: University of Minnesota Press, 1957. x + 287 p.
   Willard C. Olson, "Developmental Psychology," *Encyclopedia of Educational Research.* Edited by Chester W. Harris. Third Edition. New York: The Macmillan Co., 1960. p. 370–75.
[2] John E. Anderson, "Methods of Child Psychology," *Manual of Child Psychology.* Second Edition. Edited by Leonard Carmichael. New York: John Wiley & Sons, 1954. p. 18–19.

2. Products of the child in the form of permanent records, including drawings, letters, and compositions

3. Records on file at home, school, and in a variety of agencies, covering school achievement, birth certificates, and health records

4. Introspections of the child

5. Memories of the child, or of the adult of his own earlier life, as based on the recording of conscious memories or of getting at more deeply buried memories by a free-association process or projective methods

6. Memories of the child's life as retained by those who have been associated with him

7. Measures of the parents, siblings, and other relatives of the child or of the environment, culture, or background in which he develops—a source that actually does not provide direct information concerning the child.

In describing the stages of maturity from 10 to 16, Gesell and associates have used the following sources of information:[3]

Developmental evaluation
    Developmental examination—naturalistic observations, organization and consistency of performance of simple tasks, standardized psychometric tests, projective techniques
    Visual examination—case history, visual analysis, visual skills
    Physical growth evaluation—observations of response to situation, standard physical-growth measures, standardized physique photographs
Subject interview
    Topics covering emotions, sense of self, interpersonal relationships, activities and interests, self-care and routines, action system, school, ethical sense, philosophical outlook
Teacher interview.

CROSS-SECTION AND LONGITUDINAL TECHNIQUES

The cross-section technique requires at least a single measurement for each individual within the particular groups represented, as when height is measured for each pupil in the first six grades of a public-school system. The central tendency for each of the six grades can be calculated, the result representing "norms" of growth in height or growth trends from grade to grade or year to year, although these central tendencies are not appropriate "norms" of growth in height for an individual child. The cross-section technique has the advantage of gathering the data promptly, as in measuring at one time the height of children in the first six grades, rather than waiting for the pupils in the first grade to grow in height through a period of six years (a longitudinal technique),

[3] Arnold Gesell, Frances L. Ilg, and Louise B. Ames, *Youth: The Years from Ten to Sixteen.* New York: Harper & Brothers, 1956. p. 506–7.

although cross-section studies present special problems in sampling and statistical procedure.[4]

In following growth in height of a particular group of children or of an individual through a period of months or years by the longitudinal method, the resulting series of measurements represents growth sequences for the same group or the same individual. The longitudinal approach is considered a sounder method than the cross-section technique, although the former involves an expenditure of time and resources in waiting a period of months or years for growth to take place. While problems of sampling and statistical procedure sometimes are perplexing in cross-section studies, there are other problems related to unpredictable and uncontrollable selective elimination in longitudinal investigations, because of the casualties of death, illness, moving of families, and changes in the cooperation of children and parents. The longitudinal technique provides a significant picture of growth not present in the successive cross sections of development for different groups, since the latter do not represent the developmental stages of an individual child. For example, the cross-section approach, on an age basis, groups together at the thirteen-year level girls who are well past puberty and other girls who are some months away from puberty. Therefore, it is incorrect to say that the average increment in height for this group of thirteen-year-old girls is typical, since a preadolescent girl at this age will have a much smaller gain in height than an adolescent girl who is passing through her stage of most rapid growth. Growth curves for adolescent groups tend to "smooth" this period and to conceal the usual spurt in height during adolescence, whereas individual curves at this period reveal a rapid increment in growth.

Fairly broad problems of procedure arise in the study of child behavior and development:[5]

1. Since the subjects are children, we must know their characteristics, language, and psychology.

2. We are unable to control the environment of a child over any reasonably long period of time, which means that controls over the events in the child's life are frequently inadequate in longitudinal studies.

3. We face ethical problems, particularly if some deception of the child is necessary in the interest of research.

4. Both ethical and practical problems are present in securing subjects, and in working with the homes and with schools and institutions.

[4] Norman L. Munn, *The Evolution and Growth of Human Behavior.* Boston: Houghton Mifflin Co., 1955. p. 7–9.

[5] Alfred L. Baldwin, "The Study of Child Behavior and Development," *Handbook of Research Methods in Child Development.* Edited by Paul H. Mussen. New York: John Wiley & Sons, 1960. Chapter 1.

Although wider use of the longitudinal method has been recommended, rather specific precautions are necessary in dealing with certain difficulties, some of which are common to cross-section studies.[6]

1. Difficulties in population sampling, such as the selective elimination of many of the original subjects during the course of a long-term investigation

2. Maintenance of satisfactory working relationships among subjects, parents, schools, and investigators, particularly as personnel changes take place with the passing of time

3. Motivation of children to demonstrate full rather than perfunctory performance, a real challenge in the case of repeated testing over a period of months or years

4. Systematic errors of measurement in the administration or scoring of tests, mental or physical

5. Noncomparability or uncertain psychological equivalence of tests used at different age levels, especially when the time span is from early childhood to adolescence

6. Unequal experience of groups in terms of factors affecting the results of the measurement used, but not affecting the trait itself; for example, variation in previous experience with standardized tests

7. Recording and manipulation of data; for example, work of graduate students probably not as accurate and efficient as a highly trained permanent staff or skilled punch-card operators and statistical clerks

8. Mistakes of interpretation resulting from failure to take account of the principle of regression, particularly in its effects on measurements of gain or loss.

Bell, in partial solution of some of the difficulties of the longitudinal technique, has suggested a method of combining the cross-section and longitudinal techniques in such a manner that long-range developmental changes may be estimated in a relatively short period of time.[7] He has recommended that groups be selected so that final measurements on a younger group could be made at the same age as the initial measurements of the next-older group; for example, a longitudinal study that normally would take eight years might be accomplished over a two-year period if four slightly overlapping age groups were selected. Both absolute measurements and directions of development could be ascertained and used to help answer the question of whether age changes only were involved. Such a short-cut method would be especially helpful in study-

[6] Florence L. Goodenough, "Some Special Problems of Nature-Nurture Research," *Intelligence: Its Nature and Nurture*. Thirty-ninth Yearbook of the National Society for the Study of Education, Part I. Bloomington, Ill.: Public School Publishing Co., 1940. p. 367–84.

W. F. Dearborn and J. W. M. Rothney, *Predicting the Child's Development*. Cambridge, Mass.: Sci-Art Publishers, 1941. p. 58–79.

[7] Kai Jensen, "Physical Growth," in "Growth, Development, and Learning." *Review of Educational Research* 25: 369–414; December 1955.

ing transient populations or relatively uncooperative groups, and
wherever extensive study leads to undesirable contamination of the population universe, as well as to point up special problems and to obtain
initial results to further experimental design in longitudinal studies.

LONGITUDINAL STUDY OF CULTURAL GROWTH[8]

The "age-unit method," adopted and modified from the longitudinal
study of human development, has been suggested for describing quantitatively the growth-maturity-senescence cycles of an economic, political,
or entire cultural system and for analyzing the relationships among their
component parts. Tentative examples of factors that might enter into
the determination of an economic age, a political age, and a cultural age
are suggested below. Some of these ages, like height age in the study
of human development, appear and are measurable from the time the
organism (economy, political system, or cultural group) first exists as a
separately definable entity. Others, like dental age in the child, represent
late emerging characteristics and cannot be measured individually or
averaged into an "organismic age" until they first appear.

    Political age
        Behavior controls age
            Sacredness-secularness age
            Legal codification age
            Universality of legal applicability age
            Normative (moral) integration age
        Public works age
            Flood control age
            Road construction age
        Political unit age
        Taxation age
            Tax incidence age
            Tax utilization age
        Inclusiveness of "in-group" age (definition of "we the people")
        Defense-militarization age
        Governmental age
            Political participation age
            Functional division of governmental age
            Inclusiveness of governmental control age
            Determination of power incidence age
    Economic age
        Specialization of labor age
        Producing unit age

    [8] Thomas E. Parsons, "A Longitudinal Approach to the Study of Cultural
Growth." *Social Forces* 34: 34–41; October 1955.

Tool (machine) production age
Productivity per unit-of-work age
Food source age
Food processing age
Product diversification age
Surplus goods age
Savings age
Investment age
Human conservation age
Wealth distribution age
Commercial exchange age
    Universality of exchange system age
    Credit extension age
    Banking age
Taxation age

Cultural age (Would include many of the component ages of Political age and Economic age plus others, some of which are suggested below. A list of universal culture traits might well provide both a systematic organization of subages and a theoretical framework within which to interpret or interrelate them.)
Sanitation age
Literary age
Graphic arts age
Architectural-structural age
Systematization of knowledge age
Population control age
Communication age
Transportation age.

This "age-unit method" consists essentially of:

(*a*) operationally defining the class of political, economic, social, or cultural divisions within which development is to be analyzed; (*b*) defining —again operationally, if possible—the cultural (etc.) subdivisions to be studied and the unitary structural or functional composition of these subdivisions for each developmental variable or growth factor under investigation; (*c*) determining (by direct measurement if possible) the units which comprise each growth factor within each cultural (etc.) subdivision; (*d*) repeating the latter operation at regular intervals through time; (*e*) computing age norms, or means of the obtained status values for each of the representative growth factors in the cultural (etc.) system at each chronological age (or point in time since the system's defined beginning) for which reliable data are available; (*f*) expressing the average measured status of each cultural (etc.) subdivision— and of each component growth factor within each subdivision—as the mean chronological age at which that status is attained within the culture (etc.) as a whole; and (*g*) plotting the obtained status values for all the growth factors and their means (within each subdivision being studied) as serial points on a grid which calibrates chronological time along the abscissa and equal time units of average growth (interpreted as units of time required to reach normal status in any growth factor) along the ordinate.[9]

CROSS-CULTURAL METHOD[10]

The cross-cultural method has been in existence since approximately the 1880's, but not until recently has either its scope or its value been recognized, and there have been relatively few studies utilizing this method. Early examples of cross-cultural studies include: development of laws of marriage and descent, relationships between certain social institutions and stages of economic development, and constructs relating to kinship derived from evolutionary theory. In spite of the very limited amount of published research, however, the cross-cultural method has greatly influenced behavioral science and has proved a sensitive methodology for interdisciplinary research in the behavioral sciences. This approach employs statistical techniques to test theory and recently has had a major interest in matters of personality development of different cultures.

Since the late 1930's, interest has increased in an interdisciplinary approach to behavioral science, as indicated by attempts to pool the evidence and theory from the fields of anthropology, psychoanalysis, and experimental psychology. Examples of cross-cultural studies during recent years include developmental investigations of: patterns of sexual behavior, relationship between the drinking of alcoholic beverages and anxiety, kinship terminology and its relation to certain phenomena (forms of marriage, descent, and social structure), relationship between sorcery and social control, relationship between the education of the child and art forms, relationship between the content of myths and education as these both relate to aggression, relationship between certain child-training variables and need achievement, and relationship between various

[9] Quoted from *ibid.*

[10] George W. Goethals and John W. M. Whiting, "Research Methods: The Cross-Cultural Method," in "Methodology of Educational Research." *Review of Educational Research* 27: 441–48; December 1957.

Bert Kaplan, Editor, *Studying Personality Cross-culturally.* Evanston, Ill.: Row, Peterson, 1961. x + 687 p.

Gardner Lindzey, *Projective Techniques and Cross-Cultural Research.* New York: Appleton-Century-Crofts, 1962. ix + 339 p.

William Line and Margery R. King, "Cross-Cultural Research." *Journal of Educational Sociology* 29: 281–91; March 1956.

Carl Murchison, Editor, "Cross-Cultural Research and Methodology." *Journal of Social Psychology* 47: 157–405; May 1958.

William Van Til, "Intercultural Education," *Encyclopedia of Educational Research.* Edited by Chester W. Harris. Third Edition. New York: The Macmillan Co., 1960. p. 718–24.

techniques of education and the development of superego and other manifestations of personality.

One of the criticisms of cross-cultural studies relates to use of ethnographic sources written at different times by people with a variety of backgrounds and personal predilections. It is obvious that ethnographies already in existence cannot be completely rewritten, but such materials can be brought up to date in relation to a strict set of criteria. Criticisms of this method have been met by anthropologists and behavioral scientists in general through provision of appropriate training, so that a group of anthropologists may collect field data in the same way, after having the benefit of methodological training (before going into the field). Anthropology may contribute especially to the methods of studying child rearing through: (1) the concept of the culture complex, with its analysis of values, beliefs, techniques, justifications, and rationalizations; and (2) comparative study of child life in non-European societies, with identification of important variables that may have been overlooked and may prove useful in prediction of behavior.[11]

In keeping with these new safeguards relating to existing data and to the collection of new information, recent cross-cultural studies with developmental implications have dealt with such problems as the following: techniques of education and the development of the superego from a sample of three cultures; relationship between pregnancy taboos, family structure, and dietary regulations; relationship of initiation ceremonies to child-training practices and to aspects of the kinship organization of various cultures; and relationship between kinship, education, and forms of marriage.

The implications of the cross-cultural method for educational research indicate that there is a broad range of methods or patterns by which a child may be brought up, that we must be aware of both the virtues and the limitations of the untrained observer, and that there are ways of training persons to look at the phenomena of behavior with a strategy of reason, logic, and objectivity. The evidence from cross-cultural research is important in socializing the child as the school faces problems involving the emotions of both the individual child and of groups of children as they come together. This approach should help education correct the mistake of remaining "culture bound."[12]

A review of the pertinent research concerning the related topic of cultural differences includes the following classification of subjects: race

[11] John W. M. Whiting and Beatrice B. Whiting, "Contributions of Anthropology to the Methods of Studying Child Rearing," *Handbook of Research Methods in Child Development*. Edited by Paul H. Mussen. New York: John Wiley & Sons, 1960. Chapter 21.

[12] Robert R. Sears, Eleanor E. Maccoby, and Harry Levin, *Patterns of Child Rearing*. Evanston, Ill.: Row, Peterson and Co., 1957. 549 p.

and culture; group differences in behavior, in terms of race mixture and cultural assimilation, group differences and age, regional differences and migration, long-range effects of cultural change, and schooling and intelligence; culture and personality, including comparative surveys of national character, comprehensive studies of single cultures, and investigations of social class; levels of cultural differentials; cross-cultural testing; and group differences and the individual.[13]

In applying the results of cross-cultural research to school and instructional problems, cross-cultural education may be defined as the "changes in perception, in evaluation, and in action occurring in individuals socialized in one culture as a result of their sojourn for educational purposes in a foreign culture."[14]

DEVELOPMENTAL TECHNIQUES IN RELATION TO OTHER METHODS

Certain types of genetic or developmental studies use methods similar to the techniques employed in other types of research. The cross-section approach, in terms of the data secured for each age group, is similar to a descriptive-survey investigation of status.[15] Genetic studies make extensive use of the data-gathering methods described in the chapter on descriptive-survey studies.

Both genetic and historical investigations are interested in the sequence or development of events, with genetic studies emphasizing growth sequences and a forward movement, while historical research involves the entire range of human events and a backward movement by means of documents and remains. The genetic and historical approaches most nearly meet in certain types of biography or autobiography with emphasis on the growth and development of the individual.[16]

Genetic investigations that use the co-twin control technique[17] in studying development are similar to experimentation. Some experimental factor affecting development is present for one twin, while his mate

[13] Anne Anastasi, "Cultural Differences," *Encyclopedia of Educational Research.* Edited by Chester W. Harris. Third Edition. New York: The Macmillan Co., 1960. p. 350–58.

[14] Simon N. Herman and Erling Schild, "Contexts for the Study of Cross-Cultural Education." *Journal of Social Psychology* 52: 231–50; November 1960.

[15] Roger G. Barker and Herbert F. Wright, *Midwest and Its Children:* The Psychological Ecology of an American Town. Evanston, Ill.: Row, Peterson and Co., 1955. vii + 532 p. Also see Herbert F. Wright, "Psychological Development in Midwest." *Child Development* 27: 265–86; July 1956.

Lewis M. Terman and Melita H. Oden, *The Gifted Child Grows Up:* Genetic Studies of Genius. Stanford, Calif.: Stanford University Press, 1947. xiv + 450 p.

[16] Harry L. Hollingworth, *Leta Stetter Hollingworth.* Lincoln: University of Nebraska Press, 1943. 204 p.

[17] Morton M. Hunt, "Doctor Kallmann's 7000 Twins." *Saturday Evening Post* 227: 20–21, 80–82; November 6, 1954. Co-twin control and genetics.

serves as the control. For example, one twin may be taught to climb the stairs, while the other proceeds to the activity of stair-climbing whenever he reaches his own stage of "readiness."

Genetic and case-clinical studies are similar in certain investigations of growth or development of an individual child, adolescent, or adult over a period of time.[18] Another example of a type of investigation where genetic and case studies meet is a series of cases concerned chiefly with diagnosis of defects and deviations of child development in such clinical areas as amentia, endocrine disorders, convulsive disorders, neurological behavior, cerebral injury, special sensory handicaps, prematurity, precocity, and environmental retardation.[19]

During the 1950's and later, studies of the intellectual growth of children increasingly applied projective methods, especially drawing and painting, as a means of exploring the more subtle changes in the child's inner world of thoughts and feelings; for example, doll play and spontaneous drawings and paintings in studying the emotional experiences and personality development of children. Other techniques for study of personality development include observation of behavior, interviews, questionnaires, personal documents, rating scales, certain psychometric and sociometric instruments, and the projective techniques of word association, story telling, play, psychodrama, and picture methods.[20]

The techniques of growth studies vary with the age of the subjects: for infants—experiments, direct measurements, observations, one-way vision screen, the Gesell observation dome, and motion-picture recording; preschool children—direct observation and experiments; older children and adolescents—paper-and-pencil tests, indirect measurement tech-

[18] Robert J. Havighurst, *Human Development and Education*. New York: Longmans, Green and Co., 1953. p. 177–253. Three cases.

Harold E. Jones. *Development in Adolescence*. New York: Appleton-Century-Crofts, 1943. 161 p. Development of one boy over a period of seven years.

For a highly detailed, contrasting study of behavior covering only one day, see Roger G. Barker and Herbert F. Wright, *One Boy's Day: A Specimen Record of Behavior*. New York: Harper & Brothers, 1951. x + 435 p.

Lois B. Murphy and Others, *Personality in Young Children*. 2 vols. New York: Basic Books, 1956. Volume 2 is a detailed study of "Colin, A Normal Child," from his second through his fifth year.

Robert W. White, *Lives in Progress: A Study of the Natural Growth of Personality*. New York: Dryden Press, 1952. 376 p. Presents, interprets, and compares the lives (case studies) of three normal people.

[19] Arnold Gesell and Catherine S. Amatruda, *Developmental Diagnosis*. New York: Harper & Brothers, 1947. xvi + 496 p.

[20] Lawrence E. Abt and Leopold Bellak, Editors, *Projective Psychology: Clinical Approaches to the Total Personality*. New York: Alfred A. Knopf, 1950. xvii + 485 + xiv p.

Harold H. Anderson and Gladys L. Anderson, Editors, *An Introduction to Projective Techniques. . . .* New York: Prentice-Hall, 1951. xxiv + 720 p.

Lydia Jackson and Kathleen M. Todd, *Child Treatment and the Therapy of Play*. Second Edition. New York: Ronald Press, 1950. xii + 159 p.

niques, one-way vision screen, recording of individual behavior in a social setting, and sociometric techniques in dramatic-play situations and in diagramming social relationships.[21]

PRINCIPLES FOR ANALYSIS AND INTERPRETATION

Principles of Child Development

Certain principles of child development, which may be classified under the following abbreviated headings, are helpful as background for discussion of the several aspects of human growth and development:[22]

1. Developmental objectives
2. Levels of maturity
3. Differential rates of maturing
4. Variability in rate of maturing
5. Variability in differential rates of maturing
6. Differential developmental pre-eminence at various stages of growth
7. "Wholeheartedness and gradation" in emotional development
8. Indigenous motivation or spontaneous use, as a feature of growing ability
9. The principle of anticipation
10. "Laying by" or shedding as a feature of development
11. Developmental revision of habits
12. Differentiation and integration
    a. Individuation
    b. Progression from generalized to more localized response
    c. Incorporation of separately practiced operations into larger activity systems
13. Priority of "large" over "small" muscular activities in certain sections of the body
14. Interaction between various aspects of growth
15. Vicarious extension of experience
16. Early establishment of some of the basic features of personality structure
17. The play of complementary and potentially conflicting forces
    a. Dependence—independence
    b. Self-centered and "outgoing" tendencies.

Initial Stage

In interpreting growth and development, certain stages and processes are significant.[23] The beginning or initial stage of development is

[21] John E. Anderson, *op. cit.*, p. 32–33.

[22] Arthur T. Jersild and Charlotte Fehlman, "Child Development and the Curriculum: Some General Principles." *Journal of Experimental Education* 12: 130–42; December 1943.

[23] Elizabeth M. Fuller, "Early Childhood Education," *Encyclopedia of Educa-*

important in genetic research. The initial stages of certain types of behavior in infancy are commonly as follows: in the first quarter of the first year he gains control of the muscles that move his eyes; second quarter, reaches out for things; third quarter, sits; fourth quarter, stands upright; second year, walks and runs, and articulates words and phrases; and in the third year, speaks in sentences, using words as tools of thought.[24]

Quantitative and Qualitative Changes

Growth or development is both quantitative and qualitative. Growth in vocabulary involves both the total number of words used (a quantitative change) and the effectiveness of usage in speaking or writing (a relatively qualitative phase of development). Qualitative changes in growth commonly are expressed in descriptive terms; for example, at different stages of development an infant commonly responds to the mirror situation as follows: at 40 weeks, smiles at his mirror image; at 52 weeks, approaches his mirror image socially and even vocalizes; and at 56 weeks, brings his face close to his image, sometimes kissing it.[25]

Trends and Patterns

A basic continuity characterizes human psychological development, in the sense that patterns of personality and adjustment once established tend to persist over long periods of time, although environmental or constitutional factors or circumstances, under certain conditions, might alter the growth trends of particular individuals. The interrelatedness of developmental trends is noted in the positive correlation of desirable traits and in a certain unity of growth. Although in physical and social interaction, and possibly in intelligence, some alteration in direction or rate of growth is associated with pubescence, anything approaching reorganization of personality has not been demonstrated. The characteristics of any age group, such as adolescents, must be evaluated in the perspective of what has gone before and what follows.[26]

---

tional Research. Edited by Chester W. Harris. Third Edition. New York: The Macmillan Co., 1960. p. 385–96.

William E. Martin and Paul H. Mussen, "Infancy and Early Childhood," *Encyclopedia of Educational Research,* p. 696–700.

[24] Arnold Gesell and Others, *The First Five Years of Life.* New York: Harper & Brothers, 1940. p. 13.

[25] Arnold Gesell and Helen Thompson, *The Psychology of Early Growth.* New York: The Macmillan Co., 1938. p. 158–63.

[26] Raymond G. Kuhlen, "Adolescence," *Encyclopedia of Educational Research.* Edited by Chester W. Harris. Third Edition. New York: The Macmillan Co., 1960. p. 24–29.

Paul H. Mussen and William E. Martin, "Childhood and Preadolescence," *Encyclopedia of Educational Research,* p. 194–98.

All growth probably is substantially gradual rather than irregular or in spurts, when due consideration is given to the relatively long period of preliminary preparation, as in walking without aid. The stages of behavior that ordinarily precede walking without aid include: at 32 weeks, in sitting the infant leans forward passively, although he sits erect for a brief period, and standing he supports his entire weight, but he leans forward with considerable hip flexion; at 40 weeks, when prone he pushes with his hands and regresses, and when standing supports himself by holding the crib side-rail; at 48 weeks, when prone he creeps, and unaided pulls himself to standing, cruises sidewise holding onto the crib rail, and may even walk forward if both hands are held; and at 56 weeks, he stands alone at least momentarily.[27] There are exceptions to the concept or principle of gradual development, such as the familiar growth spurt at adolescence, and even an occasional reversal, as illustrated by a decrease in the neck girth during the infant's first year.

Stages of Growth and Integration

Reasonable unity or integration in development prevails at a particular stage of growth, although there are many exceptions. The normal boy of 10 has reached similar stages of development, intellectually, educationally, socially, and physically. On the other hand, an exceptional boy of 10 may be small in physical size but will answer questions on a quiz show at the college level in science and mathematics. Another exception to the concept of integrated growth at a particular stage is the adolescent boy who may be 6 feet in height but quite immature socially and emotionally. The vestibule of the ear is of adult size at birth, but the heart has not fully completed its growth at the age of 20. As a general rule, the several aspects of development tend to cluster around a "center of gravity of growth" for the individual.

Individuality of Growth

Although there are stages of maturation and behavior that reveal basic or common trends in development, not even identical twins grow up in exactly the same way. Individuality of behavior in motor activity relates to such items as output of energy, bodily activity and fatigability, and postural demeanor, with the latter noted to determine whether it is tense, relaxed, poised, steady, or variable. Adaptive behavior varies in terms of insight, inquisitiveness, originality, decisiveness, and initiative. Language is characterized by individual differences in articulation, flow of speech, inflections, inhibitions, conversational rapport, and expressive-

[27] Arnold Gesell and Helen Thompson, *op. cit.*, p. 156–62.

ness. Personal-social behavior reflects variations in emotional vitality; motivation; reaction to success, failure, and fatigue; reaction to novelty and surprise; and sense of humor.[28]

Limits of Growth and Old Age

The upper limits of physical growth or performance can be determined with considerable precision, as in height or speed of running, but little is known concerning maximum mental development or performance. It may be that "quantitative" growth of intelligence continues until 18 or 19 years or even later, although qualitative and functional development of intelligence in terms of vocabulary, information, and insight or power in contrast to speed of reaction probably continues well beyond the age of 20.

Lehman's studies of the relationship between creativity or production of "masterpieces" and age indicate that most creative work of talented individuals is done at a relatively early age. To many persons this is a disturbing fact, because psychologically it would mean that a scientist, scholar, or artist does not develop creatively in the sense of producing "masterpieces" after thirty-nine or forty and that there is a very limited relationship between science (or creativity) and experience. In other words, it would seem that more experience does not help the scientist in contributing creatively to science. A possible explanation is found in the biographies of individual great chemists and other scientists, indicating that, as these able men grew older, administrative and public duties absorbed an increasing amount of the time and energy that previously had been applied to scientific work. This explanation would indicate that age in itself is not necessarily a cause for creative decline.[29] In his book, *Age and Achievement*, Lehman lists sixteen general causative factors that helped to account for his statistical findings.

It has also been suggested that as the total output of science has increased, the percentage of research or scholarly literature cited by his-

[28] Arnold Gesell and Others, *The First Five Years of Life*. New York: Harper & Brothers, 1940. p. 296–308.

Arnold Gesell and Others, *Biographies of Child Development*. New York: Paul B. Hoeber, 1939. p. 13–309.

[29] Eduard Farber, "Creativity and Age." *Science* 128: 676; September 19, 1958. Also see:

Harvey C. Lehman, "Creativity and Age." *Science* 128: 676, 678; September 19, 1958.

Harvey C. Lehman, "The Chemist's Most Creative Years." *Science* 127: 1213–22; May 23, 1958. The 2500 ablest of the world's chemists attained their maximum production rate at ages 30 through 34.

Harvey C. Lehman, *Age and Achievement*. Princeton: Princeton University Press, 1953. xiv + 358 p.

Harvey C. Lehman, "The Age Decrement in Outstanding Scientific Creativity." *American Psychologist* 15: 128–34; February 1960.

torians has declined. (Frequency of citation in the literature is used as one method of determining creativity.) This may be due to the limitations of the historians and of book size rather than to age changes in the creativity of scientists. The honor of having one's work mentioned in histories or included in historical anthologies may have been bestowed to a diminishing proportion of the publications of successive decades, which would mean that citation in histories of science has become more difficult to attain for young and old alike. In other words, a scientist's quantity and quality of output may have remained approximately constant through the decades of his life, but the increasing difficulty of securing citation during the later decades of his life (the recent decades of the twentieth century) may give the false impression of a decline in creativity or productivity.[30]

A good example of problems in discovery and development of talent and creativity is available in the field of psychology. In view of the fact that for a sample of significant contributors to psychology, only 4 per cent had thought of psychology as a career when in high school and only 23 per cent when in the first two years of college, it has been urged that we find ways for earlier discovery and development of talent in psychology. Among older psychologists, one reason for relatively late development of interest in the field was the fact that psychology was not usually offered in their time before the junior year of college. E. L. Thorndike declared that he had no "memory of having heard or seen the word psychology until my junior year at Wesleyan University when I took a required course in it." A few budding psychologists had earlier interests, but no courses were available; for example, Hunter at the age of 15 had purchased and read Darwin's *Origin of Species* and at 17 became interested in psychology after a preparatory school roommate lent him a text in the field. Pillsbury wrote that when 14 and in the second year of high school he had chanced upon a copy of Carpenter's *Mental Physiology* in his father's library, read it with great interest, and declared that he would like to specialize in psychology; however, not until upper class work with Wolfe at Nebraska did that interest really get underway. At the age of 14 or 15 Cyril Burt was reading Ward's article on psychology in the *Encyclopaedia Britannica* and starting manuscript notes "which proposed to cover the whole range of human character-qualities." Terman described observations he had made, while still a boy, regarding memory and afterimages. Jastrow, Judd, Hunter, and E. L. Thorndike obtained the doctorate when 23 and Washburne when only 22. In spite of late choice of field, notable early American psychologists tended to get into

[30] Wayne Dennis, "The Age Decrement in Outstanding Scientific Contributions: Fact or Artifact?" *American Psychologist* 13: 457–60; August 1958.

their career at a young age: four obtained the undergraduate degree at 19, and the doctorate often took only three years, Judd using only two.[31]

In terms of physical and physiological development, adulthood is reached soon after the age of 20, followed by a few years at the peak of physical efficiency, and then some physical deterioration actually beginning as early as the late 20's, as is well known in the athletic sports. The peak of physical maturity and physiological equilibrium are lost in part only a few years after attainment. Fortunately, the relatively early deterioration of the anatomical and physiological functions may be offset by creative imagination, enriched experience, and good judgment, thus permitting the intellect to operate in a socially effective manner. Changes in test performances of a quantitative sort during maturity and old age may be offset by qualitative aspects of intellectual performance. It is well known that senescence or disease may produce marked changes in behavior and even disintegration of personality.

There is the remarkable story of a man who graduated from medical school at the age of 64, after earning seven other degrees: chiropody, bachelor of law, bachelor of science, two master's diplomas, doctor of philosophy, and doctor of judicial science. To cite another example of further growth and development at an advanced age, an eminent state commissioner of education after retiring went through law school and practiced law in his 70's. It would be interesting and profitable to follow the growth, development, and experience for a month or a year of a first-year teacher, a new supervisor, or a beginner in school administration.

During the 1950's and later there was increased study of the psychological and social adjustment of people as they grow older, but the concept of adjustment as applied to adults in a modern society is so complex that these studies have merely served to outline the problem and to suggest some useful approaches to it, leaving a thorough exploration to the future. An important characteristic of current research in gerontology is the amount of study being devoted to middle age rather than to old age. This signifies an interest in the process of aging and in knowledge which will provide a basis for a preventive mental hygiene that will help people make a better adjustment in their later years. The studies of aging in relation to social and psychological adjustment during the 1950's and later may be classified under the following broad headings: meaning and scope of adjustment in the later years, measurement of psychological adjustment in later maturity, adjustment and social relations, increased social isolation, income and standard of living, living

[31] S. L. Pressey, "Toward Earlier Creativity in Psychology." *American Psychologist* 15: 124–27; February 1960.

conditions and personal adjustment, retirement, public attitudes about aging, health and adjustment, changes in intellectual and physical capacities, motivation and learning, and education for aging. We have done better in studying problems of disease, housing, and economics than in providing a developmental psychology of the later years in terms of learning, perception, and personality.[32]

A recent review of research in the field of geriatrics considers aging in relation to: psychobiology; the individual organism; antomation; problem solving; motivation; social interests and needs, and emotional reactions; confidence and caution; and expectations, set, and attitude toward change.[33]

Scientists study psychological adjustment for two general purposes: the purely scientific purpose of getting an accurate description of the behavior of people, and to discover how to help people become happier, more successful in their pursuit of the goals of life, or better adjusted. Both purposes are illustrated in recent research on adjustment in the later years.[34]

Pressey and Kuhlen's book emphasizes psychological development during the later years, with appropriate graphs and tables in a textual presentation which has been carefully organized:[35]

The warp of the fabric is the genetic or age order of development. Starting with infancy and following through age by age to senescence, growth is mapped in successive chapters on its physical side, then its intellectual, its educational, its emotional and motivational, its moral-religious, its interpersonal-social, its familial. The woof in the weave is the recognition of individual differences in most of the functions and at most of the stages, and their exploitation and interpretation against the background of individual history. . . .

The most nearly central theme of this book is a sort of longitudinal holism (as well as the currently well-accepted cross-sectional holism), a life-span, cradle-to-grave perspective. Even where the problems of old age are being canvassed, the reader is reminded that that period of life with its subculture and subsociety—the period which needs to be rescued from the "inane placidities of the Florida trailer camp or the narrow evangelism of

[32] Sidney L. Pressey, "Adulthood and Old Age," *Encyclopedia of Educational Research.* Edited by Chester W. Harris. Third Edition. New York: The Macmillan Co., 1960. p. 42–47.

[33] David P. Ausubel and Others, "Aging and Psychological Adjustment: Problem Solving and Motivation," in "Growth, Development, and Learning." *Review of Educational Research* 31: 487–99; December 1961.

[34] Robert J. Havighurst and Betty E. Orr, "Aging and Psychological Adjustment," in "Growth, Development, and Learning." *Review of Educational Research* 25: 477–86; December 1955.

[35] Quoted from review by John F. Dashiell, *Contemporary Psychology* 2: 265–66; October 1957, of Sidney L. Pressey and Raymond G. Kuhlen, *Psychological Development Through the Life Span.* New York: Harper & Brothers, 1957. xxiii + 654 p.

certain religious groups"—must be seen in its continuity with childhood, youth, and maturity. . . .

Scattered through the chapters there are such queries as: Do the biological drives resume their earlier primary importance for motivation in the advanced years? Is the dichotomy of work versus play especially false in those years? What are the actual effects upon people—at all ages—of the ready-made fantasies stimulated by TV and other mass media? The age-trends toward conservatism: what are possible remedies? The age-changes in marital adjustment are highly multiple and complex: how may that relationship be kept optimal? And finally the all-pervading question: can one hope to approximate Browning's wistful insight?

> "Grow old along with me.
> The best is yet to be:
> The last of life for which the first
> was made."

Diagnosis and Prognosis[36]

Interest in developmental diagnosis and causation came later than the investigations limited to determination of growth norms or sequences. A common error in identifying causation is failure to recognize the combined effects of two or more causal factors that are interrelated functionally, as illustrated by the difficulty of separating the influence of nature from nurture on achievement. The causal factors that affect growth and development include: race; age; sex; familial heredity; prenatal conditions; birth trauma; birth order; maternal age at pregnancy; endocrine factors; nutritional factors; health factors; disease and infections; seasonal conditions; atmospheric conditions (temperature, humidity, and pressure); national-racial culture; socioeconomic status; educational agencies; social pressure; family and neighborhood; acquaintances and friends; intelligence; knowledge; experience, exercise, and training; interests and motivation; and emotional adjustments.

Interest and progress in the area of developmental diagnosis are illustrated by a full-length treatise which presents in some detail a wide range of diagnostic problems: techniques for the developmental examination of behavior and norms of development; diagnosis of the defects and deviations of development (amentia, endocrine disorders, convulsive

---

[36] Leona M. Bayer and Nancy Bayley, *Growth Diagnosis: Selected Methods for Interpreting and Predicting Physical Development from One Year to Maturity*. Chicago: University of Chicago Press, 1959. xiv + 241 p.

Max L. Hutt, "Diagnosis," *Encyclopedia of Educational Research*. Edited by Chester W. Harris. Third Edition. New York: Macmillan Co., 1960. p. 376–80.

Goldine C. Gleser, "Prediction," *Encyclopedia of Educational Research*, p. 1038–46.

disorders, neurological diagnosis of infant behavior, cerebral injury, special sensory handicaps, prematurity, precocity, environmental retardation, and clinical aspects of child adoption); and protection of early child development, as related to diagnosis, guidance, and developmental supervision.[37]

The discussion in this chapter relating to causal factors affecting physical and mental growth suggests the difficulties of developmental prognosis and prediction. Prediction in such areas as constancy of the I.Q., height, time of maturity, and age at which growth will cease is possible only to the extent that valid techniques or instruments of measurement are available, that early development provides a stable base from which subsequent growth proceeds, and that later development is affected by the same causal factors as operated in the earlier stages of growth. As indicated earlier in this chapter, it is much simpler to predict in the area of physical growth and performance than in the fields of mentality and personality development.

DEVELOPMENTAL TASKS AND STAGES OF MATURITY

During the 1950's the developmental-task concept was applied to the field of education. This concept evolved from the research on child and adolescent development during the 1930's and resulted in a science of human development cutting across disciplines in the biological and the social sciences. More recently this concept has been explored on the basis of psychological and sociological research on attitudes and social roles, and also has been applied to adulthood and old age.

A developmental task is one which "arises at or about a certain period in the life of the individual, successful achievement of which leads to his happiness and to success with later tasks, while failure leads to unhappiness in the individual, disapproval by society, and difficulty with later tasks.[38] Such tasks arise from three sources: physical maturation, cultural pressure (the expectations of society), and individual aspirations or values.

To cite an example, the central task of adolescence, "achieving identity," includes the following developmental tasks: learning a masculine or feminine social role, accepting one's body, achieving emotional independence of parents and other adults, selecting and preparing for an occupation, and achieving a scale of values and an ethical system to live by.

[37] Arnold Gesell and Catherine S. Amatruda, *op. cit.*
[38] Robert J. Havighurst, "Research on the Developmental-Task Concept." *School Review* 64: 215–23; May 1956.

By way of illustration, the developmental tasks of middle childhood include:[39]

1. Learning physical skills necessary for ordinary games
2. Building wholesome attitudes toward oneself as a growing organism
3. Learning to get along with age-mates
4. Learning an appropriate masculine or feminine social role
5. Developing fundamental skills in reading, writing, and calculating
6. Developing concepts necessary for everyday living
7. Developing conscience, morality, and a scale of values
8. Achieving personal independence
9. Developing attitudes toward social groups and institutions.

Gesell and associates have outlined maturity traits and gradients of growth:[40]

1. *Total action system:* physical growth, sex interest, health, tensional outlets, response to the examination and interview
2. *Self-care and routines:* eating, sleep, bath, clothes, care of room, money, and work
3. *Emotions:* in general, anger, worries and fears, humor, affectivity, self-assertion, expressing feelings
4. *The growing self:* in general, self-evaluation, wishes and inclinations, the future
5. *Interpersonal relationships:* mother-child, father-child, siblings, family, same-sex friends, opposite-sex friends, crushes, parties
6. *Activities and interests:* outdoor activities, indoor activities, clubs and camps, reading, radio, television, phonograph, movies
7. *School life:* in general, school subjects and work, teacher-child relationship
8. *Ethical sense:* right and wrong, sense of fairness, response to reason, honesty, swearing, drinking, smoking
9. *Philosophical outlook:* time and space, death and deity.

As an illustration of stages of development, the changes in "likes" from ten to sixteen are as follows:[41]

Ten: "My mother and father, of course," is the outstanding answer to the question: "What do you like best in the world?" "Horses" comes next in frequency.

[39] Robert J. Havighurst, *Human Development and Education.* New York: Longmans, Green and Co., 1953. p. 25–41.
[40] Arnold Gesell, Frances L. Ilg, and Louise B. Ames, *Youth:* The Years from Ten to Sixteen. New York: Harper & Brothers, 1956. p. 35.
Also see Louise B. Ames, "Arnold L. Gesell: 'Behavior Has Shape'." *Science* 134: 266–67; July 28, 1961.
[41] *Ibid.,* p. 372–75.

Eleven: As at ten years, "my mother and father" are mentioned most often as things liked best, and again "horses" is second in frequency. Few other likes are mentioned, except eating and travel.

Twelve: Mother and father still lead as best liked of anything, and animals of some kind—cats, dogs, horses—are next in frequency of mention. Sports have come in strongly, and eating, dancing, and reading are other favored activities. Nice clothes and "my home" are among the things most liked.

Thirteen: A real change appears at thirteen—great variety of likes occurs, and parents have dropped out in mention of best liked. Friends of the opposite sex are now most often mentioned, and are followed in frequency by eating, "my home," and automobiles. Items mentioned for the first time at thirteen include: a good time, the United States, peace and quiet, luxury, and popular music.

Fourteen: Fourteen's likes seem to be broad-ranging. Sports and friends of the opposite sex now lead in frequency, followed by travel and music. Likes first mentioned at fourteen include: knowledge, art and literature, just living, shelter.

Fifteen: Again, as at thirteen, great individual variation appears, with no two "best likes" alike. Among items mentioned are: reading, sailing, art, literature, just living. For the first time, security is named as a thing liked best.

Sixteen: Great individual variety of likes, and many Sixteens find it difficult to indicate the thing they like best. Only one mentioned material objects ("car and radio"), while others have more general preferences, such as work, communication, "having other people like me."

An example of four stages of maturity in using measuring instruments, with specific applications to the school curriculum, is as follows:

Early Childhood: Becoming acquainted with common measuring instruments—Using ruler to measure paper, wood for construction; measuring curtains, wallpaper for playhouse; measuring paper for mural; helping fill aquarium; telling time; reading thermometer; finding dates on calendar; figuring how many more days before special holiday or excursion; keeping chart of weight or height; using such measures as cupful, spoonful, pint, quart, in following recipes; learning to tell time.

Later Childhood: Using common measuring instruments effectively—Using yardstick, ruler effectively; deciding whether ruler, tape measure, or yardstick is most suitable to measure given distances; finding how to use stop watch; investigating uses of compass in telling direction; finding how to use pints, quarts, other measuring instruments in the home; using scales to weigh self, other objects; reading speedometer; reading thermometer, barometer; making charts, maps, scale drawings; developing simple time chart in social studies.

Youth: Extending the range and variety of measuring instruments used —Using stop watch; using efficiently protractor or compass; using kitchen utensils to measure ingredients; laying out basketball court; using a T square for construction activities; using transit, angle mirror or other instruments for measuring heights or distances; using fine scales in experimental work;

reading gasoline gauge, speedometer, and other indicators on car; reading directions from compass; using color charts; adjusting shutter and lens speed on camera; reading barometer; interpreting different types of thermometers, metric and other scales.

Adulthood: Using instruments of measurement appropriately in a variety of situations of adult life—Using precise instruments appropriate to one's vocation; recognizing when inaccurate instruments might throw measurements off, when more accurate instruments are needed; interpreting statements about industrial processes requiring precision measures; using surveying instruments; using scales in grocery store, scales to weigh self, children; reading utility meters; reading clinical thermometers; using barometer and thermometer to make weather predictions; using scale on light meter, other photographic equipment; reading automobile gauges.[42]

EXAMPLES AND APPLICATIONS

In a large measure, developmental and growth studies have been centralized and co-ordinated through such university centers as California at Berkeley, Columbia, Chicago, Harvard, Iowa, Michigan, Minnesota, Stanford, and Yale,[43] as illustrated in the footnotes and bibliography of this chapter. Another example of a center is found in the work of the Fels Research Institute for the Study of Human Development at Antioch College, which was founded to study human growth and development from the prenatal period through maturity by the longitudinal method of research, by means of repeated measurements and observations of the same children over long periods of time. More than 300 children from Yellow Springs and neighboring communities have participated in the program of investigation, with staff members in the fields of biochemistry, physical growth, psychophysiology, and psychology engaged in experimental and cross-section research, as well as longitudinal investigation.

Example: Genetic Studies of Genius[44]

At the time of the follow-up reported in this volume, most of the subjects of the Gifted Child Study had reached their mid-forties. Like the preceding

[42] Quoted from Florence B. Stratemeyer, Hamden L. Forkner, Margaret G. McKim, and A. Harry Passow, *Developing a Curriculum for Modern Living.* Second Edition. New York: Bureau of Publications, Teachers College, Columbia University, 1957. p. 208–9.

[43] Lois M. Stolz, "Youth: The Gesell Institute and Its Latest Study." *Contemporary Psychology* 3: 10–15; January 1958. Reviews the projects in child development completed at Yale University.

[44] Quoted from review by Anne Anastasi, *Contemporary Psychology* 5: 46–47; February 1960, of Lewis M. Terman and Melita H. Oden, *The Gifted Group at Mid-Life:* Thirty-Five Years' Follow-Up of the Superior Child. Genetic Studies of Genius, Vol. 5. Stanford, Calif.: Stanford University Press, 1959. xvi + 187 p.

volume, this book is complete in itself, providing a summary of the earlier stages of the project in the first two chapters. The remaining chapters are devoted to the results of the third major follow-up, including test, questionnaire, and interview data on the gifted subjects, their spouses, and their offspring. Field data were gathered in 1950-52, thirty years after the initiation of the study, and were supplemented in 1955 through a mail questionnaire. The unparalleled amount of cooperation obtained in this project is indicated by the fact that 95% of the 1437 living subjects participated actively in the field study. . . .

Terman's own participation in the project which he started in 1921 and with which he was so closely identified ended with his death in 1956. The present volume was completed by Mrs. Oden, who served as research associate on the project since 1927. Through Terman's foresight, however, arrangements for the continuation of the study had been made before his death. This unique aspect of the project has been aptly characterized by Robert R. Sears, its present research director, in the following words: "We can be grateful for the courage and vision of the man who finally broke the barrier of the limited lifetime allotted to any one researcher, and got under way a study of man that will encompass the span of the *subjects'* lives, not just those of the researchers."

Physical Growth[45]

Physical growth is a biological process that involves rates, directions, and patterns of change and development affected by a variety of diverse and complex external and internal factors and causes. It encompasses a diversity of detectable and measurable changes in size, shape, or function occurring in living organisms with the passage of time. Many scientific disciplines study physical growth from a variety of angles at different levels with increasingly refined and ingenious methods and techniques. Challenging and rewarding fields for study have included: genetic origins and backgrounds; reproduction; cell multiplication; protein synthesis; the role of chemical excitors and inhibitors; cell migration; prenatal development; birth phenomena; developmental history of special tissues, organs, and intact organisms; increases in body measurements and changes in shape; comparative growth of groups, interindividual and intraindividual growth; and environmental conditioners and impacts.[46]

Mental Development[47]

Before the middle of the present century, investigations of mental development dealt primarily with the period of childhood and adoles-

[45] Kai Jensen, "Physical Development," *Encyclopedia of Educational Research.* Edited by Chester W. Harris. Third Edition. New York: The Macmillan Co., 1960. p. 964–71.

Ruth B. Glassow, "Motor Development," *Encyclopedia of Educational Research,* p. 901–4.

[46] Kai Jensen, *op. cit.*

[47] Samuel R. Pinneau and Harold E. Jones, "Mental Development in Infancy

cence. Longitudinal studies now have begun to provide information on age changes later in the life span of individuals first tested in childhood or adolescence. During the 1950's and later research workers showed an active interest in the consistency of test performance at different ages and in factors related to change in test performance; effect of environmental variables on mental development; role of emotional and motivational factors; extent to which I.Q. changes represent true changes in relative standing or are attributable instead to test construction, test standardization, or other psychometric factors; group and individual differences; test performance of institutional and defective children; studies of various socioeconomic and ethnic groups; differential responses of groups with different physical and mental disorders; and mental development of the infant in relation to predictive value of tests given in infancy. The topics under which the studies of mental development during the 1950's and later were reviewed include the following: abilities at different developmental levels, adult mental abilities, constancy of the I.Q., intelligence and achievement, sex differences in intelligence, intelligence and socioeconomic status, differences among ethnic groups, bilingualism, genetic influences on intelligence, institutionalized and defective children, mental abilities in psychiatric groups, intelligence and personal and social adjustment, and mental, physical, and physiological relationships.

Learning

A recent review of investigations on growth and development takes the position that such research can be interpreted most meaningfully to the educational specialist if considered in relation to classroom learning.[48]

Developmental trends during the life span—particularly those of a cognitive nature, but not excluding trends in social, emotional, and personality development—are obviously relevant. Since these trends influence the cognitive, motivational, interpersonal, and social determinants of classroom learning at every age, they must be taken into account by all persons concerned with teaching and curriculum development.

Perceptual and cognitive development . . . have greater relevance for cognitive aspects of classroom learning than do social, emotional, and personality development. After a quarter-century of virtual neglect, during which educational and developmental psychologists have emphasized personality and

---

and Childhood and Mental Abilities in Adult Life," in "Growth, Development, and Learning." *Review of Educational Research* 25: 415–37; December 1955.

Nancy Bayley, "Mental Development," *Encyclopedia of Educational Research.* Edited by Chester W. Harris. Third Edition. New York: The Macmillan Co., 1960. p. 817–22.

John B. Carroll, "Language Development," *Encyclopedia of Educational Research*, p. 744–50.

[48] Quoted from David P. Ausubel and Others, "Growth, Development, and Learning." *Review of Educational Research* 31: 449–50; December 1961.

social development in teaching and research, cognitive development has emerged as an important focus of research and general interest for the educator.

The development of a universally accepted definition of learning is greatly needed and would not necessarily limit either the number or variety of studies or the differences in perceptual or theoretical framework of the investigators. An acceptance of such a definition, however, not only would provide a more effective opportunity to synthesize for the use of research but would also enable the investigator to make contributions more in harmony with the total field than at present. Although the name used to identify a particular phenomenon is not of significance in itself, the assumptions upon which experimentation is based are highly significant. It is often easier to make an assumption from the name given than from the reality itself.

Apparatus and procedures are now available for careful study of children's learning, with considerable work already completed on conditioning, discrimination learning, rote verbal and motor learning, and concept formation. However, systematic study of a particular area of children's learning is still rare, with most experiments in the form of single-shot investigations rather than a series or patterns of careful, planned studies; for example, we need to analyze the learning performance of children in the relatively complex rote-learning and concept-formation situations. To cite a promising development, laboratory methods and apparatus in the form of teaching machines have been applied to the teaching of academic content, with provision for control and manipulation of the psychologically potent factors of amount of practice, immediacy of reinforcement, stimulus-presentation methods, and problem sequence.[49]

A number of trends in the literature on learning indicate that a new frame of reference is being accepted: a change from concern for facts to a concern for generalizations and laws; a change of focus from the experimenter to the learner, from emphasis on outcomes to emphasis on process, from judgment based on magnitude to that based on rate, from the cross-section to the longitudinal basis, from specifics to patterns or configurations, and from independent findings to findings related to each other. Much of the recent literature has been concerned with the learner's perception of the self-concept; understanding, transfer, and retention; problem-solving; and attitudes and values.

[49] Charles C. Spiker, "Research Methods in Children's Learning," *Handbook of Research Methods in Child Development*. Edited by Paul H. Mussen. New York: John Wiley & Sons, 1960. Chapter 9.

Personality and Social Development[50]

Modern personality theories assign a leading role in personality formation to the events of the preschool years. Although the need for knowledge and understanding of the important early processes has long been acutely experienced, the relative dearth of sound studies of early personality development indicates a hiatus between theory and observation. The scarcity of relevant studies probably is the result of several factors: a lack of technical devices for assessment of the behavior of young children comparable to the procedures currently utilized in studies of adults, and the cultural lag that permits less recognition of efforts in this area than of work in the more adequately financed and currently fashionable fields. The use of conventional psychometric devices has not proved adequate, with interest focused on projective and play techniques. The Rorschach Test has been a common projective device selected for young children, with recent studies concentrated on the normative aspects of performance. The studies of personality development in infancy and the preschool years during the 1950's and later may be classified under the headings of child-rearing practices (demographic differences and relation to development), family relationships and attitudes (mother-child relationships, early separation, father-child relationships, and sibling relationships), frustration and aggression, adjustment, behavior disorders, prematurity, hospitalization, measuring instruments, and play therapy. Recent studies of personality and social development in childhood and adolescence have been classified under the broad headings of family structure and intra-familial dynamics, aggressive behavior and delinquency, socio-sexual adjustment, adolescence, exceptional children, counseling, appraisal instruments and procedures, and personality traits, interests, and attitudes.[51]

Personality and social development during the 1950's and later received considerable attention from psychologists, psychiatrists, sociolo-

---

[50] Arthur R. Delong, "Learning," in "Growth, Development, and Learning." *Review of Educational Research* 25: 438–52; December 1955.

J. Murray Lee and Others, "Growth, Development, and Learning." *Review of Educational Research* 28: 433–74; December 1958.

[51] Louis P. Thorpe and Virginia Johnson, "Personality and Social Development in Childhood and Adolescence," in "Growth, Development, and Learning." *Review of Educational Research* 28: 422–32; December 1958.

Harold H. Anderson, Charles Hanley, and John R. Hurley, "Personality Development in Infancy and the Preschool Years," in "Growth, Development, and Learning." *Review of Educational Research* 25: 453–68; December 1955.

Robert J. Havighurst, "Social Development," *Encyclopedia of Educational Research*. Edited by Chester W. Harris. Third Edition. New York: The Macmillan Co., 1960. p. 1287–90.

David P. Ausubel, "Emotional Development," *Encyclopedia of Educational Research*, p. 448–53.

gists, and anthropologists, which suggests an interdisciplinary approach. The individual is being viewed increasingly as a unique, unified, and whole personality with the ability to act according to his own self-determination and not just in response to present and past occurrences, which places major emphasis on striving and goal-directed behavior. The investigations of the 1950's and later dealing with personality and social development during childhood and adolescence may be classified under the large headings of adolescence, juvenile delinquency, sociometric investigations, relationship to academic success, and techniques for evaluation.[52]

In the literature of personality development of children, recurring pitfalls and errors include the following:[53]

1. Reliance on purely empirical approaches to the construction and validation of measuring techniques without prior and continuing conceptual clarification of the precise variable or variables to be measured
2. Failure to consider and control the extraneous variables that may in fact be measured by a particular technique
3. Reliance on measurements by a single technique applied in a single situation often far removed from the context in which the variable appears in the day-to-day life of the child.

Encouraging evidence of methodological ingenuity in studying personality development is present in the following trends:

1. A trend away from traditional mechanistic methods of test construction, with their single-measure indices of reliability and validity, toward multiple approaches for establishing the construct validity of the theory underlying the measuring instrument
2. Investigation of a particular variable simultaneously through fantasy and overt behavior with the aim not merely of demonstrating a positive correlation between the two but of exploring the situational conditions and processes that appear to account both for the continuities and discontinuities in the two spheres of expression
3. The effort to supplement traditional objective and projective instruments with systematic behavioral observations and experimental procedures that are sufficiently simple and attractive to be applicable to children but permit controlled manipulation of situational factors
4. The articulation of social and cultural variables into the procedures employed for the appraisal of personality characteristics.

[52] Cameron W. Meredith, "Personality and Social Development During Childhood and Adolescence," in "Growth, Development, and Learning." *Review of Educational Research* 25: 469–76; December 1955.

[53] Urie Bronfenbrenner and Henry N. Ricciuti, "The Appraisal of Personality Characteristics in Children," *Handbook of Research Methods in Child Development*. Edited by Paul H. Mussen. New York: John Wiley & Sons, 1960. Chapter 18.

As a goal for the future, incorporation of the attitudes and values of children into more general developmental theory would be valuable to both developmental and social psychology. Concepts of attitudes and values have proved useful in investigating the social contexts of children, and should be explored further in intrafamilial contexts—the effects of parental handling upon children's attitudes and value systems, and the interactive effects of children's attitudes and values and parental handling upon other consequents in child development.[54]

CONCLUDING STATEMENT

Nearly 6,000 references are listed in the ten issues of the *Review of Educational Research* devoted to growth and development, with much of this research sponsored in child-study divisions of higher institutions and with helpful support from the foundations. These resources, however, are not adequate for the expensive and time-consuming longitudinal investigations, which suggests the need for public interest and support, including the cooperation of teachers, administrators, parents, and children. The concepts, procedures, and applications of developmental or growth investigations may be summarized briefly as follows:

1. An interest in origin, direction, trend, rate, pattern, limit, and decline of growth. The concept of development is fundamentally biological and has been most commonly associated with the organization of living structures and life processes, although a developmental concept sometimes is applied to physical systems, cultures, social institutions, or systems of ideas, and has been applied to educational, psychological, sociological, anthropological, historical, economic, political, artistic, and aesthetic phenomena.

2. Encouragement of carefully planned longitudinal investigations, and improved sampling procedures in cross-section studies. The cross-section technique requires at least a single measurement for each individual, as in the first six grades of a public-school system. In following growth in height of a particular group of children or of an individual through a period of months or years by the longitudinal method, the resulting series of measurements represents growth sequences for the same group or the same individual.

3. Application of the longitudinal approach to study of the growth-maturity-senescence cycles of an economic, political, or entire cultural system. Some of these ages, like height age in the study of human development, appear and are measurable from the time the organism (economy, political system, or cultural group) first exists as a separately definable entity. Others, like dental age in the child, represent late emerging characteristics and cannot be measured individually or averaged into an "organismic age" until they first appear.

4. Use of the cross-cultural method in the behavioral sciences, with statistical techniques employed to test theory, and recently with a major interest

[54] Marian R. Yarrow, "The Measurement of Children's Attitudes and Values," *Handbook of Research Methods in Child Development*, Chapter 16.

in matters of personality development in different cultures. Anthropology may contribute especially to the methods of studying child rearing through: (a) the concept of the culture complex, with its analysis of values, beliefs, techniques, justifications, and rationalizations; and (b) comparative study of child life in non-European societies, with identification of important variables that may have been overlooked and may prove useful in prediction of behavior.

5. Formulation of basic principles for analysis and interpretation of genetic data. A basic continuity characterizes human psychological development, in the sense that patterns of personality and adjustment once established tend to persist over long periods of time, although environmental or constitutional factors or circumstances, under certain conditions, might alter the growth trends of particular individuals. The interrelatedness of developmental trends is noted in the positive correlation of desirable traits and in a certain unity of growth.

6. Further progress in identification of maturity traits and gradients of growth, stages of development or maturity, and developmental tasks. A developmental task is one which "arises at or about a certain period in the life of the individual, successful achievement of which leads to his happiness and to success with later tasks, while failure leads to unhappiness in the individual, disapproval by society, and difficulty with later tasks."[55]

7. Increased interest and recently devised procedures in certain major areas of development (physical, mental, social, personality, learning, and old age). Apparatus and procedures are now available for careful study of children's learning, with considerable work already completed on conditioning, discrimination learning, rote verbal and motor learning, and concept formation. As a goal for the future, incorporation of the attitudes and values of children into more general developmental theory would be valuable to both developmental and social psychology.

SELECTED REFERENCES

ALMY, Millie. *Child Development.* New York: Henry Holt and Co., 1955. xvii + 490 p. (Chapters 3 and 4 deal with procedures and problems in studying child development.)

ANDERSON, Harold H., and Others. "Growth, Development, and Learning." *Review of Educational Research* 25: 365-540; December 1955.

ANDERSON, John E. *The Psychology of Development and Personal Adjustment.* New York: Henry Holt and Co., 1949. xvi + 720 p.

AUSUBEL, David P. *Theory and Problems of Adolescent Development.* New York: Grune and Stratton, 1954. 600 p.

AUSUBEL, David P. *Theory and Problems of Child Development.* New York: Grune and Stratton, 1958. xiv + 650 p.

AUSUBEL, David P., and Others. "Growth, Development, and Learning." *Review of Educational Research* 31: 445-572; December 1961.

[55] Robert J. Havighurst, "Research on the Developmental-Task Concept." *School Review* 64: 215-23; May 1956.

BALDWIN, Alfred L. *Behavior and Development in Childhood.* New York: Dryden Press, 1955. xviii + 620 p.

BALLER, W. R. *Readings in the Psychology of Human Growth and Development.* New York: Holt, Rinehart, and Winston, 1962. xiv + 689 p.

BALLER, W. R., and CHARLES, D. C. *The Psychology of Human Growth and Development.* New York: Holt, Rinehart, and Winston, 1961. xvi + 432 p.

BARKER, Roger G., and WRIGHT, Herbert F. *Midwest and Its Children:* The Psychological Ecology of an American Town. Evanston, Ill.: Row, Peterson and Co., 1955. vii + 532 p.

BARKER, Roger G., and WRIGHT, Herbert F. *One Boy's Day:* A Specimen Record of Behavior. New York: Harper & Brothers, 1951. x + 435 p.

BARRON, Milton L. *The Aging American:* On Introduction to Social Gerontology and Geriatrics. New York: Thomas Y. Crowell Co., 1961. xvii + 269 p.

BAYER, Leona M., and BAYLEY, Nancy. *Growth Diagnosis:* Selected Methods for Interpreting and Predicting Physical Development from One Year to Maturity. Chicago: The University of Chicago Press, 1959. xvi + 241 p.

BAYLEY, Nancy. "Individual Patterns of Development." *Child Development* 27: 45-74; March 1956.

BERNARD, Harold W. *Adolescent Development in American Culture.* Yonkers-on-Hudson: World Book Co., 1957. xii + 644 p.

BERNARD, Harold W. *Human Development in Western Culture.* Boston: Allyn and Bacon, 1962. 445 p.

BIJOU, Sidney W., and BAER, Donald M. *Child Development:* Vol. 1, A Systematic and Empirical Theory. New York: Appleton-Century-Crofts, 1961. v + 90 p.

BIRREN, J. E., Editor. *Handbook of Aging and the Individual:* Psychological and Biological Aspects. Chicago: The University of Chicago Press, 1960. xii + 939 p.

BLAIR, Arthur W., and BURTON, William H. *Growth and Development of the Preadolescent.* New York: Appleton-Century-Crofts, 1951. viii + 221 p.

BLOS, Peter. *On Adolescence:* A Psychoanalytic Interpretation. New York: Free Press of Glencoe, 1962. 269 p.

BOSSARD, J. H. S., and BOLL, Eleanor S. *The Sociology of Child Development.* Third Edition. New York: Harper & Brothers, 1960. xiii + 706 p.

BRECKENRIDGE, Marian E., and VINCENT, E. Lee. *Child Development:* Physical and Psychological Growth through Adolescence. Fourth Edition. Philadelphia: W. B. Saunders, 1960. xiv + 648 p.

BREEN, Leonard Z. "Some Problems of Research in the Field of Aging." *Sociology and Social Research* 41: 412-16; July-August 1957.

BURLINGHAM, Dorothy. *Twins:* A Study of Three Pairs of Identical Twins. New York: International Universities Press, 1953. x + 92 p. + 30 developmental charts.

CARMICHAEL, Leonard, Editor. *Manual of Child Psychology.* Second Edition. New York: John Wiley & Sons, 1954. ix + 1295 p.

COLE, Luella. *Psychology of Adolescence.* Fifth Edition. New York: Rinehart, 1959. xviii + 718 p.

COLEMAN, J. S., and Others. *The Adolescent Society:* The Social Life of the

Teenager and Its Impact on Education. New York: Free Press of Glencoe, 1961. xvi + 368 p.

CORNELL, Ethel L., and ARMSTRONG, Charles M. "Forms of Mental Growth Patterns Revealed by Reanalysis of the Harvard Growth Data." *Child Development* 26: 169-204; September 1955.

CROW, L. D., and CROW, Alice. *Adolescent Development and Adjustment.* New York: McGraw-Hill Book Co., 1956. xiv + 555 p.

CROW, L. D., and CROW, Alice. *Child Development and Adjustment:* A Study of Child Psychology. New York: The Macmillan Co., 1962. xi + 514 p.

CROW, L. D., and CROW, Alice, Editors. *Readings in Child and Adolescent Psychology.* New York: Longmans, Green, 1961. xiv + 592 p.

CRUZE, Wendell W. *Adolescent Psychology and Development.* New York: Ronald Press, 1953. 584 p.

DEWEY, Richard, and HUMBER, W. J. *The Development of Human Behavior.* New York: The Macmillan Co., 1951. 832 p.

DONAHUE, Wilma T., Editor. *Education for Later Maturity:* A Handbook. New York: Whiteside, and William Morrow, 1955. xiii + 338 p.

DUNN, L. C., Editor. *Genetics in the 20th Century.* New York: The Macmillan Co., 1951. xi + 634 p.

DUVALL, Evelyn M. *Family Development.* Philadelphia: J. B. Lippincott Co., 1957. vii + 533 p.

ENGLISH, H. B. *Dynamics of Child Development.* New York: Holt, Rinehart, and Winston, 1961. xvi + 461 p.

ESSERT, Paul L., and Others. "Adult Education." *Review of Educational Research* 23: 191-283; June 1953.

FOREST, Ilse. *Child Development.* New York: McGraw-Hill Book Co., 1954. 286 p.

FRAIBERG, Selma H. *The Magic Years:* Understanding and Handling the Problems of Early Childhood. New York: Charles Scribner's Sons, 1959. xiv + 305 p.

GARN, Stanley M., and SHAMIR, Zvi. *Methods for Research in Human Growth.* Springfield, Ill.: Charles C Thomas, 1958. 132 p.

GARRISON, Karl C. *Growth and Development.* New York: Longmans, Green and Co., 1952. xii + 559 p.

GARRISON, Karl C. *Psychology of Adolescence.* Fourth Edition. New York: Prentice-Hall, 1951. 510 p.

GESELL, Arnold. *Infant Development:* The Embryology of Early Human Behavior. New York: Harper & Brothers, 1952. 108 p.

GESELL, Arnold, and AMATRUDA, Catherine S. *Developmental Diagnosis:* Normal and Abnormal Child Development, Clinical Methods and Practical Applications. Revised Edition. New York: Harper & Brothers, 1947. xvi + 496 p.

GESELL, Arnold, ILG, Frances L., and AMES, Louise B. *Youth:* The Years from Ten to Sixteen. New York: Harper & Brothers, 1956. xv + 542 p.

GILBERT, Jeanne G. *Understanding Old Age.* New York: Ronald Press, 1953. 442 p. (Detailed treatment of gerontology; important physical aspects of the aging process and the intellectual, emotional, and psychosexual changes that take place in later years; normal and abnormal aging; 26 case histories based on the author's professional experience.)

GILBERT, Luther C. "Genetic Study of Eye Movements in Reading." *Elementary School Journal* 59: 328-35; March 1959.

GOOD, Carter V., and SCATES, Douglas E. *Methods of Research:* Educational, Psychological, Sociological. New York: Appleton-Century-Crofts, 1954. p. 800-831.

GOODENOUGH, Florence L., and TYLER, Leona E. *Developmental Psychology:* An Introduction to the Study of Human Behavior. Third Edition. New York: Appleton-Century-Crofts, 1959. xx + 552 p.

HARRIS, D. B., Editor. *The Concept of Development:* An Issue in the Study of Human Behavior. Minneapolis: University of Minnesota Press, 1957. x + 287 p.

HAVIGHURST, Robert J. *Human Development and Education.* New York: Longmans, Green and Co., 1953. ix + 338 p.

HAVIGHURST, Robert J. "Research on the Developmental-Task Concept." *School Review* 64: 215-23; May 1956.

HAVIGHURST, Robert J., and ALBRECHT, Ruth. *Older People.* New York: Longmans, Green and Co., 1953. xvi + 415 p.

HAWKES, Glenn R., and PEASE, Damaris. *Behavior and Development from 5 to 12.* New York: Harper & Brothers, 1962. 375 p.

HOCH, Paul H., and ZUBIN, Joseph, Editors. *Psychopathology of Aging.* New York: Grune and Stratton, 1961. v + 321 p.

HORROCKS, John E. *The Psychology of Adolescence:* Behavior and Development. Second Edition. Boston: Houghton Mifflin Co., 1962. xv + 711 p.

HURLOCK, Elizabeth B. *Adolescent Development.* Second Edition. New York: McGraw-Hill Book Co., 1955. 590 p.

HURLOCK, Elizabeth B. *Child Development.* Second Edition. New York: McGraw-Hill Book Co., 1950. xvi + 669 p.

HURLOCK, Elizabeth B. *Developmental Psychology.* Second Edition. New York: McGraw-Hill Book Co., 1959. 645 p.

HUTT, M. L., and GIBBY, R. G. *The Child:* Development and Adjustment. Boston. Allyn and Bacon, 1959. xiv + 401 p.

HUXLEY, Julian. *Evolution in Action.* New York: Harper & Brothers, 1953. 182 p.

ILG, Frances L., and AMES, Louise B. *Child Behavior.* New York: Harper & Brothers, 1955. xi + 364 p.

JERSILD, Arthur T. *Child Psychology.* Fifth Edition. Englewood Cliffs. N. J.: Prentice-Hall, 1960. xxii + 506 p.

JERSILD, Arthur T. *The Psychology of Adolescence.* New York: The Macmillan Co., 1957. xii + 438 p.

KIELL, Norman. *The Adolescent Through Fiction:* A Psychological Approach. New York: International Universities Press, 1959. 345 p.

KINSEY, A. C., and Others. *Sexual Behavior in the Human Male.* Philadelphia: W. B. Saunders Co., 1958. xvi + 804 p.

KINSEY, A. C., and Others. *Sexual Behavior in the Human Female.* Philadelphia: W. B. Saunders Co., 1953. xxx + 842 p.

KUHLEN, Raymond G. *The Psychology of Adolescent Development.* New York: Harper & Brothers, 1952. xvii + 675 p.

KUHLEN, Raymond G., and THOMPSON, George G. *Psychological Studies of Human Development.* New York: Appleton-Century-Crofts, 1952. 533 p.

LANDIS, Paul H. *Adolescence and Youth:* The Process of Maturing. Second Edition. New York: McGraw-Hill Book Co., 1952. xii + 461 p.

LANDRETH, Catherine. *The Psychology of Early Childhood.* New York: Alfred A. Knopf, 1958. xviii + 412 + xiii p.

LANDY, David. *Tropical Childhood:* Cultural Transmission and Learning in a Rural Puerto Rican Village. Chapel Hill: University of North Carolina Press, 1959. xii + 291 p.

LEHMAN, Harvey C. *Age and Achievement.* Princeton: Princeton University Press, 1953. xi + 358 p.

LINDZEY, Gardner. *Projective Techniques and Cross-Cultural Research.* New York: Appleton-Century-Crofts, 1962. ix + 339 p.

LINE, William, and KING, Margery R. "Cross-Cultural Research." *Journal of Educational Sociology* 29: 281-91; March 1956.

MALM, Marguerite, and JAMISON, Olis G. *Adolescence.* New York: McGraw-Hill Book Co., 1953. 512 p.

MARTIN, Phyllis C., and VINCENT, Elizabeth L. *Human Development.* New York: Ronald Press, 1960. vi + 541 p.

MARTIN, William E., and STENDLER, Celia B. *Child Behavior and Development.* Revised edition of *Child Development,* 1953. New York: Harcourt, Brace, 1959. xxii + 618 p.

MARTIN, William E., and STENDLER, Celia B. *Readings in Child Development.* New York: Harcourt, Brace and Co., 1954. 513 p.

McCANDLESS, B. R. *Children and Adolescents:* Behavior and Development. New York: Holt, Rinehart, and Winston, 1961. x + 531 p.

McCORD, Joan, and McCORD, William. "Cultural Stereotypes and the Validity of Interviews for Research in Child Development." *Child Development* 32: 171-85; March 1961.

MEREDITH, Howard V. "Methods of Studying Physical Growth," *Handbook of Research Methods in Child Development.* Edited by Paul H. Mussen. New York: John Wiley and Sons, 1960. Chapter 5.

MERRY, Frieda K., and MERRY, Ralph V. *The First Two Decades of Life.* Second Edition. New York: Harper & Brothers, 1958. 626 p.

MILLARD, Cecil V. *Case Inventory for the Study of Child Development.* Minneapolis: Burgess Publishing Co., 1950. 29 p.

MILLARD, Cecil V. *Child Growth and Development in the Elementary School Years.* Boston: D. C. Heath and Co., 1951. xiv + 511 p.

MILLARD, Cecil V. *School and Child:* A Case History. East Lansing: Michigan State College Press, 1954. xv + 210 p.

MILLARD, Cecil V., and ROTHNEY, John W. M. *The Elementary School Child:* A Book of Cases. New York: Dryden Press, 1957. xii + 660 p. (Case histories of development, including a developmental curve, achievement record, elementary-school marks, mental characteristics, mental-test results, observation notes, and teachers' summaries.)

MOHR, G. J., and DESPRES, Marian A. *The Stormy Decade:* Adolescence. New York: Random House, 1958. 272 p.

MONTAGUE, M. F. ASHLEY. *The Direction of Human Development:* Biological and Social Bases. New York: Harper & Brothers, 1955. 404 p.

MUNN, Norman L. *The Evolution and Growth of Human Behavior.* Boston: Houghton Mifflin Co., 1955. xi + 525 p.

MURASE, Kenneth. "Cross-Cultural Education: Some Implications for Social Work." *Social Service Review* 33: 43-54; March 1959.

MURPHY, Lois B., and Others. *Personality in Young Children.* 2 vols. New York: Basic Books, 1956. (Volume 2 is a detailed study of "Colin, A Normal Child," from his second through his fifth year.)

MUSSEN, Paul H., Editor. *Handbook of Research Methods in Child Development.* New York: John Wiley & Sons, 1960. x + 1061 p. For an especially analytical review see Robert R. Sears, *Contemporary Psychology* 6: 385-88; November 1961.

MUSSEN, Paul H., and CONGER, John J. *Child Development and Personality.* New York: Harper & Brothers, 1956. xii + 569 p.

OGBURN, William F., and BOSE, Nirmal K. "On the Trail of the Wolf-Children." *Genetic Psychology Monographs* 60: 117-93; August 1959.

OLSON, W. C. *Child Development.* Second Edition. Boston: D. C. Heath, 1959. xii + 497 p.

PARSONS, Thomas E. "A Longitudinal Approach to the Study of Cultural Growth." *Social Forces* 34: 34-41; October 1955.

PATTERSON, Franklin, and Associates. *The Adolescent Citizen.* Glencoe, Ill.: Free Press, 1960. xii + 387 p.

PIKUNAS, Justin, and ALBRECHT, E. J. *Psychology of Human Development.* New York: McGraw-Hill Book Co., 1961. xiv + 346 p.

PINNER, Frank A., JACOBS, Paul, and SELZNICK, Philip. *Old Age and Political Behavior:* A Case Study. Berkeley: University of California Press, 1959. xi + 352 p.

PRESSEY, S. L., and KUHLEN, R. G. *Psychological Development Through the Life Span.* New York: Harper & Brothers, 1957. xxiii + 654 p.

RAMSEY, Charles E., and COLLAZO, Jenaro. "Some Problems of Cross-Cultural Measurement." *Rural Sociology* 25: 91-106; March 1960.

READ, Margaret. *Children of Their Fathers:* Growing Up Among the Ngoni of Nyasaland. New Haven, Conn.: Yale University Press, 1960. 176 p.

RODD, William G. "A Cross-Cultural Study of Taiwan's Schools." *Journal of Social Psychology* 50: 3-36; August 1959.

ROGERS, Dorothy. *The Psychology of Adolescence.* New York: Appleton-Century-Crofts, 1962. 600 p.

SARNOFF, Irving, and Others. "A Cross-Cultural Study of Anxiety Among American and English School Children." *Journal of Educational Psychology* 49: 129-36; June 1958.

SCHNEIDERS, A. A. *Personality Development and Adjustment in Adolescence.* Milwaukee: Bruce Publishing Co., 1960. x + 473 p.

SEIDMAN, J. M., Editor. *The Adolescent:* A Book of Readings. Revised Edition. New York: Holt, Rinehart and Winston, 1960. x + 870 p.

SHOCK, N. W. *Trends in Gerontology.* Second Edition. Stanford, Calif.: Stanford University Press, 1957. viii + 214 p.

SIGEL, Irving E. "The Need for Conceptualization in Research on Child Development." *Child Development* 27: 241-52; June 1956.

SONTAG, Lester W., BAKER, Charles T., and NELSON, Virginia L. *Mental Growth and Personality Development:* A Longitudinal Study. Monographs of the Society for Research in Child Development, Vol. 23, Serial No. 68, No. 2, 1958. Lafayette, Ind.: Child Development Publications, Purdue University, 1958. 143 p.

STEPHENS, J. M. *Educational Psychology:* The Study of Educational Growth. New York: Henry Holt and Co., 1951. xxiii + 692 p.

STEVENS, S. S., Editor. "Growth and Development," *Handbook of Experimental Psychology.* New York: John Wiley & Sons, 1951. p. 236-386.

STONE, A. A., and ONQUE, Gloria C. *Longitudinal Studies of Child Personality:* Abstracts with Index. Cambridge, Mass.: Harvard University Press for the Commonwealth Fund, 1959. xvi + 314 p.

STONE, L. J., and CHURCH, Joseph. *Childhood and Adolescence:* A Psychology of the Growing Person. New York: Random House, 1957. xvii + 456 p.

STOTT, L. H. *The Longitudinal Study of Individual Development.* Detroit: Merrill-Palmer School, 1955. x + 115 p.

STRANG, Ruth. *The Adolescent Views Himself:* A Psychology of Adolescence. New York: McGraw-Hill Book Co., 1957. xiv + 581 p.

STRANG, Ruth. *Introduction to Child Study.* Fourth Edition. New York: The Macmillan Co., 1959. xxii + 544 p.

STUART, Harold C., and PRUGH, Dane G., Editors. *The Healthy Child:* His Physical, Psychological, and Social Development. Cambridge, Mass.: Harvard University Press, 1960. xvi + 507 p.

SUCHMAN, J. Richard. *Observation and Analysis in Child Development:* A Laboratory Manual. New York: Harcourt, Brace and Co., 1959. x + 276 p.

SYMONDS, P. M., and JENSEN, A. R. *From Adolescent to Adult.* New York: Columbia University Press, 1961. xiv + 413 p.

TERMAN, Lewis M., and ODEN, Melita H. *The Gifted Child Grows Up:* Genetic Studies of Genius. Stanford, Calif.: Stanford University Press, 1947. xiv + 450 p.

TERRELL, Glenn. "The Need for Simplicity in Research in Child Psychology." *Child Development* 29: 303-10; June 1958.

THOMPSON, George. *Child Psychology.* Second Edition. Boston: Houghton Mifflin Co., 1962. 714 p.

THORPE, Louis P. *Child Psychology and Development.* Second Edition. New York: Ronald Press, 1955. 700 p.

THORPE, Louis P., and CRUZE, Wendell W. *Developmental Psychology.* New York: Ronald Press, 1956. v + 670 p.

TIBBITTS, Clark, Editor. *Handbook of Social Gerontology:* Societal Aspect of Aging. Chicago: The University of Chicago Press, 1960. xx + 770 p.

TIBBITTS, Clark, and DONAHUE, Wilma, Editors. *Aging in Today's Society.* Englewood Cliffs, N.J.: Prentice-Hall, 1960. xxv + 418 p.

TRAVERS, R. M. W. *An Introduction to Educational Research.* New York: The Macmillan Co., 1958. Chapter 12.

VINCENT, Elizabeth L., and MARTIN, Phyllis C. *Human Psychological Development.* New York: Ronald Press Co., 1961. vi + 522 p.

WAGONER, Lovisa C., and CASTELLANOS, J. M. *Observation of Young Children, Their Behavior, Their Teaching.* Revised Edition. Oakland, Calif.: L. C. Wagoner, Mills College, 1951. 142 p.

WATSON, Ernest H., and LOWERY, George H. *Growth and Development of Children.* Chicago: Year Book Publications, 1951. 260 p.

WATSON, Robert I. *Psychology of the Child:* Personal, Social, and Disturbed Child Development. New York: John Wiley & Sons, 1959. ix + 662 p.

WATTENBERG, W. W. *The Adolescent Years.* New York: Harcourt, Brace and Co., 1955. 510 p.

WHITE, Robert W. *Lives in Progress:* A Study of the Natural Growth of Personality. New York: Dryden Press, 1952. 376 p. (Presents, interprets, and compares the lives or case studies of three normal people.)

WHITING, John W. M. "The Cross-Cultural Method," *Handbook of Social Psychology:* Theory and Method. Vol. 1. Edited by Gardner Lindzey. Cambridge, Mass.: Addison-Wesley Publishing Co., 1954. p. 523-31.

WIENER, Norbert. *Ex-Prodigy:* My Childhood and Youth. New York: Simon and Schuster, 1953. xii + 309 p.

WILES, Kimball, and Others. "The Educational Program: Adolescence." *Review of Educational Research* 24: 1-104; February 1954. (Chapter 11 lists needed research.)

WOLFE, Kurt. *The Biological, Sociological and Psychological Aspects of Aging.* Springfield, Ill.: Charles C Thomas, 1959. 95 p.

WRIGHT, Herbert F. "Psychological Development in Midwest." *Child Development* 27: 265-86; July 1956.

ZUBEK, John P., and SOLBERG, Patricia A. *Human Development.* New York: McGraw-Hill Book Co., 1954. 478 p.

CHAPTER SEVEN

Clinical and Case Studies: Individuals, Institutions, and Communities

This chapter presents the several types of case study, applications and uses of clinical and case techniques, sequence or stages in case study and case work (symptoms, examination and history, diagnosis, therapy, and follow-up), clinical and case records, ethical standards, relationship between case-clinical and statistical methods, and illustrative case histories.

TYPES OF CASE STUDY

The basic approach of the case study is to deal with all pertinent aspects of one thing or situation, with the unit for study an individual, a social institution or agency such as a family or a hospital, or a community or cultural group such as a rural village, a steel town, or a trailer camp, as illustrated by numerous titles in the chapter bibliography. The case is some phase of the life history of the unit of attention, or it may represent the entire life process.

Case studies of individuals may be an autobiography of a mental patient or of a criminal, a personal account of a psychoanalysis, a biography of child development, an autobiography of an evolving philosophy and psychology of teaching, or the childhood and youth of a prodigy.

Case studies have been made of such social institutions or agencies as the family, marriage, a higher institution of learning, a hospital clinic, and a movie.

Case studies of communities or cultural groups have included such units as a rural village, an industrial community, a war-boom community, a factory setting, a ghetto, and a trailer camp. Many community studies mentioned in the chapter on descriptive-survey research may also serve as examples of the case approach.

A distinction sometimes is made between case study, case work, and case method. From the point of view of research, case study means intensive investigation of the case unit, especially with respect to initial status or symptoms, collection of explanatory data, and diagnosis or identification of causal factors, looking toward remedial or developmental treatment. Case work frequently is interpreted as the process of therapy and follow-up in relation to developmental, adjustment, or remedial procedures. Although case study and case work frequently are done by different persons or agencies, they are complementary. The case method of instruction is a plan of organizing and presenting materials in such fields as law, medicine, social work, psychology, and education, based on case materials produced through case-study investigation.

APPLICATIONS AND USES

Case-study procedures have been extensively followed in such fields as law and juvenile delinquency, medicine, psychiatry, psychology, education, counseling and guidance, anthropology, sociology, social work, economics, business administration, political science, and journalism. Although case study was once limited primarily to problems of maladjustment, such as truancy or failure in school, a broken or poverty-stricken home, or an underprivileged or malfunctioning community, this approach more recently has been extended to investigation of normal or bright children, successful institutions and agencies, and well-organized communities or effectively functioning cultural groups. Case study has been helpful in providing classifications or categories of individuals referred to such agencies as a bureau of juvenile research or a juvenile court; information on social and institutional group patterns in families, schools, and communities; case materials for teaching purposes; supplementary interpretations and illustrations for statistical findings; and generalizations through the accumulation of careful case reports, especially in the field of medicine.

The usefulness of the clinical and case approach may be illustrated by the field of clinical psychology in general, and more specifically by personality study and counseling psychology. Clinical psychologists perform a variety of services in many settings, dealing with a wide range of human problems. However, within this apparent diversity of clinical psychology there is considerable unity. Psychologists first try to achieve an understanding, based on the hypotheses and techniques of their professional field of knowledge. Then they apply their understanding, so as to help the people help themselves, with such activities frequently labeled "diagnosis" and "therapy." Clinical psychology has grown not so much by the invention of new basic functions as by the extension and development of fundamental procedures; for example, in the diagnostic area, methods for assessing and describing broader aspects of personality are supplementing the older techniques for testing intelligence and school achievement.[1]

Clinical psychology has been of service in a variety of centers and settings, as represented by especially long-standing service in the psychological clinic at the University of Pennsylvania, the Institute for Juvenile Research for the State of Illinois, the Training School at Vineland in New Jersey, Worcester State Hospital, the Menninger Foundation, and the Wichita Guidance Center. Government agencies with large-scale programs of clinical psychology include the Veterans Administration, United States Army, United States Navy, United States Air Force, and the Public Health Service. Clinical centers concerned primarily with mental-health problems are represented by the medical school psychiatric clinic, the psychological-service center, private clinical practice, the old-age counseling center, the clinic for alcoholics, the student-counseling bureau, and industrial-employee counseling. Clinical centers dealing chiefly with antisocial behavior include the municipal court, the juvenile court and youth authority program, the training school for delinquents, and prison. Clinical centers concerned primarily with educative, remedial, and rehabilitative problems include the rehabilitation center, school system, reading clinic, hearing clinic, and speech clinic.

Factors that have played a compelling part in promoting clinical and case studies of personality are as follows:

(1) a national situation (press) consisting of an increased awareness of an increasing incidence of mental illness; (2) in response to this invasion of the field of mental illness by humanitarians (need to relieve suffering), by social reformers (need to correct societal defects), and by scientists (need for knowledge and understanding), and as a result of these forces, the construction of new and enlarged hospitals and clinics with facilities for research under the direction of psychiatrists; (3) technical developments within the field of psychology—the perfection of intelligence tests, word-association tests, projective tests, etc., also the accomplishments of applied psychologists in World Wars I and II; (4) in recognition of their technical abilities, the creation of jobs in hospitals and clinics affording livelihood to clinical psychologists; (5) the acquisition by psychologists of certain medical principles and practices, especially the case method.[2]

[1] Eli A. Rubinstein and Maurice Lorr, Editors, *Survey of Clinical Practice in Psychology.* New York: International Universities Press, 1954. xvii + 363 p.

[2] Quoted from Arthur Burton and Robert E. Harris, Editors, *Clinical Studies of Personality.* Vol. 2 of Case Histories in Clinical and Abnormal Psychology. New York: Harper & Brothers, 1955. p. 12–13.

Counseling psychology is a specialty within the area broadly designated as applied psychology, and utilizes concepts, tools, and techniques also used by several other specialty groups, notably social, personnel, and clinical psychology. Historically, counseling psychology has drawn upon three distinct movements: vocational guidance, psychological measurement, and personality development.

Currently, the specialty of counseling psychology is approaching a balance among emphases upon contributions to (a) the development of an individual's inner life, (b) the individual's achievement of harmony with his environment, and (c) the influencing of society to recognize individual differences and to encourage the fullest development of all persons within it. Although counseling psychology leaves to other psychologists the major responsibility for treating psychological disasters, the counseling psychologists may be found working in the full range of social settings. He has unique resources, e.g., tests and other methods of psychological evaluation, for helping individuals to achieve harmonious relationships with their environments. He is willing to work directly with other persons and groups with whom his clients must deal outside of the counseling office. His goal is to further the fullest possible self-realization of those who live in a particular social setting.[3]

In many instances case study is supplementary to or related to other investigational procedures. The life history of an individual, of an institution, or of a community resembles historical research in sources and techniques. Case investigation uses many of the data-gathering instruments described in the chapter on descriptive-survey studies. Case and genetic investigations of an individual have common interests in growth and development, although ordinarily the direction of movement in case study is backward, whereas in genetic research the movement is forward as growth takes place.

SEQUENCE OR STAGES IN CASE STUDY AND CASE WORK

The characteristics and skills of case study and case work include the following items:[4]

1. Continuity of data and procedure. Although continuity in gathering evidence, diagnosis, and therapy is a logical sequence, in a concrete life situation the movement may be shuttle-like. While interviewing an individual to gather information, certain treatment may take place, or during adjustment or therapeutic procedures, additional evidence may be secured.

[3] Quoted from Harold B. Pepinsky and Others, "Counseling Psychology as a Specialty." *American Psychologist* 11: 282–85; June 1956.
[4] Gordon Hamilton, *Theory and Practice of Social Case Work*. Second Edition. New York: Columbia University Press, 1951. vii + 328 p.

2. Completeness and validity of data, including symptoms relating to initial status, examination results (psychophysical, health, educational, and mental), and health, school, family, and social history.

3. Synthesis in the form of an adequate diagnosis which identifies causal factors, with a prognosis that points toward therapy in the form of corrective treatment or developmental procedures. The social skills of case work or of adjustment procedures include social insight, empathy, and a positive social behavior; ability to communicate by transmitting an experience or sharing a common experience; co-operation and participation in working with others; and effective counseling and guidance. It is recognized that the concepts of non-directive or client-centered therapy tend to minimize the process of diagnosis as a basis for therapy.[5]

4. Confidential recording and relationships, as exemplified in the field of medicine.

Expressed in one way, the standards of case study and case work are similar to the major requirements of clinical psychology: high levels of academic and professional qualifications for the worker, a practitioner who is familiar with the trends of recent research even though not actually engaged in investigation, and sound ethics emphasizing long-term aims by way of service to society.[6]

The cycle of complementary steps in case study and case work is as follows:[7]

1. Recognition and determination of the status of the phenomenon to be investigated; for example, reading disability.

2. Collection of data relating to the factors or circumstances associated with the given phenomenon; factors associated with learning difficulty or reading disability may be physical, intellectual, pedagogical, emotional, social, or environmental.

3. Diagnosis or identification of causal factors as a basis for remedial or developmental treatment; defective vision may be the cause of difficulty in reading.

4. Application of remedial or adjustment measures; correctly fitted glasses may remove the cause of the poor performance in reading.

5. Subsequent follow-up to determine the effectiveness of the corrective or developmental measures applied.

INITIAL STATUS OR SYMPTOMS OF THE CASE

The first step in case study is to identify the unit for investigation in the form of some aspect of behavior, or phase of the life process, or

[5] Carl R. Rogers, *Client-Centered Therapy:* Its Current Practice, Implications, and Theory. Boston: Houghton Mifflin Co., 1951. xii + 560 p.

[6] L. A. Pennington and Irwin A. Berg, Editors, *An Introduction to Clinical Psychology.* Second Edition. New York: Ronald Press, 1954. p. 22.

[7] Carter V. Good and Douglas E. Scates, *Methods of Research:* Educational, Psychological, Sociological. New York: Appleton-Century-Crofts, 1954. p. 732–33.

need-situation, as in truancy, delinquency, exceptional talent, or a broken home. Whereas the case has commonly centered on the need-situation as the unit of attention, client-centered or nondirective therapy has focused attention on the individual or subject. With increased knowledge and improved techniques, cases in new areas have been identified for corrective or developmental treatment; for example, in the field of special education recognizing in turn the need for therapy of the physically handicapped, then cases of low mentality, special talents, and deficiencies in the school subjects, and later the various types of social maladjustment involving personality difficulties and behavior disorders. With increased knowledge, cases of child delinquency have become subdivided to represent such problems as parental rejection, parental overprotection, poverty and low social status, emotional immaturity, and rebellion against authority. It is not possible even to count the several types of cases for remedial or developmental attention until the scope of the various categories is defined as a basis for labeling a child as exceptional: the extent of deficiency necessary in vision or hearing to be labeled subnormal, the level of general intelligence or of special talent to be considered superior, and the line between normality and social, emotional, personality, or behavior disorders. Many of the data-gathering instruments and procedures discussed in the chapter on descriptive-survey research are available for the first step of case study and also for later steps, especially in collection of data through the examination and case history.

EXAMINATION AND HISTORY AS SOURCES OF DATA

Determination or identification of the status of the situation or unit of attention leads into the collection of data through the examination and life history, which suggests that the first and second steps of case study are supplementary. The emphasis in the second stage, however, is on evidence that may serve as a basis for diagnosis through identification of the explanatory or causal factors. This step in case study has available for use the several descriptive-survey instruments and procedures, as well as the life history, biography, autobiography, letters, and diaries. The case study usually includes an examination[8] of psychophysical, health, educational, and mentality factors, as well as a health, school, family, and social history. Certain of the common testing instruments may be characterized briefly.

Testing Instruments

Intelligence-testing in modern clinical psychology is far more than the automatic administration of routine test procedures. It involves a

[8] Cecil V. Millard, *Case Inventory for the Study of Child Development*. Minneapolis: Burgess Publishing Co., 1950. 29 p.

judicious choice of instruments, precise knowledge of the characteristics of intelligence scales, skill in interpreting test results, ability to evaluate the results of highly controversial research, and formulation of insightful hypotheses to account for a patient's behavior. In short, the clinician is both a proficient laboratory experimenter and an impartial, understanding observer of human behavior.[9]

From personality, interest, and achievement tests the clinician secures information which often can be gathered from no other source. Scores from these inventories may suggest hypotheses to the clinical psychologist, who must then verify them and integrate his data into an adequate descriptive picture of his patient for the purposes of diagnostic, prognostic, and treatment problems.

Projective methods utilize ambiguous stimuli to which subjects are encouraged to respond freely in their own way, as illustrated by ink blots, pictures, art and drama media, and paper-and-pencil techniques. It is assumed that attention is selective and that perception is motivated by the wishes and attitudes of the responding person, with the result that the content perceived and the manner of organizing the material reveal significant dynamic aspects of personality (useful for diagnosis, prognosis, and research).[10]

Life History

As sources of data for case study, from an analytical rather than a historical approach, more frequent and better use may well be made of such personal documents as the life history, biography, autobiography, diaries and journals, letters, records of dreams, and expressive interviews. Such personal materials include retrospective autobiographies, contemporaneous life histories, and episodic and topical documents. Data obtained from personal documents may make a contribution by way of supplementing ecological and statistical information, so as to provide a more inclusive interpretation of the problem, and may serve as a basis for prediction of human behavior.

As a longitudinal observation of culture, the life history emphasizes the natural history of the individual, his reactions to early social stimuli which have led to development of attitudes and values, evolution of a philosophy of life, personal experiences, anecdotes, mental and social conflicts, crises, adjustments, accommodations, and release of tensions. As an intimate personal document or confession which records through introspection inward stresses and attitudes rather than external events, the life history differs from the usual autobiography secured from famous persons (with one eye on publication). The life history, dealing with indi-

[9] L. A. Pennington and Irwin A. Berg, Editors, *op. cit.*, p. 154–55, 181.
[10] *Ibid.*, p. 215.

viduals who have encountered mental and social crises or conflict situations, does not stress judgments of merit. The subject may tell his own story or an interviewer may record the life history, as "a deliberate attempt to define the growth of a person in a cultural milieu and to make theoretical sense of it." Basic criteria for evaluating the life-history approach are as follows:[11]

1. The subject must be viewed as a specimen in a cultural series.
2. The organic motors of action ascribed must be socially relevant.
3. The peculiar role of the family group in transmitting the culture must be recognized.
4. The specific method of elaboration of organic materials into social behavior must be shown.
5. The continuous related character of experience from childhood through adulthood must be stressed.
6. The social situation must be carefully and continuously specified as a factor.
7. The life-history material itself must be organized and conceptualized.

The purposes and procedures of a particular life history or autobiography may be generally helpful as background for understanding this approach:[12]

1. To prepare a relatively full and reliable account of an individual's experience and development from birth on, or a comprehensive life history emphasizing personality problems
2. To accumulate and arrange in natural order a socially and culturally oriented record of an individual in a "primitive society" for the purpose of developing and checking certain hypotheses in the field of culture
3. To attempt at least a partial interpretation of the individual's development and behavior
4. To utilize the investigation for the formulation of generalizations and the testing of theories in the field of individual behavior with respect to society and culture (reserved for further study).

Autobiography, Biography, and Diaries

Autobiography, biography, and diaries have been resorted to frequently as sources in historical studies. Autobiography as historical narration and the diaries of distinguished persons who have anticipated pub-

[11] John Dollard, *Criteria for the Life History.* New Haven: Yale University Press, 1935. p. 3. Reprinted in 1949 by Peter Smith.
Pauline V. Young, *Scientific Social Surveys and Research.* Third Edition. Englewood Cliffs, N. J.: Prentice-Hall, 1956. p. 230–39.
[12] Leo W. Simmons, Editor, *Sun Chief:* The Autobiography of a Hopi Indian. New Haven: Yale University Press, for the Institute of Human Relations, 1942. xii + 460 p.

lication usually have been relatively formal documents. The movement in autobiography and biography is backward (written in retrospect), whereas the movement in a diary is forward, with entries recorded as events take place. Autobiography contributes to case study through providing the life history of an individual, a tribe, race, or community; is helpful in studying reticent or resistant persons; is economical for use in groups; and may serve therapeutic purposes for the subject by release of tensions and insight into his own life. Diaries kept without undue concern for publication may reveal interests, desires, tensions, and conflicts not apparent in the more formal autobiography (usually written for publication), although the persons who keep diaries and permit their use are a rather select group of individuals. The general principles of historical research apply in dealing with personal documents.

To cite as an example the autobiography of an educator, Spaulding has written in two volumes what is substantially his life history to the end of his administrative work in the public schools. The first volume[13] carries the story to the completion of his graduate study in Europe and at Clark University, including early life on a farm in New Hampshire, schooling in the district and college-preparatory schools in New England, four years at Amherst College, a doctoral program at the University of Leipzig, and postdoctoral year at Clark University. The second volume[14] is substantially an anecdotal history or case study of the development of the city superintendency during the first quarter of the twentieth century. It is the story of the evolution and application of a philosophy of education to the organization and administration of the public schools. The individual probably is not fully aware of the pattern and sources of his own philosophy until he attempts what Spaulding has done in his autobiography or life history.

Another autobiography is the story of an 81-year-old man who began to teach at the age of seventeen in a one-teacher school in Pennsylvania in 1891. His long years of service were as teacher, principal, superintendent, and teacher or executive in 17 American colleges in 10 states, as author, organizer of professional groups, editor, and lecturer before many thousands of educational and professional groups. The autobiography is to a considerable extent an anecdotal history of education and of the education of teachers, covering almost the entire modern period of educational history and teacher education during the twentieth century. Here are the beginnings of teaching as a profession, the development of small local school systems, the struggles of boards of education on professional problems, the efforts of school administrators to profes-

[13] Frank E. Spaulding, *One School Administrator's Philosophy: Its Development*. New York: Exposition Press, 1952. 352 p.

[14] Frank E. Spaulding, *School Superintendent in Action in Five Cities*. Rindge, N. H.: Richard R. Smith, 1955. xx + 699 p.

sionalize their staffs in larger cities, and the organization of a program to prepare the professors who staff the teachers colleges.[15]

An especially interesting group of personal documents is an approach to the history of psychology through the autobiographies of eminent psychologists.[16]

Yet another example is the autobiography of a schizophrenic, although this description may be inaccurate, since the author set out to prove that he was never "insane" and perhaps not even mentally ill; yet he does demonstrate that mental illness is misunderstood and badly mistreated even in some of our better hospitals.

As a case history the book does not arouse the same clinical interest and speculative excitement that come with a reading of Schreber's *Memoirs,* or the autobiography written by Sechehaye's patient, or comparable documents by Beers, Custance, and others; but as a very human and moving statement of a young man's struggle to maintain personal integrity and dignity in the face of a practical, well-meaning, but uncomprehending world, [it] will touch deeply every reader. It is difficult to say whether the author succeeds better in demonstrating that the ideas and beliefs of non-inmates of mental institutions are just as irrational as his own, or that he is entitled to maintain his own irrational beliefs without undue interference by authority, however well intentioned. Certainly he presents a dramatic and often frightening picture of what it means to someone who has lost his way in the world to be suddenly confronted by the loving therapeutic zeal involved in hospitalization, electric shock, insulin convulsions, and medical logic. The reader, whether professional or otherwise, is bound to experience that compassion and uneasiness which come with sharing intimately in the life-and-death struggle which is psychosis.[17]

A book of nine word portraits or type-persons or case histories may offer suggestions for similar studies of the teacher, supervisor, administrator, or professor. Bauer and his colleague have created type-persons as they live, think, and act in the Soviet milieu. The data are true, based on interviews with escaped refugees from the Soviet Union, who have reported their own experiences and have revealed their knowledge of conditions within their motherland. The portraits are fiction, composites of the data collected, with the smallest amount of fabrication necessary to make them into stories. The nine synthesized types of persons are: the student (three of them), the woman collective farmer, the woman doctor, the Party secretary, the housewife, the writer, the factory director,

[15] Ambrose L. Suhrie, *Teacher of Teachers.* Rindge, N. H.: Richard R. Smith, 1955. 418 p.

[16] Herbert S. Langfeld and Others, Editors, *A History of Psychology in Autobiography,* Vol. 4. Worcester, Mass.: Clark University Press, 1952. xii + 356 p.

Edwin G. Boring, *Psychologist at Large.* New York: Basic Books, 1961. 371 p.

[17] Quoted from the review by Milton Wexler, *Contemporary Psychology* 1: 306; October 1956, of William L. Moore, *The Mind in Chains:* The Autobiography of a Schizophrenic. New York: Exposition Press, 1955. 315 p.

the tractor driver, and the secret police agent. These portraits are not actual case histories, nor are they even exactly fiction, since the characteristics of the people and the events of their stories are always subordinated to the facts of the records; the persons themselves are synthesized types.[18]

An application of psychoanalytic psychology to the biographical data of famous creative individuals has the two purposes of comprehending the subject of the biography in terms of the dynamic forces of his developmental experience, and of understanding the nature of the creative man and the creative process. For these purposes, the main value of psychoanalytic psychology lies in its ability to analyze and to structure meaningfully highly complex and diverse biographical information, by way of establishing cause-and-effect relationships between the data of infancy, childhood, and adult life.[19]

The biography of an imposing imposter deals with a man, Ferdinand W. Demara, who attained unusual publicity and notoriety. The story leaves many aspects of Demara's behavior only partly explained, but the author had to depend largely on what the subject chose to tell, and Demara was at one time or another in the interviews temperamental, recalcitrant, grandiose, or unpredictable. The early part of the subject's life, from birth through adolescence, is too briefly told to provide adequate clues to the powerful inner forces and to the family relationships that underlie his later behavior and difficulties.

With this brief picture of his childhood, we can begin, at least, to speculate on the "why's" of Demara's behavior. We can understand something of the little boy who found his dreams of omnipotence made into reality by his father and then was never able to give up this easy way of achieving power, status, and self-esteem. We can ask questions about the man who is continually seeking an identity in new roles, desperately avoiding the original intense identification with a glorious father who, overnight, met disaster. And we can begin to understand the overpowering guilt ("I'm rotten through and through!") over his fantasied responsibility for father's disastrous fall that makes it necessary for him to always be caught and disgraced in the end.

Postscript: Mr. Demara, when last heard from, was in Hollywood, the true land of make-believe, making a film in which he plays eight roles and supervising the filming of his own biography.[20]

---

[18] Review by Edwin G. Boring, *Contemporary Psychology* 1: 149; May 1956, of Raymond A. Bauer and Edward Wasiolek, *Nine Soviet Portraits*. New York: John Wiley & Sons, 1955. ix + 190 p.

[19] Edward Hitschmann, *Great Men:* Psychoanalytic Studies. New York: International Universities Press, 1956. xiii + 278 p.

[20] Quoted from review by John H. Porter, *Contemporary Psychology* 5: 255–56; August 1960, of Robert Crichton, *The Great Impostor*. New York: Randon House, 1959. 218 p.

CAUSATION AND DIAGNOSIS[21]

Diagnosis seeks to formulate a theory or hypothesis of causation, pointed toward the adjustment or development of the individual, institution, or community. Diagnosis and treatment may at times be parallel or even move shuttle-like. Diagnosis is prognostic in recommending therapy, and when adjustment procedures fail, further search for causal factors and a second diagnosis may be necessary. If adjustment proves only temporary, as revealed in the last step of follow-up, further diagnosis and therapy are indicated. For evidence, diagnosis depends on the data gathered in the earlier phases of case study. It has already been indicated in this chapter that nondirective or client-centered therapy minimizes the diagnostic process in advance of psychotherapy, although recognizing the basic necessity for physical diagnosis in dealing with organic disease.[22]

Adequate diagnosis[23] of difficulties must meet certain basic requirements relating to significant objectives, valid evidence of strengths and weaknesses, objectivity, reliability, specificity, comparable and exact data, practicability, and expertness. Most of the data-gathering instruments and procedures described in the chapter on descriptive-survey research can be adapted to provide evidence on which successful diagnosis rests. Diagnosis as an aspect of case study, like other research approaches, finds the problem of causation complex and perplexing. To cite examples, factors that may be associated with learning difficulty are physical, intellectual, pedagogical, emotional, social, and environmental. Causes of poor performance in reading may be perceptual (visual and auditory), motor, intellectual, linguistic, emotional, and methodological. Factors affecting the behavior of the problem child may be hereditary, physical, mental, familial, economic, cultural, social, and educational. Defects and deviations of development may be in the form of amentia, endocrine disorders, convulsive disorders, neurological defects, cerebral injury, special sensory handicaps, prematurity, precocity, and environmental retardation.[24] It usually is necessary to look beneath the surface to find the basic

[21] Max L. Hutt, "Diagnosis," *Encyclopedia of Educational Research.* Edited by Chester W. Harris. Third Edition. New York: The Macmillan Co., 1960. p. 376–80.

Goldine C. Gleser, "Prediction," *Encyclopedia of Educational Research,* p. 1038–46.

Cora Kasius, Editor, *A Comparison of Diagnostic and Functional Casework Concepts.* New York: Family Service Association of New York, 1950. 169 p.

Robert I. Watson, *The Clinical Method in Psychology.* New York: Harper & Brothers, 1951. p. 21–153, 527–761.

[22] Carl R. Rogers, *op. cit.,* p. 219–28.

[23] Robert I. Watson, Editor, "Diagnostic Methods," *Readings in the Clinical Method in Psychology.* New York: Harper & Brothers, 1949. p. 183–443.

Gordon Hamilton, *op. cit.,* p. 213–36.

[24] Arnold Gesell and Catherine S. Amatruda, *Developmental Diagnosis:* Normal and Abnormal Child Development, Clinical Methods and Practical Applications. Revised Edition. New York: Harper & Brothers, 1947. xvi + 496 p.

or primary cause of maladjustment; on the surface we may see only a secondary, tertiary, or contributory cause or condition. For example, difficulty in reading as a primary cause of maladjustment may lead to failure in the school subjects, truancy, and misbehavior (probably only secondary or tertiary factors in this instance).

To cite an example in the area of counseling, school psychologists, guidance specialists, and school social workers need a common knowledge of psychological principles and of educational aims and practices. It is highly desirable that school psychologists be equipped, like competent high-school counselors, to do diagnostic and counseling work. It is equally desirable that counselors, deans, and visiting teachers be better trained in the psychological principles and techniques that are appropriate. The school psychologist may well be an educationally oriented clinical psychologist, in contrast to the medically oriented clinical psychologist, who serves as a diagnostician, therapist, and consultant in the preventive and alleviative work of adjustment.[25]

THERAPY AND DEVELOPMENTAL ADJUSTMENT

Purposes

The purpose of diagnosis is realized in some form of effective therapy or developmental adjustment. Therapy and follow-up sometimes are labeled as case work, as distinguished from case study or case investigation, and in many instances these later steps are the work of other specialists (as in medicine). It has been indicated earlier that there is no sharp division between the earlier steps of case investigation and diagnosis, and the later phases of therapy and follow-up. In gathering information through the examination and case history, certain treatment or therapy may be possible, and in the stage of treatment additional evidence may appear. The supplementary and cooperative relationships of the specialists engaged in the several steps of case study and case work may be illustrated by the type of conference frequently arranged for planning the therapy of the problem child, with participation by such workers and agencies as the clinic staff, school, visiting teacher, court, probation officer, child-placing agency, family agency, and children's institution.

Frequently, complex or multiple causation of maladjustment may lead to a diagnosis and to therapy requiring the cooperation of a number of specialists. Child-guidance clinics and mental-hygiene programs, working with problem and delinquent children, have combined the resources

[25] Review by Donald E. Super, *Contemporary Psychology* 2: 35–37; February 1957, of Stanley S. Marzolf, *Psychological Diagnosis and Counseling in the Schools.* New York: Henry Holt and Co., 1956. xiv + 401 p.

of psychiatrists, physicians, psychologists, social workers, sociologists, and sometimes teachers and specialists in the field of education. Adequate treatment in child guidance requires the cooperation of clinic, community, home, school, case-working organization, recreational program, and child-placement agency.

The primary purpose of therapy is development of the potentialities of the individual for growth and improvement. In a learning situation this means focusing of attention on the pupil in relation to a specific difficulty or opportunity for growth rather than on the formal organization of a subject of instruction as such. To cite another illustration, the purposes of social treatment or therapy are concerned with preventing social breakdown, conserving strength, restoring social function, making life more comfortable or compensating, creating opportunities for growth and development, and increasing the capacity for self-direction and social contribution.[26] More specific examples of assistance given to a client by a case worker would include financial aid, help in seeking employment, facilitating health plans, entrance into an appropriate group activity, and modifying the attitudes of associates.

Preventive Measures and Self-Help

Adjustment procedures are outlined in this chapter with recognition of the desirability of preventive measures,[27] as illustrated by current emphases in medicine, dentistry, and the field of health in general. Regular physical and health examinations, including the testing of sight and hearing, may indicate corrective measures which will prevent later maladjustments. Effective programs of education, work, recreation, and guidance in school, home, community, church, and other social institutions and agencies will do much to prevent the maladjustment known as the "youth problem," including juvenile delinquency.

In all forms of therapy, the importance of self-help is recognized, as illustrated by the patient's will or desire to recover from an illness. This basic principle of therapy or treatment is recognized in such concepts as encouraging the subject in his own efforts, thinking things through together, and increasing the capacity for self-understanding and self-direction.

Favorable mental attitudes on the part of specialists, parents, and child contribute materially to the process of therapy. Effective remedial

[26] Gordon Hamilton, *op. cit.*, p. 237–70.

[27] Sheldon Glueck and Eleanor Glueck, *Delinquents in the Making:* Paths to Prevention. New York: Harper & Brothers, 1952. viii + 214 p.

Pauline V. Young, *Social Treatment in Probation and Delinquency:* Treatise and Casebook for Court Workers, Probation Officers, and Other Child Welfare Workers. Revised Edition. New York: McGraw-Hill Book Co., 1952. xxvi + 536 p.

or developmental treatment is based on genuine concern for the well-being of the child or client, cordial relationships of mutual confidence, and understanding and control of prejudices and emotional reactions. Favorable initial attitudes are especially significant in short contacts, as in large school systems and social transient work, where critical decisions may be made in one or two brief interviews; for example, employment of a teacher or arrangements to return a young traveler to her distant home.

The principle of self-help in the process of therapy is illustrated by nondirective or client-centered procedures, which have revealed certain improvements in the subject:[28]

1. Change or movement in therapy, as revealed in the type of verbal comment presented by the client; for example, from talk about his problems and symptoms, to insightful statements showing some self-understanding of relationship between his past and current behavior, to discussion of new actions in accord with his new understanding of the situation.

2. Change in the client's perception of and attitude toward self: (a) sees himself as a more adequate person, with increased worth and greater possibility of meeting life; (b) draws on more experiential data, thus achieving a more realistic appraisal of himself, his relationships, and environment; (c) tends to place the basis of standards or values within himself rather than in the experience or perceptual object.[29]

Treatment of Learning Difficulties

Basic principles underlying therapy or treatment of learning difficulties are as follows:[30]

1. Treatment must be based on a diagnosis.
   a. Locate weaknesses that require correction.
   b. Establish the type of treatment needed.
   c. Clearly formulate the remedial program.
   d. Modify the program as may be advisable.
   e. Use a variety of remedial techniques.
   f. The child should help formulate the program of treatment.
2. The child's personal worth must be considered.
   a. Avoid stigmatizing pupils in classification and grouping.
   b. Consider the child's emotional state.
   c. Correct faulty attitudes.
   d. Recognize the importance of group as well as individual work.

[28] Carl R. Rogers, op. cit., p. 131–96.

[29] Robert I. Watson, The Clinical Method in Psychology, op. cit., p. 21–153, 527–761.

[30] Leo J. Brueckner and Guy L. Bond, The Diagnosis and Treatment of Learning Difficulties. New York: Appleton-Century-Crofts, 1955. p. 77–100.

3. Corrective treatment must be individualized.
   a. Outcomes and methods should be commensurate with the child's ability.
   b. Treatment should be specific and not general.
   c. Fatigue should be noted and practice spaced.
4. The program must be well motivated and encouraging to the child.
   a. The teacher must be optimistic.
   b. Success of the student must be emphasized.
   c. Errors should be pointed out in a positive way.
   d. Growth should be made apparent to the child.
   e. Treatment should not conflict with other enjoyable activities.
   f. Purpose should always be established.
   g. The results of the learning experience should be utilized and evaluated.
5. Materials and exercises must be carefully selected.
   a. Materials must be suitable in level of difficulty and type.
   b. Materials must be suitable in interest and format.
   c. Materials must be abundant and not artificial.
6. The entire environment of the child must be considered.
   a. Adjustments must be made in the child's school program.
   b. The home environment must be favorable.
7. Continuous evaluations must be made.
   a. A cumulative record must be kept.
   b. A follow-up is necessary.
8. Sound teaching procedures must be utilized in the treatment of learning difficulties.

Principles and Techniques of Psychotherapy

Psychotherapy involves difficulties, in that our diagnostic instruments fall short of desirable standards of validity and reliability. We are uncomfortably aware of elements of truth behind the facetious characterization of psychotherapy as "the art of applying a science which does not yet exist," although our therapeutic anxiety is relieved somewhat by dependence on the best available techniques and procedures of psychodiagnosis.[31]

Psychotherapy is limited or handicapped by the tendency of some clinicians, teachers, and students to overemphasize certain approaches at the expense of others, thus failing to recognize at least three major sources of error in therapy:[32]

1. No single approach to psychotherapy has been found that can explain the behavior of all individuals or is pertinent to all persons.

[31] Paul E. Meehl, "The Cognitive Activity of the Clinician." *American Psychologist* 15: 19–27; January 1960.

[32] James L. McCary and Daniel E. Sheer, Editors, *Six Approaches to Psychotherapy.* New York: Dryden Press, 1955. p. 4–5.

2. An individual with a specific problem may fail to respond to a single type of therapy; as the individual's needs change the therapeutic techniques must be changed, if the patient is to derive maximum benefit.

3. Since therapists differ in personality structure, need systems, and value systems, the therapeutic techniques must be suited to the needs of the therapist.

Psychological research has identified the wide range of individual differences in physical, intellectual, pedagogical, emotional, social, and environmental factors that must be considered in diagnosis and therapy. To illustrate by a specific example, variations in the treatment of children with individual problems of adjustment include: (1) change of environment through the foster home or institutional placement; (2) modification of environment through adjustments in the parents' attitudes, family relationships, school and instructional program, clubs, groups, and camps; and (3) treatment of the individual through a variety of therapeutic approaches, including psychoanalysis, nondirective interviewing and therapy, group psychotherapy, projective techniques, play therapy, physical treatment, occupational therapy, psychodrama, sociodrama, and hypnodrama.

The variety and complexity of the problems of clinical and case study may be illustrated in further detail from the field of psychotherapy. The varieties of psychotherapy include supportive therapy, insight therapy with re-educative goals, and insight therapy with reconstructive goals.[33]

Among the techniques and procedures utilized in supportive therapy are guidance, environmental manipulation, externalization of interests, reassurance, prestige suggestion, pressure and coercion, persuasion, emotional catharsis and desensitization, muscular relaxation, hydrotherapy, drug therapy, shock and convulsive therapy, and inspirational group therapy.

Insight therapy with re-educative therapeutic approaches includes "relationship therapy," "attitude therapy," distributive analysis and synthesis, interview psychotherapy, therapeutic counseling, therapeutic casework, reconditioning, re-educative group therapy, semantic therapy, and bibliotherapy.

Insight therapy with reconstructive goals includes the three main "types": "Freudian psychoanalysis," "non-Freudian psychoanalysis," and "psychoanalytically oriented psychotherapy."

Supportive, re-educative, and reconstructive therapies have certain similarities and differences with respect to the duration of therapy, fre-

[33] Lewis R. Wolberg, The Technique of Psychotherapy. New York: Grune and Stratton, 1954. xiv + 869 p.

quency of visits, taking of detailed histories, routine psychologic examinations, kinds of communications obtained from the patient, general activity of the therapist, frequency of advice-giving to the patient, handling of transference, general relationship of the patient to the therapist, physical position of the patient during therapy, handling of dream material, and adjuncts utilized during treatment.

The beginning phase of treatment in psychotherapy includes a number of problems relating to the initial interview: the first contact with the patient, collating essential data, making a diagnosis, formulating the tentative dynamics, estimating the prognosis, estimating the patient's general condition, making practical arrangements for psychotherapy, securing essential consultations, and dealing with inadequate motivation.

The principal techniques by which the therapist helps the patient in the acquisition of insight include interview procedures, free association, dream analysis, and the examination of attitudes toward the therapist (including transference).

In the terminal phase of psychotherapy, success is judged from the standpoint of the patient, of society, and of the therapist, and in terms of the "ideal" objectives of mental health.

Adjunctive aids in psychotherapy include group therapy, hypnotherapy, narcotherapy, and bibliotherapy.

Among the emergencies that sometimes develop during psychotherapy which require prompt and cautious handling are: suicidal attempts; psychotic attacks; excitement, overactivity, and antisocial behavior; panic states; acute alcoholic intoxication; acute barbiturate poisoning; severe psychosomatic symptoms; and intercurrent incurable somatic illness.

Certain kinds of conditions make extensive therapeutic objectives difficult to achieve, and require specific techniques or combinations of methods, especially in dealing with problems often encountered in the treatment of the different neurotic, psychophysiologic, personality, and psychotic disorders.

The variety of techniques in psychotherapy is illustrated in convenient form by the following list of "supportive" methods.[34] An equally long list of "reconstructive" methods has been compiled by the same authors.

1. Bibliotherapy	7. Environmental manipulation
2. Color therapy	8. Hypnotherapy
3. Conditioned-reflex therapy	9. Inspirational group therapy
4. Correction of physical defects	10. Motivational procedures (such as rewards and punishments)
5. Dance therapy	
6. Desensitization	11. Music therapy

[34] James L. McCary and Daniel E. Sheer, *op. cit.*, p. 3.

12. Narcotherapy	20. Reassurance
13. Negative practice	21. Recreation
14. Occupational therapy	22. Re-education
15. Persuasion and reasoning	23. Religious approaches
16. Physiotherapy	24. Rest
17. Placebos	25. Suggestion and advice
18. Pressure and coercion	26. Selected types of group therapy
19. Progressive relaxation	27. Verbal catharsis and abreaction.

Group psychotherapy has been used to good effect with patients suffering from a variety of psychosomatic disorders and with addicts, alcoholics, stutterers, unmarried mothers, mothers of emotionally disturbed children, delinquents, and the aged. It has been of value in mental hospitals, child guidance, family service, marital counseling agencies, community mental-health programs, and industry. As a rule, group psychotherapists have been more willing than individual therapists to record their sessions by mechanical and observational methods, which augurs well for improvement of the therapeutic process and for future development of group psychotherapy.[35]

The literature of the 1950's and later includes dozens of full-length treatments of therapy, as listed in the chapter bibliography.

FOLLOW-UP

The final stage in case and clinical work is follow-up to determine whether the treatment is successful, as illustrated by the physician's attention to the patient during the stage of convalescence. Failure to make satisfactory progress following treatment may require a new diagnosis and another form of therapy. It is common to utilize the techniques of experimentation in evaluating the success of treatment, especially in the field of medicine. By way of example of follow-up, case study has been used as one approach in following a group of bright children over a period of years through school into maturity.[36] The school, home, and other environmental conditions may be thought of as the therapy or treatment for the bright children, with a follow-up to determine the adjustment of the subjects after reaching maturity.

---

[35] Review by Norman A. Polansky, *Social Service Review* 30: 372–73; September 1956, of S. R. Slavson, Editor, *The Fields of Group Psychotherapy*. New York: International Universities Press, 1956. xiii + 338 p.

[36] Lewis M. Terman and Melita H. Oden, *The Gifted Child Grows Up:* Genetic Studies of Genius. Stanford, Calif.: Stanford University Press, 1947. xiv + 450 p.

CLINICAL AND CASE RECORDS[37]

Desirable Characteristics

Adequate case records serve useful purposes in treatment, especially when the regular worker or client moves to another locality, or when a case is reopened; as a medium for study of social problems; and for instructional materials in training students. Adequate records possess the attributes of accuracy and objectivity, conciseness and clarity, ease of reference and visibility, and uniformity and "up-to-dateness," with suitable provision for cumulative recording of interviews, the narrative, letters, anecdotal information, summaries, and interpretation and treatment.

Accuracy goes beyond the recording of information as received to insure the correctness of the data in relation to the truth, as discussed in the chapter on the historical method (with respect to the reliability of witnesses and the criticism of documents).

Effective recording in case study, like adequate reporting in any area of investigation, must be an active process of attention and discriminating selection from a considerable mass of materials, with a balance to strike somewhere between the completeness necessary for objectivity and the brevity essential for clarity. Many of the comments of the chapter on technical reporting and of the section on note-taking in the chapter on library usage are appropriate and suggestive in case-recording and in the preparation of case reports. Uniformity of records within the agency, institution, or school system, and between similar social or educational services in different territories, facilitates research, interchange of information, and ready use.

With respect to the recording of interviews in case study, the discussions of interviewing and of mechanical techniques of observation and recording in the descriptive-survey chapter are pertinent. In social case-recording, the narrative usually begins with the first interview. When conditions are favorable, the first interview should be reasonably complete. It is relatively simple to record information concerning identity, address, legal residence, financial status, and units of food, shelter, or education, but both interviewing and recording become more complex in dealing with human relationships and with the related process and movement within the interview.

The narrative or running record in case study may be entered either chronologically or topically, or by some appropriate combination, as discussed in the chapter on historical writing. In chronological recording,

[37] Gordon Hamilton, *Principles of Social Case Recording.* New York: Columbia University Press, 1946. vii + 142 p.

Kenneth R. Hammond and Jeremiah M. Allen, *Writing Clinical Reports.* New York: Prentice-Hall, 1953. p. 169–231.

the contacts and interviews are entered in diary fashion as they occur, although some marginal headings may give a superficial appearance of topical organization. The chronological narrative may have large subdivisions corresponding approximately with the case-study stages of initial status, examination, diagnosis, therapy, and follow-up. These large headings also are suitable for topical or thematic organization of materials. Topical recording combines and condenses information from a number of contacts or interviews under such large themes as family and home setting, neighborhood and group life, cultural background, education, recreational activities and interests, health, mental attitude, occupation, and income and resources. Topical recording presents original data or subject matter, whereas the several types of "summaries" condense and point up material which has previously appeared in the record.

Since letters and written reports frequently serve as substitutes for direct contacts in the form of personal visits and interviews, they are an important part of case records, especially as a medium of communication between social-work, medical, clinical, legal, and educational agencies. Letters and reports today stress the immediate situation and the therapy or adjustment rather than present a complete summary of the case. Certain forms or blanks have been developed for routine types of communication between agencies, especially between the public schools and other social agencies.

Cumulative and Anecdotal Records[38]

Clinical work and case study, as well as counseling in the schools, depend to a large extent on the data in cumulative records, including

[38] Wendell C. Allen, *Cumulative Pupil Records:* A Plan for Staff Study and Improvement of Cumulative Pupil Records in Secondary Schools. New York: Teachers College, Columbia University, 1943. 69 p.

Joan Bollenbacher, "Student Records and Reports—Elementary and Secondary," *Encyclopedia of Educational Research.* Edited by Chester W. Harris. Third Edition. New York: The Macmillan Co., 1960. p. 1437–41.

Melvene D. Hardee, "Student Records and Reports—College and University," *Encyclopedia of Educational Research,* p. 1433–36.

A. E. Hamalainen, *An Appraisal of Anecdotal Records.* Contributions to Education, No. 891. New York: Teachers College, Columbia University, 1943. 88 p.

Gordon Hamilton, *Principles of Social Case Recording.* New York: Columbia University Press, 1946. vii + 142 p.

Gordon Hamilton, *Theory and Practice of Social Case Work.* Second Edition. New York: Columbia University Press, 1951. p. 133–41.

Kenneth R. Hammond and Jeremiah M. Allen, *op. cit.*

Judith I. Krugman and J. Wayne Wrightstone, *A Guide to the Use of Anecdotal Records.* Educational Research Bulletin of the Bureau of Reference, Research and Statistics, No. 11. New York: Board of Education, May 1949. 33 p.

A. E. Traxler, *The Nature and Use of Anecdotal Records.* Revised Edition. Educational Records Supplementary Bulletin *D.* New York: Educational Record Bureau, 1949. p. 4–8.

anecdotal records. The cumulative record is maintained for a client or pupil over a considerable period of time, usually a number of years, with additions to the record at relatively frequent intervals; for example, marks in the school subjects, educational and aptitude test scores, social and character ratings, school attendance, health, home conditions and family history, participation in the activities program, interests, and attitudes. Cumulative records are useful in meeting instructional needs, for discovery of causes of behavior difficulties and failures, identification of talents and special abilities, placement, and counseling on a variety of problems.

To summarize in more detail, important items as a part of cumulative records[39] include:

1. *Autobiography, including family background, home and neighborhood environment.*—The family and cultural background, as shown by the autobiography, has considerable bearing on the pupil's immediate achievement in school and his future education and vocational plans. From such information teachers and counselors may often gain insight of great value in working with the pupil and his parents.

2. *Health history, including physical and medical examination data.*—Properly evaluated, such material may have a direct bearing on the pupil's school progress and future plans. For the evaluation of such data, the school teaching and guidance staff and the school nurse depend on the school physician or the pupil's physician.

3. *Standardized test records.*—Many records of test data are incomplete in the information necessary later to identify the test used. Space should be provided for the name of the test, form, grade level of the test, norms used, date administered, and any special conditions that might affect the results. Marked answer sheets or test booklets are sometimes helpful. With complete records, trends in class achievement can be observed and studied. For example, teacher's marks on essay-type tests and class work run consistently higher for girls than marks for boys, but scores on standardized tests usually reverse the direction of superiority—a finding that emphasizes the need for both kinds of data in cumulative record files.

4. *School marks.*—Class marks and standardized test results are not to be regarded as duplicative. Marks often reflect the presence and the influence of many personality factors of educational significance that impartial and objective standardized tests do not measure.

5. *Anecdotal items.*—Short descriptions of observed behavior supply evidence of character, personality, attitudes, and interests. No interpretation is given. A number of these on the same student can be helpful to a record user in spotting difficulties.

6. *Participation in cocurricular activities.*—A pupil's participation in cocurricular activities should be recorded, such as music and dramatic clubs and

[39] Quoted from Royce E. Brewster, "The Cumulative Record." *School Life* 42: 16–17; September 1959.

athletics. Positions of leadership as indicated by offices he has held should also be included.

7. *Work experience.*—Such work as delivering papers, baby sitting, clerking in a store, or other employment and helping in church bazaars and in scout organizations should be included.

In filing all pertinent information concerning the individual in one place as a unit, a folder is essential for samples of school work, test forms, behavior deviations, and adjustment or treatment procedures. Child-guidance clinics, for example, have sought especially to integrate into a unit record the medical, psychological, psychiatric, social, and also the school evidence.

Anecdotal materials have come to be a significant part of the cumulative record. A type of cumulative individual record which emphasizes episodes of behavior important in the development of character or personality is known as the anecdotal-behavior journal. These anecdotes include not only maladjustment, but also positive and constructive episodes, the admirable behavior of well-adjusted pupils, and the outstanding accomplishments of the superior or talented. The anecdote as a revealing episode of conduct is in the form of a word picture or verbal snapshot. To be most helpful, anecdotes should possess the characteristics of objectivity, factual emphasis, clarity, and subjectivity (in the sense that an artistically composed photograph is subjective, with a center of attention and with subordination of inconsequential details). Anecdotal records serve useful purposes by way of mutual understanding between faculty and pupils, counseling relationships, curriculum development, appraisal of outcomes, and case instruction in professional programs for preparation of teachers and others.

Although highly standardized or formalized procedures are incompatible with the nature of anecdotal recording, certain steps or sequential stages are desirable in introducing the plan into a school:[40]

1. Enlisting the cooperation of the faculty, including counselors, and development of an understanding and acceptance of the ideal of individualized education.

2. Deciding how much should be expected of observers who write anecdotes, possibly a reasonable minimum number per week.

3. Preparing forms, which are usually very simple, as illustrated by forms in current use; an outline adapted to most situations provides blank spaces for identifying the pupil, class, and observer, with separate columns for date, incident, and comment.

4. Obtaining the original records, including a plan for jotting down the name of the pupil and an appropriate catch word at the time of the incident,

[40] Judith I. Krugman and J. Wayne Wrightstone, *op. cit.,* p. 8–14, 23–24.
Arthur E. Traxler, *op. cit.,* p. 9–22.

with a period set aside toward the end of the day for recording the anecdotes concerning significant behavior episodes observed during the day; a reasonable, although not equal, distribution of anecdotes among the pupils is desirable.

5. Central filing, as emphasized in the earlier discussions of cumulative records, in order that incidents described by different observers over a period of time may be assembled and compared to note trends.

6. Periodic summarizing, preferably under topical headings, as recommended earlier in the discussion of case-recording.

Certain precautions and procedures are essential in dealing with problems which frequently arise in the preparation of anecdotes:[41]

1. Accuracy and objectivity in observation and in recording are imperative, as emphasized in the discussion of case-recording; statements of opinion must be separated from the report of the incident itself.

2. Anecdotal records should not be used as a defense mechanism by the teacher to justify some action on his part, such as loss of temper or harsh discipline.

3. In many instances, a brief description of the background against which a behavior incident occurred is necessary, since there is a grave danger of misinterpretation in isolating an episode from its social setting.

4. In summarizing and interpreting anecdotal records, one must be on guard against acceptance of a relatively small number of anecdotes as a valid picture of the total behavior pattern of the pupil; an understandable picture is based on some degree of repetition of similar behavior reported from a number of situations in different areas of conduct.

5. As in case study in general, anecdotal records must have professional and confidential treatment, in order that unfortunate behavior incidents may not prejudice the future adjustment and success of the pupils represented.

6. A workable plan for handling the load of clerical work and for summarizing anecdotes is necessary before a school commits itself to the writing of anecdotes.

7. Urgent needs for adjustment, as revealed through anecdotes, should not encourage hasty generalizations and should not be used as excuses for short cuts in personality adaptation, which is usually a long-term process.

8. Observers should strive to record evidence of growth and favorable adjustment even more diligently than examples of undesirable behavior.

9. Teachers must be on guard against overemphasizing inconsistencies in behavior or incidents that are not at all typical of the behavior of the particular pupil; sometimes behavior at the beginning of the school year is atypical, although anecdotes recorded during the first few weeks may possess some significance as single incidents for understanding the pupil; however, without repetition episodes give little insight for determining developmental patterns of behavior, and deviations cannot be recognized until the usual patterns have been established through a repetition of incidents in different situations.

[41] Judith I. Krugman and J. Wayne Wrightstone, *op. cit.*, p. 3–5, 15–20.
Arthur E. Traxler, *op. cit.*, p. 22–26.

ETHICAL STANDARDS[42]

Since the primary function of records is to render treatment of the case more effective in terms of adjustment of the client, and to serve community interests in dealing with social problems, the ethical implications of case-recording are important. It may be wise to omit personal or nonessential information of a confidential nature that throws little light on diagnosis and therapy, although other possibilities or alternatives are to inform the client in advance of the nature and use of case records, to label such personal material "confidential," or to assume that all case records are confidential and will be so treated. Problems arise in deciding what use to make of evidence concerning the efficiency of staff members, the mistakes of fellow workers, and the policies of the agency or institution. Accuracy and objectivity require that the facts be entered in the record, where they usually speak for themselves, and may prove useful in improvement of both staff and program. Workers must keep within their own bounds of training and experience in making diagnoses and interpretations; for example, a teacher may communicate certain objective facts concerning a pupil's health or mental level, but diagnosis and treatment usually must be left to the physician or psychologist. Safeguarding of confidential records is a heavy responsibility, and ordinarily professional workers will not risk using case records outside the office where they are filed.

An extensive summary of ethical principles formulated for psychology is generally applicable to other clinical fields, especially in the diagnosis and treatment relationships with the client.[43]

As to diagnosis and therapy, a serious quandary may confront clinical psychologists both in the operation of a clinic and in the administration of a training program for graduate students. To what extent may one clinical installation or another be unintentionally sacrificing the treatment of patients to their use as data in experiments or to their manipulation through recordings and observations for the training of the students, with only marginal thought given to the welfare of the patient?[44]

It is generally accepted that almost every question in clinical psychology, certainly almost every proposition in connection with psychotherapy, cries for experimental study and for the verification of psychotherapeutic hypotheses.

[42] Nicholas Hobbs and Others, *Ethical Standards of Psychologists*. Washington: American Psychological Association, 1953. xv + 171 p.

A. M. Lee, "Responsibilities in Sociological Research." *Sociology and Social Research* 37: 367–74; July-August 1953. Ethics of sociology.

[43] *Ethical Standards of Psychologists: A Summary of Ethical Principles*. Washington: American Psychological Association, 1953. 19 p.

[44] Quoted from Harriet E. O'Shea, "Research and Training: Are They Sometimes Sirens Leading Therapy Astray?" *Journal of Psychology* 48: 103–5; July 1959.

The question then is whether there are precautions which should be followed rigidly to avoid destroying the very thing that it is hoped to study, namely, the progress of the patient in the relationship between the patient and his therapist. . . .

Perhaps what is needed is for clinical psychologists as a group to evolve a clear set of criteria which they can use, or at least strong guide lines which can be followed, to determine whether a patient's ethical rights are actually being observed and to determine whether sound therapy is occurring or has been lost in the struggle for research gains and for the training of therapists in a professional activity which may at least partially have vanished from the clinic.

RELATION BETWEEN CASE-CLINICAL AND STATISTICAL METHODS

A major problem of methodology in clinical psychology is to determine the relation between the clinical and the statistical or actuarial methods of prediction. In the actuarial or statistical type of prediction, we may classify the subject on the basis of objective facts from his life history, his scores on psychometric tests, behavior ratings or check lists, or possibly subjective judgments secured from interviews. We check this classification against a statistical or actuarial table which gives the statistical frequencies of behavior of various sorts for persons belonging to the particular class.

In the clinical or case-study method of prediction, we may arrive at some psychological hypothesis regarding the structure and dynamics of a particular individual, on the basis of interview impressions, other data from the life history, and possibly certain psychometric information, as in a psychiatric staff conference.

Various terms are applied to the method or approach preferred; for example, those who favor the statistical method have referred to it as "operational, communicable, verifiable, public, objective, reliable, behavioral, testable, rigorous, scientific, precise, careful, trustworthy, experimental, quantitative, down-to-earth, hardheaded, empirical, mathematical, and sound." Those who dislike the statistical method have labeled it as "mechanical, atomistic, additive, cut-and-dried, artificial, unreal, arbitrary, incomplete, dead, pedantic, fractionated, trivial, forced, static, superficial, rigid, sterile, academic, oversimplified, pseudoscientific, and blind."

The clinical method, on the other hand, is labeled by its proponents as "dynamic, global, meaningful, holistic, subtle, sympathetic, configural, patterned, organized, rich, deep, genuine, sensitive, sophisticated, real, living, concrete, natural, true to life, and understanding." The critics of the clinical method are likely to view it is "mystical, transcendent, metaphysical, supermundane, vague, hazy, subjective, unscientific, unreliable, crude, private, unverifiable, qualitative, primitive, prescientific, sloppy, uncontrolled, careless, verbalistic, intuitive, and muddleheaded."[45]

It is a common error to group together the terms *quantitative, statistical,* and *experimental,* setting them in opposition to *qualitative, clinical,* and *nonexperimental.* Some phenomena of behavior cannot be studied satisfactorily in the laboratory, and some quantification of clinical evidence is desirable. What we need is a balanced approach in selecting techniques appropriate for the problem at hand.

Can a clinician, as an applied member of the field of psychology, call himself a scientist? Students find themselves caught in this dilemma, generally about the beginning of their second graduate year, and prove to be an irritating source of questions like: "How can I be a scientist when the obvious fact is that in the clinic I have very little control over all of the variables in operation?"[46]

Those of us in the position of educating and training clinicians must face such inquiries with each new group of graduate students after they have learned the facts of life: that clinical psychology is a *science.* What can we answer them? . . .

In brief, the view here propounded does not consider the clinical office as the appropriate situation for validating certain hypotheses. If one is studying the nature of therapy, then naturally one must validate hunches relating to therapeutic behavioral change in this context. This is what process studies are concerned with. However, though a fruitful source of hypotheses, the clinical relationship should not be considered as the necessary and sufficient criterion for the validation of personality theory. This is so because to date research findings suggest that, no matter what theory the clinician subscribes to and phrases his interpretations in terms of, client changes in behavior and "insights" always serve to validate the theory held by the clinican. This is probably because of other variables functioning in the therapeutic situation than the variables of the clinician's theory of personality (e.g., suggestion), and such extratheoretical variables should be studied in their own right as process studies attempt to do.

Problems result when the clinician takes the client's behavior, made on the basis of the client's personal procedural evidence—an unreliable criterion at best—as *necessarily* validating the clinical interpretation. Personality theories have been developed this way. Many of the constructs so postulated and "clinically validated" have stood up in subsequent experimentation, but many have not. The behavioral change of the client *may* be consistent with a valid principle, but not necessarily so; and we should never rest our case with

[45] Paul E. Meehl, *Clinical Versus Statistical Prediction:* A Theoretical Analysis and a Review of the Evidence. Minneapolis: University of Minnesota Press, 1954. p. 3–9, 136–38.

[46] Quoted from Joseph F. Rychlak, "Clinical Psychology and the Nature of Evidence." *American Psychologist* 14: 642–48; October 1959.

merely clinical evidence. Clinical practice is a truly fruitful source of hypotheses and may even be viewed as a kind of pretesting; but we should always submit our theories to extraclinical test, particularly since they make reference to life beyond the therapy room. Designing the crucial experiment is a problem in its own right; but we are speaking here of attitude, and in principle we should assume that all relevant experiments can someday be carried out.

By continually accepting therapeutic change as validating theoretical hypotheses we have both learned much and consistently confused issues. This is the reason why clinicians are and must remain scientists, must subject their hypotheses to public trial, and must keep in touch with other points of view (the larger body of scientific knowledge). And the clinical student need not be confused, for he can be a scientist to the extent that he follows such a program. This is nothing more than anyone with an interest in people and a desire to be correct could be expected to do. If he prefers to abstract himself from the larger scientific community, to neglect the research literature, to deride the attempts of his peers to validate some of the notions "he knows" can never be validated, he certainly cannot be considered a scientist. Again, the decision is with him.

ILLUSTRATIONS OF CASE HISTORIES

Students of psychology have not been fully trained to construct adequate case histories, to gather the relevant information and to organize and interpret the findings. Other factors have interfered with the development of a library of case histories (normal and abnormal), including the conditions that make it difficult to obtain the data necessary for an understanding of any personality:[47]

1. Every life is long and complicated to the psychologist, and many hours are required for the exploration of even a few segments of it.
2. Man's power to recall his past is limited.
3. Man tends to guard his reputation when scientific scrutiny seeks to look at some crucial area of his secret life.
4. The psychologist's conscience, acknowledging that every man is entitled to his privacy, forbids unscrupulous intrusions.

Additional factors which have interfered with building a body of case histories are the difficulties in making dependable observations under clinical or experimental conditions, in formulating correct interpretations, in publication of a revealing, recognizable portrait of a still living person, and in finding a publisher and an audience.

In spite of the difficulties in producing adequate case histories, the dozens of book-length treatments in the chapter bibliography contain hundreds of illustrative case and clinical studies in such fields as educa-

[47] Arthur Burton and Robert E. Harris, *op. cit.*, p. 15–16.

tion, psychology, psychiatry, mental hygiene, guidance and counseling, therapy, behavior problems and delinquency, child development, social work, and sociology. A number of the earlier examples of community or village surveys may also be classified as case studies (Chapter 5).

Examples: Five Primitive and Peasant Societies[48]

The publication of the books under review now makes it possible for students and laymen to own first-hand accounts of five primitive and peasant societies, whereas earlier such source materials were either expensive or (mostly) unavailable except in major libraries. These "case studies" are useful, too, not only because they are much cheaper than the usual ethnological monograph, but also because they have been written especially for this series, which envisages a readership composed of non-professionals. Hence, they are all much more readable than the monographs which ordinarily are laden with esoteric detail.

Each book stands alone, of interest in its own right, and can be purchased separately. It is apparent, however, that the series has aims of its own. The five books together provide an ethnological "scatter"; that is, the student benefits by studying cultures which are distinct from one another as types and are also widely separated geographically.

Despite the diversity represented, however, the series does not lend itself well to cross-cultural comparisons nor does it elicit generalizations. The aim of the series is not to provide comparative materials, but instead each work is written around its own independent theme or focus—each is a distinctive "case." There is space here to mention briefly the themes, but not to evaluate. Fortunately, each author is a foremost authority on the peoples discussed.

Barnett's contribution, as suggested by its title, presents Palauan culture in behavioral episodes and in terms of the experiences and feelings of particular persons. It therefore gives the reader a feeling for the functioning culture so that it seems more "real" as well as more interesting than in the usual monographic writing. Beattie's account of Bunyoro is focused on the past history of this African kingdom as this is related to its present (and rapidly changing) condition. Hart and Pilling are able to contrast the Tiwi at two stages of modern acculturative change. Hart studied them in 1928-1929 and

[48] H. G. Barnett, *Being a Palauan.* New York: Henry Holt and Co., 1960. vii + 87 p.

John Beattie, *Bunyoro:* An African Kingdom. New York: Henry Holt and Co., 1960. ix + 86 p.

C. W. M. Hart and Arnold R. Pilling, *The Tiwi of North Australia.* New York: Henry Holt and Co., 1960. ix + 118 p.

E. Adamson Hoebel, *The Cheyennes:* Indians of the Great Plains. New York: Henry Holt and Co., 1960. vii + 103 p.

Oscar Lewis, *Tepoztlan:* Village in Mexico. New York: Henry Holt and Co., 1960. viii + 104 p.

Quoted from review by Elman R. Service, *American Sociological Review* 25: 777–78; October 1960.

Pilling in 1953-1954, making for an unusual collaborative account of Australian aborigines who are, in any case, always of interest. Hoebel presents the Cheyenne in a more standardized set of ethnographic descriptive categories than those employed by the other authors, and as a consequence the reader feels that it is a rather fuller account of the total culture, however boiled down; it is not focused on some particular problem or interest. Lewis' book, on the other hand, puts the peasants of Tepoztlan in a much broader and deeper context than do any of the others. He sees them as part of Mexico, the New World, and Spain; he also gives historical perspective from pre-Columbian to modern times, with particular consideration for the effects of the striking technological changes of recent years. I should remark, finally, that however distinct from one another in organization and focus, all the books succeed in various ways in including the more essential descriptive data.

Example: Childhood Emotional Disabilities[49]

The cases presented in this volume include a wide range of disorders, although they are not necessarily a representative sample of the range of child disabilities that one commonly encounters in a child-guidance clinic. Each case opens with a developmental history and a brief description of the emotional interrelationships within the family, which is followed by a detailed account of the collaborative treatment that includes the child and the simultaneous treatment of one or both parents. Considerable case material, interspersed with interpretative comment, is presented to illustrate therapeutic methods and patterns of family dynamics. Although little direct verbatim material is included, the abstracts of the therapeutic sessions seem to convey adequately the flavor of the therapeutic interaction. Reading through these cases one is impressed with the therapists' sensitivity to the patients' needs and the considerable flexibility in treatment. At a time when therapeutic rituals and rule-of-thumb methods are prevalent, these papers make for refreshing and instructive reading. Unfortunately, apart from the therapists' general impressions, little attempt is made to evaluate the procedures and outcomes through the use of data external to the therapeutic process.

Most of our clinical methods and classification systems have been designed primarily for the purpose of individual diagnosis and few adequate procedures have been developed for yielding a family diagnosis. The articles in this volume demonstrate how the case method can be used successfully to give a comprehensive picture of the constellation of intrafamily relationships and the changes in the family pattern during treatment. The limitations of the case method, nevertheless, tend to make these papers better as a source of hypotheses for more definitive studies than as a source of systematic knowledge about family disturbances.

[49] Quoted from review by Albert Bandura, *Contemporary Psychology* 2: 14–15; January 1957, of George E. Gardner, Editor, *Case Studies in Childhood Emotional Disabilities*. Vol. 2. New York: American Orthopsychiatric Association, 1956. vii + 368 p.

The types of disorders and problems represented in these cases are as follows:

Collaborative treatment of mother and boy with fecal retention, soiling, and a school phobia

The planned return of a placed child to own family

The defense mechanisms of a six-year-old

The use of a therapeutic nursery school in cooperation with clinical treatment of an acute separation problem

Pupils psychologically absent from school

The dynamics of encopresis

On the significance of the anal phase in pediatrics and child psychiatry

Brother identification in an adolescent girl

The dynamic significance of the mother-child relationship in the case of a young delinquent with psychotic mechanisms

Ego treatment causing structural change in personality

Is trying enough? A report of treatment during the latency period of a girl with atypical development

The psychological problems of the congenitally blind child

Two phases in the treatment of a hyperactive, destructive boy

Treatment of the adolescent delinquent

A technical problem in the beginning phase of psychotherapy with a borderline psychotic child.

Example: Therapy for Families[50]

Families in Treatment is based on data collected from 34 families who were seen in therapy at the Child Study Center at the Institute of the Pennsylvania Hospital in Philadelphia, apparently a fairly typical child-guidance clinic. The families in the sample were mostly members of the middle-income group, professional, and predominantly Jewish. The children's problems covered the range of neurotic disturbances and character disorders. Most of the child patients were boys. The average number of treatment sessions was between 20 and 30—with mother and child treated concurrently and lesser attention paid to the father. While the therapy staff comprised one senior child psychiatrist, eight Fellows in Child Psychiatry, and six social workers, the book deals primarily with the treatment conducted by the social workers, three of whom had considerable professional experience, the remaining three having relatively little (one year or less). The theoretical orientation was mainly psychoanalytic.

The study is focused upon the analysis of electrically recorded descriptions of interpersonal experience, obtained from therapists, parents, and children. Somewhat arbitrarily the third, sixteenth, and thirtieth interviews were

---

[50] Quoted from review by Hans H. Strupp, *Contemporary Psychology* 5: 264–65; August 1960, of Erika Chance, *Families in Treatment:* From the Viewpoint of the Patient, the Clinician, and the Researcher. New York: Basic Books, 1959. xviii + 234 p.

chosen as samples of the early, middle, and terminal phases of the treatment. The analysis of the data gathered during one year required another four years. Indeed, a test of the researcher's endurance!

What changes take place? Can the changes be anticipated by the therapist? How do the patients perceive the therapist? To what extent do descriptions of the problem by different members of the family coincide? How do the mutual expectations of patients and therapists influence the course of therapy? Are the prognostic expectations of the therapist borne out? Is there a difference between experienced and inexperienced therapists in this regard? These are but a few of the questions to which this book addresses itself.

Example: Three Patients in One[51]

A bewildered young woman sought treatment for severe headaches. She turned out to be three patients in one. Her two psychiatrists studied their patient with the best traditional care together with special checks and modern methods. Evidently these authors, like a number of their predecessors in the field, were completely surprised to find that their patient was a multiple personality. They tested every possibility of play-acting, escape, fraud, and fun. They avoided reading accounts of other cases while working with this one. They scrutinized their own interests and asked themselves, after Bernheim, "Who is hypnotizing whom?" They checked the patient's statements with statements from the same personality, other personalities, relatives, friends, other observers, and records. They observed naive persons' reactions to the several personalities; they exhibited the several personalities to professional colleagues for interpretation; and, from experts who knew as little as possible about the patient, for each personality they obtained interpretations of the handwriting, the results of intelligence tests, projective tests, and Osgood and Luria's semantic differential test. They obtained electroencephalograms, sound recordings and sound films.

The recordings and sound films the authors used as part of the therapy. The case, like a number of the earlier ones in the literature, was worked through to an excellent synthesis; one which, though the authors say they cannot be sure about this, seems durable.

The entire study supports the observations of prior authors about multiple personality: the build-up of meanings that can make for stress; conflicts in childhood and maturity; lapses, relevant sleepwalking; neurotic symptoms; hallucinations engendered by a co-conscious personality; transitional syncopes; various amnesias; the several personalities' differences in facial expression, manner, voice, speech, handwriting, interests, thought, character, and maturity; between personalities, barriers neither perfect nor wholly unchanging; one-way amnesia between certain personalities, and mutual amnesia, for a time, between others; each personality's striving to function as fully as possible;

[51] Quoted from review by William S. Taylor, *Contemporary Psychology* 2: 289–90; November 1957, of Corbett H. Thigpen and Hervey M. Cleckley, *The Three Faces of Eve*. New York: McGraw-Hill Book Co., 1957. ix + 308 p.

Evelyn Lancaster with James Poling, *The Final Face of Eve*. New York: McGraw-Hill Book Co., 1958. x + 290 p.

use of hypnosis to recover dreams, other memories, and larger organizations; light on psychotherapy; the changing, growing self; the integrative role of an inclusive interest; and the throes of coalescence or synthesis.

The findings are thought new, to the effect that one of the personalities, Eve Black, could not be hypnotized; one, Jane, emerged with mature powers, general orientation, and language, but with no specific memories; each of the most disparate personalities, Eve White and Eve Black, was sad at having to "die," and the most inclusive of the three personalities, Jane, was sad to "lose" her erstwhile "sisters." New too, and significant, are the special methods of study as applied to multiple personality, and the whole picture of a contemporary young woman, with her playfulness, selfishness, affection, humanity, idealism, and practical judgment most revealingly tried, segregated, and finally synthesized in a normal urge to live as a mature person.

Example: Case Study of a Y.M.C.A.[52]

Institutions find it relatively easy to experiment with phases of their life and to make improvements in segments of their work. The distinctive quality of the San Francisco Y.M.C.A. project is its comprehensiveness. Many different things are described as having been done as parts of a common design and with resolute effort to deal with the institution as a totality. Depending on tested and known processes, it would have been possible to improve membership enlistment, equipment, group procedures, instruction materials, supervision, parent participation, appraisal of results, public relations, administration, or other aspects of the life and work of this Y.M.C.A. Any such single venture would have been commendable. We know, however, that the *total life* of an institution—a school, a house, a church, a community, or a Christian Association—is a major determiner of the nature of its influence. Various aspects or segments of institutional life are each intrinsically important, but all are interrelated in a manner that determines the real significance of each and of the organization as a whole. Here is described an earnest attempt to change an Association as a whole—its goals, its methods, its administration—and that comprehensive factor, its *total climate*. All who compose the institution—members, leaders, supervisors, administrators, officers, related families, and community supporters—will, it is hoped and planned, come to hold those common expectations composing the climate which is the effective determiner of quality.

Each aspect of the San Francisco Y.M.C.A. takes on new dimensions when seen in the context of the whole. Each development is made in the light of a new perspective on the Association as a totality, and that outlook makes distinctive demands on every phase of the project.

The threefold character of this project is revealing of the manner in

[52] Roy Sorenson and Hedley S. Dimock, *A Case Study in Institutional Change.* New York: Association Press, 1955. p. vii–viii.

which dependable change comes in an institution. Concepts have been re-thought and have taken on a living reality for all involved. Steps in transition—how to get from where we are to new positions—have been carefully taken with the best of procedures for re-education. Records have been kept all along the way. These steps are interrelated—they do not come in an orderly sequence but each is seen and described clearly. Each makes its vital contribution to the adventure as a whole.

Example: An Institute of Social Welfare[53]

Old Age and Political Behavior is a case study of the California Institute of Social Welfare (CISW), a semi-interest-group, semi-mass-movement type of organization which champions the various causes of aged pensioners in California. It contains data which will be of use to sociologists interested in reform movements, techniques of propaganda and mass communication, and problems of leadership and membership.

The study contains historical information on old-age movements in California, the CIWS, and the charismatic leadership of George McLain, its founder and leader. A sample of members, when contrasted with a control group of non-members, shows that, while both groups are quite similar, members tend to experience more intense "status-anxiety" and are also "slightly privileged." The book contains descriptions of mass media and other devices used to reach the CISW's membership as well as a typology of membership ranging from most to least involved. Finally, there is a description of the political action of both the CISW and the "Opposition" and an account of the process of change in the CISW's form from that of a rather disreputable California reform movement to a fairly respectable lobby lodged in the nation's capital.

The authors made use of various methods of social research, the chief of which was a questionnaire mailed both to CISW members and non-members. It is hardly necessary to belabor the issue of the shortcomings of the mailed questionnaire: the authors point out that, of 4,969 questionnaires mailed to members, there were 2,224 responses and, of 3,430 mailed to non-members, only 915 replied. In addition to the questionnaires, intensive interviews were administered to forty-two relatively active members. However, no sample of non-members was interviewed. Content analyses of letters from members, radio speeches, and institute publications were also carried out.

Example: A Selling Group[54]

This study describes the behavior pattern emerging from the inter-personal relations of the members of a small group of 20 salesgirls. It

[53] Quoted from review by Ruth Granick, *American Journal of Sociology* 66: 306–7; November 1960, of Frank A. Pinner, Paul Jacobs, and Philip Selznick, *Old Age and Political Behavior: A Case Study*. Berkeley: University of California Press, 1959. xi + 352 p.

[54] George F. F. Lombard, *Behavior in a Selling Group: A Case Study of Interpersonal Relations in a Department Store*. Boston: Harvard University Graduate School of Business Administration, 1955. p. v–vi.

describes the relation of these emergent behavior patterns to the need satisfaction of the particular members of the group and to the achievement of the group's purposes. The emergent behavior patterns satisfied the personal need of each girl to maintain her beliefs about herself and also secured organized purposes in ways considered unusually successful by both the salesgirls and the executives concerned. Nevertheless, the group processes through which these results were obtained made difficult changes of behavior that would have resulted in more satisfaction to either customers or salesgirls. Indeed, the girls' beliefs brought it about that in most instances when one of them changed her behavior in these ways, she would be punished for the change.

The study regards the assumptions about behavior underlying the executives' evaluations of service as the single most important influence restricting the development of new behavior patterns in the department as a whole. The executives' need to maintain their beliefs about themselves by behaving in conformity to the existing logics of management made it difficult for them to examine and change these assumptions.

The conclusions of the study point to a need for the re-education of executives in sensitivity to group behavior patterns and in awareness of the effects of their own behavior on others.

Example: Personnel Security[55]

The 50 cases presented here have been collected in the course of a study of several hundred cases arising under the various Federal personnel security programs. These histories are collected, with the consent of the employees involved, from the files of the lawyers who advised or represented them. The reports are of necessity incomplete, because the Government file, which was not released to the employee, was also not available to our interviewers. While we realize that the usefulness of a study of this kind is circumscribed by the limitations on the available material, we feel that it will provide useful and indeed essential material for an understanding of how the security programs operate from day to day. We have tried to eliminate possible bias, by employing carefully selected lawyer-interviewers; by relying in the main on documentary materials, such as the written charges, the employee's written response, and the transcript of the hearing; and by identifying information based on statements by the employee or his counsel.

The 50 cases in this collection are taken from a current total of 230 cases from 12 cities. In each instance, the employee is asked, through his

[55] Adam Yarmolinsky, Compiler, *Case Studies in Personnel Security*. Washington: Bureau of National Affairs, 1955. p. iii. The cases include government civilian employees, industrial employees, military personnel, port security, and international organization employees.

lawyer, whether he would be willing to release the report of his case for general distribution, and the cases appearing here are among those in which such a release has been obtained.

Example: Personnel and Industrial Relations[56]

Two different types of materials have been included in the book. Forty-four cases, each written around a situation which actually occurred in a business concern, provide facts and information which give the student practice in developing his ability to think through a problem. There is no single solution to any of these problems. It should be emphasized that the most important benefits gained by the student will not come from whatever solution is decided upon, but rather from the opportunity to discuss and analyze problem situations.

The second part of the book consists of seven summary case problems in which the student evolves a complete personnel program from the individual cases he has been studying. Thus the student learns to look at a situation objectively, to plan logically sound solutions, and to use intelligent initiative, ingenuity, and imagination. The cases and problems deal with personnel programming, personnel research and standards, employment, training and development, health and medical care, safety, employee services, and employee relations.

Example: Case Study of a Factory Group[57]

This report is a study of behavior in an industrial work group. The group, consisting of fourteen workers and their foreman, formed one department of a small instrument manufacturing company. It was referred to as "the machine shop." The purpose is to demonstrate through description and diagnosis how social organization in a group develops from the web of work and nonwork behavior. We want to demonstrate why this social organization is so important to the men involved and to the enterprise for which they work. We also want to show, however, that social organization can become "frozen" unless leadership is exercised to challenge the adaptive capacities of individuals and their group.

The plan for our field work was simple in design, but difficult in execution. The data we wanted to get consisted of actual behavior in the group and how the men perceived this behavior. The major method for research was observation, informal interviewing, and examination of

---

[56] Edgar G. Williams and John F. Mee, *Cases and Problems in Personnel and Industrial Relations*. New York: Ronald Press, 1955. p. iii.

[57] Abraham Zaleznik, *Worker Satisfaction and Development: A Case Study of Work and Social Behavior in a Factory Group*. Boston: Harvard University Graduate School of Business Administration, 1956. p. 1, 2, 5, 9–10.

records where appropriate. The methodology was similar to that followed by the social anthropologist in field work. Over a period of almost six months we spent part of each workday in the shop and part in recording data and in discussion with colleagues. The data were present in the group itself and available to all members, with the possible exception of the information in the personnel records. But, to lift up these data, to fit them into a consistent pattern of behavior and to see their significance required some understanding of theoretical material on small group behavior as well as skill in observation and diagnosis.

From this analysis, we attempt to restate the central problem for the administration of work groups. This problem is two-fold: First, how can work groups be helped to develop an effective social organization? Second, how can the ingredients for growth and creativity be introduced to prevent the social organization from becoming static?

Example: Methods of Operations Research[58]

Although not explicitly advertised as such, this book is a collection of articles on the methods of operations research, written at an elementary level that is suitable for engineers and management personnel. There are introductory articles on the general philosophy and methodology of operations research and specific articles on such techniques as linear programming, queueing theory, theory of games, simulation studies, information theory, and other systems methods. Finally there is a collection of case studies. The chief defect in these articles is a tendency to verbosity on the part of some of the contributors.

By far the most fascinating and persuasive section is that on case studies. Of particular interest is an article by Zimmerman on the simulation of tactical war games; the discussion follows the course of a particular game step by step. Other articles detail studies on the operation of a hospital and a newspaper and analyze the cost and value of reports in a telephone company.

An article by Ellis Johnson (reprinted from the *Journal of Operations Research*) on operations research in the world crisis in science and technology goes far to illustrate the limitations of overenthusiastic applications of operations research considerations.

Example: A College[59]

This is a case study of the first four years of San Jose Junior College, in the process of assuming its initial structure and of meeting the needs of a new

---

[58] Quoted from review by George Weiss, *Science* 132: 543; August 26, 1960, of Charles D. Flagle, Jr., William H. Huggins, and Robert H. Roy, *Operations Research and Systems Engineering*. Baltimore, Md.: Johns Hopkins Press, 1960. x + 889 p. Reprinted from *Science* by permission.

[59] Burton R. Clark, *The Open Door College: A Case Study*. New York: McGraw-Hill Book Co., 1960. xvi + 208 p.

type of student body, including the characteristics of the college, job requirements of the teacher, orientation of the administrative staff, and aptitude of the
students. More specifically, the study deals with the pressures of modern
society affecting students and curriculum programs, essential elements shaping
the "personality" of the college, administrative setting in a local public school
district, aims and ambitions of the students, formal organization of the college,
composition of administrative and instructional staff, and the role of the junior
college in a system of higher education. The data were collected through informal interviews, observation, analysis of documents, and questionnaires.

Example: The Ineffective Soldier[60]

Volume II, *Breakdown and Recovery*, is a collection of 79 dramatically
told case histories, chosen to illustrate how factors in the life of the soldier
bear on whether he breaks down and, if he does, whether he recovers. It has a
good list of the resources within the individual that help mental health: stamina,
good intelligence, a desire to get ahead, generous and understanding parents, a
self-reliant and capable wife, and good stabilizing work. Beyond these—for military life—the support or lack of support a man received from his peer group and
from the military organization itself and the severity and duration of the stress
he was exposed to are of importance.

Because the stories are brief, they are oversimplified. Some of the points
illustrated through the thumb-nail case histories will seem self-evident to the
psychologists who were there. But the lessons learned in one military generation, like those in one academic generation, often have to be learned again later
through hard experience, and spelling out the obvious may then help. This
volume should be full of lessons for currently active military psychologists and
psychiatrists and those working in the Veterans Administration.

CONCLUDING STATEMENT

Significant trends and emphases in clinical and case study may be
summarized briefly as follows:

1. Extension of the case approach to include study of social institutions or
agencies and communities or cultural groups: a college, a hospital clinic, a
rural village, or an industrial community.

2. Application and use in a number of professional fields and to a wide
range of human problems: law and juvenile delinquency, medicine, psychiatry,
psychology, education, counseling and guidance, anthropology, sociology, social
work, economics, business administration, political science, and journalism.

3. Recognition of the complementary functions of the several stages in
case study and case work: initial status and symptoms, examination and history,
diagnosis, therapy, and follow-up.

[60] Eli Ginzberg and Others, *The Ineffective Soldier. Breakdown and Recovery*,
Vol. 2. New York: Columbia University Press, 1959. xx + 284 p.

4. Fuller and better use of such personal documents as the life history, autobiography, biography, diaries and journals, letters, records of dreams, and expressive interviews. Data obtained from personal documents may make a contribution by way of supplementing ecological and statistical information, so as to provide a more inclusive interpretation of the problem, and may serve as a basis for prediction of human behavior.

5. Recognition of the significance of multiple causation in diagnosis and of the corresponding need for a variety of therapeutic techniques. It usually is necessary to look beneath the surface to find the basic or primary cause of maladjustment; on the surface we may see only a secondary, tertiary, or contributory cause or condition. Frequently, complex or multiple causation of maladjustment may lead to a diagnosis and to therapy requiring the cooperation of a number of specialists.

6. A concept of therapy as development of the potentialities of the individual for growth and improvement, including adjustment procedures in the form of preventive measures, self-help, and client-centered techniques. In all forms of therapy, the importance of self-help is recognized, as illustrated by the patient's will or desire to recover from an illness.

7. Development and application of a variety of methods of psychotherapy, including group therapy. Psychotherapy involves difficulties in that our diagnostic instruments fall short of desirable standards of validity and reliability. We are uncomfortably aware of elements of truth behind the facetious characterization of psychotherapy as "the art of applying a science which does not yet exist," although our therapeutic anxiety is relieved somewhat by dependence on the best available techniques and procedures of psychodiagnosis.

8. Further improvement in case records, as well as wider use of cumulative and anecdotal records, with a place for autobiography, health history, test scores, school marks, cocurricular activities, and work experience.

9. Formulation of ethical principles or standards, particularly in the field of psychology, but with applications to other clinical and case areas (especially in diagnosis and treatment). Since the primary function of records is to render treatment of the case more effective in terms of adjustment of the client, and to serve community interests in dealing with social problems, the ethical implications of case-recording are important.

10. Recognition of the supplementary functions of case-clinical and statistical methods. It is a common error to group together the terms *quantitative, statistical,* and *experimental,* setting them in opposition to *qualitative, clinical,* and *nonexperimental.* Some phenomena of behavior cannot be studied satisfactorily in the laboratory, and some quantification of clinical evidence is desirable. What we need is a balanced approach in selecting techniques appropriate for the problem at hand.

11. Appearance of a considerable body of case-history material, in spite of certain difficulties in producing and publishing adequate case histories, in such fields as education, psychology, psychiatry, mental hygiene, guidance and counseling, therapy, behavior problems and delinquency, child development, social work, and sociology.

SELECTED REFERENCES

ABRAHAMSON, Arthur C., Editor. *Social Work Practice in Canada:* Case Records and Examples for Study and Teaching. Vancouver: School of Social Work, University of British Columbia, 1955. 252 p.

ABT, Lawrence E., and BELLAK, Leopold, Editors. *Projective Psychology:* Clinical Approaches to the Total Personality. New York: Grove Press, 1959. xviii + 486 + xiv p.

ABT, Lawrence E., and RIESS, B. F., Editors. *Progress in Clinical Psychology.* Vol. 4. New York: Grune and Stratton, 1960. x + 181 p.

ADAMS, James F. *Problems in Counseling:* A Case Study Approach. New York: The Macmillan Co., 1962. 164 p.

ADAMS, Leonard P., and ARONSON, Robert L. *Workers and Industrial Change:* A Case Study of Labor Mobility. Ithaca, N. Y.: New York State School of Industrial and Labor Relations, Cornell University, 1957. xi + 209 p.

ADAMS, R. N., and PREISS, J. J., Editors. *Human Organization Research:* Field Relations and Techniques. Homewood, Ill.: Dorsey Press, for the Society for Applied Anthropology, 1960. xviii + 456 p.

ALLBAUGH, Leland G. *Crete:* A Case Study of an Underdeveloped Area. Princeton: Princeton University Press, 1953. 592 p.

ALLEN, R. M. *Personality Assessment Procedures:* Psychometric, Projective, and Other Approaches. New York: Harper & Brothers, 1958. xi + 541 p.

ANDERSON, Harold H., and ANDERSON, Gladys L., Editors. *An Introduction to Projective Techniques.* . . . New York: Prentice-Hall, 1951. xxiv + 720 p.

ANDREWS, Kenneth R., Editor. *Human Relations and Administration; The Case Method of Teaching:* An Interim Statement. Cambridge: Harvard University Press, 1953. xvi + 271 p.

ANTHONY, Joseph.*The Invisible Curtain:* Psychoanalytic Cases of Louis Montgomery. New York: Rinehart & Co., 1957. 250 p.

APTEKAR, Herbert H. *The Dynamics of Casework and Counseling.* Boston: Houghton Mifflin Co., 1955. 262 p.

ARGYRIS, Chris. *Diagnosing Human Relations in Organization:* A Case Study of a Hospital. New Haven: Labor and Management Center, Yale University, 1956. vii + 120 p.

BACH, George R. *Intensive Group Psychotherapy.* New York: Ronald Press, 1954. xi + 446 p.

BAKER, John W., and HOLZWORTH, Annette. "Social Histories of Successful and Unsuccessful Children." *Child Development* 32: 135-49; March 1961.

BAKWIN, Harry, and BAKWIN, Ruth M. *Clinical Treatment of Behavior Disorders in Children.* Philadelphia: W. B. Saunders Co., 1953. xi + 495 p.

BALSER, Benjamin H., Editor. *Psychotherapy of the Adolescent.* New York: International Universities Press, 1957. 270 p.

BARRY, Ruth, and Others. *Case Studies in College Student-Staff Relationships.* New York: Bureau of Publications, Teachers College, Columbia University, 1956. ix + 117 p.

BAUER, Raymond A., and WASIOLEK, Edward. *Nine Soviet Portraits.* New York: John Wiley & Sons, 1955. ix + 190 p.

BAUER, Ronald C. *Cases in College Administration.* New York: Columbia University Press, 1955. 213 p.

BELLER, E. Kuno. *Clinical Process.* New York: Free Press of Glencoe, 1962. xx + 394 p.

BELLOWS, Roger M. *Case Problems in Personnel Management.* Dubuque, Ia.: William C. Brown and Co., 1955. 148 p.

BENNETT, IVY. *Delinquent and Neurotic Children:* A Comparative Study with One Hundred Case Histories. New York: Basic Books, 1961. xii + 532 p.

BERKMAN, Herman G. *The Delineation and Structure of Rental Housing Areas:* A Milwaukee Case Study. Wisconsin Commerce Reports, Vol. 4, No. 5. Madison: University of Wisconsin School of Commerce and Bureau of Business Research and Service, 1956. 144 p.

BERNSTEIN, Arnold. *On the Nature of Psychotherapy.* Garden City, N. Y.: Doubleday & Co., 1954. ix + 36 p.

BERRIEN, F. K., and BASH, Wendell H. *Human Relations:* Comments and Cases. Second Edition. New York: Harper & Brothers, 1957. xii + 564 p.

BETTELHEIM, Bruno. *Paul and Mary:* Two Case Histories From "Truants From Life." Garden City, N. Y.: Doubleday, 1961. xxx + 435 p.

BETTELHEIM, Bruno. *Truants From Life.* Glencoe, Ill.: Free Press, 1955. 511 p.

BIESTEK, Felix P. *The Casework Relationship.* Chicago: Loyola University Press, 1957. 149 p.

BLAESSER, Willard W., and CROOKSTON, Burns B. "Student Personnel Work— College and University," *Encyclopedia of Educational Research.* Edited by Chester W. Harris. Third Edition. New York: Macmillan Co., 1960. p. 1415-25.

BLAU, T. H. *Private Practice in Clinical Psychology.* New York: Appleton-Century-Crofts, 1959. x + 184 p.

BLAIR, G. M. *Diagnostic and Remedial Teaching.* New York: The Macmillan Co., 1956. xvi + 409 p.

BLOCH, Herbert A., and FLYNN, Frank T. *Delinquency:* The Juvenile Offender in America Today. New York: Random House, 1956. xii + 612 p. (Two cases are reported at some length.)

BORGATTA, Edgar F., FANSHEL, David, and MEYER, H. J. *Social Workers' Perceptions of Clients:* A Study of the Caseload of a Social Agency. New York: Russell Sage Foundation, 1960. 92 p.

BRACKENBURY, Robert L. *Getting Down to Cases:* A Problems Approach to Educational Philosophizing. New York: G. P. Putnam's Sons, 1959. 222 p.

BRAMELD, Theodore. "Explicit and Implicit Culture in Puerto Rico: A Case Study in Educational Anthropology." *Harvard Educational Review* 28: 197-213; Summer 1958.

BRAMMER, Lawrence M., and SHOSTROM, Everett L. *Therapeutic Psychology:* Fundamentals of Counseling and Psychotherapy. Englewood Cliffs, N.J.: Prentice-Hall, 1960. xvii + 447 p.

BRAUN, John R., Editor. *Clinical Psychology in Transition.* Cleveland: Howard Allen, 1961. ix + 211 p.

BROWER, Daniel, and ABT, Lawrence E., Editors. *Progress in Clinical Psychology*. Vol. 2. New York: Grune and Stratton, 1956. viii + 364 p.

BUCHHEIMER, Arnold, and BALOGH, Sara C. *The Counseling Relationship: A Casebook*. Chicago: Science Research Associates, 1962. vii + 234 p.

BURCH, Thomas K. "Postwar Japan: A Case Study in Population Policy and Social Disorganization." *American Catholic Sociological Review* 19: 45-53; March 1958.

BURTON, Arthur, Editor. *Case Studies in Counseling and Psychotherapy*. Englewood Cliffs, N. J.: Prentice-Hall, 1959. x + 431 p.

BURTON, Arthur, Editor. *Psychotherapy of the Psychoses*. New York: Basic Books, 1961. x + 386 p.

BURTON, Arthur, and HARRIS, R. E., Editors. *Clinical Studies of Personality*. Vol. 2. Case Histories in Clinical and Abnormal Psychology. New York: Harper & Brothers, 1955. xiii + 836 p.

BYCHOWSKI, Gustav, and DESPERT, J. Louise, Editors. *Specialized Techniques in Psychotherapy*. New York: Basic Books, 1958. xii + 371 p.

CALHOON, Richard P., NOLAND, E. Williams, and WHITEHALL, Arthur M., Jr. *Cases on Human Relations in Management*. New York: McGraw-Hill Book Co., 1958. 444 p.

CALLIS, Robert, and Others. *A Casebook of Counseling*. New York: Appleton-Century-Crofts, 1955. ix + 352 p.

CARR, A. C., and Others. *The Prediction of Overt Behavior Through the Use of Projective Techniques*. Springfield, Ill.: Charles C Thomas, 1960. xii + 177 p.

CASAGRANDE, Joseph B., Editor. *In the Company of Man:* Twenty Portraits by Anthropologists. New York: Harper & Brothers, 1960. xvi + 540 p. (Social types found in diverse cultures around the world.)

"Casework with the Aging." *Social Casework* 42: 215-90; May-June 1961.

CAUDILL, William. *The Psychiatric Hospital as a Small Society*. Cambridge, Mass.: Harvard University Press, for the Commonwealth Fund, 1958. xxii + 406 p.

CHANCE, Erika. *Families in Treatment*. New York: Basic Books, 1959. xviii + 234 p. (From the viewpoint of the patient, clinician, and research worker.)

COHEN, Y. A. *Social Structure and Personality:* A Casebook. New York: Holt, Rinehart, and Winston, 1961. xiv + 528 p.

COLBY, Kenneth. *A Primer for Psychotherapists*. New York: Ronald Press, 1951. viii + 167 p.

CORSINI, Raymond J. *Methods of Group Psychotherapy*. New York: McGraw-Hill Book Co., 1957. xi + 251 p.

CULBERTSON, Jack. "The Case for Cases in the Study of Administration." *Educational Administration and Supervision* 42: 420-27; November 1956.

CURTI, Merle. *The Making of an American Community:* A Case History of Democracy in a Frontier County. Stanford: Stanford University Press, 1959. vii + 483 p.

DAUGHERTY, William E. *A Psychological Warfare Casebook*. Baltimore: Johns

Hopkins Press, 1958. xxiii + 880 p. (Seventy-three collected readings on psychological warfare, largely case descriptions of specific events.)

DE GRAZIA, Sebastian. *Errors of Psychotherapy.* Garden City, N. Y.: Doubleday & Co., 1952. 288 p.

DELLIS, N. P., and STONE, H. K., Editors. *The Training of Psychotherapists: A Multidisciplinary Approach.* Baton Rouge: Louisiana State University Press, 1961. xii + 195 p.

DEUTSCH, Felix, and MURPHY, William F. *The Clinical Interview.* Vol. 1, *Diagnosis.* New York: International Universities Press, 1954. 613 p.

DEUTSCH, Felix, and MURPHY, William F. *The Clinical Interview.* Vol. 2, *Therapy.* New York: International Universities Press, 1955. 335 p.

DEVEREUX, George. *Therapeutic Education:* Its Theoretical Bases and Practice. New York: Harper & Brothers, 1956. xxviii + 435 p. (Includes 77 brief cases.)

DOHRMAN, H. T. *California Cult:* The Story of "Mankind United." Boston: Beacon Press, 1958. xi + 163 p. (A case study based on interviews, observations, and documentary materials.)

DOLLARD, John. *Criteria for the Life History.* New Haven: Yale University Press, 1935. vi + 288 p. Reprinted in 1949 by Peter Smith.

DOLLARD, John, AULD, Frank, and WHITE, Alice. *Steps in Psychotherapy.* New York: The Macmillan Co., 1953. 222 p.

DOLLARD, John, and MILLER, Neal E. *Personality and Psychotherapy:* An Analysis in Terms of Learning, Thinking, and Culture. New York: McGraw-Hill Book Co., 1950. xiii + 488 p.

EARL, C. J. C. *Subnormal Personalities:* Their Clinical Investigation and Assessment. Baltimore: Williams and Wilkins Co., 1961. v + 338 p.

EKSTEIN, Rudolf, and WALLERSTEIN, R. S. *The Teaching and Learning of Psychotherapy.* New York: Basic Books, 1958. xvi + 334 p.

ELIASBERG, Wladimir G. *Psychotherapy and Society.* New York: Philosophical Library, 1959. xviii + 223 p.

ERICKSON, Clifford E. *Counseling Interview.* New York: Prentice-Hall, 1950. 174 p.

ERIKSON, E. H. *Young Man Luther:* A Study in Psychoanalysis and History. New York: W. W. Norton, 1958. 288 p.

Ethical Standards of Psychologists: A Summary of Ethical Principles. Washington: American Psychological Association, 1953. 19 p.

EVANS, Jean. *Three Men:* An Experiment in the Biography of Emotion. New York: Alfred A. Knopf, 1954. xviii + 298 p. (Case reports.)

EWALT, J. R., STRECKER, E. A., and EBAUGH, F. G. *Practical Clinical Psychology.* Eighth Edition. New York: McGraw-Hill Book Co., 1957. xiv + 457 p.

EYSENCK, H. J., Editor. *Handbook of Abnormal Psychology.* New York: Basic Books, 1961. xvi + 816 p.

FAATZ, Anita J. *The Nature of Choice in Casework Process.* Chapel Hill: University of North Carolina Press, 1953. vii + 141 p.

FANSHELL, David. *An Overview of One Agency's Casework Operation.* New York: Family Service Association of America, 1958. 318 p.

FINDLEY, Warren G. "Student Personnel Work—Elementary and Secondary," *Encyclopedia of Educational Research*. Edited by Chester W. Harris. Third Edition. New York: The Macmillan Co., 1960. p. 1427-32.

FINK, Arthur E., WILSON, Everett E., and CONOVER, Merrill B. *The Field of Social Work*. Third Edition. New York: Henry Holt and Co., 1955. ix + 630 p.

FISHER, V. E. *The Meaning and Practice of Psychotherapy*. New York: The Macmillan Co., 1950. xv + 411 p.

FOOTE, Estelle. *Six Children*. Springfield, Ill.: Charles C Thomas, 1956. ix + 317 p. (Psychiatric case studies.)

FOULKES, S. H., and ANTHONY, E. J. *Group Psychotherapy*: The Psycho-Analytic Approach. Baltimore: Penguin Books, 1957. 263 p.

FRANCIS, Roy G., and STONE, Robert C. *Service and Procedure in Bureaucracy*: A Case Study. Minneapolis: University of Minnesota Press, 1956. vi + 201 p. (Empirical study of a public employment agency.)

FRIEDLANDER, Walter A., Editor. *Concepts and Methods of Social Work*. Englewood Cliffs, N. J.: Prentice-Hall, 1958. ix + 308 p.

FRIEND, Maurice R., and Others. "The Historical Development of Family Diagnosis." *Social Service Review* 34: 2-18; March 1960.

FRINGS, John, KRATOVIL, Ruth, and POLEMIS, Bernice. *An Assessment of Social Case Recording*. New York: Family Service Association of America, 1958. 151 p.

FROMM-REICHMANN, Frieda. *Principles of Intensive Psychotherapy*. Chicago: The University of Chicago Press, 1950. xv + 246 p.

FROMM-REICHMANN, Frieda, and MORENO, J. L., Editors. *Progress in Psychotherapy*. New York: Grune and Stratton, 1956. xii + 352 p.

GARDNER, George E., Editor. *Case Studies in Childhood Emotional Disabilities*. Vol. 2. New York: American Orthopsychiatric Association, 1956. vii + 368 p.

GARFIELD, Sol L. *Introductory Clinical Psychology*: An Overview of the Functions, Methods, and Problems of Contemporary Clinical Psychology. New York: The Macmillan Co., 1957. xiii + 469 p.

GEE, Wilson. *Social Science Research Methods*. New York: Appleton-Century-Crofts, 1950. p. 230-51.

GERBER, Israel. *Man On a Pendulum*: A Case History of an Invert Presented by a Religious Counselor. New York: American Press, 1956. 320 p.

GESELL, Arnold, and AMATRUDA, Catherine S. *Developmental Diagnosis*: Normal and Abnormal Child Development, Clinical Methods and Practical Applications. Revised Edition. New York: Harper & Brothers, 1947. xvi + 496 p.

GILBERT, Jeanne G. *Understanding Old Age*. New York: Ronald Press, 1953. 442 p. (Twenty-six case histories based on the author's professional experience.)

GINOTT, Haim G. *Group Psychotherapy with Children*: The Theory and Practice of Play Therapy. New York: McGraw-Hill Book Co., 1961. xvi + 208 p.

GINZBERG, Eli, and BRAY, Douglas W. *The Uneducated*. New York: Columbia

University Press, 1953. xxv + 246 p. (Case histories from civilian and military life.)

GLICKMAN, Esther. *Child Placement through Clinically Oriented Casework.* New York: Columbia University Press, 1957. xii + 448 p.

GLUECK, Sheldon, and GLUECK, Eleanor. *Delinquents in the Making:* Paths to Prevention. New York: Harper & Brothers, 1952. viii + 214 p.

GLUECK, Sheldon, and GLUECK, Eleanor. *Unraveling Juvenile Delinquency.* New York: Commonwealth Fund, 1950. xv + 399 p.

GONDOR, Emery I. *Art and Play Therapy.* Garden City, N.Y.: Doubleday & Co., 1954. x + 61 p.

GOOD, Carter V., and SCATES, Douglas E. *Methods of Research:* Educational, Psychological, Sociological. New York: Appleton-Century-Crofts, 1954. p. 726-99.

GOODE, William J., and HATT, Paul K. *Methods in Social Research.* New York: McGraw-Hill Book Co., 1952. p. 330-40.

GORDON, Henrietta L. *Casework Services for Children:* Principles and Practices. Boston: Houghton Mifflin Co., 1956. xii + 493 p.

GORLOW, L., HOCH, E. L., and TELSCHOW, E. *The Nature of Nondirective Group Psychotherapy.* New York: Bureau of Publications, Teachers College, Columbia University, 1952. viii + 143 p.

GREENACRE, Phyllis. *Swift and Carroll:* A Psychoanalytic Study of Two Lives. New York: International Universities Press, 1955. 306 p.

GROSS, Neal, MASON, Ward S., and McEACHERN, Alexander W. *Explorations in Role Analysis:* Studies of the School Superintendency Role. New York: John Wiley & Sons, 1958. 379 p.

GULICK, John. *Social Structure and Culture Change in a Lebanese Village.* Viking Fund Publications in Anthropology, Number Twenty-One. New York: Wenner-Gren Foundation for Anthropological Research, 1955. 191 p.

GULLAHORN, John T. "Teaching by the Case Method." *School Review* 67: 448-60; Winter 1959.

GUNTRIP, Henry. *Psychotherapy and Religion.* New York: Harper & Brothers, 1957. 206 p.

HADLEY, J. M. *Clinical and Counseling Psychology.* New York: Alfred A. Knopf, 1958. xv + 682 + xix p.

HAHN, Milton E., and MACLEAN, Malcolm S. *General Clinical Counseling in Educational Institutions.* New York: McGraw-Hill Book Co., 1950. xi + 375 p.

HAMILTON, Gordon. *Principles of Social Case Recording.* New York: Columbia University Press, 1946. vii + 142 p.

HAMILTON, Gordon. *Psychotherapy in Child Guidance.* New York: Columbia University Press, 1947. 340 p.

HAMILTON, Gordon. *Theory and Practice of Social Case Work.* Revised Edition. New York: Columbia University Press, 1951. vii + 328 p.

HAMMER, E. F., Editor. *The Clinical Application of Projective Drawings.* Springfield, Ill.: Charles C Thomas, 1958. xxii + 663 p.

HAMMOND, Kenneth R., and ALLEN, Jeremiah M. *Writing Clinical Reports.* New York: Prentice-Hall, 1953. 288 p.

HARRELL, T. W., and RUSMORE, J. T. *A Casebook in Industrial and Personnel Psychology.* New York: Rinehart and Co., 1958. v + 89 p.

HARRIS, Myron W., and WHITE, Mary A. *The School Psychologist.* New York: Harper & Brothers, 1961. 431 p.

HARRISON, Paul M. *Authority and Power in the Free Church Tradition:* A Social Case Study of the American Baptist Convention. Princeton, N.J.: Princeton University Press, 1959. xix + 248 p. (Case study of the contrast between doctrine and actual organization.)

HARROWER, Molly. *The Practice of Clinical Psychology.* Springfield, Ill.: Charles C Thomas, 1961. xiv + 321 p.

HARROWER, Molly, and Others. *Creative Variations in the Projective Techniques.* Springfield, Ill.: Charles C Thomas, 1960. viii + 138 p.

HARTLEY, E. L., and WIEBE, G. D. *Casebook in Social Processes.* New York: Thomas Y. Crowell, 1960. x + 534 p.

HAVIGHURST, Robert J. *Human Development and Education.* New York: Longmans, Green and Co., 1953. p. 177-253.

HAVIGHURST, Robert J., and MORGAN, H. Gerthon. *The Social History of a War-Boom Community.* New York: Longmans, Green and Co., 1951. xix + 356 p.

HENRY, William E. "Projective Techniques," *Handbook of Research Methods in Child Development.* Edited by Paul H. Mussen. New York: John Wiley & Sons, 1960. Chapter 15.

HINCKLEY, Robert G., and HERMANN, Lydia. *Group Treatment in Psychotherapy.* Minneapolis: University of Minnesota Press, 1951. 136 p.

HITSCHMANN, Edward. *Great Men:* Psychoanalytic Studies. New York: International Universities Press, 1956. xiii + 278 p.

HOBBS, Nicholas, and Others. *Ethical Standards of Psychologists.* Washington: American Psychological Association, 1953. xv + 171 p.

HODGES, Wayne. *Company and Community:* Case Studies in Industry-City Relationships. New York: Harper & Brothers, 1958. 224 p.

HOLLIS, Ernest V., and TAYLOR, Alice L. *Social Work Education in the United States:* Report of a Study Made for the National Council on Social Work Education. New York: Columbia University Press, 1951. xviii + 422 p.

HUGHES, Helen M., Editor. *The Fantastic Lodge:* The Autobiography of a Girl Drug Addict. Boston: Houghton Mifflin Co., 1961. x + 267 p.

HUNT, William A. *The Clinical Psychologist.* Springfield, Ill.: Charles C Thomas, 1956. xi + 206 p.

INGHAM, Harrington V., and LOVE, Leonore R. *The Process of Psychotherapy.* New York: McGraw-Hill Book Co., 1954. ix + 270 p.

JACKSON, Lydia, and TODD, Kathleen M. *Child Treatment and the Therapy of Play.* Second Edition. New York: Ronald Press, 1950. xii + 159 p.

JACOBSON, Eugene, and SCHLACHTER, Stanley, Editors. "Cross-National Research: A Case Study." *Journal of Social Issues* 10: 2-68; 1954.

JACQUES, Elliott. *The Changing Culture of a Factory.* New York: Dryden Press, 1952. xxi + 341 p. (Three-year case study of the psychological and social forces affecting the group life, morale, and productivity of a London industrial community; includes description, diagnosis, and treatment.)

JENKINS, Gladys G., SHACTER, Helen, and BAUER, William W. *These Are Your Children*. Expanded Edition. Chicago: Scott, Foresman and Co., 1953. 320 p. (Numerous case studies.)

JONES, Maxwell. *The Therapeutic Community*. New York: Basic Books, 1953. 727 p.

JOURARD, Sidney M. *Personal Adjustment:* An Approach through the Study of Healthy Personality. New York: The Macmillan Co., 1958. 462 p.

KAHN, T. C., and GIFFEN, M. B. *Psychological Techniques in Diagnosis and Evaluation*. New York: Pergamon Press, 1960. xii + 164 p.

KARDINER, Abram, and OVESEY, Lionel. *The Mark of Oppression:* A Psychosocial Study of the American Negro. New York: W. W. Norton and Co., 1951. xvii + 396 p. (Case histories of 25 American Negroes.)

KASIUS, Cora, Editor. *A Comparison of Diagnostic and Functional Casework Concepts*. New York: Family Service Association of New York, 1950. 169 p.

KATZENELBOGEN, Solomon. *Analyzing Psychotherapy*. New York: Philosophical Library, 1958. 126 p.

KENT, Grace H. *Mental Tests in Clinics for Children*. New York: D. Van Nostrand, 1950. xii + 180 p.

KIMBALL, Solon T., and PEARSALL, Marion. *The Talladega Story:* A Study in Community Process. University, Ala.: University of Alabama Press, 1954. xxxii + 259 p.

KING, Clarence. *Working with People in Small Communities:* Case Records of Community Development in Different Countries. New York: Harper & Brothers, 1959. vii + 130 p. (Case studies, mostly from underdeveloped countries, of programs of community action.)

KINSEY, A. C., and Others. *Sexual Behavior in the Human Female*. Philadelphia: W. B. Saunders Co., 1953. xxx + 842 p.

KINSEY, A. C., and Others. *Sexual Behavior in the Human Male*. Philadelphia: W. B. Saunders Co., 1948. xvi + 804 p.

KIRKPATRICK, Clifford. *The Family:* As Process and Institution. New York: Ronald Press, 1955. viii + 651 p.

KLEIN, Leo, as told to Edward Uhlan. *You Are Not Alone:* Psychological Case Histories. New York: Exposition Press, 1959. 180 p.

KLEIN, Melanie. *Narrative of a Child Analysis:* The Conduct of the Psychoanalysis of Children as Seen in the Treatment of a Ten Year Old Boy. New York: Basic Books, 1961. 496 p.

KOLAJA, Jiri. *A Polish Factory:* A Case Study of Workers' Participation in Decision Making. Lexington, Ky.: University of Kentucky Press, 1960. xviii + 157 p.

KORNBERG, Leonard. *A Class for Disturbed Children:* A Case Study and Its Meaning for Education. New York: Teachers College, Columbia University, 1955. viii + 157 p.

KRAMER, Edith. *Art Therapy in a Children's Community:* A Study of the

Function of Art Therapy in the Treatment Program of Wiltwyck School for Boys. Springfield, Ill.: Charles C Thomas, 1958. xvii + 238 p.

KRUGER, Judith. *My Fight for Sanity*. Philadelphia: Chilton Co., 1959. 244 p.

KVARACEUS, William C. "Behavior Problems," *Encyclopedia of Educational Research*. Edited by Chester W. Harris. Third Edition. New York: The Macmillan Co., 1960. p. 137-42.

KVARACEUS, William. "Delinquency," *Encyclopedia of Educational Research*. Edited by Chester W. Harris. Third Edition. New York: The Macmillan Co., 1960. p. 365-69.

LADD, Edward T., and SAYRES, William C. *Social Aspects of Education*: A Casebook. Englewood Cliffs, N.J.: Prentice-Hall, 1962. xi + 388 p.

LANCASTER, Evelyn, and POLING, James. *The Final Face of Eve*. New York: McGraw-Hill Book Co., 1958. x + 290 p.

LANGFELD, Herbert S., and Others, Editors. *A History of Psychology in Autobiography*. Vol. 4. Worcester, Mass.: Clark University Press, 1952. xii + 356 p.

LAWRENCE, P. R. *The Changing of Organizational Behavior Patterns*: A Case Study of Decentralization. Boston: Division of Research, Graduate School of Business Administration, Harvard University, 1958. xi + 237 p.

LEARY, Timothy. *Interpersonal Diagnosis of Personality*. New York: Ronald Press, 1957. xix + 518 p.

LEVITT, Eugene E. *Clinical Research Design and Analysis in the Behavioral Sciences*. Springfield, Ill.: Charles C Thomas, 1961. xxii + 199 p.

LEWIS, Oscar. *The Children of Sanchez*: Autobiography of a Mexican Family. New York: Random House, 1961. xxxi + 499 p.

LEWIS, Oscar. *Five Families*: Mexican Case Studies in the Culture of Poverty. New York: Basic Books, 1959. xvi + 351 p.

LIPPMAN, Hyman S. *Treatment of the Child in Emotional Conflict*. New York: McGraw-Hill Book Co., 1956. x + 298 p.

LOUTTIT, C. M., and Others. *Clinical Psychology of Exceptional Children*. Third Edition. New York: Harper & Brothers, 1957. xii + 573 p.

LOWENSTEIN, Edith. *The Alien and the Immigration Law*: A Study of 1,446 Cases Arising under the Immigration and Naturalization Laws of the United States. New York: Common Council for American Unity by Oceana Publications, 1958. xii + 388 p.

LURIE, Nancy O., Editor. *Mountain Wolf Woman, Sister of Crashing Thunder*: The Autobiography of a Winnebago Indian. Ann Arbor: University of Michigan Press, 1961. xx + 142 p.

MARZOLF, S. S. *Psychological Diagnosis and Counseling in the Schools*. New York: Henry Holt and Co., 1956. xiv + 401 p.

MASSERMAN, Jules H., Editor. *Current Psychiatric Therapies*. Vol. 1 (1961). New York: Grune and Stratton, 1961. x + 246 p.

MASSERMAN, Jules H., Editor. *Psychoanalysis and Social Process*. Science and Psychoanalysis, Vol. 4. New York: Grune and Stratten, 1961. xii + 196 p.

MASSERMAN, Jules H. *Science and Psychoanalysis*: Integrative Studies. Vol. 1. New York: Grune and Stratton, 1958. vi + 201 p.

MASSERMAN, Jules H., and MORENO, J. L., Editors. *Progress in Psychotherapy*:

Anxiety and Therapy. Vol. 2. New York: Grune and Stratton, 1957. viii + 264 p.

MASSERMAN, Jules H., and MORENO, J. L., Editors. *Progress in Psychotherapy:* Techniques of Psychotherapy. Vol. 3. New York: Grune and Stratton, 1958. x + 324 p.

MASSERMAN, Jules H., and MORENO, J. L., Editors. *Progress in Psychotherapy:* Social Psychotherapy. Vol. 4. New York: Grune and Stratton, 1959. xii + 361 p.

MASSERMAN, Jules H., and MORENO, J. L., Editors. *Progress in Psychotherapy:* Review and Integrations. Vol. 5. New York: Grune and Stratton, 1960. x + 262 p.

McCARY, James L., Editor. *Six Approaches to Psychotherapy.* New York: Dryden Press, 1955. vii + 402 p.

McCORD, Joan, and McCORD, William. *Psychotherapy and Delinquency.* New York: Grune and Stratton, 1956. + 230 p. (Evaluation of therapy with seriously disturbed delinquents.)

McCORMICK, Mary J. *Diagnostic Casework in the Thomistic Pattern.* New York: Columbia University Press, 1954. xiv + 239 p.

MEEHL, Paul E. *Clinical Versus Statistical Prediction:* A Theoretical Analysis and a Review of the Evidence. Minneapolis: University of Minnesota Press, 1954. x + 149 p.

MIDELFORT, C. F. *The Family in Psychotherapy.* New York: McGraw-Hill Book Co., 1957. 203 p.

MILES, Arthur P. *American Social Work Theory:* A Critique and a Proposal. New York: Harper & Brothers, 1954. 246 p.

MILLARD, Cecil V. *Case Inventory for the Study of Child Development.* Minneapolis: Burgess Publishing Co., 1950. 29 p.

MILLARD, Cecil V. *School and Child:* A Case History. East Lansing: Michigan State College Press, 1954. xvi + 221 p.

MILLARD, Cecil V., and ROTHNEY, J. W. M. *The Elementary School Child:* A Book of Cases. New York: Dryden Press, 1957. xii + 660 p.

MINTZ, S. W. *Worker in the Cane:* A Puerto Rican Life History. New Haven: Yale University Press, 1960. xiv + 288 p.

MORENO, J. L., in collaboration with MORENO, Z. T. *Psychodrama:* Foundations of Psychotherapy. Vol. 2. Beacon, N.Y.: Beacon House, 1959. vi + 238 p.

MORENO, J. L., and ENNEIS, J. M. *Hypnodrama and Psychodrama.* Beacon, N.Y.: Beacon House, 1950. 56 p.

MORRIS, Cherry, Editor. *Social Case-work in Great Britain.* London: Faber and Faber, 1950. 223 p.

MOSHER, Arthur T. *Case Study of the Agricultural Program of Acar in Brazil.* Washington: National Planning Association (Technical Cooperation in Latin America), 1955. xiv + 63 p.

MOUSTAKAS, Clark E. *Children in Play Therapy:* A Key to Understanding Normal and Disturbed Emotions. New York: McGraw-Hill Book Co., 1953. ix + 218 p.

MOUSTAKAS, Clark E. *Psychotherapy With Children:* The Living Relationship. New York: Harper & Brothers, 1959. xx + 324 p. (Case studies.)

MOWRER, O. H., and Others. *Psychotherapy:* Theory and Research. New York: Ronald Press, 1953. xviii + 700 p.

MUDD, Emily H., and Others, Editors. *Marriage Counseling:* A Casebook. New York: Association Press, 1958. 488 p.

MURPHY, Lois B., and Others. *Personality in Young Children.* 2 vols. New York: Basic Books, 1956. (Volume 2 is a detailed study of "Colin, A Normal Child," from his second through his fifth year.)

NATENBERG, Maurice. *The Case History of Sigmund Freud:* A Psychobiography. Chicago: Regent House, 1955. 245 p.

NEA Research Division for the NEA Committee on Tax Education and School Finance, *Action in State Equalization; Case Studies:* Equalization of Property Tax Assessments in Selected States. Washington: NEA, 1959. 45 p.

NEWLAND, T. Ernest. "Psychological Services—Elementary and Secondary," *Encyclopedia of Educational Research.* Edited by Chester W. Harris. Third Edition. New York: The Macmillan Co., 1960. p. 1067-73.

OSTROVSKY, E. S. *Father to the Child:* Case Studies of the Experiences of a Male Teacher with Young Children. New York: G. P. Putnam's Sons, 1959. xviii + 173 p.

PARAD, Howard J., Editor. *Ego Psychology and Dynamic Casework:* Papers from the Smith College School for Social Work. New York: Family Service Association of America, 1958. 282 p.

PATTERSON, C. H. *Counseling and Psychotherapy:* Theory and Practice. New York: Harper & Brothers, 1959. xii + 322 p.

PATTERSON, T. T. *Glasgow Limited:* A Case-Study in Industrial War and Peace. Social and Economic Studies No. 7 of the Department of Social and Economic Research, University of Glasgow. London: Cambridge University Press, 1960. x + 243 p.

PAUL, Benjamin D., Editor, and MILLER, Walter B. *Health, Culture, and Community:* Case Studies of Public Reactions to Health Programs. New York: Russell Sage Foundation, 1955. viii + 493 p.

PEARSALL, Marion. *Little Smoky Ridge:* The Natural History of a Southern Appalachian Neighborhood. University: University of Alabama Press, 1959. xii + 205 p. (Field study of a rural Appalachian community.)

PECK, Harris B., and BELLSMITH, Virginia. *Treatment of the Delinquent Adolescent:* Group and Individual Therapy with Parent and Child. New York: Family Service Association of America, 1954. 147 p.

PENNINGTON, L. A., and BERG, Irwin A. *An Introduction to Clinical Psychology.* Second Edition. New York: Ronald Press, 1954. viii + 709 p.

PEPINSKY, Harold B., and PEPINSKY, Pauline N. *Counseling Theory and Practice.* New York: Ronald Press, 1954. viii + 307 p.

PERLMAN, Helen H. *Social Casework:* A Problem-solving Process. Chicago: The University of Chicago Press, 1957. xv + 268 p.

PHILLIPS, Ewing L. *Psychotherapy:* A Modern Theory and Practice. Englewood Cliffs, N.J.: Prentice-Hall, 1956. xviii + 334 p.

PHILLIPS, Helen U. *Essentials of Social Group Work Skill.* New York: Association Press, 1957. x + 180 p.

PITTMAN, David J., and GORDON, C. Wayne. *Revolving Door:* A Study of the Chronic Police Case Inebriate. Monographs of the Yale Center of Alcohol Studies, No. 2. Glencoe, Ill.: Free Press, 1958. xx + 154 p.

POLANSKY, Norman A., Editor. *Social Work Research.* Chicago: The University of Chicago Press, 1960. vii + 306 p. (Fourteen papers constituting a manual of research methods for social workers.)

POLLAK, Otto, and Others. *Social Science and Psychotherapy for Children.* New York: Russell Sage Foundation, 1952. 242 p.

PORTER, E. H., Jr. *An Introduction to Therapeutic Counseling.* Boston: Houghton Mifflin Co., 1950. xi + 223 p. (Extracts from cases serve as a test for counselors.)

POWDERMAKER, Florence B., and FRANK, Jerome D. *Group Psychotherapy:* Studies in Methodology of Research and Therapy. Cambridge: Harvard University Press, 1953. xv + 615 p. (Report of a group psychotherapy research project of the U. S. Veterans Administration.)

QUEEN, Stuart A., and ADAMS, John B. *The Family in Various Cultures:* A Survey of Eleven Family Systems in Eleven Cultural and Historical Settings throughout the World. Philadelphia: J. B. Lippincott Co., 1952. vii + 280 p.

RABIN, A. I., and HAWORTH, Mary R., Editors. *Projective Techniques With Children.* New York: Grune and Stratton, 1960. xiv + 392 p.

RAIMY, Victor C., Editor. *Training in Clinical Psychology.* New York: Prentice-Hall, 1950. xix + 253 p.

RAPOPORT, R. N., and Others. *Community as a Doctor:* New Perspectives on a Therapeutic Community. Springfield, Ill.: Charles C Thomas, 1961. x + 325 p.

RASEY, Marie I. *It Takes Time:* An Autobiography of the Teaching Profession. New York: Harper & Brothers, 1953. x + 204 p. (Case history of an evolving philosophy and psychology of teaching.)

ROE, Anne. *A Psychological Study of Eminent Biologists.* Washington: American Psychological Association, 1951. iii + 68 p. (Reports data from the life histories and from three psychological tests of twenty eminent research biologists.)

ROGERS, Carl R. *On Becoming a Person:* A Therapist's View of Psychotherapy. Boston: Houghton Mifflin Co., 1961. xii + 420 p.

ROGERS, Carl R. *Client-Centered Therapy.* Boston: Houghton Mifflin Co., 1951. xii + 560 p.

ROGERS, Carl R., and DYMOND, Rosalind F., Editors. *Psychotherapy and Personality Change.* Co-ordinated Research Studies in the Client-Centered Approach. Chicago: The University of Chicago Press, 1954. x + 446 p.

RONKEN, Harriet O., and LAWRENCE, Paul R. *Administering Changes:* A Case Study of Human Relations in a Factory. Boston: Harvard University, 1952. xvii + 324 p.

ROSEN, Elizabeth. *Dance in Psychotherapy.* New York: Bureau of Publications, Teachers College, Columbia University, 1957. xx + 178 p.

ROSS, A. O. *The Practice of Clinical Child Psychology.* New York: Grune and Stratton, 1959. x + 275 p.

ROSS, G. Robert, and FEDER, Daniel D. "Psychological Services—College and

University," *Encyclopedia of Educational Research.* Edited by Chester W. Harris. Third Edition. New York: The Macmillan Co., 1960. p. 1063-66.

Ross, M. G. *Case Histories in Community Organization.* New York: Harper & Brothers, 1958. ix + 259 p.

Rubinstein, Eli A., and Lorr, Maurice, Editors. *Survey of Clinical Practice in Psychology.* New York: International Universities Press, 1954. xvii + 363 p.

Ruesch, Jurgen. *Therapeutic Communication.* New York: W. W. Norton, 1961. xv + 480 p.

Sarason, Seymour B. *The Clinical Interaction.* New York: Harper & Brothers, 1954. x + 425 p.

Sargent, Cyril G., and Belisle, Eugene L. *Educational Administration:* Cases and Concepts. Boston: Houghton Mifflin Co., 1955. xiii + 474 p.

Sayles, Leonard R. *Behavior of Industrial Work Groups:* Prediction and Control. New York: John Wiley & Sons, 1958. viii + 182 p. (A theory of work groups based on case studies of three hundred groups in thirty factories.)

Schary, Dore. *Case History of a Movie.* New York: Random House, 1950. xix + 242 p.

Scott, Andrew M., and Wallace, Earle. *Politics, U.S.A.:* Cases on the American Democratic Process. New York: The Macmillan Co., 1961. xii + 571 p. (A book of readings for use in courses on government.)

Seagle, William. *Acquitted of Murder.* Chicago: Henry Regnery Co., 1958. 257 p. (Case studies of criminals, attempting to demonstrate that there are too many loopholes in the criminal law.)

Sechrest, Carolyn A. *New Dimensions in Counseling Students:* A Case Approach. New York: Bureau of Publications, Teachers College, Columbia University, 1958. viii + 119 p.

Seeley, John R., and Others. *Community Chest:* A Case Study in Philanthropy. Toronto: University of Toronto Press, 1957. 593 p.

Seward, Georgene. *Psychotherapy and Culture Conflict.* With Case Studies by Judd Marmor. New York: Ronald Press, 1956. ix + 299 p.

Seward, Georgene, Editor. *Clinical Studies in Culture Conflict.* New York: Ronald Press, 1958. 587 p.

Shaffer, G. Wilson, and Lazarus, Richard S. *Fundamental Concepts in Clinical Psychology.* New York: McGraw-Hill Book Co., 1952. 540 p.

Shaffer, L. F., and Shoben, E. J., Jr. *The Psychology of Adjustment.* Second Edition. Boston: Houghton Mifflin Co., 1956. xxi + 672 p.

Shostrom, Everett L. *Therapeutic Psychology:* Fundamentals of Counseling and Psychotherapy. Englewood Cliffs, N.J.: Prentice-Hall, 1960. 447 p.

Sills, David L. *The Volunteers—Means and Ends in a National Organization.* Glencoe, Ill.: Free Press, 1958. xx + 320 p. (Case study of the National Foundation for Infantile Paralysis.)

Slavson, S. R. *Analytic Group Psychotherapy with Children, Adolescents, and Adults.* New York: Columbia University Press, 1950. ix + 275 p.

Slavson, S. R. *Child Psychotherapy.* New York: Columbia University Press, 1952. 332 p.

SLAVSON, S. R. *An Introduction to Group Therapy.* New York: International Universities Press, 1953. xvi + 352 p.

SLAVSON, S. R., Editor. *The Fields of Group Psychotherapy.* New York: International Universities Press, 1956. xiii + 338 p.

SLOTKIN, J. S. *The Peyote Religion:* A Study in Indian-White Relations. Glencoe, Ill.: Free Press, 1956. vii + 195 p. (Ethnohistorical case study using sociological approach.)

SNYDER, William U. *The Psychotherapy Relationship.* New York: The Macmillan Co., 1961. xiv + 418 p.

SORENSON, Roy, and DIMOCK, Hedley S. *Designing Education in Values:* A Case Study in Institutional Change. New York: Association Press, 1955. xiv + 365 p. (Change in San Francisco Y.M.C.A.)

SPAULDING, Frank E. *One School Administrator's Philosophy:* Its Development. New York: Exposition Press, 1952. 352 p.

SPICER, Edward H., Editor. *Human Problems in Technological Change:* A Casebook. New York: Russell Sage Foundation, 1952. 301 p.

SPOTNITZ, Hyman. *The Couch and the Circle:* A Story of Group Psychotherapy. New York: Alfred A. Knopf, 1961. xii + 274 p.

STACY, Chalmers L., and DeMARTINO, Manfred F., Editors. *Counseling and Psychotherapy with the Mentally Retarded:* A Book of Readings. Glencoe, Ill.: Free Press, 1957. 478 p.

STEIN, Harold, Editor. *Public Administration and Policy Development:* A Case Book. New York: Harcourt, Brace and Co., 1952. 860 p. (Applied to the area of public administration, including the executive branches of the federal, state, and local governments; for example, a case study of the Office of Education Library.)

STEIN, M. I., Editor. *Contemporary Psychotherapies.* New York: Free Press of Glencoe, 1961. x + 386 p.

STEWART, David A. *Preface to Empathy.* New York: Philosophical Library, 1956. 157 p.

STRANG, Ruth. *Group Work in Education.* New York: Harper & Brothers, 1958. x + 322 p.

STRUPP, H. H. *Psychotherapists in Action:* Explorations of the Therapist's Contribution to the Treatment Process. New York: Grune and Stratton, 1960. xiv + 338 p.

SULLIVAN, Harry S. *Clinical Studies in Psychiatry.* Edited by Helen S. Perry, Mary L. Gawel, and Martha Gibbon. New York: W. W. Norton and Co., 1956. 386 p.

SULLIVAN, Harry S. *The Psychiatric Interview.* New York: W. W. Norton and Co., 1954. 246 p.

SYMONDS, P. M. *Dynamics of Psychotherapy:* Principles. Vol. 1. New York: Grune and Stratton, 1956. 224 p.

SYMONDS, P. M. *Dynamics of Psychotherapy:* The Psychology of Personality Change. Vol. 2: Process. New York: Grune and Stratton, 1957. xlv + 175-398 p.

SYMONDS, P. M. *Dynamics of Psychotherapy:* The Psychology of Personality Change. Vol. 3: Procedures. New York: Grune and Stratton, 1958. xxxv + 399-607 (209) p.

TABA, Hilda, BRADY, Elizabeth H., and ROBINSON, John T. *Elementary Curriculum in Intergroup Relations:* Case Studies in Instruction. Washington: American Council on Education, 1950. xiii + 248 p.

TAFT, Jessie. *Otto Rank:* A Biographical Study. New York: Julian Press, 1958. xix + 299 p.

TALBERT, Robert H. *Cowtown—Metropolis:* Case Study of a City's Growth and Structure. Fort Worth: Texas Christian University, 1956. xvii + 274 p.

TATE, H. Clay. *Building a Better Home Town:* A Program of Community Self-Analysis and Self-Help. New York: Harper & Brothers, 1954. xvi + 236 p.

TATUM, Edward L. "A Case History in Biological Research." *Science* 129: 1711-15; June 26, 1959. (Chance and the exchange of ideas played roles in the discovery that genes control biochemical events.)

TROW, William C. "Group Processes," *Encyclopedia of Educational Research.* Edited by Chester W. Harris. Third Edition. New York: The Macmillan Co., 1960. p. 602-11.

TRUMAN, David B. *The Congressional Party:* A Case Study. New York: John Wiley & Sons, 1959. xii + 336 p. (Study of party structure in the Eighty-First Congress, based on statistical analysis of roll-call votes.)

TUMIN, Melvin M. *Caste in a Peasant Society:* A Case Study in the Dynamics of Caste. Princeton: Princeton University Press, 1952. 300 p.

VIRTUE, Maxine B. *Family Cases in Court:* A Group of Four Court Studies Dealing with Judicial Administration. Durham, N.C.: Duke University Press, 1956. xxxvii + 291 p.

WALKER, Charles R. *Steeltown:* An Industrial Case History of the Conflict between Progress and Security. New York: Harper & Brothers, 1950. xv + 284 p. (Case study of an industrial town, with relation to a decision of the steel company to abandon the town and the plant; one of a series of studies on decision-making.)

WALKER, Charles R. *Toward the Automatic Factory:* A Case Study of Men and Machines. New Haven: Yale University Press, 1957. xxii + 232 p.

WALLEN, Richard W. *Clinical Psychology:* The Study of Persons. New York: McGraw-Hill Book Co., 1956. 400 p.

WARREN, James V. *Methods in Medical Research.* Volume 7. Chicago: Educational Year Book, 1958. 250 p.

WARTERS, Jane. *Techniques of Counseling.* New York: McGraw-Hill Book Co., 1954. viii + 384 p. (A number of chapters on observational, descriptive-survey, and case techniques.)

WATKINS, J. G. *General Psychotherapy:* An Outline and Study Guide. Springfield, Ill.: Charles C Thomas, 1960. xviii + 255 p.

WATSON, Robert I. "Child Guidance Clinics," *Encyclopedia of Educational Research.* Edited by Chester W. Harris. Third Edition. New York: The Macmillan Co., 1960. p. 192-94.

WATSON, Robert I. *The Clinical Method in Psychology.* New York: Harper & Brothers, 1951. xii + 779 p.

WEINBERG, Henry, and HIRE, A. W. *Casebook in Abnormal Psychology.* New York: Alfred A. Knopf, 1956. 320 p.

WELLEMEYER, J. F., Jr., Editor. *Compensation on the Campus:* Case Studies of College and University Faculty Compensation Practices. Washington: National Education Association, 1961. viii + 528 p. (Case studies from fourteen campuses.)

WHITAKER, Carl A., and MALONE, Thomas P. *The Roots of Psychotherapy.* Philadelphia: Blakiston Co., 1953. xvii + 236 p.

WHITE, Mary A., and HARRIS, M. W. *The School Psychologist.* New York: Harper & Brothers, 1961. x + 431 p.

WHITE, Robert W. *The Abnormal Personality.* Second Edition. New York: Ronald Press, 1956. 644 p. (Illustrated by case histories.)

WHITE, Robert W. *Lives in Progress:* A Study of the Natural Growth of Personality. New York: Dryden Press, 1952. 376 p. (Presents, interprets, and compares the lives, case studies, of three normal people.)

WILLIAMS, Edgar G., and MEE, John G. *Cases and Problems in Personnel and Industrial Relations.* New York: Ronald Press, 1955. 204 p.

WILMER, Harry. *Social Psychiatry in Action:* A Therapeutic Community. Springfield, Ill.: Charles C Thomas, 1958. xxiii + 373 p. (Account of an experimental psychiatric ward in a naval hospital and a therapy program based on the programs of Maxwell Jones and T. P. Rees.)

WINTER, Edward H. *Beyond the Mountains of the Moon:* The Lives of Four Africans. Urbana: University of Illinois Press, 1959. xii + 276 p. (The lives of four members of the Amba tribe in Uganda as recorded, verbatim, by the author, including his general conclusions.)

WOLBERG, L. R. *Technique of Psychotherapy.* New York: Grune and Stratton, 1954. xiv + 869 p.

WOLFF, Werner, Editor. *Projective and Expressive Methods of Personality Investigation.* New York: Grune and Stratton, 1950. 76 p.

WOLFF, Werner. *Success in Psychotherapy.* New York: Grune and Stratton, 1952. 196 p.

WOOLF, Maurice D., and WOOLF, Jeanne A. *Remedial Reading:* Teaching and Treatment. New York: McGraw-Hill Book Co., 1957. viii + 424 p. (Includes case reports.)

WRENN, C. Gilbert, and PARKER, Clyde A. "Counseling Theory,"*Encyclopedia of Educational Research.* Edited by Chester W. Harris. Third Edition. New York: The Macmillan Co., 1960. p. 341-48.

YARMOLINSKY, Adam, Compiler. *Case Studies in Personnel Security.* Washington: Bureau of National Affairs, 1955. ix + 310 p.

YOUNG, Pauline V. *Scientific Social Surveys and Research.* Third Edition. Englewood Cliffs, N.J.: Prentice-Hall, 1956. Chapters 10, 15-18.

YOUNG, Pauline V. *Social Treatment in Probation and Delinquency:* Treatise and Casebook for Court Workers, Probation Officers, and Other Child Welfare Workers. Second Edition. New York: McGraw-Hill Book Co., 1952. xxvi + 536 p.

ZALEZNIK, Abraham. *Worker Satisfaction and Development:* A Case Study of Work and Social Behavior in a Factory Group. Boston: Harvard University Graduate School of Business Administration, 1956. xv + 148 p.

CHAPTER EIGHT

Experimental and Quasi-Experimental Designs

This chapter on experimentation includes the topics of independent and dependent variables, control of variables, validity of experimental designs, pre-experimental designs, true experimental designs, quasi-experimental designs, other special classifications of experimental designs, inference and generalization, training for experimentation, appropriate standards and problems for experimental investigation, role of the teacher in classroom experimentation, ethics, relations of experimentation to other research techniques, and instrumentation.

Since the typical reader of this book is a graduate student in his first year or two of study following the bachelor's degree, with only limited training in statistics, measurement, and quantitative methods, this chapter is a descriptive account of controlled experimentation. The statistical and mathematical details of experimental design are treated fully in the references listed in the chapter bibliography. Such concepts are commonly presented in a second-level statistics course. In presenting the several types of experimental design, the limitations of older methods of experimentation (one group, parallel group, and rotation group) and of exhaustive person-for-person matching or pairing have been recognized, these techniques having given way to the newer methods of statistics and experimental design.

VARIABLES IN CONTROLLED EXPERIMENTATION

Independent and Dependent Variables

Experimentation differs from descriptive-survey methods and from other techniques of investigation, in that the experimenter has some degree of control over the variables involved and the conditions under which the variables are observed. The relationship between socioeconomic status and opinion on some issue can be determined by a survey investigation through appropriate observation (questionnaire, interview, or some other appropriate data-gathering instrument). In this instance the two variables, socioeconomic status and opinion, are fixed, and the investigator has no control over the variables; he does not manipulate or change either socioeconomic status or opinion.[1]

In experimentation the investigator controls (manipulates or changes) certain independent variables and observes the changes that take place in the form of dependent variables. The investigator may wish to note the effect of a film strip or a lecture (an independent variable) on the performance of the subjects, as measured by an appropriate test (a dependent variable). To cite other examples of the simplest form of experimentation, involving an independent variable and at least one dependent variable, a blow (independent or experimental variable) delivered to the patellar tendon of the bended knee causes the leg to straighten (dependent variable or result). An independent or experimental variable (a loud noise producing the condition of being startled) may result in an increase in arterial pulse rate, perspiration, and an increased diameter of the pupils of the subject's eyes (dependent variables or results).[2]

In a well-known experiment,[3] Dr. Jonas Salk tested polio vaccine in 1954, first on animals and then on human beings. It was a large-scale experiment, including children from every part of the United States, especially from areas where there was a high incidence of polio. Three injections of vaccine were given to 440,000 school children, placebo or "dummy" shots were given to 210,000 youngsters as a control group, and no injections at all to approximately 1,180,000 children as a second control group. To achieve maximum similarity of conditions for the experimental and control groups, each bottle of injection material was made to appear exactly alike, with identification by a code number which was known only to the scientists who planned the experiment but not to the doctors who injected the vaccine. Many experts in statistics and experimental design aided in planning the experiment and analyzing the results, including information on age, sex, the area in which the child lived, the kind of health and educational facilities available, and other related data.

Many hundreds and even thousands of other examples of experiments may be found in the references of the chapter bibliography, the *En-*

[1] Allen L. Edwards, "Experiments: Their Planning and Execution," *Handbook of Social Psychology:* Theory and Method. Vol. 1. Edited by Gardner Lindzey. Cambridge, Mass.: Addison-Wesley Publishing Co., 1954. p. 260–61.

[2] John C. Townsend, *Introduction to Experimental Method:* For Psychology and the Social Sciences. New York: McGraw-Hill Book Co., 1953. p. 52–57.

[3] Philip Goldstein, *How to Do an Experiment.* New York: Harcourt, Brace and Co., 1957. p. 44–46.

cyclopedia of Educational Research, Review of Educational Research, Psychological Abstracts, and *Annual Review of Psychology.*

Control of Variables

In experimentation the investigator seeks to control variables for three purposes: to isolate the determiners of activity or behavior individually and in combinations; to vary them as magnitudes either singly or in combinations; and to describe quantitatively the extent of their expression and their interacting effects, again, either as single determiners or as combinations of determiners.[4]

Single-Variable Experimentation. The simple and narrow concept of the "rule of the single variable" was formulated at a time in the earlier period of experimentation when it was believed that all variables (independent) must be held constant except one, with a "one-to-one" correspondence between a particular cause and a specific effect, as when one end of a lever is pushed down, the other end goes up (a predictable amount). Today many specialists in statistics and experimental design regard such a theory of causation as narrow and mechanical, and as characteristic of past investigations in physical science, since the efficient statistical methods and experimental designs now available make it possible to handle several independent variables in the same design and to have as many dependent variables as may seem necessary:

. . . The seventeenth, eighteenth, and nineteenth centuries formed the period in which physical science learned how to analyze two-variable problems. Thus during that three hundred years, science developed the experimental and analytical techniques for handling problems in which one quantity say, a gas pressure—depends primarily upon a second quantity—say, the volume of the gas. . . . These two-variable problems are essentially simple in structure, and precisely for the reason that the theories or the experiments related to them need deal with only two quantities, changes in one of which cause changes in the other.[5]

Multivariate Experimentation. While this simple type of experimental design contributed to progress in the earlier stages of physical science, scientists more recently have gone beyond the simple two-variable problems to attack problems involving a large number of factors, resulting in

[4] Clarence W. Brown and Edwin E. Ghiselli, *Scientific Method in Psychology.* New York: McGraw-Hill Book Co., 1955. p. 76.

[5] Quoted from Warren Weaver, Editor, *The Scientists Speak.* New York: Boni and Gaer, 1947. p. 1, 2.

Warren Weaver, "A Quarter Century in the Natural Sciences," in *The President's Review, Rockefeller Foundation Annual Report, 1958.* New York: The Foundation, 1958. p. 7–122.

statements of probability. Certain complex problems of the human and behavioral sciences do not lend themselves to either the ordinary experiment or the probability approach, and await solution through some appropriate combination of statistical and experimental methods.

To cite an illustration, experiments may be multivariate in either or both of two senses:[6]

More than one "independent" variable (sex, school grade, method of teaching arithmetic, style of printing type, size of printing type, etc.) may be incorporated into the design and/or more than one "dependent" variable (number of errors, speed, number right, various tests, etc.) may be employed.

Control in the Social and Behavioral Sciences. The characteristics of the social object and the social context of the experimenter are sufficiently different from experimentation in the physical sciences to warrant special consideration. There are differences between physical data and social data which must be considered before the experimental method is carried over bodily from physical science to social science. The social scientist encounters difficulties in holding extraneous influences constant, and is seldom in a position to remove these influences physically, although society sometimes creates situations in which such extraneous influences are physically held constant. In taking over the experimental method from the older sciences, the social scientist is compelled to examine it in terms of problems and assumptions in relation to the specific social problem for investigation.[7]

The personality and expectation of the experimenter are a source of bias in experimental work. Studies in experimenter bias have shown that experimenters are able to obtain from their human or animal subjects the data that the experimenters want, need, or expect to get. Therefore, we are challenged to learn more about the social psychology of the experimental situation and its focal unit, the experimenter-subject relationship. To cite a specific example, certain "interpersonal" relationships or effects have been present in research on conditioning in animals. For the human experimental subject, the artificiality of the experimental setting and the student's knowledge that he is participating in an experiment may generate a higher-order problem-solving task in which the procedures and experimental treatment are reacted to not only for their simple stimulus values, but also for clues in discovering the investigator's intent, with possible development of attitudes of play-acting, outguessing,

[6] Quoted from Donald T. Campbell and Julian C. Stanley, "Experimental and Quasi-Experimental Designs for Research on Teaching," *Handbook of Research on Teaching.* Edited by N. L. Gage. Chicago: Rand McNally, 1963. Chapter 5.

[7] Arnold M. Rose, "Conditions of the Social Science Experiment," *Theory and Method in the Social Sciences.* Minneapolis: University of Minnesota Press, 1954. p. 273–81.

or up-for-inspection (attitudes unrepresentative of the normal school setting).[8]

We should not overemphasize the familiar complaint, however, that the kind of control possible in the laboratory is impossible in the world at large. Human behavior is controlled in a number of ways. The genetic constitution of the individual and his personal history to date play a part in the determination of behavior, as does the social environment, which is man-made. There are many instances outside the laboratory in which independent variables may be freely manipulated with respect to human behavior; for example, the nursery, certain types of schools, and corrective and penal institutions, where the degree of control may be great, although there are certain legal and ethical restrictions. In such situations as education, industry, law, public affairs, and government the control is not so likely to be lodged in a single person or agency. Sometimes this control has been managed in such a way as to bring sorrow to the individual and to society.[9]

Factors Requiring Control. Among the factors, variables, or determiners of behavior requiring control in psychological and educational investigations are the following:[10]

Schooling: academic incentives, level of success in different areas of subjects, amount of training in different areas, curriculum likes and dislikes, speed and accuracy of work in different fields or subjects

Skills: sports, hobbies, musical instruments, mechanical; physical handicaps

Maturity: chronological, physiological, psychological, developmental experience in special areas

Culture: foreign language and ideologies, American, regional

Social activities and experiences: likes and dislikes, participation in activities (social, sports, hobbies)

Physiological factors: physiological development, emotional development, general physical well-being, specific physical impairments, susceptibility to particular diseases, level of energy output.

Control Through Physical Manipulation. In certain types of experimentation, particularly in psychology, control of variables may be effected through some form of physical manipulation:[11]

[8] Robert Rosenthal and Others, "Subjects' Perception of Their Experimenter under Conditions of Experimenter Bias," *Perceptual and Motor Skills.* Missoula, Montana: Southern Universities Press, 1960. p. 325–31.

[9] B. F. Skinner, *Cumulative Record.* New York: Appleton-Century-Crofts, 1959. p. 223–57.

[10] Clarence W. Brown and Edwin E. Ghiselli, *op. cit.,* p. 80–82.

[11] *Ibid.,* p. 82–83.

John C. Townsend, *op. cit.,* p. 64–67.

Mechanical means: insulating material for sound-proofing a room, a light-proof room, or a tachistoscope for exposing perceptual stimuli

Electrical means: generation of sounds for experiments in hearing, screening out a distracting noise, or use of telechron and other constant speed motors for driving apparatus, controlling relays, and measuring time intervals

Surgical means: surgical removal of glands, such as the thyroid or the adrenals

Pharmacological means: drugs, change of diet, or feeding of gland extracts, as illustrated by use of dilantin in the treatment of epilepsy.

Control Through Selection. Control of variables through selection enables the experimenter to achieve results not possible through the method of physical manipulation of the determining variables:[12]

Selection of materials: for example, in studying the relation between the amount of material to be learned and the time required for learning, to provide (select) a sufficiently large number of units of material which are comparable in terms of the ease of learning. Any difference in the difficulty of the material would introduce a spurious factor which might affect the speed of learning.

Selection of subjects: to consider such factors as experience, age, ability, interest, attitude.

Selection of data: as illustrated by such primary sources as the records of public institutions, collections of vital statistics, government census reports, and certain types of records for institutions where the behavior of the subjects could not be subjected to experimental control (as in a reform school or a state prison).

Control over Intraprocedural Factors. In psychological and educational experimentation, determinant variable factors (intraprocedural factors) sometimes are present within the experimental procedures themselves. Certain techniqus of control over potentially disturbing intraprocedural factors, with examples of physical-response factors, are as follows:[13]

1. Equal exposure of the subject to the experimental conditions: equal time to work; or time required to complete the task and the nature and number of errors committed

2. Minimizing the contribution of the spatial arrangement of procedural factors: spatial relation of the apparatus to the subject, or the direction of the adjustive movement (right-left or left-right)

3. Minimizing the contribution of temporal factors within an experimental sitting: time intervals between trials in most conditioning experiments of a few seconds, and time intervals of a number of hours in some maze experiments

[12] Clarence W. Brown and Edwin E. Ghiselli, *op. cit.,* p. 84–85.
[13] *Ibid.,* p. 280–86.

4. Minimizing the contribution of factors arising from the order of the experimental conditions: counterbalancing of the temporal order of conditions in experiments in memory and in work involving carrying forward practice or fatigue effects from one gradation or condition to another

5. Counterbalancing of the order of experimental conditions through their random assignment to subjects: similar to counterbalancing experimental conditions in time.

The importance of randomization may be illustrated simply. If the problem is to divide 30 pupils in a class into a control group of 15 and an experimental group of the same size, with 5 seats to a row, the experimenter might consider taking all pupils in the first three rows for one group and all pupils in the last three rows for the other group. However, if girls commonly sit near the front of the room and boys near the rear, possible sex interests and achievements in arithmetic might bias the experiment from the beginning.

Another procedure would be to place the 30 names in a hat or bowl, each on a separate slip, shuffle them thoroughly, and then draw out 15 names. Another less desirable plan is to alphabetize the 30 names, and place the odd-numbered pupils in one group and the even-numbered persons in the other group. The best method is to number the pupils from 1 through 30 (or from 0 through 29) and draw 15 numbers within this range from a table of random numbers.[14]

DEVELOPMENT AND VALIDITY OF EXPERIMENTAL DESIGNS

Historical Development of Experimental Designs

Helen Walker summarizes concisely the development of the literature of experimental design during a third of a century:[15]

From Thorndike on, many individual research workers were vividly aware of the danger of bias and took great precautions to keep extraneous factors from influencing the outcome of their work, but many others were not so careful. McCall's *How to Experiment in Education,* published in 1923, was probably the first book dealing explicitly with this important matter and apparently had a tonic effect upon educational research. Before the first issue of the *Review* at least 15 books on research methods in education appeared, most of them showing McCall's influence.[16]

[14] Julian C. Stanley, "Controlled Experimentation in the Classroom." *Journal of Experimental Education* 25: 195–201; March 1957.

[15] Quoted from Helen M. Walker, "Methods of Research," in "Twenty-five Years of Educational Research." *Review of Educational Research* 26: 323–43; June 1956.

[16] W. A. McCall, *How to Experiment in Education.* New York: The Macmillan Co., 1923. 282 p.

Fisher's *Design of Experiments,* 1935, introduced novel ideas and patterns which made use of the technic of analysis of variance.[17] To the statistician, design means primarily the decision as to what subjects shall be employed, how many, and how distributed over the categories with which a study is concerned. Fisher showed how the design must control the analysis, and startled his readers by the statement, now generally accepted, that an "unfortunate consequence only ensues when a method of diminishing the real errors is adopted, unaccompanied by their elimination in the statistical analysis." This was a blow to research workers who had spent long hours in matching subjects but had not taken account of that matching in their statistical treatment of the data.

The first paper on research designs in the *Review,* by C. C. Peters,[18] appeared in December 1945. A very considerable development took place in the next three years, so that in the 1948 issue Lev was able to discuss randomized blocks, Latin squares, factorial designs, and split-plot designs and to quote 51 studies applying such designs to educational research.[19] In December 1951, a chapter of 15 pages by Norton and Lindquist had as its chief purpose "to draw attention to some of the more serious or more frequently recurring errors that are currently being made in experimental design and analysis in educational research," and commented that "on the whole, the authors have been none too favorably impressed with the general quality of contemporary educational research so far as experimental design and analysis are concerned."[20] In December 1954, there was a separate chapter by Kogan on applications of variance-covariance designs.[21]

The era of exhaustive person-to-person matching appears now to be over. The newer statistical methods at the same time facilitate more efficient use of data, make possible greater economy in design, and require that the statistician shall have a part in the initial planning of a study before the data are gathered.

Stanley's concise summary of the literature on experimental design, appearing during the middle 1950's, supplements Walker's review, indicates the complexity of the concepts, and emphasizes the extensive training needed to understand the rudiments of experimental design:

Many of the contributions to experimental design during the past three years should be incorporated rapidly into statistics textbooks designed for students in education and psychology. Authors of such books need the ability and willingness to translate into simpler but still accurate form relevant mate-

[17] R. A. Fisher, *The Design of Experiments.* Sixth Edition. New York: Hafner Publishing Corp., 1951. xv + 244 p.

[18] C. C. Peters and Others, "Research Methods and Designs." *Review of Educational Research* 15: 377-93; December 1945.

[19] Joseph Lev, "Research Methods and Designs." *Review of Educational Research* 18: 410-23; December 1948.

[20] Dee W. Norton and Everet F. Lindquist, "Applications of Experimental Design and Analysis." *Review of Educational Research* 21: 350-67; December 1951.

[21] Leonard S. Kogan, "Applications of Variance-Covariance Designs in Educational Research," in "Statistical Methodology in Educational Research." *Review of Educational Research* 24: 439-47; December 1954.

rial published by mathematical statisticians. Then by studying for at least a year, and preferably longer, under a well-qualified instructor, graduate students may come to understand the rudiments of experimental design. To do less than this and still hope for properly designed experiments is asking for a miracle.[22]

Validity of Experimental Designs

Certain factors jeopardize the validity of various experimental designs. As background for consideration of these factors, it is fundamental to distinguish between *internal* validity and *external* validity.[23]

Internal validity is the basic minimum without which any experiment is uninterpretable: did in fact the experimental treatments make a difference in this specific experimental instance? *External validity* asks the question of *generalizability:* to what populations, settings, treatment variables, and measurement variables can this effect be generalized? Both types of criteria are obviously important, even though they are frequently at odds in that features increasing one may jeopardize the other. While *internal validity* is the *sine qua non,* and while the question of *external validity,* like the question of inductive inference, is never completely answerable, the selection of designs strong in both types of validity is obviously our ideal. This is particularly the case for research in teaching, in which generalization to applied settings of known character is the desideratum.

Internal Validity. As to internal validity, certain classes of extraneous variables, if not controlled in the experimental design, might produce effects confounded with the effect of the experimental stimulus.

History: During the time span between the two observations or measurements, many events have occurred in addition to the experimental variable or event. Although experimental isolation, through the employment of experimental settings in which all extraneous stimuli are eliminated, may be approximated in physical and biological research, such control is difficult or even impossible in social psychology and in other social sciences.

Maturation: Certain effects are systematic with the passage of time and not, like history, a function of the specific events involved. Between the two observations the subjects may have grown older, hungrier, or tireder, and these conditions may have produced the difference between the two observations or measurements, independently of the experimental

[22] Quoted from Julian C. Stanley, "Research Methods: Experimental Design," in "Methodology of Educational Research." *Review of Educational Research* 27: 449–59; December 1957.

Also see Raymond O. Collier, Jr., and Donald L. Meyer, "Research Methods: Experimental Design and Analysis," in "The Methodology of Educational Research." *Review of Educational Research* 30: 430-39; December 1960.

[23] Quoted from Donald T. Campbell and Julian C. Stanley, *op. cit.,* Chapter 5.

variable. While maturation is unlikely to be a source of change in the typical brief experiment in the psychology laboratory, it has been a real problem in research in child development, social psychology, and education.

Testing: The effect of testing itself may explain the difference between the two observations, apart from the effect of the experimental variable. In many instances persons taking a test for the second time make scores systematically different from individuals taking a test for the first time; for example, a second mean for intelligence tests may run as much as 5 I.Q. points higher than the first one. In general, any measurement procedure which makes the subject self-conscious or aware of the fact of the experiment may introduce an effect other than the experimental variable or event; for example, measurement of weight, introduced into a experimental design involving adult American women, probably would stimulate weight reduction (through the mere process of noting weight) apart from any experimental variable involving food or nutrition.

Instrumentation and instrument decay: This variable may be illustrated by the fatiguing of spring scales. In educational and social psychology, education, and other social fields, fatiguing is an especially acute problem when human beings are part of the measuring apparatus or procedure, as in the case of judges, observers, raters, or coders. The two observations may differ because the raters have become more experienced, more fatigued, better adapted, or informed about the purpose of the experiment. Conditions are especially crude when observers or interviewers or coders are different for the two observations.

Statistical regression: Shifts toward the mean may occur owing to random imperfections of the measuring instrument or random instability within the population, as reflected in the test-retest reliability. Regression operates where groups have been selected on the basis of their extreme scores. In general, regression operates like maturation, in that the effects increase systematically with the time interval between the two observations or measurements. Failure to control this factor results in especially serious mistakes of interpretation in remedial research.

Differential selection of respondents: Biases may result in differential selection of respondents for the comparison groups.

Experimental mortality: Differential loss of respondents from the comparison groups may be confounded with the effect of the experimental variable. Even though the groups may have been equivalent at some prior time, differences between the two observations may result because individuals have dropped out, as illustrated in studies seeking to compare the attitudes of college freshmen and college seniors.

External Validity. The factors jeopardizing external validity or representativeness are as follows:[24]

The *reactive* or *interaction effect* of *testing*, in which a pretest might increase or decrease the respondent's sensitivity or responsiveness to the experimental variable and thus make the results obtained for a pretested population unrepresentative of the effects of the experimental variable for the unpretested universe from which the experimental respondents were selected.

The *interaction* effects of *selection* biases and the *experimental variable.*

Reactive effects of experimental arrangements, which would preclude generalization about the effect of the experimental variable upon persons being exposed to it in nonexperimental settings.

Multiple-treatment interference, a problem wherever multiple treatments are applied to the same respondents, and a particular problem for one-group designs.

PRE-EXPERIMENTAL DESIGNS[25]

One-Shot Case Study

Much research in social science has relied upon the *"one-shot" case study,* in which a single individual or group is studied in detail only once, subsequent to some agent or treatment presumed to cause change, and in which the observations are attributed to exposure to some prior situation. This design does not merit the title of an experiment, since the minimum of useful scientific information involves at least one formal comparison and therefore at least two careful observations. Such studies would be much more valuable if the one set of observations were reduced by half, with the saved time and effort directed to investigation in equal detail of an appropriate comparison instance. In these "one-shot" case studies, "standardized" tests provide very limited help, since the numerous rival sources of difference other than the so-called experimental variable render the "standard-test" reference group almost useless as a "control group." On the same grounds, comparison of a present case study with potential future ones for experimental purposes would seem equally hopeless.

One-Group Pretest-Posttest Design

The *one-group pretest-posttest design* provides for one formal comparison of two observations and is still widely used. In this design, how-

[24] Quoted from Donald T. Campbell and Julian C. Stanley, *op. cit.,* Chapter 5.
[25] *Ibid.*

Donald T. Campbell, "Factors Relevant to the Validity of Experiments in Social Settings." *Psychological Bulletin* 54: 297–312; July 1957. This helpful analysis and the preceding reference are the basis for the review of pre-experimental, true experimental, and quasi-experimental designs on succeeding pages of this chapter.

ever, several confounded extraneous variables may be left uncontrolled so as to jeopardize internal validity and thus become rival explanations of any difference between the two observations or measurements, confounded with the possible effect of the experimental variable or event. These uncontrolled variables might include the effect of history, maturation, testing, instrumentation, and statistical regression, as described earlier in this chapter.

Static Group Comparison

Another pre-experimental design is the *static group comparison,* in which there is a comparison of a group which has experienced the experimental variable with a group which has not, for the purpose of establishing the effect of the variable or event. In this design, there is no means of certifying that the groups were equivalent at some prior time. The prevalence of this design in the social sciences and its weaknesses have been recognized. Any difference between the two observations might have come about through biased selection or recruitment of the persons making up the groups, or they might have differed without the effect of the experimental variable. Exposure to the experimental variable may have been voluntary, and therefore the two groups have an inevitable systematic difference on the factors determining the choice involved, a difference which no amount of matching can remove. Experimental mortality may have produced differences in the groups due to differential dropout of persons from the groups. Thus, two groups once identical may differ later because of selective dropout of subjects, as in seeking to determine the effects of a college education by comparing measures on freshmen (without the experimental variable) with seniors (who have encountered the experimental variable). If such a study should conclude that first-year women are more beautiful than seniors, we would inquire concerning the chances for a beautiful girl to finish college before marriage and recommend an experimental design in which the *same* girls are compared as freshmen and as seniors. Other examples of this type of comparison include: school systems requiring the bachelor's degree of teachers versus those not requiring it, students in classes given speed-reading training versus those not receiving it, and persons hearing a particular TV program versus those not hearing it.

TRUE EXPERIMENTAL DESIGNS[26]

Pretest-Posttest Control Group Design

The difficulties of confounded extraneous variables in the pre-experimental designs led psychologists during the first quarter of the

[26] Donald T. Campbell, *op. cit.*
Donald T. Campbell and Julian C. Stanley, *op. cit.*, Chapter 5.

twentieth century to search for true experimental designs. The *pretest-posttest control group design* (the most widely used) was formed by adding a control group to the one-group pretest-posttest design. This experimental design seeks to control the main effects of history, maturation, testing, instrument decay, regression, selection, and mortality. If the differences between the two observations for the experimental group are due to intervening historical events, then they should also show up in the results for the control group, although there may be certain complications in achieving control. If the respondents operate as groups, with only one experimental session and one control session, then there is no control over the unique internal histories of the groups, possibly involving a chance distracting factor appearing in one or the other group. If only one experimenter is involved, he ordinarily cannot make a simultaneous initial observation or measurement for the two groups and likewise cannot make a second or end measurement of the two groups at the same time. If two experimenters are available, one working with the experimental respondents, and the other with the control subjects, differences between the two experimenters probably introduce extraneous variable factors. Therefore, for a true experiment, the experimental and control groups should be tested and exposed individually or in small subgroups, with sessions of both types temporally and spatially intermixed.

If maturation or testing contributes to a difference between the two observations, this should appear also in the results of the control group. To make sure the design controls for instrument decay, it is necessary to use the same experimenter or a small-session approximation to the simultaneity needed for controlling historical events. Therefore the running of the experimental group and the control group at different times is ruled out; otherwise the observers may have become more experienced, more hurried, more careless, or the equipment or apparatus changed in some respect. When more than one experimenter or observer is used, counterbalancing the experimenter, time, and group is desirable, with the balanced Latin square frequently serving a useful purpose.

Although regression is controlled in the design as a whole, secondary analyses of effects may be made for extreme pretest scores in both experimental and control groups.

Selection is handled by the sampling equivalence insured through the randomization employed in assigning persons to groups, supplemented by matching procedures, with the initial observations of the experimental and control groups serving as a check on possible sampling differences.

With respect to experimental mortality, if the experimental and control groups do not differ in the number of lost cases or in their pretest scores, the experiment can be judged internally valid on this point. However, mortality reduces generalization of effects, as applied to the original population from which the groups were selected.

Although the pretest-posttest control group design was highly regarded in the social sciences for some thirty years, by 1940 serious criticism was voiced, in the form of an interaction effect of testing. The effects of history, maturation, and testing, in the language of analysis of variance, are main effects, manifesting themselves in mean differences independently of the presence of other variables, and capable of adding on to other effects, including the effect of the experimental variable. In contrast, interaction effect (a joint effect) may occur even when no main effects are present; for example, applied to the testing variable, the interaction effect might involve not a shift due solely or directly to the measurement process, but rather a sensitization of subjects to the experimental variable.

As a concrete example of interaction it is pertinent to cite the NORC study of a United Nations information campaign in Cincinnati, in which two equivalent samples of a thousand each were drawn from the city's population. After one of these samples was interviewed, Cincinnati was subjected to an intensive publicity campaign using the various mass media of communication, including special features in the newspapers and on the radio, bus cards, and public lectures. At the end of two months the second sample of 1,000 persons was interviewed and the results compared with the first 1,000. There were no differences between the two groups except that the second group was somewhat more pessimistic about the likelihood of Russia's co-operation for world peace, which could be attributed to history rather than to the publicity campaign in Cincinnati. As a result of the publicity campaign of two months, the second sample was no better informed than the first about the United Nations, nor had it been sensitive to the publicity campaign itself. The initial sample was reinterviewed, at the same time that the second sample was interviewed (after the publicity campaign), with the first group showing significant attitude changes, a high degree of awareness of the campaign, and important increases in information. The interaction effect was in the form of sensitizing the initial group (through the initial interview) to the topic of the United Nations, so as to make the subsequent publicity campaign effective for them.[27]

Four-Group Design

A *four-group design* has been suggested by Solomon to control the problem of interaction effects.[28] This design involves adding to the

[27] Shirley A. Star and Helen M. Hughes, "Report on an Educational Campaign: The Cincinnati Plan for the United Nations." *American Journal of Sociology* 55: 389–400; January 1950.

[28] Richard L. Solomon, "An Extension of Control Group Design." *Psychological Bulletin* 46: 137–50; March 1949.

traditional two-group experiment two groups that are not pretested. The design enables the experimenter to control and measure both the main and interaction effects of testing, and the main effects of a composite of maturation and history. These possibilities recommend the design highly to social scientists, with a deservedly higher prestige than the preceding design. It represents the first formal design consideration of external-validity factors.

Posttest-Only Control Group Design

The *posttest-only control group design* is disturbing to many investigators in education and psychology, because the concept of the pretest has become firmly fixed in the thinking of many such research workers, although the pretest is not actually essential to true experimental designs. For psychological reasons it is difficult to give up "knowing for sure" that the experimental and control groups were "equal" before the differential experimental treatment, whereas actually randomization without the pretest is the most adequate all-purpose assurance of lack of initial biases between groups. To cite an example, in research in the primary grades we frequently must experiment with methods for the initial introduction of entirely new subject matter, for which pretests in the ordinary sense do not exist and are impossible.

The *posttest-only control group design* is illustrated by Fisher's typical agricultural experiment,[29] which involves no pretest; equivalent plots of ground receive different experimental treatments, and the subsequent yields are measured. To cite an illustration in a social area, by way of testing the influence of a motion picture upon attitudes, two randomly assigned audiences would be selected, one exposed to the movie, and the attitudes of each audience measured subsequently for the first time. This design has been criticized as vulnerable to selection bias, especially where random assignment is not possible. Where naturally aggregated units such as classes are employed intact, these should be used in large numbers and assigned at random to the experimental and control conditions. If but one or two intact classrooms are available for each experimental treatment, the pretest-posttest control group design is preferable. Other advantages of the pretest-posttest control group design over the posttest-only control group design are in terms of greater precision, dealing with experimental mortality (through comparing pretest scores of lost cases in both experimental and control groups), and studying the relationship of pretest attitudes to kind and amount of change. For the posttest-only control group design, there are certain social settings in which it is feasible; for example, whenever the social contact

[29] R. A. Fisher, *op. cit.*

represented by the experimental variable is made to single individuals or to small groups, and where the response to that stimulus can be identified in terms of individuals or type of exposure to the experimental variable (as illustrated by direct mail and door-to-door contacts).

It is traditional in discussions of experimental design in psychology, education, and such social fields as sociology to think of exposure to the experimental variable as opposed to absence of the experimental variable. While this condition may be possible in the stimulus-isolated laboratory in the physical sciences, it is difficult to think of a setting in the social sciences as empty of potentially change-inducing stimuli. The experience of the control group, in social experimentation, may be described as another type of exposure to the experimental variable (a control experience) rather than complete absence of an experimental variable. Frequently, in the social areas, we are not so much interested in the qualitative fact of effect or no-effect as in the degree of effect for varying degrees of the experimental variable, which leads to designs in which multiple groups are used, each with a different degree of the experimental variable. When different degrees of the experimental variable are given to the same group, with different groups receiving the variable in different orders, the technique of counterbalancing is essential.

It is necessary to test for effects extended in time, since the longer-range effects of persuasive experimental variables may be qualitatively as well as quantitatively different from immediate effects. Experiments may be designed to measure the effect of the experimental variable at extended periods of time by adding two separate groups for each post-test period (including the additional control group). The additional control group is necessary; otherwise the effects of intervening history, maturation, instrument decay, regression, and mortality are confounded with the delayed effects of the experimental variable.

QUASI-EXPERIMENTAL DESIGNS[30]

The investigator may introduce into many natural social settings something like experimental design in scheduling the data-collecting procedures, even through he lacks the full control over scheduling of experimental stimuli that would make a true experiment possible. Such quasi-experimental designs in appropriate social settings may be encouraged, with full awareness of the specific variables not controlled in the particular design, even though there are serious risks by way of spurious confirmation of inadequate misdirection of subsequent research efforts and by

[30] Donald T. Campbell, op. cit.
Donald T. Campbell and Julian C. Stanley, op. cit., Chapter 5.

waste of publication space. It is a question of using the tools we have for these natural social settings until more efficient designs are developed.

Single-Group Experimental Designs

The *times-series design* involves the presence of a periodic measurement process on some group or individual and the introduction of an experimental change into this time series of measurements, the results of which are indicated by a discontinuity in the measurements recorded in the time-series.

The *equivalent time-samples design* is a form of the time-series experiment with the repeated introduction of the experimental variable, and is useful where the effect of the experimental variable is anticipated to be of transient or reversible character, as sometimes found in studies of learning, work production, conditioning, and physiological reaction.

The *equivalent-materials design* resembles the equivalent time-samples design, involving equivalence of samples of materials to which the experimental variables under comparison are applied; for example, massed versus distributed practice.

Multi-Group Experimental Designs

A common experimental design, the *nonequivalent control group design,* involves an experimental group and a control group both given a pretest and a posttest, but without pre-experimental sampling equivalence for the two groups. Examples are naturally assembled collectives such as classrooms, which are similar but yet require the pretest.

Counterbalanced designs (sometimes described by the terms "rotation," "crossover," or "switch-over") seek to achieve experimental control or precision by entering all respondents (or settings) into all treatments, with the Latin-square arrangement typically employed in counterbalancing.

The *separate-sample pretest-posttest design* may be used for large populations such as cities, factories, schools, and military units, where the investigator cannot randomly segregate subgroups for differential experimental treatment, but can exercise experimental control through random assignment procedures.

The *separate-sample pretest-posttest control group design* is possible when to the preceding design may be added a control group (comparable if not equivalent) from which the experimental variable can be withheld.

In the *multiple time-series design,* the investigator of major administrative change by use of time-series data may seek out a similar institution not undergoing the experimental variable, from which to collect a similar "control" time series (ideally with the experimental variable assigned randomly).

Other Quasi-Experimental Designs

The *recurrent institutional cycle design* is labeled as "patched-up," in that the investigator in field research may start with an inadequate design and then add specific features to control for one or another of the recurrent sources of invalidity, often resulting in an inelegant accumulation of precautionary checks and lacking the intrinsic symmetry of the true experimental designs.

Regression-discontinuity analysis is a design developed in a situation where ex post facto designs were previously being used. To cite a possible example, if a foundation interested in improving higher education makes a large grant to a college to study the impact of the school on its students, what are the results ten years later?

Ex post facto design refers to efforts to simulate experimentation through certain procedures, especially as developed in the field of sociology, and represents one of the most extended efforts toward quasi-experimental design, although subject to grave errors in both sociology and education. To cite examples of such studies: the effect of high-school education on success and community adjustment ten years later, and the effect of housing on juvenile delinquency (tracing the earlier records of families before they became residents of a public-housing project, in order to compare the incidence of juvenile delinquency).

Another quasi-experimental design involves *correlation;* for example, between heavy smoking and lung cancer.

Panel studies in their simplest survey form represent observations at a single point in time, commonly offering to the respondent the opportunity to classify himself as having been exposed to the experimental variable or not so exposed, typically with correlations between "seeing the program" and "buying the product."

OTHER CLASSIFICATIONS OF EXPERIMENTAL DESIGNS

The techniques of the recent statistical approaches and forms of experimental design are beyond the scope of an introductory, descriptive account of research methodology, but these methods may be illustrated further by a list of the significant chapter headings[31] of a comprehensive

[31] William G. Cochran and Gertrude M. Cox, *Experimental Designs.* Second Edition. New York: John Wiley & Sons, 1957. xiv + 611 p. Also see:

Walter T. Federer, *Experimental Design:* Theory and Application. New York: The Macmillan Co., 1955. xix + 544 + 47 p.

Oscar Kempthorne, *The Design and Analysis of Experiments.* New York: John Wiley & Sons, 1952. xix + 631 p.

E. F. Lindquist, *Design and Analysis of Experiments in Psychology and Education.* Boston: Houghton Mifflin Co., 1953. xix + 393 p.

book in this field. Study of such concepts usually is preceded by an introductory course in statistical method.

Completely Randomized, Randomized Block, and Latin Square Designs
Factorial Experiments
Confounding
Factorial Experiments in Fractional Replication
Factorial Experiments with Main Effects Confounded: Split-Plot Designs
Factorial Experiments Confounded in Quasi-Latin Squares
Methods for Study of Response Surfaces
Balanced and Partially Balanced Incomplete Block Designs
Lattice Designs
Incomplete Block Designs
Lattice Squares
Incomplete Latin Squares.

To cite another approach, by way of classification of 1,000 experiments in education, dating from 1909 to 1952, and in many instances
representing outmoded procedures, Shannon has identified seventeen
headings or types:[32]

Groups of subjects
　In single formation
　　　1. Treated once, not in series (or in series with the same act
　　　　 repeated and no changing factor involved), and perhaps
　　　　 with comparison with earlier practice or with the mode of
　　　　 practice
　　　2. Treated in series with a changing factor and with compari-
　　　　 son from stage to stage
　In parallel formation
　　　3. Equivalent, with a single variable
　　　4. Not known to be equivalent, with a single variable
　　　5. Known not to be equivalent, usually with no variable factor,
　　　　 to determine the degree of nonequivalence in performance
　In reversed formation
　　　6. Equivalent, with a single variable
　　　7. Not known to be equivalent, with a single variable
　　　8. Known not to be equivalent
Single subjects
　In single formation
　　　9. Treated once, not in series (or in series with the same act
　　　　 repeated and no changing factor involved), and perhaps

Benton J. Underwood, "Research Design," *Psychological Research.* New York:
Appleton-Century-Crofts, 1957. p. 85–173.

Benjamin Winer, *Statistical Principles in Experimental Designs.* New York:
McGraw-Hill Book Co., 1962. v + 672 p.

[32] J. R. Shannon, "Experiments in Education: A New Pattern and Frequency of
Types." *Journal of Educational Research* 48: 81–93; October 1954.

with comparison with earlier practice or with the mode of
practice
10. Treated in series with a changing factor and with comparison from stage to stage
In parallel formation
11. Equivalent, with a single variable
12. Not known to be equivalent, with a single variable
13. Known not to be equivalent, usually with no variable factor,
to determine the degree of nonequivalence in performance
In reversed formation
14. Equivalent, with a single variable
15. Not known to be equivalent
16. Known not to be equivalent
Materials and instruments
17. Materials, material facilities, or instruments relating to
schools or to formal instruction (inanimate objects or procedures rather than live subjects either as individuals or in
groups).

Shannon found that the majority of the experiments in education
have been in the area of teaching methods. The prevailing types of experimental procedure or technique have been parallel groups, with the groups
not known to be equivalent (but apparently presumed to be approximately so) or with the experimental factors so well controlled, according
to Shannon, that the groups were known to be equivalent in the significant
characteristics involved. The single-group type has been second in frequency of use in educational experimentation.

To summarize the essential characteristics of a good experimental
design:[33]

1. It will insure that the observed treatment effects are unbiased estimates
of the true effects. (The term *treatment* refers to any induced or selected variation in the experimental procedures or conditions whose effect is to be observed
and evaluated.)

2. It will permit a quantitative description of the precision of the observed
treatment effects regarded as estimates of the "true" effects.

3. It will insure that the observed treatment effects will have whatever
degree of precision is required by the broader purposes of the experiment.

4. It will make possible an objective test of a specific hypothesis concerning the true effects.

5. It will be efficient.

INFERENCE AND GENERALIZATION

Statisticians and experts in experimental design[34] frequently are asked
for advice about making inferences from the results of experiments,

[33] E. F. Lindquist, *op. cit.*, p. 1, 6–7.
[34] William G. Cochran and Gertrude M. Cox, *op. cit.*, p. 9–11.

sometimes after the investigation has been completed. Since the making of sound inferences depends on the way in which the experiment was carried out, the time to think about statistical inference and to seek advice is when the experiment is being planned. The statistician or expert in experimental design can make a valuable contribution beyond advice on some technical matter of statistical theory by getting the investigator to explain clearly why he is doing the experiment, to justify the experimental treatments whose effects he proposes to compare, and to defend his claim that the completed treatment will enable its objectives to be realized. The statement of objectives may assume the form of the questions to be answered, the hypotheses to be tested, or the effects to be estimated. (A general treatment of the formulation and testing of hypotheses has been presented in the chapter on the development of the problem.)

In experimentation, generalization beyond the specific group studied can be made only to other comparable groups; for example, if certain results are found when male college students are subjects, to what extent would this result hold true for female subjects, for high-school subjects, or for older subjects? If a specified amount of fertilizer applied to units of land in a section of Iowa results in greater production of corn than any other specified amount of fertilizer tested, to what extent could a generalization be made for land units in a different part of Iowa or in Nebraska? In this instance the varying amounts of fertilizer represent an independent variable, and the yield of corn a dependent variable. Soil differences may represent important independent variables in the sense that they are related to the results obtained from the applications of the different amounts of fertilizer; a particular amount of fertilizer may work well with certain kinds of land and have little or no effect when applied to other kinds.[35]

EVALUATION OF EDUCATIONAL EXPERIMENTATION

Obstacles to controlled experimentation in the field of education and in the classroom include three factors: the very limited training for experimentation offered in the field of education, as compared with prolonged exposure of doctoral candidates in psychology to experimental psychology, statistics, and measurement; the relatively small amount of experimentation done by professors of education; and the neutral or even negative attitude toward experimentation on the part of many school administrators and parents.

[35] Allen L. Edwards, *op. cit.*, p. 265.

Training for Experimentation

It is essential for the graduate student or investigator interested in controlled experimentation to have the necessary training in statistics (especially the analysis of variance) and research methods before attempting to design an experiment, and to work closely from the beginning with a competent specialist. One answer is to take courses in statistics and experimental design usually offered in the psychology departments of major universities and relatively less frequently in graduate departments of education. It is common for experts in experimental design in education and psychology to consult each other and the mathematical statisticians. Although the specialist in experimental design may not know the investigator's subject-matter field thoroughly, he can point out logical flaws and methodological imperfections that might nullify otherwise commendable efforts. A number of the book-length treatises in the chapter bibliography are used as texts in experimental-design courses in psychology and education.

A critical comment on controlled experimentation in the classroom points out that we have neglected this technique to our great detriment:

Most decisions about methods have been based upon colloquial, anecdotal, or administrative considerations rather than experimentation. Seldom are adequate control groups incorporated into classroom experiments. The necessity for long-range experimental design is not usually appreciated by teachers and administrators. The principle of randomness is often misunderstood or ignored in favor of elaborate matching, which has several disadvantages. Worst of all, few teachers, including those with doctoral degrees, get even minimal training for modern experimentation. Our professional literature is virtually devoid of well controlled experimental studies in the classroom. We continue to pool ignorance via conferences, questionnaires, rating scales, opinionnaires, and ineffective correlational studies, all of which are valuable for certain purposes, but not sufficient in themselves.[36]

Appropriate Standards and Problems for Experimental Study

A critical comment on the educational research of the second quarter of the present century, including experimentation, indicates the need for adequate standards of investigation and the overemphasis on purely local, trivial, or temporary problems. The suggestion is made that members of such groups as the American Educational Research Association can do much as individuals and as members of the organization to improve the quality and influence of educational research.

[36] Quoted from Julian C. Stanley, "Controlled Experimentation in the Classroom." *Journal of Experimental Education* 25: 195–201; March 1957.

The fetish of empiricism leads to elaborate and expensive attempts to demonstrate experimentally, at rather modest levels of confidence, hypotheses whose truth could be defended on rational grounds with much greater degrees of certainty. Is it necessary, for example, to demonstrate experimentally that a teacher who gives some time to individual instruction in a large class has more time available for individual instruction per pupil if the class becomes smaller? Is it even necessary to show experimentally that a teacher, unused to spending much time in individual instruction because of the pressure of large classes, will not automatically begin to do more individual instruction when the size of her class is reduced? The techniques used in educational research studies are frequently inadequate. Specific testable hypotheses are not identified before the experiment begins. There is too much tendency to seek global answers to complex questions such as, "Is teaching by television effective?" There is too easy yielding in the face of difficulties of adequate experimental control— too many woefully inadequate studies whose only defense is that this was the best that could be done under the circumstances. Because of the nature of the problems studied, and the techniques employed, the findings of many educational research studies are of temporary local value only, or contradictory and inconclusive.[37]

As indicated above, at times zeal for experimentation may become a fetish. There is a place for the exercise of good judgment in attempting to bring about social and educational improvements, without seeking an answer through controlled experimentation, as illustrated by Andrew Carnegie's establishment of libraries and Abraham Flexner's reform of medical education. To provide teachers with a better knowledge of their subject matter is a worthwhile activity, but to secure and analyze such evaluative data as can be gathered may prove more costly than the results justify. A pertinent example of a project that does not lend itself to experimental evaluation is the program of the American Association for the Advancement of Science and the National Science Foundation, which involves sending sets of books about science and scientists to more than 100 high schools, mainly to schools with meager library facilities of their own.

We can get records of how many times each book was withdrawn. We can get the judgments of teachers about the usefulness of the program. But the real purpose of the traveling libraries is to supplement the library and teaching resources of the schools and, we hope, to stimulate a few bright students and help them to decide whether or not they want to become scientists. Because we do not know any feasible method of finding out how successfully we accomplish this real purpose, we are not planning to make

[37] Quoted from Robert L. Ebel, "The Role of Educational Research." *AERA Newsletter* 9: 1–2; January 1958.

Also see J. G. Taylor, "Experimental Design: A Cloak for Intellectual Sterility." *British Journal of Psychology* 49: 106–16; May 1958. Maintains that there is a dearth of serious theorizing and an excess of trivial experimentation.

elaborate evaluative studies. The project seems well worth doing, but we shall have to rely on unverified judgments in deciding whether or not it is worth continuing.[38]

We must always remember, however, that experimentation is the only valid procedure for settling disputes concerning educational practice, for verifying educational improvements, and for establishing a tradition or setting in which improvements can be introduced without the danger of a "faddish discard of old wisdom in favor of inferior novelties." It is true that we need to avoid a recurrence of the pessimism concerning controlled experimentation, beginning in the latter part of the 1930's and following the overoptimism of the 1920's. We must increase our time-perspective to recognize that continuous, multiple experimentation is more typical of science than once-and-for-all definitive experiments; that experiments need replication and cross validation under other times and conditions; and that "crucial" experiments which pit opposing theories are not likely to have clearcut outcomes in the behavioral and social sciences.

The claims made for the rate and degree of progress which would result from experiment were grandiosely overoptimistic and were accompanied by an unjustified depreciation of nonexperimental wisdom. The initial advocates assumed that progress in teaching technology had been slow *just because* scientific method had not been applied; they assumed traditional practice was incompetent, just because it had not been produced by experimentation. When in fact experiments often proved to be tedious, equivocal, of undependable replicability, and confirming of pre-scientific wisdom, the overoptimistic grounds upon which experimentation had been justified were undercut, and a disillusioned rejection or neglect took place.

This disillusionment was shared by both observer and participant in experimentation. For the experimenters, a personal avoidance-conditioning to experimentation can be noted. For the usual highly-motivated researcher the nonconfirmation of a cherished hypothesis is actively painful. As a biological and psychological animal, the experimenter is subject to laws of learning which lead him inevitably to associate this pain with the contiguous stimuli and events. These stimuli are the experimental process itself, more vividly and directly than the "true" source of frustration, i.e., the inadequate theory, and may thus lead, perhaps unconsciously, to the avoidance or rejection of the experimental process. If, as seems likely, the ecology of our science is one in which there are many more available wrong responses than correct ones, we may anticipate that most experiments will be disappointing. We must somehow inoculate young experimenters against this effect, and in general must justify experimentation on more pessimistic grounds—not as a panacea, but rather as the only available route to cumulative progress. We must instill in our

[38] Quoted from Dael Wolfle, "The Fetish of Experiment." *Science* 125: 177; February 1, 1957. Reprinted from *Science* by permission.

students the expectation of tedium and disappointment and the duty of thorough persistence, by now so well achieved in the biological and physical sciences. We must expand our students' vow of poverty to include not only the willingness to accept poverty of finances, but also a poverty of experimental results.[39]

Classroom Experimentation and the Teacher

As a setting for experimentation the classroom is a complex human situation. The pupils in a classroom act not only as individuals, but together react as a social system. The school is a part of the political subdivision and of a community of educational institutions. The school itself is a system, of which the classroom is a part. Within the classroom many sources (sometimes unseen) are at work—a reference group to which each individual feels himself accountable, a pedagogical tradition that dictates subject matter and method, and a culture (societal needs, the peer culture, and the professional culture represented by the school and the teacher).[40]

Since experimentation is the most difficult and technically exacting research method for studying human and behavioral problems, if teachers do not understand the scientific spirit of inquiry and the requirements of controlled experimentation, they may make departures from the rules and design prescribed for the experiment. The teacher's values, attitudes, interests, motives, and sentiments may affect the procedure and results, since the natural inclination of the teacher is to try to "help" the pupils, the experiment, and investigator appear in the best possible light. Certainly it seems desirable for the classroom teacher to have a knowledge of the fundamentals of experimental methods and of illustrative investigations, but not to attempt formal experimental studies without the counsel of an appropriate expert in statistics and experimental design. Objective, impartial participation by teachers in appropriate experimentation should have a stimulating effect on both teachers and pupils and cultivate a spirit of exploration in the adventure of teaching (a personal value or by-product of the experiment).

Ethics

We must recognize that, as scientific inquiry pushes toward the limits of research on human behavior, some danger to the subjects and related legal and moral problems may be involved:

[39] Quoted from Donald T. Campbell and Julian C. Stanley, *op. cit.*, Chapter 5.
[40] Arthur W. Foshay and James A. Hall, *Research for Curriculum Improvement.* 1957 Yearbook. Washington: Association for Supervision and Curriculum Development, National Education Association, 1957. p. 8–11.

It is the nature of scientific inquiry to push towards the limits of the phenomena being studied, and the limits of research on human behavior will surely entail some danger to the subjects. As a current example, what kinds of performance can be expected of an astronaut in the super-solitary confinement of space? Under what circumstances will integrated, rational behavior break down? Such questions can be answered only by putting experimental subjects under real stress, and the subjects who volunteer to help find the answers, even under simulated and earth-bound conditions, are running some risk of personal damage. So are subjects in studies of other types of stress, fatigue, or the factors that induce abnormal mental states.

Most discussions of the legal and moral problems of the use of human subjects have been written from the medical point of view. Medicine has the most experience with human subjects, but in several respects the medical experience provides a quite inadequate guide. In testing a new medical or surgical technique on human patients it is customary to explain the nature of the technique, its possible dangers, and its possible beneficial results, and to secure the patient's consent before the new technique is tried. In psychological research, neither explanation nor consent can be so easily handled. Explanation of the nature or prospective results of a psychological experiment may vitiate the results. And if the experiment cannot be fully and honestly explained, to what has the subject consented? Or has he in fact consented at all?

There is another difference. A new medicine or operative technique is ordinarily tried out on ill patients who may themselves be directly benefited. In contrast, research of the type being considered must frequently be carried out on normal and healthy subjects who may never directly benefit from the experiment. Clearly the differences are too great to allow using the precedents of the physician-patient relationship as a total guide in handling the problems of the experimenter-subject relationship.

[One legal analysis offers] a partial solution with the concept of "liability without fault." Under this concept, if a subject is damaged as a result of participation in a psychological experiment he would be entitled to be made whole, through treatment or rehabilitation, or to receive compensatory damages. Thus the subject would be protected. The experimenter would also be protected. He would not be considered to be at fault, but rather to have been acting in the interest of society. Thus society, through appropriate government channels, would assume the costs of rehabilitation or compensation just as society, also through government channels, supports most of the experimentation for which the concept of liability without fault would be appropriate.

Some practical problems remain, such as which experimenters would be protected and how psychological damage would be assessed. But the fact that such details and the underlying legal and moral issues are being seriously considered constitutes somber evidence that scientific inquiry will prove increasingly powerful in gaining knowledge of man himself.[41]

[41] Quoted from Dael Wolfle, "Research with Human Subjects." *Science* 132: 989; October 14, 1960. Reprinted from *Science* by permission.

In the behavioral sciences many of the techniques for manipulation of variables involve deception, prevarication, and misdirection of the subject. In working with human subjects the experimenter is obligated to keep in mind his responsibilities to the subject and the ethics of experimentation. One of the difficulties in classroom experimentation is that the subjects are children, who for ethical reasons must not be subjected to conditions that may harm them. The investigator may be handicapped by the popular attitude of "no experimenting with children." The experimenter should perform some service for the subjects in exchange for their help; for example, to give the subjects (if mature enough to comprehend) a full explanation at the conclusion of the experiment, even though it may require more time for explanation and discussion than it took to do the experiment. If this explanation is well done, the subjects will feel that they have learned something and have not wasted their time.[42]

A somewhat more comprehensive analysis of the obligations and ethics involved in the "human" study of human beings includes: the need for consent to the research by both observer and subject, control of the individual and cultural bias of the observer or experimenter, protection of both the subject and experimenter from the effects of cruelty (and safeguarding from ill effects other human beings not directly involved in the observations), effect of the research methods on the behavior observed, and protection of science itself from any possible loss of confidence or respect.

The growth of importance of the study of human behavior raises a host of new ethical problems, at the head of which I would place the need for consent to the research by both observer and subject. Studies of the behavior of animals other than man introduced a double set of problems: how to control the tendency of the human observer to anthropomorphize, and so distort his observations, and how to protect both the animal and the experimenter from the effects of cruelty. In debates on the issue of cruelty it is usually recognized that callousness toward a living thing may produce suffering in the experimental subject, but it is less often recognized that it may produce moral deterioration in the experimenter.

Further problems arise when living human beings are studied in their natural habitats, in laboratories, or in partially simulated situations. The observer or experimenter must control his individual and cultural bias at the same time that he uses his membership in the species and in a culture as tools of research. He must systematically allow for the effect of his research methods on the behavior he is observing. He must protect his subjects from damage during and subsequent to his investigations. He must protect his particular

[42] Leon Festinger and Daniel Katz, *Research Methods in the Behavioral Sciences.* New York: Dryden Press, 1953. p. 170.

scientific discipline and science in general from any loss of confidence that might make future scientific work more difficult. *And* he must protect from ill effects other human beings who are not involved in his particular set of observations.

The first two of these ethical and scientific imperatives are reasonably well understood, although many natural scientists may not be fully conversant with the various disciplined ways in which individual and cultural bias are allowed for—through, for example, allowance for countertransference in psychiatry or the employment of different observational methods with comparison groups. . . . Much more specific safeguards are needed to protect the subjects of research, sometimes in terms of their own identity, sometimes in terms of their capacity to trust themselves or to trust other individuals of higher status. In regard to loss of confidence, there is a general recognition that a social investigator should not infuriate the local citizenry or outrage the board of trustees of a university by his research methods or the way in which he presents his results.

But the last requirement is one on which scientists have not yet adequately come to terms. The question can be stated simply: Is it scientifically and ethically permissible to deceive the subjects of research by disguising oneself as a "participant observer," or by introducing stooges into an experiment, or by making use of long-distance television or hidden microphones or other devices for concealed observation? When a human being is introduced who is consciously distorting his position, the material of the research is inevitably jeopardized, and the results always are put in question as the "participant"— introduced as a "psychotic" into a mental ward or as a "fanatic" into a flying-saucer cult group—gives his subjects false clues of a nonverbal nature and produces distortions which cannot be traced in his results. Concealed instruments of observation may not distort the subjects' course of action, but the subsequent revelation of their presence—as in the jury room that was tapped for sociological purposes—damages the trust both of the original participants and of all others who come to know about it. The deception violates the conventions of privacy and human dignity and casts scientists in the role of spies, intelligence agents, Peeping Toms, and versions of Big Brother. Furthermore, it damages science by cutting short attempts to construct methods of research that would responsibly enhance, rather than destroy, human trust.[43]

To cite another specific example, the Houston, Texas, School Board ordered certain answer sheets for tests destroyed, because of complaints from parents about the intimate nature of some test items. This action precipitated a controversy concerning freedom of investigation and the ethics of invading the privacy of the individual:

When the student of behavior works in a xenophobic and individualistic community, he cannot assume that his scientifically honorable intentions will be considered morally justifiable by those whom he seeks to help. Even though the scientist says, in effect, "I am studying you, and asking you these questions,

[43] Quoted from Margaret Mead, "The Human Study of Human Beings." *Science* 133: 163; January 20, 1961. Reprinted from *Science* by permission.

for your own good," his subject may respond, "It is part of my 'good' that you desist from your intrusion of my privacy."

As with all such conflicts in ethics (in ultimate values), facts are irrelevant —and consequences too.[44]

While many of the institutes or agencies devoted to study of the child maintain child populations and facilities for research purposes, it is frequently necessary to seek access to the children and resources of other agencies—schools, hospitals, and institutions for the disturbed, handicapped, or retarded. Although the public school rarely has been under any mandate or obligation to cooperate with the university investigator, the response usually has been favorable to the student of child-related research interests. However, in order to avoid complications, many of the larger school systems have assigned to an administrative officer the task of reviewing research proposals and providing the necessary contacts with principals, teachers, and children, thus making certain that the proposed study is compatible with the routine, regulations, practices, and responsibilities of the particular school system. A comparable reciprocating arrangement in the university has been less frequent.[45]

EXPERIMENTATION IN RELATION TO OTHER TECHNIQUES

Psychometric and Statistical Research

Some investigators differentiate between experimental research and psychometric research (studies in which psychometric techniques are used to investigate relations between variables, but excluding such procedures in assessing individuals for clinical or other applied psychological work). Since experimental and psychometric techniques are basically similar in purpose, they can be combined in areas traditionally restricted to one or the other:

In an investigation of the relation between, let us say, reaction time and alcoholic content of blood, variations in alcoholic content of blood are likely to be produced experimentally by feeding comparable groups of subjects different amounts of alcohol. The groups are treated in different ways, subjected to different conditions. On the other hand, in studying the relation between memory and intelligence, for example, variations in intelligence are obtained psychometrically by selecting individuals who vary with respect to scores on an intelligence test. In both cases we vary each of at least two variables in order to determine the relation between them, but the method of

[44] Quoted from Gwynn Nettler, "Test Burning in Texas." *American Psychologist* 14: 682–83; November 1959.

[45] Alfred Castaneda and Leila S. Fahel, "The Relationship Between the Psychological Investigator and the Public Schools." *American Psychologist* 16: 201–3; April 1961.

producing variation is different. In experimental investigations the investigator produces variation by changing the external environment, or internal state, or both, of his subjects. In psychometric research no attempt is made to produce any change in the individual subject. Rather, the subject is assumed to stay put with respect to the property (e.g., intelligence) in which the investigator is interested, and variation in that property is obtained by selecting individuals who differ with respect to it. The experimentalist obtains variation by subjecting a given group of subjects to different experimental conditions, the psychometric researcher achieves it by moving from individual to individual.[46]

It is not enough for the two disciplines of correlational psychology and experimental psychology to borrow from each other. Although correlational psychology studies only variance among organisms, and experimental psychology investigates only variance among treatments, a united discipline will study both of these and will also be concerned with the otherwise neglected interactions between organismic and treatment variables:[47]

There was a time when experimental psychologists concerned themselves wholly with general, nonindividual constructs, and correlational psychologists sought laws wholly within developmental variables. More and more, nowadays, their investigations are coming to bear on the same targets. One psychologist measures ego involvement by a personality test and compares the behavior of high- and low-scoring subjects. Another psychologist heightens ego involvement experimentally in one of two equated groups and studies the consequent differences in behavior. Both investigators can test the same theoretical propositions, and to the extent that their results agree they may regard both procedures as embodiments of the same construct. . . .

In both applied work and general scientific work, psychology requires combined, not parallel, labors from our two historic disciplines. In this common labor, they will almost certainly become one, with a common theory, a common method, and common recommendations for social betterment. In the search for interactions we will invent new treatment dimensions and discover new dimensions of the organism. We will come to realize that organism and treatment are an inseparable pair and that no psychologist can dismiss one or the other as error variance.

Despite our specializations, every scientific psychologist must take the same scene into his field of vision. Clark Hull, three sentences before the end of his *Essentials of Behavior*, voiced just this need. Because of delay in developing methodology, he said, individual differences have played little part in behavior theory, and "a sizeable segment of behavioral science remains

[46] Quoted from Dalbir Bindra and Ivan H. Scheier, "The Relation Between Psychometric and Experimental Research in Psychology." *American Psychologist* 9: 69–71; February 1954.

[47] Quoted from Lee J. Cronbach, "The Two Disciplines of Scientific Psychology." *American Psychologist* 12: 671–84; November 1957.

practically untouched."[48] This untouched segment contains the question we really want to put to Nature, and she will never answer until our two disciplines ask it in a single voice.

We are reminded that statistical and experimental methods represent one approach to problems but not the only scientific method, although the prestige of statistics and experimentation is great, in part deriving from the high repute of mathematics and logic. Strong professional societies are devoted to the advancement of mathematics and statistics, and hundreds of technical books and journals in the fields of statistics and experimentation are published annually. We must keep in mind, however, that important parts of the scientific process do not now lend themselves to mathematical, logical, or any other formal treatment, as illustrated particularly by certain of the studies cited in the chapter on case and clinical techniques.

Statistical techniques serve a useful function, but they have acquired a purely honorific status which may be troublesome. Their presence or absence has become a shibboleth to be used in distinguishing between good and bad work. Because measures of behavior have been highly variable, we have come to trust only results obtained from large numbers of subjects. Because some workers have intentionally or unconsciously reported only selected favorable instances, we have come to put a high value on research which is planned in advance and reported in its entirety. Because measures have behaved capriciously, we have come to value skillfully deductive theories which restore order. But although large groups, planned experiments, and valid theorizing are associated with significant scientific results, it does not follow that nothing can be achieved in their absence.[49]

It has been emphasized in the literature of the past decade that all statistical techniques are tools which should be fitted to the experiment's requirements, and that the statistical tail should never be permitted to wag the experimental dog:[50]

It is evident that the requirements for statistics vary greatly from one area of research to another, and our concern here is twofold: first, that adequate recognition be given to such diversity in any attempt to specify the minimum preparation to be expected of doctoral candidates; secondly, that formal statistical training should not be such as to obscure, in the student's mind, the desirability of simple procedures and direct experimental (instead of statistical) control wherever feasible. It seems possible to us that heavy emphasis on

[48] C. L. Hull, *Essentials of Behavior*. New Haven: Yale University Press, 1951. p. 116.

[49] Quoted from B. F. Skinner, "A Case History in Scientific Method." *American Psychologist* 11: 221–33; May 1956.

[50] Quoted from Donald W. Taylor and Others, "Education for Research in Psychology." *American Psychologist* 14: 167–79; April, 1959.

complex "design of experiment" procedures at an early stage of training may give the student a false conception of the art of research and may tend to induce as well a kind of perfectionism that can act as a positive barrier to fertility of invention or flexibility of thinking. Somehow the student must learn to find and use the methods appropriate to his problem—to avoid limiting his choice of problems to those which can be handled by methods with which he is familiar or by which he is overly impressed.

A caricature of the preparation of a hypothetical thesis with an experimental approach and certain statistical aspects is biting in its humor, but is well worth our attention:

1. Skim through the paragraph headings and summaries of articles in the last couple of issues of the *Journal of Abnormal and Social Psychology, Journal of Consulting Psychology,* the *Journal of Projective Techniques,* and *Journal of Personality.* This is known as *surveying the literature.*

2. Select the measurement device most frequently used in recent work (preferably one that is self-administering and requires no effort to score or interpret, like the Taylor Manifest Anxiety Scale). This assures your study of *timeliness, topical relevance, and publishability.*

3. Find some other fashionable instrument or procedure with which the first has never been correlated, also preferably one that gives a quantitative, objectively derived score. State that this score will be adopted as a measure of *self-actualization,* or some other fine sounding and not too easily defined concept, and note that, when you say "self-actualization," you mean it only in the restricted sense of your test's score. This puts your work on a sound *operational basis.*

4. Get a group of subjects—any old subjects who happen to be available. Divide them into an experimental and a control group, taking elaborate precautions to match them for mean age and years of schooling, whether these variables have anything to do with your problem or not. This procedure solves all of the problems of *experimental design.*

5. Give the two tests to both groups, scaring hell out of the experimental group by solemnly assuring them that your dependent variable is a test of intelligence, leadership, innate decency, and sexual potency and that they have all scored below second percentile and you are sorry but you feel honor bound to report them to the dean. This process, called *experimentally manipulating the independent variable,* is really good clean fun because after the papers are handed in you tell them that it was just a little trick, all for science.

6. Then you correlate X with Y under your experimental and control conditions, reporting the coefficient and its PE to four decimal places. This shows you to be a *rigorous, mathematically* exact sort of scientist.

7. If your correlations are not quite different enough, rescrutinize the data to make sure that you have not inadvertently included subjects who were *insufficiently motivated,* and eliminate the ones who were fouling up the results.

8. Now write it all up, predicting whatever finding you happen to get, which makes it permissible for you to use one-tailed tests of significance

throughout. Make it as long, ponderous, and dull as possible; dedicate it jointly to your spouse and your advisor, "without whose help this work could not have been completed," and you are in.[51]

The Experimental Clinician or Flight from the Laboratory

Many graduate students in psychology (and some in education) have experienced frustration in attempting to mold themselves in the image of the "experimental clinician." The graduate student seeks to find some appropriate middle ground in his training and profession between the goal of research as the pursuit of understanding and the ideal of service as the welfare of the client. (The relationship of the clinical and statistical approaches to problem-solving has been discussed in the chapter on clinical and case studies.)

To many, there appears to be an irreconcilable schism between the rather rigid, controlled methodology of the experimentalist, on the one hand, and the flexible, eclectic approach extolled as the clinician's *modus operandi,* on the other. And many feel that this schism will never be reached. It appears to be the logical dividing line between two mental attitudes which, although possibly lying on a continuum, form the polar aspects of this continuum with no present-day intermediate steps. It is the difference between a data-centered and a client-centered approach, between a research-centered and a service-centered attitude which makes the difference here. . . .

When an experimental psychologist sets about experimenting, he is quite careful to control rigidly his variables, to manipulate precisely his parameters, and to adhere religiously to an explicit procedure. Emulating the mother science, he strives to approach the situation of quantitatively plotting the concomitant changes in a dependent variable against the measured changes in an independent variable. Adherence to stated rules, quantification, and explicit control are the hallmarks of the experimental psychologist's procedure, and this is as it should be. Summarily stated, then, this is the experimental methodology as taught in our universities. When results are presented, they are presented, with confidence, as a function of the stated conditions, i.e., the manipulated variables.

But the other half of our "experimental clinician" faces problems of its own. In a client-centered, service-oriented profession the clinician is opportuned to follow the lead of his patient, to be flexible, and to consider the patient first and society second. Multidimensional manipulation of variable complexes, clinical intuition, and qualitative insights are the hallmarks of clinical psychology. This is the psychotherapeutic methodology as taught in our universities today.[52]

[51] Quoted from Robert R. Holt, "Researchmanship or How to Write a Dissertation in Clinical Psychology Without Really Trying." *American Psychologist* 14: 151; March 1959.

[52] Quoted from Lawrence N. Solomon, "The Paradox of the Experimental Clinician." *American Psychologist* 10: 170–71; April 1955.

The student's predicament is shared by the profession of psychology as a whole. Psychologists have yet to learn how to test in the laboratory the induced hypotheses of the therapy room and to develop a theoretical framework which will deductively support both clinical insight and experimental inquiry.[53]

Near the middle of the present century many graduate students and some professors were turning to social, personal, clinical, and applied psychology. Movements competing with experimental psychology for the attention of professors and graduate students, or even encouraging "flight from the laboratory," included statistical specialization and machine tabulation, mathematical models, case histories, psychoanalysis and the organization of personality, and over-popularization of psychological concepts and language. At that time there was a familiar caricature of the experimental psychologist which runs something like this:

He is first of all an apparatus man, who spends a good share of his time tinkering with sundry pieces of equipment which never quite work to his satisfaction. He investigates only problems which he calls appropriate to the laboratory. He cannot study learning as part of the complex and subtle interplay of behavior and environment in everyday life, so he confines himself to the memorizing of meaningless words presented with clocklike regularity in a standard aperture. He cannot bring love or hate or envy into the laboratory, so he investigates reactions to garter snakes and pistol shots. The only strong motives he knows are his own, for his subjects perform merely to oblige him or because they are required to do so as part of a course they are taking. (In an exceptional case, if he "has a grant," they may be paid seventy-five cents an hour.) He remains an experimental psychologist only so long as his problems have no practical value; that is how he stays pure. If his field suddenly becomes important for industry or the public weal, then he becomes an industrial or applied psychologist and does the whole thing over again in no time at all with better and more expensive apparatus. He works only with amenable subjects—that is to say, with subjects in whom no one is really interested: white rats or dogs or human beings who have stepped out of their normal lives and into a laboratory frame as standard organisms.[54]

This picture of the experimental psychologist is not amusing to the thoughtful student of education and psychology. Until past the middle of the twentieth century, parts of it were perhaps too close to the truth to be funny. Psychologists with a broader interest in the affairs of men have sometimes grown impatient with their experimental associates and often have resented the historical seniority and prestige of the experimental field. Experimental psychologists themselves in increasing num-

[53] George A. Kelly, "I Itch Too." *American Psychologist* 10: 172–73; April 1955.
[54] Quoted from B. F. Skinner, *Cumulative Record*. New York: Appleton-Century-Crofts, 1959. p. 223.

bers have become uncertain of their scientific position and in some numbers have turned to other fields of psychological endeavor. The field of scholarship and research, however, should place in high priority the survival of experimental psychology as a field of investigation and should assure its ultimate position with respect to other branches of psychology. Certain factors have contributed to our doubts concerning experimental psychology. In defining or delimiting the scope of experimental psychology there is no reason to suppose that this field is concerned chiefly with such limited areas as sensory processes, reaction times, and certain limited learning situations; as a matter of fact, experimentation is now common in every field of human behavior. The experimental psychologist is no longer distinguished by the fact that he uses apparatus; use of apparatus may improve an experiment, but must not be confused with experimentation itself. Since the experimental psychologist is no longer distinguished by a special field of research, by technical equipment, or by laboratory simplification of conditions, his statements or conclusions must not necessarily be considered any more reliable than those of other research specialists and scholars.[55]

One view or prediction is that educational psychology will attract a relatively large number of the new research workers in psychology during the decade ahead, just as clinical psychology did in the 1940's and 1950's.

Educational psychology will be for psychology during the '60s and '70s what clinical psychology was during the '40s and '50s. Education will be the locus of the next massive development of psychology's resources for scientific research and social usefulness. Just as clinical psychology has attracted the chief part of psychology's new research workers, in the decade or two ahead, a major share of the research and professional work of psychologists will be attracted to educational psychology.

Some psychologists will wring their hands at these likelihoods. Educational psychology, they say, will only be further distracted from its proper goal —more and better research—by this new growth. Rather than "professional" activity, aimed directly at building our financial and manpower resources, what we need is more of the lonely thinking and creating that alone can restore educational psychology to the heights it occupied in the days of Thorndike and Judd.

Others have long been impatient for this new growth to begin. They say the signs of these new trends are now easily seen. Federal and state governments, foundations, and the most prestigious circles of American society and science have in recent years been paying new attention to educational psychology. Social forces ranging in scope from the cold war to the fight over phonics have converged to make education—and with it, educational psychology—the center of American hope. We cannot turn our backs on the problems that our new responsibilities bring.

[55] *Ibid.*

Obviously, the ideal resolution is that we need both: (a) more and better research and (b) more and better professional action.[56]

Observational or Descriptive-Survey Studies

For certain purposes direct observation of a descriptive-survey type may prove more rewarding than controlled experimentation, as in noting the particular stimuli in a complex social setting to which the individual child reacts, consistency of reaction for an individual, and variability in response between the different members of the group. From this point of view, controlled experiments in laboratories and in many classrooms are regarded as artificial or unnatural. Some observational studies may even satisfy the requirements of controlled observation, in that certain controls are used in selecting the room, equipment, children, stimuli, and observers. The simpler technique of observation of behavior, as compared with controlled experimentation, is useful in securing accurate running accounts of what happens from day to day in teaching a group of children some complex skill, generalization, or attitude.

On the other hand, if the experimenter succeeds in controlling the conditions under which an event occurs, he has certain advantages over an observer who simply watches the course of events without exercising any control: the experimenter can make the event occur when he wishes; he can repeat his observation under the same conditions for verification; and he can vary the conditions systematically and note the variation in results.

Psychologists sometimes have used the term *qualitative* in contrast to *quantitative* in discussing experimentation. Woodworth points out that certain important variables are qualitative rather than quantitative: the role of the different senses in revealing the environment as an important psychological problem; training with "understanding" differs from routine drill; an animal will approach one object and avoid another; and a human subject likes one odor and dislikes another. "How could chemistry ever have become quantitative without first being interested in the various kinds of elements and compounds? A qualitative survey is often necessary to show up the important problems and suggest hypotheses for more exact testing."[57]

Examples may be cited of other investigational techniques used in conjunction with experimentation, actually as part of the experimental design. Use of eye-movement photography, for the purpose of establishing central tendencies, is descriptive-survey in character, but may become

[56] Quoted from N. L. Gage, *Newsletter,* Division of Educational Psychology, A. P. A., November, 1961, p. 1.

[57] Robert S. Woodworth and Harold Schlosberg, *Experimental Psychology.* Revised Edition. New York: Henry Holt and Co., 1954. p. 6–7.

a first step in experimentation when reading content is varied (from prose to poetry to written problems in arithmetic). As a co-twin control technique, using identical twins, one infant may be taught to climb the stairs, while the other waits until he has reached a stage of stair-climbing "readiness." This study may be so analyzed and reported as to possess the characteristics of case-study and genetic procedures, as well as experimentation.

INSTRUMENTATION

Instruments play an important part in modern science, technology, and business organization, and also in the design of controlled experimentation (with relatively greater use in psychological research than in educational experiments). Achievements made possible by modern instruments include the development of sensing devices capable of operating under extreme conditions and sensitive to physical changes far beyond the range of human sense organs, computing machines of extreme rapidity, and devices for automatic control of machining and assembling operations. Many current discoveries would have been impossible without the aid of the specially designed instruments made possible by modern technology. Improved instruments are essential for research progress in the future. Scientists can expect and even demand more assistance from machines in handling scientific data, including the processes or techniques of integrated and electronic data-processing.[58] The numerous instruments for mechanical recording and for data-gathering, as described in the chapter on descriptive-survey studies, are available for use in controlled experimentation.

Instruments may be thought of as unifying elements which help self-centered disciplines shed their isolationism. The scientist who produces instruments for research is recognized among his fellows, especially in the cooperative efforts of interdisciplinary research. An instrument for scientific use is a physical means for observation and experimentation directed to securing and utilizing information, and may be one of several types:[59]

1. A device in which known physical principles are applied to increase one's perceptivity of natural phenomena, or to render observable otherwise completely elusive phenomena. It is an amplifier for sensory perception.

[58] Graham DuShane, "Instruments and Man." *Science* 124: 771; October 26, 1956.

Karl F. Heumann, "Data Processing for Scientists." *Science* 124: 773–77; October 26, 1956.

[59] Quoted from Paul E. Klopsteg, "The Indispensable Tools of Science." *Science* 132: 1913–22; December 30, 1960. Reprinted from *Science* by permission.

2. Means for measuring whatever attributes of a physical entity are susceptible of quantitative treatment. It provides numbers which uniquely describe the characteristics observed.

3. Means by which response to a condition may be recorded, or applied to the condition which elicits the response. It makes possible the automatic control of a condition, as in a servomechanism.

4. Means by which recorded information may be treated and processed to make it accessible to evaluation, thereby vastly decreasing the drudgery of manipulating data, or, indeed, making their evaluation feasible.

One form of instrumentation in educational research is found in the relatively new devices commonly known as teaching machines, including a multiple-choice machine (with an automated learning graph), a machine for discrimination training, a disk machine (commonly intended to increase rate of learning), an automatic random-access recording microfilm and motion-picture projector to present frames in any order, computers, language-laboratory equipment, and a relatively simple write-in machine. The more traditional forms of instrumentation developed in experimental psychology include:

(a) Behavior recording systems (polygraph), (b) timing and counting (clock, electronic counter), (c) audition (audio oscillator), (d) vision (light meter, color plate), (e) other senses (anasthesiometer), (f) human learning and perception (memory drum, stereoscope), and (g) bioelectricity (electroencephalogram and galvanic skin response).[60]

As suggested above, the electronic computer has greatly advanced the procedures of automation in data processing and calculation, making possible new methods in many areas of research, although detailed discussion of these techniques is beyond the scope of this book.[61]

[60] Quoted from Edward B. Fry, "Research Tools: Instrumentation in Educational Research," in "The Methodology of Educational Research." *Review of Educational Research* 30: 513–21; December 1960.

Lawrence M. Stolurow, "Teaching Machines and Special Education." *Educational and Psychological Measurement* 20: 429–48; Autumn 1960.

[61] "The Computer and Educational Research: A Symposium." *Harvard Educational Review* 31: 235–63; Summer 1961.

E. Wayne Martin, Jr., and Dale J. Hall, "Data Processing: Automation in Calculation," in "The Methodology of Educational Research." *Review of Educational Research* 30: 522–35; December 1960.

Franz L. Alt, Editor, *Advances in Computers.* Vol. 1. New York: Academic Press, 1960. x + 316 p.

Andrew D. Booth, Editor, *Progress in Automation.* Vol. 1. New York: Academic Press, 1960. viii + 231 p.

Harold Borko, Editor, *Computer Applications in the Behavioral Sciences.* Englewood Cliffs, N.J.: Prentice-Hall, 1962. 633 p.

John F. Davison, *Programming for Digital Computers.* New York: Gordon and Breach, 1961. xi + 175 p.

Robert H. Gregory and Richard L. Van Horn, *Automatic Data-Processing Sys-*

It was early recognized by some psychologists, including Helmholtz, that elaborate instrumentation was not so important as the human mind and the insight of the teacher or investigator:

> As a teacher, he [Helmholtz] seems to have rather disdained the current trend toward spectacular methods in the teaching of science. According to contemporary writers, the custom of the time was for each scientist to try to outdo all other scientists in this respect: they used huge charts that could be raised and lowered mechanically, a darkened auditorium for showing slides, large models of the eye and the ear, and "hundreds of animals, large and small . . . sacrificed, and in one case even a horse . . . introduced to show heart action." Textbooks were "almost useless . . . except for review"; the trend was all toward demonstration, and several assistants were kept continually occupied by each lecturer in preparing for the next day's lecture. One chemistry laboratory—that of Kolbe—was decorated with the motto: "God made the world according to number, weight, and measure."

> Helmholtz apparently left these elaborate demonstrations to his assistants and taught a small group of advanced students with no other aid than a blackboard. On this he would work out complicated equations, sometimes finding errors in his calculations, and always preferring to work out problems as he went along rather than to prepare every lecture beforehand. According to Hall, he had a habit of thinking out loud in lecture room and laboratory, and he used to spend some hours each day discussing experiments with his student assistants. But all these attributes, which might seem progressive today, apparently could not eradicate the impression—at least as far as Hall was concerned—that Helmholtz was a man "far more gifted in discovery than in teaching."[62]

CONCLUDING STATEMENT

In experimentation the investigator controls (manipulates or changes) certain independent variables and observes the changes that take place in the form of dependent variables. The "rule of the single variable" is now considered a narrow and mechanical theory of causation. The efficient statistical methods and experimental designs of today make it possible to handle several independent variables in the same design and to have as many dependent variables as may seem necessary. These true experimental designs have been developed by psychologists and others who sought to overcome the difficulties of confounded ex-

---

tems: Principles and Procedures. San Francisco, Calif.: Wadsworth, 1960. xii + 705 p.

Anthony Ralston and Herbert S. Wilf, Editors, *Mathematical Methods for Digital Computers.* New York: John Wiley & Sons, 1960. xi + 293 p.

George P. Shultz and Thomas L. Whisler, Editors, *Management Organization and the Computer.* Glencoe, Ill.: Free Press, 1960. xvii + 257 p.

[62] Quoted from Howard Gruber and Valmai Gruber, "Hermann von Helmholtz: Nineteenth-Century Polymorph." *Scientific Monthly* 83: 92–99; August 1956.

G. S. Hall, *Founders of Modern Psychology.* New York: Appleton-Century-Crofts, 1924. vii + 470 p.

traneous variables in the pre-experimental designs widely used during the first quarter of the twentieth century and even later.

We should not overemphasize the familiar complaint that the kind of control possible in the laboratory is impossible in the world at large. Human behavior is controlled in a number of ways. The genetic constitution of the individual and his personal history to date play a part in the determination of behavior, as does the social environment, which is man-made. There are many instances outside the laboratory in which independent variables may be freely manipulated with respect to human behavior; for example, the nursery, certain types of schools, corrective and penal institutions, where the degree of control may be great, although there are certain legal and ethical restrictions. In such situations as education, industry, law, public affairs, and government the control is not so likely to be lodged in a single person or agency, but at times has brought sorrow to the individual and to society.

Obstacles to controlled experimentation in the field of education and in the classroom involve three factors: limited graduate training for experimentation in the field of education, relatively little experimentation by professors of education, and a neutral or even negative attitude toward experimentation on the part of many school administrators and parents. It is essential that the graduate student or investigator interested in controlled experimentation have the necessary training in statistics (especially the analysis of variance) and in research methods before attempting to design an experiment, and that he work closely from the beginning with a competent specialist. It has been emphasized in the literature of the past decade that all statistical techniques are tools which should be fitted to the experimenter's requirements, and that the statistical tail should never be permitted to wag the experimental dog.

At times, zeal for experimentation has become a fetish. There is a place for the exercise of good judgment and logic in attempting to bring about social and educational improvements, without insisting on an answer through controlled experimentation. Near the middle of the present century many graduate students and some professors were turning to social, personal, clinical, and applied psychology for answers to their questions. Movements competing with experimental psychology for the attention of professors and graduate students or even encouraging "flight from the laboratory" included statistical specialization and machine tabulation, mathematical models, case histories, psychoanalysis and the organization of personality, and over-popularization of psychological concepts and language.

If teachers do not understand the scientific spirit of inquiry and the requirements of controlled experimentation, they may invalidate an investigation as the result of departures from the rules and design prescribed for the experiment. Objective, impartial participation by teachers in appropriate experimentation should have a stimulating effect on both teachers and pupils as a personal value or byproduct of the experiment.

We must recognize that, as scientific inquiry pushes toward the limits of research on human behavior, some danger to the subjects and related legal and moral problems may be involved. Sometimes parents and others complain about the intimate nature of some test items, resulting in controversy concerning freedom of investigation and the ethics of invading the privacy of the individual.

Instruments may be thought of as unifying elements which help self-centered disciplines shed their isolationism. The scientist who produces instruments for research and experimentation is recognized among his fellows, especially in the cooperative efforts of interdisciplinary research. An instrument for scientific use is a physical means for observation and experimentation directed to securing and utilizing information, and may be one of several types. We may be reminded again, however, that the most important instrument for research is the mind of man.

SELECTED REFERENCES

ACKOFF, Russell L. *The Design of Social Research*. Chicago: The University of Chicago Press, 1953. xi + 420 p.

American Association for Health, Physical Education, and Recreation. *Research Methods Applied to Health, Physical Education, and Recreation*. Revised Edition. Washington: The Association, National Education Association, 1952. p. 182-203, 254-314.

ANDERSON, John E. "Methods of Child Psychology," *Manual of Child Psychology*. Second Edition. Edited by Leonard Carmichael. New York: John Wiley & Sons, 1954. p. 44-52.

ANDREAS, Burton G. *Experimental Psychology*. New York: John Wiley & Sons, 1960. xii + 595 p.

ANDREWS, T. C., Editor. *Methods of Psychology*. New York: John Wiley & Sons, 1948. xiv + 716 p.

BAKER, L. M. *General Experimental Psychology:* An Introduction to Principles. New York: Oxford University Press, 1960. xiv + 420 p.

BARTLEY, S. Howard. *Beginning Experimental Psychology*. New York: McGraw-Hill Book Co., 1950. viii + 483 p.

BEVERIDGE, William I. B. *The Art of Scientific Investigation*. New York: W. W. Norton and Co., 1950. 171 p.

BIJOU, Sidney W., and BAER, Donald M. "The Laboratory-Experimental Study of Child Behavior," *Handbook of Research Methods in Child Development*. Edited by Paul H. Mussen. New York: John Wiley & Sons, 1960. Chapter 4.

BORING, Edwin G. *A History of Experimental Psychology*. Second Edition. New York: Appleton-Century-Crofts, 1950. xxi + 777 p.

Brown, Clarence W., and Ghiselli, Edwin E. *Scientific Method in Psychology.* New York: McGraw-Hill Book Co., 1955. xii + 368 p.

Brown, Clinton C., and Saucer, Rayford T. *Electronic Instrumentation for the Behavioral Sciences.* Springfield, Ill.: Charles C Thomas, 1958. 176 p.

Brownell, W. A. "Critique of Research on Learning and on Instruction in the School," *Graduate Study in Education,* p. 52-66. Fiftieth Yearbook, National Society for the Study of Education, Part 1. Chicago: The University of Chicago Press, 1951. 369 p.

Bruce, William F. "Experimentalist Orientation Toward Educational Theory." *Educational Administration and Supervision* 45: 63-76; March 1959.

Brunswik, Egon. *Perception and the Representative Design of Psychological Experiments.* Berkeley: University of California Press, 1956. xii + 154 p.

Brunswik, Egon. *Systematic and Representative Design of Psychological Experiments.* Berkeley: University of California Press, 1947. 60 p.

Bugelski, B. R. *A First Course in Experimental Psychology.* New York: Henry Holt and Co., 1951. xxiii + 421 p.

Buros, Oscar K., Editor. *The Fourth Mental Measurements Yearbook.* Highland Park, N.J.: Gryphon Press, 1953. 1,189 p.

Buros, Oscar K., Editor. *The Fifth Mental Measurements Yearbook.* Highland Park, N.J.: Gryphon Press, 1959. 1,292 p.

Campbell, Donald T. "Factors Relevant to the Validity of Experiments in Social Settings." *Psychological Bulletin* 54: 297-312; July 1957.

Chapanis, Alphonse. *Research Techniques in Human Engineering.* Baltimore: Johns Hopkins Press, 1959. Chapters 5, 6.

Chapin, F. Stuart. *Experimental Designs in Sociological Research.* Revised Edition. New York: Harper & Brothers, 1955. xxii + 295 p.

Cochran, William G., and Cox, Gertrude M. *Experimental Designs.* Second Edition. New York: John Wiley & Sons, 1957. xiv + 611 p.

Collier, Raymond O., Jr., and Elam, S. M., Editors. *Research Design and Analysis:* Second Annual Phi Delta Kappa Symposium on Educational Research. Bloomington, Ind.: Phi Delta Kappa, 1961. viii + 208 p.

Collier, Raymond O., Jr., and Meyer, Donald L. "Research Methods: Experimental Design and Analysis," in "The Methodology of Educational Research." *Review of Educational Research* 30: 430-39; December 1960.

Cox, D. R. *Planning of Experiments.* New York: John Wiley & Sons, 1958. viii + 308 p.

Crafts, L. W., and Others. *Recent Experiments in Psychology.* Second Edition. New York: McGraw-Hill Book Co., 1950. xvii + 503 p.

Dennis, Wayne, Editor. *Readings in the History of Psychology.* New York: Appleton-Century-Crofts, 1948. 598 p.

Doby, John T., Editor. "Principles of Experimentation," *An Introduction to Social Research.* Harrisburg, Penn.: The Stackpole Co., 1954. p. 101-22.

Edwards, Allen L. *Experimental Design in Psychological Research.* Revised Edition. New York: Holt, Rinehart, and Winston, 1960. xvi + 398 p.

Edwards, Allen L. "Experiments: Their Planning and Execution," *Handbook of Social Psychology:* Theory and Method. Vol. 1. Edited by Gardner

Lindzey. Cambridge, Mass.: Addison-Wesley Publishing Co., 1954. p. 259-88.

FEDERER, Walter T. *Experimental Design:* Theory and Application. New York: The Macmillan Co., 1955. xix + 544 + 47 p.

FESTINGER, Leon, and KATZ, Daniel, Editors. *Research Methods in the Behavioral Sciences.* New York: Dryden Press, 1953. p. 98-172.

FINNEY, D. J. *An Introduction to the Theory of Experimental Design.* Chicago: The University of Chicago Press, 1960. 232 p.

FINNEY, D. J. *Experimental Design and Its Statistical Basis.* Chicago: The University of Chicago Press, 1955. 169 p.

FISHER, R. A. *The Design of Experiments.* Sixth Edition. New York: Hafner Publishing Corp., 1951. xv + 244 p.

FLUGEL, J. C. *A Hundred Years of Psychology.* Second Edition. New York: The Macmillan Co., 1951. 424 p.

FRY, Edward B. "Research Tools: Instrumentation in Educational Research," in "The Methodology of Educational Research." *Review of Educational Research* 30: 513-21; December 1960.

GAGE, N. L., Editor. *Handbook of Research on Teaching.* Chicago: Rand McNally, 1963. xiv + 1218 p.

GARRETT, Henry E. *Great Experiments in Psychology.* Third Edition. New York: Appleton-Century-Crofts, 1951. 400 p.

GEE, Wilson. *Social Science Research Methods.* New York: Appleton-Century-Crofts, 1950. p. 330-60.

GIBSON, Eleanor J., and OLUM, Vivian. "Experimental Methods of Studying Perception in Children," *Handbook of Research Methods in Child Development.* Edited by Paul H. Mussen. New York: John Wiley & Sons, 1960. Chapter 8.

GOLDSTEIN, Philip. *How to Do an Experiment.* New York: Harcourt, Brace and Co., 1957. 192 p.

GOOD, Carter V., and SCATES, Douglas E. *Methods of Research:* Educational, Psychological, Sociological. New York: Appleton-Century-Crofts, 1954. p. 689-725.

GOODE, William J., and HATT, Paul K. *Methods in Social Research.* New York: McGraw-Hill Book Co., 1952. p. 74-102.

GREENWOOD, Ernest. *Experimental Sociology:* A Study in Method. New York: King's Crown Press, 1945. xiii + 163 p.

GRINGS, William W. *Laboratory Instrumentation in Psychology.* Palo Alto, Calif.: National Press, 1954. vi + 282 p.

HARRIS, Chester W. "Statistical Methods," *Encyclopedia of Educational Research.* Edited by Chester W. Harris. Third Edition. New York: The Macmillan Co., 1960. p. 1397-1414.

HERRICK, Virgil E., and HARRIS, Chester W. "Handling Data," *Research for Curriculum Improvement.* 1957 Yearbook. Washington: Association for Supervision and Curriculum Development, National Education Association, 1957. p. 83-118.

HILLWAY, Tyrus. *Introduction to Research.* Boston: Houghton Mifflin Co., 1956. p. 153-74.

HUMPHREY, George. *Thinking:* An Introduction to Its Experimental Psychology. New York: John Wiley & Sons, 1951. xi + 331 p.

JAHODA, Marie, and Others. *Research Methods in the Study of Social Relations:* With Especial Emphasis on Prejudice. Vol. 1. New York: Dryden Press, 1951. p. 58-85.

KEMPTHORNE, Oscar. *The Design and Analysis of Experiments.* New York: John Wiley & Sons, 1952. xix + 631 p.

KESSEN, William. "Research Design in the Study of Developmental Problems," *Handbook of Research Methods in Child Development.* Edited by Paul H. Mussen. New York: John Wiley & Sons, 1960. Chapter 2.

LACEY, Oliver L. *Statistical Methods in Experimentation:* An Introduction. New York: The Macmillan Co., 1953. xi + 249 p.

LANGFELD, Herbert S., and Others, Editors. *A History of Psychology in Autobiography.* Vol. 4. Worcester, Mass.: Clark University Press, 1952. xii + 356 p.

LINDQUIST, E. F. *Design and Analysis of Experiments in Psychology and Education.* Boston: Houghton Mifflin Co., 1953. xix + 393 p.

MADGE, John. *The Tools of Social Science.* New York: Longmans, Green and Co., 1953. p. 254-89.

MAXWELL, A. E. *Experimental Design in Psychology and the Medical Sciences.* New York: John Wiley & Sons, 1958. 144 p.

McGUIGAN, Frank J. *Experimental Psychology:* A Methodological Approach. Englewood Cliffs, N.J.: Prentice-Hall, 1960. vi + 314 p.

MORENO, J. L. *Sociometry, Experimental Method and the Science of Society.* New York: Beacon House, 1951. xiv + 220 p.

MURPHY, Gardner. *Historical Introduction to Modern Psychology.* Revised Edition. New York: Harcourt, Brace and Co., 1949. xiv + 466 p.

O'NEIL, W. M. *An Introduction to Method in Psychology.* Melbourne, Australia: Melbourne University Press, 1957. ix + 155 p.

OSGOOD, Charles E. *Method and Theory in Experimental Psychology.* New York: Oxford University Press, 1953. vi + 800 p.

QUENOUILLE, M. H. *The Design and Analysis of Experiment.* New York: Hafner Publishing Corp., 1953. xiii + 356 p.

RAY, William S. *An Introduction to Experimental Design.* New York: The Macmillan Co., 1960. xii + 254 p.

ROBACK, A. A. *History of American Psychology.* New York: Library Publishers, 1952. xiv + 426 p.

ROSE, Arnold M. "Conditions of the Social Science Experiment," *Theory and Method in the Social Sciences.* Minneapolis: University of Minnesota Press, 1954. p. 273-81.

ROSEBOROUGH, Mary E. "Experimental Studies of Small Groups." *Psychological Bulletin* 50: 275-303; July 1953.

RUMMEL, J. Francis. *An Introduction to Research Procedures in Education.* New York: Harper & Brothers, 1958. p. 203-24.

RUSSELL, Wallace A. "An Experimental Psychology of Development: Pipe Dream or Possibility?" *The Concept of Development.* Edited by Dale B. Harris. Minneapolis: University of Minnesota Press, 1957. p. 162-74.

Russell, W. M. S., and Burch, R. L. *The Principles of Humane Experimental Technique.* London: Methuen, 1959. 252 p.

Ryan, Thomas A. "Multiple Comparisons in Psychological Research." *Psychological Bulletin* 56: 26-47; January 1959.

Scott, M. Gladys, Editor. "Laboratory Planning and Instrumentation," "The Experimental Method," *Research Methods in Health, Physical Education, Recreation.* Second Edition. Washington: American Association for Health, Physical Education, and Recreation, 1959. Chapters 6, 10, 11.

Seagoe, May V. "Educational Psychology," *Encyclopedia of Educational Research.* Edited by Chester W. Harris. Third Edition. New York: The Macmillan Co., 1960. p. 403-7.

Selltiz, Claire, and Others. "Studies Testing Causal Hypotheses," *Research Methods in Social Relations.* Revised One-Volume Edition. New York: Henry Holt and Co., 1959. Chapter 4.

Sidman, Murray. *Tactics of Scientific Research:* Evaluating Experimental Data in Psychology. New York: Basic Books, 1960. x + 428 p.

Spearman, C. E. *Psychology Down the Ages.* Vols. 1, 2. London: Macmillan and Co., 1937. xii + 454, viii + 355 p.

Stanley, Julian C. "Research Methods: Experimental Design," in Methodology of Educational Research." *Review of Educational Research* 27: 449-59; December 1957.

Stevens, S. S. "Problems and Methods of Psychophysics." *Psychological Bulletin* 55: 177-96; July 1958.

Stevens, S. S., Editor. *Handbook of Experimental Psychology.* New York: John Wiley & Sons, 1951. xi + 1436 p.

Taylor, J. G. "Experimental Design: A Cloak for Intellectual Sterility." *British Journal of Psychology* 49: 106-16; May 1958.

Tiedeman, David V. "Experimental Method," *Encyclopedia of Educational Research.* Edited by Chester W. Harris. Third Edition. New York: The Macmillan Co., 1960. p. 486-90.

Tinker, Miles A., and Russell, Wallace A. *Introduction to Methods in Experimental Psychology.* Third Edition. New York: Appleton-Century-Crofts, 1958. x + 282 p.

Townsend, John C. *Introduction to Experimental Method:* For Psychology and the Social Sciences. New York: McGraw-Hill Book Co., 1953. ix + 220 p.

Travers, R. M. W. *An Introduction to Educational Research.* New York: The Macmillan Co., 1958. Chapters 13, 14.

Underwood, Benton J. *Experimental Psychology:* An Introduction. New York: Appleton-Century-Crofts, 1949. vii + 638 p.

Underwood, Benton J. "Research Design," *Psychological Research.* New York: Appleton-Century-Crofts, 1957. p. 85-173.

Van Dalen, Deobold B. *Understanding Educational Research:* An Introduction. New York: McGraw-Hill Book Co., 1962. p. 221-48.

Walker, Helen M. *Statistical Inference.* New York: Henry Holt and Co., 1953. xi + 510 p.

WEAVER, Warren, Editor. *The Scientists Speak.* New York: Boni and Gaer, 1947. 369 p.

WILSON, E. Bright. *Introduction to Scientific Research.* New York: McGraw-Hill Book Co., 1952. 375 p.

WOODWORTH, Robert S., and SCHLOSBERG, Harold. *Experimental Psychology.* Revised Edition. New York: Henry Holt and Co., 1954. xi + 948 p.

ZIMNY, George H. *Method in Experimental Psychology.* New York: Ronald Press, 1961. x + 366 p.

CHAPTER NINE

The Technical Report, Communication, and Implementation

This chapter discusses the technical or research report in relation to communication and implementation of findings, effective use of language, major parts of the report, development of the problem, presentation of evidence, summary and conclusions, bibliographical technique, documentation, style, and readability.

COMMUNICATION AND IMPLEMENTATION[1]

The technical or research report is an exposition type of composition, with emphasis on communication of ideas and evidence in such form as to be readily understood by the reader.

Effective Use of Words

In trying to make our meanings clear, without regard for experience, it is often useless to explain words with other words, because these in turn require more words, after the fashion of the old mathematical jingle:

> Big fleas have little fleas
> On their backs to bite 'em;
> And these in turn have other fleas,
> And so *ad infinitum.*

[1] Claire Selltiz and Others, "The Application of Social Research," *Research Methods in Social Relations.* Revised One-Volume Edition. New York: Henry Holt and Co., 1959. Chapter 13.

There is no meaning beyond experience. For instance, the import of as universal a fact as the rising cost of living is fundamentally private for each and every one affected by it. No two individuals can share an identical significance; and yet, it is *discussed* on every hand and everywhere. Tennyson—remember?—had Ulysses say,

> I am a part of all that I have met;
> Yet all experience is an arch wherethro'
> Gleams that untravell'd world, whose margin fades
> Forever and forever when I move.
> And so, to be understood, if one could keep silent and only point![2]

In discussing reporting as a process of communication, it is pertinent to note Whitehead's answer when he was asked whether facts or ideas are more important; he replied: "Ideas *about* facts." In illustrating the difficulty of communication in words, Whitehead pointed out that something could be said about one's personality, but much would remain that could not be put into words. He believed that a marked limitation of philosophy is the supposition that language is an exact medium and that a verbalized philosophical idea is stated for all time; to overcome this difficulty, when ordinary verbal methods failed Plato, he came nearer to the truth by giving us a myth. When Whitehead was collaborating on a book with Bertrand Russell, the latter satisfied his craving for expression by composing directly in words and thus satisfying his ideas of things, whereas Whitehead composed in concepts and then tried to find words into which the concepts could be translated.[3]

When Polonius asked Hamlet, "What do you read, my lord?" he replied: "Words, words, words." Shakespeare also used such expressions as "mere words," "words that are no deeds," which "pay no debts." He tells us about "harsh words," "the power of the word of Caesar." He suggests that we "give sorrow words" and thus assuage "the grief that does not speak."

But whether words are good or bad, sincere or insincere, empty or full, powerful or weak, lead to deeds or do not, they are ever-present. Each day we read and speak thousands of words all combined in simple or complex patterns. Indeed the depth and breadth of our daily vocabulary furnish the best single index of our mental ability.

It is important that the schools pay close and undivided attention to the words we read or write, speak or hear. Indeed it is a critical and almost unique function of the school to foster the complicated ability of learning to read and write with fluency and grace. The schools are the agency of society for teaching specific communication skills to the young learner as well as the older one.

Therefore we can conclude that the effective use of words in reading and writing, in speaking and listening is a major job of the school. Some of

[2] Quoted from Harlan C. Koch, " 'Words' and the NCA." *North Central Association Quarterly* 33: 209–10; January 1959.

[3] *Dialogues of Alfred North Whitehead.* As Recorded by Lucien Price. New York: New American Library of World Literature, 1954. p. 149–50, 271–72, 295–96.

these words symbolize and crystallize the key concepts of our intellectual life. Others will convey our deep emotions. Some will be light, gay, and humorous. In school we work and play with words and above all—think with words.[4]

Communication in Scholarly Works

In the technical report the soundness of the data and insight in interpretation are the important considerations rather than form and style as such, although commonly there is a relationship between careful organization of materials, sound interpretation of data, and effective style. To make it possible for the reader to give undivided attention to content and interpretation, it is essential to meet standards of usage with respect to certain details of form, style, and readability. Many examples of the time requirements and other essential conditions for effective research and technical reporting are included in the chapters on formulation of the problem and on historical writing.

Darwin's treatises on evolution and natural selection are unusual examples of the time, labor, revision, and rewriting necessary, when he shifted from his original plan of a detailed two-volume work with full documentation for an audience of specialists in order to communicate his ideas to a wider public.[5]

Charles Darwin's "big book" on evolution and natural selection is still generally unknown, except for what Darwin called "my abstract"—*On the Origin of Species*—published just 100 years ago this November, 1959. The long manuscript on "Natural Selection" was already twice the length of the *Origin* and was more than two-thirds completed when Darwin's receipt of Wallace's letter outlining the same theory of evolution by natural selection interrupted Darwin's progress in writing and led to an entire change of plans for publication, involving both a reduced scale and a simplified, more popular treatment. . . .

This long manuscript, which Darwin entitled "Natural Selection," turns out to be version 3 of Darwin's book on species. Before we examine this large-scale treatment of evolution, we might consider briefly Darwin's earlier notes and sketches on the subject. Darwin had already had extensive field experience and opportunity to study the problem of the nature of species and varieties during the voyage of the Beagle, in particular the fossils of the Argentine and the peculiar tortoises, finches, and mocking thrushes of the Galapagos Islands. When he had returned and was working on his collections, he recorded in his personal diary (of which there is a copy in the Darwin scientific papers at Cambridge): "In July [1837] opened first notebook on 'Transmutation of

[4] Quoted from Edgar Dale, "Words, Words, Words." *News Letter* (Ohio State University) 25: 1–4; April 1960.

[5] Quoted from Robert C. Stauffer, " 'On the Origin of Species': An Unpublished Version." *Science* 130: 1449–52; November 27, 1959. Reprinted from *Science* by permission.

Species'—Had been greatly struck from about month of previous March on character of S. American fossils—and species on Galapagos Archipelago.—These facts origin (especially latter) of all my views." Fifteen months later Darwin conceived his theory of natural selection as a mechanism of evolution when his reading of Malthus' "Essay on Population" reminded him of Lyell's discussion of population pressure and the struggle for existence. Early in the summer of 1842 he wrote out, in pencil, a sketch of his species theory in 35 pages. This was version 1. Two years later he expanded this to a draft of 230 manuscript pages. This version 2 was completed by July 1844. (These two earliest versions were edited by Francis Darwin and published by the Cambridge University Press in 1909 as the *Foundations of the Origin of Species.*). . .

In conclusion, what can be said about the implications of Darwin's "Natural Selection"? It is tempting to speculate as to the historical outcome if Darwin had been left undisturbed and free to publish his theory in the form he originally planned. It would have been a detailed two-volume work with full documentation, appealing to an audience of specialists but probably not to a wider public. It might even have been ignored by Bishop Wilberforce and by other hostile critics in some of the great literary review journals. *Darwinism* might have been less subject to misuse by would-be scientific supporters of laissez-faire economy and of imperialism. Darwin himself, instead of having to devote months to frequent revision and qualification of the *Origin of Species,* for five more editions, might have been free to develop more extensively the concept of the economy of nature as a background for the struggle for existence, and to carry out the plan mentioned in 1859 in the *Origin of Species* in regard to the latter subject: "In my future work this subject shall be treated as it well deserves, at much greater length." In the late 19th century there might have been less "Social Darwinism" and more ecology.

On the other hand, the writings of Herbert Spencer, formerly so influential, now line the back shelves of second-hand bookstores, while the chief books of Darwin are frequently republished and are so much read that their author's name is virtually a synonym among ordinary folk for "evolution," and among sophisticates for "natural selection."

I am speaking, of course, about the way these men are received now, in the 20th century; in his own day, which was that of Darwin too, Spencer was regarded as a giant, and his *Principles of Biology* was adduced as one of the chief evidences for this high estimation. Of course this could not be on literary grounds; Spencer is no more a first-class stylist than Darwin, and it must have been content and general arrangement rather than any niceties of diction that kept readers faithful through his dozen volumes, so stuffy in their confidence, so heavy in their repetitions and summaries. But then, there is also *The Origin of Species,* winding in its periodic sentences, replete with modifiers, disclaimers, and exceptions.[6]

[6] Quoted from George K. Plochmann, "Darwin or Spencer?" *Science* 130: 1452–56; November 27, 1959. Reprinted from *Science* by permission.

These are comparatively rare instances in which a man achieves greatness in spite of a generally ineffective style of writing; John Dewey is one:

To begin with, he wrote badly—almost, indeed, as though it were a matter of principle. Most of his books were unorganized and repetitious, many of his arguments imprecise and incomplete. At times his sentences have vigor and bite. At other times we enter a sentence of Dewey's and find ourselves in a trackless thicket, from which we emerge at the other end scratched, shaken, and relieved. In Dewey's hands, even individual words play tricks on us, snarling when we expect them to purr, evaporating when we expect them to stand for something solid. Dewey did not invent his own system of notation, but he did not write in ordinary English either. With some help from his long apprenticeship in German idealism, he made ordinary English over into an artificial language.

To be sure, there was a purpose behind this semantic mayhem. Dewey had a sense of the nuances of terms and a shrewd Yankee judgment about ambiguities. He saw, or thought he saw, that many words we habitually use—including words like "experience," "reality," "true," and "good," which are fundamental in building our conception of the world and our place in it—have quite the wrong meanings attached to them as a result of their historical careers. He wanted to squeeze the wrong meanings out of these words and attach new and better meanings to them. So he used the words not as they are ordinarily used, but as he thought they ought to be used, and he frequently gave old terms new depth and power in the process.

Unfortunately, however, he did not always remember that his readers needed to be warned about what he was doing. And he frequently replaced an old ambiguity simply with a new and more troublesome polyguity. Surely, for example, it is confusing to remark, as Dewey once did, that his book *Experience and Nature* might just as easily have been called *Culture and Nature*, and that the title would not have changed its meaning with this change in its terms. Whatever the reasons may have been, Dewey wrote tortuously, inexactly, carelessly. . . .

What, then, remains? Why did Dewey make the stir that he did? What did he leave that was important, and that we can choose to forget only at a great loss to ourselves?

The answer can be found, I would suggest, only if we are prepared to look at Dewey from a point of view that is not habitual in philosophical circles today. He did not have some of the qualities which a professional philosopher ought to have. He was not an elegant thinker and not always a disciplined one. But he had a quality which can make the difference between a merely skillful philosopher and a first-rate original mind. In his own cheerful, unaggressive way, he was a visionary.

It is not easy to think of this quiet, patient man in this way. He was easygoing, unimpassioned, and temperate. He did not go in for flights of fancy or bursts of indignation or indulge in the consolations of paradox and irony like those other visionaries of his generation, Shaw and Russell. He simply kept going, year after year, sticking to his guns, insistent, indefatigable, and always returning—the sure mark of a visionary—to the same basic theme. . . .

Without vanity or pretentiousness, John Dewey made himself a spokesman for the best hopes of his generation. And to our generation he leaves the image of a man of unforced courage and honesty, living by choice in the main-stream of events, and yet rising above events to a coherent vision of what men might make of themselves. He helped us to see farther and to move more freely. It is to him as much as to anyone that we owe what belief we have that our own place in history can be an opportunity and not a fatality.[7]

John Lubbock wrote books that sold by the hundred thousand, edition after edition, published in many languages. His success is not really surprising, for he had hit on a technique then quite new and rarely copied successfully since that time, for he took the whole reading public into his confidence and never wrote down to it.

There is hardly a book of his which could not be suitably read to the family before bedtime and which does not at the same time tell the expert much that he didn't know and suggest things he had never thought of. And he kept it up. From *Prehistoric Times*, published in 1865, to *Marriage, Totemism and Religion*, in 1911, there is hardly a consecutive three-year period in which a book by him, important, influential, and extremely popular, did not appear.

Books on botany, geology, archeology, sociology, and zoology; books on economics and books on scenery; books on the pleasures of life and the history of coins—it seems incredible that books by one man on such varied subjects should be always readable and almost always of substantial scientific value, until one considers Lubbock's special advantages and abilities. He knew everybody who knew anything; he never forgot what he had heard or read or seen, and he kept to the end of his life the sense of wonder and the curiosity of childhood; he saw the relations between apparently unrelated things, and he saw, with the clarity of the successful businessman, the best thing to do next. He was the master of the wide view and the limited and attainable objective.[8]

Communicative Accuracy and Science News Writing

Scientists are cautioned against attempting, in a "popular" description of their efforts, the same precision and detail as would be appropriate in communicating with colleagues. "Communicative accuracy," or the effective accuracy of a written statement, depends primarily upon the reader's interpretation.

[7] Quoted from Charles Frankel, "John Dewey: Where He Stands." *Teacher Education Quarterly* 17: 84–94; Spring 1960.

[8] Quoted from R. J. Pumphrey, "The Forgotten Man: Sir John Lubbock." *Science* 129: 1087–92; April 24, 1959. Reprinted from *Science* by permission.

It is important for scientists to describe their activities to the public in such a way that they will be generally understandable and properly informative. This runs into the practical difficulty that some scientists, when they attempt a "popular" description of their labors and of their ideas, insist on achieving almost the same precision and completeness of statement which they would, quite properly, use in talking to their scientific colleagues. "You must not expect me to say that genes are distributed along a chromosome like different sizes and colors of beads along a string, for I have no satisfactory evidence that genes are as discrete as separate beads, and also I don't know about their sizes and shapes." Such scientists feel the urge to attach to each general statement of a popular exposition all the cautionary qualifications, all the modifying details, and all the scholarly footnotes that they would use in a technical report.

It may be helpful to suggest to such scientists that they consider the concept of "communicative accuracy." This concept rests upon the fact, not always recognized, that the effective accuracy of a written statement depends primarily upon the interpretation given to it by the reader. A statement may be said to have communicative accuracy, relative to a given audience of readers or hearers, if it fulfills two conditions. First, taking into account what the audience does and does not already know, it must take the audience closer to a correct understanding. The better an example of communicative accuracy it is, the more gain in understanding it will achieve—but the basic point is simply that it must gain ground in the right direction. Second, its inaccuracies (as judged at a more sophisticated level) must not mislead, must not be of a sort which will block subsequent and further progress toward the truth. Both of these criteria, moreover, are to be applied from the point of view of the audience, not from the more informed and properly more critical point of view of an expert.

Communicative accuracy is important to all of us all of the time. Consider the illuminating example, recently offered by a newspaper reporter, of the two men coming home from work and greeting their wives. One says, "My dear, when I look into your face, time stands still." The other remarks, "My dear, your face would stop a clock."[9]

Many science news writers and reporters say that communication would be greatly improved if the scientist would behave or act as follows:[10]

1. Be willing to cooperate with the press and society.

2. Have a better concept of the public that is to be informed. Scientists work with things. Reporters know about and write for people. The reporter's reader cannot be told what to read. If a science writer can convey the excitement of science he will get and hold the attention of the reader. The excite-

[9] Quoted from Warren Weaver, "Communicative Accuracy." *Science* 127: 499; March 7, 1958. Reprinted from *Science* by permission.

[10] Quoted from David M. Gates and John M. Parker, "Science News Writing." *Science* 133: 211–14; January 20, 1961. Reprinted from *Science* by permission.

ment factor is most important since newspapers, to be successful, must be read, and therefore a newspaper must appeal to both intellect and emotion.

3. Be willing to interpret his subject for the layman.

4. Realize that a reporter works with a deadline, not only on straight news stories but also on feature stories.

5. Recognize that newspapers contribute to civic projects, and that they need more help from scientists than they are getting at the present time. In the opinion of the science news writers this is particularly true with regard to crusades to raise teaching standards and teachers' salaries, wherein scientists, both as individuals and as groups, could work with the press better than they now do. Scientists appear not to accept enough public responsibility.

6. Realize that newspapers must crusade for 200 different things, of which science is only one.

7. Recognize a common tie between scientists and reporters; both are curious and both are skeptical.

Communication and Educational Research

The importance of communication in the field of educational research was stressed in the First International Conference on Educational Research, sponsored by the American Educational Research Association in cooperation with UNESCO. Adequate communication will contribute to the development of research and to applications of its findings in improvement of education at the personal, community, national, and international levels. Many of the sources of information and media of communication are listed in the chapter on library guides and techniques. Procedures for extending and improving communication, especially at the national and international levels, are as follows:[11]

1. Compilation and publication of a list of primary sources of information about educational research.

2. Preparation and publication of abstracts of the more important studies in certain fields of research selected because they are considered to be of international concern.

3. Compilation and publication of sources of information about research methods.

4. Clarification of technical terminology.

5. Compilation and publication of a list for all countries of sources of information about agencies of educational research, especially those which produce or publish the various types of instruments required for evaluation and measurement.

6. Greater international utilization of existing national periodicals carrying reports of research.

[11] Ben S. Morris and Others, "Communication in the Field of Educational Research," *Report of the First International Conference on Educational Research.* Educational Studies and Documents, No. 20. Paris: UNESCO, 1956. p. 10–15.

7. Development, where they do not already exist, of national centers for the collection, dissemination, and co-ordination of information about educational research and, in those national centers which already exist, a re-examination of their functions and responsibilities with respect to communication.

8. Expansion of the personal mailing list of individual research workers.

9. Widening the coverage of related studies that are reviewed before a piece of contemplated research is undertaken.

10. Use of ephemeral publications to reduce the time lag in communication.

11. More frequent movement of research workers from one country to another.

12. Greater recognition by research workers of their professional responsibility for improving the utilization of the results of research.

The foregoing procedures for extending and improving communication cover most of the techniques sometimes discussed under the topic of implementation of the results of research. The opening chapter presents a related discussion of the social responsibility of the scholar and scientist in making certain that the discoveries of research are used for the benefit of society. Scientific communication and improved relations between science and society will be advanced greatly if every practicing scientist assists in representing to the public the way in which science advances, the need for tests of the validity of conclusions, the logical processes of science, the demands for objectivity, the need for adequate and valid data, and the difference between claims and proved results (with his own research reports so written as to be models of objectivity and clarity).[12]

STRUCTURE OF THE REPORT

Standards of technical reporting and publication have taken form in a series of parts or sections that should be generally observed. These items of mechanical make-up are known as *format*. While the manuals and handbooks in the chapter bibliography are generally helpful, many publishing houses, editors of journals, and graduate schools or departments have their own sample pages, style sheets, or outlines for preparation of the book, thesis, or technical report.

Relatively short reports of less than forty or fifty pages usually do not lend themselves to a chapter form of organization, but can be divided into sections, with appropriate headings and subheadings. The parts of the longer technical report or thesis and the usual sequence are commonly

[12] Fred W. Decker, "Scientific Communications Should Be Improved." *Science* 125: 101–5; January 18, 1957.

as listed below. The several sections or subdivisions of this book may serve as examples of the different parts of the research report.[13]

Title Page
Acknowledgment (if any)
  (The terms *Preface* or *Foreword* ordinarily are used in printed books, and sometimes an *Editor's Introduction* is included.)
Table of Contents
List of Tables (if any)
List of Figures (if any)
Formulation and Definition of the Problem
  (One or more chapters dealing with such items as the problem, sources, procedure, and related literature)
Presentation and Interpretation of Data
  (Commonly divided into several chapters)
Summary and Conclusions
  (Restatement of problem, sources, and procedure; conclusions and their limitations; application and recommendations; needed research)
Bibliography
Appendix (if any)
Index (if any)
  (Customary only in printed volumes)

Preparation of the research or technical report is an aspect of the investigation that may move shuttle-like in relation to the various stages of formulation of the problem, development of the data-gathering procedure, gathering of evidence, and analysis and interpretation of data. In preference to waiting until the end of the investigation before preparing the report, first drafts of sections relating to formulation of the problem and the related literature may be prepared early in the project, and helpful notes at different stages of the study will simplify greatly preparation of the complete report.

Certain skills of outlining, briefing, and note-taking are basic to preparation of an adequate report. While the outline should be prepared before the report is written, in order to serve as a framework of organization, revision of the outline takes place as the study progresses and even as the report is being written. The brief, a more advanced stage than outlining, expresses concisely the principal statements under each topic. From the outline and brief may be phrased the appropriate headings and subheadings for the report. It is helpful to place the headings and subheadings of the outline and the different statements of the brief on separate slips of paper, in the interest of revision or rearrangement of the outline and brief. The chapters of this book may serve as illustrations of

---

[13] Carter V. Good and Douglas E. Scates, *Methods of Research:* Educational, Psychological, Sociological. New York: Appleton-Century-Crofts, 1954. p. 842.

outlining and of headings. Note-taking has been discussed in some detail in the chapter on the related literature.

The pages of this chapter in particular and of this book as a whole include many illustrations of form with respect to formulation of the problem, presentation of evidence, summarizing, conclusions, headings, footnotes, bibliographies, quotations, and other matters of format.

TITLE OF THE REPORT

The title of an investigation should be concise and as adequately descriptive as preferably two lines of space will permit. Certain forms of expression and phrasing are either redundant or superfluous; for example, aspects of, comments on, study of, investigation of, inquiry into, analysis of. Exceptions to this statement are helpful attempts to indicate the research procedure involved; for example, experimental investigation of, developmental study of, case study of. Many of the titles in the references of this book, in the *Review of Educational Research,* and in the *Encyclopedia of Educational Research* are suggestive. The particular graduate school or department usually has its own style sheet for the title page of the thesis or dissertation.

ACKNOWLEDGMENT

The terms *acknowledgment, preface,* and *foreword* are commonly used as synonyms in the preparation of graduate studies and similar typed reports, although the printed book frequently makes distinctions between these expressions. The usual designation for this preliminary part of the thesis or dissertation is acknowledgment. It is appropriate to recognize substantial assistance and cooperation in concise and temperate language, although tributes to the graduate advisory committee, librarians, typists, and clerks seem out of order.

TABLE OF CONTENTS

If the working outline and brief are logical and well organized, the design or structural pattern of the report should be clearly apparent, with the table of contents serving as a synopsis or headline display. Since the typed report or thesis usually has no index, a reasonably complete table of contents is essential for the guidance of the reader. It is advantageous for a heading in the body of the report and in the table of contents to keep within one line of space. The table of contents and the index of this book may serve illustrative purposes.

TABLES AND FIGURES

Titles of tables and figures should be listed accurately on separate pages in the front matter or section of the report, numbered consecutively in one list for tables and in another list for figures. Figures may include all types of graphic representation or illustrations, whether called graphs, charts, diagrams, maps, or photographs. Titles of tables and figures should include information concerning who, what, when, where, and how many. It is advantageous to phrase the titles concisely within two lines, avoiding such wording as "showing," "table showing," or "graph showing." Titles or legends are placed above tables and below figures.

A table is appropriate for any series of items that involve frequencies. For purposes of interpretation, it is well to confine each table to a single page, sometimes breaking up unwieldly tables into smaller tables, and placing each table in the manuscript as near the point of first reference as possible. Sometimes an especially lengthy or complex table of several or more pages can be placed to advantage in the appendix, with a shorter summary table in the body of the thesis for purposes of discussion and interpretation. A practical test of the effectiveness of a table or figure is whether it is understandable apart from the text or discussion of the technical report.

Figures should be used only when they make a real contribution to interpretation of the data or tables, never to impress the reader. The general arrangement of a figure is from left to right, and the lettering is placed so as to be easily read from the base as the bottom or sometimes from the right-hand edge of the figure as the bottom. The horizontal scale for curves usually reads from left to right, and the vertical scale from bottom to top.

The details of tabular and graphic representation are such that an adequate treatment is not possible within the limits of this chapter. Therefore, the writer of a technical report that includes tables or figures is referred to the available handbooks or manuals.[14]

[14] Darrell Huff, *How to Lie with Statistics.* New York: W. W. Norton and Co., 1954. 142 p.

R. R. Lutz, *Graphic Presentation Simplified.* New York: Funk and Wagnalls, 1949. xx + 202 p.

Rudolf Modley and Others, *Pictographs and Graphs:* How to Make and Use Them. New York: Harper & Brothers, 1952. 186 p.

Publication Manual of the American Psychological Association. 1957 Revision. Washington: The Association, 1957. 70 p.

Anna C. Rogers, *Graphic Charts Handbook.* Washington: Public Affairs Press, 1961. iv + 189 p.

Calvin F. Schmid, *Handbook of Graphic Representation.* New York: Ronald Press, 1954. vii + 316 p.

Helen M. Walker and Walter N. Durost, *Statistical Tables:* Their Structure and

FORMULATION OF THE PROBLEM

The formulation and development of the problem may require one or more chapters to present an analysis of the problem into its constituent elements, limits or scope of the study, related literature, sources of data, method or technique, technical terminology, initial assumptions, and hypotheses. Since these details have been presented at some length in the chapter on the development of the problem, only brief comment will be made at this time. If the sequence in a well-organized report is to tell the reader where he is going, take him there, and then tell him where he has been, the first purpose should be accomplished in the section devoted to formulation and development of the problem. In this sense, the introductory chapter looks forward, and also looks backward through the medium of the related literature and historical background. The opening chapter may well begin with a direct statement of the purpose of the study. This overview section of the research report may be prepared to advantage early in the investigation, with necessary revisions as the study progresses. A functional test of the effectiveness of the introductory chapter is to ask whether one who has never heard of the investigation could secure, through the statement of the problem, a satisfactory understanding of the purpose, sources of data, and technique.

BODY OF THE REPORT

The body of the research report presents the evidence. The inexperienced writer frequently leaves gaps in his report, partly because he is so familiar with the investigation that he overlooks the importance of certain details and of a unified organization for the reader. A careful outline, meaningful headings, and a brief of key statements will aid materially in developing a unified report. The body of the report varies in keeping with the content and research method represented. The historical narrative usually is presented in a series of chronological or topical chapters. The case-clinical report may have a series of chapters dealing with the different types of cases, or a number of sections on the several steps in case study and case work, or some combination of these two forms of organization of content. Unity can be promoted within a chapter and within the report as a whole through introductory, transitional, and sum-

---

Use. New York: Bureau of Publications, Teachers College, Columbia University, 1936. v + 76 p.

Walter E. Weld, *How to Chart: Facts from Figures with Graphs.* Norwood, Mass.: Codex Book Co., 1959. xiv + 218 p.

Hans Zeisel, *Say It with Figures:* How to Make Figures Make Sense—a Guide for Those Who Use and Read Statistics. Fourth Revised Edition. New York: Harper & Brothers, 1957. xviii + 257 p.

mary statements; appropriate cross references; placement of lengthy tables, questionnaires, tests, and other exhibits in the appendix; skill in handling quotations; and avoidance of overloading of the text with statistical details.

SUMMARY AND CONCLUSIONS

The chapter of summarization and conclusions looks backward, and also forward through consideration of applications, recommendations, and needed research. The final chapter should be an illustration of the adage that the whole is greater than the sum of the parts. Although chapter summaries are helpful in preparing the closing chapter, the mere process of adding these details together falls short of the synthesis or integration expected at the end of the report. The summarizing chapter is especially valuable to many readers, particularly in business and industry, who may not go outside the closing chapter (sometimes the summary is the opening section in business reports) for information concerning problem, sources of evidence, method or technique, conclusions and their limitations, applications and implementation, recommendations, and needed research. The final chapter should recapitulate the answer to the opening question or hypothesis of the study. The investigator should plainly label all instances where he has depended on his own judgment rather than directly on the data in presenting limitations, applications, recommendations, and problems for future research.

BIBLIOGRAPHY AND DOCUMENTATION

Adequate bibliographical and summarizing work as a phase of the investigation has been characterized as the "pilot" of research. This view has been emphasized in the chapters on formulation of the problem and on the library guides. The rules of professional ethics require adequate documentation of ideas and quotations from other sources. Appropriation of ideas from another author, without proper recognition, is a type of intellectual dishonesty known as plagiarism. The ethical standards of psychologists as characterized in the chapter on case-clinical studies, include principles relating to professional relationships, research, writing, and publishing. Specific examples of plagiarism or literary piracy include theft of ideas without documentation, use of figures or drawings without credit lines, direct or indirect quotations without proper documentation, and sometimes reproduction for class use of large portions of copyrighted works without permission from the publisher or author. As a general rule, permission to quote is not necessary in an unpublished thesis or typewritten report. In writing for publication, however, when quoting more than a few lines from a published source it is wise to secure permission from the copyright holder. Extremes of documentation are to be avoided; there is a common body of knowledge in each field which belongs to the discipline itself rather than to an individual author. A major purpose of direct quotations is to portray accurately the language and thought of the particular author. This book includes numerous illustrations of direct and indirect quotations and documentation (in footnotes):

Direct quotations of more than a few lines in smaller type (single space in a typed manuscript)

Shorter direct quotations within double quotation marks as part of the paragraph of discussion

Indirect quotations (paraphrasing or borrowing of ideas) without quotation marks but with appropriate documentation in footnotes.

Footnotes have several valid purposes:[15]

1. To indicate to the reader where he may find the source of a quotation or a more extended account of some subject mentioned in the text

2. To cite authority—not just any old source—in support of a statement, an opinion, or contention in the text that might be questioned by the skeptical reader

3. To direct the attention of the reader to opinions on controversial issues contrary to those expressed in the text.

Criteria for evaluating footnotes include:

1. The accuracy and precision by which the footnote guides the reader to the source

2. The reliability of the source

3. The extent to which the source satisfies and fulfills the intention of the citation.

In technical or research reports, it is common practice to place a complete bibliography of all pertinent references immediately after the summary chapter, arranged alphabetically by authors, although chapter bibliographies sometimes are listed, as illustrated in the *Review of Educational Research*. The references in the bibliography must be numbered consecutively, if a cross-reference system of citation from the body of the report to the bibliography is preferred to footnotes. In the interest of uniformity and completeness of information, it is necessary to translate references of different styles from a variety of sources into the form adopted by the particular graduate school or publisher. In this chapter and book are hundreds of illustrations of bibliographical form for the

[15] William D. Mallam, "A Focus on Footnotes." *Journal of Higher Education* 31: 99–102; February 1960.

several types of references: books not identified with a series, publications (monographs, yearbooks, and certain books) identified with a series, journals or periodicals, and unpublished studies (including theses and dissertations).

In this book the reader will find hundreds of illustrations of footnote usage, relating to such items as: consecutive numbering throughout each chapter or section of the report, listing of the author's name in normal order (rather than surname first), use of *ibid.* and *op. cit.*, and the system of cross reference to a consecutively numbered chapter bibliography. *Ibid.* is an abbreviation of *ibidem*, meaning "in the same place"; it is used when succeeding uninterrupted citations of a work occur on the same page or within the space of a few pages. *Op. cit.* is the abbreviation of *opere citato*, meaning "in the work cited"; it is used (following the author's name) when other references intervene between different citations of a particular work or when a number of pages have intervened since the work was cited in full. Some writers prefer a system of cross reference to a consecutively numbered bibliography, rather than numerous footnotes, as illustrated in the *Review of Educational Research* and *Encyclopedia of Educational Research*. John Brown's report (12: 80–90) would mean that pages 80–90 of item 12 in the bibliography contain the quotation or material cited.

APPENDIX

The appendix serves a useful purpose in providing a place for cumbersome or voluminous materials which tend to break the continuity of discussion and interpretation for the reader (in the body of the report). However, the appendix should not be made a convenient dumping ground for irrelevant materials, sometimes placed there in an attempt to impress the reader or to swell the volume of the report. The pertinent materials assigned to the appendix should be grouped in homogeneous parts, provided with appropriate numbers and headings, and listed in the table of contents. Cross references in the body of the report may be made to the appendix in connection with such materials as lengthy tables, raw data, questionnaires, schedules, interview forms, standard tests, form letters, formulas, and lengthy quotations from documents (for example, constitutions, laws, and court decisions).

STYLE AND READABILITY

The details of style, usage, and readability cannot be discussed within the scope of this chapter and must be left to the manuals, handbooks, and dictionaries listed in the chapter bibliography. The dictionaries of education, psychology, and sociology are also listed in the chapter dealing with the related literature and library guides. A number of illustrations of style are presented in the chapter on historical writing.

The manuals may be consulted for assistance in diction (the choice and use of words), phraseology (the arrangement of words in groups), and style, which is concerned with certain more general characteristics of writing, especially individuality of expression. The graduate student and others may turn to these numerous manuals and handbooks listed in the chapter bibliography for many other details of form and usage which cannot be presented within the limited scope and space of the present chapter.

Skill in proofreading of manuscripts and printer's proof is an important asset, as appropriately expressed in the following anonymous verses, probably written by some harried proofreader:

> The typographical error is a slippery thing and sly,
> You can hunt till you are dizzy, but it somehow
> will get by;
> Till the forms are off the presses it is strange how
> still it keeps;
> It shrinks down in a corner, and it never stirs or
> peeps.
> That typographical error, too small for human
> eyes,
> Till the ink is on the paper, when it grows to
> mountain size.
>
> The boss he stares with horror, then he grabs his
> hair and moans,
> The copyreader drops his head upon his hands
> and groans,
> The remainder of the issues may be clean as clean
> can be,
> But that typographical error is the only thing you
> see.

The student who is tempted to consider accurate and consistent usage of relatively minor importance may well ponder the case of the lone typewriter key that went wrong.[16]

Thxrx is nothing wrong with our typxwritxr xxcxpt for onx littlx kxy. Thx othxr forty-two work pxrfxctly. But just onx inactivx kxy makxs a diffxrxncx, doxsn't it?

For instancx, you may say to yoursxlf, "I am just onx. What I do or don't

---

[16] Quoted from *NEA Journal* 50: 70; September 1961.

do won't makx much diffxrxncx to thx National Xducation Association." But you arx wrong.

Thx Association nxxds you. Its program is incomplxtx without you. Thx nxxt timx you think you arx not important, rxmxmbxr our typxwritxr and say to yoursxlf, "I am nxxdxd vxry much as a kxy mxmbxr of an important group."

—Author unknown

Examples of Style

The young author may be reminded that certain rules of good sentence structure and word choice sometimes have been broken in order to express ideas simply and effectively, as witnessed by Lincoln's Gettysburg Address. The "corrected theme" reproduced on the next page was intended to poke a little fun at the teacher who would have writing done strictly "by rule."[17]

Scientists and research workers at times are accused of being inarticulate and at other times are charged with writing in a language that few persons can understand. A technical or research report may well use a style that is simple, direct, and effective, without ornateness or literary embellishments, but with whatever skill in language the reporter possesses. Formality in reporting should not be permitted to stifle an effective individual style of writing, although there is something about technical or research reporting which sometimes freezes the pen of an author. As illustrated in the chapter on historical writing, able scholars have varied greatly in style. Ebbinghaus and William James wrote with sufficient scientific rigor, yet in a lucid and interesting manner, with glimpses of the author as a human personality, whereas Wundt almost overwhelmed the reader with a mass of facts, arguments, and dicta. Gibbon experimented extensively before he could find a middle ground between a dull chronicle and a rhetorical declamation.

Comparison of the style of the James brothers often has been made. The most frequently repeated comparison states that Henry was a novelist who wrote like a psychologist, while William was a psychologist who wrote like a novelist.

With a bit more awareness and a little less sententiousness one would today have to ask: What kind of psychologist? Our contemporary to-do over the clandestine rendezvous of experimental and clinical psychologies makes one swallow precociously before accepting this dubiously balanced verbal bait. In the light of fuller knowledge of both Henry and William, it would be more tenable to assert that Henry was essentially a clinical psychologist who worked professionally as a novelist, while William was essentially a philosopher who

[17] R. Hugh Schrain, "Think English Is Easy Here?" *Michigan Education Journal* 34: 250; February 1, 1957.

Stanley Elam, "Think English Is Easy Here?" *Phi Delta Kappan* 41: 330–31; May 1960.

THINK ENGLISH IS EASY HERE?

Bad start- be explicit
say "eighty-seven"   *"fathers"?*

repetition of sounds — Fourscore and seven years ago, our fathers brought

forth upon this continent a new nation, conceived in lib-

erty, and dedicated to the proposition that all men are

created equal.   *not a good word*
                        "gigantic" would be better

Now we are engaged in a great civil war, testing

whether that nation, or any nation so conceived and so *you used these words before*

tr - rule 194, p.6 — dedicated, can long endure. We are met on a great battle-

too many monosyllabic words — field of that war. We have come to dedicate a portion of

that field as a final resting place for those who here

gave their lives that that nation might live. [It is alto-

gether fitting and proper that we should do this.] *trite sentence*

meaning?? — But in a larger sense we cannot dedicate, we cannot

consecrate, we cannot hallow this ground. The brave men, *use another word*

spelling!

living and dead, who struggled here, have consecrated it.

Don't you mean "subtract"?

far above our poor power to add or detract. The world will *awkward*

Rule 194 p.6 — little note nor long remember what we say here; but it can

never forget what they did here. It is for us, the living, *make up your mind!*

awkward — rather, to be dedicated here to the unfinished work which

they who fought here have thus far so nobly advanced. It *Too many "here's"*

tr. — is rather for us to be here dedicated to the great task *trite word, use "tremendous"*
                                                              Rule 74, p.89

Too many small words. Eliminate — remaining before us: that from these honored dead we take

increased devotion to that cause for which they gave the

last full measure of devotion; that we here highly resolve

that these dead shall not have died in vain; that this

nation under God, shall have a new birth of freedom; and

spelling!

that government of the people, by the people, and for the

people, shall not perish from the earth.

This theme is fair, but there is too much repetition in it. There are six "That's" in the last sentence alone. Need more variety in word choice, and your words are too simple. Try again — you are improving. C—

worked for a time professionally as a clinical psychologist. The pretty paradox, alas, vanishes, but in compensation we see the brothers re-emerge, more alive than before, from the word magician's vanishing box.[18]

In spite of his style, John Dewey was our greatest educational philosopher. His written statements have been labeled as flat and involved, "lumbering and bumbling." It provoked Justice Holmes to the famous comment: "So, methought, God would have spoken had He been inarticulate, but keenly desirous to tell you how it was." Dewey's published books, articles, and pamphlets represent a pile more than twelve feet high, but one critic declared that, if he ever wrote one quotable sentence, it got permanently lost in the pile. None of the standard books of quotations contains a single Dewey entry, yet in personal conversation and sometimes in the classroom the Vermont Yankee's native wit and shrewdness became evident. The secret of Dewey's extraordinary power to stimulate his students in the remaking of their minds probably is found in the statement of Ralph Barton Perry: "He does not feel obliged to live up to his reputation: to be impressive, witty, eloquent, or even interesting; he simply says what he thinks."[19]

Kettering's exceptional ability as a public speaker was one of his great gifts. But so unconventional was his platform manner that the reasons for his singular success are not easy to analyze. He made no pretense of being an orator nor did he have any of the mannerisms or tricks of one. His talks are like an informal chat with his audience, full of wit and wisdom. However, his thoughts and expression are stimulating, involving a knack of putting things in direct and simple terms, of using imagery and apt analogy, and of injecting illustrations, anecdotes, and humor which give his talks vividness and vigor. Many of his epigrams have been widely quoted. In the transcript of one of his addresses on the serious subject of research, parentheses occur forty-two times to indicate laughter. "Some technical reports are so dry and dusty," he would say, "that if you put a pile of them in a hydraulic press and apply millions of pounds pressure to it, not a drop of juice will run out."[20]

Greenstein's interests were broad and ranged far beyond the sciences. He was a prolific reader and in his Harvard days delighted in Dickens, especially in *Pickwick Papers*. He read widely in philosophy, theology, and biography and was something of an expert on the history of the Civil War—its battles, issues, and great men. His breadth of reading and

[18] Quoted from review by Saul Rosenzweig, "The Jameses' Stream of Consciousness." *Contemporary Psychology* 3: 250–57; September 1958, of Frederick W. Dupee, Editor, *Henry James:* Autobiography. New York: Criterion Books, 1956. xiv + 622.

[19] Harold A. Larrabee, "John Dewey as Teacher." *School and Society* 87: 378–81; October 10, 1959.

[20] T. A. Boyd, *Professional Amateur:* The Biography of Charles Franklin Kettering. New York: E. P. Dutton and Co., 1957. p. 215.

appreciation of literature must have contributed to the high quality of his own writings.[21]

STYLE AND EFFECTIVE WRITING IN PSYCHOLOGY AND EDUCATION

Elimination of carelessness and individual peculiarities from seminar reports and theses is important training for graduate students, and is at the same time good training for preparation of articles for publication.[22]

To graduate students, however, APA style seems to represent, among other things, stultifying rigidity, the height of anxiety reducing compulsivity, the severity of a harsh superego, and the epitome of the D_a personality. As is apparent, these petulant remarks have been uttered by students in clinical psychology classes. However, such emotions are probably shared by experimentalists and statisticians as well as by their more qualitatively minded colleagues.

Many graduate students have expressed the further thought that style manuals are a new straight jacket for insuring modern conformity and extinguishing the creative spark of individuality. This thought is incorrect entirely.

The exactness demanded in professional writing and the absolute assurance of the advantages of uniformity in style can be traced back to the extraordinary care with which Jewish scribes transmitted their sacred writings. In talmudic works the most exacting procedural rules were established, determining for all a uniformity of style. Between A.D. 90 and 100, a synod, convened at Jamnia, established instructions in various matters of form.

An apparently anonymous report of a conversation between a graduate student and his professorial adviser includes humorous illustrations of the simple language in the student's draft of his manuscript and the ornate language supposedly suggested by the professor:

Student: "It will be hard to provide enough schools for the children entering in 1963."

Professor: "The phenomenon of fecundity has confronted American education with a challenge of Herculean proportions. An evaluation of the implication to the tax structure of state governments in providing adequate educational facilities is a difficult and complex task."

Student: "Professor Blank's scheme of teaching reading was tried, but it did not work."

Professor: "The writer does not choose to disparage the efficacy of Professor Blank's method of teaching reading. It is not inappropriate, however, to point out that careful scrutiny of the method shows it to be what might be called ineffective."

[21] John T. Edsall, "J. P. Greenstein, Biochemist and Investigator of Cancer." *Science* 130: 83–85; July 10, 1959.

[22] Quoted from Dell Lebo, "Uniformity of Style in Professional Writing During the First Century." *American Psychologist* 14: 151–52; March 1959.

Student: "The federal government has no control over local schools."

Professor: "The federal government has no plenary jurisdiction over local school matters. Moreover, since government in the United States is administered at federal, state, and local levels, the implications to government are several, rather than single, and affect each of these three levels of government in separate and differing fashion."

Student: " 'Early to bed and early to rise, makes a man healthy, wealthy, and wise,' strikes me as an effective form of expression."

Professor: "It is better to say: 'Early retirement is a significant factor in one's physical development, pecuniary success, and intellectual stature.' "

Certain principles of readability in reporting research may be summarized as follows:[23]

1. Appeal and interest increase readability.

2. Personalization means putting human interest into the report: through a review of previous investigations as a story of other persons' successes and failures, an account of how the author collected and treated the data, illustrative cases, and deviations from central tendencies.

3. Pattern or design should be made plain to the reader.

4. Through appropriate emphasis the reader should get the important points.

5. Too great density or concentration of ideas may make reading difficult, requiring some expansion or dilution.

6. Plain words are important in making a report readable.

In summary, with respect to flexibility and individuality of style, we well may quote the first editor of *Contemporary Psychology,* a book review journal for psychologists.

For myself, I take the use of the scientific language more lightly, less rigorously, and I am glad that most of my colleagues do, too. J. J. Thomson said that a scientific activity is a policy, and he might have made his comment broader to say that all scientific activity is a policy to be accepted when it works and changed when it does not. I do not pretend to be a scientist in all my speech, nor do I want students to be. I want them to have values and purposes, to know when to escape the scientific strait jacket and also when to get a new straight jacket. There should be nothing so inflexible about science or scientific conduct or scientific language. What we want for scientists is wisdom, good judgment, the ability to speak and write English delicately and significantly, enough wisdom to break any rule when a good purpose will be supported thereby.

Urbanity never hurt a scientist yet. Using English with skill, relying on the connotations to work as they should, is less secure than the rigor of mathematics but an art capable of much greater refinement. . . .

[23] Ruth Strang, "Principles of Readability Applied to Reporting Research," *Improving Educational Research.* Washington: American Educational Research Association, 1948. p. 41–43.

In any event—say I, anthropomorphically purposive, and purposively anthropomorphic—let us not warp our young scientists by rigid rules. Always remembering that we do not wish for all to be alike, let us cultivate urbanity, wisdom, and flexibility. Let us help them to learn to speak and write well, clearly, freely, attractively and differently from one another. Let us hope they can learn to think of science as a happy way of life, not as a harsh taskmaster with a code of morals dangling at his belt.[24]

Style, Readability, and the Textbook

The textbook author faces certain dilemmas that may be present in part in writing the thesis, seminar paper, or other technical report. While the following problems of technical writing deal especially with psychology, these words of wisdom are widely applicable and may serve as a partial summary of concepts and procedures for effective research reporting in general.[25]

1. Write a unified book—give it a plot; let each chapter have a subplot; give every unit a beginning, a middle and an end; *but* remember coverage, and let not the yen for coherence select *out* significant content.

2. Write a sequential book if you can, with chapter building on chapter; *but* remember that your logical sequence may be another's chaos.

3. Emphasize a general and informed appreciation of the broad field of psychology; *but* remember that the student ought to learn also a lot of detailed facts, technical methods, and precise vocabulary.

4. Try to help the student see psychology in its intellectual and social context; *but* do not take up much space with such general material, and remember that the field may best speak for itself if only described.

5. Help the student see that psychology is the most challenging and exciting of all scientific fields; *but* stay in perspective, for it is only one of man's ways of studying man.

6. Emphasize methods, approaches, and the mature scientific attitude toward problems of behavior; these things may constitute psychology's greatest present contribution; *but* remember space, coverage, and depth.

7. Represent every special segment of psychology as best you can, for there is intellectual excitement for somebody in every one of them; *but* don't, for goodness' sake, write a catalog.

8. Write in a spritely and literate style if you can; *but* watch your dignity; the text writer's role is a stuffy one.

9. Write directly to students as you know and like them, *but* remember that you are the instructor's servant; don't interfere with his role and his function; also remember that the instructor is a gatekeeper who decides whether you shall have any access at all to his students.

[24] Quoted from Edwin G. Boring, "On Eschewing Teleology." *Science* 129: 608–10; March 6, 1959. Reprinted from *Science* by permission.
[25] Quoted from Fillmore Sanford, "How to Write a Textbook." *American Psychologist* 6: 127–28; April 1961.

10. Write to the student where he is and bring him, if you can, to where you want him to be; *but* never underestimate him on what he already knows, and don't let him get the idea that psychology is simple, for it isn't.

11. Write personally; the author is an individual and students are people; *but* authors are essentially anonymous and personality is an intrusion.

12. Write concretely, remember James and Boring; *but* remember that every informality will irritate someone and that figures of speech, however pleasant, are inherently inaccurate.

13. If a sentence comes out with a bit of humor in it, let it alone; laughing and learning are not incompatible; *but* keep humor clean, brief, relevant, and non-distracting; do not take time out to tell jokes, avoid the pachydermal, and never poke hostile fun at anybody.

14. Write to the A-student, maintain high intellectual standards, never talk down, predigest, or oversimplify; *but* remember the C-student, for he is in the vast majority and will run the world; take a bit more time to make a point, write in English wherever possible, be friendly to anyone who has had the gumption to choose to learn something about psychology.

15. Articulate the book with the arts and sciences curriculum; *but* make as many majors as you can and help prepare these for further courses in psychology.

16. Emphasize the ideas that you'd like your son to carry with him the rest of his life; *but* remember that the field of psychology is broad and that your own importances are another's trivia.

17. Don't clutter up the reader with the trappings of scholarship; *but* remember that psychology *is* a scholarly field with a rich literature and that undocumented statements are taboo. (Also, as far as you know, the uncited experiment may have been performed by a psychologist who teaches 2000 students every semester.)

18. Don't be hesitant to speculate a bit, interpret a bit or even preach a little on the virtues of science and education; *but* remember to label clearly any departure from the evidence or from established theory.

19. There is substance, significance, and great intellectual challenge in psychology, so teach it with confidence; *but* remember that it is a young science and in many areas incompletely formed; so teach it with humility and, without diffidence or apology, take the student into your confidence.

20. If you find yourself coming down with a novel approach, either to content or to method of presenting it, follow your inclinations; there is plenty of room and perhaps even need for change in our established ways of handling introductory psychology; *but* watch it, son; the accepted approaches have much to recommend them and human tolerance for novelty, even should it be of high quality, is finite.

CONCLUDING STATEMENT

As an exposition type of composition, the major purpose of the technical report is communication of ideas and evidence, with the emphasis of the interpretation on ideas about facts. In trying to make our meanings clear, without regard for experience and examples, it is often useless to explain words with other words, because these in turn require more words. There is no meaning beyond experience.

Effective communication will contribute to the development of educational investigation and to the application of research findings to improvement of education at personal, community, national, and international levels.

Preparation of the report is an integral part of the total research project which may move shuttle-like in relation to the several stages of development of the problem, gathering evidence, and analysis and interpretation of data, rather than waiting until the end of the investigation before starting the writing of the report.

In the interest of readability and communication, the technical report should have a style that is simple and direct, without rhetorical flourishes, but with every bit of language skill the reporter possesses. The young author may be reminded that certain rules of good sentence structure and word choice sometimes have been broken in order to express ideas simply and effectively. Elimination of carelessness and individual peculiarities from seminar reports and theses is important training for graduate students, and is at the same time good training for preparation of articles for publication.

SELECTED REFERENCES

ALEXANDER, Carter, and BURKE, Arvid J. *How to Locate Educational Information and Data.* Fourth Edition. New York: Bureau of Publications, Teachers College, Columbia University, 1958. p. xvii + 419.

American Association for Health, Physical Education, and Recreation. *Research Methods Applied to Health, Physical Education, and Recreation.* Revised Edition. Washington: The Association, National Education Association, 1952. p. 478-517.

BALL, John, and WILLIAMS, Cecil B. *Report Writing.* New York: Ronald Press, 1955. 407 p.

BARZUN, Jacques, and GRAFF, Henry F. *The Modern Researcher.* New York: Harcourt, Brace and Co., 1957. p. 229-354.

BEBELL, Clifford S. "Getting Meaning from Research," *Research for Curriculum Improvement.* 1957 Yearbook. Washington: Association for Supervision and Curriculum Development, National Education Association, 1957. p. 119-51.

BOAZ, Martha T., Editor. *Modern Trends in Documentation.* New York: Pergamon Press, 1959. 103 p.

CAMPBELL, W. G. *Form and Style in Thesis Writing.* Boston: Houghton Mifflin Co., 1954. vi + 114 p.

DAVIDSON, Henry A. *Guide to Medical Writing:* A Practical Manual for Physicians, Dentists, Nurses, Pharmacists. New York: Ronald Press, 1957. vii + 338 p.

DECKER, Fred W. "Scientific Communications Should Be Improved." *Science* 125: 101-5; January 18, 1957.

DUGDALE, Kathleen. *A Manual of Form for Theses and Term Reports.* Bloomington: Indiana University, 1955. vi + 58 p.

EMBERGER, Meta R., and HALL, Marian R. *Scientific Writing.* W. Earl Britton, Editor. New York: Harcourt, Brace and Co., 1955. 468 p.

ENGLISH, Horace B., and ENGLISH, Ava C. *Comprehensive Dictionary of Psychological and Psychoanalytical Terms.* New York: Longmans, Green and Co., 1958. xiv + 594 p.

Faculty of Teachers College, University of Cincinnati. *A Guide for the Preparation of Dissertations, Theses, and Field Reports.* Cincinnati: University of Cincinnati, 1952. iii + 55 p.

FAIRCHILD, H. P., Editor. *Dictionary of Sociology.* New York: Philosophical Library, 1944. viii + 342 p.

FESTINGER, Leon, and KATZ, Daniel, Editors. *Research Methods in the Behavioral Sciences.* New York: Dryden Press, 1953. p. 579-646.

FISHBEIN, Morris. *Medical Writing:* The Technic and the Art. Third Edition. New York: McGraw-Hill Book Co., 1957. 272 p.

FLESCH, Rudolf. *The Art of Plain Talk.* New York: Harper & Brothers, 1946. xiii + 210 p.

FLESCH, Rudolf. *The Art of Readable Writing.* New York: Harper & Brothers, 1949. xvi + 237 p.

FLESCH, Rudolf, and LASS, A. H. *The Way to Write.* Revised Edition. New York: Harper & Brothers, 1949. x + 342 p.

GOLDHAMMER, Keith, and ELAM, Stanley, Editors. *Dissemination and Implementation.* Third Annual Phi Delta Kappa Symposium on Educational Research. Bloomington, Ind.: Phi Delta Kappa, 1962. xi + 200 p.

GOOD, Carter V., Editor. *Dictionary of Education.* Second Edition. New York: McGraw-Hill Book Co., 1959. xxx + 676 p.

GOOD, Carter V., and SCATES, Douglas E. *Methods of Research:* Educational, Psychological, Sociological. New York: Appleton-Century-Crofts, 1954. p. 832-96.

GOODE, William J., and HATT, Paul K. *Methods in Social Research.* New York: McGraw-Hill Book Co., 1952. Chapters 3, 4, 21.

GREEVER, Garland, JONES, E. S., and JONES, Agnes L. *The Century Collegiate Handbook.* Third Edition. New York: Appleton-Century-Crofts, 1950. xv + 460 p.

HAMMOND, Kenneth R., and ALLEN, Jeremiah M. *Writing Clinical Reports.* New York: Prentice-Hall, 1953. xii + 235 p.

HARRIMAN, Philip L. *New Dictionary of Psychology.* New York: Philosophical Library, 1947. 364 p.

HARWELL, George C. *Technical Communication.* New York: The Macmillan Co., 1960. 342 p. (A textbook that is primarily intended for the engineering student; Chapters 5, 6, and 7 discuss formal and informal reports and technical articles.)

Hicks, Tyler G. *Successful Technical Writing:* Technical Articles, Papers, Reports, Instruction and Training Manuals, and Books. New York: McGraw-Hill Book Co., 1959. 305 p.

Hilbish, Florence M. A. *The Research Paper.* New York: Bookman Associates, 1952. 292 p.

Hillway, Tyrus. *Introduction to Research.* Boston: Houghton Mifflin Co., 1956. p. 231-62.

Huber, Jack T. *Report Writing in Psychology and Psychiatry.* New York: Harper & Brothers, 1961. xii + 114 p.

Huff, Darrell. *How to Lie with Statistics.* New York: W. W. Norton and Co., 1954. 142 p.

Kierzek, John M., and Gilison, Walker. *The Macmillan Handbook of English.* Fourth Edition. New York: The Macmillan Co., 1960. xxi + 489 p.

Klopfer, W. G. *The Psychological Report:* Use and Communication of Psychological Findings. New York: Grune and Stratton, 1960. x + 146 p.

Leggett, Glenn, Mead, C. David, and Charvat, William. *Prentice-Hall Handbook for Writers.* Third Edition. Englewood Cliffs, N. J.: Prentice-Hall, 1960. 524 p.

Leggett, Glenn, and Yaggy, Elinor. *Writing a Paper:* From Idea to Finished Copy. New York: Ronald Press, 1955. 192 p.

Lipson, Shirley, and Abrams, Anne W. *The College of Education Style Manual.* Revised Edition. Columbus, Ohio: College of Education, Ohio State University, 1960. v + 18 p.

Lutz, R. R. *Graphic Presentation Simplified.* New York: Funk and Wagnalls, 1949. xx + 202 p.

MacWatt, Jack. "Improving Scientific Communication." *Science* 134: 313-16; August 4, 1961. (Reprints directly available from the publisher at a reasonable fee could supplement today's journals.)

A Manual of Style. Revised and Enlarged. Chicago: The University of Chicago Press, 1949. x + 498 p.

Marder, Daniel. *The Craft of Technical Writing.* New York: The Macmillan Co., 1960. 414 p. (A discussion of the principles of rhetoric basic to the writing situations encountered by scientists and technical men.)

McCormick, Thomas C., and Francis, Roy G. *Methods of Research in the Behavioral Sciences.* New York: Harper & Brothers, 1958. Chapters 8, 10.

Menzel, Donald H., Jones, Howard M., and Boyd, Lyle G. *Writing a Technical Paper.* New York: McGraw-Hill Book Co., 1961. 141 p.

Modley, Rudolf, and Others. *Pictographs and Graphs:* How to Make and Use Them. New York: Harper & Brothers, 1952. 186 p.

Moser, C. A. *Survey Methods in Social Investigation.* New York: The Macmillan Co., 1958. Chapter 15.

Nelson, J. R. *Writing the Technical Report.* Third Edition. New York: McGraw-Hill Book Co., 1952. 350 p.

Nolen, Barbara, and Goetz, Delia. *Writers' Handbook for the Development of Educational Materials.* Office of Education Bulletin 1959, No. 19. Washington: Government Printing Office, 1959. x + 183 p.

PARTEN, Mildred. *Surveys, Polls, and Samples:* Practical Procedures. New York: Harper & Brothers, 1950. Chapter 17.

Publication Manual of the American Psychological Association. 1957 Revision. Washington: The Association, 1957. 70 p.

RHODES, Fred H. *Technical Report Writing.* Second Edition. New York: McGraw-Hill Book Co., 1961. 175 p.

ROGERS, Anna C. *Graphic Charts Handbook.* Washington: Public Affairs Press, 1961. iv + 189 p.

RUMMEL, J. Francis. *An Introduction to Research Procedures in Education.* New York: Harper & Brothers, 1958. p. 278-345.

SANDERS, Chauncey. *An Introduction to Research in English Literary History.* New York: The Macmillan Co., 1952. p. 277-315.

SCHMID, Calvin F. *Handbook of Graphic Representation.* New York: Ronald Press, 1954. vii + 316 p.

SCOTT, M. Gladys, Editor. "Writing the Research Report," *Research Methods in Health, Physical Education, Recreation.* Second Edition. Washington: American Association for Health, Physical Education, and Recreation, 1959. Chapter 16.

SELLTIZ, Claire, and Others. "The Research Report," *Research Methods in Social Relations.* Revised One-Volume Edition. New York: Henry Holt and Co., 1959. Chapter 12.

SKILLIN, Marjorie E., GAY, Robert M., and Others. *Words into Type:* A Guide in the Preparation of Manuscripts; for Writers, Editors, Proofreaders and Printers. New York: Appleton-Century-Crofts, 1948. xx + 585 p.

SOUTHER, J. W. *Technical Report Writing.* New York: John Wiley & Sons, 1957. xi + 70 p.

TRAVERS, R. M. W. *An Introduction to Educational Research.* New York: The Macmillan Co., 1958. Chapter 15.

TRELEASE, Sam F. *How to Write Scientific and Technical Papers.* Third Edition. Baltimore, Md.: Williams and Wilkins Co., 1958. 194 p.

TUTTLE, Robert E., and BROWN, C. A. *Writing Useful Reports:* Principles and Applications. New York: Appleton-Century-Crofts, 1956. xiv + 635 p.

ULMAN, Joseph N., Jr. *Technical Reporting.* Revised Edition. New York: Holt, Rinehart, and Winston, 1959. 382 p.

VAN DALEN, Deobold B. *Understanding Educational Research:* An Introduction. New York: McGraw-Hill Book Co., 1962. p. 340-82.

VAN HAGAN, Charles E. *Report Writers' Handbook.* Englewood Cliffs, N.J.: Prentice-Hall, 1961. 287 p.

WALDO, Willis H. *Better Report Writing.* New York: Reinhold Publishing Corp., 1957. 238 p.

WALKER, Helen M., and DUROST, W. N. *Statistical Tables:* Their Structure and Use. New York: Teachers College, Columbia University, 1936. viii + 76 p.

WELD, Walter E. *How to Chart:* Facts from Figures with Graphs. Norwood, Mass.: Codex Book Co., 1959. xiv + 218 p.

WELTER, Rush. *Problems of Scholarly Publication in the Humanities and Social Sciences:* A Report Prepared for the Committee on Scholarly Publication of the American Council of Learned Societies. New York: American Council of Learned Societies, 1959. xii + 81 p. (Analysis of obstacles and opportunities for scholarly publication, based on questionnaires sent to university presses and to a sample of scholars in the humanities and social sciences.)

WILLIAMS, C. B., and STEVENSON, A. H. *A Research Manual for College Studies and Papers.* Revised Edition. New York: Harper & Brothers, 1951. 194 p.

WOOLLEY, Edwin C., SCOTT, Franklin W., and BRACHER, Frederick. *College Handbook of Composition.* Sixth Edition. Boston: D. C. Heath and Co., 1958. 474 p.

ZEISEL, Hans. *Say It with Figures:* How to Make Figures Make Sense—a Guide for Those Who Use and Read Statistics. Fourth Revised Edition. New York: Harper & Brothers, 1957. xviii + 257 p.

ZETLER, Robert L., and CROUCH, W. George. *Successful Communication in Science and Industry:* Writing, Reading, and Speaking. New York: McGraw-Hill Book Co., 1961. 296 p.

Index of Names

Index of Subjects